Al-Qur'ān

A Contemporary Translation by

Ahmed Ali

Princeton University Press
Princeton, New Jersey

Published by Princeton University Press, 41 William Street,
Princeton, New Jersey 08540
In the United Kingdom: Princeton University Press, 3 Market Place,
Woodstock, Oxfordshire OX20 1SY

Copyright © 1993 by Orooj Ahmed Ali

First published 1984 by Akrash Publishing, Karachi
Second revised edition 1986, Akrash Publishing
Oxford University Press, India, 1987

Revised definitive edition, and first paperback printing,
1988 Princeton University Press
Final revised edition 1994 Princeton University Press

Ninth paperback printing, newly comprising revisions last made
by the translator, 2001 Princeton University Press

11   13   15   16   14   12

All rights reserved. Except for brief passages quoted for purposes of
review or scholarly comment, no part of this publication may be reproduced,
stored in a retrieval system, or transmitted by any means, electronic, electrical,
chemical, mechanical, optical, photocopying, recording, or otherwise, without the
prior written permission of the copyright owner. Inquiries should be addressed to the
publishers at the above-mentioned address.

This book is sold subject to the condition that it shall not,
by way of trade or otherwise, be resold or circulated in any
form of binding or cover other than that in which it is published.

Library of Congress Control Number 2001087410

ISBN 0-691-07499-2

British Library Cataloging-in-Publication Data is available

Printed on acid-free paper. ∞

www.pup.princeton.edu

Printed in the United States of America

Text designed by Shahana Ahmed Ali

Cover illustration redrawn from an illustration in the Garrett Collection of
Persian, Turkish, and Indic manuscripts, Princeton University Library

Contents

CONTENTS

CONTENTS

Acknowledgements

I HAVE MANY debts of gratitude to acknowledge, first of all to my late wife and children, Eram, Orooj, Deed and Shahana, for their love and understanding of the neglect of my obligations to them during the long years that I had been busy with this translation. I should like to acknowledge the invaluable help of my son Orooj who has worked with me from the beginning, typing out the various drafts, suggesting innumerable improvements and seeing the publication of this work through the various stages of production to its finished form; and to my daughter Shahana for designing the book.

I am indebted to my friend Saiyyad Hasan Muthanna Nadvi for his help and sparing the time to read this translation word for word with me. My thanks are due to my other friends and well-wishers, both here and abroad, for their appreciation of my enormous task.

I should like to mention my indebtedness to the following Arabic lexicons in particular:

Al-Mufridat fi Gharib al-Qur'an: Abul Qasim ar-Raghib (d. 503 H.)
Muqa' is al-Lughat: Ibn Faris (d. 395 H.)
Lisan al-'Arab: Abul Fadl Muhammad bin Mukarram (d. 711 H.)
Taj al-'Urus: Murtada az-Zabidi (d. 1205 H.)
Muhit al-Muhit: Patras Bustani.

By Way of Preface

QUR'ANIC ARABIC IS distinguished by sublimity and excellencies of sound and eloquence, rhetoric and metaphor, assonance and alliteration, onomatopoeia and rhyme, ellipse and parallelism. Its cadences and sprung rhythm, pauses and stops, imply eloquent speech and duration. Some of its stylistic beauties are untranslatable and can only be suggested. The form of metrical lines has, therefore, been adopted in this translation to convey through accent, sprung rhythm and tonal structure the sonority and rhythmic patterns of the Qur'anic language. Rhyme, in which Arabic is so rich, cannot be used in English without disastrous consequences. I have tried to bring out its solemnizing effect through assonance, alliteration and internal rhyme. Etymologically Arabic is a very complex language. Words derived from the same root branch off into different sets of meaning, and the particular shade or signification of homonymous and other words used in the Qur'an to signify entirely different things, can be fixed only with reference to the context and regard to instances of their similar use elsewhere in the Book, as well as the logic and wider world view of the Qur'an. For though the Qur'an employs poetic language the basis of expression has shifted from the metaphorical to a new dialectical and metonymic plane in which 'this' is put for 'that' expressing an inner reality where words are used in place of thoughts.

The remarkably rich poetic tradition of Pagan Arabs did not deal in abstractions and pure thought. Their poems had sung of love, camels, horses, war, hunting, the mountain and desert landscape, and the martial valour of the tribesmen. Words were used to invoke concrete, almost physical images. The Qur'an restructured the metaphorical mould through allegory, paralleling it as a rhythmical unit with the conceptual language of transcendence which acquired primary authority and universal persuasive power to conform to its conceptual standards. Hence such words as *taqwa*, *sabr*, *salat*, which were connected with physical processes or particular objects, acquired entirely new and conceptual meanings. For instance, in Pagan poetry *muttaqi* was a person who fought to preserve himself from harm, but now becomes a person who preserves himself from evil and follows the straight path, fearing God and abiding by His commands. *Sabr* meant constant effort in obtaining a desired object, and implied constancy, firmness. Hence a mountain was called *as-sabir*, and the weight put in a boat to balance it *as-saburat*, while *al-asbirat* was used for camels and goats that returned home regularly in the evening. In the Qur'an it came to mean endurance, firmness, fortitude, as in 2:153, 2:250, 3:200, and acquired the conceptual meaning of perseverance, elaborated in the statement that God is with those who are patient and persevere, 2:153, 8:65. Similarly, *salat* as *as-sala* meant middle of the back, a horse that is second in a race, and as *salia-wastala* dependence, adherence, attachment. In the Qur'an *salat* acquired the conceptual meanings of devotion, adherence to God and His commands, fulfilling one's duties and obligations as behoves an *'abd*, creature, servant, devotee of God, as integral part of *'ubudiyat*, servitude and devotion, made clear in 24:41 which underlines that every creature in the heavens and the earth knows its *salat*, duties and obligations. It also means worship as in 8:35, piety as in 11:87, and service of prayer, as in 2:238, 4:43; 101-3, 11:114, etc.

The Qur'an, thus, brings to the mind its real objects from words by invoking the images embedded in the subconscious. For though the words remain the same, they often acquire new conceptual meanings and new dimensions lying hidden in their roots, which are brought out by the Qur'an, and now form part of its linguistic and intellectual dynamism. At the same time they become removed from the *Jahiliya* which was more of an attitude of mind and culture than a state of ignorance, as well as the later world as unfolded by the changing patterns of history, thought and language, so that anyone interpreting the Qur'an on the basis of Arabic as used by Arabs today would only mislead the readers of the Book.

Nature and its phenomena that figure so prominently in the Qur'an, assume a deeper significance as signs of God. The truths presented by it have come to be recognized with advance of knowledge in our age as conforming to the laws of causation and effect which science itself is trying to understand. Some of these have been pointed out in notes appended to this translation. The Qur'an has never failed to unfold its meanings to those who seek knowledge, and has remained contemporary and a Book of the future.

My attempt has been to give renderings as faithfully as is possible within the limits of another language wholly divergent in syntax, structure and scriptural development; and every language has its nuances and metaphorical use of words. Since English has a stretchability of its own, I have made use of various shades of meaning English words also carry, to convey the connotations of Qur'anic Arabic. For those who wish to ascertain it for themselves, reference to standard dictionaries of Arabic particularly, and of English, will be found rewarding. The conscientious reader in search of the right understanding of the text will find many surprises on consulting them. For this is, strictly speaking, a translation and not an interpretation, theological or otherwise, therefore, closest to the original in meaning, endeavouring to find as effective equivalents of Arabic words as creative use of English allows.

The brackets have been used mainly to give elucidations, differentiated or implied and extended meanings of words, or to fill elliptical gaps. As names of prophets generally known to all English readers have been used, an index giving their Qur'anic equivalents has been added for easy identification. Since the diacritical marks needed for transliterating Arabic words are not provided in the composing system the super-script macrons alone have been marked by hand in the titles at the beginning of the Surahs.

I have revised the translation for this definitive edition and removed the misprints and shortcomings that had escaped notice earlier, added a few more notes, and it supersedes the earlier editions.

KARACHI : DECEMBER, 1993   AHMED ALI

1 The Prologue

Al-Fātihah: Makki

بِسۡمِ اللّٰهِ الرَّحۡمٰنِ الرَّحِيۡمِ ۝

In the name of Allah, most benevolent, ever-merciful.

ٱلۡحَمۡدُ لِلّٰهِ رَبِّ الۡعٰلَمِيۡنَ ۝

ALL PRAISE BE to Allah,*
Lord of all the worlds,
2. Most beneficent, ever-merciful,
3. King of the Day of Judgement.
4. You alone we worship, and to You
alone turn for help.
5. Guide us (O Lord) to the path that is straight,
6. The path of those You have blessed,
7. Not of those who have earned Your anger,
nor those who have gone astray.

الرَّحۡمٰنِ الرَّحِيۡمِ ۝
مٰلِكِ يَوۡمِ الدِّيۡنِ ۝
اِيَّاكَ نَعۡبُدُ وَاِيَّاكَ نَسۡتَعِيۡنُ ۝
اِهۡدِنَا الصِّرَاطَ الۡمُسۡتَقِيۡمَ ۝
صِرَاطَ الَّذِيۡنَ اَنۡعَمۡتَ عَلَيۡهِمۡ ۙ غَيۡرِ الۡمَغۡضُوۡبِ
عَلَيۡهِمۡ وَلَا الضَّآلِّيۡنَ ۝

---

* Allah is the name of the same supreme Being who is called in English God and Khuda in Persian. He is the same God the Jews and Christians worship. "Our God and your God is one," is said in the Qur'an to the people of the Book in 29:46. "Whatever name you call Him by, (Allah or Ar-Rahman), all His names are beautiful." 17:110.

2 The Cow

Al-Baqarah: Madani

In the name of Allah, most benevolent, ever-merciful.

بِسۡمِ اللهِ الرَّحۡمٰنِ الرَّحِیۡمِ ۞

ALIF LĀM MĪM.

الٓمّٓ ۚ

2. This is The Book free of doubt and involution,
a guidance for those
who preserve themselves from evil
and follow the straight path,

ذٰلِكَ الۡكِتٰبُ لَا رَيۡبَ ۛ فِیۡهِ ۛ هُدًی لِّلۡمُتَّقِیۡنَ ۙ

3. Who believe in the Unknown
and fulfil their devotional obligations,
and spend in charity
of what We have given them;

الَّذِیۡنَ یُؤۡمِنُوۡنَ بِالۡغَیۡبِ وَ یُقِیۡمُوۡنَ الصَّلٰوةَ وَ مِمَّا رَزَقۡنٰهُمۡ یُنۡفِقُوۡنَ ۙ

4. Who believe
in what has been revealed to you
and what was revealed to those before you,
and are certain of the Hereafter.

وَ الَّذِیۡنَ یُؤۡمِنُوۡنَ بِمَاۤ اُنۡزِلَ اِلَیۡكَ وَ مَاۤ اُنۡزِلَ مِنۡ قَبۡلِكَ وَ بِالۡاٰخِرَةِ هُمۡ یُوۡقِنُوۡنَ ؕ

5. They have found the guidance of their Lord
and will be successful.

اُولٰٓئِكَ عَلٰی هُدًی مِّنۡ رَّبِّهِمۡ وَ اُولٰٓئِكَ هُمُ الۡمُفۡلِحُوۡنَ ۝

6. As for those who deny,
it is all the same if you warn them or not,
they will not believe.

اِنَّ الَّذِیۡنَ كَفَرُوۡا سَوَآءٌ عَلَیۡهِمۡ ءَاَنۡذَرۡتَهُمۡ اَمۡ لَمۡ تُنۡذِرۡهُمۡ لَا یُؤۡمِنُوۡنَ ۝

7. God has sealed their hearts and ears,
and veiled their eyes.
For them is great deprivation.

خَتَمَ اللهُ عَلٰی قُلُوۡبِهِمۡ وَ عَلٰی سَمۡعِهِمۡ ؕ وَ عَلٰۤی اَبۡصَارِهِمۡ غِشَاوَةٌ ؕ وَّ لَهُمۡ عَذَابٌ عَظِیۡمٌ ۝

And there are some who, though they say:
"We believe in God and the Last Day,"
(in reality) do not believe.

وَ مِنَ النَّاسِ مَنۡ یَّقُوۡلُ اٰمَنَّا بِاللهِ وَ بِالۡیَوۡمِ الۡاٰخِرِ وَ مَا هُمۡ بِمُؤۡمِنِیۡنَ ۝

9. They (try to) deceive God
and those who believe,
yet deceive none but themselves
although they do not know.

یُخٰدِعُوۡنَ اللهَ وَ الَّذِیۡنَ اٰمَنُوۡا ۚ وَ مَا یَخۡدَعُوۡنَ اِلَّاۤ اَنۡفُسَهُمۡ وَ مَا یَشۡعُرُوۡنَ ؕ

10. Sick are their hearts,
and God adds to their malady.
For them is suffering for they lie.

فِیۡ قُلُوۡبِهِمۡ مَّرَضٌ ۙ فَزَادَهُمُ اللهُ مَرَضًا ۚ وَ لَهُمۡ عَذَابٌ اَلِیۡمٌۢ ۙ بِمَا كَانُوۡا یَكۡذِبُوۡنَ ۝

11. When asked to desist from spreading corruption

وَ اِذَا قِیۡلَ لَهُمۡ لَا تُفۡسِدُوۡا فِی الۡاَرۡضِ ۙ قَالُوۡۤا اِنَّمَا

in the land they say: "Why,
we are reformers."
12. Yet they are surely mischief-mongers,
even though they do not know.
13. When asked to believe as others do, *demands submission*
they say: "Should we believe like fools?" *and conformity*
And yet they are the fools,
even though they do not know.
14. When they meet the faithful they say:
"We believe;"
but when alone with the devils (their fellows),
they say: "We are really with you;
we were joking."
15. But God will turn the joke against them *not very merciful*
and allow them to sink deeper into evil *at all*
and wander perplexed in their wickedness.
16. They are indeed those who bartered away
good guidance for error
and gained nothing from the deal,
nor found the right way.
17. They are like a man who kindles
a fire, and when its glow
has illumined the air
God takes away their light
leaving them in the dark
where they will not be able to see.
18. They are deaf, dumb and blind,
and shall never return;
19. Or like rain pouring
from the sky which hides
within it darkness,
thunder and lightning.
They thrust their fingers into their ears
for safety against noise and death.
But God surrounds those
who believe not from all sides.
20. Verily the lightning
could snatch away their eyes.
When it flashes forth
they walk in its flare.
When darkness returns
they stand still.
And if the Lord wills so
He could take away
their hearing and sight;
surely God is all-powerful.

So, O you people,
adore your Lord who created you,
as He did those before you,
that you could take heed for yourselves
and fear Him

يَٰٓأَيُّهَا ٱلنَّاسُ ٱعۡبُدُوا۟ رَبَّكُمُ ٱلَّذِى خَلَقَكُمۡ وَٱلَّذِينَ مِن قَبۡلِكُمۡ لَعَلَّكُمۡ تَتَّقُونَ ۝

22. Who made the earth a bed for you,
the sky a canopy,
and sends forth rain from the skies
that fruits may grow —
your food and sustenance.
So, do not make
another
the equal of God
knowingly.

ٱلَّذِى جَعَلَ لَكُمُ ٱلۡأَرۡضَ فِرَٰشًا وَٱلسَّمَآءَ بِنَآءً وَأَنزَلَ مِنَ ٱلسَّمَآءِ مَآءً فَأَخۡرَجَ بِهِۦ مِنَ ٱلثَّمَرَٰتِ رِزۡقًا لَّكُمۡ فَلَا تَجۡعَلُوا۟ لِلَّهِ أَندَادًا وَأَنتُمۡ تَعۡلَمُونَ ۝

23. If you are in doubt
of what We have revealed to Our votary,
then bring a Surah like this, and call
any witness, apart from God, you like,
if you are truthful.

وَإِن كُنتُمۡ فِى رَيۡبٍ مِّمَّا نَزَّلۡنَا عَلَىٰ عَبۡدِنَا فَأۡتُوا۟ بِسُورَةٍ مِّن مِّثۡلِهِۦ وَٱدۡعُوا۟ شُهَدَآءَكُم مِّن دُونِ ٱللَّهِ إِن كُنتُمۡ صَٰدِقِينَ ۝

24. But if you cannot,
as indeed you cannot,
then guard yourselves
against the Fire
whose fuel is men and rocks,
which has been prepared
for the infidels.

فَإِن لَّمۡ تَفۡعَلُوا۟ وَلَن تَفۡعَلُوا۟ فَٱتَّقُوا۟ ٱلنَّارَ ٱلَّتِى وَقُودُهَا ٱلنَّاسُ وَٱلۡحِجَارَةُ أُعِدَّتۡ لِلۡكَٰفِرِينَ ۝

25. Announce to those
who believe
and have done good deeds,
glad tidings of gardens under which
rivers flow,
and where,
when they eat the fruits that grow,
they will say: "Indeed
they are the same as we were given before,"
so like in semblance the food would be.
And they shall have fair spouses there,
and live there abidingly.

وَبَشِّرِ ٱلَّذِينَ ءَامَنُوا۟ وَعَمِلُوا۟ ٱلصَّٰلِحَٰتِ أَنَّ لَهُمۡ جَنَّٰتٍ تَجۡرِى مِن تَحۡتِهَا ٱلۡأَنۡهَٰرُ كُلَّمَا رُزِقُوا۟ مِنۡهَا مِن ثَمَرَةٍ رِّزۡقًا قَالُوا۟ هَٰذَا ٱلَّذِى رُزِقۡنَا مِن قَبۡلُ وَأُتُوا۟ بِهِۦ مُتَشَٰبِهًا وَلَهُمۡ فِيهَآ أَزۡوَٰجٌ مُّطَهَّرَةٌ وَهُمۡ فِيهَا خَٰلِدُونَ ۝

26. God is not loath
to advance the similitude
of a gnat or a being more contemptible;
and those who believe know
whatever is from the Lord is true.
But those who disbelieve say:
"What does God mean by this parable?"
He causes some to err this way,

إِنَّ ٱللَّهَ لَا يَسۡتَحۡىِۦٓ أَن يَضۡرِبَ مَثَلًا مَّا بَعُوضَةً فَمَا فَوۡقَهَا فَأَمَّا ٱلَّذِينَ ءَامَنُوا۟ فَيَعۡلَمُونَ أَنَّهُ ٱلۡحَقُّ مِن رَّبِّهِمۡ وَأَمَّا ٱلَّذِينَ كَفَرُوا۟ فَيَقُولُونَ مَاذَآ أَرَادَ ٱللَّهُ بِهَٰذَا مَثَلًا يُضِلُّ بِهِۦ كَثِيرًا وَيَهۡدِى بِهِۦ كَثِيرًا

and some He guides;
yet He turns away none but those who transgress,
27. Who, having sealed it,
break God's covenant,
dividing what He ordained cohered;
and those who spread discord in the land
will suffer assuredly.
28. Then how can you disbelieve in God?
He gave you life when you were dead.
He will make you die again
then bring you back to life:
To Him then you will return.
29. He made for you all that lies
within the earth,
then turning to the firmament
He proportioned several skies:
He has knowledge of every thing.

Remember, when your Lord said to the angels:
"I have to place a trustee on the earth,"
they said: "Will You place one there
who would create disorder and shed blood,
while we intone Your litanies and sanctify Your name?"
And God said: "I know what you do not know."
31. Then He gave Adam knowledge of the nature
and reality of all things and every thing,
and set them before the angels and said:
"Tell Me the names of these
if you are truthful."
32. And they said: "Glory to You (O Lord),
knowledge we have none
except what You have given us,
for You are all-knowing and all-wise."
33. Then He said to Adam:
"Convey to them their names."
And when he had told them, God said:
"Did I not tell you that I
know the unknown of the heavens and the earth,
and I know what you disclose
and know what you hide?"
34. Remember, when We asked the angels to bow
in homage to Adam, they all bowed but Iblis,
who disdained and turned insolent,
and so became a disbeliever.
35. And We said to Adam: "Both you and your spouse
live in the Garden, eat freely to your fill

wherever you like, but approach not this tree*
or you will become transgressors.

36. But Satan tempted them and had them banished
from the (happy) state they were in.
And We said: "Go, one the antagonist of the other,
and live on the earth for a time ordained,
and fend for yourselves."

37. Then his Lord sent commands to Adam
and turned towards him:
Indeed He is compassionate and kind.

38. And We said to them: "Go, all of you.
When I send guidance, whoever follows it
will neither have fear nor regret;

39. But those who deny and reject Our signs
will belong to Hell**, and there abide unchanged."

O children of Israel,
remember the favours I bestowed on you.
So keep your pledge to Me, and I will mine to you,
and be fearful of Me,

41. And believe in what I have sent down
which verifies what is already with you;
and do not be the first to deny it,
nor part with it for little gain; and beware of Me.

42. Do not confuse truth with falsehood,
nor conceal the truth knowingly.

43. Be firm in devotion; give zakat*** (the due share
of your wealth for the welfare of others),
and bow with those who bow (before God).

44. Will you enjoin good deeds on the others
and forget your own selves? You also read the Scriptures,
why do you then not understand?

45. Find strength in fortitude and prayer,
which is heavy and exacting but for those
who are humble and meek,

46. Who are conscious that they have to meet their Lord,
and to Him they have to return.

Remember, O children of Israel,

---

* The story of Adam presents the allegorical odyssey of man. He is here warned against oppositions.
Shajara means opposition, mutually involved, and tree, the archetypal symbol of life. 'Aduwun means
distant, not united, hence enemy. There is a perpetual antagonism between the sexes; and man and
woman are both one another's opposite and complement, one being 'sweet', the other 'brine', (25:37).
** See note on p.72.
*** See note on zakat, p. 290.

Al-Baqarah   16

the favours I bestowed on you,
and made you exalted among the nations of the world.

وَأَنِّى فَضَّلْتُكُمْ عَلَى الْعَلَمِينَ ۝

48. Take heed of the day when no man
will be useful to man in the least,
when no intercession matter
nor ransom avail, nor help reach them.

وَاتَّقُوا يَوْمًا لَّا تَجْزِى نَفْسٌ عَن نَّفْسٍ شَيْئًا وَّلَا
يُقْبَلُ مِنْهَا شَفَاعَةٌ وَّلَا يُؤْخَذُ مِنْهَا عَدْلٌ وَّلَا
هُمْ يُنصَرُونَ ۝

49. Remember, We saved you from the Pharaoh's people
who wronged and oppressed you and slew
your sons but spared your women:
In this was a great favour from your Lord.

وَإِذْ نَجَّيْنَكُم مِّنْ الِ فِرْعَوْنَ يَسُومُونَكُمْ سُوٓءَ الْعَذَابِ
يُذَبِّحُونَ أَبْنَاءَكُمْ وَيَسْتَحْيُونَ نِسَاءَكُمْ وَفِى ذَلِكُم
بَلَاءٌ مِّن رَّبِّكُمْ عَظِيمٌ ۝

50. Remember, We parted the sea and saved you,
and drowned the men of Pharaoh before your very eyes.

وَإِذْ فَرَقْنَا بِكُمُ الْبَحْرَ فَأَنجَيْنَكُمْ وَأَغْرَقْنَا الَ فِرْعَوْنَ
وَأَنتُمْ تَنظُرُونَ ۝

51. Yet, remember, as We communed
with Moses for forty nights
you took the calf in his absence (and worshipped it),
and you did wrong.

وَإِذْ وَاعَدْنَا مُوسَى أَرْبَعِينَ لَيْلَةً ثُمَّ اتَّخَذْتُمُ الْعِجْلَ
مِنْ بَعْدِهِ وَأَنتُمْ ظَالِمُونَ ۝

52. Even so, We pardoned you
that you may be grateful.

ثُمَّ عَفَوْنَا عَنكُم مِّنْ بَعْدِ ذَلِكَ لَعَلَّكُمْ تَشْكُرُونَ ۝

53. Remember, We gave Moses the Book and Discernment
of falsehood and truth,
that you may be guided.

وَإِذْ اتَيْنَا مُوسَى الْكِتَابَ وَالْفُرْقَانَ لَعَلَّكُمْ
تَهْتَدُونَ ۝

54. Remember, Moses said: "My people, by taking this calf
you have done yourselves harm, so now turn
to your Creator in repentance, and kill your pride,
which is better with your Lord."
And (the Lord) softened towards you,
for He is all-forgiving and merciful.

وَإِذْ قَالَ مُوسَى لِقَوْمِهِ يَقَوْمِ إِنَّكُمْ ظَلَمْتُمْ أَنفُسَكُم
بِاتِّخَاذِكُمُ الْعِجْلَ فَتُوبُوٓا إِلَى بَارِئِكُمْ فَاقْتُلُوٓا أَنفُسَكُمْ
ذَلِكُمْ خَيْرٌ لَّكُمْ عِندَ بَارِئِكُمْ فَتَابَ عَلَيْكُمْ إِنَّهُ هُوَ
التَّوَّابُ الرَّحِيمُ ۝

55. Remember, when you said to Moses:
"We shall not believe in you until
we see God face to face,"
lightning struck you as you looked.

وَإِذْ قُلْتُمْ يَمُوسَى لَن نُّؤْمِنَ لَكَ حَتَّى نَرَى اللَّهَ جَهْرَةً
فَأَخَذَتْكُمُ الصَّاعِقَةُ وَأَنتُمْ تَنظُرُونَ ۝

56. Even then We revived you
after you had become senseless
that you might give thanks;

ثُمَّ بَعَثْنَكُم مِّنْ بَعْدِ مَوْتِكُمْ لَعَلَّكُمْ تَشْكُرُونَ ۝

57. And made the cloud spread shade over you,
and sent for you manna and quails
that you may eat of the good things We have made for you.
No harm was done to Us, they only harmed themselves.

وَظَلَّلْنَا عَلَيْكُمُ الْغَمَامَ وَأَنزَلْنَا عَلَيْكُمُ الْمَنَّ وَ
السَّلْوَى كُلُوا مِن طَيِّبَاتِ مَا رَزَقْنَكُمْ وَمَا ظَلَمُونَا
لَكِن كَانُوٓا أَنفُسَهُمْ يَظْلِمُونَ ۝

58. And remember, We said to you: "Enter this city,
eat wherever you like, as much as you please,
but pass through the gates in humility
and say: 'May our sins be forgiven.'"
We shall forgive your trespasses
and give those who do good
abundance.

وَإِذْ قُلْنَا ادْخُلُوا هَذِهِ الْقَرْيَةَ فَكُلُوا مِنْهَا حَيْثُ
شِئْتُمْ رَغَدًا وَادْخُلُوا الْبَابَ سُجَّدًا وَقُولُوا حِطَّةٌ
نَّغْفِرْ لَكُمْ خَطَايَاكُمْ وَسَنَزِيدُ الْمُحْسِنِينَ ۝

59. But the wicked changed and perverted

مَّدَّلَ الَّذِينَ ظَلَمُوا قَوْلًا غَيْرَ الَّذِى قِيلَ لَهُمْ

the word We had spoken to a word distorted,
and We sent from heaven
retribution on the wicked,
for they disobeyed.

And remember, when Moses asked
for water for his people,
We told him to strike
the rock with his staff, and behold,
twelve springs of gushing water gushed forth
so that each of the tribes
came to know its place of drinking.
Eat and drink, (enjoy) God's gifts,
and spread no discord in the land.
61. Remember, when you said:
"O Moses, we are tired
of eating the same food (day after day),
ask your Lord to give us fruits of the earth,
herbs and cucumbers,
grains and lentils and onions;" he said:
"Would you rather exchange what is good with what is bad?
Go then to the city, you shall have what you ask."
So they were disgraced and became indigent,
earning the anger of God,
for they disbelieved the word of God,
and slayed the prophets unjustly,
for they transgressed and rebelled.

Surely the believers and the Jews,
Nazareans* and the Sabians, whoever believes
in God and the Last Day, and whosoever does right,
shall have his reward with his Lord
and will neither have fear nor regret.
63. Remember the day We made the covenant with you
and exalted you on the Mount
and said: "Hold fast to what We have given you,
and remember what is therein
that you may take heed."
64. But you went back (on your word),
and but for the mercy and grace of God you were lost.
65. You know and have known already
those among you who had broken
the sanctity of the Sabbath, and to whom

---

* The word used for Christians in the Qur'an is *Nasara*, Nazareans, to whose hierarchy Jesus belonged;
and presents Jesus's original Nazarean position, obscured after the rise of Pauline Christianity.

We had said: "Become (like) apes despised,"
66. And whom We made an example
for the people (of the day) and those after them,
and warning for those
who fear God.
67. Remember, when Moses said to his people:
"God demands that you sacrifice a cow,"
they said: "Are you making fun of us?"
And he said: "God forbid that I be of the ignorant."
68. "Call on your Lord for us," they said, "that He might
inform us what kind she should be."
"Neither old nor young, says God, but of age in between,"
answered Moses. "So do as you are bid."
69. "Call on your Lord," they said,
"to tell us the colour of the cow."
"God says," answered Moses, "a fawn coloured cow, rich
        yellow,
well pleasing to the eye."
70. "Call on your Lord," they said, "to name its variety,
as cows be all alike to us.
If God wills we shall be guided aright."
71. And Moses said: "He says it's a cow unyoked,
nor worn out by ploughing or watering the fields,
one in good shape with no mark or blemish."
"Now have you brought us the truth," they said;
and then, after wavering, they sacrificed the cow.

Remember when you killed a man and blamed
each other for the deed, God
brought to light what you concealed.
73. We had pronounced already:
"Slay (the murderer) for (taking a life)."*
Thus God preserves life from death
and shows you His signs that you may understand.
74. Yet, in spite of this,
your hearts only hardened like rocks

---

* The use of *adribu bi-ba'diha* in the original text could literally mean "strike him with some of her,"
on the basis of which it has been taken to mean "strike it (the corpse) with some (pieces) of her (the
cow)." On the very face this seems not only far-fetched but no sanction exists for such a meaning in
the Qur'an. It also does not conform to the Qur'an's wider view of life. The word *daraba* means more
than one hundred things, 'to strike' being only one of them; and when it is combined with other words
its meaning changes altogether, as in *darab al-ma*, to swim, or *darb al-mathal*, to give an example, etc.
The meaning given here is in conformity with its use in a similar sense elsewhere in the Qur'an, e.g.
8:12 and 47:4. As for *bi-ba'diha*, its use, and meaning, are similar to *an-nafsa bin-nafs* in 5:45, and the
sanction for the meaning given here is contained in 2:178-79 and 5:32-33 which contain commands of
an imperative nature applicable in such cases as this.

Al-Baqarah   **19**

or even harder, but among rocks
are those from which rivers flow;
and there are also those which split open and water gushes
       forth;
as well as those that roll down
for fear of God.
And God is not negligent of all that you do.
75. How do you expect them to put
their faith in you,
when you know that some among them heard the word of
       God
and, having understood, perverted it
knowingly?
76. For when they meet the faithful, they say:
"We believe;"
but when among themselves, they say:
"Why do you tell them what the Lord has revealed to you?
They will only dispute it in the presence of your Lord.
Have you no sense indeed?"
77. Do they not know that God
is aware of what they hide and what they disclose?
78. Among them are heathens who know nothing of
       the Book
but only what they wish to believe,
and are only lost in fantasies.
79. But woe to them who fake the Scriptures and say:
"This is from God," so that they
might earn some profit thereby;
and woe to them for what they fake,
and woe to them for what they earn from it!
80. Yet they say: "The Fire will not touch us
for more than a few days."
Say: "Have you so received
a promise from God?" Then surely
God will not withdraw His pledge.
Or do you impute things to God
of which you have no knowledge at all?"
81. Why, they who have earned the wages of sin
and are enclosed in error,
are people of Hell,
where they will abide for ever.
82. But those who believe and do good deeds
are people of Paradise,
and shall live there forever.

Remember, when We made a covenant

with the people of Israel and said:
"Worship no one but God, and be good
to your parents and your kin,
and to orphans and the needy,
and speak of goodness to men;
observe your devotional obligations,
and give zakat (the due share of your wealth
for the welfare of others),"
you went back (on your word),
except only a few, and paid no heed.
84. And remember, when We made a covenant with you
whereby you agreed
you will neither shed blood among you
nor turn your people out of their homes,
you promised, and are witness to it too.
85. But you still kill one another, and you turn
a section of your people from their homes,
assisting one another against them
with guilt and oppression.
Yet when they are brought to you as captives
you ransom them, although
forbidden it was
to drive them away.
Do you, then, believe
a part of the Book and reject a part?
There is no other award
for them who so act but disgrace
in the world, and on the Day of Judgement
the severest of punishment;
for God is not heedless of all that you do.
86. They are those who bought the life of the world
at the cost of the life to come;
and neither will their torment decrease
nor help reach them.

Remember We gave Moses the Book
and sent after him many an apostle;
and to Jesus, son of Mary, We gave
clear evidence of the truth,
reinforcing him with divine grace.
Even so, when a messenger
brought to you what did not suit your mood
you turned haughty,
and called some imposters
and some others you slew.
88. And they say: "Our hearts are enfolded in covers."

In fact God has cursed them for their unbelief;
and only a little do they believe.

89. And when the Book was sent to them by God
verifying what had been revealed to them already —
even though before it they used to pray
for victory over the unbelievers —
and even though they recognised it when it came to them,
they renounced it.
The curse of God be on those who deny!

90. They bartered their lives ill
denying the revelation of God out of spite
that God should bestow His grace
among His votaries on whomsoever He will,
and thus earned wrath upon wrath.
The punishment for disbelievers
is ignominous.

91. And when it is said to them:
"believe in what God has sent down,"
they say: "We believe
what was sent to us, and do not believe
what has come thereafter," although
it affirms the truth they possess already.
Say: "Why have you then
been slaying God's apostles as of old,
if you do believe?"

92. Although Moses had come to you with evidence of the
        truth,
you chose the calf in his absence,
and you transgressed.

93. Remember when We took your pledge
and exalted you on the Mount
(saying :) "Hold fast
to what We have given you, firmly,
and pay heed," you said:
"We have heard and will not obey."
(The image of) the calf had sunk deep into their hearts
on account of unbelief.
Say: "Vile is your belief
if you are believers indeed!"

94. Tell them: "If you think you alone
will abide with God
to the exclusion of the rest of Mankind,
in the mansions of the world to come,
then wish for death
if what you say is true."

95. But they will surely not wish for death

because of what they had done in the past;*
and God knows the sinners well.

96. You will see they are covetous of life
more than other men,
even more than those
who practise idolatry.
Each one of them desires to live
a thousand years, although longevity *[handwritten: One who strays from the path and perverts the word of God will not go unpunished]*
will never save them from punishment,
for God sees all they do.

Say: "Whosoever is the enemy of Gabriel
who revealed the word of God to you
by the dispensation of God,
reaffirming what had been revealed before,
and is a guidance and good news
for those who believe, —
98. Whosoever is the enemy of God
and His angels and apostles,
and of Gabriel and Michael,
then God is the enemy of such unbelievers."
99. We have sent clear signs to you,
such as none can deny except those
who transgress the truth.
100. And every time they made a pledge
some of them pushed it aside,
and many of them do not believe.
101. When a messenger was sent to them by God
affirming the Books they had already received,
some of them put (His message) behind their backs
as if they had no knowledge of it. *[handwritten: they don't want to know the truth]*
102. And they follow
what devilish beings used to chant
against the authority of Solomon, though Solomon
never disbelieved
and only the devils denied, who taught sorcery to men,
which, they said, had been revealed
to the angels of Babylon, Harut and Marut,
who, however, never taught it without saying:
"We have been sent to deceive you,
so do not renounce (your faith)."
They learnt what led to discord between husband and wife.
Yet they could not harm any one

---

* Literally, 'what their hands had sent ahead', that is, the good and evil deeds.

without the dispensation of God.
And they learnt what harmed them and brought no gain.
They knew indeed
whoever bought this had no place in the world to come,
and that surely they had sold themselves
for something that was vile.
If only they had sense!
103. Had they come to believe instead,
and taken heed for themselves,
they would surely have earned from God
a far better reward.
If only they had sense!

Say not (to the Prophet), O believers:
"Have regard for us (ra'ina)," but "look at us (unzurna),"
and obey him in what he says.
Painful is the nemesis for disbelievers.
105. Those without faith among the people of the Book,
and those who worship idols,
do not wish
that good should come to you from your Lord.
But God chooses whom He likes for His grace;
and the bounty of God is infinite.
106. When We cancel a message
(sent to an earlier prophet) or throw it into oblivion,
We replace it with one better or one similar.*
Do you not know that God has power over all things?
107. Do you not know that
God's is the kingdom of the heavens and the earth,
and that there is none to save and protect you apart from God?
108. Do you too, O believers, wish to question your Apostle
as Moses was in the past?
But he who takes unbelief in exchange for belief
only strays from the right path.
109. How many of the followers of the Books
having once known the truth
desire in their hearts, out of envy,
to turn you into infidels again
even after the truth has become clear to them!
But you forbear and overlook till God fulfil His plan;
and God has power over all things.
110. Fulfil your devotional obligations and pay the zakat.
And what you send ahead of good

---

* The context clearly shows that this refers to commands sent to earlier prophets, and *not* to Prophet Muhammad. See verses preceding and following this verse. See also 16:101.

Al-Baqarah

you will find with God,
for He sees all that you do.
111. And they say: "None will go to Paradise
but the Jews and the Christians;" but this
is only wishful thinking.
Say: "Bring the proof if you are truthful."
112. Only he who surrenders to God with all his heart
and also does good, will find his reward with his Lord,
and will have no fear or regret.

The Jews say: "The Christians are not right,"
and the Christians say: "The Jews are in the wrong;"
yet both read the Scriptures;
and this is what the unread
had said too. God alone
will judge between them in their differences
on the Day of Reckoning.
114. And who is more unjust than he
who prohibits the name of God
being used in His mosques,
who hurries to despoil them even though
he has no right
to enter them except in reverence?
For them is ignominy in the world
and severe punishment in the life to come.
115. To God belong the East and the West.
Wherever you turn the glory* of God is everywhere:
All-pervading is He and all-knowing.
116. Yet they say that God has begotten a son.
May He be praised!
Indeed every thing in the heavens and the earth
belongs to Him,
and all are obedient to God.
117. Creator of the heavens and the earth from nothingness,
He has only to say when He wills a thing: "Be", and it is.
118. But those who are ignorant say:
"Why does God not speak or show us a sign?"
The same question had been asked by men before them,
who were like them in their hearts.
But to those who are firm in their faith
We have shown Our signs already.
119. And We have sent you with the truth
to give glad tidings and to warn.
You will not be questioned about those

---

* Literally face, *vajha*, the front or surface, which in the case of God would be His glory, or presence.

who are inmates of Hell.

120. The Jews and Christians will never be pleased with you
until you follow their way.
Say: "God's guidance alone is true guidance;"
for if you give in to their wishes
after having received the (Book of) knowledge from God,
then none will you have
as friend or helper to save you.

121. Those to whom We have sent down the Book,
and who read it as it should be read,
believe in it truly; but those
who deny it will be losers.

O children of Israel,
remember the favours I bestowed on you,
and made you exalted among the nations of the world.

123. Fear the day when no man will
stand up for man in the least,
and no ransom avail
nor intercession matter nor help reach.

124. Remember, when his Lord tried Abraham
by a number of commands which he fulfilled,
God said to him: "I will make you a leader among men."
And when Abraham asked: "From my progeny too?"
the Lord said: "My pledge
does not include transgressors."

125. Remember, We made the House (of Ka'bah) a place
of congregation and safe retreat,
and said: "Make the spot where Abraham stood
the place of worship;" and enjoined
upon Abraham and Ishmael
to keep Our House immaculate for those
who shall walk around it and stay in it
for contemplation and prayer,
and for bowing in adoration.

126. And when Abraham said: "O Lord,
make this a city of peace,
and give those of its citizens who believe
in God and the Last Day fruits for food,"
He answered: "To those will I also give a little
who believe not, for a time,
then drag them to Hell, a dreadful destination!"

127. And when Abraham was raising the plinth of the House
with Ishmael, (he prayed):
"Accept this from us, O Lord,
for You hear and know every thing;

128. And make us submit, O Lord, to Your will,
and our progeny a people submissive to You.
Teach us the way of worship
and forgive our trespasses,
for You are compassionate and merciful;
129. And send to them, O Lord, an apostle from among them
to impart Your messages to them,
and teach them the Book and the wisdom,
and correct them in every way;
for indeed You are mighty and wise."

Who will turn away from the creed of Abraham
but one dull of soul?
We made him the chosen one here in the world,
and one of the best in the world to come,
131. (For) when his Lord said to him: "Obey," he replied:
"I submit to the Lord of all the worlds."
132. And Abraham left this legacy to his sons,
and to Jacob, and said:
"O my sons, God has chosen this as the faith for you.
Do not die but as those who have submitted (to God)."
133. Were you present at the hour of Jacob's death?
"What will you worship after me?"
he asked his sons, and they answered:
"We shall worship your God
and the God of your fathers,
of Abraham and Ishmael and Isaac, *they bring up Ishmael a lot*
the one and only God;
and to Him we submit."
134. Those were the people, and they have passed away.
Theirs the reward for what they did,
as yours will be for what you do.
You will not be questioned about their deeds.
135. They say: "Become Jews or become Christians,
and find the right way."
Say: "No. We follow the way of Abraham
the upright, who was not an idolater."
136. Say: "We believe in God
and what has been sent down to us,
and what had been revealed
to Abraham and Ishmael
and Isaac and Jacob and their progeny,
and that which was given to Moses and Christ,
and to all other prophets by the Lord.
We make no distinction among them,
and we submit to Him."

137. If they come to believe as you did,
they will find the right path.
If they turn away
then they will only oppose;
but God will suffice you against them,
for God hears all and knows every thing.

138. "We have taken the colouring of God;
and whose shade is better than God's?
Him alone we worship."

139. Say: "Why do you dispute with us about God
when He is equally your Lord and our Lord?
To us belong our actions, to you yours;
and we are true to Him."

140. Or do you claim that Abraham and Ishmael
and Isaac and Jacob and their offspring
were Jews or Christians?
Say: "Have you more knowledge than God?"
Who is more wicked than he
who conceals the testimony he received from God?
God is not unaware of all you do.

141. They were the people, and they have passed away.
Theirs the reward for what they did,
as yours will be for what you do.
You will not be questioned about their deeds.

The foolish will now ask and say:
"What has made the faithful turn away
from the Qiblah towards which they used to pray?"
Say: "To God belong the East and the West.
He guides who so wills to the path that is straight."

143. We have made you a temperate people
that you act as witness over man,
and the Prophet as witness over you.
We decreed the Qiblah which you faced before
that We may know
who follow the Apostle and who turn away in haste.
And this was a hard (test)
except for those who were guided by God.
But God will not suffer your faith to go waste,
for God is to men full of mercy and grace.

144. We have seen you turn your face to the heavens.
We shall turn you to a Qiblah that will please you.
So turn towards the Holy Mosque,
and turn towards it wherever you be.
And those who are recipients of the Book surely know
that this is the truth from their Lord;

and God is not negligent of all that you do.
145. Even though you bring all the proof
to the people of the Book they will not face
the direction you turn to,
nor you theirs,
nor will they follow
each other's direction.
And if you follow their whims
after all the knowledge that has reached you,
then surely you will be among transgressors.
146. Those to whom We have sent down the Book
know this even as they know their sons.
Yet a section among them
conceals the truth knowingly.
147. The truth is from your Lord,
so be not among those who are sceptics.

Each has a goal to which he turns.
So strive towards piety and excel the others:
God will bring you all together
wheresoever you be.
God has power over every thing.
149. Wherever you come from
turn towards the Holy Mosque:
This in truth is from your Lord.
God is not negligent of all you do.
150. Whichever place you come from
turn towards the Holy Mosque,
and wherever you are, turn your faces towards it
so that people may have no cause
for argument against you,
except such among them as are wicked.
But do not fear them, fear Me
that I may accomplish My favours on you,
and you may find the right way perchance.
151. Even as We sent a messenger from among you
to convey Our messages to you and cleanse you,
and teach you the Book and the wisdom,
and what you did not know;
152. So, therefore, remember Me,
and I shall remember you;
and give thanks and do not be ungrateful.

O you who believe,
seek courage in fortitude and prayer,
for God is with those who are patient and persevere.

154. Do not say that those who are killed
in the way of God, are dead,
for indeed they are alive,
even though you are not aware.

155. Be sure We shall try you
with something of fear and hunger
and loss of wealth and life
and the fruits (of your labour);
but give tidings of happiness to those who have patience,

156. Who say when assailed by adversity:
"Surely we are for God, and to Him we shall return."

157. On such men are the blessings of God and His mercy,
for they are indeed on the right path.

158. Truly Safa and Marwa are the symbols of God.
Whoever goes on pilgrimage
to the House (of God), or on a holy visit,
is not guilty of wrong if he walk around them;
and he who does good of his own accord
will find appreciation with God who knows every thing.

159. They who conceal Our signs
and the guidance We have sent them
and have made clear in the Book,
are condemned of God and are condemned by those
who are worthy of condemning.

160. But those who repent and reform
and proclaim (the truth), are forgiven,
for I am forgiving and merciful.

161. But those who deny, and die disbelieving,
bear the condemnation of God
and the angels and that of all men,

162. Under which they will live, and their suffering
will neither decrease nor be respite for them.

163. Your God is one God;
there is no god other than He,
the compassionate, ever-merciful.

Creation of the heavens and the earth,
alternation of night and day,
and sailing of ships across the ocean
with what is useful to man,
and the rain that God sends from the sky enlivening
the earth that was dead,
and the scattering of beasts of all kinds upon it,
and the changing of the winds, and the clouds which remain
obedient between earth and sky,
are surely signs for the wise.

Al-Baqarah

165. And yet there are men who take others
as compeers of God,
and bestow on them love due to God;
but the love of the faithful for God is more intense.
If only the wicked could see now
the agony that they will behold
(on the Day of Resurrection), they will know
that to God belongs the power entirely!
And the punishment of God is severe.
166. When those who were followed
will disclaim those who followed them,
and see the torment
all ties between them shall be severed,
167. And the followers will say:
"Could we live but once again
we would leave them as they
have abandoned us now."
God will show them thus
their deeds, and fill them with remorse;
but never shall they find release from the Fire.

O men, eat only the things of the earth
that are lawful and good.
Do not walk in the footsteps of Satan,
your acknowledged enemy.
169. He will ask you to indulge in evil, indecency,
and to speak lies of God you cannot even conceive.
170. When it is said to them:
"Follow what God has revealed,"
they reply: "No, we shall follow only what
our fathers had practiced," —
even though their fathers had no wisdom or guidance!
171. The semblance of the infidels
is that of a man
who shouts to one that cannot hear
more than a call and a cry.
They are deaf, dumb and blind,
and they fail to understand.
172. O believers, eat what is good of the food
We have given you, and be grateful to God,
if indeed you are obedient to Him.
173. Forbidden to you are carrion and blood,
and the flesh of the swine,
and that which has been
consecrated (or killed)
in the name of any other than God.

Al-Baqarah   31

عَادٍ فَلَا إِثْمَ عَلَيْهِ إِنَّ اللَّهَ غَفُورٌ رَّحِيمٌ ۝

If one is obliged by necessity
to eat it without intending to transgress,
or reverting to it, he is not guilty of sin;
for God is forgiving and kind.
174. Those who conceal any part of the Scriptures
that God has revealed, and thus make
a little profit thereby,
take nothing but fire as food;
and God will not turn to them on the Day of Resurrection,
nor nourish them for growth;
and their doom will be painful.

إِنَّ الَّذِينَ يَكْتُمُونَ مَا أَنزَلَ اللَّهُ مِنَ الْكِتَابِ وَ
يَشْتَرُونَ بِهِ ثَمَنًا قَلِيلًا أُولَٰئِكَ مَا يَأْكُلُونَ فِي
بُطُونِهِمْ إِلَّا النَّارَ وَلَا يُكَلِّمُهُمُ اللَّهُ يَوْمَ الْقِيَامَةِ وَ
لَا يُزَكِّيهِمْ وَلَهُمْ عَذَابٌ أَلِيمٌ ۝

175. They are those who bartered away
good guidance for error, and pardon for punishment:
How great is their striving for the Fire!

أُولَٰئِكَ الَّذِينَ اشْتَرَوُا الضَّلَالَةَ بِالْهُدَىٰ وَالْعَذَابَ
بِالْمَغْفِرَةِ ۚ فَمَا أَصْبَرَهُمْ عَلَى النَّارِ ۝

176. That is because God has revealed
the Book containing the truth;
but those who are at variance about it
have gone astray in their contrariness.

ذَٰلِكَ بِأَنَّ اللَّهَ نَزَّلَ الْكِتَابَ بِالْحَقِّ ۗ وَإِنَّ
الَّذِينَ اخْتَلَفُوا فِي الْكِتَابِ لَفِي شِقَاقٍ
بَعِيدٍ ۝

Piety does not lie in turning your face
to East or West:
Piety lies in believing in God,
the Last Day and the angels,
the Scriptures and the prophets,
and disbursing your wealth out of love for God
among your kin and the orphans,
the wayfarers and mendicants,
freeing the slaves, observing your devotional obligations,
and in paying the zakat and fulfilling a pledge you have given,
and being patient in hardship, adversity,
and times of peril.
These are the men who affirm the truth,
and they are those who follow the straight path.

لَيْسَ الْبِرَّ أَن تُوَلُّوا وُجُوهَكُمْ قِبَلَ الْمَشْرِقِ وَ
الْمَغْرِبِ وَلَٰكِنَّ الْبِرَّ مَنْ آمَنَ بِاللَّهِ وَالْيَوْمِ الْآخِرِ
وَالْمَلَائِكَةِ وَالْكِتَابِ وَالنَّبِيِّينَ وَآتَى الْمَالَ عَلَىٰ حُبِّهِ
ذَوِي الْقُرْبَىٰ وَالْيَتَامَىٰ وَالْمَسَاكِينَ وَابْنَ السَّبِيلِ
وَالسَّائِلِينَ وَفِي الرِّقَابِ وَأَقَامَ الصَّلَاةَ وَآتَى الزَّكَاةَ
وَالْمُوفُونَ بِعَهْدِهِمْ إِذَا عَاهَدُوا وَالصَّابِرِينَ فِي
الْبَأْسَاءِ وَالضَّرَّاءِ وَحِينَ الْبَأْسِ أُولَٰئِكَ الَّذِينَ
صَدَقُوا وَأُولَٰئِكَ هُمُ الْمُتَّقُونَ ۝

178. O believers, ordained for you is retribution
for the murdered,
(whether) a free man (is guilty)
of (the murder of) a free man, or a slave of a slave,
or a woman of a woman.
But he who is pardoned some of it* by his brother
should be dealt with equity,
and recompense (for blood) paid with a grace.
This is a concession from your Lord and a kindness.
He who transgresses in spite of it
shall suffer painful punishment.

يَا أَيُّهَا الَّذِينَ آمَنُوا كُتِبَ عَلَيْكُمُ الْقِصَاصُ فِي الْقَتْلَى
الْحُرُّ بِالْحُرِّ وَالْعَبْدُ بِالْعَبْدِ وَالْأُنثَىٰ بِالْأُنثَىٰ فَمَنْ
عُفِيَ لَهُ مِنْ أَخِيهِ شَيْءٌ فَاتِّبَاعٌ بِالْمَعْرُوفِ وَأَدَاءٌ
إِلَيْهِ بِإِحْسَانٍ ذَٰلِكَ تَخْفِيفٌ مِّن رَّبِّكُمْ وَرَحْمَةٌ
فَمَنِ اعْتَدَىٰ بَعْدَ ذَٰلِكَ فَلَهُ عَذَابٌ أَلِيمٌ ۝

---

* This does not refer to the punishment but blood-money. See 4:92.

179. In retribution there is life (and preservation).
O men of sense, you may haply take heed for yourselves.
180. It is ordained that when any one of you
nears death, and he owns goods and chattels,
he should bequeath them equitably
to his parents and next of kin.
This is binding on those who are upright and fear God.
181. And any one who changes the will, having heard it,
shall be guilty and accountable;
for God hears all and knows every thing.
182. He who suspects wrong or partialilty
on the part of the testator
and brings about a settlement,
does not incur any guilt,
for God is verily forgiving and merciful.

O believers, fasting is enjoined on you
as it was on those before you,
so that you might become righteous.
184. Fast a (fixed) number of days,
but if someone is ill or is travelling
(he should complete) the number of days (he had missed);
and those who find it hard to fast
should expiate by feeding a poor person.
For the good they do with a little harship is better for men.
And if you fast it is good for you,
if you knew.
185. Ramadan is the month in which the Qur'an was revealed
as guidance to man and clear proof of the guidance,
and criterion (of falsehood and truth).
So when you see the new moon you should fast the whole
        month;
but a person who is ill or travelling
(and fails to do so) should fast on other days,
as God wishes ease and not hardship for you,
so that you complete the (fixed) number (of fasts),
and give glory to God
for the guidance, and be grateful.
186. When My devotees enquire of you about Me,
I am near, and answer the call
of every supplicant when he calls.
It behoves them to hearken to Me
and believe in Me
that they may follow the right path.
187. You are allowed to sleep with your wives
on the nights of the fast:

They are your dress as you are theirs.
God is aware you were cheating yourselves,
so He turned to you and pardoned you.
So now you may have intercourse with them,
and seek what God has ordained for you.
Eat and drink until the white thread
of dawn appears clear from the dark line,
then fast until the night falls;
and abstain from your wives (when you have decided)
to stay in the mosques for assiduous devotion.
These are the bounds fixed by God,
so keep well within them.
So does God make His signs clear to men
that they may take heed for themselves.
188. And do not consume each other's wealth in vain,
nor offer it to men in authority with intent
of usurping unlawfully and knowingly
a part of the wealth of others.

They ask you of the new moons.
Say: "These are periods set for men (to reckon) time,
and for pilgrimage."
Piety does not lie in entering the house through the back
    door,*
for the pious man is he who follows the straight path.
Enter the house through the main gate,**
and obey God. You may haply find success.
190. Fight those in the way of God who fight you,
but do not be aggressive:
God does not like aggressors.
191. And fight those (who fight you) wheresoever you find
    them,
and expel them from the place
they had turned you out from.
Oppression is worse than killing.
Do not fight them by the Holy Mosque
unless they fight you there.
If they do, then slay them:
Such is the requital for unbelievers.
192. But if they desist, God is forgiving and kind.

----

* It means the same thing as is meant by the English expression 'through the back door,' i.e. clandestinely. Here it has more than one implication, as the verse deals with the new moon and reckoning "periods," e.g. the period of fasting, a woman's monthly courses, etc.

** That is, seek attainment through the right way. See Razi and Lane.

Al-Baqarah   34

193. Fight them till sedition comes to end,
and the law of God (prevails).
If they desist, then cease to be hostile,
except against those who oppress.

194. (Fighting during) the holy month
(if the sanctity) of the holy month (is violated)
is (just) retribution.
So if you are oppressed,
oppress those who oppress you to the same degree,
and fear God, and know that God
is with those who are pious
and follow the right path.

195. Spend in the way of God,
and do not seek destruction at your own hands.
So do good;
for God loves those who do good.

196. Perform the pilgrimage and holy visit ('Umra, to Makkah)
in the service of God.
But if you are prevented, send an offering
which you can afford as sacrifice,
and do not shave your heads until
the offering has reached the place of sacrifice.
But if you are sick or have ailment of the scalp
(preventing the shaving of hair),
then offer expiation by fasting
or else giving alms or a sacrificial offering.
When you have security, then those of you who wish
to perform the holy visit along with the pilgrimage,
should make a sacrifice according to their means.
But he who has nothing,
should fast for three days during the pilgrimage
and seven on return, completing ten.
This applies to him whose family does not live
near the Holy Mosque.
Have fear of God, and remember that God
is severe in punishment.

Known are the months of pilgrimage.
If one resolves to perform the pilgrimage in these months,
let him not indulge in concupiscence, sin or quarrel.
And the good you do shall be known to God.
Provide for the journey,
and the best of provisions is piety.
O men of understanding, obey Me.

198. It is no sin to seek the favours of your Lord (by trading).
When you start from 'Arafat in a concourse,

remember God at the monument that is sacred
(al-Mash'ar al-haram),
and remember Him as He has shown you the way,
for in the olden days you were a people astray.
199. Then move with the crowd impetuously,
and pray God to forgive you your sins.
God is surely forgiving and kind.
200. When you have finished the rites and ceremonies,
remember God as you do your fathers,
in fact with a greater devotion.
There are some who say:
"Give us, O Lord, in the world;"
but they will forego their share in the life to come.
201. But some there are who pray:
"Give us of good in the world, O Lord,
and give us of good in the life to come,
and suffer us not to suffer the torment of Hell."
202. They are those who will surely have their share
of whatsoever they have earned;
for God is swift at the reckoning.
203. Remember God during the stated days;
but if a person comes away after two days,
it will not be a sin; and if one tarries,
he will not transgress, if he keep away from evil.
Follow the law of God, and remember
that you will have to gather before Him in the end.
204. There is a man who talks well
of the world to your pleasing,
and makes God witness to what is in his heart,
yet he is the most contentious;
205. For when his back is turned
he goes about spreading disorder in the land,
destroying fields and flocks;
but God does not love disorder.
206. Whenever he is told: "Obey God,"
his arrogance leads him to more sin;
and sufficient for him shall be Hell:
How evil a place of wide expanse!
207. And there is a man who is willing to sell
even his soul to win the favour of God;
and God is compassionate to His creatures.
208. O believers, come to full submission to God.
Do not follow in the footsteps of Satan
your acknowledged foe.
209. If you falter even after Our signs
have reached you, then do not forget

Al-Baqarah

that God is all-powerful and all-wise.
210. Are they waiting for God to appear
in the balconies of clouds
with a host of angels,
and the matter to be settled?
But all things rest
with God in the end.

Ask the children of Israel
how many a clear sign We had given them.
But if one changes the favour of God
after having received it, then remember,
God is severe in revenge.
212. Enamoured are the unbelievers
of the life of this world,
and scoff at the faithful.
But those who keep from evil and follow the straight path
will have a higher place than they
on the Day of Reckoning;
for God gives in measure without number
whomsoever He will.
213. Men belonged to a single community,
and God sent them messengers
to give them happy tidings and warnings,
and sent the Book with them containing the truth
to judge between them in matters of dispute;
but only those who received it differed
after receiving clear proofs,
on account of waywardness
(and jealousies) among them.
Then God by His dispensation showed those who believed
the way to the truth about which they were differing;
for God shows whom He please
the path that is straight.
214. Do you think you will find your way to Paradise
even though you have not known
what the others before you have gone through?
They had suffered affliction and loss,
and were shaken and tossed about
so that even the Apostle
had to cry out with his followers:
"When will the help of God arrive?"
Remember, the help of God is ever at hand.
215. They ask you of what they should give in charity.
Tell them: "What you can spare of your wealth
as should benefit the parents, the relatives,

the orphans, the needy, the wayfarers,
for God is not unaware of the good deeds that you do.''
216. Enjoined on you is fighting,
and this you abhor.
You may dislike a thing
yet it may be good for you;
or a thing may haply please you
but may be bad for you.
Only God has knowledge, and you do not know.

They ask you of war in the holy month.
Tell them: "To fight in that month is a great sin.
But a greater sin in the eyes of God
is to hinder people from the way of God,
and not to believe in Him,
and to bar access to the Holy Mosque
and turn people out of its precincts;
and oppression is worse than killing.
They will always seek war against you
till they turn you away from your faith, if they can.
But those of you who turn back on their faith
and die disbelieving
will have wasted their deeds
in this world and the next.
They are inmates of Hell,
and shall there abide for ever.
218. Surely those who believe,
and those who leave their homes
and fight in the way of God,
may hope for His benevolence,
for God is forgiving and kind.
219. They ask you of (intoxicants,) wine and gambling.
Tell them: "There is great enervation though profit in them*
for men; but their enervation is greater than benefit.
And they ask you what they should give.
Tell them: "The utmost you can spare."
So does God reveal His signs: You may haply reflect
220. On this world and the next.
And they ask you about the orphans.
Tell them: "Improving their lot is much better; and if
you take interest in their affairs, they are your brethren;
and God is aware who are corrupt and who are honest;
and if He had pleased

---

* The basic meaning of *ithm* is enervation (*Taj* and Ibn Faris) of which the wine of Paradise is free:
52:23.

He could surely have imposed on you hardship,
for God is all-powerful and all-wise.
221. Do not marry idolatrous women
unless they join the faith.
A maid servant who is a believer
is better than an idolatress
even though you may like her.
And do not marry your daughters to idolaters
until they accept the faith.
A servant who is a believer is better than an idolater
even though you may like him.
They invite you to Hell, but God
calls you to Paradise and pardon by His grace.
And He makes His signs manifest that men
may haply take heed.

They ask you about menstruation.
Tell them: "This is a period of stress.
So keep away from women in this state
till they are relieved of it.
When they are free of it, you may go to them
as God has enjoined.
For God loves those who seek pardon,
and those who are clean."
223. Women are like fields for you;
so seed them as you intend,
but plan the future in advance.
And fear God, and remember,
you have to face Him in the end.
So convey glad tidings to those who believe.
224. Do not implicate God in your oaths
to avoid doing good and being pious
and keeping peace among men,
for God hears all and knows every thing.
225. God will not call you to account
for that which is senseless in your oaths,
but only for what is in your hearts;
for God is forgiving and forbearing.
226. Those who swear to keep away from their wives
(with intent of divorcing them)
have four months of grace;
then if they reconcile (during this period),
surely God is forgiving and kind.
227. And if they are bent on divorce,
God hears all and knows every thing.
228. Women who are divorced have to wait

البقرة ٢ سيقول ٢

for three monthly periods,
and if they believe in God and the Last Day
they must not hide unlawfully
what God has formed within their wombs.
Their husbands would do well
to take them back in that case,
if they wish to be reconciled.
Women also have recognised rights as men have,
though men have an edge over them.
But God is all-mighty and all-wise.

Divorce is (revokable) two times (after pronouncement),
after which (there are two ways open for husbands),
either (to) keep (the wives) honourably,
or part with them in a decent way.
You are not allowed to take away the least
of what you have given your wives,
unless both of you fear that you
would not be able to keep within the limits set by God.
If you fear you cannot maintain the bounds fixed by God,
there will be no blame on either if the woman redeems herself.
Do not exceed the limits of God,
for those who exceed the bounds set by God
are transgressors.

230. If a man divorces her again (a third time), she becomes
unlawful for him (and he cannot remarry her) until
she has married another man.
Then if he divorces her there is no harm
if the two unite again if they think
they will keep within the bounds set by God
and made clear for those who understand.

231. When you have divorced your wives,
and they have reached the end of the period of waiting,
then keep them honourably (by revoking the divorce),
or let them go with honour,
and do not detain them with the intent of harassing
lest you should transgress.
He who does so will wrong himself.
Do not mock the decrees of God,
and remember the favours God has bestowed on you,
and revealed to you the Book and the Law
to warn you of the consequences of doing wrong.
Have fear of God, and remember,
God is cognisant of every thing.

When you have divorced your wives

and they have completed the fixed term (of waiting),
do not stop them from marrying other men
if it is agreed between them honourably.
This warning is for those among you who believe
in God and the Last Day.
This is both proper and right for you,
for God knows and you do not know.

233. The mothers should suckle their babies for a period
of two years for those (fathers) who wish
that they should complete the suckling,
in which case they should feed them
and clothe them in a befitting way;
but no soul should be compelled beyond capacity,
neither the mother made to suffer for the child
nor the father for his offspring.
The same holds good for the heir of the father (if he dies).
If they wish to wean the child by mutual consent
there is no harm.
And if you wish to engage a wet nurse you may do so
if you pay her an agreed amount as is customary.
But fear God, and remember
that God sees all that you do.

234. Wives of men who die among you should wait
(after their husbands' death) for four months and ten days;
and when the term is over there is no sin
if they do what they like with themselves honourably,
for God is aware of all that you do.

235. There is no harm in proposing in secret
to (any of) these women,
or keeping the intention to yourself:
God is aware that you will keep them in mind.
Yet do not make a promise in secret,
unless you speak in a manner that is proper;
and do not resolve upon marriage
till the fixed term of waiting is over.
Remember that God knows what is in your hearts;
so be fearful of Him, and remember
that God is forgiving and forbearing.

There is no sin in divorcing your wives
before the consummation of marriage
or settling the dowry;
but then provide adequately for them,
the affluent according to their means,
the poor in accordance with theirs as is befitting.
This is surely the duty of those who do good.

237. And if you divorce them
before the consummation of marriage,
but after settling the dowry,
then half the settled dowry must be paid, unless
the woman forgoes it, or the person
who holds the bond of marriage pays the full amount.
And if the man pays the whole, it is nearer to piety.
But do not forget to be good to each other,
and remember that God sees all that you do.
238. Be wakeful of your service of prayer,
and the midmost service;
and honour God by standing before Him in devotion.
239. If you fear (war or danger), pray while standing
or on horseback; but when you have safety again
remember God, for He taught you what you did not know.
240. Those among you about to die leaving wives behind,
should bequeath a year's maintenance and lodging for them,
without expelling them from home. But if they leave
(of their own accord), you will not be blamed
for what they do with themselves in their own rights.
God is all-mighty and all-wise.
241. Making a fair provision for women who are divorced
is the duty of those who are God-fearing and pious.*
242. So does God pronounce His decrees
that you may understand.

Have you never thought of men
who went out of their homes as a measure of safety against
        death,
and they were thousands,
to whom God said: "Die," then restored them to life?**
Indeed God bestows His blessings on men;
only most men are not grateful.
244. Fight in the way of God, and remember
that God hears all and knows every thing.
245. Who will give a goodly loan to God
which He might double many times?
For God withholds and enlarges, and to Him you will return.
246. Have you thought of the elders of Israel
after Moses, and how they said to their apostle:
"Set up a king for us, then we shall fight
in the way of God?" He replied: "This too is possible
that when commanded to fight you may not fight at all."

---

* See 33:28, where the prophet is commanded to provide his wives handsomely on divorce.
** 'Die' here refers to moral death, and 'life' to regeneration.

They said: "How is it we should not fight
in the way of God when we
have been driven from our homes
and deprived of our sons?"
But when they were ordered to fight they turned away,
except for a few;
yet God knows the sinners.
247. And when their prophet said to them:
"God has raised Saul king over you,"
they said: "How can he be king
over us when we
have greater right to kingship than he,
for he does not even possess abundant wealth?"
"God has chosen him in preference to you," said the prophet
"and given him much more wisdom and prowess; and God
gives authority to whomsoever He will:
God is infinite and all-wise."
248. Their prophet said to them:
"The sign of his kingship will be that you will come to have
a heart* full of peace and tranquility from your Lord
and the legacy left by Moses' and Aaron's family
supported by angels.
This shall be a token for you
if you really believe."

When Saul led his armies, he said:
"God will test you by a stream.
Whoever drinks its water will not be of me;
but those who do not drink shall be on my side.
The only exception will be those
who scoop up a palmful of water with their hands."
And but for a few they all drank of its water.
When they had crossed it,
and those who believed with him,
they said: "We have no strength
to combat Goliath and his forces today.
But those who believed they have to face their Lord,
said: "Many a time has a small band defeated
a large horde by the will of God.
God is with those who are patient (and persevere)."

---

* The word *tabut* has generally been translated as 'ark', being taken, perhaps under Rabbinical influences, for the Ark of the Covenant mentioned in the Old Testament of the Bible. Raghib, however, says it also means 'heart' and 'breast'. *Lisan al-'Arab* supports this view, and Zamakhshari and Baidawi also offer this meaning. The context and the next two verses (249 and 250) bear out the validity of adopting this translation.

تلك الرسل ٣   البقرة ٢

250. And when they were facing Goliath and his hordes
they prayed: "O Lord, give us endurance and steady our steps,
and help us against the deniers of truth."
251. By the will of God they defeated them,
and David killed Goliath,
and God gave him kingship and wisdom,
and taught him whatsoever He pleased.
If God did not make men deter one another
this earth would indeed be depraved.
But gracious is God to the people of the world.
252. These are the messages of God.
We recite them to you in all truth,
as indeed you are one of the apostles.
253. Of all these apostles
We have favoured some over the others.
God has addressed some of them,
and the stations of some have been exalted over the others.
And to Jesus, son of Mary, We gave tokens,
and reinforced him with divine grace.
If God had so willed
those who came after them would never have contended
when clear signs had come to them.
But dissensions arose,
some believed, some denied.
And if God had willed
they would never have fought among themselves.
But God does whatsoever He please.

O believers, expend
of what We have given you
before the day arrives
on which there will be no barter,
and no friendship or intercession matter,
and those who are disbelievers will be sinners.
255. God: There is no god but He,
the living, eternal, self-subsisting, ever sustaining.
Neither does somnolence affect Him nor sleep.
To Him belongs all
that is in the heavens and the earth;
and who can intercede with Him except by His leave?
Known to Him is all that is present before men
and what is hidden
(in time past and time future),
and not even a little of His knowledge can they grasp
except what He will.
His seat extends over heavens and the earth,

and He tires not protecting them:
He alone is all high and supreme.
256. There is no compulsion in matter of faith.
Distinct is the way of guidance now from error.
He who turns away from the forces of evil
and believes in God, will surely hold fast
to a handle that is strong and unbreakable,
for God hears all and knows every thing.
257. God is the friend of those who believe,
and leads them out of darkness into light;
but the patrons of infidels are idols and devils
who lead them from light into darkness.
They are the residents of Hell,
and will there for ever abide.

Have you thought of the man who argued
with Abraham about his Lord because
God had given him a kingdom? When Abraham said:
"My Lord is the giver of life and death," he replied:
"I am the giver of life and death."
And Abraham said: "God makes the sun rise from the East;
so you make it rise from the West,"
and dumbfounded was the infidel.
God does not guide those who are unjust.
259. Or take the man who passed by a town
which lay destroyed upside down. He said:
"How can God restore this city now that it is destroyed?"
So God made him die for a hundred years,
then brought him back to life, and inquired:
"How long did you stay in this state?"
"A day or less than a day," he replied.
"No," He said, "you were dead a hundred years,
yet look at your victuals, they have not decomposed;
and look at your ass!
We shall make you a warning for men.
And regard the bones, how We raise them
and clothe them with flesh."
When this became clear to him, the man said:
"Indeed God has power over all things."
260. Remember, when Abraham said: "O Lord,
show me how you raise the dead,"
He said: "What! Do you not believe?"
"I do," answered Abraham. "I only ask for my heart's
          assurance."
(The Lord) said: "Trap four birds and tame them,
then put each of them

Al-Baqarah

on a (separate) hill, and call them,
and they will come flying to you.
Know that God is all-powerful and all-wise."

The semblance of those who expend
their wealth in the way of God
is that of a grain of corn
from which grow seven ears,
each ear containing a hundred grains.
Truly God increases for whomsoever He will,
for God is infinite and all-wise.
262. Those who spend in the way of God,
and having spent do not boast or give pain
(by word or deed),
will get their reward from their Lord,
and will neither have fear nor regret.
263. Saying a word that is kind, and forgiving
is better than charity that hurts.
(Do not forget that) God is affluent and kind.
264. O believers, do not nullify your charity
by giving to oblige and flaunting (your favours)
like a man who spends of his wealth
only to show off,
but does not believe in God and the Last Day.
His semblance is that of a rock covered with earth
which is washed away by rain
exposing the hard rock bare. So they gain
nothing from their earnings.
God does not guide a people who do not believe.
265. But the semblance of those who expend
their wealth to please God
with firm and resolute hearts,
is like a garden on a height
on which the rain falls and it yields
its fruits twice as much;
and even if the rain does not fall
the dew will suffice.
For God sees all that you do.
266. Does any of you wish to have an orchard
full of date-palm trees and vines,
and streams of running water and fruits of all kinds,
and then old age should overtake him
while his children are small,
and a scorching whirlwind
should smite and burn it down?
Thus God makes His signs clear to you

that you may reflect.

O believers, give in charity what is good
of the things you have earned,
and of what you produce from the earth;
and do not choose to give what is bad as alms,
that is, things you would not like to accept yourself
except with some condescension.
Remember that God is affluent and praiseworthy.
268. Satan threatens you with want,
and orders you (to commit) shameful acts.
But God promises His pardon and grace,
for God is bounteous and all-knowing.
269. He gives wisdom whomsoever He please;
and those who are bestowed wisdom
get good in abundance.
Yet none remembers this save men of wisdom.
270. Whatsoever you give away in alms or vow as offering,
is all known to God;
but the wicked will have none to help them.
271. If you give alms openly, it is well;
but if you do it secretly and give
to the poor, that is better.
This will absolve you of some of your sins;
and God is cognisant of all you do.
272. It is not for you to guide them:
God guides whom He will.
Whatever you spend you will do so for yourself,
for you will do so to seek the way that leads to God;
and what you spend in charity
you will get back in full,
and no wrong will be done to you.
273. (Give to) the needy who are engaged
in the service of God
who are not able to move about in the land,
whom the ignorant consider to be affluent
as they refrain from asking.
You can know them from their faces
for they do not ask of men importunately.
God is surely cognisant of good things that you spend.

Those who spend of their wealth in the way of God,
day and night, in secret or openly,
have their reward with their Lord,
and have nothing to fear or regret.
275. Those who live on usury will not rise (on Doomsday)

but like a man possessed of the devil and demented.
This because they say
that trading is like usury.*⟩
But trade has been sanctioned and usury forbidden by God.
Those who are warned by their Lord and desist
will keep (what they have taken of interest) already,
and the matter will rest with God.
But those who revert to it again
are the residents of Hell
where they will abide for ever.

276. God takes away (gain) from usury,
but adds (profit) to charity;
and God does not love the ungrateful and sinners.

277. Those who believe and do good deeds,
and fulfil their devotional obligations and pay the zakat,
have their reward with their Lord,
and will have neither fear nor regret.

278. O believers, fear God and forego
the interest that is owing,
if you really believe.

279. If you do not, beware
of war on the part of God and His Apostle.
But if you repent, you shall keep your principal.
Oppress none and no one will oppress you.

280. If a debtor is in want, give him time until
his circumstances improve; but if you forego (the debt)
as charity, that will be to your good,
if you really understand.

281. Have fear of the day when you go back to God.
Then each will be paid back in full his reward,
and no one will be wronged.

O believers, when you negotiate a debt
for a fixed term**, draw up an agreement in writing,
though better it would be
to have a scribe write it faithfully down;
and no scribe should refuse to write as God has taught him,
and write what the borrower dictates,
and have fear of God, his Lord, and not leave out a thing.
If the borrower is deficient of mind or infirm,
or unable to explain, let the guardian explain judiciously;
and have two of your men to act as witnesses; but if two men
are not available, then a man and two women you approve,**

---

* For *riba* see note 1 on page 50.
** See note 2 on page 50.

so that in case one of them is confused the other may prompt
    her.
When the witnesses are summoned they should not refuse (to
    come).
But do not neglect to draw up a contract, big or small,
with the time fixed for paying back the debt.
This is more equitable in the eyes of God,
and better as evidence and best for avoiding doubt.
But if it is a deal about some merchandise
requiring transaction face to face,
there is no harm if no (contract is drawn up) in writing.
Have witnesses to the deal, (and make sure)
that the scribe or the witness is not harmed.
If he is, it would surely be sinful on your part.
And have fear of God,
for God gives you knowledge,
and God is aware of every thing.
283. If you are on a journey and cannot find a scribe,
pledge your goods (against the Loan);
and if one trusts the other,
then let him who is trusted
deliver the thing entrusted,
and have fear of God, his Lord.
Do not suppress any evidence,
for he who conceals evidence is sinful of heart;
and God is aware of all you do.

To God belongs all
that is in the heavens and the earth;
and whether you reveal
what is in your heart or conceal it,
you will have to account for it to God
who will pardon whom He please and punish whom He will,
for God has the power over all things.
285. The Prophet believes
in what has been revealed to him by his Lord,
and so do the faithful.
Each one believes
in God and His angels, His Books and the prophets,
and We make no distinction between the apostles.
For they say: "We hear and obey, and we seek
Your forgiveness, O Lord,
for to You we shall journey in the end."
286. God does not burden a soul beyond capacity.
Each will enjoy what (good) he earns,
as indeed each will suffer from (the wrong) he does.

Punish us not, O Lord, if we fail to remember
or lapse into error.
Burden us not, O Lord, with a burden
as You did those before us.
Impose not upon us a burden, O Lord, we cannot carry.
Overlook our trespasses and forgive us,
and have mercy upon us;
You are our Lord and Master,
help us against the clan of unbelievers.

مَا اكْتَسَبَتْ رَبَّنَا لَا تُؤَاخِذْنَا إِن نَّسِينَا أَوْ أَخْطَأْنَا

رَبَّنَا وَلَا تَحْمِلْ عَلَيْنَا إِصْرًا كَمَا حَمَلْتَهُ عَلَى الَّذِينَ

مِن قَبْلِنَا رَبَّنَا وَلَا تُحَمِّلْنَا مَا لَا طَاقَةَ لَنَا بِهِ ۖ وَ

اعْفُ عَنَّا وَاغْفِرْ لَنَا وَارْحَمْنَا أَنتَ مَوْلَانَا

فَانصُرْنَا عَلَى الْقَوْمِ الْكَافِرِينَ ۩

Note on *Riba*, v. 275.
Riba (root RBW). *Raba, yarbu,* multiplying, increase, swell, expand (beyond the natural or original size), as in 22:5; excess such as surplus that comes to the surface like scum, as in 13:17; *rabiyun,* increased hold that overpowers, as in 69:10; *arba,* more than the other, as in 16:92: *Taj* and *Muhit.* All this points to unnatural or artificial increase. It is first mentioned in a Makki Surah, 30:39, as lending money on interest to increase one's capital through others' wealth; and is explained at 2:275 as the opposite of trade, and at 3:130 as doubling and redoubling. By suffocating a person's freedom of action and independence—another meaning of *riba* being asthma—it results in oppression, and is condemned in strongest possible terms and forbidden.

Since other possibilities of exploitative manipulations of people's needs and constraints exist, the word acquired a special significance in the Quranic order, so that its conceptual ramifications extend to other forms of lending and borrowing, even such as lending ten pounds of grain and demanding eleven on return. But today, in the clash of Islamic thought and Western practice, the word has become a subject of polemics, mainly through corruption in the process of translation. The Arabic of the Qur'an is pre-Quranic in its etymological and historical perspectives, and the sense of many words is altered when rendered in terms of modern Arabic. The same is true of the Bible where 'usury', the exact equivalent of *riba* in English, had originally, and formerly, meant "interest of any kind on money lent," has been changed, by accident or design, to mean "iniquitous or illegal interest on a loan," (Chambers 1901 edn.), and 'usurer' has been changed from its original Biblical sense of "money-lender for interest;" and altered in modern (American) versions of the Bible including that of King James Version of 1611 to "money-changer" as in Mark:11:15; or to "exchangers", as in Matthew: 25:27.

Note on verse 282
The verse deals with a special kind of monetary transaction, as the word *dain* signifies. Generally translated as 'debt' *dain* also means, as here, 'bill of hand', which would be called 'Letter of Credit' today. The conditions of an LC can be very tricky and complicated, and are often missed even by experienced businessmen and legal experts. That is why, perhaps, the Qur'an emphasises that the terms of the contract should be written down, preferably by a well-versed scribe, who would today be equivalent to a lawyer. There being no established courts of law at that time, the Qur'an suggests a further safeguard of having witnesses to the deal, namely, two men, and in case two men are not available, one man and two women of whom only one, in reality, is the witness, the other being just her helper *in case* she gets confused. That is why the role of the second woman is so clearly defined. These precautions have not been suggested in the case of a simple transaction face to face about merchandise, mentioned in the later part of the verse, and the simple way of pledging the goods against the loan is considered sufficient. The presence of two women does not mean that both are witnesses, or that the evidence of one woman is half of that of a man. In no other place in the Qur'an two women have been suggested as witnesses except here, because this is a case of a special transaction and women, not being adepts at business, were more likely to get confused than men.

3 The Family of Imrān

Al-ʿImrān: Madani

In the name of Allah, most benevolent, ever-merciful.

ALIF LĀM MĪM.
2. God: there is no god but He,
the living, eternal, self-subsisting, ever sustaining.
3. He has verily revealed to you this Book,
in truth and confirmation
of the Books revealed before,
as indeed He had revealed
the Torah and the Gospel
4. Before this as guidance for men,
and has sent the criterion (of falsehood and truth).
As for those who deny the signs of God,
the punishment is severe;
for God is all powerful and great His requital.
5. There is nothing in the earth and the heavens
that is hidden from God.
6. He shapes you in the womb
of the mother as He wills.
There is no god but He,
the all-mighty and all-wise.
7. He has sent down this Book which contains
some verses that are categorical
and basic to the Book,
and others allegorical.
But those who are twisted of mind
look for verses metaphorical,
seeking deviation
and giving to them interpretations of their own;
but none knows their meaning except God;
and those who are steeped in knowledge affirm:
"We believe in them as all of them are from the Lord."
But only those who have wisdom understand.
8. "Let us not go astray, O Lord,
having guided us already.
Bestow on us Your blessings

Al-ʿImrān

for You are the benevolent.
9. You will gather mankind together, O Lord,
on a day that is certain to come,
and God does not fail in His promise."

As for those who deny,
neither their wealth nor their children
will help them in the least against God.
They shall be but faggots for (the fire of) Hell,*
11. Like the people of the Pharoah,
and those before them, who rejected Our signs,
and were punished for their sins by God;
and the punishment of God is severe.
12. So tell the disbelievers:
"You will surely be subdued
and driven to Hell:
How bad a preparation!"
13. There was a token for you in the two armies
which clashed (in the battle of Badr),
one fighting for God, the other of unbelievers who saw
with their own eyes the faithful to be
two times as many as they,
for God reinforces with His help whomsoever He will.
In this is a lesson for those who have eyes.
14. Enamoured are the people
of the lust of (earthly) pleasures,
of women and of children
and hoarded heaps of gold and silver,
well-bred horses, and tilled land and cattle,
all (vain) goods and chattels of the life of this world,
while the best of abodes is with God.
15. Say: "Shall I tell you of (things) even better?
With the Lord are gardens with running streams of water
for those who keep from evil and follow the straight path,
where they will live unchanged
with the purest of companions and blessings of God."
And under God's eyes are devotees who say:
16. "O Lord, we believe;
forgive our trespasses and save us the torment of Hell."
17. They are the patient,
the sincere and devout, full of charity,
who pray for forgiveness in the hours of dawn.
18. God is witness there is no god but He,

----

* See note at the end of the Surah.

and so are the angels and men full of learning.
He is the upholder of justice.
There is no god but He,
the mighty and all-wise.
19. The true way with God is peace;
and the people of the Book did not differ
until knowledge (of this revelation) had come to them,
out of mutual opposition.
But those who deny the signs of God (should remember)
He is swift in the reckoning.
20. Even then if they argue, tell them:
"I have bowed in submission to God,
and so have my followers."
And tell the people of the Book and the Arabs:
"Do you submit?" If they do,
they will find the right path;
if they turn away,
your duty is to deliver the message.
And God keeps an eye on His votaries.

To those who deny the signs of God,
and slay the apostles unjustly,
and slay the upholders of justice,
give news of painful punishment.
22. Their good deeds will be wasted in this world
and in the next,
and none will they have to help them.
23. Have you not seen the people who have received
a part of Revelation who are called
to the Book of God that it may judge
(in their disputes) between them?
But some, being averse turn away,
24. For they say:
"The Fire will not touch us
for more than a few days."
They have been deceived by the lies
they have themselves fabricated,
and stray from their faith.
25. How shall it be when We gather them together
on a day that is certain to come,
when each will receive his reward
without (favour or) wrong?
26. Say: "O Lord of all dominions,
You give whom it pleases You the kingdom,
and You take away the power from whosoever You will;
You exalt whom You please and debase whom You will.

All goodness is Yours (entirely). Indeed
You have the power over all things.
27. You make the night succeed the day, the day succeed the
     night,
raise the living from the dead,
the dead from the living,
and give whomsoever You please,
and in measure without number."
28. Those who believe should not take unbelievers
as their friends
in preference to those who believe —
and whoever does so should have no (expectations) of God —
unless to safeguard yourselves against them.
But God commands you to beware of Him,
for to God you will journey in the end.
29. Say: "Whether you conceal or reveal
whatsoever is in your hearts
it is all known to God, as is known to Him all
that is in the heavens and the earth;
and God has the power over all things."
30. On the day when every man will find
whatever of good he has earned and of evil,
and is confronted with it, he shall wish
that a distance appeared
between him and that day —
(that it were far away).
God bids you beware of Him,
though compassionate is God to His votaries.

Say: "If you love God then follow me
that God may love you and forgive your faults;
for God is forgiving and kind."
32. Say: "Obey God and His Messenger;"
and if they refuse (then remember)
God does not love disbelievers.
33. God had chosen Adam and Noah and the families
of Abraham and 'Imran in preference to others.
34. They were descendants of one another;
and God hears all and knows every thing.
35. Remember, when the wife of 'Imran prayed: "O Lord,
I offer what I carry in my womb
in dedication to Your service, accept it,
for You hear all and know every thing."
36. And when she had given birth to the child, she said:
"O Lord, I have delivered but a girl."
— But God knew better what she had delivered:

A boy could not be as that girl was.
"I have named her Mary," (she said),
"and I give her into Your keeping.
Preserve her and her children
from Satan the ostracized."
37. Her Lord accepted her graciously,
and she grew up with excellence,
and was given into the care of Zachariah.
Whenever Zachariah came to see her
in the chamber,
he found her provided with food, and he asked:
"Where has this come from, O Mary?"
And she said: "From God who gives food in abundance
to whomsoever He will."
38. Then prayed Zachariah to his Lord:
"O Lord, bestow on me offspring,
virtuous and good,
for You answer all prayers."
39. Then the angels said to him
as he stood in the chamber at prayer:
"God sends you good tidings of John who will confirm
a thing from God
and be noble, continent, and a prophet,
and one of those who are upright and do good."
40. "How can I have a son, O Lord," he said,
"for I am old and my wife is barren?"
"Thus," came the answer; "God does as He wills."
41. And Zachariah said: "Give me a token, O Lord."
"The token will be," was the reply, "that you
will speak to no man for three days
except by signs; and remember your Lord much, and pray
at evening and sunrise."

The angels said: "O Mary, indeed God has favoured you
and made you immaculate, and chosen you
from all the women of the world.
43. So adore your Lord, O Mary, and pay homage
and bow with those who bow in prayer."
44. This is news of the Unknown
that We send you, for you were not there
when they cast lots with quills (to determine)
who should take care of Mary,
nor when they disputed it.
45. When the angels said: "O Mary,
God gives you news of a thing from Him, for rejoicing,
(news of one) whose name will be Messiah,

Jesus, son of Mary,
illustrious in this world and the next,
and one among the honoured,
46. Who will speak to the people when in the cradle▪
and when in the prime of life,
and will be among the upright and doers of good."
47. She said: "How can I have a son, O Lord,
when no man has touched me?" He said:
"That is how God creates what He wills.
When He decrees a thing, He says 'Be', and it is.
48. He will teach him the Law and the judgement,
and the Torah and the Gospel,
49. And he will be Apostle to the children of Israel, (saying:)
'I have come to you with a prodigy from your Lord
that I will fashion the state of destiny* out of mire for you,
and breathe (a new spirit) into it, and (you) will rise
by the will of God.
I will heal the blind and the leper**, and infuse
life into the dead, by the leave of God.
I will tell you what you devour
and what you hoard in your homes.
In this will be a portent for you if you do believe.
50. I (have come to) confirm the truth of the Torah
which was sent down before me,
and make certain things lawful
which have been forbidden until now;
and I come to you with a sign from your Lord;
so be fearful of God and follow me.
51. Surely God is my Lord, and your Lord,
so worship Him;
and this is the right path.' "
52. When Jesus perceived their unbelief he asked:

---

* Apart from 'bird' and other things, *tair* also means 'omen' as in 7:131, 27:47, 36:19, and 'actions'
or 'good or evil fate' – 'the register of deeds' – as in 17:13. It also means 'destiny' or 'fortune'. As
Apostle to the Jews at a time when their state was most deplorable (see verse 112 of this Surah),
Jesus instilled new life into them, and raised them up from the mire.
** The word used here is *abras,* one suffering from lukoderma, a disease that discolours the skin,
and not *judham,* leprosy, in which fingers and toes rot and drop off, the leper, unlike a person with
lukoderma being held in horror and shunned like an untouchable. It seems lukoderma has been
confused with leprosy under evangelical influences, and *abras* has been invariably translated as leper.
Metaphorically, however, leprosy means to have one misfortune added to another. See Duncan Forbes'
Hindustani-English Dictionary (London, 1866) under *korh,* leprosy. Ibn Faris says that *al-biras* means
'barren portions of the desert', whence the metaphorical meaning of misfortune.
The Qur'an compares moral crimes to diseases, and calls those guilty of them 'deaf, dumb and
blind' as in 2:18, and 'diseased of heart' as in 2:10, and even 'dead' as in 27:80. That is why the Scripture
is called 'a healing' as in 41:44. The meanings of blind, leper and dead have, therefore, to be taken
in their metaphorical sense and not literally. ▪ For v. 46, see note on p. 261.

Al-'Imran   56

"Who will help me in the way of God?"
"We," the disciples answered,
"shall be the helpers of God.
We believe in God; and you be our witness
that we submit and obey.
53. O Lord, we believe in Your revelations
and follow this Apostle.
Enroll us among the witnesses."
54. But they (the unbelievers) contrived a plot,
and God did the like;
and God's plan is the best.

When God said: "O Jesus, I will take you to Myself
and exalt you, and rid you of the infidels,
and hold those who follow you
above those who disbelieve till the Day of Resurrection.
You have then to come back to Me
when I will judge between you
in what you were at variance." *
56. Those who are infidels
will surely receive severe punishment
both in this world and the next;
and none will they have to help (or save) them.
57. But those who believe and do good deeds
shall be given their recompense in full;
but God does not love the unjust.
58. These verses that We read to you
are signs and reminder full of wisdom.
59. For God the likeness of Jesus is as that of Adam
whom He fashioned out of dust and said "Be" and he was.
60. This is the truth from your Lord,
so do not be in doubt.
61. Tell those who dispute this with you
even after the knowledge that has reached you:
"Come, let us gather our sons and your sons,
our women and your women, ourselves and yourselves,
and pray and solicit God to condemn those who lie."
62. And this verily is the true account.
There is no god but God,
and God is all-mighty and all-wise.
63. If they turn away (remember)
God knows the mischief-mongers.

Tell them: "O people of the Book,

----

* The reference is, to dissensions among the Jewish people, such as the Essenes and the Jews in general.

let us come to an agreement
on that which is common between us,
that we worship no one but God,
and make none His compeer,
and that none of us take any others
for lord apart from God."
If they turn away you tell them:
"Bear witness that we submit to Him."
65. O people of the Book,
why dispute about Abraham?
The Torah and the Gospel
were sent down after him:
Do you not understand?
66. Remember you are those
who disputed the things you knew;
so wherefore dispute about things you do not know?
And God has the knowledge, while you do not know.
67. Neither was Abraham a Jew nor a Christian,
but upright and obedient, and not an idolater.
68. Of all men the nearest to Abraham are those
who follow him, and then this Prophet and the faithful;
and God is the protector of all believers.
69. Some among the people of the Book
wish to lead you astray,
yet they lead none astray but themselves,
though they do not realise.
70. O people of the Book,
why do you disbelieve
the signs of God having witnessed them yourselves?
71. O people of the Book,
why do you mix the false with the true,
and hide the truth knowingly?

A section of the people of the Book say:
"Believe in the morning what has been
revealed to the faithful,
and deny in the evening;
they might perhaps turn back;
73. And do not believe those who do not belong to your
    faith."
Say: "True guidance is the guidance of God —
that any may be given
the like of what has been given you."
Will they argue with you before your Lord?
Say: "God's is the bounty. He gives whomsoever He please,
for He is infinite and all-wise."

Al-'Imran

74. He may choose whom He likes for His favours,
for great is His bounty.
75. There are some among the people of the Book
who return a whole treasure entrusted to them;
yet some there are who do not give back a dinar
until you demand and insist,
because they say: "It is not a sin for us
to (usurp) the rights of the Arabs."
Yet they lie against God, and they know it.
76. But certainly whoever keeps his promise
and follows the right path (will be blessed),
for God loves those who shun evil and follow the right course.
77. Those who trade on the promises of God,
and who purchase a little gain from their oaths,
will have no share in the life to come.
God will not address or even regard them
on the Day of Resurrection, nor perfect them,
and their suffering will be painful.
78. Among them is a section which distorts in reading
the Scripture in a way that though
it sounds like the Scripture, in fact it is not;
yet they say it is from God, when they know it is not;
and they lie about God, and knowingly.
79. It is not for a mortal to whom God reveals
the Book and the judgement and the prophethood
to say to the people: "Be my votaries instead of God's,"
but (to say): "Become learned in divine law,
by virtue of teaching and studying the Book."
80. He will surely not bid you make the angels and the
prophets
your lords. Would he order you disbelief
after you have submitted (and accepted the law of God)?

Remember when God covenanted the prophets (and
said):
"If after I have given you the Law and the judgement
there comes an apostle to you who confirms
the truth already with you,
you will surely believe him and help him;"
and asked: "Do you accept and agree
to the terms of My covenant?"
They said: "We accept."
"Then you be witness," said God,
"and I shall be witness with you.
82. Then any one who turns away
will be a transgressor."

83. Do they seek another way than God's?
But whosoever is in the heavens and the earth
is submissive to God and obedient (to Him),
by choice or constraint,
and will be returned to Him.
84. Say: "We believe in God,
and in what has been revealed to us,
and in what had been sent down
to Abraham and Ishmael
and Isaac and Jacob and their offspring,
and what had been revealed
to Moses and to Jesus
and to all other prophets by their Lord.
We make no distinction between them,
and we submit to Him and obey."
85. And whoever seeks a way
other than submission to God,
it will not be accepted from him,
and he will be a loser in the world to come.
86. How can God show the way to those who,
having come to faith, turned away,
even though they had borne witness
that the Messenger was true,
and the clear signs had reached them?
God does not show the unrighteous the way.
87. For such the requital is the curse of God
and the angels and of men.
88. They shall live under it,
and none of their agony decrease
nor be respite for them.
89. But those who repent and reform,
God is surely forgiving and merciful.
90. Those who deny, having once come to faith,
and persist in denial, will not have
their repentance accepted,
for they have gone astray.
91. From those who deny and die disbelieving
will never be accepted an earthful of gold
if proferred by them as ransom.
For them is grievous punishment,
and none will help them.

Y ou will never come to piety unless
you spend of things you love;
and whatever you spend is known to God.
93. To the children of Israel was lawful all food

except what Israel forbade himself
before the Torah was revealed.
Say: "Bring the Torah and recite it,
if what you say is true."
94. And anyone who fabricates lies about God even after this
is wicked indeed.
95. Say: "God has veritably spoken the truth.
So now follow the way of Abraham
the upright, who was not of idolaters."
96. The first House of God to be set up for men
was at Bakkah the blessed,
a guidance for the people of the world.
97. It contains clear signs, and the spot
where Abraham had stood.
And anyone who enters it
will find security.
And whosoever can afford should visit the House
on a pilgrimage as duty to God.
Whosoever denies, should remember
that God is independent of the peoples of the world.
98. Say: "O people of the Book,
why do you reject the word of God
when God is a witness to all that you do?"
99. Then say: "O people of the Book,
why do you turn the believers away
from the path of God,
looking for obliquities in the way
when you are witness to it?
And God is aware of all that you do."
100. O believers, if you follow
what some of the people of the Book say,
it will turn you into unbelievers
even after you have come to belief.
101. And how can you disbelieve? To you
are being recited the messages of God,
and His Prophet is among you.
And whosoever holds fast to God
shall verily be guided to the path that is straight.

O believers, fear God as He should be feared,
and do not die but submitting (to Him).
103. Hold on firmly together to the rope of God,
and be not divided among yourselves, and remember
the favours God bestowed on you
when you were one another's foe
and He reconciled your hearts,

and you turned into brethren through His grace.
You had stood on the edge of a pit of fire
and He saved you from it, thus revealing
to you His clear signs
that you may find the right way perchance.
104. So let there be a body among you
who may call to the good,
enjoin what is esteemed
and forbid what is odious.
They are those who will be successful.
105. So be not like those who became disunited
and differed among themselves
after clear proofs had come to them.
For them is great suffering.
106. On the Day when some faces would be bright,
and some others will be black (with despair),
those with black faces (will be told):
"Having come to the faith you denied it;
now taste therefore the penalty for you disbelieved."
107. And those with bright faces
shall be under God's grace
and enjoy it for ever.
108. These are the commandments of God
We recite to you verily;
God does not wish
injustice to the creatures of the world.
109. For to God belongs all
that is in the heavens and the earth,
and to God do all things return.

Of all the communities raised among men you are the
     best,
enjoining the good, forbidding the wrong,
and believing in God.
If the people of the Book
had come to believe it was best for them;
but only some believe, and transgressors are many.
111. They will do you no harm but annoyance;
and if they fight you they will only turn their backs,
then no help will reach them.
112. Degraded they shall live wheresoever they be
unless they make an alliance with God and alliance with men,
for they have incurred the anger of God,
and misery overhangs them.
That is because
they denied the signs of God

Al-'Imran

and killed the prophets unjustly,
and rebelled, and went beyond the limit.
113. Yet all of them are not alike.
Among the people of the Book is a section upright, who recite
the scriptures in the hours of the night
and bow in adoration and pray,
114. And believe in God and the Last Day,
and enjoin what is good
and forbid what is wrong,
and who hasten to give in charity:
they are among the upright and the doers of good.
115. And the good they do will not go unaccepted;
for God is aware of those who keep away from evil.
116. As for those who disbelieve,
neither wealth nor children
will avail them in the least against God.
They are the residents of Hell
where they will live for ever.
117. What they spend in the life of this world
is like a frosty wind which smites and destroys
the crops of a people who had wronged themselves.
God did not wrong them,
they wronged themselves.
118. O believers, do not make others except your own people
your confidants.
They will spare no effort to ruin you:
They surely desire your annihilation.
Hate is on their tongues,
and what they hide in their hearts is worse.
We have shown you the signs if you have sense.
119. Just think! You hold them as your friends
but they do not,
even though you believe in all the Scriptures.
When they meet you they say: "We believe;"
but when they are alone
they bite their fingers in rage.
Say: "Die of your rage. God is aware
of the secrets of the hearts."
120. If good comes your way, they are vexed;
but if evil befalls you they are pleased and rejoice;
yet if you are patient
and guard yourselves against evil,
their cunning will not harm you in the least,
for whatsoever they do
is well within the reach of God.

Al-'Imran

Remember when you set forth in the morning from
   your house
assigning the faithful positions for the battle,
God heard everything and knew all.
122. When two of your bands were about to lose heart
God befriended them;
and in Him should the faithful place their trust.
123. For God had helped you during the Battle of Badr
at a time when you were helpless.
So act in compliance with the laws of God;
you may well be grateful.
124. Remember when you said to the faithful:
"Is it not sufficient that your Lord
should send for your help
three thousand angels from the heavens?
125. Indeed if you are patient and take heed for yourselves,
and the (enemy) come rushing at you suddenly
your Lord will send even five thousand angels
on chargers sweeping down."
126. And God did not do so but as good tidings for you,
and to reassure your hearts —
for victory comes from God alone,
the all-mighty and all-wise —
127. In order that He may cut off a part of unbelievers
or overthrow them, and they turn back in frustration.
128. You have no say in the matter
if He pardon them or punish them,
for they are unjust.
129. To God belongs all
that is in the heavens and the earth:
He may pardon whom He please
and punish whom He will.
Yet God is forgiving and kind.

O you who believe, do not practice usury,
charging doubled and redoubled (interest);
but have fear of God:
you may well attain your goal.
131. Keep away from the Fire prepared for the infidels;
132. Obey God and the Prophet,
that you may be treated with mercy.
133. And hasten for the pardon of your Lord,
and for Paradise extending
over the heavens and the earth, laid out for those
who take heed for themselves and fear God,
134. Who expend both in joy and tribulation,

who suppress their anger and pardon their fellowmen;
and God loves those who are upright and do good,

135. And those who, if they commit a shameful act
or some wrong against themselves, remember God
and seek forgiveness for their sins:
For who can forgive except God?
They should not be perverse about their doings,
knowingly.

136. Their recompense is pardon by their Lord,
and gardens with streams of running water
where they will abide for ever.
How fair is the recompense of those who act!

137. There have been many dispensations before you;
so travel in the land and see
what befell those who denied the truth.

138. This is a clear declaration for mankind, and a guidance
and a warning for those who preserve themselves from evil.

139. So do not lose heart or be grieved,
for you will surely prevail if you are believers.

140. If you have been wounded
they too have suffered a wound.
We cause this alternation
of night and day in the affairs of men
so that God may know those who believe,
taking some as witness (of truth) from your ranks,
for God does not like those who are unjust.

141. This is so that God may try the faithful and destroy
the unbelievers.

142. Do you think you will go to Paradise
while God does not know who among you
strive and persist?

143. You had wished to know death
before you faced it (in battle);
so now you have seen it before your own eyes.

Muhammad is only a messenger;
and many a messenger has gone before him.
So what if he dies or is killed!
Will you turn back and go away in haste?
But he who turns back and goes away in haste
will do no harm to God.
But God will reward those
who give thanks (and are grateful).

145. No one can die before his appointed term except
in accordance with the law of God.
And to him who desires a reward in this world,

وَمَن يُرِدْ ثَوَابَ الْآخِرَةِ نُؤْتِهِ مِنْهَا وَسَنَجْزِي
الشَّاكِرِينَ ۝

We shall give it;
and to him who desires a reward in the life to come,
We shall do that.
We shall certainly reward those who are grateful.
146. Many a seeker after God
has fought in the way of God
by the side of many an apostle,
undaunted (by disaster),
and did not disgrace themselves;
— verily God loves those who are steadfast.

وَكَأَيِّن مِّن نَّبِيٍّ قَتَلَ مَعَهُ رِبِّيُّونَ كَثِيرٌ
فَمَا وَهَنُوا لِمَا أَصَابَهُمْ فِي سَبِيلِ اللَّهِ
وَمَا ضَعُفُوا وَمَا اسْتَكَانُوا وَاللَّهُ يُحِبُّ
الصَّابِرِينَ ۝

147. Nor did they say aught but: "O our Lord,
forgive us our sins and excesses in our acts,
and steady our steps,
and help us against unbelieving people."

وَمَا كَانَ قَوْلَهُمْ إِلَّا أَن قَالُوا رَبَّنَا اغْفِرْ لَنَا
ذُنُوبَنَا وَإِسْرَافَنَا فِي أَمْرِنَا وَثَبِّتْ أَقْدَامَنَا
وَانصُرْنَا عَلَى الْقَوْمِ الْكَافِرِينَ ۝

148. So God rewarded them in this world,
and a better reward awaits them in the next;
for God loves those who do good.

فَآتَاهُمُ اللَّهُ ثَوَابَ الدُّنْيَا وَحُسْنَ ثَوَابِ
الْآخِرَةِ وَاللَّهُ يُحِبُّ الْمُحْسِنِينَ ۝

O believers, if you listen to the infidels
they will make you turn your backs, and you
will be the losers.
150. But God is your protector,
and He is the best of helpers.
151. We shall strike terror into the hearts
of unbelievers
for ascribing compeers to God
for which He has sent down no sanction.
Hell is their residence,
the evil abode of the unjust.

يَا أَيُّهَا الَّذِينَ آمَنُوا إِن تُطِيعُوا الَّذِينَ كَفَرُوا
يَرُدُّوكُمْ عَلَى أَعْقَابِكُمْ فَتَنقَلِبُوا خَاسِرِينَ ۝
بَلِ اللَّهُ مَوْلَاكُمْ وَهُوَ خَيْرُ النَّاصِرِينَ ۝
سَنُلْقِي فِي قُلُوبِ الَّذِينَ كَفَرُوا الرُّعْبَ بِمَا
أَشْرَكُوا بِاللَّهِ مَا لَمْ يُنَزِّلْ بِهِ سُلْطَانًا وَمَأْوَاهُمُ
النَّارُ وَبِئْسَ مَثْوَى الظَّالِمِينَ ۝

152. The promise made to you by God was verified
when you destroyed (the foe) by His leave,
until you were unmanned and disputed the order,
and thus disobeyed (the Apostle) even after
He had brought you in sight of (victory) you longed for.
Some of you desired this world,
and some of you the next.
Then He put you to flight before (them)
in order to try you.
But (now) He has forgiven you,
for surely God is kind to the faithful.
153. Remember, as you were rushing up (the hill)
without turning back to look,
though the Prophet was calling you from the rear,
He requited you with anguish for an anguish
that you do not fret for missed opportunity
and what befell you,

وَلَقَدْ صَدَقَكُمُ اللَّهُ وَعْدَهُ إِذْ تَحُسُّونَهُم بِإِذْنِهِ
حَتَّى إِذَا فَشِلْتُمْ وَتَنَازَعْتُمْ فِي الْأَمْرِ وَعَصَيْتُم
مِّن بَعْدِ مَا أَرَاكُم مَّا تُحِبُّونَ مِنكُم مَّن يُرِيدُ الدُّنْيَا
وَمِنكُم مَّن يُرِيدُ الْآخِرَةَ ثُمَّ صَرَفَكُمْ عَنْهُمْ
لِيَبْتَلِيَكُمْ وَلَقَدْ عَفَا عَنكُمْ وَاللَّهُ ذُو فَضْلٍ
عَلَى الْمُؤْمِنِينَ ۝

إِذْ تُصْعِدُونَ وَلَا تَلْوُونَ عَلَى أَحَدٍ وَالرَّسُولُ
يَدْعُوكُمْ فِي أُخْرَاكُمْ فَأَثَابَكُمْ غَمًّا بِغَمٍّ لِّكَيْلَا
تَحْزَنُوا عَلَى مَا فَاتَكُمْ وَلَا مَا أَصَابَكُمْ وَاللَّهُ

for God is aware of all that you do.

154. Then after affliction He sent you a drowsiness
as comes after security, overwhelming some among you,
and making some anxious for themselves,
and made them think thoughts of pagan ignorance;
and they said:
"Have we a say in any affair?"
Say: "All affairs rest with God."
They hide in their hearts
what they do not disclose to you.
They say: "If we had a say in the affair
we would not have been killed in this place."
Tell them: "Even had you stayed at home,
those of you who were ordained to fight
would have gone
to their place of (eternal) rest.
God had to try them to bring out
what they concealed in their breasts,
and to bring out the secrets of their hearts,
for God knows your innermost thoughts.

155. All those among you who turned
their backs on the day the two armies clashed (at 'Uhud)
were surely induced by Satan to fail in their duty
because of their sinful deeds.
But God has already forgiven them,
for God is forgiving and kind.

O you who believe, do not be
like those who deny,
and say of their brethren
(who died) travelling in the land
or fighting:
"Had they stayed with us here
they would not have died
or been killed." This happened so that God
may fill their hearts with grief.
God is the giver of life and death
and sees all that you do.

157. If you are killed in the cause of God or you die,
the forgiveness and mercy of God are better
than all that you amass.

158. And if you die or are killed,
even so it is to God that you will return.

159. It was through God's mercy that you dealt
with them gently; for had you been stern and hard of heart
they would surely have broken away from you.

So pardon them and pray that forgiveness be theirs,
and seek their counsel in all affairs.
And when you have come to a decision
place your trust in God alone,
for He loves those who place their trust in Him.

160. If God is there to help you
none will overcome you;
and if He forsake you,
who will help you other than Him?
So only in God should the faithful place their trust.

161. It is not for a prophet to be false;
and whoever is false
will indeed bring his falsehood with him
on the Day of Reckoning
when each will receive his reward
without favour or wrong.

162. Is a man who has followed the pleasure of God
the same as he who has incurred His wrath,
whose abode is surely Hell, a dreadful place?

163. There are different ranks with God,
And God sees every thing you do.

164. God has favoured the faithful
by sending an apostle to them
from among themselves,
who recites to them His messages, and reforms
and teaches them the Law and the judgement,
for they were clearly in error before.

165. How is it that when misfortune befell you,
you said: "Where has this come from?"
— even though you had inflicted
disaster twice as great on (the enemy).
Say: "This has come from your own selves."
Surely God has power over all things.

166. What you suffered on the day the two armies had met
was by God's dispensation,
so that He may distinguish the faithful,

167. And may distinguish the hypocrites who were told:
"Fight in the way of God, or defend yourselves,"
and who had replied: "If we knew of the fight
we would have followed you."
They were nearer unbelief than faith on that day,
and they said with their tongues
what was not in their hearts;
but God is aware of what they hide.

168. To those who sit at home and say of their brothers:
"They would never have been killed had they listened to us,"

Al-'Imran

say: "Drive away death from your midst
if what you say is true."
169. Never think that those
who are killed in the way of God are dead.
They are alive, getting succour from their Lord,
170. Rejoicing at what God has given them of His grace,
and happy for those who are trying to overtake them
but have not joined them yet,
and who will have no fear or regret.
171. They rejoice at the kindness and mercy of God;
and God does not suffer
the wages of the faithful to go waste.

Those who obeyed the call of God and His Messenger,
even after they were wounded, and took heed for themselves,
shall indeed have an ample reward, —
173. Those who were told: "They have gathered
an army, beware," and their faith increased and they said:
"God is sufficient for us, and the best of protectors,"
174. And returned with God's favour and grace without harm,
for they attended the pleasure of God;
and great is the benevolence of God.
175. It is no one but Satan who frightens you with his allies.
But do not fear him, fear Me, if indeed you are believers.
176. And do not be grieved by those
who rush into disbelief.
They do no harm to God;
and God will not give them
any share in the life to come,
and their torment shall be great.
177. Those who barter unbelief for faith,
will not harm God in the least,
and the punishment for them will be painful.
178. The unbelievers must not think
that the respite We give them augurs well.
We do so that they sink
deeper into sin,
and suffer an ignominious doom.
179. God will not leave the believers in the state they are in
till He has sifted the evil from the good;
nor will God reveal the secrets of the Unknown.
He chooses (for this) from His apostles whom He will.
So believe in God and the prophets,
for if you believe and fear the displeasure of God
your reward will be great.
180. Let not those who are niggardly of things

that God has given them of His largesse
think that this is good for them. In fact, it is worse;
for what they grudged
will be hung around their necks
on the Day of Resurrection.
To God belong the heavens and the earth,
and God is aware of all you do.

God has indeed heard the words of those who said:
"God is a pauper whereas we are rich."
We shall make a note of their words,
and the murders of the prophets they committed unjustly,
and say to them: "Now taste the agony of burning."
182. This is (requital) for the deeds you had committed,
for God is not unjust to any of His creatures.
183. To those who say: "God has ordained
that we should not believe
an apostle who does not bring burnt offerings,"*
say: "Many an apostle had come to you before me
with manifest proofs, even with what you mention;
then why did you kill them if you were men of truth?"
184. If they call you a liar (remember)
so had other apostles been called before you,
who had come with clear signs and Scriptures
and the Book enlightening.
185. Every soul will know the taste of death.
You will get your recompense in full
on the Day of Resurrection;
and he who is spared the Fire
and finds his way to Paradise
will meet his desire.
As for the life of this world,
it is nothing but a merchandise of vanity.
186. You will, nonetheless, be tried
with your wealth and life,
and will hear many untoward things
from the followers of former Books and the infidels.
But if you endure with patience
and follow the straight path, it will surely (accord)
with God's fixed resolve about human affairs.
187. And remember when God took a promise from the people
of the Book
to make its (truth) known to mankind.

---

* Literally 'which fire will consume'.

and not keep back any part of it,
they set aside (the pledge),
and sold it away for a little gain;
but how wretched the bargain that they made!
188. Think not that those who exult
at what they have done, and who love to be praised
for what they have not done,
shall escape the punishment,
for grievous indeed will be their doom.
189. For God's is the kingdom of the heavens and the earth,
and God's is the power over all things.

In the creation of the heavens and the earth,
the alternation of night and day,
are signs for the wise.
191. Those who honour God in meditation,
standing or sitting or lying on their sides,
who reflect and contemplate
on the creation of the heavens and the earth,
(and say) : "Not in vain have You made them.
All praise be to You,
O Lord, preserve us
from the torment of Hell.
192. Whoever, O Lord, should be cast into Hell
shall be verily disgraced;
and the sinners shall have none
to help (or save) them.
193. We have heard, O our Lord, the crier call
inviting us to faith (and announcing):
'Believe in your Lord.'
O our Lord, to faith we have come,
so forgive our trespasses,
deliver us from sin,
and grant us (the glory of) death with the just.
194. Give us what You promised, O Lord, through Your
     prophets;
and put us not to shame on the Day of Reckoning,
for never do You go back on Your promise."
195. The Lord heard their prayer and answered:
"I suffer not the good deeds of any to go waste,
be he a man or a woman: The one of you is of the other.
And those who were deprived of their homes
or banished in My cause,
and who fought and were killed,
I shall blot out their sins and admit them indeed
into gardens with rippling streams."

ال عمران ٣   لن تنالوا

— A recompense from God,
and the best of rewards is with God.

196. Be not deceived by the comings and goings
of unbelievers in the land.

197. Their commerce is but short-lived, and then
their abode shall be Hell: And what an evil abode!

198. But those who are pious and obedient to their Lord,
will have gardens with streams of running water
where they will abide as guests of God;
and what is with God
is best for the pious.

199. Certainly among the people of the Book
are some who believe in God
and in what has been revealed to you
and had been revealed to them;
and they bow in humility before God,
and do not trade for paltry gain
the signs of God. Their reward
is verily with their Lord;
and swift is the reckoning of God!

200. So you who believe,
have endurance in suffering,
be patient and persevere,
strengthen each other and be firm,
and be pious and fear God
that you may find success.

Note on verse 10

* Hell. The word *Jahannam* is of Hebraic origin, consisting of *ji*, valley, and *Hannam*; and meant the Valley of Hannam, south of Jerusalem, where in ancient times human sacrifices were made to Moluk, the deity of the 'Ammuniyin, and burnt, thus signifying the altar of humanity's sacrifice. In the Qur'an, Heaven and Hell are not eternal kingdoms as in the Bible, but contingent to and coterminous with the heavens and the earth, as is evident from verses 106 to 108 of Surah 11:

And those who are doomed, will be in Hell:
For them will be sobbing and sighing,
where they will dwell so long as heaven and earth endure.
Verily your Lord does as He wills.
Those who are blessed will be in Paradise,
where they will dwell so long as heaven and earth survive. . . .

As Paradise is a state of ultimate bliss, enjoyably wordly, so is Hell described as "the fire kindled by God which penetrates the hearts. It vaults them over in extending columns," in 104:6-9. It is, thus, a sacred archetypal symbol, carrying both a moral and psycho-social meaning within its tautology and an eschatological ultimacy.

So is *Yaum-al-Hashr,* the Day of Resurrection, the completion and consummation of life on earth. In the metonymy of the Qur'an resurrection signifies the rising of the dead so that each could feel in person the effects of his good and evil deeds done on earth. See *Hujjat Allah al-Baligha* by Shah Waliullah.

4 The Women

An-Nisā': Madani

In the name of Allah, most benevolent, ever-merciful.

بِسْمِ اللهِ الرَّحْمٰنِ الرَّحِيْمِ

O MEN, FEAR your Lord
who created you from a single cell,*
and from it created its mate,
and from the two of them dispersed men and women
(male and female) in multitudes.
So fear God in whose name you ask
of one another (the bond of) relationships.**
God surely keeps watch over you.
2. Give to the orphans their possessions,
and do not replace things of your own which are bad
with things which are good among theirs, and do not
intermix their goods with your own and make use of them,
for this is a grievous crime.
3. If you fear you cannot be equitable to orphan girls
(in your charge, or misuse their persons), then marry
women who are lawful for you,*** two, three, or four;
but if you fear you cannot treat so many with equity,
marry only one, or a maid or captive.****
This is better than being iniquitous.
4. Give to women their dowers willingly,
but if they forego part of it themselves,
then use it to your advantage.
5. Do not entrust (their) property God has given you
to maintain (on trust), to those who are immature;

---

* See note 1 on page 96.
** See note 2 on page 96.
*** See note 3 on page 96.
**** Literally 'what your right hands possess.' *Milk* (root MLK), possession, has been used for 'marrying' *(Taj-al-'urus)* and *amlikah* for 'given in marraige.' 'Ayesha is reported saying: *Malakani rasul Allah,* the Prophet of God married me.' The expression is used in the Qur'an for women one has married, as here and in 33:52, as well as for captives of war, subordinates, and maid servants and slaves. *Aiman-u-kum,* your right hands, has also been used for pledging in marraige, as in 4:33. The verse also virtually restricts the number of wives to one, for treating even two with absolute equality is well-nigh impossible.

but feed them and clothe them from it,
and speak to them with kindness.
6. And test (and try) the orphans
until they are of marriageable age.
If you find they have acquired sound judgement,
then hand over their property to them;
but devour not their wealth,
nor use it up hastily out of fear
that soon they will grow up (and demand it).
And (the guardian) who is rich should abstain
from spending much (of their wealth);
and he who is poor
should use only as much as is fair.
And when you give back their possessions
have this witnessed, (and remember)
that God is sufficient to take all account.
7. Men have a share in what the parents and relatives
leave behind at death;
and women have a share
in what the parents and relatives leave behind.
Be it large or small
a legal share is fixed.
8. And when the relatives and orphans and the needy
collect at the time of the division (of property)
provide for them too,
and talk kindly to them.
9. Let people fear the day when they leave
small children behind them unprovided,
and how concerned they would be for them.
So fear God and say the right things to them.
10. Those who devour the possessions
of the orphans unjustly
devour only fire,
and will surely burn in Hell.

As for the children, God decrees
that the share of the male
is equivalent to that of two females.
If they consist of women only,
and of them more than two,
they will get two-thirds of the inheritance;
but in case there is one, she will inherit one half.
The parents will each inherit a sixth of the estate
if it happens the deceased has left a child;
but if he has left no children,
and his parents are his heirs,

then the mother will inherit one-third;
but if he has left brothers,
the mother will inherit one-sixth
after payment of legacies and debts.
Of parents and children
you do not know who are more useful to you.
These are the decrees of God who knows all and is wise.
12. Your share in the property the wives leave behind
is half if they die without an issue,
but in case they have left children,
then your share is one-fourth after the payment
of legacies and debts; and your wife shall inherit
one-fourth of what you leave at death if you die childless,
if not, she will get one-eighth of what you leave behind
after payment of legacies and debts.
If a man or a woman should die
without leaving either children or parents behind
but have brother and sister,
they shall each inherit one-sixth.
In case there are more, they will share
one-third of the estate after payment of legacies and debts
without prejudice to others.
This is the decree of God who knows all and is kind.
13. These are the limits set by God,
and those who follow the commandments of God
and the Prophet, will indeed be admitted
to gardens with streams of water running by,
where they will for ever abide;
and this will be success supreme.
14. Those who disobey God and the Prophet
and exceed the bounds of law,
will be taken to Hell and abide there for ever
and shall suffer despicable punishment.

If any of your women is guilty of unnatural offence,
bring four of your witnesses to give evidence;
if they testify against them, retain them in the houses*
until death overtakes them or God
provides some other way for them.

---

* The meaning of this verse resides in key words, *masaka* and *bai't*, pl. *buyut*. *Masaka* means to retain; and *imsak* has been used in the Qur'an in the sense of keeping within the bond of marriage. See 2:229 where *imsak* has been used for keeping as wives, as antonym of *tasrih*. *Bai't* means a place where one takes shelter at night, hence, house or home. *Al-bai't* means to marry; *Taj*, as *baitur-rajul* means a man's wife, also his family.

16. If two (men) among you are guilty of such acts
then punish both of them.
But if they repent and reform, let them be,
for God accepts repentance and is merciful.
17. God does accept repentance, but only
of those who are guilty of an evil out of ignorance
yet quickly repent,
and God turns to them again,
for God is all-knowing and all-wise.
18. But (He does not accept) the repentance of those
who continue indulging in evil
until death draws near
and they say: "We now repent;" nor of those
who die disbelieving.
For them We have a grievous retribution in wait.
19. O believers, you are not allowed to take perforce
the women (of dead relatives) into your heritage,
or tyrannise over them
in order to deprive them of what you have given them,
unless they are guilty of open adultery.
Live with them with tolerance and justice
even if you do not care for them.
For it may well be you may not like a thing,
yet God may have endued it with much goodness.
20. If you want to take another wife
in place of the one you are married to,
then even if you have given her a talent of gold,
do not take back a thing.
Would you take it away by slandering
and using unjust means?
21. How could you do that having slept with one another,
and when they had taken a solemn pledge from you?
22. And do not wed the women your fathers had wed.
What happened in the past is now past:
It was lewd and abhorrent,
and only the way of evil.

Unlawful are your mothers and daughters
and your sisters to you,
and the sisters of your fathers and your mothers,
and the daughters of your brothers and sisters,
and foster mothers, foster sisters, and the mothers
of your wives,
and the daughters of the wives you have slept with
who are under your charge; but in case
you have not slept with them

there is no offence (if you marry their daughters);
and the wives of your own begotten sons;
and marrying two sisters is unlawful.
What happened in the past (is now past):
God is forgiving and kind.
24. Also forbidden are married women
unless they are captives (of war).
Such is the decree of God.
Lawful for you are women besides these
if you seek them with your wealth for wedlock
and not for debauchery.
Then give those of these women you have enjoyed,
the agreed dower. It will not be sinful if you
agree to something (else) by mutual consent
after having settled the dowry.
God is certainly all-knowing and all-wise.
25. If one of you cannot afford to marry
a believing gentlewoman
(let him marry) a maid who is a believer.
God is aware of your faith:
The one of you is of the other;
so marry them with the consent of their people,
and give them an appropriate dowry.
They are women (seeking) wedlock, and not lechery,
nor secretly looking for paramours.
But if they are married and guilty of adultery,
inflict on them half the punishment (enjoined) for gentlewomen.
This is for those who are afraid
of doing wrong.
In case they can wait, it is better for them.
God is forgiving and kind.

God wishes to make it clear to you
and guide you through the example of earlier people,
and to forgive you, for God
is all-knowing and all-wise.
27. God likes to turn to you, but those
who are lost in the pleasures of the flesh
wish to turn you astray, far away.
28. God would like to lighten your burden,
for man was created weak.
29. O believers, you should not usurp
unjustly the wealth of each other,
but trade by mutual consent;
and do not destroy yourselves.
God is merciful to you.

والمحصنته النِسَاءُ

30. If someone does so through oppression
or injustice,
We shall cast him into Hell:
This is how (the Law of) God works inevitably.
31. If you keep away from the deadly sins
that have been forbidden,
We shall efface your faults,
and lead you to a place of honour.
32. Do not covet what God has favoured some with
more than He has some others.
Men have a share in what they earn,
and women have theirs in what they earn.
Ask God for His favours. Surely
God has knowledge of every thing.
33. For each We have appointed heirs
to what parents and relatives leave behind.
And to those you have given your pledge in marriage
give their share,
for God is witness to every thing.

Men are the support of women as God
gives some more means than others, and because
they spend of their wealth (to provide for them).
So women who are virtuous are obedient to God*
and guard the hidden as God has guarded it.
As for women you feel are averse,**
talk to them suasively;
then leave them alone in bed (without molesting them)
and go to bed with them (when they are willing).***
If they open out to you, do not seek an excuse
for blaming them. Surely God is sublime and great.

---

* Qawwam (root QWM) in line 1 does not mean lord or master, but provider of food and necessities of life, and through its form qaim, to take care of; and qanitat only means devoted or obedient to God, as in 2:116, 16:120, 33:35, etc. See Taj. Al-ghaib similarly means the unknown, unseen, and the hidden as here.

** Nushuz: Apart from rising up, ill treatment, it also means aversion to an act, and has been used in this sense here as in 4: 128 for men's aversion.

*** For the three words fa 'izu, wahjaru, and wadribu in the original, translated here 'talk to them suasively,' 'leave them alone (in bed — fi 'l-madaje),' and 'have intercourse', respectively, see Raghib, Lisan al-'Arab and Zamakhshari. Raghib in his Al-Mufridat fi Gharib al-Qur'an gives the meanings of these words with special reference to this verse. Fa-'izu, he says, means to 'talk to them so persuasively as to melt their hearts.' (See also v. 63 of this Surah where it has been used in a similar sense.) Hajara, he says, means to separate body from body, and points out that the expression wahjaru hunna metaphorically means to refrain from touching or molesting them. Zamakhshari is more explicit in his Kshshaf when he says, 'do not get inside their blankets.' Raghib points out that daraba metaphorically means to have intercourse, and quotes the expression darab al-fahl an-naqah, 'the stud camel covered

35. If you fear a breach between them,
appoint one arbiter from the people of the man
and one from the people of the woman.
If they wish to have a settlement
then God will reconcile them,
for God is all-knowing and cognisant.
36. Pay homage to God, and make none His compeer,
and be good to your parents and relatives,
the orphans and the needy and the neighbours
who are your relatives,
and the neighbours who are strangers,
and the friend by your side,
the traveller and your servants and subordinates.
God does not surely love those
who are arrogant and boastful,
37. Who are miserly and bid others
to be so,
and hide what God has given them in His largesse.
We have prepared for unbelievers a shameful punishment.
38. Those who spend of their wealth to show off
and do not believe
in God and the Last Day,
take Satan as companion,
and how evil a companion (have they)!
39. Would something have befallen them
if they had believed
in God and the Last Day,
and spent of what has been given them by God?
God is fully aware of all they do.
40. God does not wrong any one,
not even the equal of an atom;
and if men do good
He multiplies it by two,
and adds a great reward of His own.
41. How shall it be when We call
witnesses from each and every people
and call you as witness over them?
42. On that day those who disbelieved
and disobeyed the Prophet,

---

the she-camel,' which is also quoted by *Lisan al-'Arab*. It cannot be taken here to mean 'to strike them (women).' This view is strengthened by the Prophet's authentic *hadith* found in a number of authorities, including Bukhari and Muslim: "Could any of you beat your wife as he would a slave, and then lie with her in the evening?" There are other traditions in Abu Da'ud, Nasa'i, Ibn Majah, Ahmad bin Hanbal and others, to the effect that he forbade the beating of *any* woman, saying: "Never beat God's handmaidens."

shall wish they were levelled with the dust,
and shall not be able to conceal
a thing from God.

O you who believe, do not perform your service of prayer
when you are intoxicated
until you are sure of what you are saying,
nor when in a state of seminal pollution,
until you have taken a bath,
except when you are travelling.
But in case you are ill or are travelling,
or you have relieved yourself of nature's call,
or cohabited with a woman,
and cannot find water,
then take wholesome dust
and pass it over your face and hands:
God is benign and forgiving.

44. Have you not seen the people who were given
a share of the Book, but who purchased
only error, and wish
that you also go astray?

45. But God knows your enemies well:
and sufficient is God to protect you,
and sufficient is God for all help.

46. Some among the Jews
distort the words out of context and say
(in place of the right words):
"We have heard and do not obey;"
and, "hear without hearing," and "listen to us,"
twisting their tongues and reviling the faith.
But if they had said: "We have heard and obey,"
and, "hear and regard us,"
it would have been better for them
and more appropriate.
But God has disgraced them for their lack of belief;
and so only a few of them believe.

47. O people of the Book, believe
in what We have revealed,
which confirms what is already with you,
before We disfigure your visages
and turn your faces about and curse you,
as We did with those who had broken the Sabbath;
and what God decrees comes to pass.

48. God does not forgive that compeers
be ascribed to Him, though He may
forgive aught else if He please.

And he who ascribes compeers to God
is guilty of the gravest sin.
49. Have you not seen the people who
call themselves pure?
Yet God purifies whom He pleases,
and none shall be wronged
even the breadth of a thread.
50. See how they fabricate lies about God,
which is a clear sin.

Have you not seen those who were given
a portion of the Book, who believe
in false deities and evil powers,
and say of unbelievers:
"These are better guided than those who believe."
52. They are the ones who were cursed by God;
and those who are cursed by God
will have none to protect them.
53. Have they a share in the kingdom? (If they had,)
they would never have given an iota to the people.
54. Are they so envious of others
for what God has given them of His bounty?
So We had given the Book and the Law
to Abraham's family, and given them great dominion.
55. Then some of them believed in it,
and some turned away from it;
yet sufficient is Hell, the flaming Fire!
56. And those who disbelieve Our revelations
shall be cast into Hell;
and when their skin is burnt up and singed,
We shall give them a new coat that they may go on
tasting the agony of punishment,
for God is all-mighty and all-wise.
57. But those who believe and do good deeds
We shall admit into gardens
with streams of running water, where they will abide for ever,
with fairest of companions and coolest of shades.
58. God enjoins that you render to the owners
what is held in trust with you,
and that when you judge among the people
do so equitably.
Noble are the counsels of God,
and God hears all and sees everything.
59. O you who believe, obey God and the Prophet
and those in authority among you;
and if you are at variance over something,

والمحصنته   النِّسَاءِ

refer it to God and the Messenger,
if you believe in God and the Last Day.
This is good for you and the best of settlements.

اللهِ وَالرَّسُولِ اِنْ كُنْتُمْ تُؤْمِنُونَ بِاللّٰهِ وَالْيَوْمِ
الْاٰخِرِ ذٰلِكَ خَيْرٌ وَّاَحْسَنُ تَاْوِيْلًا ۞

Have you never seen those who aver
they believe in what has been revealed to you
and had been to others before you,
yet desire to turn for judgement to evil powers,
even though they have been commanded
to disbelieve in them?
Satan only wishes to lead them astray, far away.
61. When they are told:
"Come to that which God has revealed,
and to the Prophet,"
you should see the hypocrites,
how they hesitate and turn their faces away.
62. How shall it be when they suffer
misfortunes for their own misdeeds?
Then they will come to you
swearing by God and saying:
"We wish for nothing but good and amity."
63. The secrets of the hearts of these people
are well known to God.
So leave them alone, and counsel them
and speak to them eloquent words
that would touch their very souls.
64. We have sent no apostle but that he should be obeyed
by the will of God.
If they had come to you after wronging themselves
and asked forgiveness of God,
and you had also asked forgiveness for them,
they would surely have found God
forgiving and merciful.
65. Indeed, by your Lord, they will not believe
till they make you adjudge in their disputes
and find no constraint in their minds about your decisions
and accept them with full acquiescence.
66. If We had commanded them to lay down their lives
and to go forth from their homes,
only a few would have obeyed;
though had they followed
what they had been commanded
it would surely have been good for them
and the strengthening of their faith.
67. And We would have bestowed on them
a great reward of Our own,

اَلَمْ تَرَ اِلَى الَّذِيْنَ يَزْعُمُوْنَ اَنَّهُمْ اٰمَنُوْا بِمَا اُنْزِلَ
اِلَيْكَ وَمَا اُنْزِلَ مِنْ قَبْلِكَ يُرِيْدُوْنَ اَنْ يَّتَحَاكَمُوْا
اِلَى الطَّاغُوْتِ وَقَدْ اُمِرُوْا اَنْ يَّكْفُرُوْا بِهٖ وَيُرِيْدُ
الشَّيْطٰنُ اَنْ يُّضِلَّهُمْ ضَلٰلًا بَعِيْدًا ۞

وَاِذَا قِيْلَ لَهُمْ تَعَالَوْا اِلٰى مَا اَنْزَلَ اللّٰهُ وَاِلَى الرَّسُوْلِ
رَاَيْتَ الْمُنٰفِقِيْنَ يَصُدُّوْنَ عَنْكَ صُدُوْدًا ۞

فَكَيْفَ اِذَا اَصَابَتْهُمْ مُّصِيْبَةٌ بِمَا قَدَّمَتْ اَيْدِيْهِمْ
ثُمَّ جَآءُوْكَ يَحْلِفُوْنَ بِاللّٰهِ اِنْ اَرَدْنَا اِلَّا اِحْسَانًا
وَّتَوْفِيْقًا ۞

اُولٰئِكَ الَّذِيْنَ يَعْلَمُ اللّٰهُ مَا فِيْ قُلُوْبِهِمْ فَاَعْرِضْ
عَنْهُمْ وَعِظْهُمْ وَقُلْ لَّهُمْ فِيْ اَنْفُسِهِمْ قَوْلًا بَلِيْغًا ۞

وَمَا اَرْسَلْنَا مِنْ رَّسُوْلٍ اِلَّا لِيُطَاعَ بِاِذْنِ اللّٰهِ وَلَوْ
اَنَّهُمْ اِذْ ظَّلَمُوْا اَنْفُسَهُمْ جَآءُوْكَ فَاسْتَغْفَرُوا اللّٰهَ وَ
اسْتَغْفَرَ لَهُمُ الرَّسُوْلُ لَوَجَدُوا اللّٰهَ تَوَّابًا رَّحِيْمًا ۞

فَلَا وَرَبِّكَ لَا يُؤْمِنُوْنَ حَتّٰى يُحَكِّمُوْكَ فِيْمَا شَجَرَ بَيْنَهُمْ
ثُمَّ لَا يَجِدُوْا فِيْ اَنْفُسِهِمْ حَرَجًا مِّمَّا قَضَيْتَ وَيُسَلِّمُوْا
تَسْلِيْمًا ۞

وَلَوْ اَنَّا كَتَبْنَا عَلَيْهِمْ اَنِ اقْتُلُوْا اَنْفُسَكُمْ اَوِ
اخْرُجُوْا مِنْ دِيَارِكُمْ مَّا فَعَلُوْهُ اِلَّا قَلِيْلٌ مِّنْهُمْ
وَلَوْ اَنَّهُمْ فَعَلُوْا مَا يُوْعَظُوْنَ بِهٖ لَكَانَ خَيْرًا لَّهُمْ
وَاَشَدَّ تَثْبِيْتًا ۞
وَّاِذًا لَّاٰتَيْنٰهُمْ مِّنْ لَّدُنَّا اَجْرًا عَظِيْمًا ۞

والمحصنٰته   النسآء   والمحصنٰته

68. And led them to the path that is straight.
69. Those who obey God and the Prophet
are with those who are blessed by God, —
the prophets, the sincere and the trustful,
the martyrs and the upright;
and how excellent a company are they!
70. This is a favour from God;
and sufficient is God, the all-knowing.

O believers, take precautions,
and advance in detachments, or go
all together in a body.
72. Someone among you will surely lag behind,
and if calamity should befall you, will say:
"God was gracious to me that I was not among them."
73. But if success comes to you from God
he will say, as though
no love existed between you and him:
"I wish I were with them,
for I would have certainly
met with great success."
74. Those who barter the life of this world for the next
should fight in the way of God.
And We shall bestow on him
who fights in the way of God,
whether he is killed or is victorious, a glorious reward.
75. What has come upon you
that you fight not in the cause of God and for the oppressed,
men, women and children,
who pray: "Get us out of this city, O Lord,
whose people are oppressors;
so send us a friend by Your will,
and send us a helper."
76. Those who believe
fight in the way of God;
and those who do not,
only fight for the powers of evil;
so you should fight the allies of Satan.
Surely the stratagem of Satan is ineffective.

Have you not seen the people who were told:
"Hold back your hands (from attacking),
observe your devotional obligations
and pay the zakat?"
But when they were commanded to fight,
behold, a section among them were filled

with fear of men as though it were the fear of God
and even more, and said: "O Lord,
why did you make war compulsory for us?
Why did you not allow us to live a little more?"
Say to them:
"How short-lived is the commerce of this world;
but that of the next
is best for those who fear God;
and you will not be wronged the breadth of a thread."
78. Death will overtake you wheresoever you be,
even in the mightiest of towers.
Yet if some good comes their way
they say: "It is from God;"
and if it is evil that befalls them, they say:
"It is indeed from you." Say to them:
"Every thing is from God."
O, what has come upon the people
that even this they fail to understand!
79. What comes to you of good
is verily from God;
and what comes to you of ill
is from your own self (your actions).
We have sent you as apostle to all mankind;
and God is sufficient as witness.
80. He who obeys the Apostle obeys God;
and if some turn away (remember)
We have not sent you as warden over them.
81. They say: "We obey;"
but when they leave your company, a section of them
discuss at night other things than you had said;
but God takes note of what they discuss.
So turn aside from them and trust in God;
and God is sufficient as protector.
82. Do they not ponder over the Qur'an?
Had it been the word of any other but God
they would surely have found
a good deal of variation in it.
83. And when any tidings of peace or war come to them
they spread the news around. Had they gone
to the Prophet or those in authority among them,
then those who check and scrutinise would have known it.
And but for the favour of God and His mercy
you would certainly have followed Satan, except a few.
84. So fight on in the way of God
(irrespective of the others).
You cannot compel any one except your own self;

والمحصنٰت ه   النساء

but urge the believers to fight.
It may well be that God
will keep back the might of the infidels,
for God's might is greater, and severe His punishment.
85. He who intercedes in a good cause
will surely have a share in the recompense;
and he who abets an evil act
will share the burden thereof;
for God (equates and) is watchful of all things.
86. When you are greeted with a greeting,
then greet with one fairer,
or repeat the same greeting.
For God takes account of all things.
87. God: There is no god but He.
He will gather you together
on the Day of Resurrection
which is certain to come;
and whose word is truer than God's?

H ow is it that you
are divided in two factions **about** the hypocrites?
God has routed them
for what they were doing.
Do you wish to guide him to the path
whom God has allowed to go astray?
As for him whom God allows to go astray
you will not find a way.
89. They wish you to become disbelievers as they are,
so that you should become like them.
Therefore hold them not as friends
until they go out of their homes
in the way of God.
If they do not, seize them wherever they are
and do away with them.
Do not make them your friends or allies,
90. Except those who take refuge
with a people allied to you,
or those who, weary of fighting you or their people,
come over to you.
If God had so willed
He would surely have given them power over you,
and they would have fought you.
If they keep aloof and do not fight, and offer peace,
God has left you no reason to fight them.
91. You will also find persons who,
while wishing to live in peace

with you as well as with their own people,
turn to civil war
the moment they are called to it.
If they do not keep away from you,
nor offer you peace nor restrain their hands,
seize them and kill them wherever they are.
We have given you a clear sanction against them.

It is not for a believer to take a believer's life
except by mistake;
and he who kills a believer by mistake
should free a slave who is a believer,
and pay blood-money to the victim's family
unless they forego it as an act of charity.
If he belonged to a community
hostile to you but was himself a believer,
then a slave who is a believer should be freed.
In case he belonged to a people with whom you have a treaty,
then give blood-money to his family
and free a believing slave.
But he who has no means (to do so)
should fast for a period of two months continuously
to have his sins forgiven by God,
and God is all-knowing and all-wise.
93. Any one who kills a believer intentionally
will be cast into Hell
to abide there for ever,
and suffer God's anger and damnation.
For him a greater punishment awaits.
94. O believers, when you go out on a journey
in the way of God, be discreet
and do not say to anyone who greets you in peace:
"You are not a believer."
You desire the gain of earthly life,
but there are prizes in plenty with God.
You were also like him (an unbeliever) in the past,
but God has been gracious to you.
So be careful and discreet,
for God is aware of what you do.
95. The faithful who sit idle,
other than those who are disabled,
are not equal to those
who fight in the way of God
with their wealth and lives.
God has exalted those in rank
who fight for the faith

والمحصنته السّآء

with their wealth and souls
over those who sit idle.
Though God's promise of good is for all,
He has granted His favour of the highest reward
to those who struggle
in preference to those who sit at home.
96. For them are higher ranks with God,
and forgiveness and grace;
and God is forgiving and kind.

As for those whose souls
are taken by the angels (at death)
while in a state of unbelief,
they will be asked by the angels:
"What (state) were you in?"
They will answer: "We were oppressed in the land."
And the angels will say: "Was not God's earth
large enough for you to migrate?"
Their abode will be Hell, and what an evil destination!
98. But those who are helpless, men, women and children,
who can neither contrive a plan
nor do they know the way,
99. May well hope for the mercy of God;
and God is full of mercy and grace.
100. Whosoever leaves his country in duty to God
will find many places of refuge, and abundance
on the earth.
And he who leaves his home and becomes
an emigre in the way of God and His Messenger,
and death overtake him,
is sure to receive his reward from God;
for God is forgiving and kind.

When you travel in the land
there is no sin if you curtail your service of prayer
if you fear the unbelievers may harass you,
for indeed your open enemies are the infidels.
102. When you are among them,
and have to lead the service of prayer,
let one group stand up with you,
but let them keep their arms.
After they have paid their homage they should go to the rear,
and let the group which has not done so yet
offer their service of prayer with you,
remaining cautious and armed.
The infidels wish to find you neglectful of your arms

and provisions, to attack you unawares.
It will not be a sin
if you put aside your arms
when you are troubled by rain, or you are ill;
but take full precautions.
God has reserved for infidels
a despicable punishment.
103. If you are late in performing your service of prayer
honour God by remembering Him,
standing or sitting or lying on your sides.
And when you have security
perform your act of prayer befittingly;
and praying at fixed hours is prescribed for the faithful.
104. And do not be chary of pursuing them.
If you suffer, they shall also suffer like you.
But while you have hope (of success) from God,
they have none.
Surely God is all-knowing and all-wise.

We have sent down to you the Book
containing the truth, in whose light
you should judge among the people
as God has shown you,
and do not be a contender
for deceivers.
106. And seek God's forgiveness,
for God is surely forgiving and kind.
107. Do not argue for those
who harbour deceit in their hearts,
for God does not love the treacherous and the iniquitous.
108. They try to hide from (men),
but they cannot hide from God
who is with them at night when they discuss
such matters as He does not approve;
but what they do is well within the compass of God.
109. Well, you are those who pleaded for them
in the life of this world;
but who will plead for them on the Day of Resurrection
or be their security?
110. He who does evil or acts against his own interests
(by disbelieving), then prays for God's forgiveness,
will find God compassionate and merciful.
111. He who earns the wages of sin
does so for himself;
and God is aware of everything and is wise.
112. He who commits a mistake or iniquity

والمحصنات٤ النساء٤

and ascribes it to one who is innocent,
is guilty of calumny and brazen sin.

But for the mercy of God and His grace
you would certainly have been misled by a section of them;
yet they could not mislead you but themselves alone,
and could do you no harm,
for God has revealed to you the Book and the Law,
and taught you what you did not know.
Great have been the blessings of God on you.
114. Their confidential counsels are seldom for the good,
save of those who talk of charity
or goodness or peace among men.
Whosoever does so for the pleasure of God,
We shall give him an ample reward.
115. And he who opposes the Prophet
even after the way has become clear to him,
and follows a path other than the way of believers,
We shall lead him to what he has chosen for himself,
and shall take him to Hell: How evil a journey's end!

God does not forgive
that compeers be ascribed to Him,
and absolves all else whatsoever He will.
And he who associates compeers with God
has indeed wandered far astray.
117. In His place they invoke
only females (the pagan deities);
and instead of Him they invoke Satan the obstinate rebel
118. Who was condemned by God and who said:
"I shall take from Thy creatures
my determinate share,
119. And mislead them and tempt them,
and order them to slit the ears of animals;
and order them to alter God's creation."
He who holds Satan as friend in place of God
will assuredly be damned to perdition.
120. Whatever the promises he makes,
whatever the desires he enkindles,
and whatever the hopes Satan rouses in them,
are no more than delusion.
121. For such the abode is only Hell
from which they will find no escape.
122. But those who believe and do good deeds
We shall admit into gardens with streams of running water
where they will abide for ever.

True is the promise of God;
and whose word could be truer than God's?
123. It is neither dependent on your wishes,
nor the wishes of the people of the Book,
(but) whosoever does ill will be punished for it,
and will find no protector or friend apart from God;
124. But he who performs good deeds,
whether man or a woman,
and is a believer,
will surely enter Paradise,
and none shall be deprived
even of an iota of his reward.
125. Whose way is better
than that of the man who has submitted to God,
and does good, and who follows
the creed of Abraham the upright?
And God chose Abraham as friend.
126. And all that is in the heavens and the earth
belongs to God;
and everything is well within the compass of God.

And they ask you for judgement about women.
Tell them: "God has given you instructions about them.
You also read them in the Book
concerning orphaned women (in your charge)
to whom you deny their ordained rights
and yet wish to take them in marriage, as well as
in respect of helpless children,
that you should be just in the matter of orphans."
The good you do is known to God.
128. If a woman fears aversion from her husband,
or ill treatment,
there is no harm if they make a peaceful settlement;
and peace is an excellent thing.
But men keep self-interest uppermost.
Yet if you do good and fear God,
God is cognisant of all that you do.
129. Howsoever you may try
you will never be able to treat
your wives equally.
But do not incline (to one) exclusively
and leave (the other) suspended (as it were).
Yet if you do the right thing and are just,
God is verily forgiving and kind.
130. If both (decide to) separate,
God in His largesse will provide for them;

for God is infinite and all-wise.

131. All that is in the heavens and the earth
belongs to God.
We had commanded those
who received the Book before you,
and have commanded you too, to obey the laws of God.
Even if you deny, surely
all that is in the heavens and the earth
belongs to God;
and God is self-sufficient and praise-worthy.

132. For all that is in the heavens and the earth
belongs to God;
and God is sufficient as guardian.

133. He could take you away if He will, O men,
and replace you with others:
God has the power to do so.

134. Whosoever desires a reward of this world (should
        remember)
that with God are rewards of this world and the next;
and God hears all and sees every thing.

O you who believe, be custodians of justice
(and) witnesses for God,
even though against yourselves
or your parents or your relatives.
Whether a man be rich or poor, God
is his greater well-wisher than you.
So follow not the behests of lust
lest you swerve from justice;
and if you prevaricate or avoid (giving evidence),
God is cognisant of all that you do.

136. O believers, believe in God and His Messenger
and the Book He has revealed to His Apostle,
and the Books revealed before.
But he who believes not
in God and His angels
and the Books and the prophets
and the Last Day, has wandered far away.

137. Those who accept the faith, then disbelieve,
then return to it, and deny once again
and increase in disbelief,
will not be forgiven by God or be guided by Him.

138. Give tidings to the hypocrites
that painful is their doom.

139. Do those who take unbelievers as their friends
in preference to the faithful

seek power from them?
But all power belongs to God.
140. You have been commanded in the Book
that whensoever you hear
God's messages denied or derided,
do not sit in that company until
they begin talking of other things,
or you will be no different from them.
Indeed God will put
the hypocrites and infidels together in Hell.
141. Those who wait to see what befalls you, say
in case success comes to you from God:
"Were we not with you?"
But if fortune favours the infidels,
they say: "Did we not overpower you,
and yet protected you against the believers?"
But God will judge between you on the Day of Resurrection;
and God will never give the unbelievers
a way over the faithful.

The hypocrites try to deceive God,
but He (leads them to) deceive themselves,
When they stand up for performing the service of prayer
they do so indolently, only for show,
and remember God but little,
143. Wavering between the two,
neither with these nor with those.
For them who are not given the guidance by God,
you will never find a way.
144. O believers, do not hold unbelievers as friends
in preference to the faithful.
Do you want to proffer a clear proof
of your own guilt before God?
145. The hypocrites will be in the lowest depths of Hell,
and you will find none to help them.
146. But those who repent and amend,
and hold firmly to God,
and are sincere and wholly obedient to God,
are surely with the faithful;
and God will bestow on the faithful
a great reward.
147. Why should God punish you
if you acknowledge the truth and believe?
God is responsive to gratitude and is cognisant.
148. God does not like ill (of others) spoken about,
except by him who has been wronged.

For God hears all and knows everything.

149. Whether you do some good openly or in secret,
or forgive an ill done to you, (know) that God
is forgiving and all-powerful.

150. Those who believe not in God and His apostles,
and desire to differentiate
between God and His messengers,
and say: "We believe in some and not in the others,"
and wish to find a way (between affirmation and denial),

151. Are verily the real unbelievers.
And We have reserved for unbelievers
an ignominious punishment.

152. But those who believe in God and His apostles
and make no distinction among any of them,
will be given by Him their recompense;
for God is forgiving and kind.

The people of the Book demand of you
to bring for them a book from heaven.
But of Moses they had asked a bigger thing,
and demanded: "Show us God face to face."
They were struck by lightning then
as punishment for their wickedness.
Even then they made the calf,
when clear signs had reached them.
Still We forgave them
and gave Moses clear authority.

154. We exalted them on the Mount,
and they gave a solemn pledge, and We said to them:
"Enter the gates submissively," and told them:
"Do not break the Sabbath,"
and took a solemn pledge from them.

155. So (they were punished) for breaking the covenant
and disbelieving the signs of God,
and for killing the prophets unjustly, and saying:
"Our hearts are enfolded in covers,"
(though) in fact God had sealed them
because of their unbelief;
so they do not believe except a few;

156. And because they denied
and spoke dreadful calumnies of Mary;

157. And for saying: "We killed the Christ, Jesus, son of Mary,
who was an apostle of God;"
but they neither killed nor crucified him,
though it so appeared to them.
Those who disagree in the matter

are only lost in doubt. They have no knowledge about it
other than conjecture,
for surely they did not kill him,
158. But God raised him up (in position)*
and closer to Himself; and God is all-mighty and all-wise.
159. There is not one among the people of the Book
who will not believe in it before his death;
and he will be a witness over them
on the Day of Resurrection.
160. Because of the wickedness of some among the Jews,
and because they obstructed people from the way of God,
We forbade them many things
which were lawful for them;
161. And because they practised usury
although it had been forbidden them;
and for usurping others' wealth unjustly.
For those who are unbelievers among them
We have reserved
a painful punishment.
162. But to the learned among them,
and the believers who affirm
what has been revealed to you
and was revealed to those before you,
and to those who fulfil their devotional obligations,
who pay the zakat
and believe in God and the Last Day,
We shall give a great reward.

We have sent revelations to you as We sent
revelations to Noah and the prophets (who came) after him;
and We sent revelations to Abraham
and Ishmael and Isaac and Jacob, and their offspring,
and to Jesus and Job,
and to Jonah and Aaron and Solomon,
and to David We gave the Book of Psalms,
164. And to many an apostle We have mentioned before,
and to many other apostles We have not mentioned to you;
and to Moses God spoke directly.
165. All these apostles of good news and admonition
were sent so that after the apostles
men may have no argument against God.
God is all-powerful and all-wise.
166. God is Himself witness to what has been revealed to you,
and revealed with His knowledge,

-----

* For similar meaning of rafa'a see 19:57, 40:15, 56:23, 94:4.

and the angels are witness;
and God is sufficient as witness.
167. Those who denied and turned away
from the path of God,
have wandered far astray.
168. Those who deny and transgress
will not be forgiven by God,
nor be shown the way
169. Except to Hell,
where they will abide for ever;
and this is how (the law of God) works inevitably.
170. O men, the Apostle has now come to you,
bringing the truth from your Lord;
so believe for your own good;
but if you deny (then remember)
that all that is in the heavens and the earth
belongs to God;
and God is all-knowing and all-wise.
171. O people of the Book,
do not be fanatical in your faith,
and say nothing but the truth about God.
The Messiah who is Jesus, son of Mary,
was only an apostle of God, and a command of His
which He sent to Mary,
as a mercy from Him.
So believe in God and His apostles,
and do not call Him 'Trinity'.
Abstain from this for your own good;
for God is only one God,
and far from His glory is it
to beget a son.
All that is in the heavens and the earth
belongs to Him;
and sufficient is God for all help.

The Christ will never disdain
to be a votary of God,
nor will the angels close to Him.
And those who disdain
to serve Him and are proud (should remember)
that they will all go back to Him in the end.
173. Then those who believed and earned good deeds
will be given their recompense in full,
and even more out of grace.
But those who disdain and who boast
will receive a painful punishment.

An-Nisa

They will find none except God
to help them or save them.
174. O men, you have received
infallible proof from your Lord,
and We have sent down a beacon light to you.
175. So those who believe in God and hold fast to Him
shall indeed be received
into His mercy and His grace,
and be guided to Him the straight path.
176. They ask you for judgement about 'Kalalah'
(a man who dies childless). Say:
"God has given a decision in the matter of inheritance."
If a man dies and leaves no child behind
but have a sister, she will get a half of what he owned,
as he would have done the whole of what she possessed
if she had died a childless person. In case he has two sisters
then they will get two-thirds of the heritage.
But if he has both brothers and sisters,
the male will inherit a share equal to that of two females.
God makes this manifest to you lest you wander astray,
for God has knowledge of every thing.

I. V.1. This should be viewed in the light of God's throne being in the beginning "on the waters," 11:7, where 'throne' stands for authority, control, being the symbol of sovereign power, and affirmations that "all living things were created from water," 21:30, 24:45, including man, 25:54; that man was created from *tin,* loam or clay, 32:7, then from *nutfah,* that is semen or sperm, 16:4 etc. Biologically, the earliest form of life was the amoeba, a unicellular animal found in water; and all living organisms consist of cells. "We created you from a single cell (which is what the sperm is), and from it (note use of neuter gender) created its mate; and from the two dispersed men and women (male and female) in multitudes." Since *nafs* means more than one hundred things, including essence, sub-tance, vital principle, blood etc., it has enough amplitude to include 'cell' among its meanings, the concept of 'cell' being unknown to ancient etymologists to be indentified by them, but has been made clear by modern science. One of the many functions of cells is to produce hormones which govern every aspect of human experience. A cell is a complete unit, in itself a *nafs.* The cellular origin of sexes also gives absolute equality to women, which is emphasised throughout the Qur'an. At the same time, the *arham* or bond of relationships, and the symbiosis implied in the verse, become more significant when we consider the scientific fact that "the most spectacular symbionts of all are the mitochondria in all our cells, direct descendants of ancient bacteria . . ." (Dr. Lewis Thomas: The Way the World Works: Readers Digest, Nov. 1983). These bacteria are present in the *tin* from which man was created (32:7), and which also transmit genes, the metaphorical meaning of *tin* being man's essential quality and nature. Verse 54 of Surah 25 has special significance in this context as it contains a clear indication of the genetic element, discussed in footnote 2 on page 311. See also notes on pp. 505 and 515 which are connected with this subject.
2. Literally, *arham,* pl. of *rahm,* the womb, primordial symbol of the Mother, vessel of human repro-duction, goddess of early man, under whose feet lies Paradise. Hence the metaphorical meaning of relationships. See also note 2 on page 311.
3. That is, those outside the prohibited categories mentioned in verses 22-23. At the same time, marriage with "two, three, or four" is conditional on the fear of behaving inequitably with, or tempta-tion of misusing, the orphan, or husbandless girls in their charge.

5 The Feast

Al-Mā'idah: Madani

In the name of Allah, most benevolent, ever-merciful.

بِسْمِ اللهِ الرَّحْمٰنِ الرَّحِيْمِ ٠

O YOU WHO believe,
fulfil your obligations.
Made lawful (as food) for you are animals
except those mentioned (here);
but unlawful during Pilgrimage is game.
God ordains whatsoever He wills.
2. O you who believe,
do not violate the (sanctity of) offerings to God,
nor the rites of the holy month,
nor sacrificial cattle with garlands
(that are brought to the Ka'bah),
nor of the people who flock to the Holy House seeking
the bounties of their Lord, and His pleasure.
Hunt when you have laid aside the robe of the pilgrim.
And do not let your hatred
of a people who had barred you from the Holy Mosque
lead you to aggression.
But help one another in goodness and piety,
and do not assist in crime and rebellion,
and fear God. Surely
God is severe in punishment.
3. Forbidden you is carrion and blood,
and the flesh of the swine,
and whatsoever has been killed
in the name of some other than God,
and whatever has been strangled, or killed
by a blow or a fall, or by goring,
or that which has been mauled by wild beasts
unless slaughtered while still alive;
and that which has been slaughtered
at altars is forbidden,
and also dividing the meat
by casting lots with arrows.
All this is sinful.

Today the unbelievers have lost every hope
of (despoiling) your creed;
so do not fear them, fear Me.
Today I have perfected your system of belief
and bestowed My favours upon you in full,
and have chosen submission (al-Islam) as the creed for you.
If one of you is driven by hunger
(to eat the forbidden)
without the evil intent of sinning,
then God is forgiving and kind.
4. They ask you what is lawful for them.
Say:"All things are lawful for you that are clean,
and what the trained hunting animals take for you
as you have trained them in the light of God's teachings,
but read over them the name of God,
and fear (straying from the path of) God,
for God is swift in the reckoning."
5. On this day all things that are clean
have been made lawful for you;
and made lawful for you
is the food of the people of the Book,
as your food is made lawful for them.
And lawful are the chaste Muslim women,
and the women of the people of the Book who are chaste,
(for marriage) and not fornication or liaison,
if you give them their dowries.
Useless shall be rendered the acts
of those who turn back on their faith,
and they will be among the losers in the life to come.

O believers, when you stand up for the service of prayer
wash your faces and hands up to elbows,
and also wipe your heads,
and wash your feet up to the ankles.
If you are in a state of seminal pollution,
then bathe and purify yourself well.
But in case you are ill or are travelling,
or you have satisfied the call of nature,
or have slept with a woman,
and you cannot find water,
then take wholesome dust
and pass it over your face and your hands,
for God does not wish to impose any hardship on you.
He wishes to purify you,
and grace you with His favours in full
so that you may be grateful.

7. Remember the favours He bestowed on you,
and the covenant He cemented with you,
when you said: "We have heard and obey."
Have fear of God,
for He knows the secrets of your heart.
8. O you who believe,
stand up as witnesses for God in all fairness,
and do not let the hatred of a people
deviate you from justice.
Be just: This is closest to piety;
and beware of God. Surely
God is aware of all you do.
9. God has made a promise of forgiveness and the highest
reward
to those who believe and perform good deeds.
10. But those who disbelieve and deny Our revelations
are the people of Hell.
11. O believers, remember the favours God bestowed on you
when a people raised their hands against you
and He restrained their hands.
So fear God;
and the faithful should place their trust in God.

God covenanted the people of Israel
and raised twelve leaders among them,
and said: "I shall verily be with you.
If you fulfil your devotional obligations, pay the zakat
and believe in My apostles and support them,
and give a goodly loan to God,
I shall certainly absolve you of your evil,
and admit you to gardens with streams of running water.
But whosoever among you denies after this,
will have wandered away from the right path."
13. When they dishonoured their pledge
We condemned them, and hardened their hearts.
So they distort the words of the Scripture out of context,
and have forgotten some of what they were warned against.
You will always hear of treachery on their part
except that of a few.
But forbear and forgive them,
for God loves those who do good.
14. We had taken the pledge of those also
who call themselves Christians.
But they too forgot to take advantage
of the warning they were given.
So We have caused enmity and hatred among them

to last till the Day of Resurrection,
when God will inform them
of what they were doing.
15. O people of the Book,
Our Apostle has come to you, announcing
many things of the Scriptures that you have suppressed,
passing over some others.
To you has come light and a clear Book from God
16. Through which God will lead those
who follow His pleasure
to the path of peace,
and guide them out of darkness into light by His will,
and to the path that is straight.
17. Verily they are unbelievers who say:
"The Messiah, son of Mary, is God."
You ask them: "Who could prevail against God
if He had chosen to destroy the Messiah, son of Mary,
and his mother, and the rest of mankind?"
For God's is the kingdom
of the heavens and the earth
and whatsoever lies between them.
He creates what He please, for God
has the power over all things.
18. Say the Jews and the Christians:
"We are sons of God and beloved of Him."
Say: "Why does He punish you then for your sins?
No: You are only mortals, of His creation."
He can punish whom He please and pardon whom He will,
for God's is the kingdom
of the heavens and the earth
and all that lies between them,
and everything will go back to Him.
19. O you people of the Book,
Our Apostle has come to you
when apostles had ceased to come long ago,
lest you said: "There did not come to us
any messenger of good news or of warnings."
So now there has reached you
a bearer of good tidings and of warnings;
for God has the power over all things.

Remember when Moses said to his people:
"O my people, remember the favours that God bestowed on
            you
when He appointed apostles from among you,
and made you kings and gave you

what had never been given to any one in the world.
21. Enter then, my people, the Holy Land
that God has ordained for you,
and do not turn back, or you will suffer."
22. They said: "O Moses, in that land
live a people who are formidable;
we shall never go there until they leave.
We shall enter when they go away."
23. Then two of the men who feared (God),
and to whom God was gracious, said to them:
"Charge and rush the gate.
If you enter, you will surely be victorious.
And place your trust in God if you truly believe."
24. They said: "O Moses, we shall never, never enter
so long as they are there.
Go you and your Lord to fight them;
we stay here."
25. Said (Moses): "O Lord, I have control
over none but myself and my brother;
so distinguish between us and these, the wicked people."
26. (And God) said: "Then verily this land
is forbidden them for forty years, and they
shall wander perplexed over the earth.
So do not grieve for these, the wicked people."

Narrate to them exactly
the tale of the two sons of Adam.
When each of them offered a sacrifice (to God),
that of one was accepted,
and that of the other was not.
Said (the one): "I will murder you,"
and the other replied: "God only accepts
from those who are upright and preserve themselves from evil.
28. If you raise your hand to kill me,
I will raise not mine to kill you,
for I fear God, the Lord of all the worlds;
29. I would rather you suffered the punishment
for sinning against me, and for your own sin,
and became an inmate of Hell.
And that is the requital for the unjust."
30. Then the other was induced by his passion
to murder his brother, and he killed him,
and became one of the damned.
31. Then God sent a raven which scratched the ground
in order to show him how to hide
the nakedness of his brother.

أكُون مِثْلَ هٰذَا الْغُرَابِ فَأُوَارِيَ سَوْءَةَ أَخِي
فَأَصْبَحَ مِنَ النَّادِمِينَ ۝

"Alas, the woe," said he, "that I could not be
even like the raven and hide
the nakedness of my brother,"
and was filled with remorse.
32. That is why We decreed for the children of Israel
that whosoever kills a human being,
except (as punishment) for murder
or for spreading corruption in the land,
it shall be like killing all humanity;
and whosoever saves a life,
saves the entire human race.
Our apostles brought clear proofs to them;
but even after that most of them
committed excesses in the land.
33. The punishment for those
who wage war against God and His Prophet,
and perpetrate disorders in the land,
is to kill or hang them,
or have a hand on one side
and a foot on the other cut off,
or banish them from the land.
Such is their disgrace in the world,
and in the Hereafter
their doom shall be dreadful.
34. But those who repent before they are subdued
should know that God is forgiving and kind.

O you who believe, follow the path shown to you by God,
and seek the way of proximity to Him,
and struggle in His way:
you may have success.
36. As for unbelievers, if they possess
the riches of the whole earth, and two times more,
and offer it as ransom for release
from the torments of the Day of Resurrection,
it will not be accepted from them,
and their punishment will surely be painful.
37. They would like to escape from the Fire,
but will never succeed,
and their suffering will be constant.
38. As for the thief, whether man or woman,
cut* his hand as punishment from God
for what he had done; and God is all mighty and all wise.
39. But those who repent after a crime and reform,

_____

* See note 2 on p. 113

shall be forgiven by God,
for God is forgiving and kind.
40. Do you not know that God's is the kingdom
of the heavens and the earth?
He punishes whom He will,
and pardons whom He please,
for God has the power over all things.
41. Be not grieved, O Apostle, by those
who hasten to outrace others in denial,
and say with their tongues: "We believe,"
but do not believe in their hearts.
And those of the Jews who listen to tell lies,
and spy on behalf of others
who do not come to you, and who
distort the words (of the Torah) out of context, and say:
'If you are given (what we say is true) accept it;
but if you are not given it, beware."
You cannot intercede with God for him
whom God would not show the way.
These are the people whose hearts
God does not wish to purify.
For them is ignominy in this world
and punishment untold in the next —
42. Eavesdropping for telling lies, earning through unlawful
                                    means!
So, if they come to you, judge between them or decline.
And if you decline, they can do you no harm;
but if you judge, you should do so with justice,
for God loves those who are just.
43. But why should they make you a judge
when the Torah is with them which contains
the Law of God? Even then they turn away.
They are those who will never believe.

We sent down the Torah which contains
guidance and light, in accordance with which
the prophets who were obedient (to God)
gave instructions to the Jews, as did
the rabbis and priests, for they were
the custodians and witnesses of God's writ.
So, therefore, do not fear men, fear Me,
and barter not My messages away for a paltry gain.
Those who do not judge
by God's revelations are infidels indeed.
45. And there (in the Torah) We had ordained for them
a life for a life, and an eye for an eye,

and a nose for a nose, and an ear for an ear,
and a tooth for a tooth, and for wounds
retribution, though he who forgoes it
out of charity, atones for his sins.
And those who do not judge
by God's revelations are unjust.
46. Later, in the train (of the prophets),
We sent Jesus, son of Mary, confirming the Torah
which had been (sent down) before him,
and gave him the Gospel containing guidance and light,
which corroborated the earlier Torah,
a guidance and warning for those who
preserve themselves from evil and follow the straight path.
47. Let the people of the Gospel judge
by what has been revealed in it by God.
And those who do not judge
in accordance with what God has revealed are transgressors.
48. And to you We have revealed
the Book containing the truth,
confirming the earlier revelations,
and preserving them (from change and corruption).
So judge between them by what has been revealed
by God, and do not follow their whims,
side-stepping the truth that has reached you.
To each of you We have given a law
and a way and a pattern of life.
If God had pleased He could surely have made you
one people (professing one faith).
But He wished to try and test you
by that which He gave you.
So try to excel in good deeds.
To Him will you all return in the end,
when He will tell you of what you were at variance.
49. Judge between them in the light
of what has been revealed
by God, and do not follow their whims,
and beware of them lest they lead you away
from the guidance sent down to you by God.
If they turn away, then know
that God is sure to punish them for some of their sins;
and many of them are transgressors.
50. Do they seek a judgement of the days of pagan ignorance?
But who could be a better judge than God
for those who are firm in their faith?

O believers, do not hold Jews and Christians

as your allies. They are allies of one another;
and anyone who makes them his friends
is surely one of them;
and God does not guide the unjust.
52. You will notice that those
whose hearts are afflicted with sickness (of doubt)
only hasten to join them and say:
"We fear lest misfortune should surround us."
It may well be that God may soon send (you)
success, or other command of His.
Then will they be repentant
of what they had concealed in their hearts.
53. Then the believers will say: "Are these the people
who had sworn by God on solemn oath
and said: "We are surely with you?"
Wasted have been all their deeds,
and losers they remain.
54. O believers, any one of you who turns back on his faith
(should remember) that God
could verily bring (in your place) another people
whom He would love as they would love Him,
gentle with believers, unbending with infidels,
who would strive in the way of God,
unafraid of blame by any slanderer.
Such is the favour of God which He bestows
on whomsoever He will.
God is Infinite and all-knowing.
55. Your only friends are God and His Messenger,
and those who believe and are steadfast in devotion,
who pay the zakat and bow in homage (before God).
56. And those who take God and His Prophet
and the faithful as their friends
are indeed men of God,
who will surely be victorious.

O believers, do not make friends
with those who mock and make a sport of your faith,
who were given the Book before you,
and with unbelievers;
and fear God if you truly believe;
58. (Nor make friends with) those
who, when you call (the faithful) to prayer,
make mock of it and jest,
because they do not understand.
59. Say to them: "O people of the Book,
what reason have you for disliking us

other than that we believe
in God and what has been sent down to us,
and was sent down before,
and because most of you are disobedient?''
60. Say: ''Shall I inform you
who will receive the worst chastisement from God?
They who were condemned by God,
and on whom fell His wrath,
and those who were turned to apes and swine,
and those who worship the powers of evil.
They are in the worse gradation,
and farthest away from the right path.''
61. When they come to you they say: ''We believe;''
but unbelieving they came and unbelieving go;
and God is aware of what they conceal in their hearts.
62. You will see among them many
who rush into sin and wickedness,
and devour unlawful gain.
How evil are the things they do!
63. Why do not their rabbis and priests
prohibit them from talking of sinful things
and from devouring unlawful gain?
Evil are the acts they commit!
64. The Jews say: ''Bound are the hands of God.''
Tied be their own hands, and damned may they be
for saying what they say!
In fact, both His hands are open wide:
He spends of His bounty in any way He please.
But what your Lord has revealed to you
will only increase
their rebellion and unbelief.
So We have caused enmity and hatred among them
(which will last) till the Day of Resurrection.
As often as they ignite the fires of war
they are extinguished by God.
Yet they rush around to spread
corruption in the land;
but God does not love those who are corrupt.
65. If the people of the Book had believed and feared,
We would surely have absolved them of their sins,
and admitted them to gardens of delight.
66. And if they had followed the teachings of the Torah
and the Gospel, and what has been
sent down to them by their Lord,
they would surely have enjoyed (blessings)
from the heavens above

and the earth below their feet.
Some among them are moderate,
but evil is what most of them do!

O Prophet, announce
what has reached you from your Lord,
for if you do not,
you will not have delivered His message.
God will preserve you from (the mischief of) men;
for God does not guide those
who do not believe.
68. Say to them: "O people of the Book,
you have no ground (for argument)
until you follow the Torah and the Gospel
and what has been revealed
to you by your Lord."
But what has been revealed to you by your Lord
will surely increase
rebellion and unbelief in many;
so do not grieve for those who do not believe.
69. All those who believe,
and the Jews and the Sabians and the Christians,
in fact any one who believes in God and the Last Day,
and performs good deeds,
will have nothing to fear or regret.
70. We had taken a solemn pledge from the children of Israel,
and sent messengers to them;
but whenever an apostle came to them bringing
what did not suit their mood,
they called one imposter, another they slew,
71. And imagined that no trials would befall them;
and they turned deaf and blind (to the truth).
But God still turned to them;
yet many of them turned blind and deaf again;
but God sees every thing they do.
72. They are surely infidels who say:
"God is the Christ, son of Mary."
But the Christ had only said:
"O children of Israel, worship God
who is my Lord and your Lord."
Whosoever associates a compeer with God,
will have Paradise denied to him by God,
and his abode shall be Hell;
and the sinners will have none to help them.
73. Disbelievers are they surely who say:
"God is the third of the trinity;"

but there is no god other than God the one.
And if they do not desist from saying what they say,
then indeed those among them
who persist in disbelief
will suffer painful punishment.
74. Why do they not turn to God and ask His forgiveness?
God is forgiving and kind.
75. The Christ, son of Mary, was but an apostle,
and many apostles had (come and) gone before him;
and his mother was a woman of truth.
They both ate the (same) food (as men).
Behold, how We show men clear signs,
and behold, how they wander astray!
76. Tell them: "Leaving God aside, will you worship
something that has no power over your loss or gain?"
But God is all-hearing and all-knowing.
77. Tell them: "O people of the Book, do not overstep
the bounds of truth in your beliefs,
and follow not the wishes of a people who had erred before,
and led many others astray,
and wandered away from the right path."

Cursed were disbelievers
among the children of Israel
by David and Jesus, son of Mary,
because they rebelled and transgressed the bounds.
79. They did not restrain one another
from the wicked things they used to do;
and vile were the things that they were doing!
80. You can see among them many
allying themselves with the infidels.
Vile it was what they sent ahead of them,
so that God's indignation came upon them;
and torment will they suffer an eternity.
81. If they had believed
in God and the Prophet and what had been revealed to him,
they would never have held them as allies;
and many among them are transgressors.
82. You will find the Jews and idolaters
most excessive in hatred of those who believe;
and the closest in love to the faithful
are the people who say: "We are the followers of Christ,"
because there are priests and monks among them,
and they are not arrogant.
83. For when they listen to what has been revealed
to this Apostle, you can see their eyes brim over with tears

Al-Ma'idah

at the truth which they recognise, and say:
"O Lord, we believe; put us down
among those who bear witness (to the truth).
84. And why should we not believe in God
and what has come down to us of the truth?
And we hope to be admitted by our Lord
among those who are upright and do good?"
85 God will reward them for saying so
with gardens where streams flow by,
where they will live for ever.
This is the recompense of those who do good.
86. But those who disbelieve and deny Our revelations
are residents of Hell.

O believers, do not forbid the good things
God has made lawful for you;
and do not transgress.
God does not love transgressors.
88. Eat what is lawful and good
of the provisions God has bestowed on you,
and fear God in whom you believe.
89. God does not punish you
but for what you swear in earnest.
The expiation (for breaking an oath)
is feeding ten persons who are poor,
with food that you give your own families,
or clothing them, or freeing a slave.
But he who cannot do so
should fast for three days.
This is the expiation for an oath
when you have sworn it.
So abide by your oaths.
Thus God makes His commandments clear to you:
You may perhaps be grateful.
90. O believers, this wine and gambling,
these idols, and these arrows you use for divination,
are all acts of Satan; so keep away from them.
You may haply prosper.
91. Satan only wishes to create among you
enmity and hatred through wine and gambling,
and to divert you from the remembrance of God and prayer.
Will you therefore not desist?
92. Obey God and the Prophet, and beware.
If you turn away, remember,
that the duty of Our Apostle
is to give you a clear warning.

Al-Ma'idah

93. Those who believe and perform good deeds
will not be held guilty
for what they have eaten (in the past)
if they fear God and believe,
and do good things
and are conscious (of God) and believe,
and still fear and do good,
for God loves those who do good.

O you who believe, God will surely try you
with the game that you take with your hands or your lances,
in order to know who fear Him unseen.
Whosoever transgress after this
will suffer grievous punishment.
95. O you who believe, do not kill game
when you are on pilgrimage.
And anyone among you who does so on purpose
should offer livestock of equivalent value, determined
by two honourable persons among you, (as atonement),
to be brought to the Ka'bah as an offering;
or else expiate by giving food to the poor,
or its equivalent in fasting,
so that he may realise the gravity of his deed.
God has forgiven what has happened in the past;
but any one who does so again
will be punished by God.
And God is severe in requital.
96. Lawful is all game of the water for you,
and eating of it as food, so that you
and the travellers may benefit by it.
But unlawful is game of the jungle
when you are on pilgrimage.
Fear God before whom you have to gather in the end.
97. God has made the Ka'bah, the Sacred House,
a means of support for mankind,
as also the holy month, the sacrificial offerings,
and consecrated cattle, so that you may understand
that known to God is all that is in the heavens and the earth,
and God has knowledge of every thing.
98. Know that the punishment of God is severe,
but that God is also forgiving and kind.
99. It is for the Prophet to convey the message:
God knows what you reveal and what you hide.
100. Tell them: "The unclean and the pure
are not equal,
even though the abundance of the unclean

may be pleasing to you."
So fear God, O men of wisdom;
you may haply find success.

O believers, do not ask about things which,
if made known to you, may vex you.
But if you ask about them
when the Qur'an is being revealed
they will be unfolded to you.
God has overlooked (your failings) in this (respect),
for God is forgiving and forbearing.
102. Such things were asked by a people before you,
but they disbelieved them afterwards.
103. God has not sanctioned Baheerah or Sa'ibah,
Waseelah or Hām*.
The unbelievers fabricate lies of God,
for many of them are devoid of sense.
104. When you say to them: "Come to what
God has revealed, and the Prophet," they say:
"Sufficient to us is the faith
that our fathers had followed," even though
their fathers had no knowledge or guidance.
105. O you who believe, on you rests (the responsibility)
for your own selves.
If you follow the right path those who have gone astray
will not be able to do you harm.
To God have all of you to return,
when He will tell you what you were doing
106. O you who believe, let two honest men among you
be witness when you dictate your last will and testament
as (the hour of) death draws near;
and if death approaches while you are on a journey,
two men other than yours.
Detain them after the service of prayer,
and if you doubt their word
make them swear by God that :
"We shall not take a bribe even though it be offered
by a near relative, nor hide the testimony of God,
for then we shall surely be sinful."
107. If it transpires they have concealed the truth,
two of those who are immediately concerned
should take their place and swear by God:
"Our testimony is truer than theirs.

---

* Names of consecrated animals which were dedicated to pagan deities and were allowed to roam freely without molestation.

We have stated no more (than the truth),
or else we shall be unjust."
108. It is thus likely that men
will bear witness rightly,
or else fear that their oaths
may be disproved by oaths given after them.
So fear God, and do not forget
that God does not guide the iniquitous.

The day God will gather the apostles and ask:
"What answer was made to you?"
They will say: "We know not.
You alone know the secrets unknown."
110. And when God will say: "O Jesus, son of Mary,
remember the favours I bestowed on you
and your mother, and reinforced you
with divine grace that you spoke to men
when in the cradle, and when in the prime of life;
when I taught you the law and the judgement
and the Torah and the Gospel;
when you formed the state
of your people's destiny* out of mire
and you breathed (a new spirit) into it,
and they rose by My leave;
when you healed the blind by My leave, and the leper*;
when you put life into the dead by My will;
and when I held back the children of Israel from you
when you brought to them My signs,
and the disbelievers among them said:
"Surely these are nothing but pure magic."
111. And when I inspired the disciples (through Jesus)
to believe in Me and My apostle, they said:
"We believe, and You bear witness that we submit."
112. When the disciples said: "O Jesus, son of Mary,
could your Lord send down for us a table laid with food?"
he said: "Fear God, if indeed you believe."
113. They said: "We should like to eat of it
to reassure our hearts and to know
that it's the truth you have told us,
and that we should be witness to it."
114. Said Jesus, son of Mary. "O God, our Lord,
send down a table well laid out with food from the skies
so that this day may be a day of feast
for the earlier among us and the later,

---

* See note 1 for destiny, and note 2 on leprosy on page 56.

and a token from You.
Give us our (daily) bread,
for You are the best of all givers of food."
115. And said God: "I shall send it down to you;
but if any of you disbelieve after this,
I shall inflict such punishment on him as I never
shall inflict on any other creature."

And when God will ask: "O Jesus, son of Mary,
did you say to mankind:
'Worship me and my mother as two deities apart from God?' "
(Jesus) will answer: "Halleluja.
Could I say what I knew I had no right (to say)?
Had I said it You would surely have known,
for You know what is in my heart
though I know not what You have.*
You alone know the secrets unknown.
117. I said nought to them but what You commanded me:
Worship God, my Lord and your Lord.
And so long as I dwelt with them
I was witness over their actions.
And after my life had been done,
You were their keeper;
and You are a witness over all things.
118. If You punish them, indeed they are Your creatures;
if You pardon them, indeed You are mighty and wise."
119. God will say: "This is the day
when the truthful shall profit by their truthfulness.
For them will be gardens with streams running by,
where they will for ever abide."
God will accept them, and they
will be gratified in (obeying) Him.
This will surely be happiness supreme.
120. To God belongs all that is in the heavens and the earth,
and His the power over every thing.

---

*Ibn Faris says that *nafs* also means knowledge and wisdom.

2. Note on v. 38, p. 102. *Qata'a* means to cut, but when used with different nouns it means different things idiomatically, for which see Raghib and *Taj al-'urus,* such as to stop someone from speaking when used with *lisan,* tongue, or cut off the road when used with *sabil,* or become hopeless when used with *rajul,* man, etc. In 12:31, for instance, *qatta'na aidihunna* means they wounded their hands or stopped peeling fruit, *not* cut off their hands. Hence here, in v. 38, it could also mean to stop their hands from stealing by adopting deterrent means, for the next verse, 39, speaks of repentance and forgiveness with overtones of rehabilitation, which would be lost if the hands were cut off completely or amputated. Similarly in v. 33 *tuqatta'a* could mean restrain them by putting fetters on one hand and one leg. During the Umayyad caliphate the punishment for theft was flogging.

Al-Ma'idah   113

6 The Cattle

Al-An'ām: Makki

In the name of Allah, most benevolent, ever-merciful.

ALL PRAISE BE to God
who created the heavens and the earth,
and ordained darkness and light.
Yet the unbelievers make
the others equal of their Lord.
2. It is He who created you from clay
then determined a term (of life) for you,
and a term (is fixed) with Him. Even then you doubt.
3. He is God in the heavens and the earth.
He knows what you hide and bring out into the open,
and knows what you earn (of good and evil).
4. Yet no sign of their Lord comes to them
but they turn away from it.
5. So they disbelieved the truth when it came to them;
but they will soon come to know
the reality of what they had ridiculed.
6. Do they not see how many generations We laid low
before them, whom We had firmly established in the land
as We have not established you,
and showered abundant rain on them,
and made rivers lap at their feet,
yet whom We destroyed for their sins,
and raised new generations after them?
7. Even if We had sent you a transcript on paper
which they could feel with their hands,
the unbelievers would have said:
"This is nothing but clear sorcery."
8. They say: "How is it no angel was sent down to him?"
Had We sent an angel down
the matter would have come to end,
and they would have had no respite.
9. Even if We had sent down an angel as messenger
he would have appeared in the garb of a man
and filled them with confusion, like the one

they are filled with.

10. Surely the apostles have been mocked before you;
but what they had mocked
rebounded on the mockers themselves.

Say: "Travel in the land and see
what happened to those who disbelieved."

12. And ask: "To whom belongs
what is in the heavens and the earth?"
Say: "To God."
He has prescribed grace for Himself.
He will gather you on the Day of Resurrection
which is certain to come.
Only they who are lost of soul
will not come to believe.

13. Whatsoever dwells in the night and day belongs to Him.
He is all-hearing and all-knowing.

14. Say: "Should I find some other protector besides God
the Creator of the heavens and the earth,
who nourishes all and is nourished by none?
Say: "I am commanded to be the first
to submit to Him, and not be an idolater."

15. Say: "If I disobey my Lord, I fear
the punishment of a grievous Day."

16. Whosoever is spared that Day
will surely have mercy shown to him,
and this will be a clear triumph.

17. If God sends you harm,
there is no one but He who can take it away;
and if He bring you good,
surely He has power over every thing.

18. It is He who prevails over His creatures,
and He is all-wise and aware.

19. Ask: "Of all things what is most vital as evidence?"
Say: "God (who) is witness between you and me
that this Qur'an has been revealed to me that I
may warn you on its strength,
and those whom it reaches.
Do you really bear witness
there are other gods with God?"
Tell them: "I bear no such witness."
Say: "Verily He is the only God,
and I am clear of what you associate (with Him)."

20. Those to whom We have given the Book
know it distinctly as they know their sons;
but those who are lost of soul do not believe.

Al-An'am　　　　　　　　　　　　　　　　　115

And who is more wicked than he
who invents lies about God or denies His revelations?
Surely the wicked will not succeed.
22. The day We shall gather all of them together
and say to those who ascribe (partners to God):
"Where are the compeers who you claimed
(were equal to God)?"
23. Then their excuse will be but to say:
"By God our Lord, we were not idolaters."
24. You will see how they will lie against themselves,
and all their slanderings will be vain.
25. There are some among them who listen to you;
but We have put a covering on their hearts
so that they fail to understand it,
and a deafness appears in their ears. Even if they saw
all the signs they would not believe in them;
and even when they come to you to dispute with you,
the unbelievers say: "This is nothing but fables of antiquity."
26. And they forbid others from (believing in) it,
and themselves keep away from it.
But they ruin none but themselves,
and do not understand.
27. If you should see them when they are stood before the
  Fire,
they will say: "Ah would that we were sent back (to the
  world)!
We shall not deny the signs of our Lord,
and be among those who believe."
28. But no. What they were hiding
has now become clear to them.
If they were sent back they would surely return
to what had been forbidden them,
for surely they are liars.
29. They say: "There is no other life but that of this world,
and we will not be raised (from the dead)."
30. If you see them
when they are put before their Lord,
He will say to them: "Is not this the truth?"
They will answer: "Indeed, by our Lord."
He will say: "Then taste the agony
of punishment for what you had denied."

They are surely lost who call
the meeting with God a lie.
When the Hour comes upon them unawares,
they will say: "Alas, we neglected it!"

and carry their burdens on their backs:
How evil the burden they will carry!
32. As for the life of this world,
it is nothing but a frolic and frivolity.
The final abode is the best
for those who are pious and fear God.
Do you not comprehend?
33. We know what they say distresses you.
It is not you in fact they accuse of lies,
but the wicked deny the revelations of God!
34. Many an apostle has been accused of lies before you.
Yet they bore with fortitude
the falsehoods and the hurt
until Our help arrived.
There is no changing the word of God:
The news of (past) apostles has come to you already.
35. If their aversion still weighs upon you,
seek out a tunnel (going deep) into the earth,
or a ladder reaching out to the skies,
and bring them a sign: (Even then they will not believe).
If God had willed
He would have brought them all to the right path.
So be not like the pagans.
36. Only they will respond who can hear.
As for the dead, raised they will be by God,
then to Him they will be returned.
37. They say: "How is it no miracle was sent down
to him from his Lord?"
Say: "God certainly has power to send down a miracle;
but most men cannot understand."
38. There is not a thing that moves on the earth,
no bird that flies on its wings,
but has a community of its own like yours.
There is nothing that We have left out
from recording.
Then they will all be gathered before their Lord.
39. Those who deny Our revelations
are deaf, dumb, and lost in the dark.
God sends whosoever He wills astray,
and leads whom He will to the straight path.
40. Say: "Have you thought if the punishment of God
or the Hour (of Doom) came upon you,
would you call to any other than God?
Answer, if you are men of truth."
41. No: You will call to Him alone;
and He will, if He please,

remove (the distress) for which you had called Him;
and forget those you associate
as compeers (with Him).

We have indeed sent (apostles)
to many a people before you,
and inflicted upon them hardships and afflictions
so that they might submit.
43. Then why did they not submit
when Our punishment came upon them?
But their hearts were hardened,
and Satan made things they were doing
look attractive to them.
44. When they had become oblivious
of what they were warned,
We opened wide the gates
of every thing to them;
yet as they rejoiced at what they were given,
We caught them unawares,
and they were filled with despair.
45. Thus were the wicked people
rooted out of existence to the last.
All praise be to God,
the Lord of all the worlds.
46. Say: "Imagine if God takes away
your hearing and sight, and sets a seal on your hearts,
what deity other than God will restore them to you?"
See how We inflect Our signs:
Even then they turn aside.
47. Say: "Imagine if the punishment of God
were to come unawares, or openly,
who will perish but the evil-doers?"
48. We do not send apostles but to give
good tidings and to warn.
Then those who believe or reform
will have neither fear nor regret.
49. But those who deny Our messages
will be seized by nemesis for being disobedient.
50. Tell them: "I do not say that I possess
the treasures of God, or have knowledge of the Unknown,
or that I am an angel.
I only follow what is sent down to me."
And say: "How can a blind man
and a man who can see, be alike?
Will you not reflect?"

Warn those who fear, through this (Qur'an),
that they will be gathered before their Lord,
and they will have none to protect or intercede for them
apart from Him. They may haply take heed for themselves.
52. Do not turn away those who supplicate their Lord
morning and evening, seeking His magnificence.
You are not accountable for them in the least,
nor they for you at all.
If you drive them away you will only be unjust.
53. Thus do We try men through one another
so that they may ask:
"Are these the ones of all of us
who have been favoured by God?"
Does God not know who are the grateful?
54. When those who believe in Our revelations
come to you, say to them: "Peace on you."
Your Lord has prescribed grace for Himself,
so that in case one of you commits evil out of ignorance,
then feels repentant and reforms,
He may be forgiving and kind.
55. Thus distinctly do We explain
Our signs that the way of sinners may become distinct.

Tell them: "I am forbidden to worship those
you invoke apart from God."
And say: "I will not follow your wishes.
If I do, I shall be lost and not be
one of those who follow the right path."
57. Tell them: "A clear proof has come to me from my Lord,
and Him you deny.
But what you wish to be hastened
is not within my power.
The judgement is only God's.
He unfolds the Truth,
and is the best of judges."
58. Say: "If what you wish to be hastened
were in my power,
all matters between you and me would have been settled;
God is cognisant of those who are unjust."
59. He has the keys of the Unknown.
No one but He has knowledge;
He knows what is on the land and in the sea.
Not a leaf falls without His knowledge,
nor a grain in the darkest (recess) of the earth,
nor any thing green or seared
that is not recorded in the open book (of nature).

واذا سمعوا   الانعام ٦

60. It is He indeed who sends you to death at night,
and knows what you do in the day,
then makes you rise with it again in order that
the fixed term of life be fulfilled.
Then to Him you will be returned
when He will tell you what you did.

He has power over His creatures, and appoints
guardians to watch over them.
When death comes to one of you,
Our messengers take away his soul,
and do not falter.
62. Then they are taken to God,
their real lord and master.
His indeed is the judgement;
and He is swift at reckoning.
63. Ask: "Who is it who comes to your rescue
in the darkness of the desert and the sea,
and whom you supplicate humbly and unseen:
'If You deliver us from this,
we shall indeed be grateful?' "
64. Say: "God delivers you from this and every calamity.
Even then you ascribe compeers (to Him)!"
65. Say: "He has power to send you retribution
from the skies above,
or the earth beneath your feet,
or confound you with divisions among you,
and give one the taste
of the vengeance of the other."
See, how distinctly We explain Our signs
that they may understand.
66. This (Book) has been called by your people
a falsehood though it is the truth.
Say: "I am not a warden over you."
67. A time is fixed for every prophecy;
you will come to know in time.
68. When you see them argue about Our messages,
withdraw from their company
until they begin to talk of other things.
In case the Devil makes you forget,
leave the company of these unjust people
the moment you remember this.
69. As for the heedful and devout, they are not
accountable for them, but should give advice:
They may haply come to fear God.
70. Leave those alone

Al-An'am   120

who have made a sport and frolic of their faith,
and have been seduced by the life of this world.
Remind them hereby lest a man
is doomed for what he has done.
He will have none to help him,
or intercede for him, other than God;
and even if he offer all the ransoms
they will not be accepted from him.
They are those who will be destroyed by their own acts.
There will be scalding water to drink for them
and painful punishment,
for they had disbelieved.

Say: "Should we call in place of God
one who can neither help nor do us harm,
and turn back after having been guided by God,
like a man beguiled by the devils
who wanders perplexed in the wilderness
while his friends call him back to the right path,
saying: 'Come to us, this way?' "
Say: "God's guidance is (true) guidance,
and we have been commanded
to submit to the Lord of all the worlds.
72. Observe (your) devotional obligations and fear (God),
for it is He before whom you will be gathered (in the end)."
73. It is He who created the heavens and the earth
with a definite purpose. The day
He will say "Be," it will be.
His word is the truth,
His alone the power on the Day
when the blast of the trumpet will be sounded.
He knows the hidden and the visible.
He is all-prudent and all-knowing.
74. Remember when Abraham said to Azar, his father:
"Why do you take idols for God?
I certainly find you and your people in error."
75. Thus We showed to Abraham the visible
and invisible world of the heavens and the earth,
that he could be among those who believe.
76. When the night came with her covering of darkness
he saw a star,
and (Azar, his father) said: "This is my Lord."
But when the star set, (Abraham) said:
"I love not those that wane."
77. When (Azar) saw the moon rise all aglow,
he said: "This is my Lord."

But even as the moon set, (Abraham) said:
"If my Lord had not shown me the way
I would surely have gone astray."
78. When (Azar) saw the sun rise all resplendent,
he said: "My Lord is surely this,
and the greatest of them all."
But the sun also set, and (Abraham) said:
"O my people, I am through
with those you associate (with God).
79. I have truly turned my face
towards Him who created the heavens and the earth:
I have chosen one way and am not an idolater."
80. His people argued, and he said:
"Do you argue with me about God?
He has guided me already,
and I fear not what you associate with Him,
unless my Lord wills,
for held within the knowledge of my Lord is every thing.
Will you not reflect?
81. And why should I fear those you associate with Him
when you fear not associating others with God
for which He has sent down no sanction?
Tell me, whose way is the way of peace,
if you have the knowledge?
82. They alone have peace who believe and do not intermix
belief with denial,
and are guided on the right path."

This is the argument
We gave to Abraham against his people.
We exalt whosoever We please in rank by degrees.
Your Lord is wise and all-knowing.
84. And We gave him Isaac and Jacob and guided them,
as We had guided Noah before them,
and of his descendants, David and Solomon
and Job and Joseph and Moses and Aaron.
Thus We reward those who are upright and do good.
85. Zachariah and John We guided,
and guided Jesus and Elias
who were all among the upright.
86. We gave guidance to Ishmael,
Elisha and Jonah and Lot;
And We favoured them over the other people of the world,
87. As We did some of their fathers
and progeny and brethren, and chose them,
and showed them the right path.

Al-An'am

88. This is God's guidance:
He gives among His creatures whom He will.
If they had associated others with Him,
surely vain would have been all they did.
89. Those were the people to whom We gave
the Book and the Law and the Prophethood.
But if they reject these things
We shall entrust them to a people who will not deny.
90. Those were the people who were guided by God;
so follow their way.
Say: "I ask no recompense of you for this.
It is but a reminder for all the people of the world."

But they failed to make a just estimation of God
when they said: "He did not reveal to any man any thing."
Ask them: "Who then revealed the Book that Moses brought, —
a guidance and light for men, —
which you treat as sheafs of paper,
which you display, yet conceal a great deal,
though through it you were taught things
you did not know before,
nor even your fathers knew?"
Say: "God," and leave them
to the sport of engaging in vain discourse.
92. And this (Qur'an) is another Book that We have revealed,
blessed, affirming the earlier (revelations),
so that you may warn the people of (Makkah) the town of
                                        towns,
and those who live around it.
Those who believe in the life to come shall believe in it
and be watchful of their moral obligations.
93. Who is more vile than he
who slanders God of falsehood,
or says: "Revelation came to me,"
when no such revelation came to him;
or one who claims: "I can reveal
the like of what has been sent down by God?"
If you could see the evil creatures
in the agony of death
with the angels thrusting forward their hands
(saying): "Yield up your souls:
This day you will suffer ignominious punishment
for uttering lies about God and rejecting
His signs with arrogance."
94. "You have come before Us all alone," (God will say),
"as when you were created first,

leaving behind all that We had bestowed on you.
We do not see your intercessors with you
who, you imagined, had partnership with you.
Shattered lie your ties with them now,
and gone are the claims you made.''

Indeed it is God
who splits up the seed and the kernel,
and brings forth the living from the dead,
the dead from the living.
This is God:
So whither do you stray?
96. He ushers in the dawn,
and made the night for rest,
the sun and moon a computation.
Such is the measure appointed by Him,
the omnipotent and all-wise.
97. It is He who made the stars
by which you reckon your way
through the darkness of the desert and the sea.
Distinct have We made Our signs
for those who recognise.
98. It is He who produced you from a single cell,
and appointed a place of sojourning,
(the womb of the mother),
and a place of depositing,
(the grave).
How clear have We made Our signs
for those who understand.
99. It is He who sends down water from the skies,
and brings out of it every thing that grows,
the green foliage,
the grain lying close,
the date palm trees with clusters of dates,
and the gardens of grapes, and of olives and pomegranates,
so similar yet so unlike.
Look at the fruits, how they appear
on the trees, and they ripen.
In all these are signs for those who believe.
100. Yet they ascribe to jinns a partnership with God,
although He created them;
and they ascribe to Him sons and daughters,
without possessing any knowledge.
All praise be to Him. He is much too exalted
for things they associate (with Him).

Creator of the heavens and the earth from nothingness,
how could He have a son
when He has no mate?
He created all things,
and has knowledge of all things.
102. This is God, your Lord;
there is no god but He,
the creator of all things.
So pay homage to Him,
for He takes care of every thing.
103. No eyes can penetrate Him,
but He penetrates all eyes,
and He knows all the mysteries,
for He is all-knowing.
104. To you have come signs from your Lord,
(and the light of understanding).
So any one who sees (and understands)
does so for himself,
and any one who turns blind
shall suffer the consequences alone.
(Say:) "I am not a guardian over you
(to make you understand)."
105. Thus in varied ways
We explain Our signs
so that they may say: "You have been instructed,"
and that We might make it clear
to those who understand.
106. So follow what is sent down to you by your Lord,
for homage is due to no one but God,
and turn away from idolaters.
107. Had He willed they would not have been idolaters.
We have not appointed you their guardian,
nor are you their pleader.
108. Do not revile those who invoke
others apart from God, lest they begin
to revile God out of malice and ignorance.
We have made attractive their deeds to every people.
They have to go back to their Lord,
when He will tell them what they used to do.
109. They solemnly swear by God:
"If a sign comes to us
we shall certainly believe in it."
Tell them: "The signs are with God."
Yet for all you know
they will not believe if the signs came to them.
110. We shall turn their hearts and their eyes,

for they did not believe them at the very first,
and leave them to wander perplexed in bewilderment.

Even if We send down the angels to them,
and the dead should speak to them,
and We gather all things before their eyes,
they will not believe, unless God should will,
for most of them are ignorant.
112. That is how We have made for each apostle
opponents, the satans among men and jinns,
who inspire one another with deceitful talk.
But if your Lord had willed they would not have done so.
Pay no attention to them and to what they fabricate.
113. Let those who do not believe in the life to come,
listen to it and be pleased with it,
and let them gain what they may gain.
114. (Say): "Then should I seek (the source of) law
elsewhere than God,
when it is He who has revealed this Book to you,
which distinctly explains (every thing)?"
Those to whom We have given the Book know it has been
sent by your Lord in truth. So be not a sceptic.
115. Perfected are the laws of your Lord in truth and justice,
and there is no changing His laws.
He is all-hearing and all-knowing.
116. If you follow the majority of people on the earth,
they will lead you astray from the path of God,
for they follow only conjecture and surmise.
117. Your Lord surely knows those who have strayed
from his path, and knows those who are rightly guided.*
118. Eat only that over which the name of God
has been pronounced, if you truly believe in His commands.
119. And why should you not eat of that
over which the name of God has been pronounced,
when He has made it distinctly clear
what is forbidden, unless you are constrained to do so.
Surely many (men) mislead others into following
their vain desires through lack of knowledge.
Your Lord certainly knows the transgressors.
120. Discard both the visible and invisible sin.
For those who sin will be punished for what they have done.

---

* vv. 112-17 centre round falsification of belief and the laws of the Qur'an. The true believers
uphold the Qur'an wholly and completely. The hypocrites and false believers only profess belief in
it, but spread frivolous stories, *lahv-al-hadith* (31:6) and make the Qur'an *mahjura*, ineffectual by
shackling it (25:30) with laws derived from fabricated traditions, customs, hearsay, and their own,
man-made laws which are held more sacrosanct, thus imposing their own concept of morality on it.

121. Do not eat of that over which
God's name has not been pronounced,
for that would amount to exceeding the limits of law.
Certainly the devils inspire their proteges
to dispute with you:
If you obey them, you will surely become an idolater.

Can he who was lifeless, to whom We gave life,
and gave him a light
in whose glow he walks among men,
be like him who is used to darkness
from which he can never emerge?
Thus have been their doings made attractive to unbelievers.

123. And thus have We placed in every city
the greatest of the sinners to contrive and deceive;
yet they contrive against no one but themselves
even though they do not know.

124. Every time a sign comes to them
they say: "We shall never believe till what God's apostles
had been given comes to us."
God knows best where to direct His messages.
A degradation will befall the sinners
and chastisement from God for deceiving.

125. Thus God guides whomsoever He please
by opening wide his breast to surrender;
and straitens the breasts of those He allows to go astray,
(who feel suffocated) as if they were ascending the skies.
Thus will God punish those who do not believe.

126. This is the straight path of your Lord.
Distinct have We made Our signs
for those who reflect.

127. For them is an abode of peace with their Lord.
He will be their defender as reward for what they did.

128. On the day He will gather them together,
(He will say:) "O you assembly of jinns,
you made great use of men."
But their proteges among men will say:
"O our Lord, we lived a life of mutual gain,
but have now reached the term You ordained for us."
"Your abode is Hell," He will say,
"where you will dwell for ever,
unless God please otherwise."
Verily your Lord is wise and all-knowing.

129. Thus do We place some sinners over others
as requital for their deeds.

O you assembly of jinns and men, *
did not apostles come to you
from among you, communicating My signs
to you, bringing warnings
of this your day (of Doom)?''
They will answer: "We bear witness to our sins.''
They were surely deluded by the life of the world,
and bore witness against themselves
because they were unbelievers.

131. And this (so that it may be clear) that your Lord
does not destroy towns and cities arbitrarily
while the citizens remain unaware.

132. Every one has his place according to his deeds,
for your Lord is not negligent of what you do.

133. Your Lord is all-sufficient and full of benevolence.
He can take you away if He please,
and make whom He will succeed you,
as He had raised you from the progeny of others.

134. The promise that was made to you
is bound to be fulfilled.
It is not in your power to defeat it.

135. Tell them: "O my people,
go on acting on your part,
I am acting on mine.
You will soon know whose is the guerdon of life to come.''
The wicked will not succeed.

136. They allocate a share
from God's own created fields and cattle
to God, and they say: "This is God's'' —
or so they think — "and that, of the compeers of God,''
so that what belongs to the compeers
does not reach God, but that which is God's
may reach the compeers (set up by them).
How bad is the judgement that they make!

137. In the same way have their companions shown
many unbelievers the killing of their children as desirable
in order to ruin them and falsify their faith.
If God had so willed they would never have done so.
Leave them to their falsehoods.

138. They also say: "These cattle and these crops
are consecrated. None may eat of them other than those
we permit,'' — so they assert.
"And the use of these cattle is forbidden for carrying burden.''

---

* *Jinn* means to hide, used both for invisible forces and beings, as in 26:210 and 37:158, and nomadic
tribes, as here. *Ins* is also used for settled tribes, as in 2:60.

They do not pronounce the name of God on certain animals,
inventing lies against Him.
He will punish them for what they fabricate.
139. And they say: "Whatever is in the wombs
of these cattle is only meant for men and forbidden our women;
but in case it should be still-born both could eat it."
God will punish them for what they assert.
He is all-wise and all-knowing.
140. They will surely perish who kill their offspring
in ignorance foolhardily,
and forbid the food that God has given them
by fabricating lies against God.
Misguided are they surely,
and will never come to guidance.

It is He who grew the gardens, trellised and bowered,
and palm trees and land sown with corn
and many other seeds,
and olives and pomegranates,
alike and yet unlike.
So eat of their fruit when they are in fruit,
and give on the day of harvesting
His due, and do not be
extravagant,
for God does not love those who are prodigal.
142. He has created beasts of burden and cattle for slaughter.
So eat of what God has given you for food,
and do not walk in the footsteps of Satan
who is surely your declared enemy.
143. There are eight pairs,
two of the species of sheep and two of goats.
Ask them which has He forbidden,
the two males or the two females,
or what the females carry in their wombs?
Produce the sanction if you are truthful.
144. And there are two of camels and two of oxen.
Ask them: "Which has He forbidden,
the two males or the two females,
or what the females carry in their wombs?"
Were you present at the time God issued this command?"
Who then could be more wicked than he
who fabricates a lie and ascribes it to God
to mislead men, without any knowledge?
God does not guide the miscreants.

You tell them: "In all the commands revealed to me

I find nothing which
men have been forbidden to eat except carrion
and running blood and flesh of the swine for it is unclean,
or meat consecrated in the name of some other than God,
which is profane.
But if one is constrained to eat of these
without craving or reverting to it,
then surely your Lord is forgiving and kind."
146. We made unlawful for the Jews
all animals with claws or nails,
and the fat of the oxen and sheep,
except that on their backs or their intestines,
or which remains attached to their bones.
This was the punishment for their insubordination;
and what We say is true.
147. If they call you a liar,
tell them infinite is the mercy of your Lord;
but His vengeance will not be turned back from the sinners.
148. But the idolaters say: "If God had so willed
we would not have associated (others with Him),
nor would have our fathers,
nor would we have forbidden any thing."
So had others denied before them, and had to taste
Our punishment in the end.
Ask them: "Have you any knowledge? Then display it.
You follow nothing but conjecture,
and are nothing but liars."
149. Say: "To God belongs the consummate argument. Had
        He willed
He would surely have guided all of you aright."
150. Tell them: "Bring your witnesses to testify
that God has forbidden this (and this)."
Then even if they testify,
you should not testify with them;
and do not follow the wishes of those who deny Our signs
and believe not in the Hereafter,
and make others the equal of their Lord.

Tell them: "Come, I will read out what your Lord
has made binding on you:
That you make none the equal of God,
and be good to your parents,
and do not abandon your children out of poverty,
for We give you food and We shall provide for them;
and avoid what is shameful, whether open or hidden,
and do not take a life which God has forbidden,

unless for some just cause.
These things has God enjoined on you.
Haply you may understand.
152. Do not spend the belongings of the orphans
but for their betterment,
until they come of age;
and give in full measure, and weigh justly on the balance.
God does not burden a soul beyond capacity.
When you say a thing, let it be just,
even though the matter relate to a relative of yours,
and fulfil a promise made to God.
These are the things that He has enjoined
that you may take heed.
153. (He has further commanded:) 'This is My straight path,
so walk along it, and do not follow other ways,
lest you should turn away from the right one.'
All this has He commanded.
You may perhaps take heed for yourselves."
154. To that end We gave the Book
to Moses, a perfect law,
distinctly explaining all things,
and a guidance and grace, so that they should believe
in the meeting with their Lord.

Blessed is this Book We have revealed;
so follow it and preserve yourself from evil
that you may qualify for grace,
156. Lest you say: "The Book that was sent before
was meant only for two groups;
we were not aware of their teachings;"
157. Or that: "Had the Book been sent down to us
we would surely have been guided better than they."
So you have now received from your Lord
a clear proof and a guidance and grace.
Then who is more wicked than he
who denies the signs of God
and turns away from them?
We shall punish those severely
who turn away: A requital indeed
for having turned aside.
158. What are the people waiting for?
For the angels to come down,
or your Lord to appear,
or some signs from your Lord?
The day when certain signs appear from your Lord,
the embracing of faith shall not be of any avail

to one who did not come to belief at first,
or who did not perform good deeds
by virtue of his faith.
Tell them: "Wait on, we are waiting too
(for the good and evil to become distinct)."

159. As for those who have created schisms
in their order, and formed different sects,
you have no concern with them.
Their affair is with God.
He will tell them the truth
of what they were doing.

160. He who does a good deed will receive
ten times its worth;
and he who does evil
will be requited to an equal degree;
and no one will be wronged.

161. Tell them: "My Lord has directed me to a path
that is straight, a supreme law,
the creed of Abraham the upright
who was not an idolater."

162. Tell them: "My service and sacrifice, my life and my
        death,
are all of them for God,
the creator and Lord of all the worlds.

163. No equal has He,
I am commanded (to declare),
and that I am the first to submit."

164. Say: "Shall I search
for another lord apart from God
when He is the only Lord of all and every thing?"
Each soul earns (what it earns) for itself,
and no man shall bear another's burden.
You have to go back to your Lord in the end
when He will tell you
about the things you disputed.

165. It is He who made you trustees on the earth,
and exalted some in rank over others
in order to try you
by what He has given you.
Indeed your Lord's retribution is swift,
yet He is forgiving and kind.

7 Wall between Heaven and Hell

Al-A'rāf: Makki

In the name of Allah, most benevolent, ever-merciful.

ALIF LĀM MĪM SĀD.
2. This Book has been sent down to you;
so do not hesitate to warn
(the unbelievers) through it,
and remind the faithful.
3. Follow what has been revealed to you
by your Lord, and do not follow
any other lord apart from Him.
Yet little do you care to remember.
4. Many a habitation have We laid low before:
Our retribution came upon them in the night
or in the midst of siesta at noon.
5. And when Our punishment overtook them
they had nothing to say except crying out:
"We have indeed been sinners."
6. (On the Day of Reckoning) We shall question the people
to whom We had sent Our apostles,
(if they followed their teachings),
and will question the apostles.
7. We shall recount (their deeds) to them with knowledge,
for We were never absent (and saw all they did).
8. And the weighing will be just on that Day.
Then those whose (deeds) are heavier in the balance
will find fulfilment,
9. And those whose (deeds) are lighter in the scale
shall perish
for violating Our signs.
10. We settled you on the earth,
and provided means of livelihood for you in it;
but little are the thanks you give.

Verily We created you and gave you form and shape,
and ordered the angels to bow
before Adam in homage;

and they all bowed but Iblis
who was not among those who bowed.
12. "What prevented you" (said God),
"from bowing (before Adam) at My bidding?"
"I am better than him," said he.
"You created me from fire, and him from clay."
13. So God said: "Descend.
You have no right to be insolent here.
Go, and away; you are one of the damned."
14. "Grant me respite," said he,
"till the raising of the dead."
15. And God said: "You have the respite."
16. "Since You led me into error," said Iblis,
"I shall lie in wait for them along Your straight path.
17. And I shall come upon them
from the front and behind, right and left;
and You will not find among them many
who would give thanks."
18. "Begone," said (God), "contemptible and rejected!
As for those who follow you,
I shall fill up Hell with all of you.
19. And you, O Adam, and your spouse,
live in the Garden and eat your fill
wheresoever you like, but do not approach this tree,
or you will become iniquitous."
20. But Satan suggested (evil) to them,
in order to reveal their hidden parts
of which they were not aware (till then),
and said: "Your Lord has forbidden you (to go near) this tree
that you may not become angels or immortal."
21. Then he said to them on oath:
"I am your sincere friend;"
22. And led them (to the tree) by deceit.
When they tasted (the fruit) of the tree
their disgrace became exposed to them; and they patched
the leaves of the Garden to hide it.
And the Lord said to them: "Did I not
forbid you this tree? And I told you
that Satan was your open enemy."
23. They said: "O our Lord,
we have wronged ourselves.
If You do not forgive us and have mercy upon us,
we shall certainly be lost."
24. "Go," said God, "one the antagonist of the other, and live
on the earth for a time ordained,
and fend for yourselves.

Al-A'raf

25. You will live there, and there will you die," He said,
"and be raised from there (on the Day of Doom)."

قَالَ فِيهَا تَحْيَوْنَ وَفِيهَا تَمُوتُونَ وَمِنْهَا تُخْرَجُونَ ۝

O sons of Adam, We have revealed to you
a dress that would both hide your nakedness and be
an adornment, but
the raiment of piety is best.
This is one of the tokens of God:
You may haply reflect.

يَبَنِى آدَمَ قَدْ اَنْزَلْنَا عَلَيْكُمْ لِبَاسًا يُّوَارِى سَوْاٰتِكُمْ وَرِيْشًا وَلِبَاسُ التَّقْوٰى ذٰلِكَ خَيْرٌ ذٰلِكَ مِنْ اٰيٰتِ اللّٰهِ لَعَلَّهُمْ يَذَّكَّرُونَ ۝

27. O sons of Adam, let not Satan beguile you
as he did your parents out of Eden,
and made them disrobe to expose their disgrace to them.
For he and his host
can see you from where you cannot see them.
We have made the devils the friends of those
who do not believe,

يَبَنِى آدَمَ لَا يَفْتِنَنَّكُمُ الشَّيْطٰنُ كَمَا اَخْرَجَ اَبَوَيْكُمْ مِّنَ الْجَنَّةِ يَنْزِعُ عَنْهُمَا لِبَاسَهُمَا لِيُرِيَهُمَا سَوْاٰتِهِمَا اِنَّهُ يَرٰىكُمْ هُوَ وَقَبِيْلُهُ مِنْ حَيْثُ لَا تَرَوْنَهُمْ اِنَّا جَعَلْنَا الشَّيٰطِيْنَ اَوْلِيَاءَ لِلَّذِيْنَ لَا يُؤْمِنُونَ ۝

28. Who say when they commit shameful acts:
"Our ancestors used to do so,
and God has enjoined us to do the same."
Say to them: "God never enjoins
a conduct that is shameful.
You impute such lies to God as you do not know."

وَاِذَا فَعَلُوْا فَاحِشَةً قَالُوْا وَجَدْنَا عَلَيْهَا اٰبَاءَنَا وَاللّٰهُ اَمَرَنَا بِهَا قُلْ اِنَّ اللّٰهَ لَا يَأْمُرُ بِالْفَحْشَاءِ اَتَقُوْلُوْنَ عَلَى اللّٰهِ مَا لَا تَعْلَمُونَ ۝

29. Tell them: "My Lord has enjoined
piety, devotion in all acts of worship,
and calling upon Him with exclusive obedience.
For you will be reverted back
to what you were (when) created first."

قُلْ اَمَرَ رَبِّى بِالْقِسْطِ وَاَقِيْمُوْا وُجُوْهَكُمْ عِنْدَ كُلِّ مَسْجِدٍ وَّادْعُوْهُ مُخْلِصِيْنَ لَهُ الدِّيْنَ كَمَا بَدَاَكُمْ تَعُوْدُوْنَ ۝

30. A section (among them) were guided,
a section were bound to go astray,
(for) instead of God they took
the devils as their friends;
yet they think
they are on the right path.

فَرِيْقًا هَدٰى وَفَرِيْقًا حَقَّ عَلَيْهِمُ الضَّلٰلَةُ اِنَّهُمُ اتَّخَذُوا الشَّيٰطِيْنَ اَوْلِيَاءَ مِنْ دُوْنِ اللّٰهِ وَيَحْسَبُوْنَ اَنَّهُمْ مُّهْتَدُوْنَ ۝

31. O sons of Adam, attire yourselves
at every time of worship;
eat and drink, but do not be wasteful,
for God does not like the prodigals.

يَبَنِى آدَمَ خُذُوْا زِيْنَتَكُمْ عِنْدَ كُلِّ مَسْجِدٍ وَّكُلُوْا وَاشْرَبُوْا وَلَا تُسْرِفُوْا اِنَّهُ لَا يُحِبُّ الْمُسْرِفِيْنَ ۝

Ask them: "Who forbids you attire that God
has given to His creatures,
and the good things that He has provided?"
Tell them: "They are (meant) for believers in the world,
and will be theirs on the Day of Judgement."
That is how We explain Our signs
to those who know.

قُلْ مَنْ حَرَّمَ زِيْنَةَ اللّٰهِ الَّتِى اَخْرَجَ لِعِبَادِهِ وَالطَّيِّبٰتِ مِنَ الرِّزْقِ قُلْ هِىَ لِلَّذِيْنَ اٰمَنُوْا فِى الْحَيٰوةِ الدُّنْيَا خَالِصَةً يَّوْمَ الْقِيٰمَةِ كَذٰلِكَ نُفَصِّلُ الْاٰيٰتِ لِقَوْمٍ يَّعْلَمُونَ ۝

33. Tell them: "My Lord has forbidden

قُلْ اِنَّمَا حَرَّمَ رَبِّىَ الْفَوَاحِشَ مَا ظَهَرَ مِنْهَا وَمَا بَطَنَ

repugnant acts, whether open or disguised,
sin and unjust oppression, associating others with God,
of which He has sent down no authority,
and saying things of God of which you have no knowledge.''

34. A term is fixed for every people;
and when their appointed time is come
there will neither be a moment's delay nor haste.

35. O sons of Adam, when apostles come to you
from among you, who convey My messages,
then those who take heed and amend
will have neither fear nor regret.

36. But those who deny Our signs and disdain them,
shall belong to Hell,
where they will abide for ever.

37. Who could be more wicked than he
who imputes lies to God or denies His revelations?
Such as these will receive what is declared in the Book,
and when Our angels come to draw out their souls and ask:
"Where are they you worshipped other than God?"
They will answer: "They have left us and fled;"
and bear witness against themselves for being infidels.

38. "Enter then the Fire," will God say,
"with the past generations of jinns and men."
On entering each batch will condemn the other;
and when all of them shall have entered
one after the other,
the last to come will say of those
who had come before them:
"O our Lord, they are the ones who led us astray;
so give them double chastisement in the Fire."
He will answer: "For all it will be double;
but this you do not know."

39. Then the former will say to the latter:
"You have no privilege over us.
So taste the punishment for what you had done."

Verily for those who deny Our signs
and turn away in haughtiness from them,
the gates of heaven shall not be opened,
nor will they enter Paradise,
not till the camel passes through the needle's eye.
That is how We requite the transgressors:

41. For them is a flooring of Hell and a covering (of fire).
That is how We requite the iniquitous.

42. As for those who believe and do good,
We never burden a soul beyond capacity.

They are men of Paradise
where they will abide for ever.
43. Whatever the rancour they may have in their hearts
We shall (cleanse and) remove.
Streams of running water shall ripple at their feet,
and they will say: "We are grateful to God
for guiding us here.
Never would we have been guided
if God had not shown us the way.
The apostles of our Lord had indeed brought the truth."
And the cry shall resound: "This is Paradise
you have inherited as meed for your deeds."
44. And the inmates of Paradise
will call to the residents of Hell:
"We have found that the promise made to us
by our Lord was true.
Have you also found the promise of your Lord to be true?"
They will answer: "Yes (it is so)."
Then a crier will call from among them:
"The curse of God be on the vile,
45. Who obstruct those who follow the path of God
and try to make it oblique,
who do not believe in the life to come."
46. There will be a veil between them, and on the wall
will be the men (of al-A'raf)
who will recognise everyone by their distinguishing marks,
and will call to the inmates of Paradise:
"Peace on you,"
without having entered it themselves
though hoping to do so.
47. When their eyes fall on the inmates of Hell
they will say: "O Lord, do not place us
in the crowd of the vile."

Recognising them by their marks
the men of al-A'raf
will call (to the inmates of Hell):
"Of what use was your amassing (of wealth)
of which you were proud?"
49. (Then pointing to the inmates of Paradise, they will say):
"Are they not those of whom you had sworn and said:
'God will not have mercy on them?'
(And yet they have been told,) 'Enter Paradise
where you will have no fear or regret.' "
50. Those in Hell will call to the inmates of Paradise:
"Pour a little water over us,

Al-A'raf

or give us a little of what God has given you.''
They will answer: "God has verily forbidden these
to those who denied the truth,
51. Who made a sport and frolic of their faith
and were lured by the life of the world.''
As they had forgotten the meeting of this Day
so shall We neglect them today
for having rejected Our signs.
52. Indeed We had brought to them a Book
distinct, replete with knowledge,
and guidance and grace for men who believe.
53. Are they waiting for the exposition
of what it speaks of?
The day that (Reality) is unravelled,
the people who had lost sight of it will say:
"The apostles of our Lord had indeed brought the truth.
Do we have any one to intercede for us?
If only we could go back to the world,
we would act otherwise.''
Indeed they have caused themselves harm,
and the lies they concocted did not help.

Surely your Lord is God
who created the heavens and the earth
in six spans of time,
then assumed all power.
He covers up the day with night which comes
chasing it fast;
and the sun and moon and the stars
are subject to His command.
It is His to create and enjoin.
Blessed be God,
the Lord of all the worlds.
55. Pray to your Lord in humility and unseen.
He does not love the iniquitous.
56. And do not corrupt the land
after it has been reformed;
and pray to Him in awe and expectation.
The blessing of God is at hand
for those who do good.
57. Indeed it is He who sends the winds
as harbingers of auspicious news
announcing His beneficence,
bringing heavy clouds which We drive
towards a region lying dead,
and send down rain, and raise

all kinds of fruits.
So shall We raise the dead
that you may think and reflect.
58. The soil that is good
produces (rich) crops by the will of its Lord,
and that which is bad
yields only what is poor.
So do We explain Our signs
in different ways
to people who give thanks.

We sent Noah to his people,
and he said: "O people worship God;
you have no other god but He; for I fear
the retribution of the great Day may fall on you."
60. The elders of his people replied:
"We see clearly that you have gone astray."
61. "I have not gone astray, O my people," he said,
"but have been sent by my Lord,
the creator of all the worlds.
62. I bring to you the messages of my Lord,
and give you sincere advice,
for I know from God what you do not know.
63. Do you wonder that a warning has come to you
from your Lord through a man who is one of you,
and warns you to take heed for yourselves and fear God?
You might be treated with mercy."
64. But they called him a liar,
and We saved him and those with him in the Ark,
and drowned the others who rejected Our signs,
for they were a people purblind.

And We sent Hud, their brother, to the people of 'Ad.
He said: "O you people, worship God,
for you have no other god but He.
Will you not take heed for yourselves?"
66. The chiefs of his people who were infidels replied:
"We find you full of folly, and a liar to boot."
67. "I am not a fool, O people," he answered,
"but have been sent by the Lord of all the worlds.
68. I bring to you the messages of my Lord.
I am your sincere friend.
69. Do you wonder that a warning has come to you from
       your Lord
through a man who is one of you and warns you?
Remember, He made you leaders

after the people of Noah, and gave you
a greater increase in your stature.
So think of the favours of God;
you may haply be blessed."
70. They answered: "Have you come to say to us
that we should worship only one God,
abandoning those our ancestors had worshipped?
If so, bring on us what you threaten us with,
if what you say is true."
71. He replied: "You have already been beset
with punishment and the wrath of God.
Why dispute with me about names
invented by you and your ancestors
for which no sanction was sent down?
So wait (for what is to come),
I am waiting with you."
72. Then We saved him and those on his side
by Our grace, and destroyed to the very last
those who rejected Our signs and denied the truth.

We sent to Thamud their brother Ṣaleh.
"O you people," said he, "worship God,
for you have no other god but He.
Clear proof has come to you already from your Lord,
and this she-camel of God is the token for you.
Leave her free to graze upon God's earth,
and do not molest her
lest a grievous punishment should befall you.
74. Remember, how you were made leaders
after the people of 'Ad,
and were settled on the land
so that you could construct on the plains
palaces, and carve dwellings out of mountains.
So think of the favours of God, and do not act
with corruption in the land."
75. The chiefs among the people who were arrogant
towards the weaker ones among them who believed,
asked: "Do you really know that Saleh
has been sent by his Lord?"
They said: "Indeed we believe in the message he has brought."
76. Those who were arrogant answered:
"We do not believe in what you believe."
77. Then they hamstrung the she-camel and rebelled
against the command of their Lord,
and said: "Bring, O Saleh, on us the affliction you promise,
if you are one of the sent ones."

78. Then they were seized by an earthquake,
and lay overturned on the ground in their homes in the morning.
79. Ṣaleh turned away from them and said:
"O my people, I conveyed to you
the message of my Lord and warned you;
but you do not like those who wish you well."
80. And We sent Lot, who said to his people:
"Why do you commit this lecherous act
which none in the world has committed before?
81. In preference to women
you satisfy your lust with men.
Indeed you are a people who are guilty of excess."
82. His people made no answer, and only said:
"Drive them out of the city. They profess to be pure."
83. But We saved him and his family, except for his wife
who was one of those who stayed behind.
84. And We rained down on them a shower (of stones).
So witness the end of sinners!

Remember, We sent to Midian their brother Shu'aib.
"O you people," he said, "worship God,
for you have no other god but He.
Clear proof has come to you from your Lord;
so give in full measure and full weight;
do not keep back from people what is theirs,
and do not corrupt the land
after it has been reformed.
This is best for you if you believe.
86. Do not lie in ambush to intimidate
and divert from the path of God
those who believe in Him,
nor seek obliquity in it.
Remember the day when you were few
and He increased your numbers.
So consider the fate of those who were evil.
87. If some of you believe what has been sent through me,
and some of you do not,
have patience until God decide between us,
for He is the best of all judges."
88. The arrogant leaders of the people replied:
"We shall drive you away from our land, O Shu'aib,
and those who are with you, unless
you come back to your faith."
But he remarked: "Even if we are disgusted with it?
89. We shall only be guilty of blaspheming God
if we accept your way

having been delivered from it by Him.
We cannot come back to your creed
unless God, our Lord, should please.
Encompassed within the knowledge of our Lord
is everything;
and in God alone do we place our trust.
O Lord, adjudge between us and our people equitably,
for you are the best of adjudicators."
90. The chiefs among his people who did not believe
said (to them): "If you follow Shu'aib and his way
you will surely be ruined."
91. Then they were seized by an earthquake,
and lay overturned on the ground in their homes in the morning.
92. They who called Shu'aib a liar (disappeared)
as though they had never existed;
and those who called Shu'aib a liar
were the ones who were ruined!
93. So Shu'aib turned away from them and said:
"O people, I conveyed to you
the message of my Lord, and warned you.
(But you paid no heed). How can I grieve
for a people who do not believe?"

There is not a region to which We sent a prophet
and did not inflict upon its people adversity and hardship
so that they may submit.
95. But when We changed hardship to ease,
and they rose and prospered,
(they forgot Our favours) and said:
"Our ancestors had also known suffering and joy."
So We caught them unawares.
96. But if the people of these regions had believed
and feared God,
We would surely have showered on them
blessings of the heavens and the earth;
but they only denied,
and We punished them for their deeds.
97. Are the people of the region so secure
that they lie asleep unaware
as Our punishment overtakes them?
98. Or, are the people of the towns so unafraid
that (even when) Our retribution comes upon them
in the hours of the morning
they remain engrossed in sport and play?
99. Can they remain secure against the plan of God?
Only they feel secure against the plan of God

who are certain of being ruined.

Do not the people who inherited the earth
from the (earlier) inhabitants perceive
that We could afflict them too for their sins if We pleased,
and put seals on their hearts
that they may not hear (the voice of truth)?
101. These were the (earlier) habitations whose accounts
We have given to you.
Their apostles came with clear proofs,
but they did not believe what they once denied.
That is how God seals
the hearts of those who do not believe.
102. We did not find many of them
faithful to their promises,
and found many of them disobedient.
103. So We sent Moses with miracles after (these apostles)
to the Pharaoh and his nobles,
but they behaved with them high-handedly.
See then the end of the authors of evil.
104. Moses said: "O Pharaoh, I have been sent
by the Lord of all the worlds;
105. I am duty bound to speak nothing of God but the truth.
I have brought from your Lord a clear sign;
so let the people of Israel depart with me."
106. He said: "If you have brought a sign then display it,
if what you say is true."
107. At this Moses threw down his staff,
and lo, it became a live serpent.
108. And he drew forth his hand,
and behold, it looked white to those who beheld it.

The nobles of Pharaoh said:
"He surely is a clever magician.
110. He wishes to drive you away from the land.
So what do you advise?"
111. They said: "Put him and his brother off (awhile)
and send out heralds to the cities
112. To bring all the wise magicians to you."
113. The magicians came to the Pharaoh and said:
"Is there reward for us if we succeed?"
114. "Yes," said he, "you will be among the honoured."
115. So they said: "O Moses, you may cast your spell first,
or we shall cast ours."
116. "You cast it first," answered Moses.
When they cast their spell, they bewitched

the eyes of the people and petrified them
by conjuring up a great charm.
117. We said to Moses: "Throw down your staff;"
and it swallowed up their conjurations in no time.
118. Thus the truth was upheld,
and the falsehood that they practised was exposed.
119. Thus there and then they were vanquished
and overthrown, humiliated.
120. The sorcerers fell to the ground in homage,
121. And said: "We have come to believe
in the Lord of all the worlds,
122. The Lord of Moses and Aaron."
123. But Pharaoh said: "You have come to accept
belief in Him without my permission!
This surely is a plot you have hatched to expel
the people from the land. You will soon come to know.
124. I will have your hands and feet on alternate sides
cut off, and have you all crucified."
125. They answered: "We have (in any case)
to go back to our Lord.
126. The only reason you have to hate us is
that we believed in the signs of our Lord
as they came to us.
O our Lord, give us sufficient endurance
that we may die submitting (to You)."

And the leaders of Pharaoh's people said to him:
"Would you allow Moses and his people to create
disorder in the land and discard you and your gods?"
He replied: "We shall now slay their sons
and spare their women, and subdue them."
128. Said Moses to his people: "Invoke the help of God
and be firm. The earth belongs to God: He can make
whom He wills among His creatures inherit it.
The future is theirs who take heed for themselves."
129. They said: "We were oppressed before you came,
and have been since you have come to us."
He answered: "It may well be that soon
God may destroy your enemy
and make you inherit the land,
and then see how you behave."

We afflicted the people of Pharaoh with famine
and dearth of everything that they might take heed.
131. Yet when good came their way they said:
"It is our due;"

but when misfortune befell them they put
the omen down to Moses and those who were with him.
But surely the omen was with God,
yet most of them did not understand.

132. They said: "Whatsoever the sign you have brought
to deceive us, we shall not believe in you."

133. So We let loose on them floods and locusts,
and vermin, frogs and blood — how many different signs.
But they still remained arrogant,
for they were a people full of sin.

134. Yet when punishment overtook them, they said:
"O Moses, invoke your Lord for us
as you have been enjoined.
If the torment is removed,
we shall certainly believe in you and let
the people of Israel go with you."

135. But no sooner was the punishment withdrawn for a time
to enable them to make good their promise
than they broke it.

136. So We took vengeance on them, and drowned them in the
        sea
for rejecting Our signs and not heeding them.

137. We then made the people who were weak (and oppressed)
successors of the land to the East and the West
which We had blessed.
Thus the fair promise of your Lord
to the children of Israel was fulfilled,
for they were patient in adversity;
and whatsoever the Pharaoh and his people had fashioned,
and the structures they had raised, were destroyed.

138. When We brought the children of Israel across the sea,
and they came to a people who were devoted to their idols,
they said: "O Moses, make us also a god like theirs."
"You are ignorant," he replied.

139. "These people and their ways will surely be destroyed,
for false is what they practise.

140. Do you want me to seek for you," he said,
"a god other than God,
when He has exalted you over all the nations of the world?

141. Remember (the day) when He saved you
from the people of Pharaoh who oppressed and afflicted you,
and slew your sons and spared your women.
In this was a great trial from your Lord."

We made an appointment of thirty nights
with Moses (on Mount Sinai)

Al-A'raf

to which We added ten more; so the term
set by the Lord was completed in forty nights.
Moses said to Aaron, his brother:
"Deputise for me among my people.
Dispose rightly, and do not follow the way
of the authors of evil."

143. When Moses arrived at the appointed time
and his Lord spoke to him, he said:
"O Lord, reveal Yourself to me
that I may behold You."
"You cannot behold Me," He said. "But look at the mountain:
If it remains firm in its place
you may then behold Me."
But when his Lord appeared
on the mountain in His effulgence,
it crumbled to a heap of dust,
and Moses fell unconscious.
When he came to, he said: "All glory to You. I turn
to You in repentance, and I am the first to believe."

144. Said (the Lord): "O Moses, I raised you above all men
by sending My messages and speaking to you;
so receive what I give you, and be grateful."

145. And We wrote down on tablets admonitions
and clear explanations of all things for Moses,
and ordered him: "Hold fast to them,
and command your people to observe the best in them.
I will show you the abode of the wicked.

146. I will turn those away from My signs
who behave unjustly with arrogance in the land
so that even though they see all the signs
they will not believe in them;
and if they see the path of rectitude,
will not take it to be a way;
and if they see the way of error
take it to be the (right) path.
This is so for they have called Our messages lies,
and have been heedless of them."

147. Vain are the acts of those who deny Our signs
and the meeting in the Hereafter.
Can they ever be rewarded
for anything but what they did?

In the absence of Moses his people prepared
the image of a calf from their ornaments,
which gave out the mooing of a cow.
Yet they did not see

Al-A'raf   146

it could neither speak to them
nor guide them to the right path.
Even then they took it (for a deity) and did wrong.
149. Then they were filled with remorse and saw
that they had erred and said:
"If our Lord does not forgive us we will surely be lost."
150. When Moses returned to his people,
indignant and grieved,
he said: "How wickedly you behaved in my absence.
Why must you hasten the decree of your Lord?"
And he cast aside the tablets,
and pulled his brother by the hair.
"O son of my mother," said (Aaron), "these people
took advantage of my weakness and almost killed me.
Do not let my enemies rejoice at my plight,
and do not put me down among transgressors."
151. (Moses) said: "O Lord, forgive me and my brother,
and admit us to Your grace,
for You are the most compassionate of all."

Surely those who have taken the calf (as a god)
will suffer the anger of their Lord,
and disgrace in the world.
That is how We requite those who fabricate lies.
153. Yet those who do wrong, then repent and believe,
are forgiven, for your Lord is forgiving and kind.
154. When his anger subsided Moses picked up the tablets.
Inscribed on them was guidance and grace
for those who fear their Lord.
155. Moses chose seventy of his people
for the appointment (on Mount Sinai).
When they arrived they were seized by a tremor.
(Moses) said: "O Lord, if You had so pleased
You could have annihilated them and me before this.
Will You destroy us for something the foolish among us
        have done?
This is but a trial from You whereby
You will lead whom You will astray
and guide whom You please.
You are our saviour, so forgive us
and have mercy on us,
for You are the best of forgivers.
156. Enjoin for us good in the world,
and good in the world to come.
We turn to You alone."
And the Lord said: "I punish only those whom I will,

but My mercy enfolds everything.
I shall enjoin it for those
who take heed for themselves,
who pay the zakat
and believe in My signs,
157. Who follow the messenger, the gentile Prophet,*
described in the Torah and the Gospel,
who bids things noble and forbids things vile,
makes lawful what is clean,
and prohibits what is foul,
who relieves them of their burdens,
and the yoke that lies upon them.
Those who believe and honour and help him,
and follow the light sent with him,
are those who will attain their goal."

Say: "O men,
I am verily the apostle of God to you all. His
whose kingdom extends over the heavens and the earth.
There is no god but He,
the giver of life and death. So believe
in God and the messenger, the gentile Prophet, sent by Him,
who believes in God and His messages.
Obey him; you may haply be guided aright."
159. Among the people of Moses is a section that shows
the way to the truth,
and deals justly in accordance with it.
160. We divided them into twelve (different) tribes.
When his people asked for water, We said to Moses:
"Strike the rock with your staff;" and behold,
twelve springs of water gushed forth,
so that each of the tribes
had a place of its own to drink;
and We made the clouds spread shade over them
and sent for them manna and quails (and said):
"Eat of the good things We have provided for you."
But (by disobeying) they did not harm Us,
they harmed themselves.
161. And when it was said to them:
"Live in this land and eat of its produce
wheresoever you like, and ask for remission of your sins,
but pass through the gates with submission (and not pride),
We shall forgive your trespasses,
and give to those who are righteous abundance,"

----

* See note on p. 153.

162. The wicked among them changed and perverted
the word We had spoken to a word unpronounced;
so We sent from heaven retribution on them
for all their wickedness.

فَبَدَّلَ الَّذِينَ ظَلَمُوا مِنْهُمْ قَوْلًا غَيْرَ الَّذِى قِيلَ
لَهُمْ فَأَرْسَلْنَا عَلَيْهِمْ رِجْزًا مِّنَ السَّمَاءِ بِمَا كَانُوا
يَظْلِمُونَ ۝

Enquire of them about the town situated by the sea
where, when they did not keep the Sabbath,
the fish came up to the surface of the water for them;
but on days other than the Sabbath the fish did not come.
We tried them in this way, for they were disobedient.

وَسْئَلْهُمْ عَنِ الْقَرْيَةِ الَّتِى كَانَتْ حَاضِرَةَ
الْبَحْرِ إِذْ يَعْدُونَ فِى السَّبْتِ إِذْ تَأْتِيهِمْ
حِيتَانُهُمْ يَوْمَ سَبْتِهِمْ شُرَّعًا وَيَوْمَ لَا يَسْبِتُونَ
لَا تَأْتِيهِمْ كَذَلِكَ نَبْلُوهُمْ بِمَا كَانُوا
يَفْسُقُونَ ۝

164. When a section of them said:
"Why do you admonish a people whom God
is about to destroy or to punish severely?"
They replied: "To clear ourselves of blame before your Lord,
and that they may fear God.

وَإِذْ قَالَتْ أُمَّةٌ مِّنْهُمْ لِمَ تَعِظُونَ قَوْمًا اللَّهُ
مُهْلِكُهُمْ أَوْ مُعَذِّبُهُمْ عَذَابًا شَدِيدًا قَالُوا
مَعْذِرَةً إِلَى رَبِّكُمْ وَلَعَلَّهُمْ يَتَّقُونَ ۝

165. But when they forgot to remember the warning,
We saved those who prohibited evil,
but inflicted on the wicked a dreadful punishment —
requital for their disobedience.

فَلَمَّا نَسُوا مَا ذُكِّرُوا بِهِ أَنْجَيْنَا الَّذِينَ يَنْهَوْنَ عَنِ
السُّوءِ وَأَخَذْنَا الَّذِينَ ظَلَمُوا بِعَذَابٍ بَئِيسٍ بِمَا
كَانُوا يَفْسُقُونَ ۝

166. When they persisted in doing what they had been
                forbidden,
We said to them: "Become (like) apes despised."

فَلَمَّا عَتَوْا عَنْ مَا نُهُوا عَنْهُ قُلْنَا لَهُمْ كُونُوا
قِرَدَةً خَاسِئِينَ ۝

167. And your Lord declared
He would send men against them who would inflict
dreadful suffering on them till the Day of Doom,
for your Lord is swift in retribution,
though He is certainly forgiving and kind.

وَإِذْ تَأَذَّنَ رَبُّكَ لَيَبْعَثَنَّ عَلَيْهِمْ إِلَى يَوْمِ الْقِيَامَةِ
مَنْ يَسُومُهُمْ سُوءَ الْعَذَابِ إِنَّ رَبَّكَ لَسَرِيعُ
الْعِقَابِ وَإِنَّهُ لَغَفُورٌ رَّحِيمٌ ۝

168. We dispersed them in groups over the earth,
some righteous, some otherwise;
and We tried them with good things and bad,
that they may haply turn back.

وَقَطَّعْنَاهُمْ فِى الْأَرْضِ أُمَمًا مِّنْهُمُ الصَّالِحُونَ
وَمِنْهُمْ دُونَ ذَلِكَ وَبَلَوْنَاهُمْ بِالْحَسَنَاتِ وَالسَّيِّئَاتِ
لَعَلَّهُمْ يَرْجِعُونَ ۝

169. Then after them a new generation inherited the Book.
They took to the things of this base world, and said:
"We shall (surely) be forgiven this."
Yet they will accept similar things
if they came their way again.
Had they not been covenanted in the Book
to say nothing in the name of God but the truth?
And they have read this in it.
The abode of the life to come
is better for those who fear God.
Can they not comprehend?

فَخَلَفَ مِنْ بَعْدِهِمْ خَلْفٌ وَرِثُوا الْكِتَابَ يَأْخُذُونَ
عَرَضَ هَذَا الْأَدْنَى وَيَقُولُونَ سَيُغْفَرُ لَنَا وَإِنْ
يَأْتِهِمْ عَرَضٌ مِّثْلُهُ يَأْخُذُوهُ أَلَمْ يُؤْخَذْ عَلَيْهِمْ مِّيثَاقُ
الْكِتَابِ أَنْ لَا يَقُولُوا عَلَى اللَّهِ إِلَّا الْحَقَّ وَدَرَسُوا مَا فِيهِ وَ
الدَّارُ الْآخِرَةُ خَيْرٌ لِّلَّذِينَ يَتَّقُونَ أَفَلَا تَعْقِلُونَ ۝

170. As for those who adhere to the Book
and are firm in devotion,
We shall certainly not let
the wages of those who are upright to go waste.

وَالَّذِينَ يُمَسِّكُونَ بِالْكِتَابِ وَأَقَامُوا الصَّلَاةَ إِنَّا
لَا نُضِيعُ أَجْرَ الْمُصْلِحِينَ ۝

171. The day We shook the mountain above them like an
      awning,
and they feared it would fall over them,
(We said): "Hold fast to what We have given you,
and bear in mind what is (said) therein
so that you may take heed."

When your Lord brings forth from their loins
the offspring of the children of Adam,
He makes them witnesses over themselves,
(and asks): "Am I not your Lord?"
'Indeed,' they reply. 'We bear witness,' —
lest you should say on the Day of Resurrection:
"We were not aware of this;"

173. Or, lest they should say: "It were our fathers
who had ascribed compeers to God;
we are only their offspring.
Will You destroy us for the deeds of those
who dealt in vanities?"

174. That is how We explain Our signs distinctly
so that they may come back (to the right path).

175. Relate to them the plight of the man
whom We gave Our signs, but he passed them by,
so that Satan came after him,
and he went astray.

176. We wished to exalt him,
but he loved baseness and followed his lust.
His likeness is that of a dog
who hangs out his tongue if you drive him away,
and still hangs it out if you leave him alone.
Such is the case of the people who deny Our signs.
Narrate this history to them;
they may haply reflect.

177. Evil is the case of those who deny Our signs
and wrong themselves.

178. He alone is guided whom God shows the way;
and whom He leads astray is surely lost.

179. Many of the jinns and human beings
have We destined for Hell,
who possess hearts but do not feel,
have eyes but do not see,
have ears but do not hear,
like cattle, even worse than them.
They are people unconcerned.

180. All the names of God are beautiful,
so call Him by them;

Al-A'raf   150

and leave those alone who act profanely towards His names:
They will be retributed for their deeds.
181. Yet there are among those We have created
people who lead (others) to the truth,
and act justly in its light.

We shall punish those who deny Our revelations
slowly in a way that they will not know.
183. I will just give them respite.
My plan is certainly invincible.
184. Have they not bethought themselves
their companion is not mad?
He is only a plain admonisher.
185. Have they not contemplated
the kingdom of the heavens and the earth
and everything created by God,
(to educe) that perhaps
their own term is drawing to a close?
In what lore after this would they then believe?
186. Whosoever God allows to go astray
has none to show him the way,
for He leaves them to wander perplexed in their wickedness.
187. They ask you about the Hour:
"When is its determined time?"
Say: "Only my Lord has the knowledge.
No one can reveal it except He.
Oppressive will it be for the heavens and the earth.
When it comes, it will come unawares."
They ask you about it as if you were in the know.
You tell them: "Only God has the knowledge."
But most people do not know.
188. Tell them: "I am not master of my own gain or loss
but as God may please.
If I had the knowledge of the Unknown
I would have enjoyed abundance of the good,
and no evil would have touched me.
I am only a bearer of warnings
and bringer of happy news for those who believe."

It is He who created you
from a single cell,
and from it created its mate,
that you may live as companions.
When the man covered the woman
she conceived a light burden
and carried it about.

And when she was heavy (with child)
they prayed together to their Lord:
"If You bestow a healthy son on us
we shall truly be grateful."
190. But when they were given a healthy son,
they started ascribing to other powers a share
in what God had bestowed on them.
But God is above what they ascribe to Him.
191. Do they associate those with Him
who cannot create a thing,
and are themselves created,
192. Who can neither help them,
nor help themselves?
193. If you call them to guidance
they will not follow you.
It is all the same if you call them or hold your tongue.
194. Those whom you invoke besides God
are created beings like you.
So call on them and let them answer your call,
if what you say is true.
195. Do they have feet to walk on,
or hands to hold with,
or eyes to see and ears to hear with?
Say to them: "Call your compeers,
and work out a plot against me,
and do not give me time.
196. My saviour is God
who has revealed this Book; and He
protects those who are upright;
197. While those you beseech apart from Him
cannot help you or even help themselves.
198. When you call upon them for guidance,
they do not hear.
When you think they are looking at you,
(in fact) they cannot see."
199. Cultivate tolerance, enjoin justice,
and avoid the fools.
200. If you are instigated by the Devil to evil
seek refuge in God,
for God hears all and knows every thing.
201. Verily those who fear God
think of Him when assailed
by the instigations of Satan,
and lo! they begin to understand,
202. Even though their (devilish) brothers
would like them to continue in error,

and would not desist.

203. And when you do not bring a (Qur'anic) verse to them,
they say: "Why don't you make one up?"
Say: "I follow only what my Lord reveals to me."
These (revelations) are an evident proof from your Lord,
and a guidance and grace
for those who believe.

204. When the Qur'an is recited
listen to it in silence.
You may perhaps be blessed.

205. Meditate on your Lord inwardly
with humility and trepidation,
reciting His Book softly, morning and evening,
and be not negligent.

206. Verily those who are in the presence of your Lord
are never too proud to worship and celebrate His praises,
and bow in homage to Him.

Note on *Ummi*, v.157. *Ummi* (root UMM), derived like *ummah* from *Umm* — mother, source, basis, foundation. Basically *al-ummi* means a person in a natural state as at birth. In the Qur'an it has been used for non-Jews, gentiles, heathens and non-*ahl-e-kitab*, that is, people who do not possess a Scripture, the Arabs themselves being called *ummi* in this sense in 3:75. In pre-Quranic days only the Jews and Christians were called 'people of the Book', the Arabs being called *ummi* which, however, did not mean that they were illiterate.

Its use for illiterate (and a distinct attribute of the Prophet) starts at a later date, through a misunderstanding of verse 48 of Surah 29, The Spider, read in isolation and out of context of 'the people of the Book' in section (ruku') 5 of the Surah:

> You did not read any Scripture before this,
> nor wrote one with your right hand...

The Qur'an is clearly dealing here with the conferment of the Scripture on the Prophet, thus making him and his followers a people of the Book, as until the revelation of the Qur'an the Prophet was a non-*ahl-e-kitab*, an *ummi,* and therefore neither read a Scripture nor wrote, that is, copy it with his right hand, the pen in those days being the sole means of making a copy of a book or Scripture. This, it seems, was misinterpreted to mean that he was illiterate. But the Qur'an, addressing the Prophet, says:

> Read, for your Lord is most beneficent
> Who taught by the pen,
> Taught man what he did not know. (96:3-5)

8 Spoils of War

Al-Anfāl: Madani

In the name of Allah, most benevolent, ever-merciful.

THEY ASK YOU of (benefits accruing as) spoils of war.
Tell them: "The benefits belong to God and His Messenger."
So fulfil your duty to God
and keep peace among yourselves.
Obey God and the Prophet,
if you really believe.
2. Only they are true believers
whose hearts fill up with awe
when the name of God is mentioned;
and their faith is further strengthened
when His messages are read out to them;
and those who place their trust in their Lord,
3. Who are firm in devotion,
and spend of what We have given them,
4. Are true believers.
There are for them (high) ranks with their Lord,
and pardon and noble provision.
5. As your Lord sent you from your home (to fight)
for the true cause, a section of the faithful were averse,
6. Who argued with you about the matter
even after it had become quite clear,
as if they were being pushed into (the arms of) death
as they waited.
7. Though God promised that one of two columns
(would fall to you), you desired
the one that was not armed.
But God wished to confirm the truth by His words,
and wipe the unbelievers out to the last,
8. So that Truth may be affirmed and falsehood negated,
even though the sinners be averse.
9. Remember when you prayed to your Lord for help,
He heard you and said:
"I shall send a thousand angels
following behind you for your aid."

10. He gave you the good news only to reassure your hearts,
for victory comes from God alone,
and certainly God is all-mighty and all-wise.

وَمَاجَعَلَهُ اللّٰهُ اِلَّا بُشْرٰى وَلِتَطْمَىِٕنَّ بِهٖ قُلُوبُكُمْ وَمَا
النَّصْرُ اِلَّا مِنْ عِنْدِ اللّٰهِ اِنَّ اللّٰهَ عَزِيْزٌ حَكِيْمٌ ۝

A blanketing sleep came over you
as a (measure of) security from Him,
and He sent down rain from the skies to cleanse you,
and to remove the plague of Satan,
and to strengthen your hearts and steady your steps.

اِذْ يُغَشِّيْكُمُ النُّعَاسَ اَمَنَةً مِّنْهُ وَيُنَزِّلُ عَلَيْكُمْ مِّنَ
السَّمَآءِ مَآءً لِّيُطَهِّرَكُمْ بِهٖ وَيُذْهِبَ عَنْكُمْ رِجْزَ الشَّيْطٰنِ
وَلِيَرْبِطَ عَلٰى قُلُوبِكُمْ وَيُثَبِّتَ بِهِ الْاَقْدَامَ ۝

12. And the Lord said to the angels:
"I am with you; go and strengthen the faithful.
I shall fill the hearts of infidels with terror.
So smite them on their necks and every joint,
(and incapacitate them),"

اِذْ يُوْحِيْ رَبُّكَ اِلَى الْمَلٰٓئِكَةِ اَنِّيْ مَعَكُمْ فَثَبِّتُوا الَّذِيْنَ
اٰمَنُوْا سَاُلْقِيْ فِيْ قُلُوبِ الَّذِيْنَ كَفَرُوا الرُّعْبَ فَاضْرِبُوْا
فَوْقَ الْاَعْنَاقِ وَاضْرِبُوْا مِنْهُمْ كُلَّ بَنَانٍ ۝

13. For they had opposed God and His Apostle;
but whosoever opposes God and his Apostle (should know)
that God is severe in retribution.

ذٰلِكَ بِاَنَّهُمْ شَآقُّوا اللّٰهَ وَرَسُوْلَهٗ وَمَنْ يُّشَاقِقِ
اللّٰهَ وَرَسُوْلَهٗ فَاِنَّ اللّٰهَ شَدِيْدُ الْعِقَابِ ۝

14. For you is this (punishment) to taste,
for the infidels the torment of Hell.

ذٰلِكُمْ فَذُوْقُوْهُ وَاَنَّ لِلْكٰفِرِيْنَ عَذَابَ النَّارِ ۝

15. O believers, when you meet unbelievers
on the field of battle,
do not turn your backs to them.

يٰٓاَيُّهَا الَّذِيْنَ اٰمَنُوْٓا اِذَا لَقِيْتُمُ الَّذِيْنَ كَفَرُوْا زَحْفًا
فَلَا تُوَلُّوْهُمُ الْاَدْبَارَ ۝

16. For any one who turns his back on that day,
except to manoeuvre or rally to his side,
will bring the wrath of God on himself,
and have Hell as abode;
and what an evil destination!

وَمَنْ يُّوَلِّهِمْ يَوْمَىِٕذٍ دُبُرَهٗٓ اِلَّا مُتَحَرِّفًا لِّقِتَالٍ اَوْ
مُتَحَيِّزًا اِلٰى فِئَةٍ فَقَدْ بَآءَ بِغَضَبٍ مِّنَ اللّٰهِ وَمَأْوٰىهُ
جَهَنَّمُ وَبِئْسَ الْمَصِيْرُ ۝

17. It was not you who killed them, but God did so.
You did not throw what you threw, (sand into the eyes
of the enemy at Badr), but God, to bring out the best
in the faithful by doing them a favour of His own.
God is all-hearing and all-knowing.

فَلَمْ تَقْتُلُوْهُمْ وَلٰكِنَّ اللّٰهَ قَتَلَهُمْ وَمَا رَمَيْتَ اِذْ رَمَيْتَ
وَلٰكِنَّ اللّٰهَ رَمٰى وَلِيُبْلِيَ الْمُؤْمِنِيْنَ مِنْهُ بَلَآءً حَسَنًا
اِنَّ اللّٰهَ سَمِيْعٌ عَلِيْمٌ ۝

18. That was that, but remember
God will make the plots of the unbelievers contemptible.

ذٰلِكُمْ وَاَنَّ اللّٰهَ مُوْهِنُ كَيْدِ الْكٰفِرِيْنَ ۝

19. You had asked for a judgement,
so the judgement has come to you
(in the form of victory for the faithful).
So, if you desist it will be better for you.
If you come back to it, We shall do the same,
and your forces, however large, will not be of the least avail,
for God is with those who believe.

اِنْ تَسْتَفْتِحُوْا فَقَدْ جَآءَكُمُ الْفَتْحُ وَاِنْ تَنْتَهُوْا فَهُوَ
خَيْرٌ لَّكُمْ وَاِنْ تَعُوْدُوْا نَعُدْ وَلَنْ تُغْنِيَ عَنْكُمْ فِئَتُكُمْ
شَيْئًا وَّلَوْ كَثُرَتْ وَاَنَّ اللّٰهَ مَعَ الْمُؤْمِنِيْنَ ۝

O believers, obey God and His Messenger,
and do not turn away from him when you hear (him speak);
21. And do not be like those who say: "We have heard,"
but do not hear.

يٰٓاَيُّهَا الَّذِيْنَ اٰمَنُوْٓا اَطِيْعُوا اللّٰهَ وَرَسُوْلَهٗ وَلَا تَوَلَّوْا
عَنْهُ وَاَنْتُمْ تَسْمَعُوْنَ ۝
وَلَا تَكُوْنُوْا كَالَّذِيْنَ قَالُوْا سَمِعْنَا وَهُمْ لَا يَسْمَعُوْنَ ۝

22. The worst of creatures in the eyes of God
are those who are deaf and dumb and devoid of sense.
23. If God had seen any good in them
He would surely have made them hear.
Now even if He makes them hear
they will turn away (in obduracy).
24. O believers, respond to the call of God and His Prophet
when he calls you
to what will give you life (and preservation).
Remember that God intervenes between man and his heart,
and that you will be gathered before Him.
25. Beware of sedition, which does not affect
the oppressors alone among you,
and know that the punishment of God is severe.
26. Remember, when you were few
and powerless in the land,
afraid of despoliation at the hands of men.
But then God sheltered and helped you to strength,
and provided for you good things
that you may perhaps be grateful.
27. O you who believe, do not be faithless
to God and His Apostle, nor violate
your trusts knowingly.
28. Know that your worldly possessions and your children
are just a temptation,
and that God has greater rewards with Him.

O believers, if you follow the path shown by God,
He will give you a standard (of right and wrong),
and overlook your sins, and forgive you.
God is abounding in benevolence.
30. Remember, when the infidels
contrived to make you a prisoner or to murder or expel you,
they plotted, but God also planned;
and God's plan is the best.
31. When Our messages were read out to them,
they said: "We have heard.
We could certainly compose (writings) like them if we choose.
They are but only tales of long ago."
32. They had also said: "If this be the truth from you, O God,
then rain down on us stones from the skies,
or inflict a grievous punishment upon us."
33. But God would not choose to punish them
while you are in their midst, nor afflict them
when they are seeking forgiveness.
34. But what is there so special they have

that God should not punish them
when they obstruct people from the Holy Mosque,
though they are not its (appointed) guardians?
Its guardians could be only those
who are pious and devout.
But most of them do not know.
35. Their worship in the House of God
has been no more than whistling and clapping.
So they have to taste the punishment for disbelief.
36. Those who disbelieve spend
their possessions on turning men away from God.
They will go on spending
and rue it in the end, and will be subdued.
But those who remain disbelievers
shall be gathered into Hell
37. That God may separate the bad from the good,
and link the wicked together
and cast them into Hell.
These are verily the people who will lose.

You tell the unbelievers in case they desist
whatever has happened will be forgiven them.
If they persist, they should remember
the fate of those who have gone before them.
39. So, fight them till all opposition ends,
and obedience is wholly God's.
If they desist then verily God sees all they do.
10. But if they are obstinate,
know that God is your helper and protector:
How excellent a helper,
and how excellent a protector is He!
41. Know that one-fifth of what you acquire as booty (of war)
is for God and His Apostle,
and for relatives and orphans, the poor and wayfarers,
if you truly believe in God and what We revealed
to Our votary on the day of victory over the infidels
when the two armies clashed (at Badr).
For God has the power to do any thing.
42. (That day) when you were at one end of the valley,
(the unbelievers) at the other, and the caravan
below you (on the lowland by the coast),
you would surely have declined to fight
if (the Makkans) had offered you battle.
(But the battle did take place) that God
may end the matter which had been accomplished,
so that he who had to die may perish

after a clear demonstration,
and he who had to live may survive
in the light of positive proof,
for God hears all and knows every thing.
43. God showed (the Makkans) to be few in your dream,
for if He had shown them to be many
you would surely have lost courage
and disagreed about the (wisdom) of the battle.
But God spared you this,
for He surely knows what is in the hearts of men.
44. When you faced them He made (the enemy) seem
few to you in numbers,
and made you appear fewer in their eyes,
(it was) so that God could accomplish
what had been decreed;
for all things rest with God.

O believers, when you meet an army, stand firm,
and think of God a great deal
that you may be blessed with success.
46. Obey God and His Apostle,
and do not disagree among yourselves
or you will be unmanned and lose courage. Persevere,
for God is with those who endure.
47. Do not be like those who went out of their homes
full of their own importance, ostentatiously,
trying to hinder others from the way of God.
But God encompasses all they do.
48. Satan made their deeds look alluring to them,
and said: "None will prevail over you this day,
for I shall be near at hand."
Yet when the two armies appeared face to face,
he turned back and fled, saying:
"I am not with you,
for I can see what you cannot perceive.
I fear God, for His punishment is severe."

The hypocrites, and those who had doubts in their
    hearts,
said: "Their faith has misled them."
But whoever places his trust in God
will find God mighty and wise.
50. If you could only see the infidels
as the angels draw away their souls
and strike their faces and their backs,
(saying): "Taste the torment of burning

Al-Anfal

51. For what you have brought upon yourselves.''
God is surely not unjust to His creatures,
(they are unjust to themselves).

ذٰلِكَ بِمَا قَدَّمَتْ اَيْدِيْكُمْ وَاَنَّ اللّٰهَ لَيْسَ بِظَلَّامٍ لِّلْعَبِيْدِ ۞

52. Their case is like that of Pharaoh's people,
and of those before them,
who denied the revelations of God, and were punished
for their sins by God,
and God is all powerful and severe His punishment.

كَدَاْبِ اٰلِ فِرْعَوْنَ وَالَّذِيْنَ مِنْ قَبْلِهِمْ كَفَرُوْا بِاٰيٰتِ اللّٰهِ فَاَخَذَهُمُ اللّٰهُ بِذُنُوْبِهِمْ اِنَّ اللّٰهَ قَوِيٌّ شَدِيْدُ الْعِقَابِ ۞

53. God does not withdraw a favour
bestowed upon a people
unless they change themselves,
for God hears all and knows every thing.

ذٰلِكَ بِاَنَّ اللّٰهَ لَمْ يَكُ مُغَيِّرًا نِّعْمَةً اَنْعَمَهَا عَلٰى قَوْمٍ حَتّٰى يُغَيِّرُوْا مَا بِاَنْفُسِهِمْ وَاَنَّ اللّٰهَ سَمِيْعٌ عَلِيْمٌ ۞

54. This was the case with the people of Pharaoh
and those before them,
who rejected the signs of their Lord
and were destroyed for their sins,
and We drowned the people of Pharaoh as they were
          oppressors.

كَدَاْبِ اٰلِ فِرْعَوْنَ وَالَّذِيْنَ مِنْ قَبْلِهِمْ كَذَّبُوْا بِاٰيٰتِ رَبِّهِمْ فَاَهْلَكْنٰهُمْ بِذُنُوْبِهِمْ وَاَغْرَقْنَا اٰلَ فِرْعَوْنَ وَكُلٌّ كَانُوْا ظٰلِمِيْنَ ۞

55. Verily the worst of creatures in the sight of God
are those who deny (the truth),
and will not believe.

اِنَّ شَرَّ الدَّوَآبِّ عِنْدَ اللّٰهِ الَّذِيْنَ كَفَرُوْا فَهُمْ لَا يُؤْمِنُوْنَ ۞

56. As for those with whom you have made a treaty
and who abrogate it every time, and do not fear God,

الَّذِيْنَ عٰهَدْتَّ مِنْهُمْ ثُمَّ يَنْقُضُوْنَ عَهْدَهُمْ فِيْ كُلِّ مَرَّةٍ وَّهُمْ لَا يَتَّقُوْنَ ۞

57. If you meet them in battle, inflict on them
such a defeat as would be a lesson
for those who come after them,
and that they may be warned.

فَاِمَّا تَثْقَفَنَّهُمْ فِي الْحَرْبِ فَشَرِّدْ بِهِمْ مَّنْ خَلْفَهُمْ لَعَلَّهُمْ يَذَّكَّرُوْنَ ۞

58. If you apprehend treachery from a people
(with whom you have a treaty),
retaliate by breaking off (relations) with them,
for God does not like those who are treacherous.

وَاِمَّا تَخَافَنَّ مِنْ قَوْمٍ خِيَانَةً فَانْبِذْ اِلَيْهِمْ عَلٰى سَوَآءٍ اِنَّ اللّٰهَ لَا يُحِبُّ الْخَآئِنِيْنَ ۞

The infidels should not think
that they can bypass (the law of God).
Surely they cannot get away.

وَلَا يَحْسَبَنَّ الَّذِيْنَ كَفَرُوْا سَبَقُوْا اِنَّهُمْ لَا يُعْجِزُوْنَ ۞

60. Prepare against them whatever arms and cavalry
you can muster, that you may strike terror
in (the hearts of) the enemies of God and your own,
and others besides them not known to you,
but known to God.
Whatever you spend in the way of God
will be paid back to you in full,
and no wrong will be done to you.

وَاَعِدُّوْا لَهُمْ مَّا اسْتَطَعْتُمْ مِّنْ قُوَّةٍ وَّمِنْ رِّبَاطِ الْخَيْلِ تُرْهِبُوْنَ بِهٖ عَدُوَّ اللّٰهِ وَعَدُوَّكُمْ وَاٰخَرِيْنَ مِنْ دُوْنِهِمْ لَا تَعْلَمُوْنَهُمُ اللّٰهُ يَعْلَمُهُمْ وَمَا تُنْفِقُوْا مِنْ شَيْءٍ فِيْ سَبِيْلِ اللّٰهِ يُوَفَّ اِلَيْكُمْ وَاَنْتُمْ لَا تُظْلَمُوْنَ ۞

61. But if they are inclined to peace,
make peace with them,
and have trust in God,

وَاِنْ جَنَحُوْا لِلسَّلْمِ فَاجْنَحْ لَهَا وَتَوَكَّلْ عَلَى اللّٰهِ اِنَّهٗ

for He hears all and knows every thing.
62. If they try to cheat you,
God is surely sufficient for you.
It is He who has strengthened you with His help
and with believers
63. Whose hearts He cemented with love.
You could never have united their hearts
even if you had spent
whatever (wealth) is in the earth;
but God united them with love,
for He is all-mighty and all-wise.
64. God is sufficient for you, O Prophet,
and the faithful who follow you.

O Prophet, urge the faithful to fight.
If there are twenty among you with determination
they will vanquish two hundred;
and if there are a hundred then they will vanquish
a thousand unbelievers,
for they are people devoid of understanding.
66. God has lightened your burden
as He knows you are weak:
So, if there are a hundred men
of firm determination among you,
they will vanquish two hundred;
and if there are a thousand of you they will vanquish
two thousand by the will of God,
for God is with those who are determined.
67. No apostle should take captives
until he has battled and subdued the country.
You desire the vanities of this world, but God
wills (for you the reward) of the world to come;
and God is all-mighty and all-wise.
68. Had this not been decreed by God in advance,
you would have suffered a grievous punishment
for what you took (as booty).
69. But now use such of the spoils as are lawful and good,
and fear God,
for God is forgiving and kind.

O Prophet, tell the captives you have taken:
"If God finds some good in your hearts,
He will reward you with something better
than was taken away from you, and forgive your sins,
for God is forgiving and kind."
71. If they try to deceive you, remember

they have deceived God before.
So He gave you mastery over them,
for God is all-knowing and all-wise.
72. Those who accepted the faith and set out of their homes,
and fought in the way of God wealth and soul,
and those who gave them shelter and helped them,
are friends of one another.
You are not responsible for protecting those
who embraced the faith but did not leave their homes,
until they do so.
In case they ask for your help in the name of faith,
you are duty bound to help them,
except against a people with whom you have a treaty;
for God sees all that you do.
73. Those who are infidels aid one another.
Unless you do the same
there will be discord in the land and anarchy.
74. Those who accepted the faith and abandoned their homes,
and struggled in the cause of God,
and those who gave them shelter and helped them,
are veritably true believers.
For them is forgiveness and noble sustenance.
75. Those who accepted the faith and left their homes
and fought by your side, are your brothers;
yet those who are related by blood are closer
to one another according to the decree of God.
Verily God knows every thing.

9 Repentance

At-Taubah: Madani

IMMUNITY is granted those idolators
by God and his Apostle with whom you have a treaty.
(They can) move about for four months freely in the land,
but should know they cannot escape (the law of) God,
and that God can put the unbelievers to shame.
3. A general proclamation is (made)
this day of the Greater Pilgrimage
on the part of God and His Apostle,
that God is not bound (by any contract) to idolaters,
nor is His Apostle.
It is, therefore, better for you to repent.
If you do not, remember that you cannot elude (the grip of)
        God.
So announce to those who deny the truth
the news of painful punishment,
4. Except those idolaters with whom you have a treaty,
who have not failed you in the least,
nor helped anyone against you.
Fulfil your obligations to them
during the term (of the treaty).
God loves those who take heed for themselves.
5. But when these months, prohibited (for fighting), are over,
slay the idolaters wheresoever you find them,
and take them captive or besiege them,
and lie in wait for them at every likely place.
But if they repent and fulfil their devotional obligations
and pay the zakat, then let them go their way,
for God is forgiving and kind.
6. If an idolater seeks protection,
then give him asylum that he may hear the word of God.
Then escort him to a place of safety,
for they are people who do not know.

How could there be a treaty between idolaters
and God and His Apostle,
except those you covenanted by the Sacred Mosque?

Therefore as long as they are honest with you
be correct with them, for God loves those who are godly.
8. How (can they be trusted)? If they prevail against you
they will neither observe pacts nor good faith with you.
They flatter you with their tongues, but their hearts
are averse to you, for most of them are iniquitous.
9. They barter away the words of God for a petty price,
and obstruct (others) from His path.
How evil indeed are the things they do!
10. They have no regard for kinship or treaties with believers,
for they are transgressors.
11. But if they repent and are firm in devotion
and pay the zakat, then they are your brothers in faith.
We explain Our commands distinctly for those who
        understand.
12. If they break their pledge after giving their word
and revile your faith,
fight these specimens of faithlessness,
for surely their oaths have no sanctity:
They may haply desist.
13. Will you not fight those who broke their pledge
and plotted to banish the Apostle,
and who were the first to attack you?
Are you afraid of them?
If you are believers you should fear God more.
14. Fight them so that God may punish them at your hands,
and put them to shame, and help you against them,
and heal the wounds of the hearts of believers,
15. And remove the anger from their breasts;
for God turns to whosoever desires.
God is all-knowing and all-wise.
16. Do you think you will get away
before God knows who among you
fought and did not take
anyone but God, His Apostle and the faithful,
as their friends?
God is congnisant of all that you do.

The idolaters have no right to visit the mosques of God
while bearing testimony to their disbelief.
Meaningless will be their acts,
and in Hell they will bide for ever.
18. Only those who believe in God and the Last Day,
who fulfil their devotional obligations, pay the zakat,
and fear no one but God, can visit the mosques of God.
They may hope to be among the guided.

19. Do you think that giving a drink of water
to the pilgrims and going on a visit to the Sacred Mosque,
is the same as believing in God
and the Last Day,
and striving in the cause of God?
In the eyes of God it is not the same;
and God does not show the unrighteous the way.
20. Those who accepted the faith and left their homes
and fought in the way of God, wealth and soul,
have a greater reward with God, and will be successful.
21. Their Lord announces to them news of His mercy,
acceptance, and gardens of lasting bliss
22. Which they will enjoy for ever.
Indeed God has greater rewards with Him.
23. O you who believe, do not hold your fathers and brothers
        as friends
if they hold disbelief more dear than faith;
and those of you who do so are iniquitous.
24. You tell them: "If your fathers and sons,
your brothers and wives and families and wealth,
or the business you fear may fail,
and the mansions that you love,
are dearer to you than God, His Apostle,
and struggling in His cause,
then wait until God's command arrives,
for God does not show transgressors the way."

Indeed God has helped you on many occasions,
even during the battle of Hunain,
when you were elated with joy at your numbers
which did not prove of the least avail,
so that the earth and its vast expanse
became too narrow for you,
and you turned back and retreated.
26. Then God sent down a sense of tranquility
on His Apostle and the faithful;
and sent down troops invisible
to punish the infidels.
This is the recompense of those who do not believe.
27. Yet God may turn (even) after this
to whomsoever He please,
for God is compassionate and kind.
28. O believers, the idolaters are unclean.
So they should not approach the Holy Mosque
after this year. In case you fear indigence
(from the stoppage of business with them),

then God will enrich you of His bounty if He will,
for God is all-knowing and all-wise.
29. Fight those people of the Book who do not believe
in God and the Last Day, who do not prohibit what God
and His Apostle have forbidden, nor accept divine law,
until all of them pay protective tax* in submission.

The Jews say: "Ezra is the son of God;"
the Christians say: "Christ is the son of God."
That is what they say with their tongues
following assertions made by unbelievers before them.
May they be damned by God: How perverse are they!
31. They consider their rabbis and monks and the Christ,
son of Mary, to be gods apart from God,
even though they had been enjoined to worship
only one God,
for there is no god but He.
Too holy is He for what they ascribe to Him!
32. They wish to extinguish the light of God
by uttering blasphemies;** but God will not have it so,
for He wills to perfect His light,
however the unbelievers be averse.
33. It is He who sent His Messenger
with guidance and the true faith
in order to make it superior to other systems of belief,
even though the idolaters may not like it.
34. O believers, many rabbis and priests
devour the possessions of others wrongfully,
and keep men away from the path of God.
To those who accumulate gold and silver,
and do not spend in the way of God,
announce the news of painful punishment.
35. On the day We shall heat up (their gold) on the fire of Hell
and brand their foreheads, sides and backs
(and say to them): "It is this you stored up for yourselves;
so now taste of what you had stored!"
36. The number of months with God is twelve in accordance with
God's law since the day He created the heavens and the earth.
Of these four are holy. This is the straight reckoning.
So do not exceed yourselves during them; but fight
the idolaters to the end as they fight you in like manner;
and remember, God is with those
who preserve themselves from evil and do the right.

---

* *Jaziyah* is a tax levied on non-Muslims for protection and other services.
** Literally with their mouths.

37. Intercalating a month is adding to unbelief.
The unbelievers are misguided by this,
for they take the same month to be sacred one year
and sacrilegious the next,
thus making the number of months sanctified by God
accord with theirs
in order to make what God has forbidden, lawful.
Attractive seem to them their evil deeds;
but God does not show the unbelievers the way.

What has happened to you, O believers,
that when you are asked to set out in the cause of God
your feet begin to drag?
Do you find the life of the world so pleasing
that you forget the life to come?
Yet the profit of the life of this world is but meagre
as compared to the life to come.

39. Unless you go out (to strive), God will inflict
grievous punishment on you,
and bring other people in your place,
and you will not be able to harm Him in the least,
for God has the power over all things.

40. If you do not help (the Prophet, remember)
God had helped him when the infidels
had forced him to leave (and he was) one of two.
When both of them were in the cave,
he said to his companion:
"Do not grieve, for God is with us."
Then God sent divine peace on him,
and invisible armies for his help,
and made the unbelievers' purpose abject.
Most exalted is God's word,
for God is all-mighty and all-wise.

41. O believers, go out in the cause of God,
(whether) light or heavy,
and strive in the service of God, wealth and soul.
This is better for you if you understand.

42. (O Prophet), had the gain been close at hand,
and easy the journey,
they would surely have followed you;
but hard was the journey and long the going.
Even then they swear by God (and say):
"If we had the strength we would surely
have gone out with you."
They are only ruining themselves,
for God is aware they lie.

At-Taubah   166

May God forgive you.
Why did you allow them (to stay behind)
without ascertaining who spoke the truth
and who were liars?

44. Those who believe in God and the Last Day,
do not ask your leave
to be excused from fighting wealth and soul (in the cause of
    God),
for God knows the pious and devout.

45. Only they ask (for leave)
who do not believe in God and the Last Day,
whose hearts are full of doubt;
and doubting they waver (between gain and loss).

46. If they had intended to go out (to fight)
they would surely have made preparations.
But God did not like their setting forth,
and they were held back and told:
"Stay at home with those who stay behind."

47. Had they gone out with you,
they would only have been a hindrance
and let loose confusion among you to create discord;
for there are some in your midst who spy for them.
But God knows who are the wicked.

48. They had tried to create disorder before
and intrigued against you,
but truth came out in the end and God's will prevailed,
even though they did not like it.

49. And (many a one) there is among them who says:
"Allow me (to stay back at home),
and put me not on trial."
Surely they have put themselves on trial already,
and Hell will enclose the unbelievers from all sides.

50. If good comes your way they are vexed,
but if calamity befalls you, they say:
"We had taken precautions in advance;"
and pleased, turn away.

51. Tell them: "Nothing can befall us except what God
    decrees.
Our protector is He, and in God
should the faithful place their trust."

52. Say: "Are you waiting for anything else but one
of two good things for us, (victory or martyrdom)?
Yet what we are waiting for you is
the punishment of God,
direct or through us.
So keep waiting; we are waiting with you."

53. Tell them: "You may spend (in the way of God),
whether willingly or with reluctance,
it will not be accepted from you,
for you are reprobates."

54. Nothing prevents the acceptance of what they spend
except that they do not believe in God and His Apostle,
and come to worship but languidly
and spend only grudgingly.

55. Do not marvel at their wealth and children.
God intends to punish them through these in the world;
and their souls will depart in a state of disbelief.

56. They swear by God they are with you,
though in fact they are not.
They are only a frightened lot.

57. If they find a place of shelter or a cave or hole to hide,
they will turn to it.

58. There are some among them who blame you (of partiality)
in distributing the offerings made in the name of God.
In case they receive some of these they are pleased,
if not, they are incensed.

59. They should rather have been pleased
with what God and His Prophet had given them,
and said: "God is sufficient for us;
He will give us of His largesse as will His Apostle.
We supplicate no one but God."

Charities are meant for the indigent and needy,
and those who collect and distribute them,
and those whom you wish to win over, and for redeeming
slaves (and captives) and those who are burdened with debt,
and in the cause of God, and the wayfarers: So does God ordain.
God is all-knowing and all-wise.

61. There are some among them who talk ill of the Prophet
by saying: "He listens to everyone."
Tell them: "He listens for your good,
and trusts in God and trusts the faithful,
and he is a blessing for those who believe.
For those who offend the Apostle of God
there is painful punishment."

62. They swear by God to please you;
but if they are believers it would have been worthier
to have pleased God and His Apostle.

63. Have they not realised
that anyone who opposes God and His Prophet,
will abide in Hell for ever?
And that is the worst disgrace.

64. The hypocrites fear lest a Surah is revealed
concerning them, exposing what is in their hearts.
Say to them: "Mock as much as you like;
God will surely expose what you dread."
65. But if you ask them, they will say:
"We were only gossiping and jesting."
You ask them: "Were you jesting with God,
His revelations and His messengers?"
66. Do not make excuses:
You turned unbelievers after having come to faith.
If We pardon a section of you (for being frivolous),
We shall punish the other
for being guilty (of deliberate sin).

The hypocrites (are the same) whether men or women,
the one of them being of the other.
They encourage what is bad
and dissuade from the good,
and tighten their purses (when it comes
to spending in the way of God).
Of God they are oblivious;
so He is oblivious of them.
The hypocrites are indeed transgressors.
68. God has reserved for hypocrites, whether men or women,
and for unbelievers, the fire of Hell,
where they will abide for ever.
This is sufficient for them:
They have God's condemnation and lasting torment.
69. Like those before you
who were greater in strength,
had more wealth and children
than you,
who enjoyed their lot in this world,
as you have enjoyed your share like them.
You indulge in idle talk,
as they had indulged in vain discourse.
Yet nothing of what they did remains
in this world or will in the next,
and they are the losers.
70. Has not the account of those before them come to them, —
of the people of Noah and 'Ad and Thamud,
of Abraham and Midian,
and all the habitations that were destroyed?
Their apostles had come to them with clear proofs;
and God did not surely wrong them,
they wronged themselves.

At-Taubah

71. Those who believe, men and women,
befriend one another, and enjoin
what is right and prohibit what is wrong.
They observe their devotional obligations, pay the zakat,
and obey God and His Apostle.
God will be merciful to them,
for God is all-mighty and all-wise.
72. God has promised men and women who believe
gardens with streams of running water
where they will abide for ever,
and beautiful mansions in the Garden of Eden,
and the blessings of God above all.
That will be happiness supreme.

Strive, O Prophet, against the unbelievers
and the hypocrites, and deal with them firmly.
Their final abode is Hell:
And what a wretched destination!
74. They swear by God: "We never said this."
But they surely said words disbelieving the truth,
and they turned unbelievers after having come to faith,
and designed what they could not accomplish.
They did it only out of vengeance
for God and His Apostle had enriched them
by their grace.
So, if they repent it is better for them.
If they turn away
then God would afflict them
with painful punishment in this world
and the next;
and none will they have on the face of the earth
to protect or help them.
75. Some of them made a covenant with God:
"If You give us in Your bounty
we shall give alms and be upright."
76. But when He gave them of His bounty they became
greedy, and then turned away.
77. As a consequence of breaking their promise made to God,
and telling lies, He filled their hearts with hypocrisy
which will last till the day they come before Him.
78. Have they not realised that God
knows their secrets and their confidential talk,
and that God has the knowledge of unknown things?
79. They who defame those of the believers
who give alms willingly,
and deride those who have nothing besides

At-Taubah

what they earn by their labour (to give in charity),
will be derided by God,
and will suffer painful punishment.
80. Whether you plead forgivenss for them or not,
God will not forgive them, even though
you plead seventy times,
for they disbelieved in God and His Apostle;
and God does not show transgressors the way.

Those who were left behind rejoiced
that they stayed at home against the wishes of God's Apostle,
being averse to fighting in the way of God
with their wealth and lives, and said:
"Do not go in this heat."
Tell them: "The heat of Hell is far more intense."
If only they had cared to instruct themselves!
82. So let them laugh a little,
for weep they will more
as retribution for what they have done.
83. If you come back to them by (the grace of) God,
and they seek your permission to go (to fight),
you should tell them:
"You will never go out nor fight the enemy with me any more.
You preferred to stay back on the first occasion,
so stay at home with those who stay behind."
84. Do not invoke blessings on any of them who die,
nor stand to pray at their graves,
for they disbelieved in God and His Prophet,
and died transgressors.
85. And let not their wealth and children astonish you.
God wishes to punish them through these in the world,
and their souls will depart in a state of disbelief.
86. Whenever a Surah is revealed (which says):
"Believe in God and fight along with His Prophet,"
the well-to-do among them ask for leave
to stay at home, and say:
"Leave us with those who are left behind."
87. They prefer to be with women
who (are allowed to) stay at home during war,
and their hearts are sealed;
so they fail to understand.
88. But the Prophet and those who have embraced the faith
       with him,
and have fought wealth and soul (in the way of God),
are blessed and will be successful.
89. God has provision for them of gardens with streams

At-Taubah

of running water,
where they will abide for ever.
This will be the supreme triumph.

Some Arabs of the desert came with ready excuses,
asking for leave to stay behind.
But those who had lied to God and His Prophet
stayed at home doing nothing.
So the punishment for those who disbelieve
among them will be painful.
91. No blame will attach to the old and the sick,
or those without means to spend on good acts,
if they stay behind provided they are sincere
to God and His Apostle.
There is no way to blame those who are doers of good,
for God is forgiving and kind.
92. Nor will they be blamed who came to you
for transport, to whom you said:
"I cannot find any means of conveyance for you,"
and they went away in tears,
grieving that they lacked the means
to spend (on carriage).
93. Blame will lie on those who are rich
yet ask your leave to stay behind.
They prefer to stay with women who stay at home,
and God seals their hearts; so they do not understand.
94. When you come back they will offer excuses to you.
Tell them: "Make no excuses;
we do not believe you.
God has informed us about you;
and God and His Apostle shall watch your conduct.
Then you will be brought to Him who knows
what is hidden and what is manifest.
He will tell you of what you did."
95. They will beg you in the name of God,
on your return, to forgive them;
but you keep away from them:
They are scum; their abode is Hell:
Requital for what they had done.
96. They will plead on oath that you accept them.
Even if you accept them, remember
God does not accept
people who are disobedient.
97. The village Arabs are more obstinate
in disbelief and hypocrisy,
and impervious to ordinances

At-Taubah

172

revealed to His Apostle by God;
yet God is aware of every thing and is wise.

مَآ أَنزَلَ اللّهُ عَلَىٰ رَسُولِهِ وَاللّهُ عَلِيمٌ حَكِيمٌ ۝

98. Some of these rustics take whatever they spend
in the way of God as a penalty, and wait
for an adverse turn in your fortune.
For them will be the adverse change,
as God hears all and knows every thing.

وَمِنَ الْأَعْرَابِ مَن يَتَّخِذُ مَا يُنفِقُ مَغْرَمًا وَ
يَتَرَبَّصُ بِكُمُ الدَّوَائِرَ عَلَيْهِمْ دَائِرَةُ السَّوْءِ وَاللّهُ
سَمِيعٌ عَلِيمٌ ۝

99. Yet some Arabs of the desert
believe in God and the Last Day,
and consider what they spend
to be a means of bringing them nearer to God
and the blessings of the Prophet.
This is certainly a means of achieving nearness (to God),
and God will admit them to His mercy,
for God is forgiving and kind.

وَمِنَ الْأَعْرَابِ مَن يُؤْمِنُ بِاللّهِ وَالْيَوْمِ الْآخِرِ
وَيَتَّخِذُ مَا يُنفِقُ قُرُبَاتٍ عِندَ اللّهِ وَصَلَوَاتِ
الرَّسُولِ أَلَا إِنَّهَا قُرْبَةٌ لَّهُمْ سَيُدْخِلُهُمُ اللّهُ فِي
رَحْمَتِهِ إِنَّ اللّهَ غَفُورٌ رَّحِيمٌ ۝

Those among the migrants (from Makkah)
and helpers (in Madina)
who were the first to believe,
and those who followed them in goodness,
have been accepted by God and they follow His way.
For them He has gardens with streams of running water
where they will abide for ever;
and that is happiness supreme.

وَالسَّابِقُونَ الْأَوَّلُونَ مِنَ الْمُهَاجِرِينَ وَالْأَنصَارِ
وَالَّذِينَ اتَّبَعُوهُم بِإِحْسَانٍ رَّضِيَ اللّهُ عَنْهُمْ
وَرَضُوا عَنْهُ وَأَعَدَّ لَهُمْ جَنَّاتٍ تَجْرِي تَحْتَهَا الْأَنْهَارُ
خَالِدِينَ فِيهَا أَبَدًا ذَٰلِكَ الْفَوْزُ الْعَظِيمُ ۝

101. Some of the Arabs of the desert around you are
    hypocrites,
and some of the people of Madina are stubborn in hypocrisy.
You are not aware of them; We know them,
and will punish them twice,
and they will be sent to a harrowing doom.

وَمِمَّنْ حَوْلَكُم مِّنَ الْأَعْرَابِ مُنَافِقُونَ وَمِنْ أَهْلِ
الْمَدِينَةِ مَرَدُوا عَلَى النِّفَاقِ لَا تَعْلَمُهُمْ نَحْنُ
نَعْلَمُهُمْ سَنُعَذِّبُهُم مَّرَّتَيْنِ ثُمَّ يُرَدُّونَ إِلَىٰ
عَذَابٍ عَظِيمٍ ۝

102. But there are others who admit their sins
of mixing good deeds with evil.
It may be that God will accept their repentance,
for God is forgiving and kind.

وَآخَرُونَ اعْتَرَفُوا بِذُنُوبِهِمْ خَلَطُوا عَمَلًا صَالِحًا
وَآخَرَ سَيِّئًا عَسَى اللّهُ أَن يَتُوبَ عَلَيْهِمْ إِنَّ اللّهَ
غَفُورٌ رَّحِيمٌ ۝

103. Accept the offerings they make from their wealth
in order to cleanse and purify them for progress,
and invoke blessings upon them.
Your blessings will surely bring them peace,
for God hears all and knows every thing.

خُذْ مِنْ أَمْوَالِهِمْ صَدَقَةً تُطَهِّرُهُمْ وَتُزَكِّيهِم بِهَا وَ
صَلِّ عَلَيْهِمْ إِنَّ صَلَوَاتَكَ سَكَنٌ لَّهُمْ وَاللّهُ سَمِيعٌ عَلِيمٌ ۝

104. Do they not know that God accepts
the repentance of His creatures and receives
what they offer in charity,
and that He is forgiving and kind?

أَلَمْ يَعْلَمُوا أَنَّ اللّهَ هُوَ يَقْبَلُ التَّوْبَةَ عَنْ عِبَادِهِ وَ
يَأْخُذُ الصَّدَقَاتِ وَأَنَّ اللّهَ هُوَ التَّوَّابُ الرَّحِيمُ ۝

105. Say to them: "Act. God will see your conduct,
and so will His Apostle and the faithful;
for you will in the end go back to Him

وَقُلِ اعْمَلُوا فَسَيَرَى اللّهُ عَمَلَكُمْ وَرَسُولُهُ
وَالْمُؤْمِنُونَ وَسَتُرَدُّونَ إِلَىٰ عَالِمِ الْغَيْبِ وَالشَّهَادَةِ

who knows the unknown and the known,
who will tell you of what you were doing."
106. There are still some others whose affairs
await the dispensation of God.
He may punish or pardon them,
for God is all-knowing and all-wise.
107. There are those who built a mosque
on opposition and disbelief,
and to cause rifts among the faithful,
and to serve as an outpost for those
who have warred against God and His Apostle before this.
Yet they will surely swear:
"We had only meant well."
But God is witness that they are liars.
108. Never set foot in that place.
Only a mosque whose foundations have been laid
from the very first on godliness
is worthy of your visiting it.
There you will find men who wish to be purified;
and God loves those who are pure.
109. Is the man who lays the foundations of his sanctum
on his allegiance to God and the wish to seek His favour,
better,
or he who lays the foundations of his building
on the edge of a bank eroded by water,
which will collapse with him into the fire of Hell?
But God does not guide the people
who are wilfully unjust.
110. The edifice they have built
will always fill their minds with perturbation
(which will not cease) till their hearts are rent to pieces,
for God is all-knowing and all-wise.

God has verily bought the souls and possessions
of the faithful in exchange for a promise of Paradise.
They fight in the cause of God, and kill and are killed.
This is a promise incumbent on Him,
as in the Torah, so the Gospel and the Qur'an.
And who is more true to his promise than God?
So rejoice at the bargain you have made with Him;
for this will be triumph supreme.
112. To those who repent and pay homage,
give praise and are devout, who kneel in prayer
and bow in supplication,
who enjoin good deeds and prohibit the bad,
and keep to the limits set by God,

announce the news of rejoicing to the faithful.

113. It is not worthy of the Prophet and those who believe
to seek forgiveness for those who are idolaters,
even though they may be their relatives,
after they have come to know
that they are destined for Hell.

114. As for Abraham's prayer for his father,
he was fulfilling a promise he had made to him.
Yet when it became evident to him
that (his father) was an enemy of God,
he broke away from him,
though Abraham was soft hearted and kind.

115. God never leads men astray after guiding them,
until He makes quite clear to them what they should avoid,
for God indeed knows each and every thing.

116. Verily God's is the kingdom of the heavens and the earth.
He alone is the giver of life and death;
and none do you have besides God as friend and helper.

117. God was kind to the Prophet, the emigrants,
and the helpers of the faithful
who followed him in the hour of distress.
When a section of them were about to lose courage
He turned to them in His mercy,
for He is compassionate and kind.

118. He has relented towards the three also
(who had refused to go to the battle of the Ditch)
whose case was left undecided,
and even the earth with all its expanse
had become narrow for them,
and their lives were confined,
and they came to realise
there was no refuge for them except in God.
So He softened towards them
that they may repent;
for God surely accepts repentance and is merciful.

O believers, do not stray from the path of God,
and be with those who are truthful.

120. It was not worthy of the people of Madina,
and the Arabs of the desert around them,
to abandon the Prophet of God, and to care
more for themselves than for him;
for there is no hardship or thirst or hunger
that they know in the service of God,
and no place they walk on
where walking provokes the unbelievers,

and no harm they receive from the enemy,
but is put down as a good deed in their favour.
Surely God does not let
the recompense of those who do good to go waste.
121. There is not a sum, large or small, that they spend,
not a piece of land that they traverse
(in the service of God)
which is not put down in their favour,
so that God could reward them for what they had done.
122. It is not possible for all believers to go out (to fight).
So a part of each section (of the population)
should go (to fight) in order that the others
may acquire understanding of law and divinity,
and warn their companions on return
so that they may take heed for themselves.

O believers, fight the unbelievers around you,
and let them realise that you are firm:
Remember, God is with those who are pious and obedient to
     Him.
124. When a Surah is revealed some of them remark:
"Whose faith among you has it increased?"
It does increase the faith of those who believe,
and they rejoice.
125. But it adds disbelief to disbelief
for those whose hearts are filled with doubt,
and they die disbelieving.
126. Do they not know that they are tried
every year once or twice?
Even then they do not repent and take heed.
127. Whenever a Surah is revealed
they look at each other (so as to ask):
"Is anyone looking at us?"
and then turn away.
Indeed God has turned their hearts away
(from the truth),
for they cannot discern the law of heaven.
128. To you has come an Apostle from among you.
Any sorrow that befalls you weighs upon him;
He is eager for your happiness,
full of concern for the faithful, compassionate and kind.
129. So, if they turn away, say to them:
"God is sufficient for me.
There is no God but He;
I depend on Him alone,
the Lord of the glorious Throne."

10 Jonah

Yūnus: Makki

In the name of Allah, most benevolent, ever-merciful.

ALIF LĀM RĀ.
These are the verses of the authoritative Book.
2. Are the people astonished that a man who is one of them
was commanded by Us to warn them
and to bring glad tidings
to those who believe
that they have a true precedence with their Lord?
(Yet) the unbelievers say:
"He is a clear sorcerer."
3. Your Lord is God
who created the heavens and the earth
in six spans, then assumed His power,
dispensing all affairs.
None can intercede with Him except by His leave.
He is God, your Lord,
so worship Him.
Will you not be warned?
4. To Him will you all return:
God's promise is true.
It is He who originates creation,
then will revert it, so that He may reward
those who believe and do good things in all justice.
But those who deny the truth will receive
boiling water to drink
and grievous punishment, for they disbelieved.
5. It is He who gave the sun its radiance,
the moon its lustre,
and appointed its stations
so that you may compute years and numbers.
God did not create them but with deliberation.
He distinctly explains His signs
for those who can understand.
6. In the alternation of night and day,
and all that He has created in the heavens and the earth,

are certainly signs for people who fear God.

7. As for those who do not hope to meet Us (after death),
and are content with the life of this world,
who are oblivious of Our signs,

8. Will have Hell as their abode
for what they have earned.

9. But those who believe and act for a beneficial end
will be guided by their Lord for their good faith.
At their feet shall flow streams of running water
in gardens of delight.

10. Their invocation will be:
"All glory to you, O God,"
and "Peace" will be their salutation,
and the end of their prayer (will be):
"All praise be to God,
the Lord of all the worlds."

If God were to hasten the evil,
as men try to hasten the good,
their term would come to end.
So We leave those who do not expect
to meet Us to wander perplexed in transgression.

12. When man is afflicted with adversity
he calls to Us, whether lying on his side,
or sitting or standing.
But when We take away his troubles,
he moves away, as though
he had never called to Us in affliction.
In the same way, attractive have been made
their deeds to the prodigals.

13. How many generations did We lay low before you
when they became wilfully unjust.
Their apostles had brought clear proofs to them,
yet they never believed.
So We punished the sinful people.

14. Then We appointed you leaders in the land
after them to see how you behaved.

15. When Our clear messages are recited to them,
those who do not hope to meet Us, say:
"Bring a different Qur'an, or make
amendments to this one."
Say: "It is not for me to change it of my will.
I follow (only) what is revealed to me.
If I disobey my Lord, I fear
the punishment of an awful Day."

16. Say: "Had God pleased

I would never have recited it to you,
nor would He have given you comprehension of it.
(Remember that I am one of you) and have lived
a whole life with you before (its revelation).
Even then you do not understand."

17. Who is more unjust than he
who imputes lies to God or denies His revelations?
The sinners will surely not be reprieved.

18. They worship those besides God
who cannot do them harm
or bring them gain, and say:
"These are our intercessors with God."
Say: "Do you want to inform God of things
in the heavens and the earth He does not know?"
Glorious is He, and too exalted
for what they associate with Him!

19. Men were once a community of one faith;
but they differed (and followed different ways).
Had it not been for the word
proclaimed by your Lord before,
their differences would have been resolved.

20. They say: "How is it that no sign was sent
by his Lord (to His Prophet)?"
Tell them: "Unknown things are only known to God.
So watch and wait (for the sign);
I am waiting and expecting with you."

When We let them taste Our mercy after affliction,
they contrive against Our signs.
Say: "God is swifter at contriving,"
for Our angels record everything you plan.

22. It is He who enables you to travel over land and sea.
When you sail in ships in a favourable breeze, you rejoice.
But when a gale begins to blow and the waves
dash against them from every side
they realise that they have been caught in it,
(and) they call on God in all faith:
"If You save us from this we shall ever be grateful."

23. But when He rescues them, they commit
excesses in the land unjustly again.
Your rebellion, O people,
shall recoil back on your own selves.
The joys of the world (are only ephemeral):
You have to come back to Us in the end.
We shall then inform you what you were doing.

24. The life of the world is like the rain

that waters the crops of the earth which are used
as food by men and cattle.
But when the earth is embellished
and adorned with gold,
and its tillers begin to feel
that (the crops) are under control,
Our command descends suddenly at night or in the day,
and We mow them down as though
there was nothing there yesterday.
This is how We distinctly explain
Our signs to those who think.
25. God invites you to mansions of peace,
and guides whosoever He will
to the path that is straight.
26. For those who do good
there is goodness and more,
and no blot or disgrace
will cover their faces.
They are people of Paradise,
where they will abide for ever.
27. But those who earn evil shall be punished
to an equal degree as their evil,
and they will be covered with shame,
and will have none to protect them against God:
Their faces shall be blackened as though
with patches of the night.
They are the people of Hell,
where they will abide for ever,
28. The day We shall gather them all together
We shall say to the idolaters:
"Take your stand with the compeers you worshipped
as the equals of God."
We shall then create a rift between them,
and the compeers will say:
"You did not worship us;
29. For God is sufficient as witness between us and you
we were not aware of your worship."
30. Then each will see what he had done in the past;
and they will turn to God, their true Lord,
and all the lies they had fabricated
will be of no avail to them.

Ask them: "Who gives you food and sustenance
from the skies and the earth?
Or, who is the lord of ear and eye?
And who brings forth the living from the dead,

the dead from the living?
And who directs all affairs?"
They will say: "God."
So tell them: "Why do you not fear Him?"
32. Such then is God, your true Lord;
and when truth is gone what is left but error?
So why do you turn away?
33. Thus the word of your Lord about those who disobey
comes true, that they do not believe.
34. Ask them: "Is there among the partners (you ascribe to God)
one
who first originates then reverts it?
Say: "It is God alone who first creates
and then reverts it.
So where do you stray?"
35. Ask: "Is there one among those you associate with God
who can show the way to the truth?"
Say: "It is God who shows the way to truth."
Then who is more worthy of being followed —
He who guides to the truth, or he
who cannot find the path until shown the way?
What has happened to you that you judge in such a wise?
36. Many of them follow nothing but illusion;
yet illusion cannot replace the reality.
God verily knows what they do.
37. This Qur'an is not such (a writ) as could be composed
by anyone but God.
It confirms what has been revealed before,
and is an exposition of (Heaven's) law.
Without any doubt it's from the Lord of all the worlds.
38. Do they say (of the Prophet) that: "He has composed it?"
Say to them: "Bring a Surah like this,
and call anyone apart from God you can (to help you),
if what you say is true."
39. In fact, they deny what is beyond
the reach of their knowledge,
whose explanation has not reached them yet.
So had those who have gone before them denied;
but look at the fate of the unjust!
40. Some of them will believe in it, some will not.
Your Lord knows the transgressors well.

If they (still) call you a liar, tell them:
"For me my actions, for you yours.
You are not answerable for my deeds,
nor I for what you do."

42. Some of them listen to you:
But can you make the deaf hear
who do not understand a thing?

وَمِنْهُمْ مَّن يَسْتَمِعُونَ إِلَيْكَ أَفَأَنتَ تُسْمِعُ الصُّمَّ وَلَوْ كَانُوا لَا يَعْقِلُونَ ۝

43. Some of them look toward you:
But can you show the blind the way
even when they cannot see?

وَمِنْهُم مَّن يَنظُرُ إِلَيْكَ أَفَأَنتَ تَهْدِي الْعُمْىَ وَلَوْ كَانُوا لَا يُبْصِرُونَ ۝

44. Surely God does not wrong anyone;
they wrong themselves.

إِنَّ اللَّهَ لَا يَظْلِمُ النَّاسَ شَيْئًا وَلَٰكِنَّ النَّاسَ أَنفُسَهُمْ يَظْلِمُونَ ۝

45. The day He will gather them together
it will appear to them
that they had lived (in the world) but an hour of day
to make each other's acquaintance.
Verily those who deny
the meeting with God
will be lost, and not find the way.

وَيَوْمَ يَحْشُرُهُمْ كَأَن لَّمْ يَلْبَثُوا إِلَّا سَاعَةً مِّنَ النَّهَارِ يَتَعَارَفُونَ بَيْنَهُمْ قَدْ خَسِرَ الَّذِينَ كَذَّبُوا بِلِقَاءِ اللَّهِ وَمَا كَانُوا مُهْتَدِينَ ۝

46. Whether We show you some of the promise
(of punishment in wait) for them,
or take you to Ourself,
their returning is to Us in the end;
and God is a witness to all they do.

وَإِمَّا نُرِيَنَّكَ بَعْضَ الَّذِي نَعِدُهُمْ أَوْ نَتَوَفَّيَنَّكَ فَإِلَيْنَا مَرْجِعُهُمْ ثُمَّ اللَّهُ شَهِيدٌ عَلَىٰ مَا يَفْعَلُونَ ۝

47. For every people there is an apostle;
and when their apostle is come
the matter is decided between them equitably,
and no one is wronged.

وَلِكُلِّ أُمَّةٍ رَّسُولٌ فَإِذَا جَاءَ رَسُولُهُمْ قُضِيَ بَيْنَهُم بِالْقِسْطِ وَهُمْ لَا يُظْلَمُونَ ۝

48. They say: "When is this promise going to come,
if what you say is true?"

وَيَقُولُونَ مَتَىٰ هَٰذَا الْوَعْدُ إِن كُنتُمْ صَادِقِينَ ۝

49. Say: "I have no power
over my own gain or loss
other than what God may please."
Every people have a certain term.
When their time is come
they can neither delay it an hour
nor advance it a moment forward.

قُل لَّا أَمْلِكُ لِنَفْسِي ضَرًّا وَلَا نَفْعًا إِلَّا مَا شَاءَ اللَّهُ لِكُلِّ أُمَّةٍ أَجَلٌ إِذَا جَاءَ أَجَلُهُمْ فَلَا يَسْتَأْخِرُونَ سَاعَةً وَلَا يَسْتَقْدِمُونَ ۝

50. Say: "Have you ever thought
if His punishment befalls you at night or in the day,
what would the sinners do to despatch it?

قُلْ أَرَأَيْتُمْ إِنْ أَتَاكُمْ عَذَابُهُ بَيَاتًا أَوْ نَهَارًا مَّاذَا يَسْتَعْجِلُ مِنْهُ الْمُجْرِمُونَ ۝

51. Will you believe it when it comes to pass?
Indeed, you will believe it then.
How impatient you were to hasten it!

أَثُمَّ إِذَا مَا وَقَعَ آمَنتُم بِهِ آلْآنَ وَقَدْ كُنتُم بِهِ تَسْتَعْجِلُونَ ۝

52. Then will the sinners be told:
"Now taste everlasting torment.
Should you be rewarded for anything else
but what you did?"

ثُمَّ قِيلَ لِلَّذِينَ ظَلَمُوا ذُوقُوا عَذَابَ الْخُلْدِ هَلْ تُجْزَوْنَ إِلَّا بِمَا كُنتُمْ تَكْسِبُونَ ۝

53. Yet they want to be informed if it is true.
Say: "By my Lord, it is the truth.
You cannot invalidate it."

وَيَسْتَنبِئُونَكَ أَحَقٌّ هُوَ قُلْ إِي وَرَبِّي إِنَّهُ لَحَقٌّ وَمَا أَنتُم بِمُعْجِزِينَ ۝

E ven if every soul that has sinned possessed
whatever is on the earth,
it would surely offer it to ransom itself,
and feel repentant on seeing the punishment.
Yet the sentence would be passed with justice,
and not one will be wronged.
55. For all that is in the heavens and the earth
belongs to God.
Remember, the promise of God is true.
But most of them do not know.
56. He is the giver of life and death,
and to Him you will return.
57. O men, a warning has come to you from your Lord,
a remedy for the (doubts) of the heart,
and a guidance and grace for those who believe.
58. Say: "It is the blessing and mercy of God;
so rejoice in it.
It is better than all that you amass."
59. Say: "Have you thought
of what God has sent you for food, of which
you have labelled some as lawful and some forbidden?"
And ask: "Has God commanded this,
or you are imputing lies to God?"
60. What do those who invent lies of God
think about the Day of Reckoning?
(Will they escape the judgement?)
In fact God is gracious to men;
but most of them are not grateful

T here is no state you are in,
whether reading from the Qur'an,
or doing something else,
but We are watching you as you are engaged in it.
There is not the weight of an atom
on the earth and in the heavens
that is hidden from your Lord,
nor is there anything smaller or greater than this
but is recorded in the perspicuous Book.
62. Remember, there is neither fear nor regret
for the friends of God.
63. Those who believe and obey God,
64. For them is good news in the life of the world
and in the life to come.
There is no changing the words of God.
That will be the great triumph.
65. You should not be grieved by what they say.

All glory is wholly for God:
He is the one who hears and knows every thing.
66. Remember, whosoever is in the heavens and the earth
belongs to God.
Those who call on others they associate with God,
follow nothing but conjecture, and only guess.
67. It is He who made the night for you to rest,
and made the day enlightening.
Indeed there are signs in this
for those who listen.
68. They say: "God has begotten a son."
Immaculate is He and self-sufficient."
Whatsoever is in the heavens and the earth
belongs to Him.
You have no proof for this (assertion):
Why do you say things of God you do not know?
69. Say: "Those who fabricate lies about God
will never succeed."
70. Let them profit by the world (while they may):
In the end they will come back to Us.
Then We shall make them taste
severe punishment for having denied (the truth).

Recount to them the story of Noah
when he said to his people:
"O people, if you find my staying with you and warning
through God's signs, unbearable to you,
know that I have reposed my trust in God.
So plan your move, and call your associates,
and make certain of your plan;
then do whatever you intend against me,
allowing me no respite.
72. If you turn away from me (remember)
I do not ask any recompense from you.
My reward is with God;
I have been commanded to be one of those who submit to
    Him."
73. Even then they denied him;
so We saved him and those with him, in the ark,
and established them in the land,
and drowned those who denied Our signs.
So think of the fate of those who were warned
(and took no heed).
74. Afterwards We sent many messengers
who brought clear proofs to their peoples.
But they were not prepared to believe

what they had once denied.
That is how We seal the hearts of the iniquitous.
75. Then after them We sent
Moses and Aaron with Our signs
to the Pharaoh and his nobles;
but they behaved arrogantly,
for they were a people full of guilt.
76. Thus, when the truth had come to them from Us,
they said: "Surely this is nothing but pure magic."
77. "You say this of the truth," said Moses,
"after it has come to you.
Is this magic?
But sorcerers do not ever prosper."
78. "Have you come," said they, "to turn us back
from what we found our ancestors doing,
so that the two of you may attain
supremacy in the land?
We shall not believe in what you say."
79. "Bring the cleverest magicians to me," said the Pharaoh.
80. So when the magicians arrived, Moses said to them:
"Cast whatever (spell) you have to cast."
81. When they had cast (their spell) Moses said:
"What you have cast is only a charm
which God will surely nullify.
God does not verily render
the deeds of evil-doers righteous.
82. God vindicates the truth by His commands,
however the sinners may dislike it."

But none of them put faith in Moses
except some youths among his people
who were nonetheless afraid
lest the Pharaoh and his nobles should persecute them;
for the Pharaoh was mighty in the land,
and guilty of excesses.
84. Moses said: "O my people, if you do believe in God
place your trust in Him if you are obedient."
85. They answered: "We have placed our trust in God.
O Lord, do not make us a target of oppression
for these tyrannical people,
86. And deliver us by Your grace
from a people who do not believe."
87. We commanded Moses and his brother:
"Build homes for your people in Egypt,
and make your houses places of worship,
perform your acts of prayer

and give happy tidings to those who believe."

88. And Moses said: "O Lord,
have You bestowed on the Pharaoh and his nobles
pomp and plenty in the life of this world
that they might mislead people from Your path?
Destroy their possessions, O Lord,
and harden their hearts
that they may not believe until
they face the painful punishment."

89. Said (the Lord): "Your prayer is answered.
Therefore persist and do not follow
the path of those who are ignorant."

90. And We brought the people of Israel across the sea,
but the Pharaoh and his army pursued them
wickedly and maliciously
till he was on the point of drowning,
and he said:
"I believe that there is no god but He
in whom the people of Israel believe,
and I submit to Him."

91. "Yes, now" (was the answer), "though before this
you were disobedient and rebellious.

92. We shall preserve your body today
that you may be a lesson for those who come after you;
as many a man is heedless of Our signs."

We gave the people of Israel a settled abode,
and bestowed good things on them to eat and use.
So they did not differ until
they came to have knowledge.
Your Lord will assuredly settle
their differences on the Day of Resurrection.

94. If you are in doubt of what We have sent down to you,
then ask those who have been reading
the Book (for a long time) before you.
The truth has indeed come to you from your Lord,
so do not be one of those who doubt,

95. And do not be one of those who deny the signs of God,
or you will be among the losers.

96. Verily those against whom the word
of your Lord is pronounced
will never believe,

97. Even though all the signs came to them,
not till they face the grievous punishment.

98. Why has there been no habitation that believed
and profited by their faith, except the people of Jonah?

When they came to believe, We removed from them
the affliction of shame in the world,
and made them prosperous for a time.
99. If your Lord had willed,
all the people on the earth
would have come to believe, one and all.
100. Are you going to compel the people to believe
except by God's dispensation?
He puts doubt in (the minds of) those
who do not think.
101. Say: "Observe all there is
in the heavens and the earth."
But signs or warnings will be of no avail
to those who do not believe.
102. Can they expect anything but what
the people before them had known?
Say: "Then wait. I am waiting with you."
103. Thus do We deliver our apostles and those who believe.
As a matter of duty We save the believers.

Say: "O men, if you have doubt about my faith, then
              (know)
I do not worship those you worship apart from God,
but I worship God who makes you die;
and I am commanded to be a believer,
105. And to set my face toward the way, as one upright,
and not be one of those
who associate others with God.
106. And not to invoke any other than God,
who can neither help nor hurt me;
for if I do, I would surely be unjust.
107. Should God bring you harm
there is none but He who could deliver you from it,
and if He wish you good
there is none who could take away His blessings:
He showers them on those of His creatures as He please,
and He is forgiving and kind."
108. Say: "O men,
the truth has come to you from your Lord,
so he who follows the right path does so for himself,
and he who goes astray errs against himself,
and I am not a guardian over you.
109. Follow what is revealed to you,
and persist until God
pronounce His judgement;
for He is the best of all judges."

11 Hūd

Hūd: Makki

In the name of Allah, most benevolent, ever-merciful.

ALIF LĀM RĀ. This is a Book
whose verses are indeclinable and distinct,
which comes from One who is most wise and all-knowing,
2. (Proclaiming) that you should worship none but God.
Verily I bring to you
from Him a message of warning and rejoicing,
3. And that you should seek
His forgiveness and turn towards Him.
He will bestow the best things of life on you
for a time ordained,
and favour those with blessings
who are worthy of grace.
But if you turn away, I fear
the punishment of a terrible Day for you.
4. To God have you to go back,
and He has power over every thing.
5. Look, how they double up their breasts
in order to hide from Him.
But when they cover themselves up with their garments,
He knows what they hide and what they expose.
Indeed, He knows the secrets of the hearts.
6. There is not a creature that moves on the earth
whose nourishment is not provided by God,
whose place of sojourning and depositing
is not known to Him.
All things conform to a manifest law.
7. It is He who created the heavens and the earth
in six spans, and has control* over the waters (of life)
so that he may bring out the best
that everyone of you could do. Yet if you said to them:
"You shall certainly be raised from the dead,"
the unbelievers will say:

---

*'*Arsh* though literally 'throne', is the seat and symbol of sovereign power, control. See also note 1, p. 96.

"This will be nothing but sorcery."
8. If We defer their punishment for a certain time,
they will say: "What is keeping it back?"
And yet, the day it comes,
they will not be able to avert it;
and what they used to laugh at
will encompass them.

If We allow man to enjoy Our favours,
and then take them away from him,
he becomes despondent and ungrateful.
10. If We let him taste Our favours after adversity,
he says: "Misfortune has left me,"
and begins to brag and exult,
11. Except those who endure with patience and do the right,
who will have pardon and a great reward.
12. You may haply omit
some of what has been revealed to you,
and may be disheartened because they say:
"Why was no treasure sent down to him,
or an angel accompanied him?"
Yet you have been sent to warn alone,
for God takes care of every thing.
13. Do they say (of the Prophet):
"He has forged (the Qur'an)?"
Say: "Then bring ten Surahs like it,
and call anyone except God to help you,
if what you say is true."
14. If they do not answer you, then know
it has been revealed
with the knowledge of God,
and that there is no god but He. (And say:)
"Will you now submit?"
15. To those who desire the life of this world
and its many allures,
We shall pay them in full for their acts herein
and will not withold any thing.
16. Yet these are the people for whom
there is nothing but Fire in the world to come.
Fruitless will be what they have fashioned,
and whatever they have done will perish.
17. Will he who has a clear proof from his Lord,
which acts as evidence from Him,
before which the Book of Moses was
a way-giver and a grace, (not believe in it)?
Whoever among the partisans does not believe in it

shall have Hell as the promised award.
So have no doubt about it,
for surely it's the truth from your Lord,
though most men may not believe.
18. Who is more wicked than he who invents lies about God?
Such men shall be arraigned before their Lord,
and the witnesses will testify:
"These are those who imputed lies to God."
Beware! The scourge of God will fall on the unjust,
19. Who obstruct others from the way of God
and seek obliquity in it,
and do not believe in the life to come.
20. They shall not weaken (the power of) God on earth,
nor find any other protector but God.
Their punishment will be doubled,
for they could neither hear nor see.
21. They are verily those who exceeded themselves,
and the (gods) they invented abandoned them.
22. Undoubtedly they will be losers in the life to come.
23. But those who believe and do things good,
and are humble before their Lord, are men of Paradise
where they will abide for ever.
24. The semblance of these two groups
is that of a man who is deaf and blind,
and the other who can hear and see.
Can they be equal?
Why do you not reflect?

We sent Noah to his people (and he said):
"I give you a clear warning.
26. Do not worship anyone but God; for I fear
the punishment of a dreadful day for you."
27. The leaders of the people who were unbelievers, replied:
"We see that you are but a man like us,
and see that none among us follows you
but the meanest and immature of judgement,
and do not see any excellence in you above us.
In fact, we think you are a liar."
28. He said: "O my people, think.
If I have a clear proof from my Lord,
and He has bestowed on me His grace,
though unknown to you,
can we force it upon you when you are averse?
29. I do not demand for it any wealth from you, O my people.
My reward is with God. And I will not
drive those away who believe.

They have also to meet their Lord.
But I see you are an ignorant people.
30. O my people, who will save me from God
if I drive them away?
Do you not understand?
31. I say not that I have the treasures of God,
or that I possess the knowledge of the unknown.
I do not claim to be an angel,
nor can I say that God
will not bestow any good on those you disdain,
for God is cognisant of what is in their hearts.
If I say this, I will surely be unjust."
32. They said: "O Noah, you have argued with us,
and disputed at length;
so bring that (retribution) you promise,
if you speak the truth."
33. He replied: "Only God will bring it on you if He please,
and you cannot prevail against Him.
34. Even if I wish to advise you aright
my counsel will not profit you if God
intend that you go astray,
for He is your Lord and to Him you will return."
35. Do they say you have fabricated it?
Tell them: "If I have fabricated it,
then mine is the guilt;
but I am clear of what you are guilty."

And Noah was informed through revelation:
"Apart from those who have come to believe already
not one of your people is going to believe.
So grieve not for what they are doing.
37. Build an ark under Our eye and as We instruct.
Do not plead for those who have been wicked,
for they shall certainly be drowned."
38. So he built the ark; and when
groups of his people passed by him,
they scoffed at him.
He said to them: "Though you laugh
at us (now), we shall laugh at you,
as you are laughing at us.
39. You will soon come to know who suffers
the punishment that would put him to shame,
and who suffers lasting torment."
40. When Our command was issued and the waters
gushed forth from the source, We said:
"Take into (the ark) a pair of every species,

and members of your family other than those
against whom the sentence has been passed already,
and those who come to believe."
But only a few believed in him.

41. And (Noah) said: "Embark. In the name of God
be its course and mooring.
My Lord is surely forgiving and kind."

42. It sailed on waves like mountains (high),
and Noah called to his son
who was separated from him:
"Embark with us, O my son,
and be not one of those who do not believe."

43. "I shall go up a mountain," he said,
"which will keep me from the water."
"There is no getting away," said Noah,
"from the decree of God today, except
for those on whom be His mercy."
And a wave came between them,
and he was among those who were drowned.

44. Then it was said: "O earth,
swallow back your water; and, O sky, desist."
And the water subsided,
and the decree was accomplished.
The ark came to rest on Judi (Mount Ararat),
and it was said: "Away with the cursed people!"

45. Noah called on his Lord and said: "O Lord,
my son is surely a member of my family,
and verily Your promise is true,
as You are the most just of all judges."

46. "O Noah", He answered, "truly he is not of your family.
He is surely the outcome of an unrighteous act.*
So ask Me not of what you do not know.
I warn you not to be one of the ignorant."

47. "Preserve me, O Lord," said (Noah), "from asking You
      that
of which I have no knowledge.
If You do not forgive me and have mercy on me
I shall be among those who perish."

48. (And the Lord) said: "O Noah, disembark
with peace and safety from Us and blessings
on you and the people with you.
As for some (of them),
We shall bestow advantages for a time,
then send a grievous punishment on them."

_____

* See 66:10.

49. This is news of the Unknown We reveal to you,
which neither you nor your people knew before.
So endure with patience. The future is for those
who keep away from evil and follow the straight path.

We sent to the people of 'Ad their brother Hud,
who said: "O my people, worship God;
you have no other god but He.
(As for the idols,) you are only inventing lies.
51. O my people, I ask no recompense of you for it:
My reward is with Him who created me.
Will you not, therefore, understand?
52. O my people, beg your Lord to forgive you,
and turn to Him in repentance.
He will send down rain in torrents for you from the skies,
and give you added strength.
So do not turn away from Him as sinners."
53. They said: "O Hud, you have come to us with no proofs.
We shall not abandon our gods
because you say so, nor believe in you.
54. All we can say is that some of our gods
have smitten you with evil."
He replied:" I call God to witness,
and you be witness too, that I am clear
of what you associate (in your affairs)
55. Apart from Him. Contrive against me
as much as you like, and give me no respite.
56. I place my trust in God who is my Lord and your Lord
There is no creature that moves on the earth
who is not held by the forelock firmly by Him.
Verily the way of my Lord is straight.
57. If you turn away, then (remember)
I have delivered to you the message I was sent with.
My Lord will put other people in your place,
and you will not be able to prevail against Him.
Indeed my Lord keeps a watch over all things."
58. So, when Our command was issued We rescued
Hud by Our grace, and those who believed, with him,
and saved them from a dreadful doom.
59. These were the people of 'Ad
who denied the word of their Lord and rebelled
against His apostles, and followed
the bidding of every perverse tyrant.
60. So they were accursed in the world,
and they will be damned on the Day of Doom.
Beware! The 'Ad turned away from their Lord.

Hud

193

Be warned! Accursed are the people of 'Ad who were Hud's.

عَادًا كَفَرُوا رَبَّهُمْ أَلَا بُعْدًا لِعَادٍ قَوْمِ هُودٍ ۞

To Thamud We sent their brother Saleh.
"O my people," he said, "worship God;
you have no other god but He.
It is He who raised you from the earth
and settled you upon it.
So beg your Lord to forgive you,
and turn to Him in repentance.
Surely my Lord is near and answers."
62. They said: "O Saleh, we had placed our hopes in you,
but you forbid us from worshipping that
which our fathers worshipped,
and we are suspicious of what you are calling us to."
63. He said: "O my people, have you considered
that if my Lord has clearly shown me the way,
and I have His blessings too,
who will save me then from God if I disobey?
You will only add to my ruin.
64. O my people, this she-camel of God is a token for you.
So leave her alone to graze on God's earth,
and do not molest her, otherwise
the swiftest punishment would befall you."
65. But they hamstrung her.
Then (Saleh) said:
"You have but three days to enjoy life in your homes.
Infallible is this promise."
66. So, when Our command (of punishment) came
We delivered Saleh by Our grace,
and those who believed, with him,
from the disgrace of that day.
Verily your Lord is mighty and powerful.
67. The sinners were seized by a blast from heaven,
and lay overturned in their homes in the morning,
68. As though they had never lived there at all.
Beware! The people of Thamud turned away from their Lord.
Beware! Accursed are the people of Thamud.

Our angels came to Abraham with good news,
and said: "Peace on you."
"Peace on you too," said Abraham,
and hastened to bring a roasted calf.
70. When they did not stretch their hands towards it
he became suspicious and afraid of them.
They said: "Do not be afraid.
We have been sent to the people of Lot."

71. His wife who stood near, laughed
as We gave her the good news of Isaac,
and after Isaac of Jacob.
72. She said: "Woe betide me! Will I give birth
when I am old and this my husband be aged?
This is indeed surprising!"
73. "Why are you surprised at the command of God?
God's mercy and blessings be upon you,
O members of this household," they said.
"Verily He is worthy of praise and glory."
74. When Abraham's fear was dispelled,
and the good news had come to him,
he pleaded for the people of Lot with Us.
75. Abraham was kind, compassionate, and penitent.
76. "Desist from pleading, O Abraham," (they said).
"Your Lord's command has verily been issued,
and a punishment that cannot be averted
is bound to fall on them."
77. So when Our angels came to Lot, he grieved for them,
and felt powerless to help them, and said:
"This is a day of sorrow."
78. His people came excited to him.
They were addicted to sin already.
Said (Lot): "O my people, these daughters of mine
are cleaner (and lawful) for you. Have fear of God,
and do not shame me before my guests.
Is there no man of discernment among you?"
79. They said: "You know we have no need for your
daughters,
and know well what we want."
80. "I wish I had the power to resist you," said (Lot),
"or powerful support."
81. (The angels) said: "O Lot,
we have verily been sent by your Lord.
They will never be able to harm you.
So, leave late at night with your family,
and none of you should turn back to look;
but your wife will suffer (the fate)
they are going to suffer.
Their hour of doom is in the morning:
Is not the morning nigh?"
82. So when the decreed moment arrived,
We turned the habitations upside down, and rained
upon them stones of hardened lava in quick succession,
83. Impressed with (the signs) of your Lord.
And such (punishment) is not far for the (other) transgressors.

Hud

We sent to Midian their brother Shu'aib.
He said: "O my people, worship God;
you have no other god but He.
So do not give in short measure nor underweigh.
I see you are prosperous, but I fear
the doom of an overwhelming Day for you.
85. So, O my people, weigh and measure with justness,
and do not withhold things due to men,
and do not spread corruption in the land, despoiling it.
86. That which is left to you by God
is better, if you are true believers;
yet I am not a warden over you."
87. They said: "O Shu'aib, does your piety teach that we
should abandon what our fathers worshipped, or desist
from doing what we like with our goods?
How gracious a man of discernment you are indeed!"
88. He said: "O my people, think.
I have a clear sign from my Lord,
who has also given me a goodly provision,
and I do not wish for myself what I forbid you:
I only wish to reform you as best I can.
My success is from God alone.
In Him I have placed my trust,
and to Him I turn.
89. O my people (I fear) lest your opposition to me
should bring you the like of what befell
the people of Noah or Hud or Saleh;
and the people of Lot
are not distant from you.
90. Beg your Lord to forgive you, and turn to Him.
Indeed my Lord is compassionate and loving."
91. They said: "O Shu'aib, much of what you say
is meaningless to us, and then (for sure)
you are powerless among us.
But for your clan we would have stoned you to death.
You have no power over us."
92. He said: "My clan seems mightier to you than God
whom you neglect and push behind your backs.
Surely what you do is within the power of my Lord.
93. Do on your part what you can, O people,
I will do what I will.
You will come to know who suffers
the punishment that would put him to shame,
and who is the liar.
So watch; I am watching with you."
94. And when Our word came to pass,

Hud

We rescued Shu'aib and those who believed, with him,
by Our grace, but those
who were wicked were seized by a punishment from heaven,
and lay overturned in their homes in the morning
95. As though they had not dwelt there at all.
Beware! Condemned were the people of Midian
as those of Thamud had been before them!

We sent Moses with Our signs and full authority
97. To the Pharaoh and his nobles,
but they followed the bidding of Pharaoh,
though the bidding of Pharaoh was unrightful.
98. He shall be at the head of his people
on the Day of Resurrection,
and drive them into Hell like cattle driven to water —
what an evil watering-place to reach!
99. Damned will they be in this world,
and on the Day of Doom
how evil the gift that they will receive!
100. These are a few accounts of settlements
that We narrate to you.
Some still survive,
and some have been mowed down.
101. We did not wrong them;
they wronged themselves.
When your Lord's chastisement descended upon them,
their gods, on whom they called apart from God,
were not of the least avail,
and all they did was only to add
to their destruction.
102. Such is the punishment of your Lord
when He seizes human settlements
in the acts of wickedness.
Surely His hold is grievous and terrible.
103. In this surely is a sign for him
who fears the torment of the Hereafter,
the day when mankind will be assembled together,
which will be a day when all things would become evident.
104. We are defering it only for a time ordained.
105. The day it comes no soul will dare
say a word but by His leave;
and some will be wretched,
some will be blessed.
106. And those who are doomed, will be in Hell:
For them will be sighing and sobbing,
107. Where they will dwell so long as heaven and earth endure,

unless your Lord will otherwise.
Verily your Lord does as He wills.
108. Those who are blessed will be in Paradise,
where they will dwell so long as heaven and earth survive,
unless your Lord wills otherwise:
This will be a gift uninterrupted.
109. So, you should not entertain any doubt
about those whom they worship:
They only worship what their fathers had worshipped before
    them.
We shall verily give them their meed
without diminution.

Verily We gave to Moses the Book,
but there was disagreement about it.
Had the decree of your Lord (delaying it)
not been issued
the matter would have been settled between them.
They are still suspicious of it and in doubt.
111. Surely your Lord will reward
everyone in accordance with his deeds.
He is certainly aware of all they do.
112. So, you and those who turned to God with you,
should walk along the straight path
as you have been commanded, and do not transgress,
for He verily sees whatsoever you do.
113. Do not lean towards the wicked,
or you will be caught in the flames of Hell,
and have none to befriend you other than God,
nor will you be given help.
114. Stand up for the service of prayer
at the two ends of day and the first watch of night.
Remember that good deeds nullify the bad.
This is a reminder for those who are observant.
115. Be steadfast, for verily God
does not let the reward of those
who are upright and do good to go waste.
116. If only there had been men endued with virtue
in the ages before you,
who could preserve men from doing evil in the world,
other than the few We saved from among them!
Those who were wicked followed that
which made them dissolute,
and became sinners.
117. Your Lord would not surely destroy unjustly
human habitations so long as the people are righteous.

118. But if your Lord had pleased
He could have made all human beings
into one community of belief.
But they would still have differed from one another,
119. Except those on whom your Lord had mercy
for which He has created them.
But fulfilled shall be the word of your Lord:
"I will fill up Hell with jinns and men."
120. The histories of apostles that We relate to you
are (meant) to strengthen your heart.
Through them has the truth come to you, and guidance,
and reminder to those who believe.
121. Say to the infidels: "Act as best you can,
we are acting too;
122. And wait (for what is to come),
we are also waiting (to see)."
123. To God belong the secrets of the heavens and the earth,
and all things will go back to Him.
So worship Him and put your trust in Him;
your Lord is not heedless of what you do.

12 Joseph

Yūsuf: Makki

وما من دابة ١٢
(١٢) سُوْرَةُ يُوْسُفَ مَكِّيَّةٌ
اٰيَاتُهَا ١١١ رُكُوْعُهَا

In the name of Allah, most benevolent, ever merciful.

ALIF LĀM RĀ.
These are the verses of the immaculate Book.
2. We have sent it down as a clear discourse
that you may understand.
3. Through the revelation of this Qur'an
We narrate the best of histories
of which you were unaware before.
4. When Joseph told his father:
"O my father, I saw eleven stars
and the sun and the moon bowing before me in homage,"
5. He said: "O son, do not narrate your dream
to your brothers, or they will plot against you.
Surely Satan is man's acknowledged foe.
6. Your Lord will choose you
and teach you to interpret events,
and confer His favours on you and the house of Jacob,
as He had done in the case of two ancestors of yours,
Abraham and Isaac, before you.
Indeed your Lord is all-knowing and all-wise."

In the story of Joseph and his brothers
are lessons for those who inquire.
8. "Surely Joseph and his brother are dearer
to our father than we," (said his half brothers),
"even though we are a well-knit band.
Our father is surely in the wrong.
9. Let us kill Joseph or cast him in some distant land
so that we may get our father's exclusive affection;
then play innocent."
10. One of them said: "If you must do so,
then do not kill Joseph,
but throw him into an unused well.
Some passing caravan may rescue him."
11. (Then going to their father) they said:

"O father, why don't you trust us with Joseph?
We are in fact his well-wishers.

12. Let him go out with us tomorrow
that he may enjoy and play.
We shall take care of him."

13. He said: "I am afraid of sending him with you
lest a wolf should devour him when you are unmindful."

14. They replied: "If a wolf should devour him
when we are there, a well-knit band,
we shall certainly be treacherous."

15. So, when they took him out they planned
to throw him into an unused well.
We revealed to Joseph: "You will tell them (one day)
of this deed when they will not apprehend it."

16. At nightfall they came to their father weeping,

17. And said: "We went racing with one another
and left Joseph to guard our things
when a wolf devoured him.
But you will not believe us even though
we tell the truth."

18. They showed him the shirt with false blood on it.
(Their father) said: "It is not so;
you have made up the story.
Yet endurance is best.
I seek the help of God alone for what you impute."

19. A caravan happened to pass, and sent
the water-carrier to bring water from the well.
He let down his bucket
(and pulled Joseph up with it).
"What luck," said the man; "here is a boy;"
and they hid him as an item of merchandise;
but what they did was known to God.

20. And they sold him as worthless
for a few paltry dirham.

The Egyptian who bought him instructed his wife:
"House him honourably. He may be of use to us.
We may even adopt him as a son."
So, We firmly established Joseph in the land,
and taught him the interpretation of dreams.
God dominated in his affairs,
though most men do not know.

22. When he reached the prime of life
We gave him wisdom and knowledge.
Thus We reward those who are good.

23. But she in whose house he resided

wished to seduce him and, closing the doors,
said: "Come into me."
"God forbid!" he said; "he is my master
who has approved my stay.
Surely those who act wrongly do not prosper."
24. But the woman desired him,
and he would have desired her
but for the indication he received from his Lord.
This was so that We may avert
both evil and lechery from him,
for he was one of Our chosen devotees.
25. Both of them raced to the door,
and she (grabbed and) rent his shirt from behind.
They met her lord outside the door.
"There is no other penalty for a man," said she,
"who wanted to outrage your wife
but imprisonment or grievous punishment."
26. (Joseph) said: "It was she who wanted to seduce me."
And a witness from her family testified:
"If the shirt is torn from the front
then the woman is speaking the truth,
and he is a liar.
27. But if the shirt is torn from behind
then she is a liar, and he speaks the truth."
28. When the husband saw the shirt torn at the back,
he said: "Surely this is a woman's ruse,
and the wiles of women are great.
29. Ignore this affair, O Joseph; and you, O woman,
ask forgiveness for your sin,
for you were surely errant."

In the city the women gossiped:
"The minister's wife longs after her page.
He has captured her heart.
We think she is in clear error."
31. When she heard their slanderings,
she sent for them and prepared a banquet,
and gave each of them a knife (for paring fruit),
and called (to Joseph): "Come out before them."
When they saw him, the women were so wonderstruck
they cut their hands,
and exclaimed: "O Lord preserve us!
He is no mortal but an honourable angel."
32. She said: "This is the one you blamed me for.
I did desire his person, but he preserved himself from sin.
Yet in case he does not do my bidding

he will be put into prison and disgraced."

33. (Joseph) prayed: "O Lord, dearer is prison
than what they invite me to.
Unless You turn their guiles away from me
I shall succumb to their charms
and thus become a pagan."

34. His Lord heard his prayer,
and averted the women's wiles from him.
He verily hears and knows every thing.

35. And yet in spite of having seen these clear proofs
they found it proper to incarcerate him for a time.

Two other youths were imprisoned along with him.
Said one of them: "I dreamt that I was pressing grapes;"
and the other: "I dreamt
that I was carrying bread on my head,
and the birds were pecking at it.
You tell us the meaning of this.
You seem to be a righteous man."

37. (Joseph) answered: "I will give you its interpretation
before the food you are served arrives.
This knowledge is one of the things my Lord has taught me.
I have given up the religion of those
who do not believe in God and deny the life to come.

38. I follow the faith of my fathers,
of Abraham and Issac and Jacob.
We cannot associate anyone with God.
This is among God's favours to us and to all mankind;
but most men are not grateful.

39. (Tell me) O fellow-prisoners,
are a number of gods better,
or one God omnipotent?

40. (What) you worship besides Him are nothing but names
that you and your fathers have assigned,
for which no sanction has been sent down by God.
Authority belongs to God alone.
He commands that you worship none but Him.
This is the right way;
but most men are ignorant.

41. O fellow-prisoners, one of you
will serve wine to your master,
the other will be crucified and the birds
will peck at his brain.
Determined is the matter of your inquiry."

42. And (Joseph) asked the man he knew would be released:
"Remember me to your lord;"

but Satan made him forget to mention this to his lord,
and Joseph remained in prison for a number of years.

One day) the king said (to his courtiers):
"I saw seven fat cows in a dream
being devoured by seven lean ones,
and seven ears of corn that were green
and seven others that were seared.
O courtiers, tell me the significance of my dream,
if you know how to interpret them."
44. "They were only confused dreams," they said;
"we do not know how to interpret them."
45. Then the servant, who of the two had been released,
remembering (Joseph), said: "I will give you its interpretation;
let me go for it."
46. (And coming to the prison) he said:
"O Joseph the truthful,
tell us (the meaning of) seven fat cows
being devoured by seven lean ones,
and seven green ears of corn and seven seared,
that I may go back to the people and tell them."
47. He said: "Sow as usual for seven years,
and after reaping leave the corn in the ears,
except the little you need for food.
48. Then there will come seven years of hardship
which will consume the grain you had laid up against them,
except a little you may have stored away.
49. This will be followed by a year of rain,
and people shall press (the grapes)."

The king said: "Bring him to me."
So when the messenger came to Joseph,
he said: "Go back to your lord and ask him:
'How fare the women who had cut their hands?'
My Lord is cognisant of their guile."
51. The king asked the women:
"What was the affair of seducing Joseph?"
"God preserve us," they said;
"we know no evil against him."
The wife of the minister said:
"The truth has now come out.
It was I who desired to seduce him,
but he is indeed a man of virtue." —
52. (At this Joseph remarked:) "From this (the Minister)
should know
that I did not betray him in his absence,

and that God does not surely let the wiles
of those who betray ever succeed.

53. But I do not wish to absolve myself,
for the soul is prone to evil,
unless my Lord have mercy.
Indeed my Lord is forgiving and kind." —

54. When the king heard this he said:
"Bring him to me. I shall take him in my special service."
When he had talked to him, he said:
"Today you are established in a rank of trust with us."

55. "Appoint me over the granaries of the land," (he said);
"I shall be a knowledgeable keeper."

56. Thus We gave Joseph authority in the land
so that he lived wherever he liked.
We bestow Our favours on whomsoever We please,
and do not allow the reward of those who are good to go
waste.

57. And certainly the recompense of the life to come
is better for those who believe and follow the right path.

The brothers of Joseph came (to Egypt) and visited
him.
He recognised them, though they did not recognise him.

59. When he had supplied their provisions, he said to them:
"Bring your (half) brother with you.
Have you not seen that I have given full measure,
and that I am the best of hosts?

60. But if you do not bring him with you,
then I shall have no grain for you,
nor should you come back to me."

61. They said: "We shall request his father,
and will certainly do that."

62. Then he ordered his servants:
"Put their money back in their packs:
They may find it on reaching home,
and perhaps come again."

63. When they returned to their father, they said:
"O father, a further measure has been denied us.
So send our brother with us that he
may bring more grain. We shall take care of him."

64. He replied: "Should I trust you with him
as I did his brother?
But God is the best of guardians,
and most merciful of all."

65. When they unpacked their goods they said:
"O father, what more can we ask?

Look, even our money has been returned.
We shall go and bring a camel-load more of grain
for our family, and take good care of our brother.
That will be an easy measure."
66. He said: "I will never send him with you
until you swear by God
that you will bring him back to me,
unless all of you are overtaken (by misfortune)."
When they had given their promise, he said:
"God is witness to our conversation."
67. (As they were leaving) their father said to them:
"O my sons, do not seek one approach
but employ different ways (of attaining your object).*
If anything should befall you from God
I shall not be able to avert it,
for all authority belongs to God.
I have placed my trust in Him,
and the trusting should rely on Him alone."
68. When they entered as their father had advised them,
nothing could avail them against (the will of) God,
yet it confirmed a premonition Jacob had,
for verily he had knowledge as We had taught him,
though most men do not know.

When they came to Joseph he made his brother his guest,
and said: "I am your brother. So do not grieve
for what they had done."
70. When he had given them their provisions he put
his goblet in his brother's saddle-bag.
Then a crier announced: "O men of the caravan,
you are thieves."
71. They turned to them and asked:
"What is it you have lost?"
72. "We cannot find the master's goblet.
Whoever comes up with it will be given
a camel-load of grain; I vouch for it."
73. They said: "We swear by God. You know we did not come
to commit any crime in the land,
nor are we thieves."
74. "What should be the punishment," they were asked,
"in case you are liars?"
75. "The punishment for that (should be)," they said,
"that he in whose luggage it is found
should be held as punishment.

----

* For the metaphorical use of gate or door (*bab*), see footnote to 2:189.

This is how we repay the wrong-doers."
76. So he searched their saddle-bags before his brother's,
then produced the cup from his brother's bag.
That is how We planned an excuse for Joseph,
for under the law of the king
he could not detain his brother
unless God so willed.
We raise the status of whom We please.
Over every man of knowledge there is one more knowing.
77. Said the brothers: "If he has stolen (no wonder),
his brother had stolen before."
But Joseph kept this secret and did not disclose it to them,
and said (to himself): "You are worse in the degree of evil,
for God knows better of what you allege."
78. They said: "O Minister, he has an aged father,
so keep one of us in his place.
We see you are a virtuous man."
79. "May God forgive us," he said, "if we hold any one
but him with whom we found our property,
or else we would be unjust."

When they despaired of (pursuading) him,
they went aside to confer.
The oldest of them said: "You know that your father
has pledged you in the name of God,
and you have been guilty of iniquity
in the case of Joseph before.
I will not leave this place unless
my father permits or God decides for me,
for He is the best of all judges.
81. So, go to your father and tell him: 'O father,
your son has committed a theft.
We bear witness to only what we know;
we could not prevent the unknown.
82. Enquire from the people of that city,
or ask the men of the caravan with whom we have come.
We are verily speaking the truth.' "
83. "No," said (the father). "You have made up the story;
but patience is best;
God may bring them back to me.
He is all-knowing and all-wise."
84. He turned away from them and cried:
"Alas for Joseph!" And his eyes turned white with grief
which he bore in silence.
85. "By God," said they, "you will never stop
thinking of Joseph till you are consumed or perish."

86. He replied: "I cry my plaint and grief to God,
and know from God what you do not know.
87. O sons, go in search of Joseph and his brother,
and do not despair of the mercy of God.
Only they despair of God's mercy who do not believe."
88. When they returned to him, they said (to Joseph):
"O Minister, calamity has befallen us and our people.
We have brought but a meagre sum,
but give us full measure as alms bestowed.
God surely rewards those who give alms."
89. He said: "Do you know what you did
to Joseph and his brother in your ignorance?"
90. They said: "Surely you are not Joseph!"
"I am Joseph," he said, "and this is my brother.
God has been gracious to us;
for God does not verily deprive those
who fear Him and are patient
of the recompense of those who are good."
91. They said: "By God, God has favoured you above us,
for we have indeed been sinners."
92. "There is no blame on you today," he said,
"May God forgive you. He is the most merciful of all.
93. Take my shirt and put it on my father's face;
his eyesight will be restored;
and bring your entire family to me."

The caravan departed (from Egypt) and Jacob said
      (at home):
"Say not that I am in my dotage,
but I get the smell of Joseph."
95. They said: "By God, you are still persisting in your old
      delusion."
96. Then, as the harbinger of happy news arrived
and put the garment over his face
his eyesight was restored.
He said: "Did I not tell you?
I know from God what you do not know."
97. Said (the sons): "O our father, pray for us
that our sins be forgiven,
for we are really sinners."
98. "I will ask my Lord to forgive you," he replied,
"for He is forgiving and kind."
99. When they went back to Joseph
he gave his father and mother a place of honour,
and said: "Enter Egypt in peace by the will of God."
100. He seated his parents by his side on the throne;

and they fell down before him in homage.
"O my father," said Joseph, "this is the meaning
of my earlier dream.
My Lord has made it come true.
He was gracious in getting me out of the prison,
and bringing you out of the desert to me
after the discord created by Satan between me and my
    brothers,
for my Lord is gracious to whomsoever He please.
He is indeed all-knowing and all-wise.
101. O my Lord, you have given me dominion
and taught me the interpretation of dreams;
O Creator of the heavens and the earth, You alone
are my saviour in this world and the world to come;
let me die submitting to You,
and place me among the upright."
102. This is news of the unknown We reveal to you,
for you were not present when Joseph's brothers
agreed on their course of action,
and devised their plot.
103. Many men will not believe howsoever you wish,
104. Even though you ask no recompense (for it).
It is only a warning for all mankind.

How many a sign there is in the heavens and the earth
which most men pass by and ignore,
106. Not only do they not believe in God,
but also associate others with Him.
107. Do they really believe
that an all-embracing punishment of God
will not come upon them, or the Day of Doom
overtake them suddenly
while they remain unaware?
108. Say: "My way, and that of my followers,
is to call you to God with full perception.
All glory to God, I am not an idolater."
109. All the apostles We had sent before you
were men of those regions,
to whom We sent Our revelations.
Have they not travelled on the earth and seen
what befell the people before them?
Surely the abode of the Hereafter
is better for those who fear straying from the right path.
Do you not understand?
110. When the apostles despaired and thought
they were made false promises, Our help arrived,

and We delivered whom We pleased;
but never will Our punishment be averted
from the sinners.
111. Verily in their accounts is a lesson for men of wisdom.
This is not a fictitious tale,
but a verification of earlier Books,
and a clear exposition of every thing,
and a guidance and grace for those who believe.

13 Thunder

Ar-Ra'd: Madani

In the name of Allah, most benevolent, ever-merciful.

بِسْمِ اللهِ الرَّحْمٰنِ الرَّحِيْمِ۞

ALIF LĀM MĪM RĀ.
These are the verses of the Scripture.
Whatsoever is sent down to you from your Lord
is the truth; but most men do not believe.
2. It is God who raised the skies
without support, as you can see,
then assumed His throne, and enthralled
the sun and the moon (so that) each
runs to a predetermined course.
He disposes all affairs,
distinctly explaining every sign
that you may be certain of the meeting
with your Lord.
3. It is He who stretched the earth
and placed upon it
stabilisers and rivers;
and made two of a pair of every fruit;
(and) He covers up the day with the night.
In these are signs for those who reflect.
4. On the earth are tracts adjoining one another,
and vineyards, fields of corn and date-palm trees,
some forked, some with single trunks,
yet all irrigated by the self-same water,
though We make
some more excellent than the others in fruit.
There are surely signs in them for those who understand.
5. If you are surprised, then astonishing is the speech
(of those who say:) "Having turned to dust
shall we be raised as a new creation?"
They are the ones who deny their Lord,
and they will have collars around their necks.
They are the inmates of Hell,
where they will abide for ever.
6. They want you to hasten the evil before the good,

even when there have been examples
of retribution before them.
Though certainly your Lord forgives human beings
for their iniquities,
your Lord is severe of retribution.
7. The unbelievers say: "Why no miracle
was sent down to him by his Lord?"
But you are only a bearer of warnings,
and a guide for every nation,

God is cognisant of what every female
carries in her womb, or what the wombs want or exceed
(of their disburdening time).
With Him all things are in determined measure.
9. He is the knower of the known and the unknown,
the mighty and most high.
10. He who keeps his secret among you is the same to Him
as he who speaks out publicly,
and he who hides himself in the night
and walks freely in the day.
11. His angels keep watch over him in succession (night and
day),
in front and behind, by God's command.
Verily God does not change
the state of a people till they change themselves.
When God intends misfortune for a people
no one can avert it,
and no saviour will they have apart from Him.
12. It is He who makes the lightning flash
for fear and hope, and raises massive clouds.
13. The thunder sings His praises,
and the angels too,
for awe of Him.
He sends thunder-bolts and strikes
whosoever He will with them:
Even then it is God they contend about!
But mighty is He in (His) power.
14. To call on Him is true (supplication).
For those they invoke other than Him
do not answer them at all,
except like a man who stretches his hands
towards the water that it reach his mouth,
but it will never reach it.
Not more than error are the prayers of infidels.
15. Whosoever is in the heavens and on earth
bows to God in submission with a will or perforce,

as do their shadows in the morning and evening.
16. Ask them: "Who is the Lord of the heavens and the earth?"
(They will) say: "God." Say: "Then why do you take
protectors besides Him who have no power
over their own gain or loss?"
Say: "Can a blind man and one who can see
be equal?
Or, darkness and light be the same?
Or, have those they have appointed equal of God
created, as He has created,
so that the (two) creations look alike to them?"
Say: "God is the creator of every thing.
He is One, the omnipotent."
17. He sends down water from the skies,
which flows in channels
according to their capacity,
with the scum borne on the surface of the torrent,
as rises the scum when metals are heated on the fire
for making ornaments and household utensils.
This is how God determines truth and falsehood.
The scum disappears like the foam on the bank,
and that which is useful to man remains on the earth.
That is how God sets forth precepts of wisdom.
18. For those who obey their Lord
is excellence.
For those who fail to obey,
the reckoning will be hard,
even if they possess and give as ransom
all that there is on the earth, and as much more;
and Hell will be their abode:
How wretched is its wide expanse!

Can a man who knows what has been revealed
to you from your Lord is the truth,
and one who cannot see, be the same?
They alone take warning who are wise,
20. Who fulfil their covenant with God
and do not break their agreement,
21. Who keep together what God has ordained held together,
and fear their Lord and dread
the hardship of the Reckoning,
22. Who persevere in seeking the way of their Lord,
who fulfil their devotional obligations,
and spend of what We have given them,
secretly or openly,
who repel evil with good:

For them is the recompense of Paradise:
23. Perpetual gardens which they will enter
with those of their fathers, spouses and children
who were virtuous and at peace,
with angels coming in through every door
24. Saying: "(Welcome,) peace on you,
for you persevered."
How excellent the recompense of Paradise!
25. As for those who break God's covenant after validating it,
and sever relations which God ordained cohered,
and spread corruption in the land,
there is condemnation for them and an evil abode.
26. God increases or decreases
the fortunes of whosoever He will,
and they rejoice in the life of this world.
Yet the life of this world
is nothing but a merchandise
as compared to the life of the next.

The unbelievers say: "How is it
that no miracle was sent down to him by his Lord?"
Say: "God leads whosoever He wills astray,
and guides whoever turns to Him in repentance.
28. Those who believe and find peace in their hearts
from the contemplation of God:
Surely there is peace of heart
in the contemplation of God!"
29. Those who believe and do the right, have happiness,
and an excellent resting place.
30. That is how We have sent you to a people
before whom many a people have come and gone,
so that you may announce to them
whatever We have revealed to you.
But they do not believe in Ar-Rahman.*
Tell them: "He is my Lord. There is no other god but He.
In Him have I placed my trust,
and to Him is my reversion."

---

* Allah and Ar-Rahman (generally translated as the Merciful) are names of the same Supreme Deity
as this verse clarifies. The Northern Arabs called Him Allah, which emphasises His qualities of Lord-
ship, omnipotence and majesty; and Ar-Rahman, perhaps an Arabised form of the Hebrew word
Rachman, was used by the Southern Arabs, which emphasised His qualities of mercy and benevolence,
as in *Rahim*, the ever-merciful. This, however, gave rise to confusion in the minds of infidels that they
were two separate deities, to which verse 60 of Surah 25 refers. In the Qur'an, Allah is used 2698
times and Ar-Rahman 51, mostly in the Makki Surahs, and only twice in Surah 2, The Cow, an early
Madani Surah, apart from its use in the invocation that heads all the Surahs except 9, where it has
been used as an adjective, but is really a proper noun with Ar-Rahim, which is another name of God.

الرعد ١٣   ومآابروج ١٣

31. Had there been a Qur'an
which could have made the mountains move,
or the earth to cleave asunder,
or the dead to speak,
yet all authority belongs to God.
Have the believers not learnt
that if God had so willed
He could have guided all mankind?
As for unbelievers, they will be visited
by misfortune endlessly for what they have done;
or it would sit in their homes
till the promised threat of God comes to pass.
Surely God does not go back on His promise.

Many an apostle have they mocked before you;
but I allowed the unbelievers respite,
then I seized them.
How severe was My punishment then!
33. Who is it who stands (watch) over every soul
for what it does?
Yet they ascribe compeers to God.
Say: "Then name them.
Or are you announcing to God what He does not know
on the earth? Or is it only empty talk?
In fact, the unbelievers' plots
are made to look attractive to them,
so that they are held back from the right path.
Whosoever God allows to go astray
has none to show him the way.
34. For them is punishment in this world;
and the punishment of the world to come
is far more severe.
They will have no one to save them from God.
35. The likeness of Paradise promised the pious and devout
is (of a garden) with streams of rippling water,
everlasting fruits and shade.
This is the recompense of those who keep away from evil;
but the recompense of those who deny the truth
is Hell.
36. Those to whom We have given the Scriptures rejoice
in what We have sent down to you;
but some of their factions reject some of it.
Tell them: "I am commanded to worship only God,
and not to associate compeers with Him.
To Him I call you, and to Him is the destination."
37. That is how We have sent down this (Qur'an)

as a code of clear judgement.
But if you follow their caprices,
now that you have been given knowledge,
you will have no friend or protector against God.

We sent many apostles before you,
and bestowed on them wives and children,
but it was not for any apostle to come up with a miracle
unless by the leave of God.
For every age there is a law.
39. God abrogates or confirms whatsoever He will,
for He has with Him the Book of Books.
40. Whether We allow you to see (the punishment)
We have promised them, or end your life
before (its execution),
it is certainly for you to convey the message;
the reckoning is for Us to do.
41. Do they not see Us advancing from all sides
into their land and reducing its frontiers?
It is for God to judge;
and there is none to reverse His judgement.
He is swift at reckoning.
42. Surely those who had gone before them had also plotted;
but God's is all the planning,
for He has knowledge of what each does.
The unbelievers will soon learn
for whom is the guerdon of Paradise.
43. Yet those who are disbelievers say:
"You are not the apostle sent (by God)."
Tell them: "God is sufficient as witness
between me and you, and he who has knowledge of the Book."

14 Abraham

Ibrahim : Makki

In the name of Allah, most benevolent, ever-merciful.

بِسْمِ اللهِ الرَّحْمٰنِ الرَّحِيْمِ۟

ALIF LĀM RĀ.
A Book We have sent down to you
that you may lead
men out of darkness into light,
by their Lord's command,
to the path of the mighty, the worthy of praise
2. God,
to whom belongs all there is in the heavens and the earth.
Woe to the unbelievers
for the terrible punishment (that awaits).
3. Those who hold the life of this world
dearer than that of the next,
who obstruct the path of God and seek
obliquity in it, have wandered far into error.
4. We never sent a messenger
who did not speak the tongue of his people,
that he may explain to them distinctly.
God leads whosoever He wills astray,
and shows whoever He wills the way:
He is all-mighty and all-wise.
5. Remember when We sent
Moses with Our signs (We said):
"Bring your people out of darkness into light,
and remind them of the visitations of God.
Indeed there are signs in this
for every steadfast, thankful soul."
6. So Moses said to his people:
"Remember the favours of God
when He saved you from the people of Pharaoh
who afflicted you with oppression, slaying your sons
but keeping alive your women,
which was a great trial from your Lord."

Remember, your Lord proclaimed:

"I shall give you more
if you are grateful; but if you are thankless
then surely My punishment is very great."

8. And Moses said: "What if you and all the people of the
world deny,
God is unconcerned and worthy of praise."

9. Has not the news of those before you,
the people of Noah and 'Ad and Thamud,
and those who came after them, come to you?
None knows (about) them except God.
Their apostles came to them with clear proofs,
but they tried to silence them and said:
"We do not believe in what you have been sent with,
and we are in doubt of what you call us to,
about which we are in disquiet."

10. Said their apostles: "Can there be doubt about God,
the originator of the heavens and the earth?
He calls you to forgive some of your sins,
and give you respite for a time ordained."
They said: "You are only men like us,
and yet you wish to turn us away
from what our fathers worshipped.
Bring to us then a clear proof."

11. Their apostles said to them:
"Indeed we are men like you,
but God bestows His favours on whomsoever He wills
among His creatures. It is not in our power
to bring a miracle for you without the leave of God.
The believers should only place their trust in God.

12. And why should we not repose our trust in God
when He has shown us our paths of duty to Him?
We shall bear with fortitude
the hardships you inflict upon us.
The trusting place their trust in God."

The unbelievers said to their apostles:
"We shall drive you out of our land,
or else you come back to our fold."
Their Lord then communicated to them:
"We shall annihilate these wicked people,

14. And establish you in their place.
This is for him who fears My station,
and dreads My commination."

15. Then (the apostles) asked of God's assistance,
and every arrogant tyrant was frustrated:

16. Before him is Hell, and he will get

Ibrahim

putrid liquid to drink.
17. He will sip it,
yet will not be able to gulp it down.
Death will crowd in upon him from every side,
but die he will not.
A terrible torment trails him.
18. Like ashes are the deeds of those
who deny their Lord, which the wind
blows away on a windy day.
They shall have no power over what they earned.
This is the farthest limit of going astray.
19. Do you not see that God has created
the heavens and the earth with ultimate reason?
If He so wills He could take you away
from the earth and raise a new creation (in your place).
20. This is well within the power of God.
21. When they will all appear before God together,
the weak will say to those who were arrogant:
"We were your followers, so can you now
save us a little from God's punishment?"
They will say: "If we had been guided by God
we would surely have shown you the way.
To lament or endure
is all the same to us now.
No getting away is there for us."

When the reckoning is over Satan will say:
"The promise that was made to you by God
was indeed a true promise;
but I went back on the promise I had made,
for I had no power over you except
to call you; and you responded to my call.
So blame me not, but blame yourselves.
Neither can I help you nor can you give me help.
I disavow your having associated me earlier (with God).
The punishment for those who are wicked is painful indeed."
23. Those who believed and did the right,
will be admitted to gardens with rivers flowing by,
where they will abide by the leave of their Lord,
with 'Peace' as their salutation.
24. Do you not see how God compares a noble act *
to a healthy tree whose roots
are firm and branches in the sky, which yields
25. By the leave of its Lord its fruit in all seasons,

_____

* See note on p. 222.

Ibrahim

God presents words of wisdom to men
that they might reflect.
26. An evil act is like a rotten tree
torn out of the earth
with no (base or) firmness.
27. With immutable words God makes the faithful dauntless
in the life of the world and the life to come,
but leads the unjust into error,
for God does as He pleases.

Have you not looked at those who repaid
God's favours with ingratitude;
who pulled their people down to ruin,
29. Hell,
where they will roast in the fire?
And what an evil repository!
30. They have appointed equals of God
to mislead people from His path.
Tell them: "Enjoy yourselves (so long as you may).
In the end you have to go to Hell."
31. Tell those of My creatures who believe:
"Observe your devotional obligations and give
of what We have given you in charity,
secretly or openly, before the Day arrives
when there will be no buying or selling
or befriending."
32. It is God who created the heavens and the earth,
and sent down rain from the sky
producing fruits for your food thereby,
and made you master of the ships that ply
in the oceans by His command,
subjected the rivers to your control,
33. And subjugated the sun and moon for you
so that they perform their tasks diligently;
and subdued the night and day for your service.
34. He gave you whatsoever you asked.
If you try to count the favours of God
you will not be able to calculate.
Man is most unjust indeed,
full of ingratitude.

Remember when Abraham prayed: "O Lord,
make this a city of peace, and preserve
me and my progeny from worshipping idols:
36. Many a man have they led astray, O Lord.
So he who follows me is truly of me;

Ibrahim

220

but as for him who disobeys me,
surely You are forgiving and kind.
37. I have settled some of my children, O Lord,
in a barren valley near Your sacred House,
so that, O our Lord, they may be constant in devotion.
So put in the hearts of men some kindness for them,
and provide fruits for them: They may haply be grateful.
38. O Lord, You have knowledge of what we hide
and what we reveal,
for nothing on the earth or in the skies
is hidden from God.
39. All praise be to God who bestowed on me
Ishmael and Isaac in old age.
Verily my Lord listens to prayer.
40. Grant, O Lord, that I and my offspring may remain
constant in devotion.
Grant, O Lord, my supplication.
41. O Lord, forgive me, my parents and the faithful
on the Day the reckoning is done.''

Think not God is oblivious of the deeds
of the wicked. He has only allowed them respite
till the Day on which
all eyes would stare aghast,
43. (And) they would hasten forward,
heads lifted upwards, gazes fixed,
and emptied out their hearts.
44. Warn the people of that Day
when the punishment would be inflicted upon them.
Then will the wicked say: "O our Lord,
give us respite a while more.
We shall heed Your call and follow the apostles."
(But they will be told,): "Are you not those
who used to swear: 'There is no reverse for us?'
45. Yet you dwelt in the dwellings of those
who had exceeded themselves, and it was evident to you
how We had dealt with them;
and We held out examples before you."
46. Still they are plotting their plots,
but evident are their plots to God,
even though they are so adroit
as to make the mountains move.
47. Think not that God
would go back on His promise (made) to the apostles.
Indeed God is mighty, the Lord of retribution.
48. The day when the earth

Ibrahim

221

will be replaced by some other than the earth,
as will be the skies,
and every one will appear
before God the one and omnipotent,
49. You will see the wicked on that day
bound together in chains.
50. Of molten pitch shall be their garments,
their faces covered with flames,
51. That God may reward each soul for its deeds.
Indeed God is swift at reckoning!
52. This is a message for mankind
that they may take a warning from it, and may know
that He is the one and only God,
and that men of wisdom may reflect.

Note on v. 24. *Kalimat,* literally 'word' stands in the Qur'an for 'act', *speaking* life into existence, explicit in *kalimat-Allah*. As soon as God speaks He transforms His word into act *Kun,* Be, and it came into *being,* showing that it was not created out of something else, other than God's command. Since one of the basic meanings of the word *kalam* is to 'wound' (Ibn Faris), *kalimat* implies action, and it is the word of God that creates, and thus, for act, action through command, though in 18:109 or 31:27, *kalimat* stands for acts and creations of God in general, inclusive of all divine words and wonders.

15 Al-Hijr

Al-Hijr: Makki

(۱۵) سُوْرَةُ الْحِجْرِ مَكِّيَّةٌ

اٰیاتها ۹۹ رُکُوْعُهَا

In the name of Allah, most benevolent, ever-merciful.

بِسْمِ اللهِ الرَّحْمٰنِ الرَّحِیْمِ

ALIF LĀM RĀ.
These are the verses of the Book
and the perspicuous oration.

الٰرٰ تِلْكَ اٰیٰتُ الْكِتٰبِ وَقُرْاٰنٍ مُّبِیْنٍ ۞

2. The unbelievers would haply like to wish
that they had submitted (and become Muslim).

رُبَمَا یَوَدُّ الَّذِیْنَ کَفَرُوْا لَوْ کَانُوْا مُسْلِمِیْنَ ۞

3. Leave them to feast and revel,
beguiled by hope; they will come to know soon.

ذَرْهُمْ یَاْکُلُوْا وَیَتَمَتَّعُوْا وَیُلْهِهِمُ الْاَمَلُ فَسَوْفَ یَعْلَمُوْنَ ۞

4. Not one habitation have We destroyed
but at the time determined for it.

وَمَا اَهْلَکْنَا مِنْ قَرْیَةٍ اِلَّا وَلَهَا کِتَابٌ مَّعْلُوْمٌ ۞

5. No people can hasten or delay
the term already fixed for them.

مَا تَسْبِقُ مِنْ اُمَّةٍ اَجَلَهَا وَمَا یَسْتَاْخِرُوْنَ ۞

6. And yet they say: "You,
to whom this Exposition has been sent
are surely possessed of the Devil.

وَقَالُوْا یٰاَیُّهَا الَّذِیْ نُزِّلَ عَلَیْهِ الذِّکْرُ اِنَّکَ لَمَجْنُوْنٌ ۞

7. If you are a man of truth,
why can't you bring the angels to us?"

لَوْ مَا تَاْتِیْنَا بِالْمَلٰٓئِکَةِ اِنْ کُنْتَ مِنَ الصّٰدِقِیْنَ ۞

8. But then We never send the angels down
save with the purpose (of enforcing their doom),
after which they will not be given more respite.

مَا نُنَزِّلُ الْمَلٰٓئِکَةَ اِلَّا بِالْحَقِّ وَمَا کَانُوْا اِذًا مُّنْظَرِیْنَ ۞

9. We have sent down this Exposition,
and We will guard it.

اِنَّا نَحْنُ نَزَّلْنَا الذِّکْرَ وَاِنَّا لَهٗ لَحٰفِظُوْنَ ۞

10. We had also sent apostles
to people of earlier persuasions.

وَلَقَدْ اَرْسَلْنَا مِنْ قَبْلِکَ فِیْ شِیَعِ الْاَوَّلِیْنَ ۞

11. But never once an apostle came to them
at whom they did not scoff.

وَمَا یَاْتِیْهِمْ مِّنْ رَّسُوْلٍ اِلَّا کَانُوْا بِهٖ یَسْتَهْزِءُوْنَ ۞

12. We place in the hearts of sinners (disbelief).

کَذٰلِکَ نَسْلُکُهٗ فِیْ قُلُوْبِ الْمُجْرِمِیْنَ ۞

13. So, they will not believe in it:
The example of former people is there.

لَا یُؤْمِنُوْنَ بِهٖ وَقَدْ خَلَتْ سُنَّةُ الْاَوَّلِیْنَ ۞

14. Even if We open a door in the heavens
and they ascend through it in broad daylight,

وَلَوْ فَتَحْنَا عَلَیْهِمْ بَابًا مِّنَ السَّمَآءِ فَظَلُّوْا فِیْهِ یَعْرُجُوْنَ ۞

15. They will say all the same:
"Our eyes were dazed (and clouded over).
We were a people ensorcelled."

لَقَالُوْٓا اِنَّمَا سُکِّرَتْ اَبْصَارُنَا بَلْ نَحْنُ قَوْمٌ مَّسْحُوْرُوْنَ ۞

We have placed the signs of the Zodiac in the sky,
and decked it out for those who can see;
17. And We have preserved it from every accursed devil,
18. Except the ones who listen on the sly, yet they
are chased away by a shooting flame.
19. We stretched the earth and placed upon it
firm stabilisers,
and made all things grow upon it balanced evenly.
20. We have provided on it sustenance for you,
and for those you cannot provide.
21. Of all things there are We have the stores,
and send them down in determined measure.
22. We send rain-impregnated winds,
and water from the sky which you drink,
but you are not the keepers of its store.
23. It is We who give life and We who give death,
and We are the One who will abide.
24. We surely know those of you who go forward
and those of you who lag behind.
25. Your Lord will surely gather them together:
Certainly He is all-wise and all-knowing.

Man We fashioned from fermented clay
dried tingling hard,
27. As We fashioned jinns before
from intense radiated heat.
28. But when your Lord said to the angels:
"I am verily going to create a human being
from fermented clay dried tingling hard;
29. And when I have fashioned him and breathed into him
of My spirit*, bow before him in homage;"
30. The angels bowed in homage in a body
31. Except Iblis. He refused to bow with the adorers.
32. "How is it, O Iblis," said (the Lord),
"you did not join those who bowed in homage?"
33. "How could I bow," said he, "before a mortal
whom You created from fermented clay dried tingling hard?"
34. "Go hence, execrable," (said the Lord), "from this place,
35. Condemned till the day of Doom!"
36. "O my Lord," said he, "give me respite
till the day the dead are raised."
37. "You are among the reprieved," (said the Lord),
38. "Till the pre-determined time."

---

* Spirit here stands for vital force which imparts to man a participating energy with nature.

39. "O my Lord," he said,
"since You have led me into error
I'll beguile them with the pleasures of the world
and lead them astray,
40. Except the chosen ones among Your creatures."
41. (To which God) said: "This way is right by Me.
42. No power shall you have over (all) My creatures
except those who fall into error and follow you,
43. For whom the ordained place is surely Hell,
44. Which has several gates, and each gate
is marked for every section of them."

Verily those who keep away from evil and follow the
      straight path
shall be in the midst of gardens and springs of water.
46. "Enter in peace and tranquility," (they will be told).
47. We shall cast out any grudge
they may have in their hearts.
(There) they will sit on couches face to face
like brothers together.
48. No weariness will come upon them,
nor will they be sent away from there.
49. Announce to My creatures that I
am indeed forgiving and kind,
50. But My punishment is surely a painful one.
51. Inform them about the matter of Abraham's guests.
52. When they came to him and said:
"Peace," he answered: "Truly we are afraid of you,"
53. "Have no fear," they said.
"We bring you news of a son full of wisdom."
54. "You bring me the good news now," he said,
"when old age has come upon me.
What good news are you giving me then?"
55. "We have given you the happy tidings of a truth," they
      replied.
"So do not be one of those who despair."
56. "Who would despair of the mercy of his Lord," he answered,
but those who go astray."
57. And asked them: "What matter, O angels, brings you here?"
58. "We have been sent," they said,
"to (punish) a sinful people,
59. Except the family of Lot whom we shall save
60. Other than his wife who, it is decreed,
will remain with those who will stay behind."

When the messengers came to the family of Lot,

62. He said: "You are people I do not know."

63. "We have come to you with news," they said,
"of what your people doubt;

64. Yet we bring to you the truth,
and we are truthful.

65. So leave with your family late in the night,
yourself remaining in the rear,
and let none turn back to look, and go
where you will be commanded."

66. We issued this command to him, for they
were going to be destroyed in the morning.

67. Then came the people of the city, exulting
at the news.

68. Said Lot: "These are my guests;
do not put me to shame,

69. And do not disgrace me.
Have some fear of God."

70. "Did we not restrain you," they said,
"from (entertaining) creatures from the outside world?"

71. "Here are my daughters," said Lot,
"if you are so active."

72. Verily by your life
they were utterly confused
in their (lustful) drunkenness.

73. So they were seized by the mighty blast
at break of day;

74. And We turned the city upside down,
and rained on them stones of hardened lava.

75. Herein are really signs for those who discern.

76. This (city) lies on a road that still survives.

77. Indeed there is a portent in this for those who believe.

78. The dwellers of the Wood (near Midian) were also wicked.

79. So We punished them too.
They are both situated by the highway, clearly visible.

The people of Al-Hijr denied Our apostles;

81. And though We had given them Our signs
they turned away from them.

82. They used to hew dwellings in the mountains
to live in security.

83. But they were seized by the mighty blast
towards the morning;

84. And all that they had done (for security)
availed them nothing.

85. We have not created but with reason
the heavens and the earth

and all that lies within them.
The Hour (of the great change) is certain to come.
So turn away (from them) with a grace.
86. Surely your Lord is the Creator and knows (every thing).
87. We have indeed given you the seven oft-repeated
    (examples)*,
and the majestic Qur'an.
88. So covet not things We have bestowed on a portion of them
    to enjoy,
and do not grieve for them,
and protect those who believe;
89. And say: "I am a distinct warner,"
90. Like (those) We had sent
to those schismatics who slandered their Books
91. And severed their Scripture into fragments.
92. By your Lord We shall question them one and all
93. About their deeds.
94. So declare to them what We have enjoined,
and turn away from idolaters.
95. We are surely sufficient to deal
with those who scoff at you,
96. Who place other gods besides God.
They will come to know soon.
97. We are well aware that you are disheartened by what they
    say.
98. But you should glorify your Lord with praises,
and be among those who bow in submission;
99. And go on worshipping your Lord
till the certainty
(of death) comes upon you.

---

* The (seven) examples from history of the people of Noah, 'Ad, Thamud, Abraham, Lot, Midian and Pharaoh, which are repeated four times all together in the Qur'an and many times in twos, threes and fours or singly. Saba'a means to make a number up to seven, and mathani means 'oft-repeated.' See Surah 20 (The Poets) and 29 (The Spider) which deal with all the seven. The verse states that God has given us the Qur'an which contains the basic laws that govern the cause of the rise and fall of nations as well as historical proofs that appear from time to time.

16 The Bees

An-Nahl: Makki

In the name of Allah, most benevolent, ever-merciful.

بِسْمِ اللهِ الرَّحْمٰنِ الرَّحِيْمِ ۞

THE DECREE of God will surely come;
so do not try to hasten it:
Too glorious and high is He
for what they associate with Him.
2. He sends the angels with revelation
by His command,
to any of His creatures as He please,
(saying): "Warn
that there is no god but I,
so fear Me."
3. He created the heavens and the earth
with reason.
Too glorious and high is He
for what they associate with Him.
4. Man He created from a drop of semen;
and still he becomes an open contender.
5. He created the cattle from whom you get
warm clothing and (other) advantages,
and some you eat.
6. There is life and cheer for you as you drive them home
in the evening, and lead them out
in the morning to graze.
7. They carry your burdens to lands so distant
you could not have reached
without much hardship.
Indeed your Lord is compassionate and kind.
8. He created horses, mules and donkeys
for riding and for splendour.
He created other things too which you do not know.
9. To God leads the right path,
though some deviate.
If He willed He could guide
you all to the right way.

أَتٰى أَمْرُ اللهِ فَلَا تَسْتَعْجِلُوهُ سُبْحٰنَهُ وَتَعٰلٰى عَمَّا يُشْرِكُوْنَ ۞

يُنَزِّلُ الْمَلٰئِكَةَ بِالرُّوْحِ مِنْ أَمْرِهٖ عَلٰى مَنْ يَّشَاءُ مِنْ عِبَادِهٖ اَنْ اَنْذِرُوْۤا اَنَّهٗ لَاۤ اِلٰهَ اِلَّاۤ اَنَا فَاتَّقُوْنِ ۞

خَلَقَ السَّمٰوٰتِ وَالْاَرْضَ بِالْحَقِّ تَعٰلٰى عَمَّا يُشْرِكُوْنَ ۞

خَلَقَ الْاِنْسَانَ مِنْ نُّطْفَةٍ فَاِذَا هُوَ خَصِيْمٌ مُّبِيْنٌ ۞

وَالْاَنْعَامَ خَلَقَهَا لَكُمْ فِيْهَا دِفْءٌ وَّمَنَافِعُ وَمِنْهَا تَاْكُلُوْنَ ۞

وَلَكُمْ فِيْهَا جَمَالٌ حِيْنَ تُرِيْحُوْنَ وَحِيْنَ تَسْرَحُوْنَ ۞

وَتَحْمِلُ اَثْقَالَكُمْ اِلٰى بَلَدٍ لَّمْ تَكُوْنُوْا بٰلِغِيْهِ اِلَّا بِشِقِّ الْاَنْفُسِ اِنَّ رَبَّكُمْ لَرَءُوْفٌ رَّحِيْمٌ ۞

وَّالْخَيْلَ وَالْبِغَالَ وَالْحَمِيْرَ لِتَرْكَبُوْهَا وَزِيْنَةً وَّ يَخْلُقُ مَا لَا تَعْلَمُوْنَ ۞

وَعَلَى اللهِ قَصْدُ السَّبِيْلِ وَمِنْهَا جَآئِرٌ وَلَوْ شَآءَ لَهَدٰىكُمْ اَجْمَعِيْنَ ۞

It is He who sends down water from the sky
of which you drink, and which
nourishes the plants you feed your cattle,
11. With which He makes crops grow,
and olives, dates and grapes
and fruits of every kind for you.
In this is a sign for those who think.
12. He harnessed the day and night for you,
as also the sun, the moon and the stars,
by His command.
In this are signs for men who understand.
13. And other things of different shades has He
produced on the earth for you.
In this are signs for those who reflect.
14. It is He who has subdued the sea that you
may eat fresh meat from it,
and obtain ornaments to wear.
You see the ships plough through it
that you may seek of His bounties and, perhaps,
be grateful.
15. He placed stablisers in the earth *
so that while it revolves you live undisturbed,
and rivers and tracks
so that you may find your way;
16. As well as many other signs,
as by the stars (you) find direction.
17. So, could one who creates
be like one who cannot?
Will you not then contemplate?
18. If you count the favours of God
you will not be able to calculate .
Assuredly God is forgiving and kind.
19. God knows what you hide and disclose.
20. As for those they call besides God,
they cannot create a thing,
and have themselves been created.
21. Dead, without life they are,
and do not know when they will be raised.

Your God is one God.
But the hearts of those who believe not in the life to come
are filled with denial, and they are puffed up with pride.
23. Surely God knows
what they hide and what they disclose.

----

* See note on page 239.

An-Nahl

He certainly does not love the proud.

24. For when they are asked:
"What has your Lord sent down?" they say:
"Tales of long ago."
25. On the Day of Resurrection they will carry
their own burden and some of the load
of those they have led astray without any knowledge.
Oh, how evil a burden they will carry!

Those who have gone before them had also conspired;
then God uprooted their structure from its foundation;
the roof fell over them from above,
and punishment came upon them
from somewhere they did not suspect.
27. On the Day of Resurrection
He will disgrace them and ask:
"Where are My compeers for whom you contended?"
Those endowed with knowledge will say:
"Shame and evil surely are for unbelievers today."
28. They whose souls are drawn out by the angels
while they are sinning,
shall offer submission:
"We did no evil."
But God knows well what you did.
29. So enter the gates of Hell,
and dwell there for ever.
How dreadful a dwelling for the haughty!
30. When those who took heed for themselves would be asked:
"What did your Lord send down?"
They will answer: "The best."
For those who do good
there is good in the world,
but certainly the abode of the next is better.
How excellent the home of the virtuous!
31. They will enter perennial gardens
with streams of water and all they wish.
Thus will the pious and devout
be rewarded.
32. When the angels receive the souls
of those who are blameless they will say:
"Peace on you. Enter Paradise
as recompense for what you did."
33. What! Do the (unbelievers) expect
that the angels should descend,
or the sentence of your Lord come to pass?
So had the people done before them;

yet God did not wrong them,
they wronged themselves.
34. The evil they perpetrated overtook them,
and what they mocked has turned upon them.

The idolaters say: "If God had willed
we would not have worshipped anything apart from Him,
nor would our fathers have done,
nor would we have forbidden any thing without His (leave)."
So had the people done before them.
Therefore it is binding on the prophets
to convey the message in clearest terms.
36. To every community We have sent an apostle
(saying:) "Worship God, and keep away
from all other deities."
Thus some of them were guided by God,
and ruin was justified on some.
Travel over the earth and see
what befell those who accused (the apostles) of lies.
37. Even if you are eager to guide them,
God does not surely guide
those who have gone astray:
They will have no one to help them.
38. They swear emphatically in the name of God
that God will not raise the dead.
On the contrary,
it is a promise incumbent on Him,
though most men do not understand,
39. For (they fear) He might make what they differed about
plain to them,
and that the infidels may realise
that they were liars.
40. Yet when We will a thing We have only to say:
"Be", and it is.

Those who left their homes in the cause of God
after having been oppressed, will be given by Us
a better place in the world,
and if they knew, the guerdon of the next
would be greater
42. (For) those who persevere
and place their trust in their Lord.
43. We sent before you none (as apostles) but men,
to whom We sent revelations.
In case you are unaware, enquire
of those who are keepers of the Oracles of God.

44. We had sent them with miracles and Books;
and We have sent to you this Reminder
so that you may explain distinctly to men
what was sent down to them:
They may haply reflect.

بِالْبَيِّنَاتِ وَالزُّبُرِ وَأَنْزَلْنَا إِلَيْكَ الذِّكْرَ لِتُبَيِّنَ
لِلنَّاسِ مَا نُزِّلَ إِلَيْهِمْ وَلَعَلَّهُمْ يَتَفَكَّرُونَ ۞

45. Have the plotters of mischief become unafraid
that God will not split the earth to swallow them,
or that punishment will not fall upon them
from somewhere they do not (even) suspect?

أَفَأَمِنَ الَّذِينَ مَكَرُوا السَّيِّئَاتِ أَنْ يَخْسِفَ اللَّهُ بِهِمُ
الْأَرْضَ أَوْ يَأْتِيَهُمُ الْعَذَابُ مِنْ حَيْثُ لَا يَشْعُرُونَ ۞

46. Or that He will not seize them as they move about,
and they will not be able to elude (His grasp);
47. Or He may seize them by diminishing their portion.
Yet your Lord is compassionate and kind.

أَوْ يَأْخُذَهُمْ فِي تَقَلُّبِهِمْ فَمَا هُمْ بِمُعْجِزِينَ ۞
أَوْ يَأْخُذَهُمْ عَلَى تَخَوُّفٍ فَإِنَّ رَبَّكُمْ لَرَؤُوفٌ رَّحِيمٌ ۞

48. Do they not see the shadows of all things God has created
incline to the right and the left,
bowing in obeisance to God?

أَوَلَمْ يَرَوْا إِلَى مَا خَلَقَ اللَّهُ مِنْ شَيْءٍ يَتَفَيَّؤُا ظِلَالُهُ
عَنِ الْيَمِينِ وَالشَّمَائِلِ سُجَّدًا لِلَّهِ وَهُمْ دَاخِرُونَ ۞

49. All things that move on the earth and in the heavens,
and the angels, bow in homage to God,
and do not behave with pride.

وَلِلَّهِ يَسْجُدُ مَا فِي السَّمَاوَاتِ وَمَا فِي الْأَرْضِ مِنْ
دَابَّةٍ وَالْمَلَائِكَةُ وَهُمْ لَا يَسْتَكْبِرُونَ ۞

50. They have fear of God for His power over them, *
and act as commanded.

يَخَافُونَ رَبَّهُمْ مِنْ فَوْقِهِمْ وَيَفْعَلُونَ مَا يُؤْمَرُونَ ۞

God says: "Do not take to two gods,
for there is only one God. So fear Me."

وَقَالَ اللَّهُ لَا تَتَّخِذُوا إِلَهَيْنِ اثْنَيْنِ إِنَّمَا هُوَ إِلَهٌ
وَاحِدٌ فَإِيَّايَ فَارْهَبُونِ ۞

52. Whatsoever is in the heavens and the earth
belongs to Him, and His the judgement for ever.
So will you fear any other than God?

وَلَهُ مَا فِي السَّمَاوَاتِ وَالْأَرْضِ وَلَهُ الدِّينُ وَاصِبًا
أَفَغَيْرَ اللَّهِ تَتَّقُونَ ۞

53. Whatsoever the blessings you enjoy
are surely from God,
and when in trouble you turn to Him in supplication.

وَمَا بِكُمْ مِنْ نِعْمَةٍ فَمِنَ اللَّهِ ثُمَّ إِذَا مَسَّكُمُ
الضُّرُّ فَإِلَيْهِ تَجْأَرُونَ ۞

54. Yet when He has delivered you from affliction,
some of you ascribe
companions to your Lord

ثُمَّ إِذَا كَشَفَ الضُّرَّ عَنْكُمْ إِذَا فَرِيقٌ مِنْكُمْ
بِرَبِّهِمْ يُشْرِكُونَ ۞

55. So as to deny what We have bestowed on them.
Well, enjoy yourselves, you will come to know soon.

لِيَكْفُرُوا بِمَا آتَيْنَاهُمْ فَتَمَتَّعُوا فَسَوْفَ تَعْلَمُونَ ۞

56. They set aside a portion of the food We have given them
for those they do not know.
By God, you will surely have to answer for all you contrive!

وَيَجْعَلُونَ لِمَا لَا يَعْلَمُونَ نَصِيبًا مِمَّا رَزَقْنَاهُمْ
تَاللَّهِ لَتُسْأَلُنَّ عَمَّا كُنْتُمْ تَفْتَرُونَ ۞

57. They attribute daughters to God, the glorious,
but for themselves whatsoever they please.

وَيَجْعَلُونَ لِلَّهِ الْبَنَاتِ سُبْحَانَهُ وَلَهُمْ مَا يَشْتَهُونَ ۞

58. Yet when news of the birth of a daughter
reaches one of them, his face is darkened,
and he is overwhelmed with silent grief,

وَإِذَا بُشِّرَ أَحَدُهُمْ بِالْأُنْثَى ظَلَّ وَجْهُهُ مُسْوَدًّا
وَهُوَ كَظِيمٌ ۞

59. And hides from people for shame at the news,
(at a loss) whether he should keep her with shame,

يَتَوَارَى مِنَ الْقَوْمِ مِنْ سُوءِ مَا بُشِّرَ بِهِ أَيُمْسِكُهُ
عَلَى هُونٍ أَمْ يَدُسُّهُ فِي التُّرَابِ أَلَا سَاءَ مَا

---
* See note 2, on p. 239.

يَحْكُمُونَ ۞

or bury her in the ground.
How bad is the judgement that they make!
60. The semblance of those
who believe not in the life to come
is that of the meanest;
but the semblance of God is the most sublime,
for He is all-mighty and all-wise.

If God were to punish men
for their inequity
He would not leave a single moving thing on earth.
Yet He gives them latitutde for a time ordained.
When that time is come,
there will not be a moment's delay
nor a moment's haste.
62. Yet they attribute to God what they find detestable;
and their tongues assert the lie
that for them is only good.
On the contrary,
there is Fire for them,
and they will be thrown into it.
63. By God, We sent apostles to many a people before you,
but Satan made their acts seem attractive to them,
and he is their friend this day,
and a painful torment awaits them.
64. We have sent down this Book to you
that you may explain to them
what it is that they are differing about,
and as guidance and a grace for those who believe.
65. God sends down water from the skies and quickens
the dead earth to a new birth.
Here is a sign for those who listen.

And surely in cattle there is a lesson for you:
We give you a drink from the extract of food
in their bellies and blood—
purest milk so delicious to drink;
67. And in fruits of the date-palm and the vine,
from which you obtain inebriating drinks and excellent food.
In this indeed are signs for those who understand.
68. Your Lord predisposed the bees
to make their hives in mountains, trees and trellices,
69. And suck from all fruits and flit
about the unrestricted paths of their Lord.
A drink of various hues comes out of their bellies
which contains medicine for men.

In this is a sign for those who reflect.
70. It is God who creates you, then makes you die;
and some reach the age of dotage
when they forget
what they had known before.
God is indeed all-knowing and all-powerful.

God has favoured some of you over others
in the means of subsistence. But those
who have been favoured with more do not give
of their means to their dependents
so that they may become equal with them.
Do they then deny God's beneficence?
72. God has provided mates for you
of your own kind,
and has bestowed on you
sons and daughters from your mates,
and has given you good things for food.
Will they even then believe in the false
and deny God's grace?
73. Yet they worship those apart from God
who cannot provide for them any sustenance
from the heavens or the earth,
nor will they have power to do so.
74. So do not invent similitudes for God.
Indeed God knows, and you do not know.
75. God presents the example of a man
who is a hired servant with no power over anything,
and another on whom We have bestowed a handsome fortune,
who spends from it in private and in public:
Can they be equal?
Praised be God! But most men do not understand.
76. God presents another example of two men,
one dumb and unable to do a thing
and is a burden on his master.
Wherever he is sent he returns
without any good (result).
Could he be equal to one who enjoins what is just,
and follows the right path?

To God belong the secrets of the heavens and the earth,
and the Hour of Doom is a matter of the winking of an eye,
even less,
for God has certainly power over all things.
78. God produced you from your mothers' wombs
knowing nothing.

An-Nahl

but gave you ears and eyes and hearts
so that you may be grateful.
79. Do you not see the birds held high
between the heavens and the earth?
Nothing holds them (aloft) but God.
There are verily signs in this for those who believe.
80. God has given you homes to live in,
and tents (made) from the hides of cattle
convenient for days of travelling and halting;
and from their wool and fur and hair
you make domestic articles and goods
that last a certain time.
81. God has given you of things created, shade,
and places of shelter in the mountains,
and clothes for protection against the heat,
and coats (of mail) for defence during war.
He thus bestows His favours on you
so that you may be grateful to Him.
82. If they still turn away, your duty is
to warn them in clear terms.
83. They do know the favours of God, and yet
they deny them,
for most of them are not grateful.

The day We shall call a witness from every people,
the unbelievers will not be allowed
to make excuses.
85. And when the wicked shall face the torment
it will not be decreased,
nor will they be reprieved.
86. When the idolaters see their partners
they will call out: "O our Lord,
these are the partners we invoked
instead of You;"
but they will retort: "You are liars."
87. They will offer submission to God that Day,
and the lies they fabricated
will not be of the least avail.
88. For those who deny the truth and obstruct
(others) from the way of God,
We shall add torment to torment
as they were perpetrating corruption.
89. Remind them of the Day when We shall call
from every people a witness against them,
and make you a witness over them,
for We have revealed to you the Book

An-Nahl

as an exposition of every thing,
and as guidance and grace and happy tidings
for those who submit.

عَلَيْكَ الْكِتَابَ تِبْيَانًا لِكُلِّ شَيْءٍ وَهُدًى وَرَحْمَةً وَبُشْرَى لِلْمُسْلِمِينَ ۞

Verily God has enjoined justice,
the doing of good, and the giving of gifts
to your relatives; and forbidden
indecency, impropriety and oppression.
He warns you so that you may remember.

إِنَّ اللَّهَ يَأْمُرُ بِالْعَدْلِ وَالْإِحْسَانِ وَإِيتَاءِ ذِي الْقُرْبَى وَيَنْهَى عَنِ الْفَحْشَاءِ وَالْمُنْكَرِ وَالْبَغْيِ يَعِظُكُمْ لَعَلَّكُمْ تَذَكَّرُونَ ۞

91. Fulfil your covenant with God, having made the covenant,
and do not break your oaths once you have sworn them,
as you have made God a witness over you.
Indeed God knows what you do.

وَأَوْفُوا بِعَهْدِ اللَّهِ إِذَا عَاهَدْتُمْ وَلَا تَنْقُضُوا الْأَيْمَانَ بَعْدَ تَوْكِيدِهَا وَقَدْ جَعَلْتُمُ اللَّهَ عَلَيْكُمْ كَفِيلًا إِنَّ اللَّهَ يَعْلَمُ مَا تَفْعَلُونَ ۞

92. And do not be like her who untwists her yarn
having spun it into durable thread.
Do not use your oaths deceitfully
because one party has ascendency over you.
God surely tries you in this way:
He will make it clear to you on the Day of Resurrection
what you were differing about.

وَلَا تَكُونُوا كَالَّتِي نَقَضَتْ غَزْلَهَا مِنْ بَعْدِ قُوَّةٍ أَنْكَاثًا تَتَّخِذُونَ أَيْمَانَكُمْ دَخَلًا بَيْنَكُمْ أَنْ تَكُونَ أُمَّةٌ هِيَ أَرْبَى مِنْ أُمَّةٍ إِنَّمَا يَبْلُوكُمُ اللَّهُ بِهِ وَلَيُبَيِّنَنَّ لَكُمْ يَوْمَ الْقِيَامَةِ مَا كُنْتُمْ فِيهِ تَخْتَلِفُونَ ۞

93. If God had pleased He would surely have made
you a single community of belief;
but He leads whosoever He wills astray,
and guides whosoever He please.
But you will surely be questioned
about what you used to do.

وَلَوْ شَاءَ اللَّهُ لَجَعَلَكُمْ أُمَّةً وَاحِدَةً وَلَكِنْ يُضِلُّ مَنْ يَشَاءُ وَيَهْدِي مَنْ يَشَاءُ وَلَتُسْأَلُنَّ عَمَّا كُنْتُمْ تَعْمَلُونَ ۞

94. So do not make your oaths a means
of deceiving one another, lest your foot
should slip after having found its hold,
and you taste of evil for having hindered (others)
from the way of God,
and suffer a grievous punishment.

وَلَا تَتَّخِذُوا أَيْمَانَكُمْ دَخَلًا بَيْنَكُمْ فَتَزِلَّ قَدَمٌ بَعْدَ ثُبُوتِهَا وَتَذُوقُوا السُّوءَ بِمَا صَدَدْتُمْ عَنْ سَبِيلِ اللَّهِ وَلَكُمْ عَذَابٌ عَظِيمٌ ۞

95. And do not trade God's covenant
for a paltry price. Remember,
what is with God is better for you,
if only you knew!

وَلَا تَشْتَرُوا بِعَهْدِ اللَّهِ ثَمَنًا قَلِيلًا إِنَّمَا عِنْدَ اللَّهِ هُوَ خَيْرٌ لَكُمْ إِنْ كُنْتُمْ تَعْلَمُونَ ۞

96. For what you possess will pass,
but what is with God will abide.
We shall certainly award those who persevere
a recompense in keeping with their deeds.

مَا عِنْدَكُمْ يَنْفَدُ وَمَا عِنْدَ اللَّهِ بَاقٍ وَلَنَجْزِيَنَّ الَّذِينَ صَبَرُوا أَجْرَهُمْ بِأَحْسَنِ مَا كَانُوا يَعْمَلُونَ ۞

97. We shall invest whosoever works for good,
whether man or woman,
with a pleasant life,
and reward them in accordance with the best
of what they have done.

مَنْ عَمِلَ صَالِحًا مِنْ ذَكَرٍ أَوْ أُنْثَى وَهُوَ مُؤْمِنٌ فَلَنُحْيِيَنَّهُ حَيَاةً طَيِّبَةً وَلَنَجْزِيَنَّهُمْ أَجْرَهُمْ بِأَحْسَنِ مَا كَانُوا يَعْمَلُونَ ۞

98. So, when you recite the Qur'an seek refuge in God

فَإِذَا قَرَأْتَ الْقُرْآنَ فَاسْتَعِذْ بِاللَّهِ مِنَ الشَّيْطَانِ

from Satan the execrable.
99. He does not have power over those
who believe and place their trust in their Lord.
100. His power is only over those
who take him as their patron, and those
who ascribe equals (to God).

When We replace a message with another —
and God knows best what He reveals —
they say: "You have made it up;" yet
most of them do not know.
102. You say: "It has been sent by divine grace
from your Lord with truth
to strengthen those who believe,
and as guidance and good news for those
who have submitted (to God)."
103. Yet We know what they say:
"It is only a man who instructs him."
The speech of the man they imply is obscure
while this is clear Arabic.
104. Those who do not believe in the words of God
are verily not guided by God.
For them is severe punishment.
105. They alone invent lies who do not believe
in the words of God,
and they are liars.
106. Whosoever denies having once believed —
unless he is forced to do so while his heart
enjoys the peace of faith —
and opens his mind to disbelief
will suffer the wrath of God.
Their punishment will be great,
107. For they loved the life of this world
more than the life to come;
and God does not guide those who do not believe.
108. They are the ones whose hearts and ears and eyes
have been sealed by God;
and these are the heedless.
109. They will surely be losers in the life to come,
110. But (to) those who were victimised and left their homes
and then fought and endured patiently, your Lord
will surely be forgiving and kind.

On the day when every soul will come
pleading for itself,
and every soul will be recompensed

for what it had done,
no one will be wronged.

112. God presents the example of a town
which enjoyed peace and security,
its provisions coming from everywhere in abundance,
but it denied the favours of God; so God
acquainted it with intimate hunger and fear
(as punishment) for what they had done.

113. An apostle came to them who was one of them,
but they called him a liar.
Then they were seized by torment
for they were sinners.

114. Eat the good and lawful of things that God has given you,
and be grateful for the bounty of God,
if you really worship Him.

115. He has forbidden carrion and blood
and the flesh of the swine,
and what has been killed
in the name of any other but God;
but if one is driven by necessity (to eat it) without craving
or reverting to it, then God is forgiving and kind.

116. Do not utter the lies your tongues make up:
"This is lawful, and this is forbidden,"
in order to impute lies to God;
for they who impute lies to God
will not find fulfilment.

117. For them there is some enjoyment,
but the punishment is painful.

118. We have already told you
what We have forbidden the Jews.
We did not wrong them,
they wronged themselves.

119. To those who do wrong out of ignorance,
then repent and correct themselves,
your Lord is indeed forgiving and kind.

Abraham was certainly a model of faith,
obedient to God and upright, and not one of idolaters,

121. Grateful to Him for His favours;
so He chose him and guided him to the path that is straight,

122. And gave him what is good in the world,
and in the Hereafter
he will be among the righteous and the good.

123. So We commanded you to follow
the way of Abraham the upright
who was not of idolaters.

124. As for the Sabbath, it was imposed on those
who had differed about it;
and your Lord will tell them on the Day of Resurrection
what it was they had differed about.
125. Call them to the path of your Lord
with wisdom and words of good advice;
and reason with them in the best way possible.
Your Lord surely knows who strays from His path,
and He knows those
who are guided the right way.
126. If you have to retaliate,
do so to the extent
you have been injured;
but if you forbear it is best for those
who bear with fortitude.
127. Endure with patience, for your endurance
is not without the help of God.
Do not grieve for them, and do not be distressed
by their plots.
128. God is verily with those
who are pious and devout,
and those who are doers of good.

---

* Note on v. 15. Stabilisers, *rawasi*, are actually mountains in the interior of the earth made evident by modern geophysicists who mapped the earth's interior. At some places they are 6 miles high and 6000 miles wide with a valley as deep and wide, situated between the liquid core and the crust of the earth. Their function is to stablise the crust and rotation of the earth. (Readers's Digest, May 1987). This description would apply to underground 'stabilisers' when used with 'so that while it revolves you live undisturbed, as here and in 21:31, 3:10, and also 77:27. In 13:3, 15:19, 27:61, 50:7 on the other hand, it has been used for mountains as stabilisers.

The four spans of earth's evolution mentioned in this connection at 41:10 are equivalent to the mineral, the vegetable and animal kingdoms, the fourth starting with the placing of man on earth which comes last as is clear from 76:1, who did not evolve from the ape but was created as an independent species like the apes themselves and all other creatures.

2. Note on v. 50. *Min Fauqihim. Fauq* means above, but when used with *min,* it means, superiority, *min fauqihim,* 'being above' them in superiority, i.e. power.

17 The Children of Israel

Bani Isrā'il: Makki

بِسُبْطِنُ الَّذِى ١٥

(١٧) سُوَرَةُ الْاِسْرَامَكِيَّة

اٰيَاتُهَا ١١١ رُكُوعُهَا

In the name of Allah, most benevolent, ever-merciful.

بِسْمِ اللهِ الرَّحْمٰنِ الرَّحِيْمِ ۟

GLORY TO HIM who took His votary
to a wide and open land* from the Sacred Mosque (at Makkah)
to the distant Mosque whose precincts We have blessed,
that We may show him some of Our signs.
Verily He is all-hearing and all-seeing.
2. We gave Moses the Book,
and made it a guidance for the children of Israel
that they should not take another protector apart from Me.
3. O you, the offspring of those We bore (in the ark)
with Noah, he was indeed a grateful votary.
4. We announced to the children of Israel in the Book:
"You will surely create disorder twice in the land,
and become exceedingly arrogant."
5. So, when the time of the first prediction came,
We sent against you Our creatures full of martial might,
who ransacked your cities;
and the prediction was fulfilled.
6. Then We gave you a chance against them,
and strengthened you with wealth and children,
and increased your numbers (and said):
7. "If you do good, you will do so for your own good;
if you do ill, you will do it for your own loss."
So, when the time of the second prediction comes,
(We shall rouse another people) to shame you,
and enter the Temple as they had done the first time,
and to destroy what they conquered utterly.
8. Your Lord may haply be merciful to you.
But if you repeat it, We shall do the same.
We have constituted Hell as prison for unbelievers.
9. Verily this Qur'an directs you to the path
that is straight, and gives happy tidings to those

----

* See Raghib and *Muhit* for meaning of *isra* generally translated as 'journey by night;' and note 2 on p. 249 for 'Our signs.'

who believe and do the right:
For them is a great reward.
10. As for those who do not believe in the Hereafter,
We have prepared a painful punishment.

Man prays for evil as he prays for good,
for man is hasty.
12. We have created night and day as two signs,
then We efface the sign of the night,
and make the sign of the day resplendent
that you may seek
the bounty of your Lord,
and know the computation of years and numbers.
We have expounded most distinctly every thing.
13. Round each man's neck We have hung his ledger of deeds,
and on the Day of Resurrection will present it
as a book spread out (and say):
14. "Read your ledger; this day
you are sufficient to take your own account.
15. He who finds the right path
does so for himself;
and he who goes astray
does so to his own loss;
and no one who carries a burden
bears another's load.
We never punish till We have sent a messenger.
16. And when We destroy a human habitation
We send Our command to (warn) its people
living a life of ease;
and when they disobey,
the sentence against them is justified,
and We destroy them utterly.
17. How many generations have We laid low
after Noah, for your Lord
knows and notices well enough
the sins of His creatures.
18. Whosoever desires what hastes away,
We hasten to give him (in this life)
as much as We please to whosoever We will; but afterwards
there is Hell for him in which he will burn,
disgraced and ostracised.
19. But he who desires the Hereafter,
and strives for it with a will, and is a believer,
will be favoured for his endeavour.
20. We bestow from the gifts of your Lord
on these and on those,

Bani Isra'il

241

for the gifts of your Lord are not restricted.
21. See, how We favour one over the other;
and in life to come are higher ranks
and favours greater still.
22. Do not set up another god with God,
or you will remain disgraced and destitute.

So your Lord has decreed: Do not worship
anyone but Him, and be good to your parents.
If one or both of them grow old in your presence,
do not say fie to them, nor reprove them,
but say gentle words to them
24. And look after them with kindness and love,
and say: "O Lord, have mercy on them
as they nourished me when I was small."
25. Your Lord knows what is in your heart.
If you are righteous, then He is indeed
forgiving to those who turn (to Him) in repentance.
26. So give to your relatives what is their due,
and to those who are needy, and the wayfarers;
and do not dissipate (your wealth)
extravagantly.
27. Those who dissipate (their wealth)
are the brethren of the devils,
and the Devil was ungrateful to his Lord.
28. If you neglect (your parents) while seeking
the bounty of your Lord, of which you are hopeful,
speak to them softly.
29. Do not be niggardly, nor so extravagant
that you may later feel reprehensive and constrained.
30. Certainly your Lord provides with open hands
whosoever He will, but according to capacity,
for He knows and watches His creatures.

Do not abandon your children out of fear of poverty.
We will provide for them and for you.
Killing them is certainly a great wrong.
32. And do not go near fornication,
as it is immoral and an evil way.
33. And do not take a life, which God has forbidden,
except in a just cause.
We have given the right (of redress)
to the heir of the person who is killed,
but he should not exceed the limits (of justice)
by slaying (the killer),
for he will be judged (by the same law).

Bani Isra'il

34. And do not touch the property of the orphans
except for bettering it,
until they come of age;
and fulfil the promise made:
You will surely be questioned about the promise.
35. Give full measure when you are measuring,
and weigh on a balanced scale.
This is better, and excellent its consequence.
36. Do not follow that of which you have no knowledge.
Verily the ear, the eye, the heart,
each will be questioned.
37. And do not strut about the land with insolence:
Surely you cannot cleave the earth,
nor attain the height of mountains in stature.
38. All these are evil and odious to your Lord.
39. This is some of the wisdom your Lord has revealed to you.
So do not take another god apart from God,
or you will be cast into Hell, reproved, ostracised.
40. Has God chosen to give you sons, and taken for Himself
daughters from among the angels?
You utter grievous things indeed!

We have explained (the truth) in various ways
in this Qur'an, that they may be warned;
but it only increased their refractoriness.
42. Say: "Had there been other gods with Him,
as they assert, they would surely have sought a way
(of opposition) against the Lord of the Throne."
43. Too glorious and high is He,
too exalted for what they say!
44. The seven skies, the earth, and all that lies within them,
sing hallelujas to Him.
There is nothing that does not chant His praises,
but you do not understand their hymns of praise.
He is verily clement and forgiving.
45. When you recite the Qur'an, We place
a hidden veil between you and those
who do not believe in the Hereafter;
46. And We put covers over their hearts
and deafness in their ears
that they should not understand it.
So when you invoke your Lord alone in the Qur'an
they turn their backs and walk away.
47. We know well with what (intent) they hear you,
for when they confer privately
the wicked say: "You follow but a man deluded."

48. See, what comparisons they coin for you,
and go astray,
and thus cannot find the way.
49. Yet they say: "When we are turned to bones and bits,
shall we be raised as a new creation?"
50. Tell them: "(Even if) you turn to stones or steel,
51. Or some other created thing which may seem to you
most difficult (to create)!"
They will then say: "Who will revert us back?"
Say: "He who originated you in the first place."
They will shake their heads at you and say:
"When will that be?"
Say: "In the near future, perhaps,
52. On the day when He will call you, and you will answer
with His praises and imagine
you did not tarry but a while."

Tell My creatures only to speak words that are good.
Verily Satan sows dissensions:
Satan is indeed the acknowledged enemy of mankind.
54. Your Lord knows you better:
He may have mercy on you if He please,
or punish you if He will.
Yet We have not sent you as warden over them.
55. Your Lord knows whoever is in the heavens and the earth.
We exalted some of the prophets over the others;
and to David We gave the Book of Psalms.
56. Say: "Call those whom you imagine to be gods
besides Him; yet they have no power
to relieve you of any distress or to avert it."
57. Those they invoke themselves seek the way
to their Lord, (striving) which one of them
shall be nearest (to Him);
and hope for His grace, and dread His punishment.
Indeed, the punishment of your Lord is to be feared!
58. There is not a habitation We shall not destroy
before the Day of Resurrection,
or not inflict severe punishment upon it.
This is in accordance with the law (of God).
59. Nothing could stop Us from sending signs
except that the earlier people
had rejected them as lies.
We sent to Thamud the she-camel as a token
to make it clear to them,
but they treated her cruelly;
and We send signs only to deter.

60. When We said to you: "Verily your Lord
circumscribes mankind," and showed you the vision
and the accursed tree of the Qur'an,
it was as a bone of contention for men.
Thus do We (instil) fear in them;
but they only transgress the more.

When We asked the angels to bow before Adam,
they all bowed but Iblis, who said:
"Can I bow before him whom You created from clay?"
62. (And) said: "Look! This is what you have honoured above
    me!
If You defer (my term) till the Day of Resurrection,
I will bring his progeny into complete subjugation,
barring a few."
63. (And God) said: "Away! Whosoever of them
follows you will surely have Hell with you as requital —
an ample recompense.
64. Mislead any of them you may with your voice,
attack them with your cavalry and soldiers on foot,
share their wealth and children with them,
and make promises to them." — But the promises of Satan
are nothing but deceit.
65. "You will surely have no power over My devotees:
Your Lord is sufficient as their protector."
66. It is your Lord who drives your ships
across the seas
that you may seek of His bounty,
He is verily kind to you.
67. When a calamity befalls you on the sea,
all those you invoke fail you except Him.
But when He brings you safely to the shore,
you turn away, for man is most ungrateful.
68. Have you then become so sure that He will not
cleave the earth and sink you in it by the shore,
or send a gale against you,
when you will not find any protector.
69. Or you feel so secure
that He will not send you back (to sea) again
or send a gravel-hurtling storm against you,
and drown you for your ingratitude?
Then you will not find any avenger against Us.
70. Indeed We have honoured the children of Adam,
and carried them over land and sea,
provided them with good things for their sustenance,
and exalted them over many of Our creatures.

The day We shall summon all men with their leaders,
whosoever is given his record in his right hand
will be able to read his account,
and none will be wronged the breadth of a thread.
72. But whoso has been blind in this world
shall be blind in the world to come,
even farther astray from the path.
73. They had almost led you away
from what has been revealed to you,
that you may invent things about Us besides those revealed,
when they would have taken you as friend.
74. If We had not kept you constant
you had almost leaned towards them.
75. In that case We would have made you taste
a double anguish of life and a double anguish of death,
and then you would not have been able to find a helper
against Us for yourself.
76. They had nearly expelled you from the land
and driven you away from it.
But then, they too would have stayed
but a little after you.
77. This has been Our way with the apostles
whom We sent before you.
You will not find any variation in Our line of action.

Observe the service of prayer
from the sun's declining from the meridian
to the darkening of the night,
and the recitation at dawn.
Indeed the Recitation at dawn is palpably evident.
79. Say a supererogatory prayer
at the hour of the first watch:
Your Lord may raise you to a most exalted station.
80. And pray: "O my Lord, let my entry be with honour,
and let my exit be with honour,
and grant me power from You
which would help (sustain) me."
81. And say: "Truth has come and flasehood nullified."
Verily falsehood is perishable.
82. What We have sent down of the Qur'an
is a healing and a grace for the faithful,
and adds only loss for the sinners.
83. When We are gracious to man
he turns away and moves aside;
yet when evil befalls him
he begins to despair.

84. Say: "Each one acts according to his disposition,
but your Lord knows well who follow the right path."

They ask you about revelation.
Say, revelation is by the command of your Lord,
and that you have been given but little knowledge.
86. If We pleased We could take away
what We have revealed to you.
Then you will not find any one
to plead for it with Us,
87. Unless your Lord have mercy.
His blessings on you are great indeed.
88. Say: "Surely if men and jinns get together
to produce the like of this (Qur'an),
they will not be able to produce the like of it,
however they might assist one another.
89. We have given examples of every kind to men
in this Qur'an in various ways, and even then
most men disdain every thing but unbelief,
90. And say: "We will not believe you until
you make a spring of water gush forth
from the earth for us;
91. Or, until you acquire an orchard of date-palm trees
and grapes, and produce rivers flowing through it;
92. Or, let chunks of sky fall over us,
as you assert (you will);
or, bring God and the angels as a surety;
93. Or, you come to possess a house of gold;
or ascend to the skies, though we shall not believe
in your having ascended
till you bring down a book for us
which we could read."
Say: "Glory to my Lord.
I am only man and a messenger."

Nothing prevented men from believing
when guidance came to them,
other than (what) they said: "Has God sent
(only) a man as messenger?"
95. Say: "If angels had peopled the earth
and walked about in peace and quiet,
We would surely have sent to them an angel as messenger."
96. Tell them: "God is sufficient witness between me and you,
for He knows His creatures well, and is well-informed."
97. He is guided whom God guides.
As for him He allows to go astray,

Bani Isra'il

you will not find a protector other than Him.
We shall raise them on the Day of Resurrection
in their own image, blind and dumb and deaf:
Their habitation will be Hell.
Every time (its fire) subsides
We will intensify its flame.
98. This will be their retribution
for having denied Our signs and said:
"Once we are turned to bones and bits,
can we be raised as a new creation?"
99. Do they not perceive that God,
who created the heavens and the earth,
has the power to create the like of them?
There is no doubt that He has fixed a term for them.
Even then the wicked disdain everything but unbelief.
100. Say: "Even if you owned the stores
of the mercy of my Lord,
you would have held them back for fear of spending them,
for man is niggardly."

We gave Moses nine clear signs;
so ask the children of Israel.
When (Moses) came to them the Pharaoh said:
"I think, O Moses, you have been deluded."
102. He replied: "You know that none
but the Lord of the heavens and the earth
has sent these (signs) as cogent proof.
I truly think, O Pharaoh, your days are done."
103. Then he sought to turn them out of the land,
but We drowned him and all his followers.
104. After this We told the children of Israel:
"Dwell in the land. When the promise of reckoning comes,
We shall bring you together from a motley crowd.
105. We have sent it down with truth,
and with truth has (the Qur'an) come down.
And We have sent you only to give good news and to warn.
106. We have divided the Qur'an into parts
that you may recite it to men
slowly, with deliberation. That is why
We sent it down by degrees.
107. Say: "Believe in it or do not believe:
Those who were given knowledge before it
bow in adoration
when it is read out to them,
108. And say: "Glory be to our Lord.
The promise of our Lord has indeed been fulfilled."

109. And weeping they kneel down,
and this increases their humility.
110. Say: "Call Him Allah or call Him Ar-Rahman;*
whatever the name you call Him by,
all His names are beautiful."
Do not say your prayers too loudly
or in too low a voice,
but follow a middle course.
111. And say: "All praise be to God
who has neither begotten a son
nor has a partner in His kingdom;
nor has He need of any one
to protect Him from ignominy.
So extol Him
by extolling His majesty."

---

* V. 110. See note to Surah 13, v. 30 on page 214.

2. Note on v.1 of this Surah. The interpretation of this verse as the Prophet's being carried by night from the sacred mosque at Makkah to al-Aqsa mosque at Jerusalem, and its association with the Prophet's ascension to heaven, me'raj, starts some two to three hundred years later with the compilations of Hadith and Tafsir. At the time of the revelation of this Surah, there was no al-Aqsa or any other mosque behind the Temple of Solomon, as Baidawi has observed. Historically, the Prophet migrated by night to Madina some 300 miles away from Makkah, and al-aqsa means distant, and mosque means a place where God is adored. Raghib and Muhit point out that the word isra as used here is not derived from sara yasri, to walk or journey by night, but from siratun, meaning God took His devotee to an open and spacious region, as-saru meaning to open out and siratun-nahar the zenith of the day. And it was at Madina where the Prophet's mission spread out to its widest horizon. As for Ascension, generally known as me'raj, it is described with precision in 53:1-18.

18   The Cave

Al-Kahf: Makki

(١٨) سُوْرَةُ الْكَهْفِ مَكِّيَّةٌ

اٰیَاتُهَا ۱۱۰ رُكُوْعُهَا

In the name of Allah, most benevolent, ever-merciful.

ALL PRAISE BE to God
who has revealed to His votary
the Book which is free of all obliquity,
2. Immutable, so that it may warn
of a severe punishment from Him;
and give happy tidings to those who believe and do the right
that there is a better reward (of Paradise) for them,
3. Where they will abide for ever;
4. And that it may warn
those who say: "God has begotten a son."
5. They have no knowledge of this,
as their fathers did not have.
How terrible are the words they utter!
They speak nothing but lies.
6. Will you kill yourself for grief of them
if they do not believe in this presentation?
7. We have made whatever exists on the earth
its adornment to test and try them
(and) know who acts better;
8. For We shall certainly turn it to barren dust.
9. Do you think the men of the cave and Ar-Raqim*
were so strange among Our signs?
10. When those young men took shelter in the cave, and
      prayed:
"O Lord, grant us Your favour
and dispose our affair aright,"
11. We sealed off their ears in the cave for a number of years,
12. Then roused them to ascertain
which of the two groups could account
for the period they had stayed.

We narrate their story to you in all truth.

---

* See note 1 on page 259.

They were a few young men who believed in their Lord;
so We gave them greater guidance.
14. And strengthened their hearts
when they stood up and said:
"Our Lord is the Lord of the heavens and the earth.
We shall invoke no god beside Him,
for we shall have uttered a blasphemy then.
15. As for these our people here,
they have taken to other gods apart from Him.
Then why do they not bring a clear authority for them?
Who is more wicked than he
who fabricates a lie against God?"
16. (And they said to each other:) "Now that you have
    withdrawn
from them and what they worship beside God,
it is better to take refuge in the cave.
Your Lord may bestow of His mercy on you,
and facilitate your affair."
17. You may well have seen when the sun came up
it moved away to the right of the cave,
and when it went down it turned away to the left,
and they stayed in its open space.
This was among the signs of God.
Whoever is guided by God follows the right path;
and whosoever goes astray
will not find a guide to show him the way.

You may have thought that they were awake,
yet they were asleep.
We made them turn right and left, while their dog
lay with his forelegs stretched across the threshold.
If you had looked at them
you would have surely turned away and fled
with horror at the sight.
19. Even so We roused them that they
may question one another.
One of them asked: "How long have you stayed here?"
They said: "A day or less than a day."
"Your Lord knows best," they said,
"how long you have stayed.
So send one of you to the town with this money of yours
to look for wholesome food and bring it for you;
but he should be careful not to let your presence known.
20. If they come to know of you
they will stone you to death,
or force you to go back to their creed;

then you will never succeed."

21. Thus did We inform the people about them
that they may know the promise of God is true,
and there is no doubt that the Hour will come.
As they were arguing among themselves
as to what should be done with them,
(some) said: "Erect a monument over them.
Their Lord is best cognisant of them."
Those who prevailed, said:
"We shall build a place of worship over their (sepulchre)."

22. Some will say: "They were three,
and their dog was the fourth;" and some
will also say: "They were five and their dog was the sixth," —
guessing in the dark. And some will even say:
"They were seven, and their dog the eighth."
Say: "My Lord alone knows best their number;
none but only a few know of them."
So do not argue about it with them but lightly,
and do not enquire about them from any one of them.

D o not say of any thing: "I will do it tomorrow,"

24. Without (adding), "if God may please;"
and think of your Lord in case you forget, and say:
"Perhaps my Lord will show me a nearer way to rectitude."

25. (It is said) they stayed in the cave three hundred years and
nine.

26. You say: "God only knows how long they stayed.
He alone knows the secrets of the heavens and the earth.
How distinctly He sees and hears!
They have no other guardian but Him,
and He does not share His authority with any one."

27. Recite what has been revealed to you of the Book of your
Lord.
There is no one who can change the word of God;
and you will not find refuge except in Him.

28. Persevere with those who call on their Lord
morning and evening, seeking His magnificence.
Do not turn your eyes away from them,
seeking the splendours of this world,
and do not follow him whose heart We have made
oblivious to Our remembrance,
who follows his own lust and exceeds the bound.

29. Say: "The truth is from your Lord:
So believe if you like,
or do not believe if you will."
We have prepared for the sinners a fire

وَإِن يَسۡتَغِيثُوا۟ يُغَاثُوا۟ بِمَآءٍ كَالۡمُهۡلِ يَشۡوِى الۡوُجُوهَ‌ بِئۡسَ الشَّرَابُ وَسَآءَتۡ مُرۡتَفَقًا ۝

which will envelope them in its tent.
If they ask for water they will be helped
to liquid like molten brass that would scald their mouths.
How evil the drink, and evil the resting-place!

30. But surely We do not let the reward
of those who believe and do the right to go waste.

إِنَّ الَّذِينَ ءَامَنُوا۟ وَعَمِلُوا۟ الصَّٰلِحَٰتِ إِنَّا لَا نُضِيعُ أَجۡرَ مَنۡ أَحۡسَنَ عَمَلًا ۝

31. There will be gardens of Eden for them, with rivers flowing
   by,
where they will be decked in bracelets of gold,
with silken robes of green and of brocades to wear,
reclining on couches.
How excellent the guerdon, and excellent the resting-place!

أُو۟لَٰٓئِكَ لَهُمۡ جَنَّٰتُ عَدۡنٍ تَجۡرِى مِن تَحۡتِهِمُ الۡأَنۡهَٰرُ يُحَلَّوۡنَ فِيهَا مِنۡ أَسَاوِرَ مِن ذَهَبٍ وَيَلۡبَسُونَ ثِيَابًا خُضۡرًا مِّن سُندُسٍ وَإِسۡتَبۡرَقٍ مُّتَّكِئِينَ فِيهَا عَلَى الۡأَرَآئِكِ‌ نِعۡمَ الثَّوَابُ وَحَسُنَتۡ مُرۡتَفَقًا ۝

Tell them the parable of two men.
We gave one two gardens of grapes
surrounded by date-palm trees,
with corn fields in between.

وَاضۡرِبۡ لَهُم مَّثَلًا رَّجُلَيۡنِ جَعَلۡنَا لِأَحَدِهِمَا جَنَّتَيۡنِ مِنۡ أَعۡنَٰبٍ وَحَفَفۡنَٰهُمَا بِنَخۡلٍ وَجَعَلۡنَا بَيۡنَهُمَا زَرۡعًا ۝

33. Each of the gardens yielded its fruit
and did not withhold the least;
and We made a stream flow in between them.

كِلۡتَا الۡجَنَّتَيۡنِ ءَاتَتۡ أُكُلَهَا وَلَمۡ تَظۡلِم مِّنۡهُ شَيۡئًا‌ وَفَجَّرۡنَا خِلَٰلَهُمَا نَهَرًا ۝

34. So he became rich.
Arguing one day with his friend he said:
"I have more wealth than you and more powerful kinsmen."

وَكَانَ لَهُۥ ثَمَرٌ فَقَالَ لِصَٰحِبِهِۦ وَهُوَ يُحَاوِرُهُۥٓ أَنَا۠ أَكۡثَرُ مِنكَ مَالًا وَأَعَزُّ نَفَرًا ۝

35. And he walked into his garden,
and, (forgetting) his limit, said:
"I cannot imagine that this will ever be ruined,

36. Nor can I think that the Hour (of Doom) will come.
And even if I am brought back to my Lord,
I will surely find a better place there than this."

وَدَخَلَ جَنَّتَهُۥ وَهُوَ ظَالِمٌ لِّنَفۡسِهِۦ قَالَ مَآ أَظُنُّ أَن تَبِيدَ هَٰذِهِۦٓ أَبَدًا ۝ وَمَآ أَظُنُّ السَّاعَةَ قَآئِمَةً وَلَئِن رُّدِدتُّ إِلَىٰ رَبِّى لَأَجِدَنَّ خَيۡرًا مِّنۡهَا مُنقَلَبًا ۝

37. Disputing with him, his companion said:
"Do you disbelieve in Him who created you
from dust, then a drop of semen,
then formed you into a man?

قَالَ لَهُۥ صَاحِبُهُۥ وَهُوَ يُحَاوِرُهُۥٓ أَكَفَرۡتَ بِالَّذِى خَلَقَكَ مِن تُرَابٍ ثُمَّ مِن نُّطۡفَةٍ ثُمَّ سَوَّىٰكَ رَجُلًا ۝

38. And He is God, my Lord,
and I do not associate any one with my Lord.

لَّٰكِنَّا۠ هُوَ اللَّهُ رَبِّى وَلَآ أُشۡرِكُ بِرَبِّىٓ أَحَدًا ۝

39. When you entered your garden, why did you not say:
'As God may please;' for no one has power except given by
   God?
Though you see me poorer in wealth and children than you,

وَلَوۡلَآ إِذۡ دَخَلۡتَ جَنَّتَكَ قُلۡتَ مَا شَآءَ اللَّهُ لَا قُوَّةَ إِلَّا بِاللَّهِ‌ إِن تَرَنِ أَنَا۠ أَقَلَّ مِنكَ مَالًا وَوَلَدًا ۝

40. Yet, my Lord may haply give me a garden
better than yours, and He may send a thunder-bolt
from the skies, and in the morning
it will be a barren plain;

فَعَسَىٰ رَبِّىٓ أَن يُؤۡتِيَنِ خَيۡرًا مِّن جَنَّتِكَ وَيُرۡسِلَ عَلَيۡهَا حُسۡبَانًا مِّنَ السَّمَآءِ فَتُصۡبِحَ صَعِيدًا زَلَقًا ۝

41. Or else of a morning its water may sink underground,
and you will not find a trace of it."

أَوۡ يُصۡبِحَ مَآؤُهَا غَوۡرًا فَلَن تَسۡتَطِيعَ لَهُۥ طَلَبًا ۝

42. And his vines were overtaken (with disaster),

وَأُحِيطَ بِثَمَرِهِۦ فَأَصۡبَحَ يُقَلِّبُ كَفَّيۡهِ عَلَىٰ مَآ أَنفَقَ

and he began to wring his hands (at the loss)
of what he had spent on them,
for the vines had fallen upon their trellises;
and he said: "Would to God that I had not
associated any one with my Lord."
43. He had no body to help him other than God,
nor was he able to save himself.
44. The jurisdiction in this province belongs to God.
His is the best reward, and His the best requital.

Present to them the example of the life of this world
so like the water We send down from the skies
that mingles with the earth to nourish its vegetation,
which then on the morrow turns to stubble
and is blown away by the wind.
God has power over every thing.
46. Wealth and children are only the gloss of this world,
but good deeds that abide are better
with your Lord for recompense,
and better for expectation.
47. The day We shall move the mountains,
and you see the earth an open plain,
We shall gather them together, leaving none behind.
48. They will be arraigned before their Lord row on row,
(and He will say): "Well, you have come to Us
as We had first created you, even though you imagined
We had fixed no time for this meeting."
49. The ledger (of their deeds) would be placed before them.
Then you will see the sinners terrified at its contents,
and say: "Alas, what a written revelation this,
which has not left unaccounted
the smallest or the greatest thing!"
They will find in it whatsoever they had done.
Your Lord does not wrong any one.

When We said to the angels:
"Bow before Adam in adoration,"
they all bowed but Iblis.
He was one of the jinns and rebelled against his Lord's
          command.
And yet you take him and his offspring as your friends
instead of Me, even though
they are your enemies.
How sad a substitute for the evil-doers!
51. I did not call them to witness
the creation of the heavens and the earth,

nor their own creation.
I would not take as helpers those who lead (men) astray.
52. The day He will say: "Call those you had called My
　　　compeers,"
they will call them, but will get no response,
and We shall place a gulf between them.
53. The sinners will see the Fire and know
that they will be thrown into it
and will not find a way of escape from it.

We have explained in various ways all things to men
in this Qur'an; but of all things
man is most contentious.
55. There is nothing to prevent men from believing
when the guidance has come to them,
and asking for their Lord's forgiveness,
unless they want the example
of earlier people visited upon them, or the punishment
to appear right before their eyes.
56. We never send apostles but to convey
happy tidings, and to warn.
But those who disbelieve contend
with false arguments to nullify the truth.
They make a mockery of My revelations
and of what they had been warned.
57. Who is more unjust than he
who, on being reminded of his Lord's revelations,
turns away from them, and forgets
the evil deeds he had committed in the past.
Verily We have placed a covering on their hearts
so that they do not understand,
and a deafness in their ears
so that however you may call them to guidance
they will never be guided aright.
58. But your Lord is forgiving, full of benevolence.
If He had pleased to punish them for their doings
He would have punished them immediately.
But a term is fixed for them
from which they will find no escape.
59. As for these habitations, We destroyed them only
when they transgressed; even so
We had fixed a time for their annihilation.

When Moses said to his servant (Joshua):
"I will not give up till I reach the confluence of two oceans,
or I will journey on and on."

61. When they reached the confluence
they forgot the fish (they had brought as food)
which swiftly made its way into the sea.

62. When they had gone past (the confluence),
Moses said to his servant:
"Give me my breakfast. I am exhausted from this journey."

63. He said: "You see, I forgot the fish
on the rock where we had stopped.
Only Satan made me forget to mention this;
but the wonder is the fish escaped to the sea."

64. Moses said: "But that is exactly what we were seeking."
So they retraced their steps.

65. Then they found one of Our votaries,
whom We had blessed
and given knowledge from Us.

66. Moses said to him: "May I attend upon you
that you may instruct me in the knowledge
you have been taught of the right way?"

67. He said: "You will not be able to bear with me.

68. How can you bear that which is beyond your
        comprehension?"

69. "You will find me patient if God wills," said Moses;
"and I will not disobey you in any thing."

70. "If you must follow me," he said, "do not ask me
any thing until I speak of it to you myself."

So they set out till they (came to the quay)
and went on board a ship
in which he made a hole, (and Moses said:)
"You have made a hole in the boat to drown its passengers?
You have done a strange thing!"

72. "Did I not tell you," he replied,
"that you will not be able to bear with me?"

73. (Moses) said: "Do not hold me for having forgotten,
and do not reprove me and make my task difficult."

74. The two went on till they came to a boy, whom he killed.
Moses exclaimed: "You have killed an innocent soul
who had taken no life. You have done a most abominable
        thing!"

75. He said: "Did I not tell you
you will not be able to bear with me?"

76. Moses said: "If I ask you any thing again
then do not keep me with you. You have my apology."

77. The two went on till they came upon some villagers,
and asked the people for food,
but they refused to entertain them.

There they found a wall that was crumbling,
which he repaired. Moses remarked:
"You could have demanded wages for it if you liked."
78. "This is the parting of our ways," he said.
"But I will now explain the things you could not bear:
79. That boat belonged to poor people
who used to toil on the sea.
I damaged it because there was a king after them
who used to seize every ship by force.
80. As for the boy, his parents were believers,
but we feared that he would harass them
with defiance and disbelief.
81. We hoped their Lord would give them a substitute
better than him in virtue and goodness.
82. As for that wall, it belonged to two orphan boys
of the city, and their treasure was buried under it.
Their father was an upright man. So your Lord
willed that on reaching the age of maturity
they should dig out their treasure as a favour from their Lord.
So, I did not do that of my own accord.
This is the explanation of things
you could not bear with patience."

They ask you about Dhu'l-Qarnain.*
84. Say: "I will cite before you his commemoration."
We gave him authority in the land
and means of accomplishing every end.
85. So he followed a certain road
86. Till he reached the point of the setting sun,
and saw it set behind a muddy lake,
and near it found a people.
We said: "O Dhu'l-Qarnain, you may either punish them
or treat them with kindness."
87. He said: "I shall punish whosoever is wicked.
He will then be sent back to his Lord
who will inflict on him a terrible punishment.
88. But he who believes and does the right
will have an excellent reward,
and we shall make things easy for him."
89. He then followed (another) road
90. Till he reached the point of the rising sun,
and saw it rise over a people for whom
We had provided no shelter against it.
91. It was so, for We were fully informed about him.

_____

* See note 2 on page 259

92. He then followed (another) road
93. Till he reached a place between two mountains,
and found this side of it a people
who understood but little of what was spoken.
94. They said: "O Dhu'l-Qarnain,
Gog and Magog* are oppressing the land.
May we pay you some tribute so that you could build
a rampart between us and them?"
95. He said: "The ability my Lord has given me is better.
So help me with your manual labour;
I will build a wall between you and them.
96. Bring me ingots of iron," (which they did) until
the space between two mountain sides was filled up.
"Blow your bellows," he said; (and they blew)
until it was red hot.
"Bring me molten brass," he said, "that I may pour over it."
97. Thus (Gog and Magog) could neither climb over it
nor dig a hole through (the rampart).
98. "This is the benevolence of my Lord," he said;
"but when the promise of my Lord comes to pass,
He will reduce it to a mound of dust;
and the promise of my Lord is true."
99. We shall leave them on that day
surging like waves pressing one against the other,
and the trumpet blast will be sounded,
when We shall gather them all together.
100. Then We shall bring Hell right before the infidels
101. Whose eyes were veiled against My warning,
and they could not hear.

Do the unbelievers think they can make My own
            creatures
their protectors against Me?
We have prepared Hell for the hospitality of infidels.
103. Say: "Shall I tell you whose labour will be wasted?
104. Theirs whose effort is misspent
in pursuit of the pleasures of the world,
even though they think they are doing good things."
105. They are those who reject the signs of their Lord,
and the meeting with Him.
So their good deeds will be fruitless,
and on the Day of Judgement We shall not
appoint any weighing for them.
106. Their requital will be Hell,

---

* See note 3 on next page.

الكهف١٨ قال الم١٦

because they disbelieved and mocked My signs and messengers.
107. But surely those who believe and do the right
will have gardens of Paradise as gift,
108. Where they will abide for ever, never wanting a change.
109. Say: "If the ocean turned to ink
for writing down the colloquy of my Lord,
the ocean itself would be exhausted
ere the words (and wonders) of my Lord come to end,
even if we brought
another like it for replenishment."
110. Say: "I am only a man like you, but it has been
communicated to me that your Lord is one and single God,
and that whosoever hopes to meet his Lord should do
what is right, and not associate
any one in the worship of his Lord."

This is the most allegorical Surah and contains allegories within allegories, and many parables.

1. The Dead Sea Scrolls and the caves in which they were found contain enough historical and archaeological evidence about the situation of these caves, and throw light on the state of religious beliefs before the appearance of Christ. There is also the famous cave near Ephesus in Turkey known as the Cave of Seven Sleepers where, it is said, seven Christians slept two hundred years to escape persecution by the Romans. There are other caves in Turkey which were similarly used by Christian priests as hiding places.

2. Many Commentators identify Dhu'l-Qarnain with Alexander of Macedon, some with kings of earlier days. But he is closest in his travels to East and West, wisdom and qualities of prophethood, to Cyrus the Great of Persia who was a contemporary of Zoroaster, whom he may well have known, as is indicated by the obviously symbolical travel to the setting and the rising sun, darkness and light. In the Bible too Cyrus is called the anointed one, with qualities similar to those attributed to Dhu' 1-Qarnain here. See Isiah, 42:1-3, and Ezra, 1-2.

3. The location of this place points to Armenia or Turkistan. Gog and Magog, in that case, would lead to the early inhabitants of what is now Soviet Russia, who were a Mongoloid people, and who eventually spread to Europe and were constantly making incursions into adjoining areas through such geographic terrain as is described here. They are mentioned in the Prophecies of Ezekiel as well as in St. John. The name Mongolia, Mungkuo in Chinese, is a compound of Mog (or Mong or Mung) which is the old name of the region, and *kuo* (pronounced *go*) which means country in Chinese, with the suffix *lia* being added though *ria* is more common, as in Manchu*ria*, Sibe*ria* and Rus*sia* where the *r* has been dropped. *Ria* and *Lia* are, however, interchangeable. The barbaric Mongols were always pressing against China on the one hand, and against Russia on the other, in search of better pastures and life. As a consequence of their raids the Chinese built the Great Wall, taking its present shape in the 3rd. century B.C. under the orders of Shih Huang Ti. It stands to reason that a wall may have also been built in Western regions in the remote past against their pressure to penetrate the fertile Mediterranean areas. Thus, Gog and Magog of the Bible and Yajuj and Majuj of the Qur'an — Hebrew Majuj and Greek Megog — would represent the two tribes of Mongolia, the Yueh Ch'i and the Mong or Meng. Now, the *ch* sound is interchangeable with *j*, and Yueh Ch'i becomes Yu-ji, Ya-ji, changing to Yajuj. Mong or Meng (also Mog or Mug) of Mongolia, become Moj, Muj or Maj through the interchangeability of *g* and *j* sounds, becoming Majuj.

19 Mary

Maryam: Makki

In the name of Allah, most benevolent, ever-merciful.

KĀF HĀ YĀ 'Ain Ṣad.
2. Commemorate the beneficence of your Lord
on Zachariah, His devotee,
3. When he called to his Lord inwardly,
4. And said: "O my Lord, my bones decay,
my head is white and hoary,
yet in calling You, O Lord,
I have never been deprived.
5. But I fear my relatives after me;
and my wife is barren.
So grant me a successor as a favour from You
6. Who will be heir to me,
and heir to the house of Jacob;
and make him obedient to You, O Lord."
7. "O Zachariah," (it was) said, "We give you good news
of a son by name of John:
To none have We attributed the name before."
8. "How can I have a son, O Lord" he said,
"when my wife is barren
and I am old and decrepit?"
9. (The angel) answered: "Thus will it be.
Your Lord said: 'This is easy for Me;
for when I brought you into being you were nothing.' "
10. He said: "O Lord, give me a token."
"Though sound," He answered, "you will not
talk to any one for three nights running."
11. So he came from the chamber to his people,
and suggested to them (by signs)
to sing the praises of the Lord morning and evening.
12. (We said:) "O John, hold fast to the Book;"
and We gave him wisdom right from boyhood,
13. And compassion from Us, and goodness.
So he was devout,
14. And kind to his parents,

وَلَمْ يَكُنْ جَبَّارًا عَصِيًّا ۝

neither arrogant nor disobedient.
15. So peace on him the day he was born,
the day he will die, and the day
that he will be raised from the dead.

وَسَلَامٌ عَلَيْهِ يَوْمَ وُلِدَ وَيَوْمَ يَمُوتُ وَيَوْمَ

يُبْعَثُ حَيًّا ۝

Commemorate Mary in the Book.
When she withdrew from her family
to a place in the East

وَاذْكُرْ فِي الْكِتَابِ مَرْيَمَ إِذِ انْتَبَذَتْ مِنْ أَهْلِهَا

مَكَانًا شَرْقِيًّا ۝

17. And took cover from them,
We sent a spirit of Ours to her who appeared
before her in the concrete form of a man.

فَاتَّخَذَتْ مِنْ دُونِهِمْ حِجَابًا فَأَرْسَلْنَا إِلَيْهَا

رُوحَنَا فَتَمَثَّلَ لَهَا بَشَرًا سَوِيًّا ۝

18. "I seek refuge in the Merciful from you,
if you fear Him," she said.

قَالَتْ إِنِّي أَعُوذُ بِالرَّحْمَنِ مِنْكَ إِنْ كُنْتَ تَقِيًّا ۝

19. He replied: "I am only a messenger from your Lord
(sent) to bestow a good son on you."

قَالَ إِنَّمَا أَنَا رَسُولُ رَبِّكِ لِأَهَبَ لَكِ غُلَامًا

زَكِيًّا ۝

20. "How can I have a son," she said,
"when no man has touched me,
nor am I sinful?"

قَالَتْ أَنَّى يَكُونُ لِي غُلَامٌ وَلَمْ يَمْسَسْنِي بَشَرٌ وَلَمْ

أَكُ بَغِيًّا ۝

21. He said: "Thus will it be.
Your Lord said: 'It is easy for Me,'
and that: 'We shall make him a sign for men
and a blessing from Us.'
This is a thing already decreed."

قَالَ كَذَلِكِ قَالَ رَبُّكِ هُوَ عَلَيَّ هَيِّنٌ وَلِنَجْعَلَهُ آيَةً

لِلنَّاسِ وَرَحْمَةً مِنَّا وَكَانَ أَمْرًا مَقْضِيًّا ۝

22. When she conceived him she went away
to a distant place.

فَحَمَلَتْهُ فَانْتَبَذَتْ بِهِ مَكَانًا قَصِيًّا ۝

23. The birth pangs led her to the trunk of a date-palm tree.
"Would that I had died before this," she said,
"and become a thing forgotten, unremembered."

فَأَجَاءَهَا الْمَخَاضُ إِلَى جِذْعِ النَّخْلَةِ قَالَتْ

يَا لَيْتَنِي مِتُّ قَبْلَ هَذَا وَكُنْتُ نَسْيًا مَنْسِيًّا ۝

24. Then (a voice) called to her from below: "Grieve not;
your Lord has made a rivulet gush forth right below you.

فَنَادَاهَا مِنْ تَحْتِهَا أَلَّا تَحْزَنِي قَدْ جَعَلَ رَبُّكِ

تَحْتَكِ سَرِيًّا ۝

25. Shake the trunk of the date-palm tree,
and it will drop ripe dates for you.

وَهُزِّي إِلَيْكِ بِجِذْعِ النَّخْلَةِ تُسَاقِطْ عَلَيْكِ رُطَبًا

جَنِيًّا ۝

26. Eat and drink, and be at peace. If you see any man,
tell him: 'I have verily vowed a fast to Ar-Rahman
and cannot speak to any one this day.' "

فَكُلِي وَاشْرَبِي وَقَرِّي عَيْنًا فَإِمَّا تَرَيِنَّ مِنَ الْبَشَرِ

أَحَدًا فَقُولِي إِنِّي نَذَرْتُ لِلرَّحْمَنِ صَوْمًا فَلَنْ

أُكَلِّمَ الْيَوْمَ إِنْسِيًّا ۝

27. Then she brought the child to her people. They exclaimed:
"O Mary, you have done a most astonishing thing!

فَأَتَتْ بِهِ قَوْمَهَا تَحْمِلُهُ قَالُوا يَا مَرْيَمُ لَقَدْ جِئْتِ

شَيْئًا فَرِيًّا ۝

28. O sister of Aaron, your father was not a wicked person,
nor your mother sinful!"

يَا أُخْتَ هَارُونَ مَا كَانَ أَبُوكِ امْرَأَ سَوْءٍ وَمَا

كَانَتْ أُمُّكِ بَغِيًّا ۝

29. But she pointed towards him. "How can we talk to one,"
they said, "who is only an infant in the cradle?"*

فَأَشَارَتْ إِلَيْهِ قَالُوا كَيْفَ نُكَلِّمُ مَنْ كَانَ فِي

الْمَهْدِ صَبِيًّا ۝

30. "I am a servant of God," he answered.

قَالَ إِنِّي عَبْدُ اللَّهِ آتَانِيَ الْكِتَابَ وَجَعَلَنِي

---

* Idiomatically a mere boy who has not shed his milk teeth. So would Jesus have appeared to the
elders of Israel, although he had already become a prophet as the next verse affirms. See Note on
page 265.

"He has given me a Book and made me a prophet,
31. And blessed me wherever I may be,
and enjoined on me worship and zakat
for as long as I live,
32. And be dutiful to my mother.
He has not made me haughty or rebellious.
33. There was peace on me the day I was born,
and will be the day I die, and on the day
I will be raised from the dead."
34. This was Jesus, son of Mary:
A true account they contend about.
35. It does not behove God to have a son.
Too immaculate is He! When He decrees a thing
He has only to say: "Be", and it is.
36. (Jesus only said:) "Surely God is my Lord and your Lord,
so worship Him.
This is the straight path."
37. Yet the sectarians differed among themselves.
Alas for the unbelievers when they see the Terrible Day!
38. How keenly would they hear and see
when they come before Us then,
even though today
the evil-doers are lost in palpable error.
39. Warn them of that day of pining
when all matters will have been settled,
though they would still be unaware
and unbelieving (of the truth).
40. Verily We shall inherit the earth
and whosoever is on it,
and to Us they will return.

Commemorate Abraham in the Book:
He was upright, a prophet.
42. Remember, when he said to his father:
"O my father, why do you worship that
which can neither hear nor see nor even profit you the least?
43. O my father, to me has come such knowledge
as never came to you.
So follow me that I may show you the right path.
44. Why do you worship Satan, O father?
Verily Satan was disobedient to Ar-Rahman.
45. O my father, I fear lest
a punishment from Ar-Rahman should befall you,
and you should become a friend of the Devil."
46. He said: "Are you averse to my gods, O Abraham?
If you do not desist, I shall have you stoned to death.

So go away for a while from me."

47. He answered: "Peace be on you. I will seek
forgiveness of my Lord for you.
He has been gracious to me.

48. I will leave you and those you invoke apart from God,
and pray to my Lord. Haply in praying to my Lord
I will not be deprived."

49. Thus, when he left them and the (idols) they worshipped,
We bestowed on him Isaac and Jacob,
and made each of them a prophet,

50. And bestowed on them some of Our blessings,
and gave them high renown.

Commemorate Moses in the Book.
He was a chosen one,
both an apostle and a prophet.

52. We called him from the right side of the Mount,
and brought him close for communion;

53. And bestowed on him his brother Aaron, a prophet,
through Our benevolence.

54. Commemorate Ishmael in the Book.
He was true of his promise, and a messenger, a prophet.

55. He enjoined on his household worship and zakat,
and he was obedient to his Lord.

56. Commemorate Enoch in the Book.
He was a truthful person and a prophet,

57. And We raised him to an exalted station.

58. These are (some of) those who were favoured by God
among the prophets of the progeny of Adam,
and of those We bore in the ark with Noah,
and the offspring of Abraham and Israel,
and of those We guided and We chose,
for they bowed weeping in adoration
when the revelations of Ar-Rahman
were recited to them.

59. But they are succeeded by a generation
who neglect their devotional obligations
and follow only earthly pleasures;
but they will reach the wrong road and meet destruction,

60. Except those who repent
and come to believe and do the right.
These will enter Paradise
and will not be wronged the least

61. In the gardens of Eden promised by Ar-Rahman
to His creatures in the unknown (future).
Verily His promise will come to pass.

Maryam

62. They will hear no vain talk there,
but only salutations of peace,
and they will have their sustenance morning and evening."

63. This is the Paradise those of Our creatures will inherit
who take heed and fear the displeasure of God.

64. "We do not come down," (will the angels say)
"but only by your Lord's command."
To Him belongs whatever lies
before us and behind us, and the space in between.
Your Lord does not ever forget:

65. Lord of the heavens and the earth
and all that lies between them.
Therefore worship Him, and be constant in His worship.
Do you know any namesake of His?

Yet man says: "When I am dead, will I come to life again?"

67. Does man not remember that before We created him
he was nothing?

68. By your Lord, We shall gather them and the devils together,
then bring them crawling on their knees around Hell.

69. We shall pull out of every section those
who were most perversely rebellious against Ar-Rahman.

70. We know best who deserve to be burnt in (the Fire).

71. There is not one among you who will not reach it.
Your Lord has made this incumbent on Himself.

72. We shall deliver those who took heed for themselves,
and leave the evil-doers kneeling there.

73. When Our lucid revelations are read out to them,
the infidels say to those who believe:
"Which of the two groups is better in standing,
and whose company is more excellent?"

74. How many generations that had far more wealth and
ostentation
have We laid low before them!

75. Say: "Ar-Rahman extends the life of those
who are astray until
they come to realise what had been promised them
was either (physical) affliction or (the terror) of Resurrection.
Then will they know who is worse in position,
and who is weak in supporters.

76. God gives greater guidance to those who are guided;
and good deeds that endure are better with your Lord
for reward, and better for consequence.

77. Have you seen him who denies Our revelations,
and says: "I will certainly be given wealth and children."

78. Has he peeped into the Unknown,

or obtained a promise from Ar-Rahman?

79. Never so. We shall certainly write down what he says,
and prolong the extent of his punishment.

80. All that he claims will revert to Us,
and he will come before Us all alone.

81. They have taken other gods apart from God
that they might be a strength to them.

82. Never. They will deny their devotion
and become their adversaries.

Do you not see that We have set
the devils against the infidels
to rouse and instigate them?

84. So, do not be hasty with them.
We are counting their number (of days).

85. The day We shall usher the righteous before Ar-Rahman
like envoys into the presence of a king,

86. And drive the wicked into Hell like cattle driven to water,

87. None will have power to intercede for them
except one who obtains a promise from Ar-Rahman.

88. They say: "God has begotten a son."

89. You have uttered a grievous thing

90. Which would cleave the skies asunder, rend the earth,
and split the mountains,

91. For they have attributed a son to Ar-Rahman,

92. When it does not behove the Merciful to have a son.

93. There is no one in the heavens and the earth
but comes before Ar-Rahman in all obedience

94. He has counted them and calculated their number.

95. Every one of them will come before Him all alone
on the Day of Resurrection.

96. Surely Ar-Rahman will show love
for those who believe and do the right.

97. So We have made this (Qur'an) easy in your tongue
that you may give good news to those who take heed,
and warn the people who are contentious.

98. How many generations have We laid low before them.
Do you see any sign of them,
or hear the least whisper of them?

---

* Note on vv. 16-30. The story of Mary first appears in 3:35-37. When she came of age, lots were
cast for selecting a sponsor or spouse for her, 3:44. It was after this that news of the birth of Jesus
was given to her by the angels, 3:45. The subsequent events are described here as a dream reality.
She brings child Jesus to her people in vv. 27-28. The nature of conversation in vv. 29-33 points to
another occassion when Jesus had become a prophet, v. 30, the time sequence showing the two
events having been telescoped, as in dream displacement.

20 Tā Hā

Tā Hā: Makki

In the name of Allah, most benevolent, ever-merciful.

Tā HĀ.

2. We have not sent down the Qur'an to you
that you should be burdened,

3. But as admonition for him who fears —

4. A revelation from Him who created
the earth and the high ascending skies,

5. The ever-merciful, established on the throne
(of authority).

6. Whatever is in the heavens and the earth
and in between them, belongs to Him,
as whatever lies under the earth.

7. Whether you say a thing aloud or inaudibly,
He has knowledge of the secret and the hidden.

8. God: There is no god but He.
To Him belong the attributes most beautiful.

9. Has the story of Moses come to you?

10. When he saw a fire he said to his family:
"You wait here. I have seen a fire.
I may haply be able to bring an ember from it,
or find direction by the fire."

11. When he approached it, a voice called out:

12. "O Moses, I am verily your Lord, so take off your shoes,
for you are in the holy plain of Towa.

13. I have chosen you, so listen to what is revealed to you.

14. I am God, and there is no god but I, so serve Me,
and observe acts of prayer to remember Me.

15. Verily the Hour (of the great change) is about to come.
I keep it secret that every soul
may be rewarded for its endeavour.

16. So do not let those who do not believe in it
and follow their vain desires, turn you away from it.

17. What is that in your right hand, O Moses?"

18. "It's my staff," he answered;
"I lean on it, and fell leaves for my goats with it,

Tā Hā

and I have other uses for it."

19. "Throw it down, O Moses," said (the Voice).
20. So he threw it down, and lo,
it became a running serpent.
21. "Catch it," said He, "and have no fear;
We shall revert it to its former state.
22. And face what is to come with patience, your hand
will not be tarnished with blame: *
Another sign
23. That We may go on showing you Our greater signs.
24. Go to the Pharaoh as he has become
exceedingly rebellious."

(M)oses) said: "O my Lord, enlarge my breast,
26. And make my mission easy.
27. Remove the defect of my tongue
28. That they may understand my speech,
29. And give me as assistant from my family
30. Aaron my brother
31. To strengthen me
32. And share my task,
33. That we may sing Your praises much,
34. And remember you a great deal.
35. Surely You know us well."
36. He answered: "Granted is your prayer, O Moses.
37. We have bestowed Our favour on you before this
38. When We told your mother what We relate:
39. 'Put him in a wooden box
and cast it in the river.
The river will cast it on the bank.
An enemy of Ours, and his, will retrieve it.'
We bestowed Our love on you
that you may be reared under Our eyes.
40. Then your sister followed you, and said
(to the people who had retrieved the child):
'Should I guide you to a person who can nurse him?'
We thus brought you back to your mother
that her heart may be cheered, and she may not grieve.
(Remember) when you killed a man
We saved you from anguish;
and tested and steeled you (in other ways).
Afterwards you sojourned for several years
with the people of Midian; then you came up to the measure,

---

* *Janaha,* hand, wing, armpit, also used for self, idiomatically means protecting, taking care of, being unafraid, etc. The metaphorical meaning of the verse have been given above.

41. And I chose you for Myself.
42. Go with My signs, you and your brother,
and do not be lax in remembering Me.
43. Then go to the Pharaoh as he has become
exceedingly rebellious.
44. Speak to him gently.
He may possibly take heed or may come to have fear."
45. They said: "O our Lord, we are really frightened lest
he behave insolently with us or become violent."
46. (The Lord) said: "Be not afraid.
I am verily with you, and I hear and see.
47. So go to him and say: 'The two of us
have indeed been sent by your Lord.
So let the children of Israel come with us,
and do not oppress them.
We have come to you with a token from your Lord.
Peace on him who follows the way of guidance.
48. It has been revealed to us
that punishment will befall him
who denies and turns away.' "
49. He asked: "Who then is that Lord of yours, O Moses?"
50. (Moses) said: "Our Lord is He who gave every thing
its natural form and directed it."
51. (The Pharaoh) said: "And what about
the former generations?"
52. (Moses) replied: "Knowledge of that is with my Lord
(recorded) in the Book.
My Lord neither errs nor forgets."
53. It is He who made the earth a bed for you,
and traced for you paths upon it,
and sends down water from the sky,
and brings out through it every kind of vegetation
54. To eat and feed your cattle.
Surely there are signs in these for those who are wise.

We created you from the earth
and will revert you back to it;
and raise you up from it a second time.
56. So We showed him all Our signs,
but he denied them and refused,
57. And said: "Have you come to us, O Moses,
to drive us out of our land with your witchery?
58. We shall certainly meet you with like magic.
So make an appointment when we and you could meet
on common ground, which neither we nor you
should fail to keep."

59. Said (Moses): "Let your meeting be on the day of the
     Feast,
and let people assemble in broad daylight."

60. After this the Pharaoh withdrew
and settled his stratagem, then came back.

61. Moses said to them: "Woe betide you.
Do not fabricate a lie against God,
or He will destroy you with some affliction.
For he who fabricates lies is doomed to failure."

62. So they discussed their strategy among themselves
and conferred privately,

63. (And) said: "These two are surely magicians.
They want to deprive you of your land with their magic,
and eradicate your distinct way (of life).

64. So prepare your strategy and come forward.
He alone shall win today who is superior."

65. They said: "Either you cast (your spell), O Moses,
or we shall cast it first."

66. Moses said: "No. You cast it first." Then it seemed to
     Moses
that by their magic their cords and rods were flying;

67. And Moses felt afraid within himself.

68. We said to him: "Fear not. You will certainly be victorious.

69. Throw down what is in your right hand:
It will swallow up what they have conjured.
For what they have fashioned is only a trick of the sorcerer;
and a sorcerer does not succeed wherever he may come."

70. The magicians, (seeing the miracle),
fell down in prostration, saying:
"We believe in the Lord of Moses and Aaron."

71. (The Pharaoh) said: "You have come to believe without
     my dispensation.
Surely he is your chief who taught you magic.
I will have your hands and feet cut off on alternate sides
and crucify you on the trunks of date-palm trees.
You will come to know whose punishment is harder and
     protracted."

72. They replied: "We cannot choose you in the face
of the clear testimony we have received,
and over Him who created us.
So do what you are determined to do. All that you would do
will only be confined to our life on earth.

73. We have certainly come to believe in our Lord
that He may forgive our trespasses
and the magic you have forced us to perform,
for God is nobler and abiding."

74. Surely for him who comes before his Lord
a sinner shall be Hell,
where he will neither die nor live.
75. But whoever comes before Him a believer
having done good deeds,
will be raised to higher stations —
76. Gardens of Eden with rippling streams,
where he will live for ever.
This is the recompense of those who achieve integrity.

We commanded Moses: "Journey by night with Our
    creatures,
and strike a dry path for them through the sea.
Do not fear being overtaken,
nor have dread of any thing."
78. Then the Pharaoh followed them with his army,
but the sea overpowered and engulfed them.
79. The Pharaoh had led his people astray,
and did not rightly guide them.
80. O children of Israel, We delivered you from your enemy,
and made a covenant with you on the right side of the Mount,
and sent down for you manna and quails,
81. (And said): "Eat of the good things We have given you for
    food,
and do not exceed the bounds (of law) in this,
or My wrath will surely fall upon you;
and he who incurs My wrath will fall into the abyss.
82. Yet I am gracious to him who repents
and believes, and does the right,
and follows the straight path.
83. What made you hurry away, O Moses, from your people?"
84. He said: "They are right behind me.
I have hastened to You, O Lord, so that You may be pleased."
85. He said: "We have put your people on trial in your absence;
and Sameri has led them astray."
86. So Moses returned to his people full of anger and regret.
"O my people," he said, "did not your Lord
make you a better promise?
Did the time of covenant seem too long to you?
Or did you wish the wrath of your Lord to fall upon you
that you broke the promise you had made to me?"
87. They said: "We did not break our promise to you of our
    own will,
but we were made to carry the loads of ornaments
belonging to the people, which we threw (into the fire),
and so did Sameri.

فَأَخْرَجَ لَهُمْ عِجْلًا جَسَدًا لَهُ خُوَارٌ فَقَالُوا هٰذَاۤ الٰهُكُمْ وَالٰهُ مُوسٰى ۪ فَنَسِىَ ۞

88. Then he produced the image of a calf which mooed like a cow.

And they said: 'This is your god and the god of Moses (whom) he has neglected."

أَفَلَا يَرَوْنَ أَلَّا يَرْجِعُ إِلَيْهِمْ قَوْلًا ۙ وَّلَا يَمْلِكُ لَهُمْ ضَرًّا وَّلَا نَفْعًا ۞

89. Did they not see that it did not give them any answer, nor had it power to do them harm or bring them gain?

وَلَقَدْ قَالَ لَهُمْ هٰرُوْنُ مِنْ قَبْلُ يٰقَوْمِ اِنَّمَا فُتِنْتُمْ بِهٖ ۚ وَاِنَّ رَبَّكُمُ الرَّحْمٰنُ فَاتَّبِعُوْنِىْ وَاَطِيْعُوْۤا اَمْرِىْ ۞

A aron had indeed told them earlier: "O my people, you are being only misled with this.
Surely your Lord is Ar-Rahman.
So follow me and obey my command."

قَالُوْا لَنْ نَّبْرَحَ عَلَيْهِ عٰكِفِيْنَ حَتّٰى يَرْجِعَ اِلَيْنَا مُوْسٰى ۞

91. They said "So long as Moses does not come back we are not going to give it up, and we will remain devoted to it."

قَالَ يٰهٰرُوْنُ مَا مَنَعَكَ اِذْ رَاَيْتَهُمْ ضَلُّوْۤا ۞ اَلَّا تَتَّبِعَنِ ۖ اَفَعَصَيْتَ اَمْرِىْ ۞

92. But (Moses) said: "O Aaron, when you saw that they had gone astray, what hindered you
93. From coming after me?
Did you not disobey my command?"
(And Moses pulled him by the hair).

قَالَ يَبْنَؤُمَّ لَا تَأْخُذْ بِلِحْيَتِىْ وَلَا بِرَأْسِىْ ۚ اِنِّىْ خَشِيْتُ اَنْ تَقُوْلَ فَرَّقْتَ بَيْنَ بَنِىْۤ اِسْرَآءِيْلَ وَلَمْ تَرْقُبْ قَوْلِىْ ۞

94. "O son of my mother," (Aaron cried),
do not pull me by my beard or my hair!
I was really afraid you may say
that I had created a rift among the children of Israel,
and did not pay heed to your command."

قَالَ فَمَا خَطْبُكَ يٰسَامِرِىُّ ۞

95. Moses asked: "O Sameri, what was the matter?"

قَالَ بَصُرْتُ بِمَا لَمْ يَبْصُرُوْا بِهٖ فَقَبَضْتُ قَبْضَةً مِّنْ اَثَرِ الرَّسُوْلِ فَنَبَذْتُهَا وَكَذٰلِكَ سَوَّلَتْ لِىْ نَفْسِىْ ۞

96. He said: "I saw what they did not see.
I picked up a handful of dust from the messenger's tracks and threw it in,
for the idea seemed attractive to me."

قَالَ فَاذْهَبْ فَاِنَّ لَكَ فِى الْحَيٰوةِ اَنْ تَقُوْلَ لَا مِسَاسَ ۖ وَاِنَّ لَكَ مَوْعِدًا لَّنْ تُخْلَفَهٗ ۚ وَانْظُرْ اِلٰۤى اِلٰهِكَ الَّذِىْ ظَلْتَ عَلَيْهِ عَاكِفًا ۖ لَّنُحَرِّقَنَّهٗ ثُمَّ لَنَنْسِفَنَّهٗ فِى الْيَمِّ نَسْفًا ۞

97. (Moses) said: "Go hence! All your life you are (cursed) to say: 'Do not touch me;'
and a threat hangs over you
which you will not be able to escape.
Look at your god to whom you are so attached:
We shall verily burn it,
and disperse its ashes into the sea.

اِنَّمَاۤ اِلٰهُكُمُ اللّٰهُ الَّذِىْ لَاۤ اِلٰهَ اِلَّا هُوَ ۚ وَسِعَ كُلَّ شَىْءٍ عِلْمًا ۞

98. Your god is only God.
There is no other god but He.
His knowledge extends over every thing."

كَذٰلِكَ نَقُصُّ عَلَيْكَ مِنْ اَنْۢبَآءِ مَا قَدْ سَبَقَ ۚ وَقَدْ اٰتَيْنٰكَ مِنْ لَّدُنَّا ذِكْرًا ۞

99. Thus do We narrate some account to you
of what has gone before,
and We have truly given you a Reminder of Our own.

مَنْ اَعْرَضَ عَنْهُ فَاِنَّهٗ يَحْمِلُ يَوْمَ الْقِيٰمَةِ وِزْرًا ۞

100. Whoever turns away from it will surely carry
a burden on the Day of Judgement,
101. And will live for ever under it.

خٰلِدِيْنَ فِيْهِ ۚ وَسَآءَ لَهُمْ يَوْمَ الْقِيٰمَةِ حِمْلًا ۞

How evil the burden they will carry on the Day of Doom!

102. The day the trumpet blast is sounded
We shall raise the sinners blind,
103. Whispering to one another:
"You have tarried but ten days."
104. We know well what they will say
when the most upright among them will say:
"You did not tarry more than a day."

They will ask you about the mountains.
Tell them: "My Lord will uproot them from the base,
106. And turn them into a level plain,
107. Over which you will see no curves or elevations.
108. That day they will follow the summoner
from whom there will be no receding;
and their voices will be hushed
before Ar-Rahman,
and you will not hear a sound
but faint shuffling.
109. On that day no intercession will matter
other than his whom Ar-Rahman
grants permission and accepts.
110. He knows what is before them and hidden from them,
but they cannot grasp it with their knowledge.
111. All heads will be bowed before the Living, the Eternal;
and whosoever bears a load of iniquity
will be full of despair.
112. But he who has done good things
and believes, will have no fear
of either being wronged or deprived.
113. That is why We have sent it down as an eloquent Qur'an,
and explained in different ways the intimidations through it
that they may haply take heed, or perhaps
it may lead them to contemplate.
114. Exalted then be God, the real King;
and do not try to anticipate the Qur'an
before the completion of its revelation,
but pray: "O Lord, give me greater knowledge."
115. We had commanded Adam before, but he disregarded it:
We found him lacking in resolution.

When We said to the angels: "Bow before Adam,"
they all bowed but Iblis, who refused.
117. So We said; "O Adam, he is truly your enemy and your
         wife's.
Do not let him have you turned out of Paradise
and come to grief.

118. Verily you will have no hunger or nakedness there,
119. Nor thirst nor exposure to the sun."
120. But then Satan tempted him by saying:
"O Adam, should I show you the tree of immortality,
and a kingdom that will never know any wane?"
121. And both ate of (its fruit),
and their hidden parts were exposed to one another,
and they patched the leaves of the garden (to hide them).
Adam disobeyed his Lord, and went astray.
122. Then his Lord chose him and relented towards him,
and showed him the way;
123. (And) said: "Go down hence together,
one the enemy of the other.
Then will guidance come to you from Me;
and whoever follows My direction
will neither be disgraced nor be miserable.
124. But he who fails to heed My warning
will have his means restricted;
and on the Day of Resurrection
We shall raise him blind."
125. He will ask: "O Lord, why have you raised me blind
when I was able to see?"
126. (God) will say: "Because Our signs came to you,
but you disregarded them.
So shall We disregard you this day."
127. And that is how We requite him who is extravagant
and does not believe the signs of his Lord;
and surely the punishment of the Hereafter
is far more severe and persistent.
128. Did they not learn from the many generations
that We destroyed before them,
whose habitations they now frequent?
Verily there are signs in this
for men of understanding.

If the decree (of respite) had not been pronounced
by your Lord, (the inevitable judgement would have ensued);
but a term is fixed (for every thing).
130. So you bear with patience what they say,
and sing the praises of your Lord
before the rising and setting of the sun,
and honour Him in the watches of the night,
and then at the two ends of day,
that you may find acceptance.
131. Do not covet what We have granted myriads of people
of the pomp and glitter of this world to tempt them.

The means your Lord has given you
are better far and more enduring.

132. Enjoin on your people service to God,
and be yourself constant in it.
We do not ask you to provide:
It is We who provide for you.
The reward is for piety and fear of God.

133. Yet they say: "Why does he not bring a sign from his
      Lord?"
Have not clear proofs come to them
in what is contained in the earlier Books?

134. If We had destroyed them by some calamity sooner
      than this,
they would have surely said: "O Lord,
if You had sent to us a messenger
we would have followed Your command
before being humbled and disgraced."

135. Say: "Each one awaits the consequence;
so you wait. You will come to know soon
who are the men of the straight path
and who have come to guidance.

21 The Prophets

Al-Anbiyā': Makki

In the name of Allah, most benevolent, ever-merciful.

بِسْمِ اللهِ الرَّحْمٰنِ الرَّحِيمِ۞

NEAR HAS COME the reckoning for men,
but they turn away in remissness.
2. Never does a new reminder come to them from their Lord
but they listen to it with dalliance.
3. Their minds are lost in frivolous pastimes;
and the evil-doers discuss secretly:
"Is he not but only a man like you?
Then why are you taken in by magic seeingly?"
4. He said: "My Lord knows whatever is spoken
in the heavens and the earth.
He hears all and knows every thing."
5. Yet they say: "These are only confused dreams,"
or rather: "He has invented them;" or: "He is only a poet.
Let him therefore bring a miracle to us
as the earlier (apostles) were sent with."
6. Not one habitation that We destroyed before them
had believed.
So how can they believe?
7. Never did We send a message before you
but through a man, whom We inspired.
If you do not know,
then ask the keepers of the oracles of God.
8. We did not make their bodies immune to hunger,
nor were they immortal.
9. Then We made Our promise good to them
and delivered whomsoever We pleased,
and destroyed the transgressors.
10. We have sent down to you a Book
which has a reminder for you.
Do you not understand?

How many habitations that were sinful
have We demolished utterly,
and raised other people after them.

12. Whensoever they sensed Our punishment
they fled from them.
13. "Do not flee; go back to your halls of pleasure
and your habitations,
so that you may be interrogated."
14. "Woe, alas," they said, "we were really sinful."
15. And this remained their lament till We mowed them down
and made them extinct.
16. We have not created the heavens and the earth,
and all that lies between them, out of fun.
17. If We had pleased to make a plaything
We could have made it Ourself,
if We had cared to do so.
18. In fact We strike the truth against the false,
which shatters it, and it disappears.
Woe to you for what you attribute (to Him)!
19. Whosoever is in the heavens and the earth
belongs to Him;
and those who are near Him do not disdain
to worship Him or weary (of His service),
20. Nor cease to endeavour praising Him night and day.
21. Or have they taken gods from the earth
who can raise the dead?
22. Had there been gods apart from God,
both (the heavens and the earth) would have been despoiled.
Much too glorious is God, the Lord of the mighty throne,
for things they assert!
23. He cannot be questioned about what He does,
but they will be questioned.
24. Have they taken gods besides God?
Say: "Then bring your proof.
Here is the Book of those who are with me,
and the Book of those who have gone before me."
But most men do not know the truth
and turn away.
25. We have not sent an apostle before you
without instructing him
that there is no god but I,
so worship Me.
26. And yet they say: "Ar-Rahman has begotten a son."
Too exalted is He!
In fact, those (they call His sons) were His honoured votaries.
27. They did not precede Him in their speech,
and acted on His command.
28. He knows what was there before them and what came
          after them;

Al-Anbiya

and they did not intercede for any one but whom He willed,
and they were filled with awe of Him.
29. If any one of them said: "I am God besides Him,"
We should award him Hell;
for this is how We requite the evil-doers.

Do not these unbelievers see
that the heavens and the earth were an integrated mass,*
then We split them and made
every living thing from water? **
Will they not believe even then?
31. We placed stabilisers in the earth
so that as it revolved with them you lived undisturbed;
and We provided passageways between them
so that men may find their way;
32. And We made the sky a well-protected roof.
Still they turn away from His signs!
33. It is He who created night and day,
the sun and the moon, revolving on its orbit.
34. We have given no man everlastingness before you.
So then if you die, will they live ever after?
35. Every soul will know the taste of death.
We tempt you with evil and with good as a trial;
and to Us you will return.
36. But when the unbelievers see you
they make fun of you (and say):
"Is this the one who mentions your gods (deridingly)?"
Yet in Ar-Rahman they disbelieve!
37. Man is made of inordinate haste.
We will show you Our signs,
then you will not desire to hasten (the punishment).
38. Yet they say: "When will the promised threat come to pass,
if you speak the truth?"
39. If only the unbelievers could apprehend the moment
when they would neither be able to ward off
the fire from their faces and their backs, nor help reach them!
40. It will come upon them unawares
confounding them, and they will not be able to keep it back,
nor will they be given respite.
41. Many apostles have been scoffed before you;
but they who scoffed were themselves caught
by what they had ridiculed.

Say: "Who guards you from Ar-Rahman

---

* See note on page 282. ** See note on page 96.

by night and by day?"
Yet from a mention of their Lord they turn away.
43. Or do they have lords of their own
besides Us who can defend them?
But they are not able to help themselves,
nor can they find protection against Us.
44. We allowed them and their fathers
time to enjoy till the very end of their lives.
Do they not see Us advancing
into the land, reducing its frontiers?
Would they still prevail?
45. Say: "I am warning you by God's command."
But the deaf do not hear the call when they are warned.
46. Even if a whiff of the Lord's chastisement
were to touch them they would surely say:
"Ah woe, alas, we were surely sinful."
47. We shall fix the scales of justice
on the Day of Resurrection,
so that none will be wronged in the least;
and even if it were equal to a mustard seed in weight
We shall take it (into account).
We are sufficient for computation.
48. We gave Moses and Aaron the Criterion,
and a light and reminder for those
who take heed for themselves,
49. Who are fearful of their Lord inwardly
and dread the Hour.
50. And this is a blessed reminder that We have sent down.
Will you then deny it?

W e had earlier given Abraham
true direction, for We knew him well.
52. When he said to his father and his people:
"What are these idols to which you cling so passionately?"
53. They replied: "We found our fathers worshipping them."
54. He said: "You and your fathers were in clear error."
55. They said: "Are you speaking in earnest,
or only jesting?"
56. He said: "In fact it was your Lord,
the Lord of the heavens and the earth, who created them;
and I bear witness to this.
57. I swear by God I will do something to your idols
when you have turned your backs and gone."
58. So he smashed them up to pieces
with the exception of the biggest,
so that they may turn to it.

Al-Anbiya

59. They asked (on return): "Who has done this to our gods?
He is surely a mischief-monger."
60. They said: "We heard a youth talk about them.
He is called Abraham."
61. "Bring him before the people," they said,
"that they may bear witness."
62. "Did you do this to our gods, O Abraham?" they enquired.
63. "No," he said. "It was done
by that chief of theirs.
Ask him in case they can speak."
64. Then they thought and observed:
"Surely you are yourselves unjust."
65. Then crestfallen (they confessed):
"Truly, as you know, they cannot speak."
66. (So Abraham) said: "Then why do you worship something
apart from God that cannot profit you or do you harm?
67. Fie on you and those you worship besides God!
Will you not understand?"
68. They said: "Burn him, and save your gods,
if you are men of action."
69. "Turn cold, O fire," We said, "and give safety to Abraham."
70. They wished to entrap him,
but We made them greater losers.
71. So We delivered him and Lot, and brought them to the
land
We had blessed for all the people.
72. And We bestowed on him Isaac,
and Jacob as an additional gift,
and made them righteous.
73. And We made them leaders to guide (the people) by Our
command;
and We inspired them to perform good deeds
and observe their moral obligations and pay the zakat;
and they obeyed Us.
74. To Lot We gave wisdom and knowledge,
and saved him from a people who acted villainously
and were certainly wicked and disobedient.
75. Thus We admitted him to Our grace.
He is surely one of the righteous.

Remember) Noah when he called to Us before this.
We heard him and saved him and those with him from great
distress;
77. And We helped him against the people
who rejected Our signs as lies.
They were a wicked people indeed,

so We drowned them one and all.
78. (Remember) David and Solomon, when they pronounced
judgement about the field which was eaten up
at night by sheep belonging to certain people.
We were witness to their judgement.
79. We made Solomon understand the case,
and bestowed on each wisdom and knowledge,
We subdued the al-jibal with David
to sing Our praises, and at-tair.*
It is We who did it.
80. And We taught him the art of making coats of mail
to shield you from each other's violence.
Will you not be grateful even then?
81. We made tempestuous winds obedient to Solomon
which blew swiftly to sail at his bidding
(with his ships) to the land We had blessed.
We are cognisant of every thing.
82. And many of the devils (We also made obedient to him)
who dived for him, and did many other things;
and We kept watch over them.
83. (Remember) Job when he called to his Lord:
"I am afflicted with distress,
and You are the most compassionate of all."
84. So We heard his cry and relieved him of the misery he was
     in.
We restored his family to him,
and along with them gave him others similar to them
as a grace from Us and reminder for those
who are obedient.
85. (Remember) Ishmael, Edris and Dhu'l-Kifl.
They were men of fortitude,
86. And they were admitted to Our grace.
Verily they were among the doers of good.
87. And (remember) Dhu 'n-Noon (Jonah of the fish),
when he went away in anger
and imagined We will not test him (with distress).
Then he called out from the darkness:
"There is no god other than You. All glory to You;
surely I was a sinner."
88. We heard his cry, and saved him from the anguish.
That is how We deliver those who believe.

---

* Although al-jibal and at-tair commonly mean mountains and birds respectively here they mean
chiefs of tribes and small kingdoms. See note on page 386. The note on page 322 may also be seen
for the metonymic use of some common nouns. Verse 81 above refers to Solomon's maritime trade
and his fleet which used to sail to Ophir down the Red Sea.

89. (Remember) Zachariah when he called to his Lord:
"Do not leave me alone (and childless),
for you are the best of givers."
90. So We heard him and gave him John,
and cured his wife (of barrenness).
These were men who vied in good deeds with one another,
and prayed to Us with love and awe,
and were meek before Us.
91. (Remember) her who preserved her chastity,
into whom We breathed a new life from Us,
and made her and her son a token for mankind.
92. Verily this your order is one order,
and I am your Lord; so worship Me.
93. But they split up the order among themselves;
(yet) all of them have to come back to Me.

So he who does the right and is a believer,
will not have his labour denied,
for We are congnisant of it.
95. It is imperative that a habitation We have destroyed
will not desist (from unbelief)
96. Until when the way is opened up for Gog and Magog
and they press from every elevated place,
97. And the certain promise (of Doom) comes near.
Then the eyes of unbelievers will be fixed in horror,
(and they will cry:) "Ah, woe betide,
we were indeed heedless of this,
and were oppressors and unjust."
98. Verily you and those you worship other than God
will be faggots for Hell; and come to it you will.
99. Had they really been gods they would not have entered it:
They will all abide in it for ever.
100. There will only be groaning for them,
and they will not hear any thing.
101. But those for whom a good reward had been fore-ordained
by Us, will be far removed from it,
102. And will not hear its hissing, and will live for ever
in the midst of what their hearts desire.
103. They will have safety from the mighty terror,
and angels will receive them, (saying:)
"This is your day which had been promised you."
104. The day We shall roll up the heavens
like a written scroll,
We shall revert it (to nothing)
as it was before We first created it.
This is a promise incumbent on Us;

We will certainly fulfil it.

105. We had prescribed in the Book of Psalms after the reminder
and admonition, that those of Our creatures who are good
will in the end rule the earth.

106. Verily there is a message in this
for people who are devout.

107. We have sent you as a benevolence
to the creatures of the world.

108. Say: "This is what has been revealed to me:
'Your God is one and only God.'
So will you bow in homage to Him?"

109. If they turn away, tell them:
"I have warned you all alike.
I do not know if what has been promised you is near
or far away.

110. He knows surely what you say aloud,
and what you hide within your breasts.

111. I do not know if this be a trial for you,
or a little advantage for a while."

112. "Judge in truth (between us), O Lord," he said.
"Our Lord is merciful,
whose help we seek
against what you attribute."

---

* Note on v. 30.

Space and matter were an integrated mass, or energy, which was 'split up' through the creative force
of the word (God's command embodied in) *Kun*, Be, (2:117) in a given moment of space-time, from
which matter, space, time had their origin. This 'splitting up' led to an explosion which has led to the
recent astro-physical theory of creation, known as the Big Bang. So would the world come to an end,
says the Qur'an, on the Day of Doom: See 82:1-2; 89;21; 99:1; 101:4-5; 102:6-7, etc.

22 The Pilgrimage

Al-Ḥajj: Madani

In the name of Allah, most benevolent, ever-merciful.

O YOU PEOPLE, fear your Lord.
The great upheaval of the Hour will indeed be terrible.
2. The day you see it
every suckling female will forget her suckling,
and every pregnant female will discharge her burden.
You will see men drunk,
yet it will not be intoxication.
The torment of God will be severe.
3. And yet there are men who contend about God
without understanding,
and follow every wayward devil
4. Who, it is inscribed, will beguile
whoever follows him,
and lead him to the torment of Hell.
5. If you have any doubt, O men,
about being raised to life again,
(remember) that We created you from dust,*
then a drop of semen, then an embryo,**
then a chewed up lump of flesh shaped and shapeless,
that We may reveal (the various steps) to you.
We keep what We please in the womb for a certain time,
then you come out as a child, then reach the prime of age.
Some of you die, some reach the age of dotage
when they forget what they knew, having known it once.
You see the earth all withered, then We send down rain
upon it, and it bestirs itself, swells,
and brings forth every kind of beauteous verdure.
6. That is so for God is the undeniable Reality.
It is He who brings the dead to life,
for He has power over every thing.
7. The Hour will come without a doubt,
and God will raise those who are dead.

----

* This refers to the evolutionary process.
** This goes on to describe the reproductive procedure.

8. Yet there are some who contend about God
without any knowledge or guidance or enlightening Book,
9. Turning their backs that they may lead
away from the path of God.
For such there is disgrace in the world,
and on the Day of Judgement
We shall make them taste the torment of burning.
10. That is on account of what you had done in the past;
yet God is not unjust to His creatures.

There are some men who worship God only from the
    margin.
If there is some profit they are content;
but if calamity befalls them
they turn about,
thus losing both this world and the next.
This is indeed a palpable loss.
12. Leaving God they pray to those
who cannot harm or profit them.
That is the limit of going astray.
13. They pray to him whose bane
is more imminent than his boon:
How bad the protector and how bad
the associate!
14. God will admit those who believe and do the right
to gardens full of rippling streams.
Verily God does as He pleases.
15. He who thinks that God will not help him in this world
and the next should stretch a rope to the sky
then cut it off and see
if his mind is relieved (of doubts) by this stratagem.*
16. That is why We have sent down these clear revelations,
for God gives guidance whomsoever He please.
17. God will judge between those who believe
and the Jews, the Sabians,** Christians and the Magians***
and the idolaters, on the Day of Judgement.
Verily God is witness to every thing.
18. Do you see how all things in heavens and the earth,
the sun, the moon, the stars, the mountains, trees and beasts,
and men in abundance, pay homage to God?
Yet there are many who deserve the punishment.
And whosoever God disgraces will have none
to raise him up in honour. God does verily as He will.
19. These two (believers and unbelievers) are disputants,

---

* See Note 1 on p. 290. ** See Note 2 and *** Note 3, on page 290.

who contend about their Lord.
But they who disbelieve
will be fitted out with garments of flames.
Boiling water will be poured down over their heads
20. Which will dissolve every thing within their bellies,
and their skins.
21. There are iron maces for them.
22. As often as they try to escape from its anguish
they would be put back into (the fire),
and taste the torment of burning.

God will surely admit those who believe and do the right
to gardens with rivers running by,
where they will be decked in bracelets of gold
and of pearls; and of silk will be their garments.
24. They will be guided with gentle words,
and guided to the commended path.
25. As for those who disbelieve,
and obstruct the way of God and the holy Mosque
which We have set down for all men,
the native and the visitor alike.
Whoever puts obstructions in this mischievously
will taste of painful punishment.

When We chose the site of the House for Abraham
(We said:) "Associate no one with Me,
and clean My House for those who will circumambulate it,
stand (in reverence), and bow in homage
27. Announce the Pilgrimage to the people.
They will come to you on foot and riding along distant roads
on lean and slender beasts,
28. In order to reach the place of advantage for them,
and to pronounce the name of God on appointed days
over cattle He has given them for food;
then eat of the meat and feed the needy and the poor.
29. Let them then attend to their persons
and complete the rites of pilgrimage,
fulfil their vows and circuit round the ancient House.
30. Apart from this, whoever respects the sacred ordinances of
        God,
will find a better reward for him with his Lord.
You are allowed to eat all cattle
except those already mentioned to you.
Avoid the repugnance of idols, and false and frivolous talk.
31. Turn uprightly to God
without ascribing compeers to Him;

for he who associates any one with God
is like a thing that falls from the sky
and is either snatched away by birds
or carried far away by the wind.
32. All this, and honouring the offerings to God,
comes from purity of heart.
33. There are advantages for you in these (cattle) up to a time,
then their place is the ancient House for sacrifice.

For every community We have ordained certain rites
that they may commemorate the name of God by reading it
over the cattle We have given them for sacrifice.
Your God is one God,
so be obedient to Him.
Give good tidings to those who bow in obedience to God,
35. Whose hearts are filled with awe
when the name of God is mentioned before them,
who endure with fortitude what befalls them,
and fulfil their moral obligations, and expend
of what We have given them.
36. We have made the camels signs of God for you.
There is good for you in this.
So pronounce the name of God over them
as they stand with their forefeet in a line.
When they have fallen (slaughtered) on their sides,
eat of (their meat) and feed those who are content with little,
and those who supplicate.
That is why We have brought them under your subjugation
so that you may be grateful.
37. It is not their meat or blood that reaches God:
It is the fealty of your heart that reaches Him.
That is why He has subjugated them to you
that you may glorify God for having shown you the way.
So give glad tidings to those who are doers of good.
38. God will certainly defend the believers.
Surely God does not like the traitors who deny the truth.

Permission is granted those (to take up arms)
who fight because they were oppressed.
God is certainly able to give help to those
40. Who were driven away from their homes
for no other reason than they said: "Our Lord is God."
And if God had not restrained some men through some others,
monastries, churches, synagogues and mosques,
where the name of God is honoured most,
would have been razed.

God will surely help those who help Him, —
Verily God is all-powerful and all-mighty, —
41. Those who would be firm in devotion, give zakat,*
and enjoin what is good and forbid what is wrong,
if We gave them authority in the land.
But the resultance of things rests with God.
42. If they accuse you of falsehood,
(remember that) the people of Noah, 'Ad and Thamud
had accused (their apostles) before,
43. And the people of Abraham and Lot,
44. And the people of Midian too.
Moses was also accused of lies.
So I allowed the infidels respite and then seized them.
How was My reprobation then!
45. How many a habitation given to wickedness have We
        destroyed,
whose roofs tumbled down, which fell into ruins.
How many a well and fortress reinforced lie abandoned!
46. Have they not travelled in the land that they could have
the heart to understand, and ears to hear?
It is not the eyes alone that do not see,
oblivious are the hearts within their breasts.
47. That is how they ask you to hasten the punishment;
but God does not go back on His promise.
Verily a day with your Lord is equal
by your reckoning to a thousand years.
48. To how many habitations did We give respite,
though given to wickedness, and then seized them.
To Me they had to come back in the end.

Tell them: "O men, it's my duty to warn you clearly."
50. For those who believe and do the right
is forgiveness and gracious provision.
51. But those who try to defeat Our signs
are people of Hell.
52. We have sent no messenger or apostle before you
with whose recitations Satan did not tamper.
Yet God abrogates what Satan interpolates;
then He confirms His revelations,
for God is all-knowing and all-wise.
53. This is in order to make the interpolations
of Satan a test for those
whose hearts are diseased and hardened:
Surely the sinners have gone far in dissent.

* See note on page 290.

54. At the same time those who have been given knowledge
may know that this is the truth from your Lord,
and come to believe in it,
and their hearts become submissive to Him.
Verily God guides those who believe, to the even path.
55. The infidels will remain in doubt about it
till the Hour overtakes them unawares, or the punishment
of the barren day destructive should come upon them.
56. The order will be God's on that Day;
He will judge between them.
Then those who had come to believe and done the right
will be in gardens of delight.
57. But those who did not believe
and called Our revelations lies,
will be given disgraceful punishment.

Those who left their homes in the way of God,
and then were killed or died,
will surely be given a better provision by God,
for God is surely the best of providers.
59. God will surely lead them to a place
with which they will be gratified.
Verily God is all-knowing and forbearing.
60. Whosoever retaliates
to the extent of injury suffered by him,
and is wronged again, will certainly be helped by God.
Verily God is forgiving and kind.
61. That is so for God
turns night into day and day into night,
for God is all-hearing and all-seeing;
62. That is so for God is the undeniable truth,
and what they invoke apart from Him is false;
yet God is all-high and supreme.
63. Do you not see how God sends down water from the sky,
and in the morning the earth turns green?
Truly God is benign and well-informed.
64. Whatsoever is in the heavens and the earth
belongs to Him.
Surely God is all-sufficing, worthy of praise.

Do you not see God has harnessed
all that is in the earth, to your service?
And the boats ply in the ocean by His command.
He holds the sky in position lest
it should fall upon the earth save by His dispensation.
Verily God is compassionate and kind to men.

66. It is He who gives you life, then makes you die;
then He will bring you back to life again.
Man is surely most ungrateful.
67. We have determined for each community
a way of worship which they follow.
So they should not contend with you in this matter;
and you should go on calling them to your Lord.
You are surely on the right path.
68. If they argue with you, tell them:
"God knows well what you are doing.
69. God will judge between you on the Day of Judgement
in what you are at variance."
70. Do you not know that God knows
whatever is in the heavens and the earth?
This is surely in accordance with the law.
This is certainly how (the law of) God works inevitably.
71. Yet they worship in place of God
that for which no authority has been sent to them,
and of which they have no knowledge.
The wicked will have none to help them.
72. When Our clear messages are read out to them
you can see denial on the faces of unbelievers.
They can hardly restrain themselves from attacking
those who recite Our revelations.
Tell them: "Should I give you news of something worse than
this? —
Hell, which God has promised the infidels.
How evil a destination!

O men, give ear to this parable:
Those you worship other than God can never create
as much as a fly, even if they get together to do so;
and if the fly were to rob them of a thing
they would not be able to snatch it away from it.
How weak the seeker and how weak the sought!
74. They do not esteem God with the right estimation.
God is surely all-powerful and all-mighty.
75. God chooses messengers from the angels and human beings.
Verily God is all-hearing and all-seeing.
76. He knows what is before them and what lies behind them,
and all things go back to God.
77. O you who believe, bow in adoration,
worship your Lord and do what is good
that you may find success.
78. Strive in the way of God with a service worthy of Him.
He has chosen you and laid no hardship on you in the way of

faith,
the faith of your forbear Abraham.
He named you Muslim earlier,
and in this (Qur'an),
in order that the Prophet be witness over you,
and you be witness over mankind.
So be firm in devotion, pay the zakat,
and hold on firmly to God.
He is your friend:
How excellent a friend is He,
how excellent a helper!

وَمَا جَعَلَ عَلَيْكُمْ فِي الدِّينِ مِنْ حَرَجٍ مِّلَّةَ

أَبِيكُمْ إِبْرَاهِيمَ هُوَ سَمَّاكُمُ الْمُسْلِمِينَ هُ مِن

قَبْلُ وَفِي هَذَا لِيَكُونَ الرَّسُولُ شَهِيدًا عَلَيْكُمْ

وَتَكُونُوا شُهَدَاءَ عَلَى النَّاسِ فَأَقِيمُوا الصَّلَوٰةَ وَ

اتُوا الزَّكَوٰةَ وَاعْتَصِمُوا بِاللَّهِ هُوَ مَوْلَىٰكُمْ فَنِعْمَ

الْمَوْلَىٰ وَنِعْمَ النَّصِيرُ ۞

---

1. Note on v. 15. This has the same connotation as the Persian proverb *asman az kuja wa risman az kuja:* where is the heaven and where is the rope? used when falsehood is opposed to truth. It shows the futility of deciding in one's mind that God will not help.
2. Another name of the Elkesaites, Jewish cult that practised baptism, which was favoured by the Essenes (1st century A.D.), called Sabians after Sobiai who was the successor of Eleksai, the founder.
3. Zoroastrians, called Magians, as relating to the Magi, pl. of Magus, Ar. *majoos.*

Note on Zakat, v. 41. *Az-zakat* means to better, to increase, as well as welfare, betterment, growth, etc, as *azka* means that which has goodness, gives nourishment, as in 18:81, or good, as in 19:19, or nourishes, as in 91:9. *Zakat* and *salat* have often been used together in the Qur'an, being the basic elements of the Qur'anic Order. Since *Salat*, discussed briefly in the Preface, stands for devotion and fulfilling one's duties and obligations arising from *'ubudiyat*, devotion, service, as *'abd*, creature or servant or slave, of God the Creator, *zakat* stands for striving for the welfare and betterment, or growth and development of mankind, as is clear from 23:4. *Zakat*, thus, constitutes the socio-economic aspect within the overall concept of *salat* as service to God in its widest connotation, as *taqwa* constitutes the moral aspect.

Being the socio-economic aspect, the dimensions of *zakat* are collective; and its purpose of nourishment, growth, betterment and welfare cannot be achieved without the participation of each individual by contributing to the common good physically or intellectually as *ita-e-zakat*, and by contributing from his wealth to enable the people or the institution, or government set up to administer the affairs of the people in an Islamic Order (whose entire income is meant for the betterment, growth and progress of the people) to utilise it for the welfare and development of the members of society and mankind, the excess going to the common treasury. That is why, even though obligatory for all Muslims the Qur'an has not prescribed any fixed amount, limit, or percentage of wealth for *zakat*.

Other contributions that are expected to be made by Muslims for the well-being of fellow-men, fall under *sadaqat*, charities, specified in 9:60 and 9:103 which include *zakat* payment of which, however, is obligatory. The category of those deserving help under *zakat*, the *mustahiqeen*, is thus delineated in 9:60, along with those entitled to receive *sadaqat*. The purpose of voluntary contributions is not only the betterment of fellow-beings but also to restrict the accumulation of wealth in a few hands, and to encourage its free flow and circulation.

Only non-Muslims are not expected to give zakat, for whom *jaziya* is prescribed. See 9:29 and note on p. 165.

23 The True Believers

Al-Mu'minūn: Makki

In the name of Allah, most benevolent, ever-merciful.

THE TRUE BELIEVERS will be successful,
2. Who are humble in their service,
3. Who shun all frivolities,
4. Who strive for betterment;
5. Who guard their sex
6. Except from their wives and women slaves of old
are free of blame,
7. But those who covet more than this
will be transgressors;
8. And those who fulfil their trusts
and keep their promises;
9. And those who are watchful of their acts of prayer.
10. These are the real gainers,
11. Who will inherit Paradise,
and live in it for ever.
12. We created man from the finest extract of clay,
13. Then We placed him as a sperm
in a firmly established lodging;
14. Then We fashioned the sperm into an embryo,
then fashioned the embryo into a shapeless lump of flesh;
then from the lump of flesh We fashioned bones,
then clothed the bones with flesh.
Thus We formed him into a new creation.
So blessed be God the best of creators.
15. And then you will certainly die,
16. Then will be raised up on the Day of Resurrection.
17. We made several highways one over the other above you.
We are not neglectful of creation.
18. We send down water from the sky in determined measure,
and store it up in the earth;
and We have power to drain it away.
19. We grow orchards of dates and grapes from it for you,
which yield fruits in abundance that you eat.
20. The tree that grows on Mount Sinai

yields oil and seasoning for those who eat.
21. There are lessons for you in the cattle
from whose bellies We give you milk to drink,
and there are other advantages that you derive from them,
and some of them you eat;
22. And you are carried on them and on boats.

We sent Noah to his people.
He said: "O my people, worship God,
for you have no other god but He.
Will you not take heed for yourselves?"
24. The chiefs of his people, who did not believe,
said: "He is only a man like you.
He wishes to acquire ascendancy over you.
If God had willed He would have sent down angels.
We never heard this from our elders.
25. He is only a man possessed;
so wait and watch him for a time."
26. "O my Lord," prayed (Noah), "help me against them,
for they accuse me of lies."
27. So We asked him to build the ark
under Our eyes and guidance, (and said):
"When Our command is issued and the source of water boils
       over,
put a pair of every species in it, and your family
except those for whom
Our sentence has been passed already;
and do not speak to Me for those who are wicked:
They will be drowned.
28. When you and those with you have boarded the ark,
say: 'All praise be to God who has delivered us
from the people who were sinful.'
29. And say: 'O Lord, disembark me in a welcome place;
You are the best of deliverers.' "
30. There were surely signs in this;
We will surely put you to the test.
31. After them We raised a new generation.
32. Then We sent to them an apostle from among them
(who said): "Worship God, for you have no other god but He.
Will you not take heed and fear God?"

The chiefs of the people who did not believe
and denied the life to come,
though We had given them good things of this life to enjoy,
(said): "He is only a mortal like you.
He eats as you do, and drinks as you drink.

Al-Mu'minun

34. So if you follow a man like yourself
you will certainly be doomed.
35. Does he give you a promise that when you are dead
and turned to dust and bones,
you will be raised to life again?
36. How far-fetched what you are promised;
37. There is only the life of this world:
We die and we live:
there is no rising from the dead for us.
38. He is just a man who invents a lie about God;
we cannot believe in him."
39. (The apostle prayed): "O Lord, deliver me,
for they accuse me of lies."
40. Answered (the Lord): "They shall wake up repenting
    soon."
41. So they were rightly seized by a mighty blast;
and We turned them into mouldy rubbish:
A good riddance of the wicked people!
42. Then after them We raised other generations.
43. No nation can live beyond its alloted time, or lag behind.
44. Then We sent Our apostles one after the other.
Every time an apostle came to a people they denied him.
So We made one follow the other (to its doom),
and turned them into bygone tales.
Cursed be the people who do not believe!
45. Then We sent Moses and his brother Aaron
with Our miracles and clear proofs
46. To Pharaoh and his nobles
who behaved with arrogance, for they were a conceited lot,
47. And said: "Should we believe in two men like yourselves,
whose people are our subjects?"
48. Then they accused them of lies,
and joined the company of those who were destroyed.
49. And We gave the Book to Moses
so that they may be guided.
50. And We made the son of Mary and his mother a sign,
and gave them shelter on an elevated ground,
sequestered, watered by a spring.

O you apostles, eat things that are clean,
and do things that are good.
We are surely cognisant of what you do.
52. Verily this your order is one order,
and I am your Lord, so fear Me.
53. But then they divided up their order into different creeds,
each section rejoicing in what it had come to have.

Al-Mu'minun

54. So leave them to their ignorance for a time.
55. Do they think that by increasing their wealth and
children
56. We are hastening to reward them for good deeds?
No. They do not comprehend.
57. Surely those who live in awe of their Lord,
58. Who believe in their Lord's revelations,
59. Who do not associate any one with their Lord,
60. Who give whatsoever they give (in His way),
and their hearts tremble with fear
that they have to go back to their Lord,
61. Are the ones who hasten to goodness and outpace the
others.
62. We do not burden a soul beyond capacity,
for We have a record that tells the truth.
No wrong will be done to any one.
63. Yet their hearts are oblivious of this; and besides,
they are busy with other things,
64. So that when We seize the affluent among them with
affliction,
they will begin to implore for help.
65. "Do not supplicate for help today;
you will not be rescued by Us;
66. For when My revelations were read out to you
you turned back on your heels and fled
67. Insolently, treating them like tales told at night."
68. Why did they not think over the message?
Or has something come to them which had not
come to their fathers?
69. Or did they not recognise their apostle,
and rejected him?
70. Or do they say that he is possessed?
In fact, he has brought the truth to them,
but most of them abhor the truth.
71. Had truth been subject to their whims
the heavens and the earth and all those within them
would have been depraved.
In fact We had sent them their reminder,
but they turned away from good advice.
72. Or do you ask of them any tribute?
In that case the tribute of your Lord is better,
for He is the best of providers.
73. You are surely calling them to the right path.
74. But those who believe not in the Hereafter
turn away from the straight path.
75. If We took compassion on them

Al-Mu'minun

and removed the affliction they are in,
they would only wander lost in confusion.
76. We had seized them with the punishment,
but they did not bow before their Lord
nor turned to Him in humility,
77. So that when at last We open up the gate
of severe punishment on them
they will be overwhelmed with despair.

It is He who gave you hearing, sight, and hearts,
but only few of you give thanks.
79. It is He who multiplied you on the earth,
and it will be before Him that you will be gathered.
80. It is He who gives you life and death,
and His the alternation of night and day.
Even then you do not understand,
81. And talk as did the people of old.
82. They say: "When we are dead and turned to dust and
                                              bones,
shall we be raised to life again?
83. We and our fathers were promised this before;
it is nothing but ancient lore!"
84. Say: "To whom does the earth and whosoever is upon it
then belong, if you know?"
85. They will say: "To God."
Say: "Then why do you not bethink yourselves?"
86. Say: "Then who is the Lord of the seven skies?
And who is the Lord of the mighty Throne?"
87. They will say: "God."
Say: "Then why do you not obey and fear Him?"
88. Say: "Whose is the sovereignty over all things,
who protects, and against whom there is no protection?
(Answer) if you have knowledge."
89. They will say: "God's."
Say: "Then why are you so deluded?"
90. In fact We have sent the truth to them,
but they are liars.
91. God has not begotten a son,
nor is there any god besides Him.
Had this been so, each god would have taken away
what he had created with him,
and some would have risen over the others.
God is much too glorious for what they
attribute (to Him)!
92. The knower of the absent and the present,
too exalted is He for what they associate (with Him)!

وَلَوْ رَحِمْنَاهُمْ وَكَشَفْنَا مَا بِهِمْ مِّن ضُرٍّ لَّلَجُّوا فِى
طُغْيَانِهِمْ يَعْمَهُونَ ۝

وَلَقَدْ أَخَذْنَاهُم بِالْعَذَابِ فَمَا اسْتَكَانُوا لِرَبِّهِمْ
وَمَا يَتَضَرَّعُونَ ۝

حَتَّىٰ إِذَا فَتَحْنَا عَلَيْهِم بَابًا ذَا عَذَابٍ شَدِيدٍ إِذَا
هُمْ فِيهِ مُبْلِسُونَ ۝

وَهُوَ الَّذِى أَنشَأَ لَكُمُ السَّمْعَ وَالْأَبْصَارَ وَالْأَفْئِدَةَ
قَلِيلًا مَّا تَشْكُرُونَ ۝

وَهُوَ الَّذِى ذَرَأَكُمْ فِى الْأَرْضِ وَإِلَيْهِ تُحْشَرُونَ ۝

وَهُوَ الَّذِى يُحْيِى وَيُمِيتُ وَلَهُ اخْتِلَافُ اللَّيْلِ وَ
النَّهَارِ أَفَلَا تَعْقِلُونَ ۝

بَلْ قَالُوا مِثْلَ مَا قَالَ الْأَوَّلُونَ ۝

قَالُوا أَإِذَا مِتْنَا وَكُنَّا تُرَابًا وَعِظَامًا أَإِنَّا
لَمَبْعُوثُونَ ۝

لَقَدْ وُعِدْنَا نَحْنُ وَآبَاؤُنَا هَٰذَا مِن قَبْلُ إِنْ
هَٰذَا إِلَّا أَسَاطِيرُ الْأَوَّلِينَ ۝

قُل لِّمَنِ الْأَرْضُ وَمَن فِيهَا إِن كُنتُمْ
تَعْلَمُونَ ۝

سَيَقُولُونَ لِلَّهِ قُلْ أَفَلَا تَذَكَّرُونَ ۝

قُلْ مَن رَّبُّ السَّمَاوَاتِ السَّبْعِ وَرَبُّ الْعَرْشِ
الْعَظِيمِ ۝

سَيَقُولُونَ لِلَّهِ قُلْ أَفَلَا تَتَّقُونَ ۝

قُلْ مَن بِيَدِهِ مَلَكُوتُ كُلِّ شَيْءٍ وَهُوَ يُجِيرُ وَلَا
يُجَارُ عَلَيْهِ إِن كُنتُمْ تَعْلَمُونَ ۝

سَيَقُولُونَ لِلَّهِ قُلْ فَأَنَّىٰ تُسْحَرُونَ ۝

بَلْ أَتَيْنَاهُم بِالْحَقِّ وَإِنَّهُمْ لَكَاذِبُونَ ۝

مَا اتَّخَذَ اللَّهُ مِن وَلَدٍ وَمَا كَانَ مَعَهُ مِنْ إِلَٰهٍ إِذًا
لَّذَهَبَ كُلُّ إِلَٰهٍ بِمَا خَلَقَ وَلَعَلَا بَعْضُهُمْ عَلَىٰ
بَعْضٍ سُبْحَانَ اللَّهِ عَمَّا يَصِفُونَ ۝

عَالِمِ الْغَيْبِ وَالشَّهَادَةِ فَتَعَالَىٰ عَمَّا يُشْرِكُونَ ۝

Say: "O Lord, if I am made to see
what has been promised them,
94. Then do not, O Lord, put me among the sinners."
95. We have certainly the power to make you see
what We have promised them.
96. Dispel evil with what is good.
We know well what they attribute (to Us).
97. Say: "My Lord, I seek refuge in You
from the evil promptings of the devils.
98. I seek refuge in You lest they come to me."
99. (But the unbelievers will persist)
until when death comes to one of them
he will say: "O Lord, send me back again
100. That I may do some good I did not do (in the world)."
Not so. These are only words he utters.
Behind them lies the intervening barrier
(stretching) to the day of their resurrection.
101. When the trumpet blast is sounded
no ties of lineage will hold among them,
nor will they ask after one another.
102. Only those whose scales are heavier in the balance
will find happiness.
103. But those whose scales are lighter
will perish and abide in Hell for ever.
104. Their faces will be scorched by flames,
and they will grin and scowl within it.
105. "Were not My messages read out to you?
But you denied them."
106. They will say: "O Lord, our misery overwhelmed us,
so we remained a people astray.
107. Get us out of this, O Lord.
If we transgress we will surely be sinful."
108. He will say: "Remain condemned in it,
and do not speak to Me.
109. There was a section among My creatures that said:
'O Lord, we believe. Forgive us and have mercy upon us,
for You are the best of the merciful.'
110. But you ridiculed them.
So much so that out of (spite) for them
you forgot to remember Me and laughed at them.
111. I have rewarded them this day for they were constant,
and they have come to attainment."
112. They will be asked: "How long did you live on the earth
in terms of years?"
113. They will say: "A day or less than a day.
Ask the enumerators of numbers."

Al-Mu'minun

114. He will say: "You stayed there only a moment, if you
knew.
115. Do you think We created you for nothing,
and that you will not return to Us?"
116. Exalted then be God, the King, the Real.
There is no god but He, the Lord of the glorious throne.
117. Whoever worships another god apart from God,
for which he holds no proof,
will have to account for it before his Lord.
Verily the unbelievers will not prosper.
118. Say: "My Lord, forgive and have mercy.
You are the best of the merciful."

قُلْ إِن لَّبِثْتُمْ إِلَّا قَلِيلًا لَّوْ أَنَّكُمْ كُنتُمْ تَعْلَمُونَ ⓜ
أَفَحَسِبْتُمْ أَنَّمَا خَلَقْنَاكُمْ عَبَثًا وَأَنَّكُمْ إِلَيْنَا لَا
تُرْجَعُونَ ⓜ
فَتَعَالَى اللَّهُ الْمَلِكُ الْحَقُّ لَا إِلَٰهَ إِلَّا هُوَ رَبُّ
الْعَرْشِ الْكَرِيمِ ⓜ
وَمَن يَدْعُ مَعَ اللَّهِ إِلَٰهًا آخَرَ لَا بُرْهَانَ لَهُ بِهِ
فَإِنَّمَا حِسَابُهُ عِندَ رَبِّهِ إِنَّهُ لَا يُفْلِحُ الْكَافِرُونَ ⓜ
وَقُل رَّبِّ اغْفِرْ وَارْحَمْ وَأَنتَ خَيْرُ الرَّاحِمِينَ ⓜ

24 The Light

An-Nūr: Madani

In the name of Allah, most benevolent, ever-merciful.

WE HAVE REVEALED this Surah and made it obligatory
as We have sent down clear injunctions in it
that you may be warned.
2. The adulteress and adulterer should be flogged
a hundred lashes each,
and no pity for them should deter you from the law of God,
if you believe in God and the Last Day;
and the punishment should be witnessed by a body of believers.
3. The adulterer can marry no one but
an adulteress or his partner (in the act)*,
and the adulteress cannot marry any
but an adulterer or her partner (in the act).
This is forbidden the believers.*
4. Those who defame chaste women
and do not bring four witnesses
should be punished with eighty lashes,
and their testimony should not be accepted afterwards,
for they are profligates,
5. Except those who repent after this and reform;
and God is surely forgiving and kind.
6. Those who accuse their wives and do not have
any witnesses except themselves,
should swear four times in the name of God,
the testimony of each such person being
that he is speaking the truth,
7. And (swear) a fifth time that if he tell a lie
the curse of God be on him.
8. The woman's punishment can be averted
if she swears four times by God as testimony
that her husband is a liar,
9. Her fifth oath being that the curse of God be on her
if her husband should be speaking the truth.
10. (This would not have been possible) if the grace
and benevolence of God were not upon you;

but God is compassionate and wise.

                                                             ﻉ تَوَّابُ حَكِيمٌ ۝

Those who spread lies
were a clique among you.
Do not think that it was bad for you:
In fact it has been good for you.
Each of them will pay for the sin he has committed,
and he who had greater share (of guilt)
will suffer grievous punishment.

12. Why did the faithful men and women not think well
of their people when they heard this, and said:
"This is a clear lie?"

13. Why did they not bring four witnesses
(in support of their charge)?
And since they did not bring the four witnesses
they are themselves liars in the sight of God.

14. Were it not for the grace of God and His mercy upon you
in this world and the next,
you would have suffered a great affliction
for the false accusation.

15. When you talked about it and said
what you did not know, and took it lightly —
though in the sight of God it was serious —

16. Why did you not say when you heard it:
"It is not for us to speak of it?
God preserve us, it is a great calumny!"

17. God counsels you not to do a thing like this,
if you are believers.

18. God explains His commands to you clearly,
for God is all-knowing and all-wise.

19. There is painful punishment in this world and the next
for those who like that immorality should spread
among the believers,
for God knows and you do not know.

20. But for the grace of God and His mercy
(much harm would have been done);
yet God is compassionate and kind.

O you who believe, do not follow
in the footsteps of Satan,
for he who follows in the footsteps of Satan
will be induced by him to what is shameful and forbidden.
But for the grace of God and His mercy upon you

---

* For v.3 (prepage) see note 1 on page 305.

none of you would have escaped undefiled;
but God makes whosoever He will grow in goodness,
for God is all-hearing and all-knowing.
22. Let not those who are men of plenty and means among you swear that they will not give
to their relatives and the poor
and those who leave their homes in the service of God.
They should forgive and overlook (their failings).
Would you not like God to forgive you?
And God is forgiving and kind.
23. Verily those who blaspheme unsuspecting chaste believing women
will be cursed in this world and the next;
and for them there will be severe punishment.
24. The day their tongues and hands and feet
bear witness to what they had done,
25. God will pay them on that day their just due in full,
and they will come to know that God
is the tangible Reality.
26. Bad women deserve bad men, and bad men are for bad women;
but good women are for good men, and good men for good women,
for they are innocent of what people say.
There is forgiveness for them and a gracious provision.

O you who believe, do not enter other houses except yours
without first asking permission and saluting the inmates.
This is better for you: You may haply take heed.
28. If you find that no one is in, then do not enter
unless you have received permission.
If you are asked to go away, turn back.
That is proper for you.
God is aware of what you do.
29. There is no harm in going into uninhabited houses
where there is some convenience for you,
as God has knowledge of what you hide and what you disclose.
30. Tell the believing men to lower their eyes
and guard their private parts. There is for them
goodness in this. God is aware of what they do.
31. Tell the believing women to lower their eyes,
guard their private parts, and not display their charms
except what is apparent outwardly,
and cover their bosoms with their veils
and not to show their finery

except to their husbands or their fathers or fathers-in-law,
their sons or step-sons, brothers, or their brothers' and sisters'
    sons,
or their women attendants or captives,
or male attendants who do not have any need (for women),
or boys not yet aware of sex.
They should not walk stamping their feet
lest they make known what they hide of their ornaments.
O believers, turn to God, every one of you,
so that you may be successful.

32. Marry off those who are single among you,
and those of your male and female servants who are righteous.
If they are poor, God will enrich them of His grace,
for God is bounteous and all-knowing.

33. Those who cannot afford to marry
should abstain from what is unlawful
until God enriches them by His grace.
And free those slaves you possess who wish to buy their
    freedom
after a written undertaking,
if you know they have some goodness,
and give them out of the riches God has given you.
Do not force your maids to prostitution
if they wish to lead married lives,
in order to get the benefits of this world
But if someone forces them, surely God (will forgive them)
after their forced helplessness,
for He is forgiving and kind.

34. We have sent down clear instructions to you,
and illustrations from (the accounts)
of those who have gone before you,
and a warning for those who take heed for themselves.

God is the light of the heavens and the earth.
The semblance of His light is that of a niche
in which is a lamp, the flame within a glass,
the glass a glittering star as it were, lit with the oil
of a blessed tree, the olive, neither of the East
nor of the West, whose oil appears to light up
even though fire touches it not, — light upon light.*
God guides to His light whom He will.
So does God advance precepts of wisdom for men,
for God has knowledge of every thing.

36. (The light is lit) in houses of worship

---

* See note on page 305.

An-Nur

يُسَبِّحُ لَهُ فِيهَا بِالْغُدُوِّ وَالْآصَالِ ۙ

which God has allowed to be raised,
and His name remembered in them.
His praises are sung there morning and evening,
37. By men not distracted from the remembrance of God
either by trade and commerce or buying and selling,
who stand by their devotional obligations
and pay the zakat, who fear the day
when hearts and eyes would flutter with trepidation

رِجَالٌ لَّا تُلْهِيهِمْ تِجَارَةٌ وَّلَا بَيْعٌ عَنْ ذِكْرِ اللّٰهِ
وَإِقَامِ الصَّلٰوةِ وَإِيتَآءِ الزَّكٰوةِ ۙ يَخَافُونَ يَوْمًا
تَتَقَلَّبُ فِيهِ الْقُلُوبُ وَالْأَبْصَارُ ۙ

38. That God may reward them for the best of their deeds,
and bestow more on them of His bounty,
for God gives whom He please without measure.

لِيَجْزِيَهُمُ اللّٰهُ أَحْسَنَ مَا عَمِلُوا وَيَزِيدَهُم مِّن
فَضْلِهٖ ۙ وَاللّٰهُ يَرْزُقُ مَن يَشَآءُ بِغَيْرِ حِسَابٍ ۝

39. As for those who disbelieve,
their deeds are like a mirage in the desert
which the thirsty takes for water
till he reaches it to find that there was nothing,
and finds God with him who settles his account,
for God is swift at the reckoning.

وَالَّذِينَ كَفَرُوا أَعْمَالُهُمْ كَسَرَابٍ بِقِيعَةٍ يَحْسَبُهُ
الظَّمْآنُ مَآءً ۙ حَتّٰى إِذَا جَآءَهُ لَمْ يَجِدْهُ شَيْئًا وَّ
وَجَدَ اللّٰهَ عِندَهُ فَوَفّٰهُ حِسَابَهُ ۙ وَاللّٰهُ سَرِيعُ
الْحِسَابِ ۝

40. Or like darkness in a wide, wide sea,
waves surging upon waves, with clouds overhanging,
darkness on darkness.
If you stretch your hand, you could hardly see it.
For him whom God does not give
any light, there is no light.

أَوْ كَظُلُمَاتٍ فِي بَحْرٍ لُّجِّيٍّ يَغْشَاهُ مَوْجٌ مِّن فَوْقِهٖ
مَوْجٌ مِّن فَوْقِهٖ سَحَابٌ ۙ ظُلُمَاتٌ بَعْضُهَا فَوْقَ بَعْضٍ
إِذَا أَخْرَجَ يَدَهُ لَمْ يَكَدْ يَرَاهَا ۙ وَمَن لَّمْ يَجْعَلِ اللّٰهُ
لَهُ نُورًا فَمَا لَهُ مِن نُّورٍ ۝

Have you not seen that all those who are in the
    heavens and the earth,
and the birds on the wing, sing the praises of God.
Each one knows its obligations and its duties,
and God knows whatever they do.

أَلَمْ تَرَ أَنَّ اللّٰهَ يُسَبِّحُ لَهُ مَن فِي السَّمٰوٰتِ وَالْأَرْضِ
وَالطَّيْرُ صَآفَّاتٍ ۙ كُلٌّ قَدْ عَلِمَ صَلَاتَهُ وَتَسْبِيحَهُ ۙ
وَاللّٰهُ عَلِيمٌ بِمَا يَفْعَلُونَ ۝

42. For God's is the kingdom of the heavens and the earth,
and the returning is to God.

وَلِلّٰهِ مُلْكُ السَّمٰوٰتِ وَالْأَرْضِ ۙ وَإِلَى اللّٰهِ الْمَصِيرُ ۝

43. Have you not seen that God drives the clouds,
then joins them together and puts them fold on fold.
Then you see the rain fall through them;
and He sends down hail from the sky where there are
    mountains of it,
and strikes those with it whom He will,
and wards it off from whomsoever He please.
His lightning could snatch away their eyes.

أَلَمْ تَرَ أَنَّ اللّٰهَ يُزْجِي سَحَابًا ثُمَّ يُؤَلِّفُ بَيْنَهُ ثُمَّ
يَجْعَلُهُ رُكَامًا فَتَرَى الْوَدْقَ يَخْرُجُ مِنْ خِلَالِهٖ ۙ وَيُنَزِّلُ
مِنَ السَّمَآءِ مِن جِبَالٍ فِيهَا مِنْ بَرَدٍ فَيُصِيبُ بِهٖ مَن
يَشَآءُ وَيَصْرِفُهُ عَن مَّن يَشَآءُ ۙ يَكَادُ سَنَا بَرْقِهٖ يَذْهَبُ
بِالْأَبْصَارِ ۝

44. It is God who alternates night and day.
There is surely a lesson in this for men of sight.

يُقَلِّبُ اللّٰهُ اللَّيْلَ وَالنَّهَارَ ۙ إِنَّ فِي ذٰلِكَ لَعِبْرَةً
لِّأُولِي الْأَبْصَارِ ۝

45. God created every moving thing from water:
One crawls on its belly,
one walks on two legs, another moves on four.
God creates whatsoever He will.
Indeed God has power over every thing.

وَاللّٰهُ خَلَقَ كُلَّ دَآبَّةٍ مِّن مَّآءٍ ۙ فَمِنْهُم مَّن يَمْشِي
عَلٰى بَطْنِهٖ ۙ وَمِنْهُم مَّن يَمْشِي عَلٰى رِجْلَيْنِ ۙ وَمِنْهُم
مَّن يَمْشِي عَلٰى أَرْبَعٍ ۙ يَخْلُقُ اللّٰهُ مَا يَشَآءُ ۙ إِنَّ
اللّٰهَ عَلٰى كُلِّ شَيْءٍ قَدِيرٌ ۝

46. We have surely sent down clear signs.
It is God who guides whom He will
to the path that is straight.

47. They say they believe in God and the Prophet,
and have come to believe,
yet a section of them turns back even after this;
and these are not believers.

48. When they are called to God and His Prophet,
that he may judge between them,
a section of them turns away.

49. Had right been on their side
they would have come to him submissively.

50. Is there a malady in their hearts,
or they are deluded, or afraid
that God and His Prophet would be unjust in dealing with
        them?
Not so; they are themselves unjust.

The answer of the believers when they are called
to God and His Apostle that he may judge between them, is:
"We hear and obey."
And they are the ones who will prosper.

52. Whoever obeys God and His Prophet,
fears God and does his duty to Him,
will surely find success.

53. They swear solemnly by God:
"If you command us we shall go forth,"
Say: "Do not swear. What is wanted is obedience, as should be.
God is certainly aware of what you do."

54. Say: "Obey God and obey the Apostle.
If you turn away, then for him is
his duty to fulfil,
and for you the burden that you carry;
yet if you obey him you will be rightly guided.
The duty of the Messenger is to convey the message clearly.

55. God has promised to make those of you
who believe and do the right, leaders in the land,
as He had made those before them,
and will establish their faith which He has chosen for them
and change their fear into security.
They will worship Me and not associate
any one with Me.
But those who disbelieve after this
will be reprobates.

56. So observe your devotional obligations, pay the zakat,
and obey the Apostle so that you may be shown mercy.

An-Nur

57. Do not think that unbelievers
will subvert (the authority of God) on earth.
Their abode is Hell; and what an evil destination!

O you who believe, let your dependants and those
who have not yet reached the age of puberty,
ask permission (to enter your presence) on three occasions:
Before the early morning prayer;
when you disrobe for the mid-day siesta;
and after prayer at night.
These are the three occasions of dishabille for you.
There is no harm if you or they visit one another
at other times (without permission).
God thus explains things to you clearly,
for God is all-knowing and all-wise.
59. When your children have reached the age of puberty,
they should similarly ask your leave (for entering)
as others did before them.
God thus clearly explains His commands to you,
for God is all-knowing and all-wise.
60. As for your women past the age of bearing children,
who have no hope of marriage, there is no harm
if they take off their outer garments,
but in such a way that they do not display their charms;
yet if they avoid this it would be better for them.
God is all-hearing and all-knowing.
61. There is no harm if the blind, the lame, the sick,
or you yourselves,
eat in your own houses or the houses of your fathers,
mothers, or your brothers' houses,
or those of your sisters, or your fathers' brothers' or sisters',
or your mothers' brothers' or sisters',
or in the houses whose care is entrusted to you,
or the houses of your friends.
There is no harm in your eating together or separately.
But when you enter the houses, salute the inmates
with a greeting in the name of God,
invoking blessings and good health.
That is how God explains things to you clearly
so that you may understand.

They alone are true believers
who believe in God and His Apostle,
and when they are with him on a matter of common concern,
do not depart without obtaining his leave.
Surely those who ask leave of you are the ones

who believe in God and His Apostle.
Therefore when they ask leave of you for personal business
give leave to those you please,
and seek God's forgiveness for them.
Surely God is forgiving and kind.
63. Do not consider your being summoned by the Apostle
to be like your summoning one another.
God knows those of you who go away surreptitiously.
So let those who act in contravention of his command take
        heed
lest a trial should befall them or a grievous punishment come
        upon them.
64. Does not every thing in the heavens and the earth
belong to God?
He surely knows what state you are in;
and on the day they go back to Him
He will tell them what they used to do,
for God has knowledge of every thing.

---

* Note on v. 3, p. 298. *Shirk*, though used in the Qur'an conceptually for associating a partner with God, basically it means to be attached to or be associated or mixed up with. *Mushrikah* (feminine gender) and *mushrik* (masculine) are the nominative forms of *sharika*, shared, participated, was a sharer, became partners. The use of a word as a concept does not abolish its etymology... The believers are forbidden to marry adulterous women unless they renounce evil and repent, for those who repent and reform are forgiven by God (3:89).

* Note on v. 35. This is the celebrated verse from which Islamic mysticism has derived much gnosis and illumination. Mansur Al-Hallaj in his *Ta-Sin* of the Prophetic Lamp identifies the lamp with the person of the Prophet in section I: "A Lamp appeared from the Light of the Unseen. It appeared and returned, and it surpassed the other lamps. It was the ruling moon, manifesting itself radiantly among the other moons. It was a star whose astrological house is in the empyrean..."
It is significant that the Surah itself is entitled Light and begins with light on etiquette in personal modesty and conduct, and ends on light on etiquette in public affairs, centring round the Prophet, with the glorification of God's Light and His majesty as its central theme.
The words *noor* and *naar* have the same root, *naar* being the intense heat of fire, and *noor* its most refined element, light. The quality of light is high-lighted here by its purity. It is well protected in a niche, and is identifiable with the Qur'an, the niche being the place where books were kept in the East, and is preserved by the chimney of glass, the person of the Prophet, and is lit by the oil of the olive, universal symbol ('neither of the East nor the West') of peace, and guidance - here symbolically the tranquil heart.

25 The Criterion

Al-Furqān: Makki

In the name of Allah, most benevolent, ever-merciful.

BLESSED IS HE who revealed
the Criterion (of right and wrong) to His votary
that it may be a warning for the world, —
2. He to whom belongs the kingdom of the heavens and the
        earth,
who has neither begotten a son
nor has He a partner in His kingdom,
(who) created every thing
and determined its exact measure.
3. Yet they choose apart from Him gods
who have not created any thing
and have themselves been created,
who possess no power over their loss or gain,
or their death or life or being raised to life again.
4. Yet the unbelievers say:
"This is nothing but a lie he has concocted
in which others have aided him."
They have come down to mischief and lies.
5. And they say: "These are fables of antiquity
he has invented, which are dictated to him
morning and evening."
6. Say: "He who knows the secrets of the heavens and the earth
has revealed it to me;
and He is surely forgiving and kind."
7. But they say: "What sort of prophet is this
who eats food and walks the market places?
Why was no angel sent to him
to act as admonisher with him?
8. Or a treasure should have been given to him,
or he should have had an orchard
from which he could eat."
And these wicked people say:
"You only follow a man ensorcelled."
9. Just see what comparisons they bring up for you!

They are lost and cannot find the way.

Blessed be He who, if He pleased,
could give you better than that, —
gardens with rivers flowing by;
and make palaces for you.
11. Yet they reject the Hour as untrue.
We have prepared a Fire for those
who deny the Resurrection.
12. When (Hell) appears to them from a distance
they will hear it raging and roaring.
13. And when they are cast within a narrow space of it
chained together, they would plead for death.
14. "Do not ask for one death but many deaths on this day."
15. Ask them: "Is this better or a garden for everlasting abode
which has been promised the pious and devout?
It would be their guerdon and their destination.
16. There will they have whatever they wish,
and there abide for ever."
This is a promise incumbent on your Lord
which will certainly be fulfilled.
17. The day He will gather them together
along with those they worshipped other than God,
He will ask them: "Did you lure these creatures of Mine away,
or did they themselves go astray?"
18. They will answer: "Glory to You. It was not worthy
            of us
to seek any protector other than You.
But You allowed them and their fathers a life of ease
until they turned oblivious of the Reminder.
They were a people impenitent.
19. (The idolaters will be told):
"Your gods have refuted your assertion.
You can neither avert (your doom) nor receive any help.
We shall make the wicked among you
taste of severe punishment."
20. We never sent before you apostles who did not eat food
and walk the market places.
We make some of you the means of trying the others.
So will you persevere?
Your Lord is always watching.

Those who do not hope to meet Us say:
"Why are no angels sent down to us,
or why do we not see our Lord?"
They are full of self-conceit

and behave with intense arrogance.
22. The day they see the angels there will be
no happy tidings for the sinners;
and they will say: "There is an insurmountable barrier!"
23. We shall turn to their deeds
and scatter them like particles of dust.
24. The inmates of Paradise will have a better abode that day,
and a better resting place.
25. The day the heavens splits asunder
with a dazzling white cloud gathering and the angels descend
in a continuous stream,
26. The real sovereignty will belong to Ar-Rahman.
How grievous will be the day for the infidels!
27. The sinner will then bite his hand and say:
"Would that I had taken the road with the Prophet.
28. Woe alas, ah would I had not taken so-and-so as friend!
29. He led me astray from the Warning
after it had come to me.
Satan always betrays man.
30. The prophet will say: "O my Lord, my people had
fettered the Qur'an."*
31. Thus do We keep opponents among the sinners for every
apostle;
yet your Lord is sufficient as a guide and helper.
32. The unbelievers say: "Why was the whole Qur'an
not sent down all at once to him?"
It was sent thus that We may keep your heart resolute.
So We enunciated it by steps and distinctly.
33. There is not an example they advance
to which We do not give you a right answer
and a better explanation.
34. Those who will be pushed faces forward into Hell
will be in a worse position, farther away from the path.

We gave Moses the Book,
and made his brother Aaron his minister,
36. Then We told them: "Go to the people
who have rejected Our signs."
Then We annihilated them completely.
37. We had drowned the people of Noah
when they had accused the apostles of lies,
and turned them into an example for men.
We have prepared a painful punishment for the wicked.
38. (As for) 'Ad, Thamud and the people of ar-Rass,
and many generations in between them,
39. We administered warnings to each of them,

and then destroyed them completely.

40. They must have surely passed by the town on which
We had rained the terrible rain of ruin.
How could they not have seen it?
Still they do not dread the Resurrection.

41. When they see you they take you only in jest:
"Is this the one whom God has sent as messenger?

42. He would have surely turned us away from our gods
if we had not adhered to them."
They will know soon who is farther away from the path
when they see the punishment!

43. Have you considered him who takes his own lust for his
     god?
Can you stand a surety for him?

44. Or do you think that most of them hear or understand?
They are no better than cattle;
in fact they are farther astray from the path.

Have you not seen how your Lord
lengthens out the shadow?
He could have kept it motionless if He liked.
Yet We make the sun its pilot to show the way.

46. Then We draw it back to Us, withdrawing it little by little.

47. It is He who made the night a covering for you;
and made sleep for rest, the day for rising.

48. It is He who sends the winds with auspicious news
in advance of His benevolence;
and We send pure water down from the sky

49. To quicken a region that was dead,
and to give it as drink to animals We have created
and to men in plenty.

50. And We distribute it among them in various ways
that they may ponder and reflect; yet most men disdain
every thing but denial and thanklessness.

51. Had We pleased We could have raised
a warner in every town.

52. So do not listen to unbelievers,
and strive against them with greater effort.

53. It is He who made two bodies of water flow side by side,
one fresh (and) sweet, the other brine (and) bitter,
and has placed an interstice, a barrier between them.

54. It is He who created man from water, then gave him
consanguinity and affinity.** Your Lord is omnipotent.

55. And yet they worship besides God

----
* See note 1 on v. 30, and ** note 2 on vv. 53-54, on p.311

Al-Furqan   309

what cannot bring them gain or do them harm.
The unbeliever has always been
an auxiliary against his Lord.
56. Yet We have not sent you but to give
good tidings and to warn.
57. Tell them: "I do not ask any recompense of you for this
other than (urging) whoever likes may take the way to his
     Lord."
58. Have trust in God the Living, who will never die,
and sing His hallelujas; for He is well aware
of the sins of His creatures.
59. He created the heavens and the earth
and all that lies between them
in six spans then assumed His authority.
He is the benevolent:
Ask those who are well-informed.
60. When you say to them: "Bow before Ar-Rahman,"
they say: "What is Ar-Rahman?
Should we adore whoever you ask us to?"
And their aversion increases further.

Blessed is He who placed in the heavens constellations
     of stars,
and placed a burning lamp in it and the luminous moon.
62. It is He who made the night and day an alternation
for him who cares to reflect and be grateful.
63. Devotees of Ar-Rahman are those
who walk with humility on the earth, and when
they are addressed by the ignorant, say: "Peace;"
64. And those who spend their nights
bowed and standing before their Lord;
65. Who say: "O our Lord, avert from us the torment of Hell:
Its punishment is surely continuous.
66. It is indeed an evil halt and an evil abode;"
67. Who are neither prodigal nor miserly in their spending
but follow a middle path;
68. Who do not invoke any god apart from God;
who do not take a life which God has forbidden
except for a cause that is just,
and do not fornicate —
and any one who does so will be punished for the crime,
69. Whose punishment will be doubled on the Day of
     Judgement,
and he will live for ever in disgrace,
70. Except those who repent and come to believe
and do the right, for whom God will turn

evil into goodness.

for God is forgiving and kind.

71. Whosoever repents and does the right,
will have turned back to God by way of repentance;

72. And those who do not give false evidence,
and if they come across unbecoming talk
ignore it and pass by in a sedate way;

73. Who, when reminded of their Lord's revelations,
do not fall for them like the deaf and blind;

74. And those who say: "O Lord, give us comfort
in our spouses and children,
and make us paragons of those who follow the straight path."

75. They will be rewarded for their perseverance
with lofty mansions in empyrean where
they will be received with greetings of peace and salutations,

76. And abide there for ever:
What an excellent destination and abode!

77. Say: "My Lord is not concerned on your account
if you do not pray to Him.
You have surely done with denying;
soon will come the inevitable judgement.

---

1. Note on v. 30. A horse or camel tied head to foot was called *mahjoor*, and the rope used for tying it, *al-hijaar*, (Taj). The Qur'an today is thus fettered by custom and tradition, hearsay reports compiled centuries later, and laws and bye-laws enacted by men, each group having its own *fiqah* and *shariah*, which are held more sacrosanct and given precedence over the uncreated Word of God, the Qur'an. See also note on p. 126.

2. Note on vv. 53-54. Apart from describing two bodies of water, verse 53 has a deeper allegorical significance and, read with v. 54, connects with v. 1 of Surah 4, The Women, and the creation of human beings from a single cell, as well as human reproduction based, again, in cellular activity (see note on p. 96). It shows the intricacy of Nature's design, the entire reproductive impulse being encoded in cells, including the genetic principle made explicit in consanguinity and affinity mentioned in v. 54, one springing from the male the other from the female, the creation of man from water (v. 54) pointing not only to 'a single cell' (4:1) but to *arham* or bond of relationships spoken therein.

The two bodies of water one sweet the other brine (v. 53) are an allegorical description of man and woman who are biologically the same, only kept distinct and apart by 'the barrier' of sex - alkaline and acid - so that man does not become woman or woman man. The sole difference between the two is of sex chromosomes and hormones which are defined as "anything produced by one cell that can get to another cell by any means and change what it does," as Wylie Vale of Salk Institute, La Jolla, California says. As a result "the lines between hormones and other body chemicals are blurring," adds Dr. Sidney Ingbar of Harvard Medical School. (Newsweek, January 12, 1987).

26 The Poets

Ash-Shu'ara: Makki

سورة الشعراء مكية ٢٦١
آياتها ٢٢٧ ركوعها

In the name of Allah, most benevolent, ever-merciful.

بسم الله الرحمن الرحيم

TĀ SĪN MĪM.

2. These are the verses of the perspicuous Book.
3. You may perhaps wear out your heart
because they do not come to belief.
4. We could send down from the heavens
a sign to them if We pleased,
before which their heads would remain bowed.
5. Never does a new reminder come to them from Ar-Rahman
but they turn away from it.
6. Surely they have done with denying;
soon will come to them the news
of what they were laughing at.
7. Do they not see the earth, how We grow
all kinds of noble things upon it?
8. Verily there are signs in this;
yet many of them do not believe.
9. Your Lord is surely mighty and merciful.

When your Lord called upon Moses:
"Go to the wicked people,
11. The people of Pharaoh. Will they not fear and take heed?"
12. He said: "O Lord, I fear that they will deny me.
13. My heart is constrained, my tongue falters,
so delegate Aaron;
14. And they have a charge (of murder) against me.
So I fear that they will kill me."
15. (It was) said: "By no means. Go with My signs, both of
you.
I am verily with you and I hear.
16. Go to the Pharaoh and tell him:
'We bring a message from the Lord of all the worlds
17. That you should send the children of Israel with us.' "
18. (The Pharaoh) said: "Did we not bring you up as a child?
And you lived a number of years of your life with us.

19. And you commited what you did,
and you are ungrateful!"
20. (Moses) replied: "I did do that and I was in the wrong,
21. So I ran away from you out of fear.
But my Lord has given me wisdom,
and made me an apostle.
22. But the favour you oblige me with
is that you have enslaved the children of Israel."
23. The Pharaoh asked: "And what is the Lord of all the worlds?"
24. (Moses) said: "The Lord of the heavens and the earth
and all that lies between them,
if you can believe."
25. (The Pharaoh) said to those around him: "Do you hear?"
26. (Moses continued): "Your Lord and the Lord
of your fathers before you."
27. (The Pharaoh) said (to his nobles): "Your apostle
who has been sent to you, is certainly mad."
28. (Moses) said: "The Lord of the East and the Lord of the West
and all that lies between them, if you have sense."
29. (The Pharaoh) said: "If you took another god apart from me
I will have you incarcerated."
30. (Moses) said: "Even though I have brought to you
something convincing?"
31. (The Pharaoh) said: "Then bring it, if you speak the truth."
32. So (Moses) cast his staff, and lo, it turned into a living serpent.
33. And he drew forth his hand, and lo,
it looked white to the beholders.

The Pharaoh) said to the chiefs around him:
"He is certainly a clever magician.
35. He wants to drive you out of your land by his magic.
So, what do you bid?"
36. They said: "Put him and his brother off awhile,
and send summoners to the cities to gather
37. And bring the ablest magicians to you."
38. So the magicians were assembled
at a stated time and place on an appointed day.
39. And the people were also asked to assemble.
40. (They said): "We may haply follow the magicians
if they are victorious."
41. When the magicians arrived, they said to the Pharaoh:
"Is there a reward for us if we are victorious?"

42. "Yes," he replied. "You will be among the honoured."
43. Moses said to them: "Cast what you have to cast."
44. So they cast their ropes and rods, and said:
"By the glory of Pharaoh, we shall be victorious."
45. Then Moses threw down his staff, and lo,
it swallowed up their conjurations.
46. Then the magicians fell prostrating in adoration,
47. And said: "We (affirm and) believe
in the Lord of all the worlds,
48. The Lord of Moses and Aaron."
49. Said (the Pharaoh): "You have come to believe in him
before I gave you leave.
He is surely your chief, who taught you magic.
You will soon come to know:
I will have your hands and feet cut off on alternate sides,
and have every one of you crucified."
50. They said: "There will be no harm.
We shall return to our Lord.
51. We certainly hope our Lord will forgive our sins
as we are the first to believe."

We said to Moses:
"Travel by night with My creatures.
You will surely be pursued."
53. Then the Pharaoh sent announcers to the cities,
54. (Proclaiming): "Surely they are a small band (of fugitives).
55. They are always harassing us.
56. But we are a fully accoutred army."
57. So We made them leave the gardens and springs of water,
58. And treasures and agreeable mansions.
59. Thus it was; and We made the children of Israel possess
them.
60. But they pursued them at sunrise.
61. When the two forces drew within seeing distance of each
other,
the people of Moses said: "We shall certainly be overtaken."
62. Moses replied: "By no means. My Lord is with me.
He will show me the way."
63. We commanded Moses: "Smite the sea with your staff."
And it parted, and every parting
was like a lofty mountain.
64. Then We brought the others to that place.
65. We delivered Moses and every one with him,
66. And We drowned the others.
67. Verily there is a sign in this,
but most of them do not believe.

68. Indeed your Lord is mighty and merciful.

Relate the news of Abraham to them.
70. When he asked his father and his people:
"What do you worship?"
71. They replied: "We worship idols
and are devoted to them."
72. (Abraham) asked: "Do they hear when you call them?
73. Or do they benefit you,
or do you harm?"
74. They said: "No. But we found our fathers doing so."
75. He said: "Have you considered what you have been
worshipping,
76. You and your fathers?
77. Yet they are my enemies
except the Lord of all the worlds
78. Who created me and showed me the way,
79. Who gives me food and drink,
80. And heals me when I am sick,
81. Who will make me die, then give me life again,
82. And who, I hope, will condone my faults
on the Day of Judgement.
83. O Lord, give me wisdom and admit me
among the righteous,
84. And uphold my name with posterity,
85. And put me among the inheritors of Paradise.
86. Forgive me and my father: He was surely among those who
went astray.
87. And do not disgrace me on the day
when they are raised from the graves,
88. The day when neither wealth nor children will be of any
avail
89. But to him who comes to God with a tranquil heart."
90. Paradise will be brought near those who take heed for
themselves
and follow the straight path;
91. And Hell made visible to those who had gone astray.
92. They will be asked: "Where are those you worshipped
93. Other than God? Can they save you or even save
themselves?"
94. They will then be thrown into Hell
with those who had gone astray
95. Together with the hordes of Iblis.
96. Disputing among themselves they will say:
97. "By God, we were plainly in error
98. In equating you with the Lord of all the worlds;

Ash-Shu'ara'

99. No one but the sinners led us astray.

100. Now we have none to intercede for us,

101. Nor any sincere friend.

102. If only we could return
and be among the believers!"

103. Verily there is a sign in this,
but many of them do not believe.

104. Verily your Lord is mighty and merciful.

The people of Noah accused the apostles of lies.

106. When their brother Noah said to them: "Will you not
take heed?

107. I have been sent as a trusted messenger to you.

108. So be fearful of God and listen to me.

109. I ask no recompense of you for it.
My reward is due from none
but the Lord of all the worlds.

110. So fear God and follow me."

111. They said: "Should we place our trust in you
when only the condemned follow you?"

112. He said: "It is not for me to know what they were doing.

113. It is for my Lord to bring them to book,
if you can understand.

114. I am certainly not one to drive away the believers.

115. I am only a plain admonisher."

116. They said: "If you do not desist, O Noah,
you will be stoned to death."

117. He prayed: "O Lord,
verily my people accuse me of lies.

118. So adjudge between me and them conclusively,
and save me and the believers who are with me."

119. So We delivered him and those with him in the loaded
ark,

120. And drowned the rest of them.

121. Verily there is a sign in this,
yet many of them do not believe.

122. But surely your Lord is mighty and merciful.

The people of 'Ad accused the messengers of lies.

124. When their brother Hud said to them: "Will you not take
heed?

125. I have been sent as a trusted messenger to you.

126. So fear God and listen to me.

127. I ask no recompense of you for it.
My reward is due from none
but the Lord of all the worlds.

128. You construct monuments on every hill in vain,

129. Erect palaces (thinking) that you will live for ever,

130. And whenever you apply force become tyrannical.

131. So be fearful of God and follow me.

132. Fear Him who has bestowed on you what you know,

133. Gave you increase of cattle and sons,

134. And orchards and springs.

135. I fear the punishment of a terrible day for you."

136. They said: "It is the same to us
if you warn us or do not warn.

137. This is just a habit of antiquated people.

138. We are not going to be damned."

139. Then they accused him of lies;
so We annihilated them.
Verily there is a sign in this,
but most of them do not believe.

140. Yet surely your Lord is mighty and merciful.

The Thamud accused the messengers of lies.

142. When their brother Saleh said to them: "Will you not
take heed?"

143. I have been sent as a trusted messenger to you.

144. So fear God and follow me.

145. I do not ask any recompense of you for this.
My reward is due from none
but the Lord of all the worlds.

146. (Do you think) you will be left secure here

147. In these gardens and these springs,

148. The fields of corn and date-palm trees
with soft and tender spathes,

149. And dwellings hewed out of mountains
ingeniously?

150. So be mindful of God and listen to me.

151. Do not follow those who are extravagant,

152. Who corrupt the land
and do not reform it."

153. They said: "Surely you are deluded.

154. You are nothing but a man like us.
Bring us a token if you speak the truth."

155. (Saleh) said: "Here is a she-camel.
She has a right of drinking water,
and you have a right of drinking it
on appointed turns.

156. Do not treat her unkindly
or the punishment of a grievous day will fall on you."

157. But they hamstrung her; and on the morrow

were repentant,
158. For they were seized by the torment.
Verily there was a sign in this,
but most of them did not believe.
159. Yet verily your Lord is mighty and merciful.

The people of Lot accused the messengers of lies.
161. When their brother Lot said to them: "Will you not take
heed?
162. I have been sent as a trusted messenger to you.
163. So fear God and listen to me.
164. I ask no recompense of you for this.
My reward is due from none
but the Lord of all the worlds.
165. Why do you go for males unlike all other creatures
166. Leaving the consorts your Lord has made for you?
But you are a people who exceed the bounds."
167. They said: "If you do not desist, O Lot,
you will be expelled (from the city)."
168. (Lot) said: "I am disgusted with your actions,"
169. (And prayed:) "O Lord, save me and my family from
what they do."
170. So We saved him and his whole family
171. Except one old woman who remained behind.
172. Then We destroyed the rest of them,
173. And rained on them a shower (of stones).
How terrible was the rain
(that fell) on those who had been warned!
174. Verily in this was a sign,
but most of them do not believe.
175. Yet surely your Lord is mighty and powerful.

The people of the Wood too called the messengers
liars.
177. When Shu'aib said to them:
"Will you not take heed?
178. I have been sent as a trusted messenger to you.
179. So fear God and follow me.
180. I ask no recompense of you for this.
My reward is due from none
but the Lord of all the worlds.
181. Give full measure and do not cheat;
182. Weigh on an even balance.
183. And do not withhold from people what belongs to them,
and do not corrupt the land;
184. And fear Him who created you and all the earlier people."

Ash-Shu'ara'

185. They said: "Surely you are deluded.
186. You are nothing but a man like us,
and we think you are a liar.
187. But in case you are speaking the truth,
then make a segment of the sky to fall upon us."
188. (Shu'aib) said: "My Lord knows well what you are doing."
189. But they denied him, and We seized them
with the torment of the Day of Shadowing
(when the cloud had rained down fire).
It was indeed the torment of a terrible day!
190. Verily in this was a sign,
but most of them do not believe.
191. Yet verily your Lord is mighty and merciful.

And this (Qur'an) is a revelation
from the Lord of all the worlds,
193. Which the trusted spirit descended with
194. To (communicate) to your heart
that you may be a warner
195. In eloquent Arabic.
196. This is (indicated) in the Books of earlier people.
197. Was it not a proof for them
that the learned men of Israel knew about this?
198. Had We revealed it to a man
of obscure tongue
199. And he had recited it to them, and they
had not believed (it would have been different)
200. Thus do We cause (unbelief) to enter
the hearts of sinners.
201. They will not believe it until
they behold the painful punishment.
202. It will come upon them unawares,
and they will not comprehend it.
203. Then will they say:
"Can we be given respite?"
204. Do they wish Us then to hasten the punishment?
205. Just think: If We let them enjoy (the good things of life)
for a few years more,
206. And then what they were promised comes upon them,
207. Of what avail shall their enjoyment be to them?
208. Never have We destroyed a habitation
till We had sent admonishers to them
209. To warn. For We are never unjust.
210. The devils did not bring it down:
211. They are not worthy of it, nor have they power.
212. They have been precluded

from hearing it.
213. So call on no other god but God,
lest you are condemned to torment;
214. And warn your near relations,
215. And take those believers under your wing
who follow you.
216. If they do not obey you, tell them:
"I am not responsible for what you do."
217. Have trust in the Mighty, the Merciful,
218. Who watches you when you get up,
219. And your movements among those who bow in homage
    to God.
220. He is all-hearing and all-knowing.
221. Should I tell you on whom the devils descend?
222. They come down to every mendacious sinner,
223. Who listens to you (for spreading rumours);
but most of them are liars.
224. As for the poets,
only those who go astray follow them.
225. Have you not seen that they wander distract in every
    valley,
226. And they say what they do not do,
227. Except those who believe and do the right,
and remember God a great deal,
who retaliate only
when they have been wronged.
Yet the oppressors will now come to know
through what reversals they will be overthrown!

27 An-Naml

An-Naml: Makki

In the name of Allah, most benevolent, ever-merciful.

TĀ SĪN. THESE are the verses of the Qur'an,
and collection of explicit laws,
2. A guidance and good tidings for the believers,
3. Who fulfil their devotional obligations,
pay the zakat, and believe with certainty
in the life to come.
4. We make their deeds attractive to those
who do not believe in the Hereafter,
so that they may wander in perplexity.
5. They are those who will suffer
the worst chastisement in this life,
and will be the greatest losers in the life to come.
6. You have been conveyed the Qur'an
from One all-wise and all-knowing.
7. (Remember) when Moses said to his family:
"I see a fire. I shall bring you news from it,
or bring an ember that you may warm yourselves."
8. But when he reached it, a voice called out:
"Blessed is He who is in the fire and all around it.
Praised be God, the Lord of all the worlds.
9. O Moses, I am that God, the mighty and all-wise.
10. Throw down your staff."
When he saw it wriggling like a serpent
he turned his back and fled without turning (to look).
"O Moses," (said the voice), "be not fearful.
Surely those sent as messengers do not fear in My presence,
11. Except those who do some wrong but afterwards
do good to make up for the wrong.
And I am forgiving and merciful.
12. Put your hand in the bosom of your shirt;
it will come out white without any blemish.
This will be one of nine tokens for the Pharaoh and his people,
who are a wicked lot indeed."
13. And when Our signs came as distinct proofs,

they said: "This is only magic."
14. And they denied them out of malice and pride,
though in their hearts they believed that they were true.
So see how was the end of evil-doers!

We gave David and Solomon knowledge;
and they said: "All praise be to God who has favoured us
over many of His creatures who believe."
16. Solomon was heir to David, and he said:
"O people, we have been taught the language of Tair,*
and have been given of every thing.
This is a clear favour indeed."
17. His armies of jinns and men and Tair
assembled, formed into ranks, (and marched)
18. Till they reached the Valley of Naml.*
Said the lady of Naml: "O Naml,
go into your dwellings lest Solomon and his hordes
should crush you unawares."
19. (Solomon) smiled, amused at her speech, and said:
"O Lord grant me that I should be grateful
for the favours You have bestowed on me and my parents,
and do good things of Your pleasing;
and admit me among Your righteous devotees by Your grace."
20. When he reviewed the Tair, he said:
"How is it I do not see Hud-hud?
Is he absent?
21. I will punish him severely, or cut his throat,
unless he bring a valid excuse."
22. But he was not long in coming, and reported:
"I have been around where you have not been.
I come from Saba with positive news.
23. I found a woman reigning over them,

---

* Since words having more than one meaning, like *naml*, *hud-hud* and *tair* have been used metonymically to stand for something quite different from what they generally mean, they have not been translated but retained in Arabic. *Naml*, for instance, means ants, but was also the name of a tribe in Syria, and Ibn Kathir in his *Tafsir* identifies *namlat*, the lady of Naml, as belonging to the tribe of Banu Shisan. Similarly, *hud-hud* means hoopoe, but was also the name of a South Yemen tribe, and men were often named after their tribes as well as birds. *Tair* is commonly used for birds, but is also applied to winged beings, yet *tayyar* means fleet-footed horse, and *at-tairan* is metaphorically used for marching impetuously to *jihad*. For some other meanings of *tair* see notes at 3:49 and 38:18-19. When king Solomon says that they had been taught the language of *tair*, he uses the word *mantiq* which is used for human speech, and man alone of all created beings is called *haivani-natiq*, speaking animal, the language of birds being called *saut*. The intention behind the use of *tair*, as of *jinn*, cannot be disregarded, and is further discussed in the note on p.386, the Surah Sad, like Sheba, Surah 34, being largely parabolical in style and narration. Knowledge of the language of *tair* implies that Tair were a conquered tribe or race and David and Solomon had knowledge of their language. Similarly *jinns* implies nomadic tribes many of whom were recruited by the king of Tyre for

and she has been favoured with every thing;
and she has a throne that is magnificent.
24. I found that she and her people worship the sun
in place of God, for Satan has made their deeds
look attractive to them and has turned them away
from the Path, so they do not find the way
25. To worship God who brings to light
what is hidden in the heavens and the earth,
and is cognisant of what you hide and what you disclose.
26. God: There is no god but He,
the Lord of the glorious throne.''
27. (Solomon) said: 'We shall see if you speak the truth
or you are a liar.
28. Take this letter from me, and deliver it to them
and withdraw, then see what reply they give in return.''
29. (The Queen said): "O nobles, a venerable letter
has been delivered to me.
30. It is from Solomon, and (says):
'In the name of Allah, Ar-Rahman, Ar-Rahim.**
31. Do not rise against me, but come to me in submission.'

Advise me, O nobles," she said, "in this matter.
I do not decide any thing until you concur.''
33. They said: "We are men of valour, and brave fighters.
It is for you to decide. So consider what you should command.''
34. She said: "Surely when kings enter a city they destroy it
and despoil the honour of its nobility.
So will they do (to us).
35. But I will send them a gift and see ***
what the envoys bring back (in return).''
36. So, when the envoys came to Solomon he said:
"Do you wish to increase my wealth?
Yet what God has given me is better

Solomon: Bible, Kings 1,5. If taken as 'knowledge of the language of birds,' it would belong to the realm of 'Faerie.' But the Qur'an is speaking metonymically, using the name of one thing for another related to it. The role of Hud-hud in this Surah is significant, and could not have been performed by a bird. In fact, it is known that the name of a prince of Midian in the days of king Solomon himself was Hud-hud; and according to Arab traditions the name of the Queen's brother or father was also Hud-hud. (See *Ard al-Qur'an* by Saiyyad Sulaiman Nadvi, Dar al-Musannifin, Azamgarh). It was by the hand of Hud-hud that the letter demanding the Queen's surrender was sent by Solomon; and it was Hud-hud who brought her throne, he alone having possessed knowledge of the letter, which verse 40 of this Surah mentions. At the same time, the metaphorical meaning of 'throne' (power, kingship) should be noted, as also the fact of the Queen's utter confusion on entering the court whose floor seemed a sheet of water to her eyes bewildered by the greatness and glory of Solomon and the splendour of his court.
** Ar-Rahman, Ar-Rahim being names of Allah, with which Sheba was familiar, have not been translated.
*** See note on p. 328.

than what He has given you.
No. Be gratified in your present.
37. Go back to them. We shall soon come with our armies
which they will not be able to face.
We shall drive them out of (the land) with ignominy,
and they will be humbled.''

اِرْجِعْ اِلَيْهِمْ فَلَنَأْتِيَنَّهُمْ بِجُنُودٍ لَّا قِبَلَ لَهُمْ بِهَا
وَلَنُخْرِجَنَّهُمْ مِّنْهَا اَذِلَّةً وَّهُمْ صٰغِرُوْنَ۝

38. He (then) said (to his courtiers): "O you nobles,
is there any one who can bring me her throne
before they come to me in submission?''

قَالَ يٰاَيُّهَا الْمَلَؤُا اَيُّكُمْ يَأْتِيْنِيْ بِعَرْشِهَا قَبْلَ اَنْ
يَّأْتُوْنِيْ مُسْلِمِيْنَ۝

39. A crafty jinn said: "I will bring it before you rise from
              your seat,
for I am strong and trustworthy.''

قَالَ عِفْرِيْتٌ مِّنَ الْجِنِّ اَنَا اٰتِيْكَ بِهٖ قَبْلَ اَنْ
تَقُوْمَ مِنْ مَّقَامِكَ وَاِنِّيْ عَلَيْهِ لَقَوِيٌّ اَمِيْنٌ۝

40. But one who had knowledge of the letter, said:
"I will bring it to you in the twinkling of an eye."
When Solomon saw it before him, (he said):
"This is by the grace of my Lord
that He may test me whether I am grateful or I am thankless.
Yet if one is grateful, he is grateful for himself,
and if one is thankless, then surely my Lord
is unconcerned and magnanimous.''

قَالَ الَّذِيْ عِنْدَهٗ عِلْمٌ مِّنَ الْكِتٰبِ اَنَا اٰتِيْكَ بِهٖ
قَبْلَ اَنْ يَّرْتَدَّ اِلَيْكَ طَرْفُكَ فَلَمَّا رَاٰهُ مُسْتَقِرًّا
عِنْدَهٗ قَالَ هٰذَا مِنْ فَضْلِ رَبِّيْ لِيَبْلُوَنِيْ ءَاَشْكُرُ
اَمْ اَكْفُرُ وَمَنْ شَكَرَ فَاِنَّمَا يَشْكُرُ لِنَفْسِهٖ وَمَنْ كَفَرَ
فَاِنَّ رَبِّيْ غَنِيٌّ كَرِيْمٌ۝

41. (Turning to his nobles) he said:
"Change the appearance of her throne.
Let us see if she is rightly guided,
or is not guided at all.''

قَالَ نَكِّرُوْا لَهَا عَرْشَهَا نَنْظُرْ اَتَهْتَدِيْ اَمْ تَكُوْنُ
مِنَ الَّذِيْنَ لَا يَهْتَدُوْنَ۝

42. When she arrived, they asked her:
"Is your throne like this?''
She said: "As though this is it.
We had come to have knowledge
and already submitted."

فَلَمَّا جَاءَتْ قِيْلَ اَهٰكَذَا عَرْشُكِ قَالَتْ كَاَنَّهٗ هُوَ
وَاُوْتِيْنَا الْعِلْمَ مِنْ قَبْلِهَا وَكُنَّا مُسْلِمِيْنَ۝

43. She was (in fact) turned away
by what she worshipped other than God,
for she came of an unbelieving people.

وَصَدَّهَا مَا كَانَتْ تَّعْبُدُ مِنْ دُوْنِ اللّٰهِ اِنَّهَا كَانَتْ
مِنْ قَوْمٍ كٰفِرِيْنَ۝

44. She was invited to enter the court.
When she saw it, she took it for a sheet of water,
and (pulling up her skirts) uncovered her legs.
(Solomon) told her: "This is paved with tiles of glass.''
"O Lord," she said, "I have wronged myself,
and I submit to the Lord of all the worlds with Solomon.''

قِيْلَ لَهَا ادْخُلِي الصَّرْحَ فَلَمَّا رَاَتْهُ حَسِبَتْهُ لُجَّةً
وَّكَشَفَتْ عَنْ سَاقَيْهَا قَالَ اِنَّهٗ صَرْحٌ مُّمَرَّدٌ مِّنْ
قَوَارِيْرَ قَالَتْ رَبِّ اِنِّيْ ظَلَمْتُ نَفْسِيْ وَاَسْلَمْتُ مَعَ
سُلَيْمٰنَ لِلّٰهِ رَبِّ الْعٰلَمِيْنَ۝

We sent to Thamud their brother Saleh
(who said): "Worship God.''
But they were divided into two groups
disputing with one another.

وَلَقَدْ اَرْسَلْنَا اِلٰى ثَمُوْدَ اَخَاهُمْ صٰلِحًا اَنِ اعْبُدُوا
اللّٰهَ فَاِذَا هُمْ فَرِيْقٰنِ يَخْتَصِمُوْنَ۝

46. (Saleh) said: "O people, why do you wish
to hasten evil rather than good?
Why not ask for God's forgiveness?

قَالَ يٰقَوْمِ لِمَ تَسْتَعْجِلُوْنَ بِالسَّيِّئَةِ قَبْلَ الْحَسَنَةِ

You may well be forgiven."

47. They said: "You betoken evil, and those with you."
(Saleh) replied: "The evil you presage can only come from God.
In reality you are a people under trial
(for your own inauspiciousness)."

48. There were in that city nine persons
who spread disorder in the land, and did not reform.

49. They said: "Let us swear by God that we will attack
Saleh and his family at night, and later tell his heirs:
'We did not see his family destroyed,
and we speak the truth.' "

50. They hatched up the plot; We also planned
without their knowledge.

51. Now see the end of their machinations:
We destroyed them and their entire people.

52. So these their habitations
lie deserted now because of their iniquities.
Verily there is a sign in this for those who understand.

53. We deliver those who believe and take heed for themselves.

54. (Remember) Lot, when he said to his people:
"Why do you indulge in obscenities when you know (it is
evil)?

55. You lust after men in place of women.
You are indeed a stolid people."

56. His people had no answer except saying:
"Expel the family of Lot from your city.
They are a people who would (rather) be pure!"

57. So We saved him and his family except his wife
who was destined to stay behind.

58. And We rained down on them a shower (of stones).
How ruinous was the rain that fell on those
who had been warned (but warned in vain)!

Say: "All praise be to God, and peace
on those of His creatures whom He has chosen."
Is God better or those they associate with Him –

60. Who created the heavens and the earth,
who sends down water from the sky for you,
with which He causes graceful gardens to grow?
It was not in your power to make trees germinate.
Is there any other god along with God.
In fact they are a people who turn away (from the truth).

61. Who then made the earth a habitable place,
and made the rivers (flow) in its valleys and dales,
and placed upon it firm stabilisers,
and kept a barrier between two bodies of water?

Is there any other god along with God?
In reality most of them do not know.
62. Who hears the cry of the anguished (soul)
when it calls to Him, and relieves its suffering?
And who made you trustees on the earth?
Is there any other god along with God?
How little it is that you reflect!
63. Who then really shows you the way
in the darkness of the desert and the sea?
And who sends breezes bringing news of His benevolence?
Is there any other god along with God?
He is far too exalted for what they associate with Him!
64. Who creates first then reverts it?
And who gives you provision from the heavens and the earth?
Is there any other god along with God?
Tell them: "Bring your proof, if you are truthful."
65. Say: "No one in the heavens and the earth
has knowledge of the unknown except God,
nor can they know when they will be raised again.
66. Still less do they comprehend the life to come.
In fact they are in doubt about it.
Still more, they are blind to it."

Those who do not believe, say:
"When we and our fathers have turned to dust,
how shall we be raised again?
68. Indeed we and our fathers had been promised this before.
It is nothing but the earlier people's lore."
69. Say: "Travel in the land and see
how (bad) was the end of sinners."
70. Do not grieve over them,
and do not be distressed by what they contrive.
71. Yet they say: "When will this promise come to pass?
(Tell us) if you speak the truth."
72. Say: "Perhaps some of what you wish to hasten
is right behind you."
73. Verily your Lord is gracious to men,
though most men are ungrateful.
74. Verily your Lord knows what lies hidden in their breasts
and what they disclose.
75. There is nothing of the hidden in the heavens and the earth
that is not recorded in the luminous Book.
76. Indeed this Qur'an explains to the children of Israel
much of what they are at variance.
77. It is a guidance and grace
for those who believe.

An-Naml

78. Surely your Lord in His wisdom will decide between them.
He is all-mighty and all-knowing.
79. So you place your trust in God.
Certainly you stand on positive truth.
80. You cannot make the dead to listen,
or the deaf to hear the call, when they have turned their backs,
81. Nor can you lead the blind when they have gone astray.
You can make none hear except those
who believe in Our signs
and have come to peace and submission.
82. When the sentence will have been passed against them,
We shall bring forth beastly brutes from the earth
who will torment them,
for men certainly do not believe Our signs.

The day We shall gather from every community
a section of those who denied Our signs,
and they will be brought (in separate groups),
84. So that when they come (before the Lord) He will say:
"Did you deny My signs without having understood them?
Or what was it that you were doing?"
85. When the sentence will have been passed
upon them for their wickedness,
they will not be able to say a word.
86. Do they not see that We made the night
for them to rest, the day to make things clear?
Indeed there are signs in this for people who believe.
87. The day the trumpet blast is sounded
whoever is in the heavens and the earth will be terrified,
save those whom God please,
and all will appear before Him in abjectness.
88. You will see the mountains and think they are firmly
       planted,
but they will pass away like flying clouds:
Artistry of God who perfected every thing.
He is indeed fully aware of what you do.
89. Whoever comes with good (deeds) will receive
better than (what he had done),
and be safe that day from terror.
90. But whosoever comes with evil
will be flung face forward into the Fire.
Can you expect reward for any thing but what you do?
91. (Say:) "I am commanded to worship the Lord
of this land He has blessed,
to whom all things belong;
and I am commanded to be one of those who submit,

92. And to recite the Qur'an."
Whoever comes to guidance does so for himself;
as for him who stays astray, tell him:
"I am only a warner."
93. Say: "All praise be to God. He will show you His signs,
and you will recognise them.
Your Lord is not heedless of what you do."

وَأَنْ أَتْلُوَا الْقُرْآنَ فَمَنِ اهْتَدَى فَإِنَّمَا يَهْتَدِى لِنَفْسِهِ وَمَن ضَلَّ فَقُلْ إِنَّمَا أَنَا مِنَ الْمُنذِرِينَ ۝

وَقُلِ الْحَمْدُ لِلَّهِ سَيُرِيكُمْ آيَاتِهِ فَتَعْرِفُونَهَا وَمَا رَبُّكَ بِغَافِلٍ عَمَّا تَعْمَلُونَ ۝

Note on v. 35. The language of the Surah being both metaphorical and metonymic, as in Surah 38, and others, the words and expressions carry a broader spectrum of meaning. Apart from the metonymic use of Hud-hud, the throne itself has been used metonymically in verses 38 and 41 for its replica as the gift sent to Solomon by the Queen, as no other single gift could have been worthy of the position and greatness of Solomon who had sent an ultimatum of surrender to the Queen. And Hud-hud had described it covetously as 'magnificent' (v. 23). Thus, when Solomon asked his courtiers to bring the Queen's throne, it was obviously this replica that was produced by 'one who had knowledge of the letter,' the jinn's plea to bring it having been ignored.

It is notable that the whole episode has the nature of ascertainment and trial, and is marked by a transcendental element, and emphasises the distinction between illusion and reality. The true and the false are high-lighted in the apostolic person of Solomon and the fact of Sheba's being a sunworshipper, the rejection of the jinn in favour of one who had knowledge, and the replica in place of the original. Illusion and reality are implicit in the altered and the real throne, and the sheet of water and the tiles of glass, the recognition of which leads to the Queen of Sheba's conversion at the hands of Solomon. There are enough indications for the wise.

28 The History

Al-Qasas: Makki

In the name of Allah, most benevolent, ever-merciful.

T_Ā SĪN MĪM.

2. These are the verses of the illuminating Book.

3. We narrate to you from the history of Moses and Pharaoh in all verity, for those who believe.

4. The Pharaoh had become high and mighty in the land, and divided the people into different classes, and impoverished one class, slaying its males and sparing its women, for he was indeed a tyrant.

5. We wished to favour those who were weak in the land and make them leaders and heirs,

6. And establish them in the country; and to make the Pharaoh, Haman and their hordes beware of what they feared from them.

7. So We conveyed to the mother of Moses: "Suckle him. If you are afraid for him, cast him in the river without any fear or regret, for We shall restore him to you, and make him an apostle."

8. Then he was picked up by the family of Pharaoh (unaware) that he would become their enemy and a cause for regret.
Surely the Pharaoh, Haman and their hordes were habitual sinners.

9. The Pharaoh's wife said: "He will be a comfort to me and to you. Do not kill him.
He may well be of some advantage to us, or we may adopt him as a son."
They were not aware (of what the future held in store).

10. The mother of Moses was perturbed in the morning. Had We not strengthened her heart to remain a believer she had almost given him away.

11. She told his sister: "Follow him."
So she kept an eye on him from a distance, unbeknown to them.

12. We made (Moses) refuse a wet nurse.
So his sister said: "Should I tell you of a household
that could bring him up for you and take care of him?"
13. Thus We restored him to his mother
that she may be tranquil and not grieve,
and know that the promise of God is true,
though most men do not know.

When he had grown up to full maturity,
We gave him wisdom and knowledge.
Thus do We recompense the doers of good.
15. He came to the city when the people were in a care-free
        mood,
and saw two men quarrelling,
one belonging to his community, the other to his enemies.
The man who belonged to his community appealed for help
against the one who belonged to the enemies.
Moses struck him a blow with his fist and finished him off.
"This is of Satan's doing," he said.
"He is certainly an enemy and a corrupter."
16. "O Lord," he prayed, "I have done wrong, forgive me."
And God forgave him.
Verily He is forgiving and kind.
17. (Moses) said: "O Lord, as You have been gracious to me
I will never aid the guilty."
18. In the morning he came to the city, fearful and hesitant.
Just then he who had asked him for help the day before
called out for help (again).
"You are indeed a meddlesome fellow," Moses said to him.
19. Then as he was about to lay hands on the one
who was their common enemy,
he cried out: "O Moses, do you want to kill me
as you killed that person yesterday?
You only want to be a tyrant in the land
and no peacemaker."
20. There came a man running from the other part of the city.
"O Moses," he said, "the chiefs are deliberating to kill you.
Go away from the city. I wish you well."
21. So he left the city, fearful and hesitant,
(and) prayed: "O Lord, deliver me from these wicked people."

Then as he turned his face to Midian, he said:
"Maybe my Lord will show me the right way."
23. And when he came to the waters of Midian
he found a crowd of people watering (their flocks),
and saw two maidens holding back (their cattle).

He asked: "What is the trouble with you?"
They said: "We cannot water our flock
till the shepherds have driven away theirs,
and our father is a very old man."
24. So he watered (their flock), and moved into the shade
and prayed:
"My Lord, I have need of whatever good you send me."
25. Then one of the (maidens) came to him walking bashfully,
(and) said: "My father invites you that he may
repay you for having watered our flock."
So, when (Moses) came to him and told him his story,
he said: "Have no fear. You have escaped from the wicked
people."
26. Said one of the maidens: "O father, employ him.
Surely the best (man) to employ is one who is strong and
honest."
27. He said: "I would like to marry one of these
two daughters of mine to you
if you agree to work for me on hire for eight years.
And if you stay on for ten, it is up to you.
I do not wish to impose any hardship on you.
God willing you will find me a man of honour."
28. (Moses) said: "This is (agreed) between you and me.
Whichever term I fulfil, no injustice will be done to me.
God is witness to our agreement."

When Moses had fulfilled the term
and was journeying with his family, he noticed a fire
on the side of the mountain.
"Wait here," he said to his family; "I have seen a fire.
I may haply bring some news from there, or an ember
that you may warm yourselves."
30. When he drew near, a voice called out to him from the tree
on the blessed spot on the right side of the valley:
"O Moses, I am verily God, the Lord of all the worlds.
31. Throw down your staff."
When he saw it wriggling like a serpent,
he turned about and fled without turning.
"O Moses, approach," (said the Voice), "and have no fear.
You will be safe.
32. Put your hand inside your shirt.
It will come out white without a tarnish of blame;
and do not be perturbed or afraid.
These are two proofs from your Lord
for the Pharaoh and his nobles.
They are certainly a rebellious people."

Al-Qasas

33. He said: "O Lord, I have killed a man of theirs,
and fear they would kill me.
34. So send my brother Aaron with me as helper
for he is more fluent than I with words,
that he should affirm me, for I fear
that they would call me a liar.''
35. (And) God said: "We shall strengthen your arm with your
   brother,
and give you power with Our signs and give you authority,
so that they will not be able to harm you.
Both of you and your followers will be victorious.''
36. But when Moses came to them with Our clear signs
they said: "This is nothing but magic he has contrived,
for we have not heard of this from our fathers of old.''
37. But Moses said: "My Lord knows well who has come
with guidance from Him,
and for whom is the guerdon of Paradise.
But surely the wicked will not prosper.''
38. The Pharaoh said: "O nobles, I am not aware
of any other lord of yours but myself.
So, O Haman, fire some clay (bricks) to build a tower for me
that I may mount up (and see)
the God of Moses; for I think he is a liar.''
39. He and his soldiers had become arrogant in the land
for no reason, and did not think
that they have to come back to Us in the end.
40. So We seized him and his hordes and threw them into the
   sea.
Behold then how was the end of the wicked!
41. We made them the leaders of those who call to Hell;
and on the Day of Judgement they will not be helped.
42. A curse lies upon them in this world,
and on the Day of Resurrection they will be despised.

After We had destroyed the earlier generations
We gave Moses the Book as evidence for mankind,
and a guidance and grace,
so that they may remember.
44. You were not there on the western side (of Mount Sinai)
when We gave the commandments to Moses,
nor were you witness (to the event).
45. We raised (many more) generations and prolonged their
   lives.
You did not live with the people of Midian,
nor recited to them Our revelations;
but We kept on sending messengers.

46. You were not present on the side of Mount Sinai
when We called. And all this (knowledge that you are given)
is by the grace of your Lord so that you may warn
a people to whom no admonisher had come before you,
that they may take heed;

47. And in case disaster comes upon them
for what they have done themselves, they should say:
"O Lord, why did You not send an apostle to us
that we should have followed Your commands,
and been with those who are believers;"

48. But when the truth came to them from Us, they said:
"Why is he not given the like of what was given to Moses?"
Did they not disbelieve before in what was given to Moses?
They said: "Both are imposters one like the other,"
and added: "We do not believe in either."

49. Say: "Then bring a Book from God
which gives better guidance than these
so that I may follow it, if you speak the truth."

50. Then, if they cannot give you an answer, know
that they are only following their lusts.
And who can be farther astray than he
who follows his lust without any guidance from God?
And certainly God does not guide an unjust people.

We have been sending word to them
that they may take a warning.

52. Those to whom We gave the Book before this
do believe in it;

53. And when it is read out to them, say:
"We believe in it. It's the truth from our Lord.
We had committed ourselves before it came."

54. These will be given their recompense twice,
for they persevered and repelled evil with good,
and spent of what We had given them.

55. When they hear idle talk they turn aside
and say: "To us our actions, to you yours.
Peace on you; we do not look for the ignorant."

56. You cannot guide any one you like:
God guides whosoever He please.
He knows best who will come to guidance.

57. They say: "If we followed your guidance
we would be driven from the land by force."
Have We not set up a sanctuary for them,
to which is brought a wealth of every thing
as provision from Us?
But most of them do not understand.

Al-Qasas

58. How many habitations that had come to boast
of their resources have We destroyed?
These their dwellings were never inhabited
except rarely after them;
and they came back to Us.
59. But your Lord does not destroy habitations
without having sent an apostle to their metropolis
to read out Our commandments to them.
We would never have destroyed cities
if their inhabitants were not given to wickedness.
60. Whatsoever has been given you is the stuff
this life is made of, and only its embellishment.
What is with your Lord is better and abiding.
Will you not understand?

Can one who was given a better promise,
which he will find come true,
be like him who was given a little enjoyment of this life,
but who will afterwards
be brought (to judgement) on the Day of Resurrection?
62. That day God will call them and ask:
"Where are they you imagined were My compeers?"
63. Those against whom the sentence is justified
will say: "O Lord, these are those we had led astray
as we had ourselves gone astray.
We clear ourselves before You:
They never worshipped us."
64. (The sinners) will be told: "Invoke your partners."
They will call on them, but they will not answer;
and they will see the torment (and wish)
if only they had come to guidance.
65. (God) will ask them on that day:
"What answer did you give the apostles?"
66. Then all news will be blacked out for them,
and they will not even ask one another.
67. But he who repents and believes and does good things
may well be among the successful.
68. Your Lord creates what He wills and chooses.
The good is not for them to choose.
Too holy and high is God for what they associate with Him.
69. Your Lord well knows what they hide in their breasts
and what they disclose.
70. He is God. There is no god but He.
His alone is praise first and last,
and His the judgement, and to Him
will you be brought back in the end.

71. Say: "Just think, if God were to cover you up with night
for ever until the Day of Doom,
what other god apart from God will give you light?
Why do you not pay heed?"
72. Say: "Just think. If God were to make the day
perpetual till the Day of Resurrection,
what other god but God would bring you night for rest?
Why do you not reflect?
73. Yet in His benevolence He made you night and day
that you may rest and seek His bounty during them,
and haply may be grateful."
74. Upon a day He will call them and ask:
"Where are they you imagined were My compeers?"
75. And We shall single out one witness from each community
and say: "Bring your proof."
Then will they know that God's is the judgement,
and what they contrived will avail them not in the least.

Verily Qarun was of Moses' people,
but he began to oppress them.
We had given him treasures, so many that a team of wrestlers
could hardly lift their keys.
His people said to him: "Do not be exultant.
God does not like those who exult.
77. So seek the abode of the Hereafter
through what God has given you,
and do not forget your part in this world.
Do good to others as God has done good to you,
and do not try to spread corruption in the land.
Surely God does not like corrupters."
78. He said: "This has come to me through my own
          acumen."
Did he not know that God had destroyed
many generations before him who possessed
far more acumen than he, and more wealth?
The sinners will not be asked about their sins.
79. Then he came before his people in all pomp;
and those enamoured of this world, said:
"Ah would that we had what Qarun has been given!
He indeed possesses great good fortune."
80. But those who knew better, said:
"Alack-a-day! God's guerdon is better for those who believe
and do the right. Only those who persevere will receive it."
81. So We opened up the earth and sunk him and his
          mansion.
There was not a body that could help him against (the will) of

يَنصُرُونَهُ مِن دُونِ اللَّهِ وَمَا كَانَ مِنَ الْمُنتَصِرِينَ ۝

God,
nor was he able to save himself.
82. Those who were envious of his position only yesterday
said on the morrow:
"Indeed God increases the fortunes
of those of His creatures as He will,
and decreases.
Had God not been gracious to us
He could have (opened up) the earth and made it swallow us.
Surely the infidels will not succeed."

وَأَصْبَحَ الَّذِينَ تَمَنَّوْا مَكَانَهُ بِالْأَمْسِ يَقُولُونَ وَيْكَأَنَّ
اللَّهَ يَبْسُطُ الرِّزْقَ لِمَن يَشَاءُ مِنْ عِبَادِهِ وَيَقْدِرُ ۚ
لَوْلَا أَن مَّنَّ اللَّهُ عَلَيْنَا لَخَسَفَ بِنَا ۖ وَيْكَأَنَّهُ لَا يُفْلِحُ
الْكَافِرُونَ ۝

We shall give the mansion of the Hereafter
to those who do not want to be haughty in the land
and spread corruption.
The future belongs to those who take heed for themselves
and follow the straight path.
84. Whoever does good will receive better than what he has
        done;
and whoever does ill shall be requited
but to the extent of what he does.
85. He who has assigned (the propagation) of the Qur'an to you
will bring you back to the destination.
Say: "My Lord knows who has come to guidance,
and who is clearly in error."
86. You did not expect that the Book would be given to you
except by the favour of your Lord.
So do not be the helper of unbelievers,
87. Nor should you let them turn you away from the
        commandments of God
once they have been delivered to you;
and call them to your Lord, and do not be an idolater,
88. And do not call on any other god apart from God.
There is no god but He.
All things will perish save His magnificence.
His is the judgement, and to Him
will you be brought back in the end.

تِلْكَ الدَّارُ الْآخِرَةُ نَجْعَلُهَا لِلَّذِينَ لَا يُرِيدُونَ عُلُوًّا
فِي الْأَرْضِ وَلَا فَسَادًا ۚ وَالْعَاقِبَةُ لِلْمُتَّقِينَ ۝

مَن جَاءَ بِالْحَسَنَةِ فَلَهُ خَيْرٌ مِّنْهَا ۖ وَمَن جَاءَ بِالسَّيِّئَةِ
فَلَا يُجْزَى الَّذِينَ عَمِلُوا السَّيِّئَاتِ إِلَّا مَا كَانُوا يَعْمَلُونَ ۝

إِنَّ الَّذِي فَرَضَ عَلَيْكَ الْقُرْآنَ لَرَادُّكَ إِلَىٰ مَعَادٍ ۚ
قُل رَّبِّي أَعْلَمُ مَن جَاءَ بِالْهُدَىٰ وَمَنْ هُوَ فِي
ضَلَالٍ مُّبِينٍ ۝
وَمَا كُنتَ تَرْجُو أَن يُلْقَىٰ إِلَيْكَ الْكِتَابُ إِلَّا رَحْمَةً
مِّن رَّبِّكَ ۖ فَلَا تَكُونَنَّ ظَهِيرًا لِّلْكَافِرِينَ ۝
وَلَا يَصُدُّنَّكَ عَنْ آيَاتِ اللَّهِ بَعْدَ إِذْ أُنزِلَتْ إِلَيْكَ ۖ
وَادْعُ إِلَىٰ رَبِّكَ ۖ وَلَا تَكُونَنَّ مِنَ الْمُشْرِكِينَ ۝

وَلَا تَدْعُ مَعَ اللَّهِ إِلَٰهًا آخَرَ ۘ لَا إِلَٰهَ إِلَّا هُوَ ۚ كُلُّ شَيْءٍ
هَالِكٌ إِلَّا وَجْهَهُ ۚ لَهُ الْحُكْمُ وَإِلَيْهِ تُرْجَعُونَ ۝

29 The Spider

Al-'Ankabūt: Makki

In the name of Allah, most benevolent, ever-merciful.

ALIF LĀM MĪM.
2. Do men think they will get away by saying: "We believe,"
and will not be tried?
3. We had tried those who were before them
so that God knew who spoke the truth, and who were liars.
4. Do those who do evil think
that they will get the better of Us?
How bad is the judgement that they make!
5. He who hopes to meet God (should know)
that God's appointed time will surely come.
He is all-hearing and all-knowing.
6. He who strives does so for himself.
Verily God is independent of the creatures of the world.
7. We shall pardon the sinful deeds of those
who believe and do the right,
and give them a reward better than their deeds.
8. We have enjoined on man to be good to his parents;
but if they try to make you associate with Me
that of which you have no knowledge, then do not obey them.
You have to come back to Us, when I will tell you
what you used to do.
9. We shall admit those who believe and do the right
among the righteous.
10. There are among men those who say: "We believe in God;"
yet if they happen to suffer in the cause of God
they take oppression by men as punishment from God.
And if help comes to them from your Lord,
they say: "We were with you."
Does not God know what is hidden in the hearts of men?
11. God will surely know the believers
and know the hypocrites.
12. Those who deny say to those who affirm:
"Follow our way; we shall carry the burden of your sins."
But they cannot carry the burden of their sins in the least.

They are liars indeed.
13. They will carry their own loads
and other loads besides their own;
and will surely be questioned
on the Day of Resurrection
about what they contrived.

We sent Noah to his people, and he lived with them
a thousand years minus fifty.
Then they were caught by the deluge
for they were evil.
15. But We saved him and those with him in the ark,
and made it a sign for the creatures of the world.
16. And (remember) Abraham who said to his people:
"Worship God and be obedient to Him.
This is better for you if you understand.
17. You worship idols in place of God
and invent lies.
Surely those you worship other than God
have no power over your means of livelihood.
So seek your sustenance from God,
and worship Him and give Him thanks.
To Him will you be brought back in the end.
18. But if you deny,
then many a people have denied before you.
The duty of the apostle is to convey
the message clearly."
19. Do they not see how God originates creation,
then reverts it back?
This is indeed how inevitably the law of God works;
20. Say: "Travel on the earth and see
how He originated creation.
Then (you will know) how God will raise the last raising
(of the dead). Surely God has power over every thing,
21. Punish whom He will,
and have mercy on whom He please.
And to Him will you be brought back in the end.
22. Escape Him you cannot either in the earth or in the sky;
and you have no friend or helper apart from God.

Those who deny the signs of God
and the meeting with Him,
cannot have hope of My mercy.
There is a painful punishment for them.
24. The people (of Abraham) had no answer except:
"Kill him or burn him;"

but God saved him from the fire.
There are lessons in this for those who believe.
25. He said: "You have taken to idols
through mutual affection in this life, in place of God,
but on the Day of Resurrection you will disown
and curse each other,
and your abode will be Hell,
and you will have none to help you."
26. Then Lot believed in him; and (Abraham) said:
"I will separate myself and take refuge in my Lord.
Surely He is all-mighty and all-wise."
27. So We bestowed on him Isaac and Jacob
and gave his progeny prophethood and scripture,
and rewarded him in this world,
and in the next he will be among the upright.
28. And (remember) Lot when he said to his people:
"You indulge in lecherous acts
which none of the creatures had done before you.
29. You commit unnatural acts with men
and cut off the way (of procreation),
and commit obscenities in your gatherings."
The only answer his people made was: "Bring
the punishment of God, if you are truthful."
30. "O Lord, help me against the wicked people," (Lot) prayed.

When Our messengers came to Abraham with good news,
they said: "We have to destroy this city
as its inhabitants have become sinful."
32. He said: "Surely Lot is there."
They answered: "We know who is there.
We are to save him and his family except his wife,
for she is one of those who will stay behind."
33. So, when Our messengers came to Lot,
he was worried on their account
as he was unable to protect them.
They said: "Have no fear or regret.
We will certainly save you and your family except your wife,
for she is one of those who will stay behind.
34. We have to bring a scourge from the heavens
on the people of this city as they are depraved."
35. Verily We have left a clear sign of this
for people of sense to see.
36. To Midian We sent their brother Shu'aib.
He said: "O people, worship God
and be ready for the Day of Resurrection.
Do no evil, and create no mischief in the land."

Al-'Ankabut

37. But they denied him and were seized
by an earthquake, and lay overturned
in their homes in the morning.
38. And (remember) 'Ad and Thamud.
It will be clear to you from their habitations
(how they were destroyed),
for Satan had made their deeds look attractive to them,
and turned them away from the path;
and yet they were a people of acumen.
39. (Remember) Qarun, Pharaoh and Haman
to whom Moses came with clear signs;
but they were haughty (and oppressed) the land.
Yet they could not run away from Us;
40. And We seized all of them for their crimes.
Against some We sent a violent wind hurling stones,
and some We seized with a mighty blast,
and some We submerged under the earth,
and some We drowned.
It was not for God to wrong them,
they wronged themselves.
41. The semblance of those who take protectors besides God
is that of the spider.
She arranges a house for herself,
but the flimsiest of houses is the spider's.
If only they had sense!
42. Verily God knows what they invoke in His place,
for He is all-mighty and all-wise.
43. These are precepts of wisdom We offer to men,
but only those who are rational understand.
44. God has created the heavens and the earth
with reason.
Surely in this is a sign for those who believe.

Recite what has been revealed to you of this Book,
and be constant in devotion. Surely prayer
keeps you away from the obscene and detestable,
but the remembrance of God is greater far;
and God knows what you do.
46. Do not argue with the people of the Book
unless in a fair way, apart from those
who act wrongly, and say to them:
"We believe what has been sent down to us,
and we believe what has been sent down to you.
Our God and your God is one,
and to Him we submit."
47. That is how We have revealed this Book to you;

Al-'Ankabut

and those to whom We have sent down the Book
will believe in it.
Only those who are infidels will deny it.
48. You did not read any Scripture before this,
nor wrote one with your right hand,
or else these dissemblers would have found a cause to doubt it.
49. In fact, in the minds of those who have intelligence
these are clear signs.
No one denies Our revelations except those who are unjust.
50. For they say: "How is it no signs
were sent down to him from his Lord?"
Say: "The signs are with God.
I am only a warner, plain and simple."
51. Is it not sufficient for them that We have revealed
the Book to you which is read out to them?
It is indeed a grace and reminder
for people who believe.

Say: "God is sufficient as witness between me and you."
He knows what is in the heavens and the earth.
It is those who believe in falsehood and disbelieve in God
who will perish.
53. They want you to hasten the punishment:
But for a time already determined
the punishment would have come upon them.
It will come upon them all too suddenly,
and they will be caught unawares.
54. They want you to hasten the punishment:
Hell will indeed surround the unbelievers.
55. The day the punishment comes upon them
from above and underneath their feet,
(God will) say: "And now taste of what you had done."
56. O My creatures who believe,
surely My earth has plenty of scope and
so worship only Me.
57. Every soul has to know the taste of death.
You will then be sent back to Us.
58. We shall admit those who believe and do the right
to empyreal gardens with rivers rippling by,
where they will abide for ever.
How excellent the guerdon of those who toil,
59. Who persevere and place their trust in their Lord.
60. How many living things there are on the earth
that do not store their food;
God provides them as well as you.
He is all-hearing and all-knowing.

Al-'Ankabut

61. If you ask them: "Who created the heavens and the earth,
and who set the sun and the moon to work?"
They will answer: "God."
Why then do they vacillate?
62. God increases the means of those of His creatures as He
    please,
or limits them for whomsoever He will.
He is certainly cognisant of every thing.
63. If you ask them: "Who sends down rain from the sky
and quickens the earth when it is dead?"
They will answer: "God."
Say: "All praise be to God."
But most of them do not understand.

The life of this world is only a sport and play.
It is surely the home of the Hereafter
that will indeed be life extended and new,
if only they knew!
65. When they board a ship they call on God,
placing their faith wholly in Him.
But when He brings them safely back to shore,
they begin to associate others with Him,
66. And deny what We had given them,
in order to go on enjoying themselves.
They will come to know soon.
67. Do they not see that We have given them a safe sanctuary,
while all around them men are being despoiled?
Do they then believe what is false,
and deny the bounty of God?
68. Who is more unjust than he
who fabricates a lie about God,
or denies the truth when it has come to him?
Is there not an abode for unbelievers in Hell?
69. We shall guide those who strive in Our cause
to the paths leading straight to Us.
Surely God is with those who do good.

30 The Romans

Ar-Rūm: Makki

In the name of Allah, most benevolent, ever-merciful.

بِسْمِ اللهِ الرَّحْمٰنِ الرَّحِیْمِ ۰

ALIF LĀM MĪM.

2. The Romans have been conquered
3. In the neighbouring land.
But having been conquered they will conquer
4. In a few years (less than ten).
God's is the imperative first and last.
On that day the believers will rejoice
5. In the help of God.
He helps whom He will;
He is all-mighty, ever-merciful.
6. It is a promise of God;
and God does not go back on His promise.
Yet most men do not understand:
7. They only know the palpable life of this world,
and are oblivious of the Hereafter.
8. Do they not think for themselves
that God did not create
the heavens and the earth and all that lies between them
without reason and a determined purpose?
But many men reject the meeting with their Lord.
9. Have they not travelled on the earth and seen
how the others before them had met their end?
They were far more powerful than them,
furrowed the earth and colonised it
far more than they;
and their apostles came to them with visible signs.
It was surely not for God to wrong them,
they wronged themselves.
10. Therefore evil was the end of those who did evil,
for they denied the signs of God and made fun of them.

God originates creation, and then will revert it,
then you will go back to Him.
12. The day the Resurrection comes

الٓمّٓ ۚ

غُلِبَتِ الرُّوْمُ ۙ

فِیْۤ اَدْنَی الْاَرْضِ وَهُمْ مِّنْۢ بَعْدِ غَلَبِهِمْ سَیَغْلِبُوْنَ ۙ

فِیْ بِضْعِ سِنِیْنَ ۬ؕ لِلهِ الْاَمْرُ مِنْ قَبْلُ وَمِنْۢ بَعْدُ ؕ

وَیَوْمَئِذٍ یَّفْرَحُ الْمُؤْمِنُوْنَ ۙ

بِنَصْرِ اللهِ ؕ یَنْصُرُ مَنْ یَّشَآءُ ؕ وَهُوَ الْعَزِیْزُ الرَّحِیْمُ ۙ

وَعْدَ اللهِ ؕ لَا یُخْلِفُ اللهُ وَعْدَهٗ وَلٰكِنَّ اَكْثَرَ النَّاسِ لَا یَعْلَمُوْنَ ۰

یَعْلَمُوْنَ ظَاهِرًا مِّنَ الْحَیٰوةِ الدُّنْیَا ۪ۖ وَهُمْ عَنِ الْاٰخِرَةِ هُمْ غٰفِلُوْنَ ۰

اَوَلَمْ یَتَفَكَّرُوْا فِیْۤ اَنْفُسِهِمْ ۫ مَا خَلَقَ اللهُ السَّمٰوٰتِ وَالْاَرْضَ وَمَا بَیْنَهُمَاۤ اِلَّا بِالْحَقِّ وَ اَجَلٍ مُّسَمًّی ؕ وَاِنَّ كَثِیْرًا مِّنَ النَّاسِ بِلِقَآئِ رَبِّهِمْ لَكٰفِرُوْنَ ۰

اَوَلَمْ یَسِیْرُوْا فِی الْاَرْضِ فَیَنْظُرُوْا كَیْفَ كَانَ عَاقِبَةُ الَّذِیْنَ مِنْ قَبْلِهِمْ ؕ كَانُوْۤا اَشَدَّ مِنْهُمْ قُوَّةً وَّاَثَارُوا الْاَرْضَ وَعَمَرُوْهَاۤ اَكْثَرَ مِمَّا عَمَرُوْهَا وَجَآءَتْهُمْ رُسُلُهُمْ بِالْبَیِّنٰتِ ؕ فَمَا كَانَ اللهُ لِیَظْلِمَهُمْ وَلٰكِنْ كَانُوْۤا اَنْفُسَهُمْ یَظْلِمُوْنَ ۰

ثُمَّ كَانَ عَاقِبَةَ الَّذِیْنَ اَسَآءُوا السُّوْٓاٰۤی اَنْ كَذَّبُوْا بِاٰیٰتِ اللهِ وَكَانُوْا بِهَا یَسْتَهْزِءُوْنَ ۰

اَللهُ یَبْدَؤُا الْخَلْقَ ثُمَّ یُعِیْدُهٗ ثُمَّ اِلَیْهِ تُرْجَعُوْنَ ۰

وَیَوْمَ تَقُوْمُ السَّاعَةُ یُبْلِسُ الْمُجْرِمُوْنَ ۰

the sinners will be overwhelmed with despair.
13. No intercessor will they have
among those they associated (with God),
and will reject their partners.
14. The day the Hour comes
they will be separated into categories.
15. Those who believed and did the right
will be feasted in a rich, well-watered meadow.
16. Those who did not believe and rejected Our signs
and the meeting in the Hereafter,
will be given over to punishment.
17. So extol God
when the evening comes and the day dawns, —
18. For His is the praise in the heavens and the earth, —
and at nightfall and the time of noon.
19. He brings the living from the dead,
the dead from the living,
and quickens the earth after it had died.
So will you be brought forth (from the dead).

Among His signs is that He created you from the earth,
and you are now human beings dispersed everywhere.
21. Another of His signs is that He created mates
of your own kind of yourselves
so that you may get peace of mind from them,
and has put love and compassion between you.
Verily there are signs in this for those who reflect.
22. Among other signs of His is the creation of the heavens
     and the earth,
and the variety of your tongues and complexions.
Surely there are signs in this for those who understand.
23. Another of His signs is the night,
a time for you to sleep,
and the day to seek His bounty.
Verily there are signs in this for those who pay heed.
24. Another of His signs is the lightning He shows
to fill you both with dread and hope,
and the water He sends down from the sky
which reawakens the earth that was dead.
There are indeed signs in this for those who have sense.
25. Another of His signs is that the heavens and the earth
stay in position by His command;
and then when He will call you once
you will come out of the earth.
26. All those who are in the heavens and the earth are His,
and they are all obedient to Him.

Ar-Rūm

27. It is He who first creates and then reverts it.
This is how His law works inevitably.
His semblance is of the most sublime
in the heavens and the earth.
He is all-mighty and all-wise.

He gives you an example from your own life:
Do you possess among your dependants any partners
in what We have bestowed on you,
so that you and they have equal (share) in it,
and that you fear them as you fear each other?
That is how We explain Our signs clearly
for those who comprehend.
29. And yet the wicked follow their own lusts without
    understanding.
Who can show the way to those
whom God allows to go astray?
None will they have to help them.
30. So keep yourself exclusively on the true way,
the creational law of God according to which
He created man with the quality of choosing right or wrong.
There is no altering of God's creation.
This is the supreme law.
But most men do not understand.
31. Turn towards Him and be dutiful to Him;
be firm in devotion, and do not become an idolater,
32. (Or) one of those who created rifts in their order
and are divided into sects,
with each group exulting in what it has (carved out for itself).
33. When misfortune befalls men
they pray to their Lord and turn to Him;
but afterwards when He has given them
a taste of His benevolence
a section of them begins to ascribe
compeers to their Lord
34. So as to deny what We have given them.
Please yourselves for a time; you will come to know soon.
35. Have We sent down a charter to them
which mentions what they associate with Him?
36. When We give men a taste of Our benevolence
they start rejoicing in it.
When misfortune befalls them
as a result of what they have done themselves,
they begin to despair.
37. Do they not see God increases or decreases
the means of whosoever He please?

Verily there are signs in this for those who believe.
38. So, give their share to the relatives, the needy,
and the wayfarers.
This is best for those who seek the way that leads to God,
and they will be successful.
39. What you give on interest to increase (your capital)
through others' wealth, does not find increase with God;
yet what you give (in alms and charity) with a pure heart,
seeking the way of God, will be doubled.
40. It is God who created you, then gave you sustenance,
then He will make you die, and bring you back to life.
Is there one among those you associate with Him
who can do the least of these things?
Too high and exalted is He for what they associate with Him!

Corruption has spread over land and sea
from what men have done themselves
that they may taste a little of what they have done:
They may haply come back (to the right path).
42. Say: "Travel on the earth and see
how came the end of those before you."
Most of them were idolaters.
43. So set your face towards the straight path
before the day arrives from God which is irreversible.
Men will be segregated on that day
44. So that he who disbelieves
will bear the consequence of his unbelief;
and he who does the right
will straighten out the way for himself,
45. So that God may reward those who believed
and did what was good, by His grace.
Surely He does not love unbelievers.
46. Among His signs are the breezes He sends
as harbingers of happy news,
so that He may allow you to taste of His mercy,
and that ships may sail by His command,
and you may seek of His bounty,
and may haply be grateful.
47. Verily We sent many apostles before you
to their people,
who brought clear signs with them.
Then We retributed those who were sinful.
It is a duty incumbent on Us to help the believers.
48. It is God who sends the breezes that raise clouds,
then spreads them over the sky as He please, fold on fold,
then you see the drops of rain issue from between them.

Ar-Rum

When He sends it down to those of His creatures as He will,
they are filled with joy,
49. Although before it came down they were despondent.
50. So consider the signs of His benevolence:
How He quickens the earth after it had become waste.
He is verily the one who will raise the dead.
He has power over every thing.
51. If We send a (blighting) wind
and they see (the earth) seared autumnal,
they would surely become ungrateful.
52. You cannot make the dead to listen
nor the deaf hear the call
when they have turned back and retreated,
53. Nor can you make the blind see the way
when they have gone astray.
You can make none hear except
those who believe Our signs and have come to submission.

It is God who created you of weakness,
then after weakness gave you strength,
then after strength will give you weakness and grey hair.
Surely He makes whatever He wills.
He is all-knowing and all-powerful.
55. The day Resurrection is set
the sinners will swear: "We did not tarry
more than an hour (and cannot be guilty)."
That is how they have always been deceived.
56. But those who were given the knowledge and belief will say:
"You have tarried, according to the Book of God,
as long as the Day of Resurrection,
and this is the Day of Resurrection,
but you do not know."
57. Their excuses will be of no avail to the sinners on that day,
and they will not be allowed to beg for favour.
58. We have offered every kind of example
here in this Qur'an to men.
Even then if you bring a verse to them,
those who disbelieve say:
"You are nothing but a liar."
59. That is how God seals the hearts of those
who do not know.
60. So have patience.
The promise of God is surely true;
and let not those who do not believe
make you relax (your endeavours).

31 Luqmān

Luqmān: Makki

In the name of Allah, most benevolent, ever-merciful.

ALIF LĀM MĪM.
2. These are the verses of the sagacious Book,
3. And a guidance and grace for those who do good,
4. Who are constant in devotion, pay the zakat,
and are certain of the Hereafter.
5. They are on guidance from their Lord,
and will prosper.
6. But among men are also those who spread
frivolous stories to mislead (others)
from the way of God, without any knowledge,
and take it lightly.
For such as these the nemesis will be shameful.
7. When Our verses are recited before them
they turn away haughtily
as though they did not hear them,
as if a deafness had come into their ears.
So give them tidings of a shameful punishment.
8. Surely for those who believe and do the right
are pleasure gardens.
9. They will abide in them for ever.
The promise of God is true;
and He is all-mighty and all-wise.
10. He created the skies without a support, as you can see,
and placed stabilisers in the earth
that you may dwell at ease as it revolves;
and dispersed on it all varieties of creatures,
and He sent down water from the skies
and grew all kinds of splendid things upon it.
11. Such is God's creation.
Show me now what those (they worship) beside Him
have created.
Surely the evil-doers are in clear error.

We bestowed wisdom on Luqman

that he may be grateful to God.
Whosoever is grateful is so for his own good,
and whoever is ungrateful (should remember) that God
is above all concern, worthy of praise.
13. (Remember) when Luqman counselled his son:
"O son, do not associate any one with God.
To associate others with God is a grievous wrong."
14. We have committed man about his parents.
His mother carries him in her womb
in weakness and debility, weaning him in two years.
So he should be grateful to Me and his parents.
To Me is the journeying back.
15. If they try to force you to associate with Me
that of which you have no knowledge,
do not obey them.
Live with them honourably in the world,
but follow the way of him who turns to Me.
Your returning is to Me in the end,
when I will tell you what you did.
16. "O my son, whatsoever it may be,
even though equal to a mustard seed in weight,
or within a rock or in the sky or in the earth,
God will bring it forth.
Verily God is perceptive, all-aware.
17. O my son, fulfil your moral obligations,
bid what is known to be right and forbid what is wrong,
and bear with patience what befalls you.
These are indeed acts of courage and resolve.
18. Do not hold men in contempt,
and do not walk with hauteur on the earth.
Verily God does not like the proud and boastful.
19. Be moderate in your bearing, and keep your voice low.
Surely the most repulsive voice is the donkey's."

Have you not seen that God has subjugated
what is in the heavens and the earth to you,
and bestowed His favours,
external and esoteric, in abundance on you?
And yet there are men who contend about God
without any knowledge or guidance or the Book enlightening.
21. When you ask them to follow what God has revealed,
they say: "No. We shall follow what we found
our ancestors following,"
— even though the devil were calling them to the torment of
    Hell!
22. He who turns his face to God in submission and does good,

holds fast to a handle that is strong;
for the resultance of things rests with God.
23. So do not let the unbelief of disbelievers grieve you.
They will be brought back to Us,
when We shall tell them what they used to do.
Whatever is in their hearts is known to God.
24. We let them enjoy themselves only for a while,
then We shall drag them to a severe punishment.
25. If you ask them: "Who created the heavens and the earth?"
They will surely answer: "God."
Say: "All praise be to God."
But most of them do not understand.
26. To God belongs what is in the heavens and the earth.
Verily He is all-sufficient, worthy of praise.
27. If all the trees of the earth were pens
and the oceans ink,
with many more oceans for replenishing them,
the colloquy of God would never come to end.
He is indeed all-mighty and all-wise.
28. Your creation and resurrection
is but like that of a single cell.
Verily He is all-hearing and all-seeing.
29. Do you not see that God makes the night succeed the day,
the day succeed the night?
And He has harnessed the sun and the moon
so that each runs its appointed course.
Surely God is aware of all you do.
30. That is so for God is the Reality,
and what they invoke other than Him is illusion.
Indeed God is all-high and supreme.

Do you not see that the ships sail in the ocean
by the grace of God, that He may show you some of His glories.
Verily there are signs in this
for those who are constant and give thanks.
32. When the waves overshadow them like a canopy,
they pray to God with all-exclusive faith in Him.
But after He has safely brought them to the shore,
there are some who vacillate between doubt and belief,
but no one rejects Our signs except those
who are perverse and disbelieve.
33. O people, fear your Lord and dread the day
when no father will avail a son,
nor son his father.
Truly the promise of God is true.
Do not be deluded by the life of this world,

وَلَا يَغُرَّنَّكُمْ بِاللَّهِ الْغَرُوْرُ ۞

and do not let the deceiver draw you away from God.
34. Only God has the knowledge of the Hour.
He sends rain from the heavens,
and knows what is in the mothers' wombs.
No one knows what he will do on the morrow;
no one knows in what land he will die.
Surely God knows and is cognisant.

إِنَّ اللَّهَ عِنْدَهُ عِلْمُ السَّاعَةِ وَيُنَزِّلُ الْغَيْثَ وَ

يَعْلَمُ مَا فِي الْأَرْحَامِ وَمَا تَدْرِيْ نَفْسٌ مَّاذَا تَكْسِبُ

غَدًا وَمَا تَدْرِيْ نَفْسٌ بِأَيِّ أَرْضٍ تَمُوْتُ إِنَّ اللَّهَ

عَلِيْمٌ خَبِيْرٌ ۞

32 As-Sajdah*

As-Sajdah: Makki

سُوْرَةُ السَّجْدَةِ مَكِّيَّةٌ (۳۲)

اٰیَاتُهَا ۳۰ رُكُوْعُهَا

In the name of Allah, most benevolent, ever-merciful.

بِسۡمِ اللّٰهِ الرَّحۡمٰنِ الرَّحِیۡمِ

ALIF LĀM MĪM.

الٓمّٓ ۟

2. The revelation of this Book free of doubt and involution
is from the Lord of all the worlds.

3. Or do they say he has fabricated it?
In fact, it is the truth from your Lord
so that you may warn the people
to whom no admonisher was sent before you.
They may haply come to guidance.

4. It is God who created the heavens and the earth
and all that lies between them,
in six spans, then assumed all authority.
You have no protector other than Him,
nor any intercessor.
Will you not be warned even then?

5. He regulates all affairs from high to low, then they rise
to perfection step by step in a (heavenly) day
whose measure is a thousand years of your reckoning.

6. Such is (He) the knower of the unknown and the known,
the mighty and the merciful,

7. Who made all things He created excellent;
and first fashioned man from clay,**

8. Then made his offspring from the extract of base fluid,

9. Then proportioned and breathed into him of His spirit,
and gave you the senses of hearing, sight and feeling.
And yet how little are the thanks you offer!

10. But they say: "When we have mingled with the earth,
shall we be created anew?"
In fact they deny the meeting with their Lord.

---

* *Sajdah* is an expression of homage peculiar to Islam. It expresses physically the worshippers' humility and sense of utter insignificance before God. It has often been translated as 'prostration' which, however, is stretching flat on the ground. In *Sajdah* one bends the knees to a sitting position, resting the palms and the forehead on the ground in one complete action, facing the Ka'bah.
** Clay and dust signify that man is made of matter. See note on page 505.

11. Say: "The angel of death appointed over you
will take away your soul,
then you will be sent back to your Lord."

If only you could see when the sinners will stand
before their Lord, heads hung low, (and say:)
"O Lord, we have seen and heard.
So send us back. We shall do the right,
for we have come to believe with certainty."
13. Had We intended We could have given
every soul its guidance;
but inevitable is My word that I will fill up Hell
with men and jinns together.
14. So now suffer. As you forgot
the meeting of this your Day of Doom,
so have We forgotten you.
Now taste the everlasting punishment for your deeds.
15. Only they believe in Our revelations
who, when they are reminded, bow in adoration,
and give praise to their Lord, and do not become arrogant.
16. Their backs do not rest on their beds,
and they pray to their Lord in fear and hope,
and spend of what We have given them (in charity).
17. No soul knows what peace and joy lie hidden from them
as reward for what they have done.
18. Is one who is a believer like one who is a transgressor?
No, they are not alike.
19. As for those who believe and do the right,
there are gardens for abode
as welcome for what they had done.
20. As for those who disobey, their abode is Hell.
Whensoever they wish to escape from it
they would be dragged back into it,
and told: "Taste the torment of the Fire
which you used to call a lie."
21. But We shall make them taste the affliction of this world
before the greater torment,
so that they may retract.
22. Who is more wicked than he
who is reminded of his Lord's revelations
yet turns away from them;
We will surely requite the sinners.

Verily We gave Moses the Book;
so be not in doubt about his having received it;
and We made it a guidance for the children of Israel.

24. When they persevered and firmly believed Our revelations
We appointed learned men among them
who guided them by Our command.
25. Surely your Lord will decide between them
about what they were at variance,
on the Day of Resurrection.
26. Did they not find guidance in the many
generations We had destroyed before them,
over whose dwellings they (now) walk?
There were indeed signs in this.
Will they even then not listen?
27. Do they not see that We drive the rain
towards a land that is dry,
then grow grain from it
which their cattle and they themselves eat?
Will they not see even then?
28. Yet they say: "When will this decree come,
if you speak the truth?"
29. Say: "Of no use will be the acceptance of belief
to unbelievers on the Day of Decision,
nor will they be granted respite.
30. Therefore turn away from them
and wait as they are waiting.

وَجَعَلْنَا مِنْهُمْ أَئِمَّةً يَهْدُونَ بِأَمْرِنَا لَمَّا صَبَرُوا
وَكَانُوا بِآيَاتِنَا يُوقِنُونَ ۝

إِنَّ رَبَّكَ هُوَ يَفْصِلُ بَيْنَهُمْ يَوْمَ الْقِيَامَةِ فِيمَا كَانُوا
فِيهِ يَخْتَلِفُونَ ۝

أَوَلَمْ يَهْدِ لَهُمْ كَمْ أَهْلَكْنَا مِن قَبْلِهِم مِّنَ الْقُرُونِ
يَمْشُونَ فِي مَسَاكِنِهِمْ إِنَّ فِي ذَٰلِكَ لَآيَاتٍ أَفَلَا
يَسْمَعُونَ ۝

أَوَلَمْ يَرَوْا أَنَّا نَسُوقُ الْمَاءَ إِلَى الْأَرْضِ الْجُرُزِ
فَنُخْرِجُ بِهِ زَرْعًا تَأْكُلُ مِنْهُ أَنْعَامُهُمْ وَأَنفُسُهُمْ
أَفَلَا يُبْصِرُونَ ۝

وَيَقُولُونَ مَتَىٰ هَٰذَا الْفَتْحُ إِن كُنتُمْ صَادِقِينَ ۝

قُلْ يَوْمَ الْفَتْحِ لَا يَنفَعُ الَّذِينَ كَفَرُوا إِيمَانُهُمْ وَلَا
هُمْ يُنظَرُونَ ۝

فَأَعْرِضْ عَنْهُمْ وَانتَظِرْ إِنَّهُم مُّنتَظِرُونَ ۝

33 The Allied Troops

Al-Ahzāb: Madani

In the name of Allah, most benevolent, ever-merciful.

O PROPHET FEAR God
and do not follow the unbelievers and the hypocrites.
2. Follow what is revealed to you by your Lord.
Verily God is all-knowing and all-wise.
3. Trust in God. God is sufficient as guardian.
4. God has not provided two hearts in the breast of a man,
nor made your wives, whom you pronounce "mothers"
(in order to divorce them), your real mothers,
nor has He made your adopted sons your real sons.
This is only what your lips pronounce.
God says what is just,
and shows the right way.
5. Call them by the names of their fathers.
This is the right course in the sight of God.
If you do not know their fathers,
they are then your brothers in religion and your friends.
It will not be a sin if you make a mistake,
unless you do so intentionally;
for God is forgiving and kind.
6. The Prophet is closer to the faithful than they are themselves;
and his wives are as their mothers.
Yet blood relations are closer to one another
according to God's decree, more than (other) believers
and the emigrants (who left their homes in the cause of God),
but you should be kind to your friends.
This is inscribed in the Book (of decrees).
7. When We made the covenant with the prophets, and with you,
as with Noah and Abraham, Moses and Jesus son of Mary,
a binding covenant,
8. (It was) so that God may ask the truthful of their sincerity.
As for the infidels, He has prepared a painful punishment for
them.

O you who believe, remember the favours of God to you

when an army came against you and We sent
a wind against them and forces that you did not see.
But God sees all that you do.

10. When they came upon you from above and below you,
when the eyes were stupefied with horror,
and hearts jumped to the throats,
and you made wild suppositions about God.

11. The faithful were sorely tried there and were shaken
completely,

12. When the hypocrites and those who were filled with doubt,
said:
"The promise of God and His Apostle was nothing but deceit."

13. When a section of them said: "O people of Yathrib,
there is no place for you here, turn back;"
and a section of them asked leave of the Prophet, saying:
"Our homes lie exposed," — while they were not exposed.
Their only intention was to run away.

14. If the (enemy) had entered the city from every side
and asked them to rise in revolt, they would have done so,
and not hesitated but a little;

15. Whereas earlier they had made a promise to God
that they would never turn their backs;
and a promise made to God is answerable.

16. Say: "Of no gain will be your running away
if you run from death or being killed,
even then you will enjoy the good things of life
but only for a while."

17. Say: "Who will save you from God
if He decide to afflict you or show you His mercy?"
They will never find a friend or helper apart from God.

18. Surely God knows who among you obstruct,
and those who say to their brethren: "Come to us,"
and go to battle but seldom,

19. Being chary of helping you.
But when danger appears you will find them looking at you
with eyes turning like a man's in the swoon of death.
Yet when the danger is past they lash you with sharp tongues,
covetous of the best (of booty). Such as these
have not come to belief.
So God nullifies whatever they have done.
This is how (the innate law of) God works inevitably.

20. They think the allied tribes have not withdrawn;
and if the allied tribes had advanced
they would have wished that they were rather
with the Arabs of the desert
asking news of you;

and had they been among you
they would have fought but just a little.

ﮎﮏ آتَيَاكُمْ وَلَوْ كَانُوا نُوافِيكُمْ مَّا انْتُواَ اِلَّا قَلِيْلَا ۩

You have indeed a noble paradigm
in the Apostle of God
for him who fears God and the Day of Resurrection,
and remembers God frequently.

22. When the faithful saw (the armies of) the allied tribes,
they said: "This is what God and His Apostle had promised us;
and God and His Apostle say the truth;"
and this enhanced their faith and obedience.

23. There are men among the faithful who have been true
to the covenant they had made with God;
and some of them fulfilled their vows (by dying in His cause),
and some still wait (prepared for death), and stand firm,

24. That God may recompense the truthful for their
          truthfulness,
and punish the hypocrites or relent
towards them, as He will.
God is surely forgiving and kind.

25. God drove the unbelievers back in their fury,
and they gained no advantage.
God was sufficient (to help) the believers in the battle.
God is all-powerful and all-mighty.

26. He made those of the people of the Book
who had helped (the tribes) descend from their forts,
and filled their hearts with dread,
so that you killed some and made many captive;

27. And He made you inherit their lands and mansions and
          wealth,
and a country you had not traversed before,
for God has power over every thing.

O Prophet, say to your wives:
"In case you desire the life and pomp of this world, come,
I will provide you handsomely, and let you go with a grace.

29. But if you desire God, His Apostle, and the joys of life to
          come,
then God has verily set apart
for those of you who are good, a great reward."

30. O wives of the Prophet, whosoever of you
commits an act of clear shamelessness,
her punishment will be doubled.
This is how (the innate law of) God works inevitably.

31. But whoever of you is obedient to God and His Apostle,
and does the right, will be given

Al-Ahzab

a two-fold reward by Us; and We have
a rich provision in readiness for her.
32. O wives of the Prophet, you are not like other women.
If you are mindful of God,
do not be too obliging in your speech, lest some one
sick of heart should covet your person;
so say only customary things.
33. Stay at home, and do not deck yourselves
with ostentation as in the days of paganism;
fulfil your devotional obligations, pay the zakat,
and obey God and His Apostle.
God desires to remove impurities from you,
O inmates of this house,
and to cleanse and bring out the best in you.
34. Remember God's revelations and the wisdom
that are recited in your homes.
God is indeed all-perceiving, well-informed.

Verily men and women who have come to submission,
men and women who are believers,
men and women who are devout,
truthful men and truthful women,
men and women with endurance,
men and women who are modest,
men and women who give alms,
men and women who observe fasting,
men and women who guard their private parts,
and those men and women who remember God a great deal,
for them God has forgiveness and a great reward.
36. No believing men and women have any choice in a matter
after God and His Apostle have decided it.
Whoever disobeys God and His Apostle
has clearly lost the way and gone astray.
37. When you said to him who had been favoured by God
and was favoured by you:
"Keep your wife to yourself and fear God,"
you were hiding something God was about to bring to light,
for you had fear of men, though you should fear God more.
And when Zaid* was through with her,
We gave her to you in marriage,
so that it may not remain a sin for the faithful
(to marry) the wives of their adopted sons

---

* A freed man, and adopted son of the Prophet, whose marraige he arranged with his cousin Zainab as an iconoclastic measure to break caste prejudices. The marraige was doomed to failure from the start.

when they are through with them.
God's command is to be fulfilled.
38. There is no constraint on the Prophet
in what God has decreed for him.
This has been the way of God with (apostles) who have gone
    before you, —
and God's command is a determined act.
39. (For) those who convey the messages of God,
and fear Him and no one else,
God is sufficient to keep account.
40. Muhammad is not the father of any man among you,
but a messenger of God, and the seal of the prophets.
God has knowledge of every thing.

O you who believe, remember God a great deal,
42. And sing His praises morning and evening.
43. It is He who sends His blessings on you,
as (do) His angels, that He may lead
you out of darkness into light,
for He is benevolent to the believers.
44. Their greeting on the day they meet Him will be: "Peace;"
and He has a generous reward ready for them.
45. O Prophet, We have sent you as a witness
and a bearer of happy tidings and an admonisher,
46. And to call (men) to God by His leave,
and as a lamp resplendent.
47. Give glad tidings to the believers that
there is great bounty for them from God.
48. Do not listen to the unbelievers and the hypocrites.
Ignore what they do to hurt you,
and put your trust in God.
God is sufficient as protector.
49. O you who believe, when you marry believing women
then divorce them before having (sexual) contact with them,
you have no right to demand
observance of the 'waiting period' of them.
But provide suitably for them, and let them go with honour.
50. We have made lawful for you, O Prophet,
wives to whom you have given their dower,
and God-given maids and captives you have married,
and the daughters
of your father's brothers and daughters of your father's sisters,
and daughters of your mother's brothers and sisters,
who migrated with you; and a believing woman
who offers herself to the Prophet
if the Prophet desires to marry her.

Al-Ahzab

This is a privilege only for you and not the other believers.
We know what We have ordained for them
about their wives and maids they possess,
so that you may be free of blame,
for God is forgiving and kind.
51. You may defer the turn of any of your wives you like,
and may take any other you desire.
There is no harm if you take any of those
(whose turn) you had deferred.
This would be better as it would gladden their hearts
and they will not grieve, and each will be happy
with what you have given her.
God knows what is in your heart,
for He is all-wise and benign.
52. No other women are lawful for you after this
except those you have married,
nor to change your present wives for other women
even though their beauty should appeal to you.
God is watchful of every thing.

O you who believe, do not enter the houses of the Prophet
for a meal without awaiting the proper time, unless asked,
and enter when you are invited, and depart
when you have eaten, and do not stay on talking.
This puts the Prophet to inconvenience,
and he feels embarrassed before you;
but God is not embarrassed in (saying) the truth.
And when you ask his wife for some thing of utility,
ask for it from behind the screen.
This is for the purity of your hearts and theirs.
It does not behove you to annoy the prophet of God,
or to ever marry his wives after him.
This would indeed be serious in the sight of God.
54. Whether you discuss a thing or conceal it,
surely God has knowledge of every thing.
55. There is no harm if they come
before their fathers or their sons,
or their brothers and their brothers' and sisters' sons,
or their women folk or captive maids they possess.
Follow the commands of God.
Verily God is witness to every thing.
56. God and His angels shower their blessings on the Prophet.
O believers, you should also send your blessings on him,
and salute him with a worthy greeting.
57. Those who offend God and His Prophet
will be damned in this world and the next.

There is a shameful punishment ready for them.
58. Those who slander believing men and women
for what they have not done,
will bear the burden of calumny and clear iniquity.

O Prophet, tell your wives and daughters,
and the women of the faithful,
to draw their wraps a little over them.
They will thus be recognised and no harm will come to them.
God is forgiving and kind.
60. If the hypocrites and perverts,
and the rumour-mongers of Madinah,
do not desist even now, We shall rouse you against them,
so they would not be able to live but a short time
in the city with you.
61. Accursed, they would be seized wherever found, and slain
mercilessly.
62. Such was the law of God among those before you;
and you will not find any change in the law of God.
63. People ask you about the Hour (of the great change).
Say: "Only God has knowledge of it.
Who knows? The Hour may be close at hand."
64. Verily God has cursed the infidels,
and prepared a blazing fire for them.
65. They will live in it for ever,
and will find no saviour or helper.
66. The day their faces would be turned on the fire (as on a
spit),
they will say: "Alas! If only we had obeyed God,
and obeyed the Prophet."
67. They will say: "O our Lord, we obeyed our leaders and the
elders,
but they only led us astray.
68. O Lord, give them a double punishment,
and put a grievous curse upon them."

O you who believe, do not be like those who maligned
Moses, whilst God cleared him of what they alleged;
and he was held in high esteem with God.
70. O you who believe, obey the commands of God,
and say straightforward things
71. That He may straighten your affairs for you
and forgive your sins;
and he who obeys God and His Prophet will be successful.
72. We had offered the Trust (of divine responsibilities)
to the heavens, the earth, the mountains,

Al-Ahzab

but they refrained from bearing the burden
and were frightened of it;
but man took it on himself.
He is a faithless ignoramus.
73. So that God punishes men and women hypocrites,
the idolaters and idolatrous women,
but He turns to faithful men and women in forgiveness,
for God is forgiving and kind.

الْجِبَالِ فَأَبَيْنَ أَن يَحْمِلْنَهَا وَأَشْفَقْنَ مِنْهَا وَحَمَلَهَا
الْإِنسَانُ إِنَّهُ كَانَ ظَلُومًا جَهُولًا ۝

لِّيُعَذِّبَ اللَّهُ الْمُنَٰفِقِينَ وَالْمُنَٰفِقَٰتِ وَالْمُشْرِكِينَ
وَالْمُشْرِكَٰتِ وَيَتُوبَ اللَّهُ عَلَى الْمُؤْمِنِينَ وَالْمُؤْمِنَٰتِ
وَكَانَ اللَّهُ غَفُورًا رَّحِيمًا ۝

34 Sheba

Sabā': Makki

In the name of Allah, most benevolent, ever-merciful.

بِسْمِ اللهِ الرَّحْمٰنِ الرَّحِيْمِ ۞

ALL PRAISE BE to God to whom belongs
whatsoever is in the heavens and the earth,
and His the praise in the world to come.
He is all-wise and all-knowing.
2. He knows whatever goes into the earth
and whatsoever issues from it,
whatsoever comes down from the sky,
and whatsoever goes up to it.
He is all-merciful, all-forgiving.
3. The unbelievers say: "There is no coming of the Hour for us."
Say: "Why not? By my Lord, the knower of the unknown,
it will certainly come for you.
Not even an atom's weight in the heavens and the earth,
or something smaller or greater than it,
is hidden from Him, and which is not
recorded in the all too manifest Book,
4. In order that He may recompense those
who have believed and done the right.
For them will be forgiveness and worthy sustenance.
5. As for those who try to subvert Our signs,
there is a punishment of painful torment.
6. Those who have been given knowledge realise
what has been revealed by the Lord is the truth,
and leads to the path of the mighty and praiseworthy (God).
7. The disbelievers say: "Shall we tell you of a man
who prophesies that when you are reduced to particles
and vanished in the dust,
you will become a new creation.
8. Has he fabricated a lie about God, or is he possessed?"
Not so; but those who believe not in the Hereafter
are themselves afflicted and far astray.
9. Do they not see what is before them and what is behind them
of the heavens and the earth?
We could cleave the earth and sink them, if We pleased,

الْحَمْدُ لِلّٰهِ الَّذِىْ لَهُ مَا فِى السَّمٰوٰتِ وَمَا فِى الْاَرْضِ
وَلَهُ الْحَمْدُ فِى الْاٰخِرَةِ وَهُوَ الْحَكِيْمُ الْخَبِيْرُ ۞
يَعْلَمُ مَا يَلِجُ فِى الْاَرْضِ وَمَا يَخْرُجُ مِنْهَا وَمَا
يَنْزِلُ مِنَ السَّمَآءِ وَمَا يَعْرُجُ فِيْهَا وَهُوَ الرَّحِيْمُ
الْغَفُوْرُ ۞

وَقَالَ الَّذِيْنَ كَفَرُوْا لَا تَأْتِيْنَا السَّاعَةُ قُلْ بَلٰى وَ
رَبِّىْ لَتَأْتِيَنَّكُمْ عٰلِمِ الْغَيْبِ لَا يَعْزُبُ عَنْهُ مِثْقَالُ
ذَرَّةٍ فِى السَّمٰوٰتِ وَلَا فِى الْاَرْضِ وَلَا اَصْغَرُ مِنْ
ذٰلِكَ وَلَا اَكْبَرُ اِلَّا فِىْ كِتٰبٍ مُبِيْنٍ ۞
لِّيَجْزِىَ الَّذِيْنَ اٰمَنُوْا وَعَمِلُوا الصّٰلِحٰتِ اُولٰٓئِكَ لَهُمْ
مَغْفِرَةٌ وَّرِزْقٌ كَرِيْمٌ ۞
وَالَّذِيْنَ سَعَوْ فِىْٓ اٰيٰتِنَا مُعٰجِزِيْنَ اُولٰٓئِكَ لَهُمْ
عَذَابٌ مِّنْ رِّجْزٍ اَلِيْمٌ ۞
وَيَرَى الَّذِيْنَ اُوْتُوا الْعِلْمَ الَّذِىْٓ اُنْزِلَ اِلَيْكَ
رَبِّكَ هُوَ الْحَقَّ وَيَهْدِىْٓ اِلٰى صِرَاطِ الْعَزِيْزِ
الْحَمِيْدِ ۞
وَقَالَ الَّذِيْنَ كَفَرُوْا هَلْ نَدُلُّكُمْ عَلٰى رَجُلٍ
يُّنَبِّئُكُمْ اِذَا مُزِّقْتُمْ كُلَّ مُمَزَّقٍ اِنَّكُمْ لَفِىْ خَلْقٍ
جَدِيْدٍ ۞
اَفْتَرٰى عَلَى اللهِ كَذِبًا اَمْ بِهٖ جِنَّةٌ بَلِ الَّذِيْنَ لَا
يُؤْمِنُوْنَ بِالْاٰخِرَةِ فِى الْعَذَابِ وَالضَّلٰلِ
الْبَعِيْدِ ۞
اَفَلَمْ يَرَوْا اِلٰى مَا بَيْنَ اَيْدِيْهِمْ وَمَا خَلْفَهُمْ مِّنَ
السَّمَآءِ وَالْاَرْضِ اِنْ نَّشَأْ نَخْسِفْ بِهِمُ الْاَرْضَ

or drop a fragment of the sky upon them.
There is surely a sign in this for every penitent creature.

اَوْ نُسْقِطْ عَلَيْهِمْ كِسَفًا مِّنَ السَّمَاءِ إِنَّ فِى ذَٰلِكَ لَآيَةً
لِّكُلِّ عَبْدٍ مُّنِيبٍ ۞

We favoured David with excellence, (and commanded):
"O Jibal and Tair, glorify the greatness of God with him."*
And We made iron pliable for him.

وَلَقَدْ اٰتَيْنَا دَاوٗدَ مِنَّا فَضْلًا يٰجِبَالُ اَوِّبِىۡ مَعَهٗ
وَالطَّيْرَ وَاَلَنَّا لَهُ الْحَدِيْدَ ۞

11. "Make long coats of mail," (We said), "and fix their links,
and do the right.
I surely see whatsoever you do."

اَنِ اعْمَلْ سٰبِغٰتٍ وَّقَدِّرْ فِى السَّرْدِ وَاعْمَلُوْا صَالِحًا
اِنِّى بِمَا تَعْمَلُوْنَ بَصِيْرٌ ۞

12. We (subjugated) the wind to Solomon.
Its morning's journey took one month,
and the evening's one month.**
We made a spring of molten brass to flow for him;
and many jinns laboured for him by the will of his Lord.
Anyone of them who turned from Our command
was made to taste the torment of blazing fire.

وَلِسُلَيْمٰنَ الرِّيْحَ غُدُوُّهَا شَهْرٌ وَّرَوَاحُهَا شَهْرٌ وَ
اَسَلْنَا لَهُ عَيْنَ الْقِطْرِ وَمِنَ الْجِنِّ مَنْ يَّعْمَلُ بَيْنَ
يَدَيْهِ بِاِذْنِ رَبِّهٖ وَمَنْ يَّزِغْ مِنْهُمْ عَنْ اَمْرِنَا نُذِقْهُ
مِنْ عَذَابِ السَّعِيْرِ ۞

13. They made for him whatever he wished,
synagogues and statues, dishes large as water-troughs,
and cauldrons firmly fixed (on ovens; and We said):
"O House of David, act, and give thanks."
But few among My creatures are thankful.

يَعْمَلُوْنَ لَهٗ مَا يَشَاءُ مِنْ مَّحَارِيْبَ وَتَمَاثِيْلَ وَ
جِفَانٍ كَالْجَوَابِ وَقُدُوْرٍ رَّاسِيٰتٍ اِعْمَلُوْا اٰلَ دَاوٗدَ
شُكْرًا وَّقَلِيْلٌ مِّنْ عِبَادِىَ الشَّكُوْرُ ۞

14. When We ordained (Solomon's) death,
none but the weevil, that was eating away his staff
(on which he rested),
pointed out to them that he was dead.
When he fell down (dead) the jinns realised
that if they had knowledge of the Unknown
they would never have suffered demeaning labour.

فَلَمَّا قَضَيْنَا عَلَيْهِ الْمَوْتَ مَا دَلَّهُمْ عَلٰى مَوْتِهٖ اِلَّا
دَابَّةُ الْاَرْضِ تَأْكُلُ مِنْسَأَتَهٗ فَلَمَّا خَرَّ تَبَيَّنَتِ
الْجِنُّ اَنْ لَّوْ كَانُوْا يَعْلَمُوْنَ الْغَيْبَ مَا لَبِثُوْا
فِى الْعَذَابِ الْمُهِيْنِ ۞

15. There was a sign for the people of Saba in their habitations:
Two gardens, on the right and left. (And they were told:)
"Eat of what your Lord has given you and be thankful.
Fair is your land, and forgiving your Lord."

لَقَدْ كَانَ لِسَبَاٍ فِى مَسْكَنِهِمْ اٰيَةٌ جَنَّتٰنِ عَنْ يَّمِيْنٍ
وَّشِمَالٍ كُلُوْا مِنْ رِّزْقِ رَبِّكُمْ وَاشْكُرُوْا لَهٗ بَلْدَةٌ
طَيِّبَةٌ وَّرَبٌّ غَفُوْرٌ ۞

16. But they turned away. So We let loose on them
the inundation of (the dyke of) al-'Arim,
replacing their gardens with two other gardens
which bore only bitter gourd, and tamarisks
and a few sparse lote-trees.

فَاَعْرَضُوْا فَاَرْسَلْنَا عَلَيْهِمْ سَيْلَ الْعَرِمِ وَبَدَّلْنٰهُمْ
بِجَنَّتَيْهِمْ جَنَّتَيْنِ ذَوَاتَيْ اُكُلٍ خَمْطٍ وَّاَثْلٍ وَّشَيْءٍ
مِّنْ سِدْرٍ قَلِيْلٍ ۞

17. That is how We requited them for their ingratitude.
We only punish those who are ungrateful.

ذٰلِكَ جَزَيْنٰهُمْ بِمَا كَفَرُوْا وَهَلْ نُجٰزِىۡ اِلَّا
الْكَفُوْرَ ۞

18. Between them and the cities We had blessed
We placed towns along the highway,
and made them stages on their journey,
(saying): "Travel between them in safety by day or by night."

وَجَعَلْنَا بَيْنَهُمْ وَبَيْنَ الْقُرَى الَّتِىۡ بٰرَكْنَا فِيْهَا
قُرًى ظَاهِرَةً وَّقَدَّرْنَا فِيْهَا السَّيْرَ سِيْرُوْا فِيْهَا
لَيَالِىَ وَاَيَّامًا اٰمِنِيْنَ ۞

---

* See notes on pp. 280 and 386.
** Morning's journey implies 'outward' and evening's 'return' journey. See also note on p. 280.

19. But they said: "O Lord, make the distance
between the stages of our journeys longer;"
but (by doing so) they wronged themselves.
So We turned them into bygone tales,
and dispersed them, scattered in all directions.
Surely there are signs in this
for those who endeavour and are grateful.
20. Thus Iblis found his supposition about them to be true;
and except for a section of believers they follow him.
21. He had no authority over them
save for the purpose of Our knowing
who believed in the world to come, and who doubted it.
For your Lord keeps a watch over every thing.

Say: "Call on those you imagine are gods apart from God.
They are not masters even of an atom's weight
in the heavens and the earth,
nor do they have a share in them,
nor is any one of them a helper (of God).
23. No intercession avails with Him
except his He allows,
so that when their hearts are freed of fear,
they ask (one another): "What did your Lord say?"
They will answer: "What is expedient.
He is the all-mighty and supreme."
24. Say: "Who gives you food from the heavens and the earth?"
Say: "God. Surely either you or we are on guidance,
or are lost in clear error."
25. Say: "You will not be questioned about the sins
that we have committed,
nor shall we be questioned about your deeds."
26. Say: "Our Lord will gather us together
and judge between us equitably,
for He is the Judge all-knowing."
27. Say: "Just show me those you associate with Him
as compeers." No, (you cannot), for He is God,
the all-mighty and all-wise."
28. We have sent you only as a bearer of good tidings
and admonisher for all mankind;
yet most people do not understand.
29. Instead they say: "When is this promise going to be,
if you speak the truth?"
30. Say: "Determined is the day of the promise,
which you can neither put back nor advance an hour."

The unbelievers say: "We do not believe in this Qur'an,

Saba'   365

nor in what was (sent) before it."
If only you could see the sinners when they are made to stand
before their Lord, blaming one another!
Those who were weak will say to those who were arrogant:
"But for you we would have certainly been believers."
32. The arrogant will say to the weak:
"Did we hold you back from guidance
after it had come to you? Certainly not.
In fact you were yourselves guilty."
33. But the weak will say to the arrogant:
"Not in the least. It was your plotting night and day
when you ordered us to disbelieve in God
and associate compeers with Him."
When they see the punishment they will express repentance.
But We shall put iron collars round the necks of infidels.
Will they be requited for anything but what they did?
34. We never sent an admonisher to a habitation
but its well-to-do people said:
"We do not believe in what you have brought."
35. And (further): "We have far more wealth and children
(than you), and we are not the ones to be punished."
36. Say: "Verily my Lord increases or restricts
the provision of whosoever He will;"
but most men do not understand.

It is not your wealth and children
that will bring you closer to Us,
except those who believe and do the right.
These will be given a two-fold reward for their deeds,
and will dwell in peace in the high empyrean.
38. But those who try to subvert Our signs
will be given over to punishment.
39. Say: "Verily my Lord increases or restricts
the provision of any of His creatures as He will,
and repays whatsoever you spend.
He is the best of all providers."
40. The day He will gather all of them together,
He will ask the angels: "Did they worship you?"
41. "God forbid!" (they will answer).
"You are our protector not they.
In fact, they worshipped the devils.
Most of them believed in them."
42. That day you will have no power
to profit or harm each other;
and We shall say to the sinners:
"Taste the punishment of Fire which you had denied."

43. When Our clear revelations are read out to them, they say:
"This is only a man who wants to turn you away
from what your fathers used to worship."
And they say: "This is nothing but a fabricated lie."
And those who do not believe say of the truth
when it has reached them:
"This is nothing but pure sorcery."
44. We did not give them any scripture to study,
nor sent any warner before you.
45. Those before them had also denied,
and they could not reach a tenth of (the possibilities)
We had given them,
and still they called My apostles liars.
How great was the change that I wrought in their condition
        then!

Say: "I urge upon you only one thing:
Stand up for God
two by two or one by one,
and think and reflect!"
There is no madness about your companion.
He is a warner against the dreadful affliction (that awaits).
47. Say: "The reward I ask is for yourself.
My reward is due from none but God;
and He is witness over every thing."
48. Say: "My Lord casts the truth:
He is the knower of things unknown."
49. Say: "The truth has come,
and falsehood had neither precedence nor will reappear."
50. Say: "If I am in error it is to my own loss;
if I am on guidance that is so
because of what my Lord reveals to me.
He is all-hearing and all-too-near."
51. If you could see when they are gripped by terror
without any escape, and are seized from close at hand
52. They will say: "We believe in it."
How could they reach it from a place of no return?
53. They had surely denied it before
and aimed without seeing from so far away.
54. A barrier shall be raised between them and what they
        desired,
as was done with their partisans before.
They too were filled with disquieting doubt.

35 The Originator

Al-Fātir: Makki

In the name of Allah, most benevolent, ever-merciful.

ALL PRAISE BE to God, the originator
of the heavens and the earth, who appointed
angels as His messengers, with wings, two, three and four.
He adds what He pleases to His creation.
He has certainly power over every thing.
2. There is none who can take away
the favours He bestows on man;
and there is none apart from Him
to restore what He has withheld.
He is all-mighty and all-wise.
3. O you people, remember the favours of God to you.
Is there any creator other than God
who gives you food from the heavens and the earth?
There is no god but He:
How then can you turn aside?
4. If they call you a liar, so have other messengers
been denied before you.
But all things will be brought back to God.
5. O you people, the promise of God is true.
So do not let the life of this world delude you,
nor let that (arch) deceiver deceive you about God.
6. Satan is certainly your enemy,
so hold him as a foe.
He only calls his faction to be
the residents of Hell.
7. For those who are unbelievers, there is severe punishment;
but for those who believe and do the right
is forgiveness and a great reward.

Can he, the evil of whose deed
is made to look attractive to him
so that he considers it good,
(be like him who is guided)?
God leads whosoever He please astray

and guides whosoever He will.
So do not waste away your self with grief for them.
God is indeed cognisant of things they do.
9. It is God who sends the winds that raise the clouds.
Then We drive the clouds towards the land that was dead,
and restore the earth to life after it had died.
So will be the Resurrection.
10. Whosoever desires honour (should remember)
that all honour is with God.
All good words ascend to Him,
and all good deeds He exalts.
As for those who are plotting evil,
there is severe punishment for them,
and their plots will be fruitless.
11. It is God who created you from dust,
then from a sperm,
then formed you into pairs.
Neither does a female conceive
nor gives birth without His knowledge;
nor do the old grow older or become younger in years
but in accordance with the law (of nature).
Indeed the law of God works inevitably.
12. Alike are not two bodies of water:
This one is sweet and fresh and pleasant to drink,
and this one brine and bitter;
yet you get fresh meat to eat from both,
and take out ornaments to wear.
You see how the ships churn through them
so that you may seek of His bounty
and, perhaps, give thanks.
13. He makes night run into day, the day run into night,
and has harnessed the sun and the moon
so that each runs to its determined course.
This is God your Lord; His is the kingdom;
and those you invoke apart from Him
are not masters even of the film on a date-palm stone.
14. You pray to them, but they do not hear your call;
and even if they heard you, they could not answer your prayer;
and on the Day of Resurrection they will deny your having
  worshipped them.
None can acquaint you (with the reality)
as He who is informed of every thing.

O men, it is you who stand in need of God.
As for God, He is above all need, worthy of praise.
16. He could take you away if He pleased.

and bring a new creation (in your place).

17. This is well within the power of God.

18. No one who carries a burden bears another's load;
and even if the burdened soul cry out for help
none will carry the least of its burden,
however close a relative it may be.
You can only warn those who fear their Lord in secret
and fulfil their devotional obligations.
Whoever grows in goodness does so for himself.
To God is the journeying back.

19. Equal are not the blind and those who can see,

20. Nor darkness and light,

21. Nor shade and heat of sunshine.

22. Equal are not the living and the dead.
Verily God makes those He will to listen;
but you cannot make those hear
who are in their graves.

23. You are only a bearer of warnings.

24. We have sent you with the truth,
to give glad tidings and to warn.
Never has there been a community
to which an admonisher was not sent.

25. If they call you a liar, so had those before them
called their apostles liars,
who had come to them with clear proofs,
scriptures and the splendent Book.

26. So We seized the unbelievers.
How great was the change I wrought in their condition then!

Do you not see how God sends
water from the sky, then We produce fruits
from it variegated in colour;
and on mountains are tracts of red and white,
in different shades and raven black.

28. And so are among men, beasts and cattle, different shades.
Only those of His creatures fear God
who have knowledge.
Verily He is all-mighty and forgiving.

29. Surely those who read the Book of God,
are firm in devotion, and spend
of what We have given them in secret or openly,
can hope for a commerce that will not decline,

30. So that He may reward them in full,
and give them a greater increase by His grace.
He is verily forgiving and rewarding.

31. What We have revealed to you of the Book is the truth,

and proves (what has been sent) before it to be true.
Verily God is informed of His creatures and sees every thing.
32. So We made those of Our creatures whom We had chosen,
heirs to the Book; but some of these exceed themselves,
and some follow the middle course,
and some surpass others in goodness by God's will,
which is the greatest blessing.
33. They will enter the gardens of Eden,
where they will be adorned
with bracelets of gold and pearls,
and of silk will be their garments.
34. They will say: "All praise be to God
who has removed all care from us.
Indeed our Lord is forgiving and rewarding,
35. Who has settled us by His grace
in the mansions of eternal rest,
where there is no labour for us,
nor does weariness come upon us."
36. As for the unbelievers, there is the fire of Hell.
It will neither consume them wholly that they should die,
nor will its torment be lessened for them.
That is how We requite the ungrateful.
37. There they will cry for help: "O Lord,
get us out that we may do the right,
and not what we used to do."
Did We not give you a long enough span of life
so that he who remembered may reflect?
And did not the warner come to you?
So now taste (the punishment).
The iniquitous will have none to help them.

Verily God knows the unknown of the heavens and
      the earth.
Indeed He knows what lies in the hearts of men.
39. He is the one who made you trustees on the earth.
So he who disbelieves, will bear the consequence of his unbelief;
but their unbelief will only increase disgust
for unbelievers in the sight of their Lord;
and their unbelief will only lead
the unbelievers to greater loss.
40. Say: "Look at the compeers you invoke apart from God.
Show me, what of the earth have they created,
or what share have they in the heavens?"
Or have We given them a Book whose testimony they possess?
Not in the least. What the unbelievers have been promising
one another is nothing but deceit.

Al-Fatir

41. Verily God holds the heavens and the earth in position
lest they deviate; and if they deviated there will be none
to hold them in place, apart from Him.
He is sagacious and forgiving.
42. The unbelievers swore on oath emphatically
that if an admonisher came to them
they would be guided better than the other communities.
But when the admonisher came to them
their aversion for the truth increased,
43. As did their arrogance in the land,
and their plotting of evil.
But their evil plots will turn back on the plotters themselves.
So can they expect any thing
but what befell the earlier people?
You will not find any change in the law of God,
nor will you find divine law mutable.
44. Have they not journeyed in the land and seen
how the end of those before them,
who were far more powerful, came about?
There is nothing in the heavens and the earth
that can defeat (the law of) God.
He is all-knowing and all-powerful.
45. If God were to seize men for their doings,
not a living being would be left upon the earth.
But He gives them respite for a time ordained.
When their time is come, surely God
will keep (the interest of) His creatures in view.

36 Yā Sīn

Yā Sīn: Makki

اياتها ... رُكوعها

In the name of Allah, most benevolent, ever-merciful.

YĀ SĪN.

2. I call to witness the Qur'an, custodian of all laws, —
3. That you are indeed one of those sent
4. On a path that is straight, —
5. A revelation from the mighty, ever-merciful (God),
6. That you may warn a people
whose ancestors had never been warned,
who are therefore heedless.
7. The sentence is surely justified against most of them,
for they do not believe.
8. We will certainly put iron collars on their necks
which will come up to their chins,
so that they will not be able to raise their heads.
9. And We shall raise a barrier in front of them
and a barrier behind them,
and cover them over
so that they will not be able to see.
10. Whether you warn them or do not warn,
it is all the same; they will not believe.
11. You can only warn him who listens to the warning
and fears Ar-Rahman secretly.
So give him good news of forgiveness and a generous reward.
12. It is We indeed who bring back the dead to life,
and write down what they send ahead (of their deeds),
and traces that they leave behind.
We keep an account of all things in a lucid register.

Narrate to them the example of the people of the city
when the messengers came to it.
14. When We sent two of them they called them liars;
so We sent a third to strengthen them.
"We have been sent to you," they said.
15. "You are only men like us," they replied;
"Ar-Rahman has not sent down any thing.

You are speaking only lies."

16. (The messengers) said: "Our Lord knows that we have been sent to you.

17. Our duty is to convey the message clearly."

18. They rejoined: "We feel you augur ill.
If you do not desist, we shall stone you to death,
and inflict a grievous punishment on you."

19. (The messengers) said: "The augury is within your own selves.
Do you (consider it a bad omen) that you should be warned?
You are a people guilty of excess."

20. Then a man came running from the other side of the city.
"O my people," he said, "follow the messengers.

21. Follow those who do not ask for any recompense of you,
and are rightly guided.

22. Why should I not worship Him who brought me into being,
to whom you will be brought back in the end?

23. Should I take other gods apart from Him,
who would neither be able to intercede for me nor save me
if Ar-Rahman brings me harm?

24. In that case I would surely be in clear error.

25. I believe in your Lord, so listen to me."

26. (But they stoned him to death.) It was said to him:
"Enter Paradise;" and he said: "If only my people knew

27. How my Lord has forgiven me
and made me one of those who are honoured!"

28. We did not send down any army against his people
from heaven, nor did We have to send one.

29. There was just one blast, and they were extinguished.

30. Alas for men! No apostle ever came to them
but they made fun of him.

31. Have they not seen how many generations
have We destroyed before them
who will not return again?

32. They will all be brought together before Us.

There is a sign in the dead earth for them
which We quicken, and produce from it grain which they eat.

34. We have laid out gardens of dates and grapes
upon it, and made springs of water flow,

35. So that they may eat of its fruit;
yet it was not done by their hands.
Then why do they not acknowledge thanks?

36. All glory to Him who created pairs of every thing
that grows from the earth, and out of themselves,

and other things they do not know.

37. And there is a sign in the night for them.
We strip off the day from it
and they are left in darkness,

38. While the sun keeps revolving in its orbit.
This is the dispensation of the mighty, all-knowing (God).

39. We have determined the stations of the moon,
so that (after its wanderings) it returns
as a dried up inflorescent spike of dates.

40. Neither can the sun overtake the moon,
nor the night outpace the day:
Each of them keeps coursing in its orbit.

41. That We bore their progeny in the laden ark
is a sign for them;

42. And We made similar vessels for them to ride.

43. We could have drowned them if We pleased,
and none would have answered their cry for help,
nor would they have been saved,

44. Unless by Our benevolence, to reap advantage for a time.

45. When it is said to them: "Beware
of what is before you and what is past,
that you may be treated with kindness;"

46. None of the signs of their Lord ever comes to them
but they turn away from it.

47. When they are told: "Spend of what God has given you,"
the unbelievers say to those who believe:
"Why should we feed those whom God should have fed if He
      pleased?"
You are only in palpable error.

48. And they say: "When will this promise come to pass,
if what you say is true?"

49. They are only waiting for a single blast
that will seize them, but they will go on contending.

50. Then they would not be able to make a will,
or go back to their people.

When the trumpet blast is sounded
they will come out of their graves
and hasten to their Lord,

52. Saying: "Ah woe, who has roused us from our sleep?"
— This is what Ar-Rahman had promised,
and whose truth the apostles had affirmed.

53. It would be but a single blast of the trumpet,
and they would all be arraigned before Us.

54. No soul will be wronged the least that Day,
nor would be recompensed

but only for what it had done.
55. Surely the inmates of Paradise
will be engaged in pastimes.
56. They and their companions will recline
on couches in the shade.
57. For them will be fruits and whatever they ask.
58. "Peace" shall be the greeting from the merciful Lord.
59. (And the guilty will be told:) "O sinners, separate
    yourselves this day.
60. Did I not commit you, O children of Adam,
not to worship Satan who is your acknowledged foe,
61. But to serve Me; (that) this is the straight path?
62. But he beguiled a great many of you.
Why did you not then understand?
63. This is the Hell that you were promised.
64. Roast in it now for having disbelieved."
65. We shall seal their lips that day;
and their hands will speak, their feet testify
to what they had done.
66. We could take away their sight if We pleased;
then they would run around to find the way:
But how then would they see?
67. And if We pleased We could paralyse them in their tracks,
and they would not be able to move forward or turn back.

Whoever reaches old age, We reverse in natural disposition.
Do they not have sense (to see)?
69. We have not taught (Muhammad) to versify,
nor is it worthy of him.
This is nothing but a reminder
and illuminating discourse,
70. So that he may warn him who is alive and feels,
and justify the word against those who do not believe.
71. Do they not see the cattle among things We have fashioned
by Our power, which they own,
72. Whom We made subservient to them
so that some of them they ride and some they eat?
73. And they derive other advantages and drinks from them.
Even then they do not offer thanks,
74. And take other gods apart from God
that they may perhaps give them help.
75. They will not be able to help them
and will be brought (to Us) as their levied troops.
76. So be not grieved by what they say.
We certainly know what they hide and disclose.
77. Does not man see We created him from a drop of semen?

Even then he becomes an open contender,
78. And applies comparisons to Us,
having forgotten his origin,
and says: "Who can put life into decayed bones?"
79. Say: "He who created you the first time.
He has knowledge of every creation,
80. Who gave you fire from a green tree,
with which you ignite the flame."
81. How can He who created the heavens and the earth
not be able to create others like them?
Why not? He is the real creator all-knowing.
82. When He wills a thing He has only to say:
"Be," and it is.
83. So all glory to Him who holds
all power over every thing, to whom
you will go back in the end.

مُوَخَصِيمٌ مُبِينٌ ۝ وَضَرَبَ لَنَا مَثَلًا وَنَسِيَ
خَلْقَهُ قَالَ مَنْ يُحْيِ الْعِظَامَ وَهِيَ رَمِيمٌ ۝
قُلْ يُحْيِيهَا الَّذِي أَنْشَأَهَا أَوَّلَ مَرَّةٍ وَهُوَ بِكُلِّ
خَلْقٍ عَلِيمٌ ۝
الَّذِي جَعَلَ لَكُمْ مِنَ الشَّجَرِ الْأَخْضَرِ نَارًا فَإِذَا
أَنْتُمْ مِنْهُ تُوقِدُونَ ۝
أَوَلَيْسَ الَّذِي خَلَقَ السَّمَوَاتِ وَالْأَرْضَ بِقَادِرٍ
عَلَى أَنْ يَخْلُقَ مِثْلَهُمْ بَلَى وَهُوَ الْخَلَّاقُ الْعَلِيمُ ۝
إِنَّمَا أَمْرُهُ إِذَا أَرَادَ شَيْئًا أَنْ يَقُولَ لَهُ كُنْ
فَيَكُونُ ۝
فَسُبْحَانَ الَّذِي بِيَدِهِ مَلَكُوتُ كُلِّ شَيْءٍ وَإِلَيْهِ
تُرْجَعُونَ ۝

37 Who Stand Arrayed in Rows

As-Sāffāt: Makki

In the name of Allah, most benevolent, ever-merciful.

I CALL TO witness those
who stand arrayed in rows,
2. And those who restrain by reprimanding,
3. And those who recite the Reminder,
4. Verily your God is One,
5. The Lord of the heavens and the earth
and all that lies between them,
and the Lord of the Easts.
6. He decked the nearest heavens* with ornaments of stars,
7. Protecting them against every wayward devil,
8. So that they are not able to listen
to the angels of higher (echelons),
and are pelted from all sides
9. And kept far away.
There is perpetual punishment for them,
10. Except those who eavesdrop and are pursued
by a shooting flame.
11. So ask them if they are more difficult to create,
or the rest We have created?
Indeed (man) We created from fermented clay.
12. Yet while you are filled with wonder, they just scoff;
13. And when they are warned they pay no heed.
14. When they see a sign, they laugh at it,
15. And say: "This is only magic.
16. When we are dead and turned to dust and bones,
how can we be raised again,
17. And our fathers too?"
18. You say: "Yes; and you will be lowly made."
19. There will only be a single jerk, and they will gape,

بِسْمِ اللهِ الرَّحْمٰنِ الرَّحِيْمِ ۝

وَالصَّٰٓفّٰتِ صَفًّا ۝ فَالزّٰجِرٰتِ زَجْرًا ۝
فَالتّٰلِيٰتِ ذِكْرًا ۝ اِنَّ اِلٰهَكُمْ لَوَاحِدٌ ۝
رَبُّ السَّمٰوٰتِ وَالْاَرْضِ وَمَا بَيْنَهُمَا وَرَبُّ
الْمَشَارِقِ ۝
اِنَّا زَيَّنَّا السَّمَاءَ الدُّنْيَا بِزِيْنَةِۨ الْكَوَاكِبِ ۝
وَحِفْظًا مِّنْ كُلِّ شَيْطٰنٍ مَّارِدٍ ۝
لَا يَسَّمَّعُوْنَ اِلَى الْمَلَاِ الْاَعْلٰى وَيُقْذَفُوْنَ مِنْ
كُلِّ جَانِبٍ ۝
دُحُوْرًا وَّلَهُمْ عَذَابٌ وَّاصِبٌ ۝
اِلَّا مَنْ خَطِفَ الْخَطْفَةَ فَاَتْبَعَهُ شِهَابٌ
ثَاقِبٌ ۝
فَاسْتَفْتِهِمْ اَهُمْ اَشَدُّ خَلْقًا اَمْ مَّنْ خَلَقْنَا ؕ اِنَّا
خَلَقْنٰهُمْ مِّنْ طِيْنٍ لَّازِبٍ ۝
بَلْ عَجِبْتَ وَيَسْخَرُوْنَ ۝
وَاِذَا ذُكِّرُوْا لَا يَذْكُرُوْنَ ۝
وَاِذَا رَاَوْا اٰيَةً يَّسْتَسْخِرُوْنَ ۝
وَقَالُوْا اِنْ هٰذَا اِلَّا سِحْرٌ مُّبِيْنٌ ۝
ءَاِذَا مِتْنَا وَكُنَّا تُرَابًا وَّعِظَامًا ءَاِنَّا لَمَبْعُوْثُوْنَ ۝
اَوَاٰبَاؤُنَا الْاَوَّلُوْنَ ۝
قُلْ نَعَمْ وَاَنْتُمْ دَاخِرُوْنَ ۝
فَاِنَّمَا هِيَ زَجْرَةٌ وَّاحِدَةٌ فَاِذَا هُمْ يَنْظُرُوْنَ ۝

---

* Read in conjunction with 41:12, and 67:3,5, that God created several skies and ingrained their functions in each, would show that our universe is the nearest in space, the others being placed farther away, with their own functions (different kind of physics and space-time). Modern scientists are reaching similar conclusions. See Andrei Linde's recent theory of many universes: Newsweek, April 20, 1987, p. 51. See also 65:12 for a number of universes.

20. And say: "Ah woe! This is the Day of Reckoning."
21. "(Yes,) this is the Day of Judgement you had called a lie."

Gather all the wicked together and their comrades,
and those they had worshipped
23. Other than God," (the angels will be told),
"then show them the way to Hell,
24. And detain them,
for they will be questioned."
25. "What is the matter with you
that you do not help each other?"
26. They will submit to questioning then,
27. And some of them will confront the others,
28. Saying: "It were you who imposed yourselves upon us."
29. They will say: "No, you were the ones who would not
        believe.
30. We had no power over you.
In fact, you were a people rebellious.
31. The sentence of our Lord has come true for us.
We have certainly to taste (the punishment),
32. For we had led you astray.
In fact we ourselves were astray."
33. So, they will become partners in punishment.
34. That is how We deal with sinners.
35. They were those who, when it was said to them,
"There is no god but God," behaved with insolence,
36. And said: "Should we abandon our gods
for the sake of an insane poet?"
37. Not in the least. He has brought the truth
and confirmed the other messengers.
38. You will indeed taste a painful punishment,
39. And be rewarded
but only for what you had done,
40. Except the chosen creatures of God,
41. Whose provision is predetermined —
42. Fruits of every kind,
and they will be honoured
43. In gardens of delight,
44. (Sitting) on couches,
face to face,
45. With cups from a flowing stream
being passed around,
46. Clear, delicious to drink,
47. Neither dulling the senses
nor intoxicating,
48. And with them maidens

وَقَالُوا يَوَيْلَنَا هٰذَا يَوْمُ الدِّينِ ۞
بَ هٰذَا يَوْمُ الْفَصْلِ الَّذِى كُنْتُمْ بِهٖ تُكَذِّبُونَ ۞
اُحْشُرُوا الَّذِينَ ظَلَمُوا وَاَزْوَاجَهُمْ وَمَا كَانُوا
يَعْبُدُونَ ۞
مِنْ دُونِ اللّٰهِ فَاهْدُوهُمْ اِلٰى صِرَاطِ الْجَحِيمِ ۞
وَقِفُوهُمْ اِنَّهُمْ مَسْئُولُونَ ۞
مَا لَكُمْ لَا تَنَاصَرُونَ ۞

بَلْ هُمُ الْيَوْمَ مُسْتَسْلِمُونَ ۞
وَاَقْبَلَ بَعْضُهُمْ عَلٰى بَعْضٍ يَتَسَاءَلُونَ ۞
قَالُوا اِنَّكُمْ كُنْتُمْ تَاْتُونَنَا عَنِ الْيَمِينِ ۞
قَالُوا بَلْ لَمْ تَكُونُوا مُؤْمِنِينَ ۞
وَمَا كَانَ لَنَا عَلَيْكُمْ مِنْ سُلْطَانٍ بَلْ كُنْتُمْ قَوْمًا طَاغِينَ ۞
فَحَقَّ عَلَيْنَا قَوْلُ رَبِّنَا اِنَّا لَذَائِقُونَ ۞
فَاَغْوَيْنَاكُمْ اِنَّا كُنَّا غَاوِينَ ۞
فَاِنَّهُمْ يَوْمَئِذٍ فِى الْعَذَابِ مُشْتَرِكُونَ ۞
اِنَّا كَذٰلِكَ نَفْعَلُ بِالْمُجْرِمِينَ ۞
اِنَّهُمْ كَانُوا اِذَا قِيلَ لَهُمْ لَا اِلٰهَ اِلَّا اللّٰهُ
يَسْتَكْبِرُونَ ۞
وَيَقُولُونَ اَئِنَّا لَتَارِكُوا اٰلِهَتِنَا لِشَاعِرٍ مَجْنُونٍ ۞
بَلْ جَاءَ بِالْحَقِّ وَصَدَّقَ الْمُرْسَلِينَ ۞

اِنَّكُمْ لَذَائِقُوا الْعَذَابِ الْاَلِيمِ ۞
وَمَا تُجْزَوْنَ اِلَّا مَا كُنْتُمْ تَعْمَلُونَ ۞
اِلَّا عِبَادَ اللّٰهِ الْمُخْلَصِينَ ۞
اُولٰئِكَ لَهُمْ رِزْقٌ مَعْلُومٌ ۞
فَوَاكِهُ ۚ وَهُمْ مُكْرَمُونَ ۞
فِى جَنَّاتِ النَّعِيمِ ۞
عَلٰى سُرُرٍ مُتَقَابِلِينَ ۞
يُطَافُ عَلَيْهِمْ بِكَاْسٍ مِنْ مَعِينٍ ۞
بَيْضَاءَ لَذَّةٍ لِلشَّارِبِينَ ۞
لَا فِيهَا غَوْلٌ وَلَا هُمْ عَنْهَا يُنْزَفُونَ ۞
وَعِنْدَهُمْ قَاصِرَاتُ الطَّرْفِ عِينٌ ۞

of modest look and large lustrous eyes,

49. Like sheltered eggs in a nest.

كَأَنَّهُنَّ بَيْضٌ مَّكْنُونٌ ۝

50. Then one turned to the other
in an enquiry.

فَأَقْبَلَ بَعْضُهُمْ عَلَىٰ بَعْضٍ يَتَسَآءَلُونَ ۝

51. Said one of the speakers: "I had a friend

52. Who used to say:
'Are you one of those
who can testify to the truth?

قَالَ قَآئِلٌ مِّنْهُمْ إِنِّي كَانَ لِي قَرِينٌ ۝

يَقُولُ أَئِنَّكَ لَمِنَ الْمُصَدِّقِينَ ۝

53. (Do you think) we would be paid back our due
when we are dead and reduced to dust and bones?'

ءَإِذَا مِتْنَا وَكُنَّا تُرَابًا وَعِظَامًا أَءِنَّا لَمَدِينُونَ ۝

54. He said: 'Will you look down?'

قَالَ هَلْ أَنتُم مُّطَّلِعُونَ ۝

55. He looked down and saw (his friend)
in the midst of Hell.

فَاطَّلَعَ فَرَآهُ فِي سَوَآءِ الْجَحِيمِ ۝

56. 'By God', he said, 'you had almost ruined me.

قَالَ تَاللّٰهِ إِن كِدتَّ لَتُرْدِينِ ۝

57. Had it not been for the grace of my Lord
I too would have been there (in Hell). ' "

وَلَوْلَا نِعْمَةُ رَبِّي لَكُنتُ مِنَ الْمُحْضَرِينَ ۝

58. (Another will say:)"Is it true,
we are not going to die

أَفَمَا نَحْنُ بِمَيِّتِينَ ۝

59. Other than our first death,
and we shall not be punished?

إِلَّا مَوْتَتَنَا الْأُولَىٰ وَمَا نَحْنُ بِمُعَذَّبِينَ ۝

60. This will indeed be great happiness.

إِنَّ هَٰذَا لَهُوَ الْفَوْزُ الْعَظِيمُ ۝

61. For this the toilers should strive."

لِمِثْلِ هَٰذَا فَلْيَعْمَلِ الْعَامِلُونَ ۝

62. Is this better or the tree of Zaqqum

أَذَٰلِكَ خَيْرٌ نُّزُلًا أَمْ شَجَرَةُ الزَّقُّومِ ۝

63. Which We have reserved
as punishment for evil-doers?

إِنَّا جَعَلْنَاهَا فِتْنَةً لِّلظَّالِمِينَ ۝

64. It is a tree that grows
at the bottom of Hell.

إِنَّهَا شَجَرَةٌ تَخْرُجُ فِي أَصْلِ الْجَحِيمِ ۝

65. Its spathes are like the prickly pear.

طَلْعُهَا كَأَنَّهُ رُءُوسُ الشَّيَاطِينِ ۝

66. They will eat and fill their bellies with it,

فَإِنَّهُمْ لَآكِلُونَ مِنْهَا فَمَالِئُونَ مِنْهَا الْبُطُونَ ۝

67. Washing it down with boiling water.

ثُمَّ إِنَّ لَهُمْ عَلَيْهَا لَشَوْبًا مِّنْ حَمِيمٍ ۝

68. Then to Hell they will surely be returned.

ثُمَّ إِنَّ مَرْجِعَهُمْ لَإِلَى الْجَحِيمِ ۝

69. They had found their fathers astray,

إِنَّهُمْ أَلْفَوْا آبَاءَهُمْ ضَالِّينَ ۝

70. Yet they hasten to follow
in their footsteps.

فَهُمْ عَلَىٰ آثَارِهِمْ يُهْرَعُونَ ۝

71. So had many an earlier people gone astray,

وَلَقَدْ ضَلَّ قَبْلَهُمْ أَكْثَرُ الْأَوَّلِينَ ۝

72. And We had sent admonishers to them.

وَلَقَدْ أَرْسَلْنَا فِيهِم مُّنذِرِينَ ۝

73. Look, then how was the end of those
who had been warned,

فَانظُرْ كَيْفَ كَانَ عَاقِبَةُ الْمُنذَرِينَ ۝

74. Other than the chosen creatures of God.

إِلَّا عِبَادَ اللّٰهِ الْمُخْلَصِينَ ۝

Noah had verily called to Us.
And how gracious was He who answered (him).

وَلَقَدْ نَادَانَا نُوحٌ فَلَنِعْمَ الْمُجِيبُونَ ۝

76. We saved him and his family
from the great affliction,

وَنَجَّيْنَاهُ وَأَهْلَهُ مِنَ الْكَرْبِ الْعَظِيمِ ۝

77. And made his progeny survive,

وَجَعَلْنَا ذُرِّيَّتَهُ هُمُ الْبَاقِينَ ۝

78. And left (his name)

وَتَرَكْنَا عَلَيْهِ فِي الْآخِرِينَ ۝

for posterity.

79. Peace on Noah among all men.
80. That is how We reward those who do good.
81. Surely he was among Our faithful creatures.
82. Afterwards We drowned the others.
83. And Abraham indeed was of his inducement,
84. When he came to his Lord with a heart
compliant,
85. When he said to his father and his people:
"What is this you worship?
86. Why do you solicit false gods instead of God?
87. What do you imagine the Lord of the worlds to be?"
88. Then he looked up at the stars (they worshipped),
89. And said: "I am sick
(of what you worship)!"
90. But they turned their backs on him
and went away.
91. Then he turned towards their gods and said:
"Why do you not eat (of these offerings)?
92. What is wrong with you that you do not speak?"
93. Then he started striking them down
with his right hand.
94. So the people descended upon him.
95. "Why do you worship these you carve yourselves," he
        asked,
96. "When God has created you and what you make?"
97. "Build a pyre for him
and throw him into the raging fire." *
98. So they contrived a plot against him,
but We made them abject.
99. And he said: "I am going away
to my Lord
who will show me the way."
100. (And he prayed:)
"O Lord, grant me a righteous son."
101. So We gave him the good news of a clement son.
102. When he was old enough to go about with him,
he said: "O my son, I dreamt that I was sacrificing you.
Consider, what you think?"
He replied: "Father, do as you are commanded.
If God pleases you will find me firm."
103. When they submitted to the will of God,
and (Abraham) laid (his son) down prostrate on his temple,

---

* According to the common belief going back to Nimrod, fire purified what it consumed.

104. We called out: "O Abraham,
105. You have fulfilled your dream."
Thus do We reward the good. —
106. That was indeed a trying test.
107. So We ransomed him
for a great sacrifice,
108. And left (his hallowed memory) for posterity.
109. Peace be on Abraham.
110. That is how We reward those
who do good.
111. He is truly among Our faithful creatures.
112. So We gave him the good news of Isaac,
apostle, who is among the righteous.
113. And We blessed him and Isaac.
Among their descendants are some who do good,
but some who wrong themselves.

We were indeed gracious to Moses and Aaron,
115. And saved them and their people
from great distress,
116. And helped them,
so they were victorious.
117. We gave them the explicit Book,
118. And showed them the straight path,
119. And left (their remembrance) for posterity.
120. Peace be on Moses and Aaron.
121. That is how We reward those who do good.
122. They are among Our faithful devotees.
123. Verily Elias is one of the apostles.
124. When he said to his people:
"Will you not be mindful of God?
125. Would you call on Baal and leave
the best of creators,
126. God, your Lord,
and the Lord of your fathers?"
127. They denied him, and will surely be brought to
        punishment,
128. Except the chosen creatures of God.
129. And We left his (memory) for posterity.
130. Peace be on Elias.
131. That is how We reward those who do good.
132. He is truly among Our faithful devotees.
133. Verily Lot was one of the apostles,
134. Wherefor We saved him and his entire family
135. Except an old woman who was one of those
who stayed behind.

As-Saffat

136. Then We destroyed the others.
137. You pass by (their habitations) in the morning
138. Or at night.
Then how is it you do not understand?

Verily Jonah is one of the apostles.
140. When he fled on the laden ship,
141. And lots were cast
(when a storm overtook them),
he was rejected, (and thrown overboard).
142. Then he was swallowed by a large fish
as he was worthy of blame.
143. Had he not been one of those
who struggled hard,
144. He would have stayed in its belly
till the day the dead are raised.
145. So We cast him, sick, on a barren shore,
146. And We made a gourd tree grow over him.
147. We sent him to a hundred thousand men
or more,
148. And they came to believe;
so We allowed them to enjoy the good things of life for an age.
149. Now ask them if their Lord has daughters,
and they sons?
150. Or did We make the angels females,
and they witnessed it?
151. Is it not a lie invented by them
when they say:
152. "God has begotten (children)?"
They are liars indeed!
153. Does He prefer sons to daughters?
154. What ails you that you judge in such a wise?
155. Why do you not reflect?
156. Or have you received some clear authority?
157. Then bring your scripture,
if what you say is true.
158. They link Him with jinns by lineage,
yet the jinns know
they will be brought before Him.
159. God is too glorious for what they ascribe to Him
160. Except His chosen creatures who do not.
161. So neither you nor those you worship
162. Can mislead anyone away from Him,
163. Except one
who is (destined) to burn in Hell.
164. "There is not one of us who does not have

As-Saffat

his appointed place," (declare the angels.)

وَإِنَّا لَنَحْنُ الصَّآفُّونَ ۝

165. "And we are truly those
who stand in rows,

166. And we are those
who sing hallelujas to Him."

وَإِنَّا لَنَحْنُ الْمُسَبِّحُونَ ۝
وَإِنْ كَانُوا لَيَقُولُونَ ۝

167. They used to say:

168. If we had the account
of earlier people with us,

لَوْ أَنَّ عِنْدَنَا ذِكْرًا مِّنَ الْأَوَّلِينَ ۝

169. We would have been
the chosen creatures of God."

لَكُنَّا عِبَادَ اللهِ الْمُخْلَصِينَ ۝

170. Yet now (that it has come)
they refuse to believe in it;
but they will come to know soon.

فَكَفَرُوا بِهِ فَسَوْفَ يَعْلَمُونَ ۝

171. Our word had already been given before
to Our votaries, the apostles,

وَلَقَدْ سَبَقَتْ كَلِمَتُنَا لِعِبَادِنَا الْمُرْسَلِينَ ۝

172. That they would be helped,

إِنَّهُمْ لَهُمُ الْمَنْصُورُونَ ۝

173. And that certainly
Our armies will be victorious.

وَإِنَّ جُنْدَنَا لَهُمُ الْغَالِبُونَ ۝

174. So you ignore them for a time

فَتَوَلَّ عَنْهُمْ حَتَّى حِينٍ ۝

175. And wait; they will come to know soon.

وَأَبْصِرْهُمْ فَسَوْفَ يُبْصِرُونَ ۝

176. Do they want to hasten Our punishment?

أَفَبِعَذَابِنَا يَسْتَعْجِلُونَ ۝

177. When it comes down on their plains,
it will be an evil dawn
for those who had been warned.

فَإِذَا نَزَلَ بِسَاحَتِهِمْ فَسَآءَ صَبَاحُ الْمُنْذَرِينَ ۝

178. So turn away from them for a time

وَتَوَلَّ عَنْهُمْ حَتَّى حِينٍ ۝

179. And watch;
they will come to know soon.

وَأَبْصِرْ فَسَوْفَ يُبْصِرُونَ ۝

180. Too glorious is your Lord,
the Lord of power,
for what they ascribe to Him.

سُبْحَانَ رَبِّكَ رَبِّ الْعِزَّةِ عَمَّا يَصِفُونَ ۝

181. So peace be on the messengers,

182. And all praise to God,
the Lord of all the worlds.

وَسَلَامٌ عَلَى الْمُرْسَلِينَ ۝
وَالْحَمْدُ لِلَّهِ رَبِّ الْعَالَمِينَ ۝

As-Saffat

38 Sad

Sād: Makki

In the name of Allah, most benevolent, ever-merciful.

SĀD. I CALL to witness the admonishing Qur'an.

2. But the unbelievers are still full of pride and hostility.

3. How many generations have We destroyed before them
who cried (for mercy) when it was too late for escape.

4. They were surprised that one of them
had come to them as warner;
and the unbelievers said: "He is a deceiving sorcerer.

5. Has he turned so many gods into one deity?
This is indeed a strange thing!"

6. And their leading chiefs said: "Remain attached to your
    gods.
There is surely some motive behind it.

7. We never heard of it in the former faith.
It is surely a fabrication.

8. To him of all of us has the Reminder been sent down?"
They are still in doubt about My admonition;
but they have not tasted My punishment yet!

9. Do they have the stores of the mercy of your Lord,
the mighty and munificent?

10. Or is the kingdom of the heavens and the earth
and all that lies between them, theirs?
Then let them climb up the ladders (to the heavens).

11. They will be one more army vanquished
among the many routed hordes.

12. Even before them the people of Noah,
'Ad, the mighty Pharoah,

13. And the Thamud, the people of Lot,
as well as the dwellers of the Wood, had denied.
These were the hordes.

14. Of all these there was not one
who did not deny the messengers.
So My retribution was justified.

They await but a single blast

which will not be repeated.

16. Still they say: "O Lord,
give us our share before the Day of Reckoning."
17. Bear with patience what they say,
and remember Our votary David, man of strength.
He surely turned to Us in penitence.
18. We subjugated the chiefs (of tribes)
to struggle day and night with him,
19. And the levied Tair.*
They were all obedient to him.
20. So We further strengthened his kingdom,
and bestowed wisdom on him,
and judgement in legal matters.
21. Have you heard of the litigants
who jumped over the wall into his chamber?
22. When they came before David, he was frightened of them.
"Do not be afraid," they said.
"The two of us are disputing the wrong one has done the other.
So judge between us with equity,
and do not be unjust,
and guide us to the right path.
23. This man here is my brother.
He has ninety and nine ewes while I have only one.
He demands that I should give him my ewe,
and wants to get the better of me in argument."
24. (David) said: "He is unjust in demanding
your ewe to add to his (many) ewes.
Many partners are surely unjust to one another,

---

* See note on p. 322 for the use of words covering different shades of meaning. The present Surah is more metonymic in its narrative and use of words. The employment of words having double meanings is continued, almost in line with *naml* (both as name of tribe and ants) and *hud-hud* (name of tribe and of individuals and hoopoe).

Jibal and *tair* are used together here always with king David as being submissive with him. Their repeated use in sentences of an almost identical nature at two other places, i.e. 21:79 and 34:10, with *ma'a* (with or along with), *sakhkhara* or *awwab* (submissive and obedient), *sabbaha* (to glorify, move swiftly or rush, return, etc.), points to the special significance they hold in the context of king David and his times full of turbulence, when he extended his power and unified the tribes and small kingdoms, under him. This policy was continued by his son Solomon, as references to David's killing Goliath and Solomon's subjugation of the prosperous kingdom of Sheba, show how David and Solomon came to occupy a legendary place in the annals of the Arabian people. See note on 27:16, p. 322.

The mention of iron being made pliable for David in 34:10, and coats of mail in 34:11, together with verse 20 of this Surah, 38, which speaks of the strengthening of his kingdom, clearly indicate martial might. This directs our attention to the obviously metonymic use of *al-jibal* and *wattaira mahshurah*. Although *jibal* commonly means mountains, it is also used for *saiyyad al-qaum*, chiefs of tribe or people, and men of knowledge or learned men. *Tair* means ever so many

except those who believe and do the right;
but there are only a few of them." **
It occurred to David that he was being tried by Us,
and he begged his Lord to forgive him,
and fell down in homage and repented.
25. So We forgave him. He has surely a high rank with Us
and an excellent place of return.
26. "O David, We have made you trustee on the earth.
So judge between men equitably,
and do not follow your lust
lest it should lead you astray from the way of God.
Surely for those who go astray
from the way of God, is severe punishment,
for having forgotten the Day of Reckoning.

We have not created the heavens and the earth
and all that lies between them, all for nothing.
Only those who deny imagine so.
So for the unbelievers there is woe from the fire.
28. Should We equate those who do the right
with those who spread corruption in the land?
Should We make those who are morally integrated
equal to those who seek disintegration?
29. We have sent down a Book to you which is blessed,
so that people may apply their minds to its revelations,
and the men of wisdom may reflect.
30. We bestowed Solomon on David
who was an excellent devotee,
for he turned to God in penitence.

---

things, as has been discussed in notes on 3:49 and 27:18. In verse 19 of the present Surah *tair* has been qualified with the adjective *mahshurah* which imparts a definite meaning and special significance to the word. Though derived from *hashara,* it does not mean simply gathered or gathered together, but summoned or commanded by authority to appear, or conscripted for military service. *Lisan al-'Arab* quotes three Traditions in which the word *yuhsharu* has been used in an identical sense: "The delegation of the tribe of Thaqif advanced the condition for peace that they will be immune from being summoned for military service." "The tribe of Najran asked for peace on the condition that they will not be summoned for purposes of war." And lastly, the *Lisan* quotes a Hadith regarding women that "they will not be summoned for war, as fighting is not compulsory for women." All this leaves no doubt that as *jibal* has been used in the sense of chiefs of tribes and principalities, *tair* has been used for either a particular tribe or a conquered race conscripted for war. The Qur'an is advancing instances from history and highlighting the roles of King David and Solomon in the history of their times.

** The meaning of the passage is clear. The reference is to one God and many gods, i.e. idolatry. David did not understand it at once. When he did, he asked for forgiveness.

31. When they brought fleet-footed chargers in the
evening to show him,
32. He said: "The love of horses* is worthy of desire to me
for the remembrance of my Lord;"
and when they were out of sight, (he said):
33. "Bring them back to me,"
and he began to rub and stroke their shanks and necks.
34. We surely tried Solomon, and placed
another body** on his throne. So he turned to God
35. Saying: "O Lord, forgive me, and give me such a dominion
as none will merit after me
You are the great bestower."
36. So we subjugated the wind to his service
which carried his merchandise wheresoever he wished;
37. And the devils — the builders and divers of all kinds,
38. And many others bound in bond.
39. "This is Our gift," (We said to him),
"so bestow freely or withhold without reckoning."
40. He has a high position with Us
and an excellent abode.

Remember Our votary Job because he called to his Lord:
"Satan has afflicted me with disease and distress."
42. "Go swiftly to the spring," (We said).
"This cold water
is for bathing and for drinking." ***
43. We restored his family to him
with others similar to them, as a blessing from Us
and a reminder for men of wisdom. —
44. "Take a handful of herbs," (We said to him),
and apply and rub them, and do not make a mistake." ****
We found him patient in adversity,
an excellent devotee, always turning in repentance.
45. Remember Our votaries Abraham, Isaac and Jacob,
men of power and insight.
46. We distinguished them for the distinct remembrance
of the abode (of the Hereafter).
47. They are the chosen ones, the excellent in Our sight.
48. And remember Ishmael, Elisha and Dhu'l-Kifl.
Every one of them is among the best.
49. This is a commemoration.
Surely for those who take heed for themselves
is an excellent place of return —

---

* & ** See notes 1 and 2 on p. 390.

*** & **** See notes 3 and 4 on p. 390.

50. Gardens of Eden with gates open wide to them, جَنّٰتِ عَدْنٍ مُّفَتَّحَةً لَّهُمُ الْاَبْوَابُ ۚ

51. Where they will take their ease,
calling for fruits in plenty, and for wine, مُتَّكِئِيْنَ فِيْهَا يَدْعُوْنَ فِيْهَا بِفَاكِهَةٍ كَثِيْرَةٍ وَّشَرَابٍ ۚ

52. With companions of modest look, the same in age, by their side. وَعِنْدَهُمْ قٰصِرٰتُ الطَّرْفِ اَتْرَابٌ ۚ

53. This is what is promised you for the Day of Reckoning. هٰذَا مَا تُوْعَدُوْنَ لِيَوْمِ الْحِسَابِ ۚ

54. This is surely Our provision never-ending. اِنَّ هٰذَا لَرِزْقُنَا مَا لَهٗ مِنْ نَّفَادٍ ۚ

55. This (for the virtuous); but for the transgressors
the evil destination, هٰذَا ۚ وَاِنَّ لِلطّٰغِيْنَ لَشَرَّ مَاٰبٍ ۚ

56. Hell, in which they will burn. How vile a resting place! جَهَنَّمَ ۚ يَصْلَوْنَهَا ۚ فَبِئْسَ الْمِهَادُ ۚ

57. There will be boiling water for them
and cold, clammy, fetid drink to taste, هٰذَا ۚ فَلْيَذُوْقُوْهُ حَمِيْمٌ وَّغَسَّاقٌ ۚ

58. And other similar torments. وَّاٰخَرُ مِنْ شَكْلِهٖۤ اَزْوَاجٌ ۚ

59. Here is a multitude rushing headlong with you.
There is no welcome for them.
They will roast in the fire. هٰذَا فَوْجٌ مُّقْتَحِمٌ مَّعَكُمْ ۚ لَا مَرْحَبًا بِهِمْ ۚ اِنَّهُمْ صَالُوا النَّارِ ۚ

60. They will say: "In fact, it is you
who will have no welcome.
It is you who brought this upon us.
What an evil place of rest!" قَالُوْا بَلْ اَنْتُمْ ۚ لَا مَرْحَبًا بِكُمْ ۚ اَنْتُمْ قَدَّمْتُمُوْهُ لَنَا ۚ فَبِئْسَ الْقَرَارُ ۚ

61. They will say: "O Lord, give him
who has brought this upon us
two times more the torment of Hell;" قَالُوْا رَبَّنَا مَنْ قَدَّمَ لَنَا هٰذَا فَزِدْهُ عَذَابًا ضِعْفًا فِى النَّارِ ۚ

62. And will add: "O what has happened to us that we do not see
the men we counted among the wicked. وَقَالُوْا مَا لَنَا لَا نَرٰى رِجَالًا كُنَّا نَعُدُّهُمْ مِّنَ الْاَشْرَارِ ۚ

63. Did we laugh at them (for nothing),
or our eyes fail to pick them out?" اَتَّخَذْنٰهُمْ سِخْرِيًّا اَمْ زَاغَتْ عَنْهُمُ الْاَبْصَارُ ۚ

64. This contending of the inmates of Hell will surely be real. اِنَّ ذٰلِكَ لَحَقٌّ تَخَاصُمُ اَهْلِ النَّارِ ۚ

Say: "I am only a warner,
and there is no other god but God,
the one, the omnipotent, قُلْ اِنَّمَاۤ اَنَا مُنْذِرٌ ۚ وَّمَا مِنْ اِلٰهٍ اِلَّا اللّٰهُ الْوَاحِدُ الْقَهَّارُ ۚ

66. Lord of the heavens and the earth
and all that lies between them,
all-mighty, all-forgiving." رَبُّ السَّمٰوٰتِ وَالْاَرْضِ وَمَا بَيْنَهُمَا الْعَزِيْزُ الْغَفَّارُ ۚ

67. Say: "This is a momentous message, قُلْ هُوَ نَبَؤٌا عَظِيْمٌ ۚ

68. To which you pay no heed. اَنْتُمْ عَنْهُ مُعْرِضُوْنَ ۚ

69. I had no knowledge of the higher Assembly
when they discussed it among themselves. مَا كَانَ لِيَ مِنْ عِلْمٍ بِالْمَلَاِ الْاَعْلٰۤى اِذْ يَخْتَصِمُوْنَ ۚ

70. Only this has been revealed to me
that I am a distinct warner. اِنْ يُّوْحٰۤى اِلَيَّ اِلَّاۤ اَنَّمَاۤ اَنَا نَذِيْرٌ مُّبِيْنٌ ۚ

71. When your Lord said to the angels:
"I am going to create a man from clay; اِذْ قَالَ رَبُّكَ لِلْمَلٰٓئِكَةِ اِنِّىْ خَالِقٌ بَشَرًا مِّنْ طِيْنٍ ۚ

72. And when I have made him and have breathed
into him of My spirit. فَاِذَا سَوَّيْتُهٗ وَنَفَخْتُ فِيْهِ مِنْ رُّوْحِيْ فَقَعُوْا لَهٗ سٰجِدِيْنَ ۚ

fall down in homage before him."

73. Then the angels bowed before him in a body,

74. Except Iblis. He was filled with pride
and turned an unbeliever.

75. Said (God): "O Iblis, what hindered you from adoring
what I created by My own authority?
Are you too proud, or too high and mighty?"

76. He said: "I am better than he.
You created me from fire, and him from clay."

77. (God) said: "Then go hence, ostracised.

78. Upon you will be My damnation
till the Day of Doom."

79. He said: "O Lord, give me respite
till the day the dead rise from their graves."

80. (God) said: "You have the respite

81. Till the appointed day."

82. He said: "By Your authority, I will lead them astray,

83. Other than the chosen ones among Your creatures."

84. (God) said: "This is right by Me,
and what I say is right.

85. I will fill up Hell with you
together with those who follow you."

86. Say: "I do not ask any compensation of you for it,
nor am I a specious pretender.

87. This is only a warning for mankind.

88. You will come to know its truth in time."

---

1. V. 32. *Khair* means what is desirable, beautiful, profitable. Arabs called their horses *khair* for their profitability. In v.33 *masaha* means rubbing or stroking, not to slash or cut off.

2. V. 34. That body or person was Ad-o-nijah, son of David by Haggith, who had himself crowned king as David lay ill in old age, even though Solomon had been nominated by David as his successor. Beth-Sheba, mother of Solomon, and David were informed of this crowning, with the result that David had Solomon seated on the throne, and Ad-o-nijah was overthrown: the Bible: I Kings I. And Solomon, therefore, turned to God in gratitude.

3. V. 42. *Urkud bi-rijlika* means to move quickly, for *rijl* means foot, and *arrakz* to run swiftly (not stamp) as in 21:12-13.

4. V. 44. *Tahnath* means here 'do not make a mistake,' though it also means sin, disobedience and taking an oath and not fulfilling it. The context, however, does not allow any other meaning but 'mistake' in this verse which is concerned with the cure of disease of a dermic nature caused, it appears, by snake bite. For *shaitan* also means snake and 'devil of the desert', hence 'thirst', indicated by the instruction to go swiftly to the spring and drink its water and bathe in it, and to rub the body with a handful of herbs, as is clear from the use of *zightha*. See *Taj* and *Raghib* for *tanath* and *zightha*.

39 The Small Groups

Az-Zumar: Makki

In the name of Allah, most benevolent, ever-merciful.

THE REVELATION OF this Book is from God,
the mighty and all-wise.
2. We have revealed to you the Scripture with exactitude;
so worship God with devotion all exclusive for Him.
3. Remember that devotion is exclusively for God.
Those who have taken protectors other than Him,
say: "We worship them that they may bring
us nearer to God."
Surely God will judge between them
in what they are differing about.
Verily God does not show the way
to an ungrateful liar.
4. Had God pleased to take a son,
He could have chosen whom He liked
from among those He has created.
Glory be to Him.
He is God, the one, the omnipotent.
5. He has created the heavens and the earth with precision.
He folds the day up over the night,
and folds the night up over the day.
He has subjugated the sun and moon,
(so that) each runs its appointed course.
Is He not all-mighty and forgiving?
6. He created you from a single cell,
then from it created its mate;
and provided eight varieties of cattle for you.
He formed you in the mother's womb,
formation after formation
in three (veils of) darkness.
He is God your Lord.
His is the kingdom.
There is no god other than He.
How then can you turn away?
7. If you are ungrateful, then remember

God is independent of you,
and He does not favour ingratitude on the part of His creatures.
If you are grateful
He will be pleased with you.
For no one who carries a burden bears another's load;
and your returning is to your Lord,
when He will tell you what you used to do.
Surely He knows what is in the hearts.
8. When man is afflicted with adversity
he turns to his Lord, and prays to Him.
But when He bestows His favour on him,
he forgets what he prayed for before,
and sets up others as compeers of God
to mislead (people) from His way.
Say: "Take advantage of your denying for a while:
You will be among the inmates of Hell."
9. Can one who prays in the watches of the night,
bowing in homage or standing attentive,
fearful of the life to come, and hoping
for the mercy of his Lord, (be like one who does not)?
Say: "Can those who know,
and those who do not know, be equal?
Only they think who are wise.

Tell them: "O my creatures who have come to belief,
have fear of displeasing your Lord.
There is good for those who do good in this world,
and productive is God's earth.
Only those who persevere
will get their reward measureless."
11. Say: "I am commanded to worship God
with obedience all-exclusive for Him;
12. And I am commanded to be the first of those who submit."
13. Say: "If I disobey my Lord, I fear
the punishment of an evil Day."
14. Say: "I worship God with devotion
all-exclusive for Him.
15. You may worship what you will apart from Him."
Say: "Surely the greatest losers will be those
who will lose their own selves and their people
on the Day of Resurrection."
Remember, this will be an all-too-evident loss.
16. Above them will be a covering of fire,
below them a cloud (of flames).
With this does God warn His creatures:
"O My creatures, fear Me."

Az-Zumar

وما لي ٣٩ الزمر ٣٩

17. There are happy tidings for those
who keep away from the worship of false gods
and turn to God in repentance.
Give glad tidings to My creatures.
18. Those who listen to the Word
and then follow the best it contains,
are the ones who have been guided by God,
and are men of wisdom.
19. Can he against whom the sentence of punishment
has been justified (be rescued)?
Can you save him who is in the Fire?
20. But for those who fear displeasing their Lord
there are lofty mansions built above mansions,
with rivers rippling past below them:
A promise of God;
(and) God does not go back on His promise.
21. Do you not see that God
sends down water from the sky,
then makes it flow in rills on the earth,
and brings forth corn from it which,
having passed through changes of shade and colour,
comes to ripen, and you see it autumnal yellow;
then He reduces it to chaff.
There are indeed lessons in this
for those who are wise.

Will he whose breast has been opened up to peace
(not be) in luminescence from his Lord?
Alas for those whose hearts
have been hardened to God's remembrance!
They wander (astray) in clear error.
23. God has sent down the very best discourse,
the Book conformable in its juxtapositions,
which makes all of those who fear their Lord, shudder.
So their hearts and bodies become receptive
to the remembrance of God.
This is the guidance of God
with which He guides whosoever He will;
but whosoever God allows to go astray
has none to show him the way.
24. Can he who will have to shield himself
against the torment of the Day of Resurrection
(be the same as one at peace)?
The evil-doers will be told: "So taste what you earned."
25. Those before them had denied,
then punishment had overtaken them

from a quarter they did not suspect.
26. Then God made them taste of disgrace in this life;
and the torment of the life to come
is greater, if they understand.
27. We have given examples of every kind for men
in this Qur'an
so that they may contemplate:
28. A clear discourse which expounds all things
without any obliquity,
so that they may take heed for themselves.
29. God advances the example of a man who is owned
(as slave in common)
by a number of men at loggerheads,
and another man who is owned by only one.
Are these two alike in attribute?
God be praised; yet many of them do not know.
30. Verily you will die, and so will they.
31. Then on the Day of Resurrection
you will dispute before your Lord.

Who does greater wrong than he
who tells a lie against God, and denies
the truth when it has come to him?
Is there no place for unbelievers in Hell?
33. He who brings the truth and verifies it, —
such are the people who are God-fearing.
34. They shall have what they wish from their Lord.
This is the recompense for the good,
35. That God may absolve them of their sins
and reward them for the best that they had done.
36. Is not God sufficient for His devotee?
Still they frighten you with others apart from Him.
Whoever God allows to go astray
has none to show him the way.
37. And none can lead him astray
who has been guided by God.
Is not God all-mighty, the lord of retribution?
38. If you ask them, "Who created the heavens and the earth?"
they will answer: "God."
Say: "Then just think. Can those whom you worship apart
from God
remove the distress God is pleased to visit upon me,
or withhold a blessing God is pleased to favour me with?"
Say: "God is all-sufficient for me.
The trusting place their trust in Him."
39. Say: "O people, act as best you can on your part,

Az-Zumar

I am acting too. You will come to know in time
40. Who suffers the shameful punishment,
and on whom falls the everlasting torment.
41. We have sent down this Book to you
with the truth for all mankind.
So, he who comes to guidance does so for himself,
and he who goes astray does so for his own loss;
on you does not lie their guardianship.

God gathers up the souls of those who die,
and of those who do not die, in their sleep;
then He keeps back those ordained for death,
and sends the others back for an appointed term.
Surely there are signs in this for those who reflect.
43. Have they appointed intercessors other than God?
Say: "Even though they have no power in the least,
nor do they understand?"
44. Say: "God's is the intercession entirely;
His is the kingdom of the heavens and the earth;
then to Him you will return."
45. When God alone is mentioned the hearts of those
who do not believe in the life to come,
are filled with resentment.
But when others are mentioned apart from God,
they begin to rejoice.
46. Say: "O God, the originator of the heavens and the earth,
the knower of the unknown and the known,
You alone will judge between Your creatures
for things they differed about."
47. Even if the sinners possessed
whatever is in the heavens and the earth, and as much more,
they would offer it to ransom themselves
from the torment of the Day of Resurrection;
yet what they did not even imagine
would appear to them from God;
48. And the evil of what they had earned
would become visible to them;
and what they used to mock
would surround them from all sides.
49. When a man is in trouble, he prays to God;
but when We bestow a favour on him
he says: "It has come to me through my acumen."
In fact, this is an illusion,
but most men do not know.
50. Those before them had also said so,
and yet nothing of what they did

availed them in the least.
51. Then the worst of what they had done overtook them.
So will the evil deeds of those who are sinners among them
recoil back on them.
They cannot get the better (of Us).
52. Do they not know that God enhances or restricts
the provision of any one He will.
Surely there are signs in this for people who believe.

Say: "O creatures of God, those of you
who have acted against your own interests
should not be disheartened of the mercy of God.
Surely God forgives all sins.
He is all-forgiving and all-merciful.
54. Turn towards your Lord and obey Him
before the punishment comes upon you
when you will not be helped.
55. Follow the best of what has been revealed
to you by your Lord
before the punishment overtakes you suddenly
and you are caught unawares,
56. Lest a soul should say: "Alas,
I was heedless of God and only laughed;"
57. Or say: "If only God had guided me
I would have been a man of fear and piety;"
58. Or say on seeing the punishment:
"If I could only return I would be among the good."
59. Why, My revelations had come to you,
but you denied them and were filled with pride,
and were among the disbelievers.
60. If you see those who had imputed lies to God
on the Day of Resurrection,
black would be their faces (with disgrace).
Is there not a place in Hell for the arrogant?
61. God would rescue those who fear Him
(and guide them) to places of safety.
Neither will evil touch them nor regret.
62. God is the creator of all things,
and He is the guarantor of all things.
63. He has the keys of the heavens and the earth;
and those who deny the revelations of God
will be losers.

Say: "O you ignorant people, do you bid me to worship
someone other than God?
65. Surely you have been commanded,

as those before you were:
"If you associate (any one with God),
wasted will be all your deeds,
and you will perish."
66. So, you should worship only God,
and be among the grateful.
67. They do not esteem God as is rightly due to Him.
The whole earth would be a fistful of His
on the Day of Resurrection,
and the heavens would be rolled up in His right hand.
Too immaculate is He and too high
for what they associate with Him!
68. When the trumpet blast is sounded
whoever is in the heavens and the earth
will swoon away, except those God please.
When the blast is sounded the second time,
they will stand up all expectant.
69. The earth will light up with the effulgence of her Lord;
and the ledger (of account)
will be placed (in each man's hand),
and the apostles and the witnesses will be called,
and judgement passed between them equitably,
and no wrong will be done to them.
70. Each soul will be paid in full for what it had done.
He is cognisant of what you do.

The unbelievers will be driven into Hell in groups
till, when they reach it and its doors are opened up,
its keepers will say to them:
"Did not apostles of your own come to you
reciting your Lord's revelations, warning you
of this your day of Doom?"
They will answer: "Yes;"
but the sentence of punishment was justified
against the unbelievers.
72. "Enter the gates of Hell," they will be told,
"and there abide for ever."
How grievous a destination for the haughty!
73. Those who were mindful of their duty to their Lord
will be driven in groups to Paradise,
till they reach it and its gates are opened,
and its keepers say to them:
"Peace be on you; you are the joyous.
So enter here to live for ever."
74. They will say: "All praise be to God
who has fulifllcd the promise He had made to us,

الزمر ٣٩   قمن اظلمرع ٢٤

and bequeathed to us this land
for dwelling in the garden wheresoever we like."
How excellent the recompense for those who act!
75. You will see the angels hover round the Throne,
singing the praises of their Lord;
and justice will be done between them equitably,
and it would be said: "All praise to God
the Lord of all the worlds."

الْأَرْضَ نَتَبَوَّأُ مِنَ الْجَنَّةِ حَيْثُ نَشَآءُ فَنِعْمَ
أَجْرُ الْعَامِلِينَ ۞

وَتَرَى الْمَلَٰٓئِكَةَ حَآفِّينَ مِنْ حَوْلِ الْعَرْشِ يُسَبِّحُونَ
بِحَمْدِ رَبِّهِمْ وَقُضِيَ بَيْنَهُم بِالْحَقِّ وَقِيلَ
الْحَمْدُ لِلَّهِ رَبِّ الْعَٰلَمِينَ ۞

40 The Believer

Al-Mū'min: **Makki**

In the name of Allah, most benevolent, ever-merciful.

HĀ MĪM.

2. The revelation of this Book is from God
the all-mighty and all-knowing,
3. Forgiver of trespasses, acceptor of repentance,
severe of retribution, lord of power.
There is no god but He.
Towards Him is your destination.
4. Only the unbelievers dispute the revelations of God.
So do not let their activities in the land
deceive you.
5. The people of Noah had denied before them,
and many factions after them.
Every nation has intrigued against its apostle
and afflicted him, and argued with false arguments
to condemn the truth.
Then I seized them.
How was then My retribution!
6. In this way the sentence of your Lord
against the infidels that they would be
the inmates of Hell, was justified.
7. The bearers of the Throne, and those around it,
sing the praises of their Lord
and believe in Him, and seek forgiveness for those who believe:
"O our Lord, Your mercy and knowledge
embrace every thing;
so forgive those who turn to You in repentance
and follow Your path; and preserve them
from the torment of Hell.
8. Admit them, O Lord, to the garden of Eden
which You promised them,
and those of their fathers, spouses and progeny
who are upright.
You are truly all-mighty and all-wise.
9. Protect them from evil;

Al-Mū'min

and whosoever You preserve from evil on that Day
shall have surely received Your mercy.
This will be the great triumph."

Those who disbelieve will certainly be told:
"God's displeasure was greater than your disgust of your selves
when you were called to belief and refused to believe."
11. They say: "O Lord, twice You made us die,
and twice You made us live.
We admit our sins.
Is there still a way out for us?"
12. This has come upon you because
when God alone was invoked you disbelieved; but when
partners were associated with Him,
you believed.
But judgement belongs to God, the all-high and supreme.
13. It is He who shows you His signs,
and sends you food from the heavens.
Yet none takes a warning except him who turns to Him.
14. So call on God with exclusive obedience,
howsoever the unbelievers may dislike it.
15. Most exalted of position, Lord of power,
He directs inspiration by His command
to any of His creatures as He will,
to warn (men) of the Day of Meeting,
16. The day when they will come out (of their graves),
with nothing of them hidden from God.
Whose then will be the kingdom? —
God's, the one, the omnipotent.
17. Each soul will be recompensed that Day
for what it had earned.
There will be no depriving on that Day.
Surely God is swift at reckoning.
18. Warn them of the coming day inevitable, when hearts
would jump to the throats, filling them with anguish.
The sinners will have neither friend nor intercessor
whose (word) will be heeded.
19. Known to Him is the treachery of the eye,
and what the breasts conceal.
20. God decides with justice.
But those they call apart from Him
can not adjudge in the least.
Verily God is all-hearing, all-perceiving.

Have they not travelled on the earth that they could see
what happened to those before them?

They were greater in strength than they,
and have left behind them traces on the earth.
Yet they were seized by God for their sins,
and had none to protect them against God.
22. This was so because their apostles came
with clear proofs to them, but they refused to believe.
So they were seized by God.
Surely God is powerful, unrelenting in retribution.
23. We sent Moses with Our signs and clear authority
24. To Pharaoh, Haman and Qarun.
But they said: "He is only a deceiving sorcerer."
25. And when he brought the truth to them from Us,
they said: "Slay the sons of those who believe with him,
and spare their women."
But the unbelievers' stratagem is bound to fail.
26. "Let me kill Moses," the Pharaoh said,
"and let him call to his Lord.
I fear that he will change your faith
and spread corruption in the land."
27. Moses said: "I seek refuge in my Lord and your Lord
from every insolent imposter
who does not believe in the Day of Reckoning."

A believer from the House of Pharaoh
who had kept his faith to himself, said:
"Will you kill a man because he says:
'My Lord is God,' when he has brought
clear signs from his Lord to you?
If he is a liar his lie will recoil back on him;
but in case he speaks the truth,
then what he predicts will befall you.
Surely God does not show the way
to the shameful liar.
29. O my people, authority is yours today
being the most powerful in the land;
but who will save us from the scourge of God
if it fall upon us?"
"I show you," said the Pharaoh, "only what I see (is right),
and guide you but to the right path."
30. But the man of belief said: "O my people,
what I fear for you is the like
of what befell the communities (of old).
31. Like the people of Noah, 'Ad and Thamud,
and those that came after them.
God does not want to be unjust to His creatures.
32. O my people, what I fear for you is the day

of gathering, crying and calling,

33. The day you will turn your backs and flee,
with none to defend you against God.
Whoever God allows to go astray
has none to show him the way.

34. Joseph had indeed come to you before with clear proofs,
but you did not cease to doubt what he had brought until
he died, when you said:
'God will not send a prophet after him.'
That is how God leads the waster, the sceptic astray.

35. Those who dispute God's revelations,
with no authority having come to them,
(are) greatly odious in the sight of God,
and the sight of those who believe.
That is how God seals
every proud and perverse heart."

36. The Pharaoh said: "O Haman, build me a lofty tower
that I may perhaps find the means

37. Of reaching the tracts of heaven
and look at the god of Moses.
though I think that he is a liar."
Thus were the evil deeds of Pharaoh
made to look attractive to him,
and he was hindered from the path.
So the stratagem of Pharaoh was bound to perish.

The man who believed said: "O my people,
follow me; I will guide you to the right path.

39. O people, the life of this world is ephemeral;
but enduring is the abode of the Hereafter.

40. Whoever does evil
will be requited in accordance with it;
but whoever does right, whether man or woman,
and is a believer,
will enter Paradise,
where they will have provision in abundance.

41. O my people, what is wrong with me
that I am calling you to preservation,
while you invite me to the Fire!

42. You are asking me to disbelieve in God,
and to associate with Him that of which I have no knowledge,
yet I invite you to the all-mighty, all-forgiving.

43. What you are calling me to is surely not
worth the calling in this world or in the next,
because our returning is to God;
and because the transgressors will be inmates of Hell.

44. You will remember what I say in time to come;
I submit my case to the judgement of God.
Surely God keeps an eye on His creatures."
45. So God preserved him from the evil they were planning;
and a dreadful doom encompassed the people of Pharaoh:
46. Fire, to which they are exposed morning and evening.
The day the Hour is proclaimed
(it will be said:) "Admit
the people of Pharaoh to the severest punishment."
47. As they will noisily argue in the Fire,
the weaker ones will say to the arrogant:
"We were your followers, so will you take over
some of our share of the fire?"
48. The arrogant will answer: "All of us are in it.
Surely God has judged between His creatures."
49. Those in the Fire will say to the warders of Hell:
"Ask your Lord to reduce the punishment by a day for us."
50. They will say: "Did not your apostles come to you
with clear proofs?"
They will answer: "Indeed, they did."
"Then pray," will (the warders) say.
But the praying of unbelievers will be all in vain.

We will certainly help Our messengers and those who
    believe,
in this world, and on the day
the witnesses take their stand,
52. The day upon which their excuses
will not benefit the evil-doers,
and the condemnation and evil abode will be theirs.
53. Verily We showed Moses the way, and bequeathed
the Book to the children of Israel,
54. A guidance and reminder for men of wisdom.
55. So persevere; the promise of God is true;
and seek forgiveness for your sins,
and chant the praises of your Lord evening and morning.
56. Verily those who argue in the matter of God's revelations,
without authority having reached them,
have nothing but pride in their hearts,
and they will not achieve their end.
So take refuge in God:
Surely He is all-hearing and all-seeing.
57. The creation of the heavens and the earth
is indeed of greater magnitude
than the creation of mankind;
but most men do not understand.

58. The blind and the seeing are surely not alike,
nor those who believe and act rightly
and those who do evil.
Little do you reflect!
59. The Hour will certainly come;
there is no mystery about it;
but most men do not believe.
60. Your Lord has said: "Call to Me
that I may answer your call.
Surely those who disdain worshipping Me
will enter Hell, disgraced."

It is God who made the night for you to rest,
the day to make things visible.
Indeed God is gracious to men,
but most men are not grateful.
62. He is God your Lord, creator of every thing.
There is no god but He.
How then do you turn away (from Him)?
63. Only they are turned away thus
who deny the signs of God.
64. It is God who made the earth a dwelling for you,
and the sky a vaulted roof,
who fashioned you and gave you excellent form
and provided you with clean and wholesome things.
He is God, your Lord.
So blessed be God, the Lord of all the worlds.
65. He is the living. There is no god but He.
Therefore pray to Him with obedience all-exclusive.
Praise be to God,
the Lord of all the worlds.
66. Say: "I am forbidden to worship those
you call apart from God,
since clear signs have come to me from my Lord,
and I am commanded to submit to the Lord of all the worlds."
67. It is He who created you from dust,
then a drop of semen, then the embryo;
afterwards He brings you forth as a child;
then you attain the age of manhood,
and then reach old age.
But some of you die before you reach the appointed term
that you may haply understand.
68. It is He who gives you life and death.
When He creates a thing, He has only to say:
"Be," and it is.

Have you not seen how those who dispute
the signs of God are turned away?
70. Those who deny the Book
and what We have sent down with Our apostles,
will soon come to know
71. When, with (iron) collars and chains around their necks,
they will be dragged
72. Through boiling water, and then burnt in the Fire.
73. They will then be asked: "Where are they
you took as partners
74. Apart from God?"
They will answer: "They have left us in the lurch and fled.
In fact it was nothing that we prayed to before."
That is how God sends the unbelievers astray.
75. "This is so because
you went about exulting wrongfully in the land,"
(will they be told), "and you were insolent.
76. So enter the gates of Hell
to abide in it for ever."
How evil the abode of the arrogant!
77. So you persevere with patience (in your mission).
The promise of God is true.
Whether We show you some of the punishment
We have promised them, or gather you up in death,
they have to come back to Us.
78. Surely We have sent apostles before you,
some of whose account We have related to you,
and that of some We have not told you
But no apostle was given a miracle
unless God dispensed.
But when the decree of God comes
the sentence is passed with justice;
and the lovers of vice and vanity
will then come to grief.

It is God who made the cattle for you
so that some you ride and some you eat.
80. There are advantages for you in them,
so that you may satisfy your needs through them,
and may be borne upon them and on ships.
81. He shows His signs.
How many of God's signs will you then deny?
82. Have they not travelled in the land and seen
how was the end of those before them
who were far more numerous than they and more strong,
and have left behind them traces on the earth.

Al-Mu'min

And yet nothing of what they did profited them.
83. For when Our apostles came to them with clear proofs,
they boasted and exulted at the knowledge they possessed;
but what they used to mock recoiled back on them,
84. So that when they saw Our might, they said:
"We believe in God the one and single,
and reject those we associated (with Him)."
85. But then their affirming served them nothing
after they had seen Our torment.
This is the law of God
that has prevailed among His creatures.
Then the unbelievers went to rack and ruin.

41 Adoration

Hā Mīm As-Sajdah: Makki

In the name of Allah, most benevolent, ever-merciful.

HĀ MĪM.

2. A revelation from the most benevolent, ever-merciful,
3. A Book whose verses have been distinguished and explained,
a lucid discourse for people who understand,
4. Announcing happy news and warnings.
And yet most of them are averse and do not listen,
5. And say: "Our hearts are immured
against what you call us to.
There is a deafness in our ears,
and a veil lies between us and you.
So act (your way), we are acting (ours)."
6. Say: "I am a man like you,
(but) it is revealed to me
that your God is one God,
so take the straight path to Him,
and ask Him to forgive your sins.
Woe to the idolaters
7. Who do not give a due share of their wealth
for the welfare of others,
and do not believe in the Hereafter.
8. But those who believe and do the right,
will have a continuing reward.

Say: "Do you refuse to believe
in Him who created the earth in two spans of time,
and set up compeers to Him,
the Lord of all the worlds?
10. He placed firm stabilisers rising above its surface,
blessed it with plenty and growth, and ingrained
the means of growing its food within it, sufficient
for all seekers, in four spans.
11. Then He turned to the heavens,
and it was smoke.
So He said to it and the earth:

Hā Mīm As-Sajdah

407

"Come with willing obedience or perforce."
They said: "We come willingly."
12. Then He created several skies in two spans,
and ingrained in each sky its function,
decking the nearest heaven with lamps, and guarded it.
This has been determined by the mighty and all-knowing.
13. If even then they turn away, tell them:
"I forewarn you of a terrible punishment
like the thunder-bolt that fell upon the 'Ad and Thamud.''
14. Their apostles came to them one after the other
(saying): "Do not worship any one but God."
They said: "If our Lord had pleased
He would have sent the angels down.
We reject what is sent with you."
15. So those who were 'Ad turned insolent unjustly
in the land, and said:
"Who is stronger than us?"
Did they not see that God who created them
was greater far in power than they?
Yet they refused to believe Our signs.
16. So We let loose on them a violent wind
for several days of distress to make them taste
a most disgraceful punishment
here in this world, and far more shameful
will be the punishment in the Hereafter,
and there will be no succour for them.
17. As for the (tribe of) Thamud, We tried to guide them,
but they preferred blindness to guidance;
then they were seized by the torment
of a humiliating punishment
as requital for their misdeeds;
18. But We saved those who believed and took heed for
      themselves.

The day the enemies of God will be gathered at the Fire
and the records of their deeds will be distributed,
20. So that when they reach it their ears and eyes and persons
will testify to what they did.
21. And they will say to their bodies:
"Why did you testify against us?"
They will answer: "God, who gave all things
power of articulation, made us speak.
It is He who created you the first time,
and to Him you will return.
22. You did not hide your (doings)
so that your ears or eyes or persons

Ha Mim As-Sajdah

should not testify against you.
In fact you thought that God did not know
the things you used to do.
23. It is this notion you had of your Lord
that caused your ruin, and you are lost."
24. Even if they are patient, their abode is Hell;
and if they beg for favour,
none will favour them.
25. We had assigned to them close companions
who made their past and present look attractive to them;
and the fate that had once befallen
the communities of jinns and men before them
was justified upon them.
They were indeed bound to perish.

The disbelievers say: "Do not listen
to this Qur'an, and shout away (its reading);
you may haply prevail."
27. We shall make the disbelievers taste
the severest punishment, and retribute them
for the worst that they had done.
28. This is the requital for God's enemies:
Hell, where they will have their lasting home,
as punishment for denying Our revelations.
29. Those who disbelieve will say: "O Lord,
show us those among the jinns and men
who had led us astray
that we may trample them underfoot
and make them wholly abject."
30. Surely the angels will come down to those who say,
'Our Lord is God' and then remain steadfast,
saying: "You should have neither fear nor regret,
but rejoice in the happy news of Paradise that has been
promised you.
31. We are your friends in this life and in the Hereafter
where you will get whatever your hearts desire,
and have whatsoever you ask for,
32. As a gift from the forgiving, ever-merciful (God)."

Whose word is better than his who calls to God
and does the right, and says:
"I am of the obedient?"
34. Good and evil are not alike.
Repel evil with what is good.
Then you will find your erstwhile enemy
like a close, affectionate friend.

Ha Mim As-Sajdah

35. Only they attain it who forbear,
and only a man of great good fortune can achieve it.
36. If the Devil incite you to evil,
seek refuge in God.
He is all-hearing and all-knowing.
37. The night and day and the sun and moon
are (only) some of His signs.
So do not bow before the sun and the moon,
but bow in homage to God who created them,
if you truly worship Him.
38. But if they become haughty (then remember)
that those who are close to your Lord
sing His praises night and day
and do not grow weary of (doing so).
39. It is among His signs that the earth you see
all barren and desolate
begins to stir and sprout
when We send down rain upon it.
Surely He who gives it life will also give life to the dead.
Indeed He has power over every thing.
40. Surely those who slander Our signs
are not hidden from Us.
Then, is he better who will be cast into Hell,
or he who will come out safe on the Day of Resurrection?
Do whatever you will, He sees whatsoever you do.
41. Those who reject the Reminder when it has come to them
(should know) that it is a Book inviolate.
42. Falsehood cannot enter it from any side:
It's a revelation from the all-wise and praiseworthy (God).
43. Nothing is said to you which had not been said
to other apostles before you.
Surely your Lord is the lord of forgiveness,
but also the lord of severe retribution.
44. If We had made it a discourse in an obscure tongue,
they would have said: "Why were its revelations
not expounded distinctly?
A foreign tongue and an Arab (audience)?"
Say: "For those who believe
it is a guidance and a healing;
but for those who do not believe
it is a deafness in the ears, and a blindness.
They are those one calls to from far away.

Verily We gave Moses the Book;
but they began to differ about it.
If the Word of your Lord had not preceded it

Ha Mīm As-Sajdah

410

the matter would have been settled between them.
They are still in doubt about it and uneasy.

46. Whoever does good does so for himself,
and whoever does wrong bears the guilt thereof.
Your Lord does no wrong to His creatures.

47. He alone has knowledge of the Hour (of change):
No fruit comes out of its spathe,
no female conceives or gives birth,
but He has knowledge of it.
The day He will call them (and ask):
"Where are the compeers (you ascribed to Me)?"
They will answer: "We profess to You
not one of us can vouch for them."

48. And those they used to worship will leave them in the
    lurch,
and they will realise there is no escape for them.

49. Man never tires of praying for good;
but if evil assails him he begins to despair.

50. If We give him a taste of Our favour
after some distress he has known,
he says: "It was my due.
I cannot imagine the Hour will come.
And even if I go back to my Lord,
there will surely still be the best for me with Him."
We shall tell those who do not believe
what they used to do,
and inflict on them a heavy punishment.

51. When We show Our favours to man
he moves away and turns aside;
but when in trouble he prays a great deal.

52. Say: "Just think. If this is from God and you deny it,
who will be in greater error
than he who is in open dissent?"

53. We will show Our signs to them
in the horizons of the external world
and within themselves,
until it becomes clear to them that it's the truth.
Is your Lord not sufficient? He is a witness over all things.

54. In truth they are in doubt
that they will ever face their Lord.
Do they not know that He surrounds all things?

Ha Mim As-Sajdah

42 Consultation

Ash-Shūrā: Makki

In the name of Allah, most benevolent, ever-merciful.

بِسْمِ اللهِ الرَّحْمٰنِ الرَّحِیْمِ ۞

Hā Mīm.

2. 'Ain Sin Qaf.

3. So has God, all-mighty and all-wise,
been revealing to you and to others before you.

4. Whatever is in the heavens and the earth,
belongs to Him.
He is all-high and supreme.

5. The skies are near to bursting asunder
above them (for awe of Him),
and the angels sing the praises of their Lord,
imploring forgiveness for the dwellers of the earth.
Is it not that God is forgiving and merciful?

6. Those who have taken protectors other than Him,
are watched over by God.
It is not for you to be their guardian.

7. We have, therefore, revealed to you the eloquent Qur'an
that you may warn the people of the Metropolis,
and those who live around it,
of the Day of Gathering, of which there is no doubt,
(when mankind would be assembled) some in Heaven, some in
      Hell.

8. If God had pleased He would have made them one
      community of belief;
but He admits whom He please to His grace;
yet the sinners have neither friend nor helper.

9. Have they taken others beside Him as protectors?
It is God who protects; it is He
who gives life to the dead,
for He has power over every thing.

In whatever matter you disagree
the ultimate judgement rests with God.
This is God, my Lord;
in Him have I placed my trust,

حٰمٓ ۞

عٓسٓقٓ ۞

كَذٰلِكَ یُوْحِیٓ اِلَیْكَ وَاِلَی الَّذِیْنَ مِنْ قَبْلِكَ ۙ
اللهُ الْعَزِیْزُ الْحَكِیْمُ ۞

لَهٗ مَا فِی السَّمٰوٰتِ وَمَا فِی الْاَرْضِ ۖ وَهُوَ الْعَلِیُّ
الْعَظِیْمُ ۞

تَكَادُ السَّمٰوٰتُ یَتَفَطَّرْنَ مِنْ فَوْقِهِنَّ وَالْمَلٰٓئِكَةُ
یُسَبِّحُوْنَ بِحَمْدِ رَبِّهِمْ وَیَسْتَغْفِرُوْنَ لِمَنْ فِی
الْاَرْضِ ۗ اَلَآ اِنَّ اللهَ هُوَ الْغَفُوْرُ الرَّحِیْمُ ۞

وَالَّذِیْنَ اتَّخَذُوْا مِنْ دُوْنِهٖٓ اَوْلِیَآءَ اللهُ حَفِیْظٌ
عَلَیْهِمْ ۖ وَمَآ اَنْتَ عَلَیْهِمْ بِوَكِیْلٍ ۞

وَكَذٰلِكَ اَوْحَیْنَآ اِلَیْكَ قُرْاٰنًا عَرَبِیًّا لِّتُنْذِرَ اُمَّ
الْقُرٰی وَمَنْ حَوْلَهَا وَتُنْذِرَ یَوْمَ الْجَمْعِ لَا رَیْبَ فِیْهِ ۚ
فَرِیْقٌ فِی الْجَنَّةِ وَفَرِیْقٌ فِی السَّعِیْرِ ۞

وَلَوْ شَآءَ اللهُ لَجَعَلَهُمْ اُمَّةً وَّاحِدَةً وَّلٰكِنْ
یُّدْخِلُ مَنْ یَّشَآءُ فِیْ رَحْمَتِهٖ ۗ وَالظّٰلِمُوْنَ مَا لَهُمْ
مِّنْ وَّلِیٍّ وَّلَا نَصِیْرٍ ۞

اَمِ اتَّخَذُوْا مِنْ دُوْنِهٖٓ اَوْلِیَآءَ ۚ فَاللهُ هُوَ الْوَلِیُّ
وَهُوَ یُحْیِ الْمَوْتٰی ۖ وَهُوَ عَلٰی كُلِّ شَیْءٍ قَدِیْرٌ ۞

وَمَا اخْتَلَفْتُمْ فِیْهِ مِنْ شَیْءٍ فَحُكْمُهٗٓ اِلَی اللهِ ۚ
ذٰلِكُمُ اللهُ رَبِّیْ عَلَیْهِ تَوَكَّلْتُ ۖ وَاِلَیْهِ اُنِیْبُ ۞

and to Him I turn.
11. Originator of the heavens and the earth,
He has made your consorts from among you,
and made pairs of cattle.
He multiplies you in this way.
There is no other like Him.
He is all-hearing and all-seeing.
12. He holds the keys of the heavens and the earth.
He increases or decreases the provision of any one He will.
He has knowledge of every thing.
13. He has laid down for you the (same) way of life and belief
which He had commended to Noah, and which
We have enjoined on you, and which
We had bequeathed to Abraham, Moses and Jesus,
so that they should maintain the order
and not be divided among themselves.
Heavy is to idolaters what you invite them to.
God chooses whom He please for Himself,
and guides to Himself whoever turns to Him.
14. Yet they did not differ about it until knowledge came to
          them,
through rivalries among themselves.
If the Word of your Lord, (staying) it for a time ordained,
had not preceded it,
the matter would have been settled among them.
But those who came to inherit the Book after them
are also in doubt and disturbed about it.
15. Yet to that (law) you should call them,
and be constant as commanded.
Do not follow their passing whims, but say:
"I believe in whatever Scripture God has revealed,
and I am commanded to act
with equivalence among you.
God is our Lord and your Lord.
To us our actions, to you your deeds.
There is no dispute between you and us.
God will gather us all together,
and to Him is our returning."
16. As for those who argue in the matter of God
after He has been fully acknowledged,
their disputing has no force with their Lord.
Upon them is (God's) anger,
and the punishment for them will be severe.
17. It is God who has sent down the Book
with the truth, and the Balance.
How do you know the Hour is not near?

Ash-Shura

18. Only they who do not believe in it wish to hasten it;
but those who believe are in fear of it,
for they know it to be true.
Surely those who are in doubt about the Hour
are wandering far astray.
19. God is gracious to His creatures, and bestows
favours on whosoever He will.
He is all-powerful and all-mighty.

Whoever desires the fruits of the Hereafter,
We shall add to his fruit.
As for him who desires the fruits of this world,
We shall give to him of these,
but he will have no share in the Hereafter.
21. Have they other associates
who have prescribed another law for them
which has not been dispensed by God?
But for the decisive Word (of God)
a sentence would have been passed amongst them.
Surely there is a grievous punishment for the ungodly.
22. You will see the evil-doers full of fear
of what they deserve,
yet it will come to pass.
But those who believe and do the right
will be in gardens of Paradise.
They will receive what they wish from their Lord;
and this will be the greatest favour.
23. This is the good news that God gives
to His creatures who believe and do good.
Say: "I ask no recompense of you for it
other than obligations of relationship."
We shall give more excellence
to him who acquires excellence.
Surely God forgives and accepts (gratitude).
24. Do they say he has fabricated a lie about God?
He could have sealed your hearts if He pleased;
but God blots out the false and vindicates the truth
by His dispensations,
for He knows the secrets of the hearts.
25. It is He who accepts repentance from His creatures
and forgives their trespasses,
for He knows what you do.
26. He answers (the prayers) of those who believe
and do good, and gives them more of His bounty.
But for the unbelievers there is severe punishment.
27. If God were to give in abundance to His creatures

they would fill the earth with oppression.
So He gives according to measure as He will.
He knows (what is good for) His creatures.
He is all-aware and all-seeing.
28. It is He who sends down rain
when they had despaired of it, and showers His benevolence.
He is the protector worthy of praise.
29. The creation of the heavens and the earth
and all the living things dispersed in them,
are a sign of His. He has the power
to gather them together when He will.

Whatever misfortune befalls you
is a consequence of your deeds;
yet He forgives much.
31. You cannot thwart Him on the earth,
and have no friend or helper apart from Him.
32. Ships sailing in the ocean like ensigns
are a sign of His.
33. He could stop the wind if He pleased,
then they would be stranded on its surface.
Surely there are signs in this
for every one who perseveres and is grateful.
34. Or He could wreck them for what they have done;
yet there is much that He pardons.
35. Let those who dispute Our signs know
that there is no way of escape for them.
90. Whatsoever you have been given
is only this life's merchandise;
but what is with God is better and more lasting
for those who believe and place their trust in their Lord,
37. Who avoid the deadly sins,
immoral acts, and forgive when they are angered,
38. Who obey the commands of their Lord
and fulfil their devotional obligations,
whose affairs are settled by mutual consultation,
who spend of what We have given them,
39. And those who defend themselves when they are wronged.
40. The retribution of evil is the equal of evil (done);
yet those who forgive and rehabilitate
will be rewarded by God.
Verily He does not like those who do wrong.
41. If one avenges himself after he has been wronged,
there is no way of blaming him.
42. Blame lies on those who oppress,
and terrorise the land unjustly.

Ash-Shura

For them there is painful punishment.
43. But he who bears with patience and forgives,
surely complies with divine resolve.

فِى الْأَرْضِ بِغَيْرِ الْحَقِّ أُولَٰٓئِكَ لَهُمْ عَذَابٌ أَلِيمٌ ۝

وَلَمَن صَبَرَ وَغَفَرَ إِنَّ ذَٰلِكَ لَمِنْ عَزْمِ الْأُمُورِ ۝

He whom God leads astray
has no one except God to protect him.
You should see the sinners when they face the punishment.
They will say: "Isn't there a way of going back?"
45. You should see them brought before the Fire,
abject in disgrace, looking stealthily.
And those who believe will say:
"They who forfeit their souls and families
on the Day of Resurrection will really be losers."
Is it not that sinners will suffer a lasting torment?
46. They will have no protector to help them other than God.
He whom God allows to go astray has no way.
47. Hearken to your Lord before the Day arrives from God
that will not be averted.
You will have no place of refuge then nor time for denying.
48. If they turn away (you are not responsible);
We have not appointed you a warden over them.
Your duty is to deliver the message.
When We let man taste of Our favours
he begins to exult;
but if misfortune befalls him,
as a consequence of his own deeds,
man is surely then ungrateful.
49. To God belongs
the kingdom of the heavens and the earth.
He creates whatsoever He wills,
bestows daughters on whosoever He will,
and gives sons to whom He choose.
50. On some He bestows both sons and daughters,
and some He leaves issueless.
He is all-knowing and all-powerful.
51. It is not given to man that God should speak
to him except by suggestion
or indirectly, or send
a messenger to convey by His command
whatsoever He please.
He is all-high and all-wise.
52. So have We revealed to you the Qur'an*
by Our command.
You did not know what the Scripture was before,
nor (the laws of) faith.
And We made it a light by which We show the way

وَمَن يُضْلِلِ اللَّهُ فَمَا لَهُ مِنْ وَلِيٍّ مِّنۢ بَعْدِهِ وَتَرَى الظَّالِمِينَ لَمَّا رَأَوُا الْعَذَابَ يَقُولُونَ هَلْ إِلَىٰ مَرَدٍّ مِّن سَبِيلٍ ۝

وَتَرَاهُمْ يُعْرَضُونَ عَلَيْهَا خَاشِعِينَ مِنَ الذُّلِّ يَنظُرُونَ مِن طَرْفٍ خَفِيٍّ وَقَالَ الَّذِينَ ءَامَنُوٓا إِنَّ الْخَاسِرِينَ الَّذِينَ خَسِرُوٓا أَنفُسَهُمْ وَأَهْلِيهِمْ يَوْمَ الْقِيَامَةِ أَلَآ إِنَّ الظَّالِمِينَ فِى عَذَابٍ مُّقِيمٍ ۝

وَمَا كَانَ لَهُم مِّنْ أَوْلِيَآءَ يَنصُرُونَهُم مِّن دُونِ اللَّهِ وَمَن يُضْلِلِ اللَّهُ فَمَا لَهُ مِن سَبِيلٍ ۝

اسْتَجِيبُوا لِرَبِّكُم مِّن قَبْلِ أَن يَأْتِىَ يَوْمٌ لَّا مَرَدَّ لَهُ مِنَ اللَّهِ مَا لَكُم مِّن مَّلْجَإٍ يَوْمَئِذٍ وَمَا لَكُم مِّن نَّكِيرٍ ۝

فَإِنْ أَعْرَضُوا فَمَآ أَرْسَلْنَٰكَ عَلَيْهِمْ حَفِيظًا إِنْ عَلَيْكَ إِلَّا الْبَلَٰغُ وَإِنَّآ إِذَآ أَذَقْنَا الْإِنسَٰنَ مِنَّا رَحْمَةً فَرِحَ بِهَا وَإِن تُصِبْهُمْ سَيِّئَةٌۢ بِمَا قَدَّمَتْ أَيْدِيهِمْ فَإِنَّ الْإِنسَٰنَ كَفُورٌ ۝

لِّلَّهِ مُلْكُ السَّمَٰوَٰتِ وَالْأَرْضِ يَخْلُقُ مَا يَشَآءُ يَهَبُ لِمَن يَشَآءُ إِنَٰثًا وَيَهَبُ لِمَن يَشَآءُ الذُّكُورَ ۝

أَوْ يُزَوِّجُهُمْ ذُكْرَانًا وَإِنَٰثًا وَيَجْعَلُ مَن يَشَآءُ عَقِيمًا إِنَّهُ عَلِيمٌ قَدِيرٌ ۝

وَمَا كَانَ لِبَشَرٍ أَن يُكَلِّمَهُ اللَّهُ إِلَّا وَحْيًا أَوْ مِن وَرَآئِ حِجَابٍ أَوْ يُرْسِلَ رَسُولًا فَيُوحِىَ بِإِذْنِهِ مَا يَشَآءُ إِنَّهُ عَلِيٌّ حَكِيمٌ ۝

وَكَذَٰلِكَ أَوْحَيْنَآ إِلَيْكَ رُوحًا مِّنْ أَمْرِنَا مَا كُنتَ تَدْرِى مَا الْكِتَٰبُ وَلَا الْإِيمَٰنُ وَلَٰكِن جَعَلْنَٰهُ نُورًا نَّهْدِى بِهِ مَن نَّشَآءُ مِنْ عِبَادِنَا وَإِنَّكَ

الشوری٤٢ الیہ یردہ۳۰

to those of Our creatures as We please;
and you certainly guide them to the right path,
53. The path of God to whom belongs
the kingdom of the heavens and the earth.
And will not all things go back to God?

---

* Note on v. 52, *Ar-rooh*. Although *ar-rooh* means so many things including rest, happiness, help, judgement and soul, it also means grace, revelation from God, and the Qur'an itself. See *Muhit al-muhit*. In 16:2, for instance, it means revelation, as also at 17:85. In verse 52 of this Surah, however, it means the Qur'an, which is made explicit by the use of *auhaina*, revealed, further clarified by: "You did not know what the Scripture was before." Similarly, in 97:4 it means *rahma*, grace, as the Qur'an was revealed on this night, vide 44:3 and 97:1, and new life, as in 21:91, 66:12.

Ash-Shura   **417**

43 Ornaments of Gold

Az-Zukhruf: Makki

In the name of Allah, most benevolent, ever-merciful.

بِسْمِ اللهِ الرَّحْمٰنِ الرَّحِيْمِ

Hā mīm.

2. I call to witness the lucent Book,

3. That We made it a distinctly lucid Qur'an
that you may understand.

4. It is inscribed in the original Book (of Books) with Us,
sublime, dispenser of (all) laws.

5. Should We have withdrawn the Reminder from you
as you are a people who exceed the bounds?

6. Many a prophet had We sent to the earlier communities,

7. But never did a prophet come
at whom they did not scoff.

8. So We destroyed far more powerful (nations) than they.
The example of earlier people is there.

9. If you ask them: "Who created the heavens and the earth?"
they will answer: "The Mighty and All-knowing created them,"

10. He who made the earth a bed for you,
and laid out tracks upon it
so that you may find the way;

11. Who sent down water in due measure
from the sky, then quickened a region that was dead —
So shall We bring you forth —

12. He who created pairs of every thing,
and fashioned for you boats and beasts on which you ride,

13. So that when you sit astride of them
and think of the bounties of your Lord,
you may say: "All glory to Him
who subjugated these for us.
We were incapable of doing so.

14. Surely we have to go back to our Lord."

15. Yet they make some of His creatures His offspring!
Man is surely most ungrateful.

Or has He taken from those He has created
daughters for Himself, and assigned sons to you?

17. Yet when news of (a daughter) they had reserved
for Ar-Rahman comes to one of them,
his face is blackened (with shame),
and he grieves in silence inwardly.
18. Can one who has been raised on ornaments
and cannot present her case coolly in a dispute
(be associated with God?)
19. Yet they have made the angels,
who are creatures of Ar-Rahman, females.
Did they witness their creation?
We shall record their testimony,
and they will be interrogated.
20. Yet they say: "If Ar-Rahman had so pleased
we would not have worshipped them."
They have no knowledge of it in the least.
They only make up lies.
21. Did We give them a Scripture before this
to which they are holding fast?
22. In fact they say: "We found our fathers
following a certain way, and are guided by their footprints."
23. Thus, We never sent an admonisher
to a settlement before you
but the decadent among them said:
"We found our fathers following this way,
and we are walking in their footsteps."
24. "Even if I bring you a better guidance," he rejoined,
"than the one you found your fathers on?"
Still they said: "We do not believe in what you have brought."
25. Then We punished them.
So look at the fate
of those who denied!

When Abraham said to his father and his people:
"I am rid of what you worship
27. Other than Him who created me.
He will show me the right way."
28. This is the legacy he left to his descendants
so that they may turn (to God).
29. In fact, I allowed them and their fathers
to enjoy this life till the truth,
and the apostle preaching it lucidly, came to them.
30. Yet when the truth had come to them, they said:
"This is sorcery.
We shall never believe in it."
31. They also said: "Why was this Qur'an
not sent down to some great man

of the two cities?"

32. Are they the ones who dispense the favour of your Lord?
It is He who apportions the means of livelihood among them
in this world, and raises some in position over the others
to make some others submissive.
The favours of your Lord are better than what they amass.

33. Had it not been that all people would become
one community (of unbelievers),
We might have given those who disbelieve in Ar-Rahman
roofs of silver for their dwellings
and (silver) stairs for mounting,

34. And doors (of silver) for their houses,
(silver) couches for reclining,

35. And ornaments of gold. But all this would have been
nothing but the vanity of this world.
The Hereafter with your Lord is for those
who take heed for themselves and follow the straight path.

We shall attach to him who goes blind
to the remembrance of Ar-Rahman a devil as companion, —

37. Surely the (devils) obstruct them from the path,
though they think they are rightly guided, —

38. Until when he comes before Us
he will say (to the devil): "Would to God
there was a distance of the East and West
between you and me, for you were an evil companion!"

39. But nothing will avail you on that day, for you were unjust,
and you will be partners in the punishment.

40. Can you make the deaf to hear, or show the blind,
and those lost in clear error, the way?

41. We shall punish them whether We take you away,

42. Or show you some of what We have promised them.
They are certainly well within Our power.

43. So hold fast to what has been revealed to you.
You are truly on the right path.

44. It is a (source) of greatness for you and your people.
You will surely be questioned about it.

45. Inquire of apostles We had sent before you
if We appointed gods to be worshipped
other than Ar-Rahman.

We sent Moses with Our signs
to the Pharaoh and his nobles.
He said: "I have been sent by the Lord of all the worlds."

47. But when he brought to them Our signs
they laughed at them,

48. (Even though) each miracle that We showed them
was greater than the other.
So We seized them with chastisement
so that they may turn back.
49. But they said: "O sorcerer, call on your Lord for us
in accordance with the compact He has made with you.
We shall certainly come to guidance."
50. Yet no sooner did We take away the affliction from them
than they broke their pledge.
51. And the Pharaoh said to his people:
"O people, is not mine the kingdom of Egypt
and these rivers that flow at my feet?
Can you still not comprehend?
52. Am I (not) better than him who is contemptible,
and cannot even express himself clearly?
53. Why were then no bracelets of gold shed upon him from
        above,
or angels sent down as a retinue with him?"
54. Thus he made light (of the matter) to his people,
and they obeyed him. They were certainly wicked.
55. But when they roused Our anger
We inflicted retributive punishment and drowned them all,
56. And made them a precedent and example
for posterity.

When the example of Mary's son
is quoted before them, your people cry out at it,
58. And say: "Are our deities better or he?"
They say this only for disputing.
Surely they are a contentious people.
59. (Jesus) was only a creature whom We favoured
and made an example for the children of Israel.
60. If We pleased We could have put
angels in place of you as trustees on the earth.
61. He is certainly the sign of the Hour (of change).
So have no doubt about it, and listen to me.
This is the straight path.
62. Let not Satan misdirect you.
He is your open enemy.
63. When Jesus came with the signs, he said:
"I have come to you with authority,
and to explain some thing about which you are at variance.
So fear God, and follow me.
64. Verily God is my Lord and your Lord;
so worship Him.
This is the straight path."

65. But the factions differed among themselves.
Woe alas to the sinners for the torment of the grievous Day!
66. Are they waiting (for any thing) but the Hour (of Doom)
which would descend upon them suddenly,
and catch them unawares?
67. Friends will turn into enemies on that day,
except those who fear and follow the straight path.

O My creatures, there will be no fear or regret
69. For (those of) you on that day
who believed in My revelations and submitted.
70. (You will) enter the garden, you and your spouses, and be
glad."
71. Golden platters and goblets will be passed around,
and every thing the heart desires and pleases the eye
will be there, where you will abide for ever.
72. This is the Paradise you will inherit
(as meed) for your deeds.
73. You will have fruits in abundance there to eat.
74. The sinners will certainly
dwell for ever in the torment of Hell.
75. It will not decrease for them; dumb with despair
they will stay in it.
76. We did not wrong them, they wronged themselves.
77. They will call (to the keeper of Hell-gate):
"O Malik, let your Lord decide our fate."
He will answer: "You are to stay."
78. We have brought to you the truth,
but most of you despise the truth.
79. Have they settled upon a plan?
We shall also settle on one.
80. Or do they think We do not hear
their secrecies and stealthy consultations?
In fact, Our messengers who attend them
record every thing.
81. Say: "If Ar-Rahman had a son
I would have been the first of worshippers."
82. All too glorious is He, Lord of the heavens and the earth,
the Lord of all power, for what they ascribe to Him!
83. Leave them to their vain discoursing and horse-play
till they come to meet their promised day (of reckoning).
84. He is God in heaven and God on earth,
and He is all-wise and all-knowing.
85. Blessed be He, who holds the kingdom
of the heavens and the earth
and all that lies between them.

He alone has knowledge of the Hour,
and to Him will you return.
86. Those they invoke apart from Him
have no power of intercession, except those
who testify to the truth and have knowledge.
87. If you ask them who created them,
they will answer: "God."
How then can they turn away?
88. And (the Prophet) will say: "O Lord,
these are certainly a people who do not believe."
89. Turn away from them and say: "Peace."
They will come to know soon.

44 Smoke

Ad-Dukhān: Makki

In the name of Allah, most benevolent, ever-merciful.

Hā Mīm.

2. The perspicuous Book is witness
3. (That) We sent it down on a night of blessing —
so that We could warn —
4. On which all affairs are sorted out and decided
5. As commands from Us.
It is indeed We who send (messengers),
6. A mercy from your Lord.
Verily He is all-hearing and all-knowing,
7. The Lord of the heavens and the earth
and all that lies between them,
if you really do believe.
8. There is no god other than He,
who gives you life and death,
your Lord and the Lord of your fathers of old.
9. Yet they are lost in doubt and play.
10. So watch for the day when the sky
begins to emit clear smoke,
11. Which would envelope mankind.
That would be a grievous affliction.
12. "O Lord, take away this torment from us,"
(they will pray); "we have come to believe."
13. How can a warning benefit them? The Apostle
who explained all things clearly had come to them,
14. But they turned away from him, and said:
"He is well-instructed, (but) possessed."
15. If We remove the torment a little,
you revert back (to misdeeds).
16. The day that We shall seize them with a grievous hold,
We will indeed castigate them.
17. We had tried the people of Pharaoh before them.
A respected prophet had come to them (saying):
18. "Deliver the creatures of God to me.
I am the trusted messenger sent to you.

19. Do not think yourselves to be above God:
I have come to you with clear authority.
20. I have taken refuge in my Lord and your Lord
against your stoning me to death.
21. If you do not believe in me, leave me alone."
22. Then he called to his Lord: "These are a sinful people."
23. "Journey by night with My devotees," (it was said);
"you will certainly be pursued.
24. (Cross and) leave the sea undisturbed.
The (pursuing) hosts will surely be drowned."
25. How many gardens and fountains did they leave behind,
26. And fields and stately mansions,
27. And the comfort they enjoyed.
28. Thus it was; and We passed them on
to another people.
29. Neither did the heavens weep for them, nor the earth,
nor were they granted respite.

So We saved the children of Israel
from degrading suffering
31. They (had experienced) under the Pharaoh.
He was certainly a tyrant, guilty of excess.
32. And We exalted them over the other people knowingly,
33. And sent them tokens to bring out the best in them.
34. Even then they say:
35. "There is no dying for us but once;
and we shall not be raised again.
36. So bring our ancestors back, if you are truthful."
37. Are they better than the people of Tubba',
and those who had lived before them,
whom We destroyed as they were sinners?
38. We have not created the heavens and the earth
and all that lies between them, out of play.
39. We created them with definite purpose;
but most of them do not understand.
40. The Day of Judgement is your promised day of meeting,
41. The day when friend will help no friend in the least,
nor will they be helped,
42. Apart from those to whom God is kind.
He is all-mighty and all-merciful.

The tree of Zaqqum will indeed be
44. The food of sinners.
45. It is like pitch. It will fume in the belly
46. As does boiling water.
47. "Seize him and drag him into the depths of Hell,"

(it will be said),

48. "Then pour over his head
the torment of scalding water."

49. "Taste it," (they will be told).
"You were indeed the mighty and noble!

50. This is certainly what you had denied."

51. Surely those who fear and follow the straight path
will be in a place of peace and security

52. In the midst of gardens and of springs,

53. Dressed in brocade and shot silk,
facing one another.

54. Just like that. We shall pair them with companions
with large black eyes.

55. They will call for every kind of fruit with satisfaction.

56. There they will not know any death
apart from the first death they had died,
and will be kept safe from the torment of Hell

57. By the beneficence of your Lord.
This will be the great success.

58. Therefore We have made this (Qur'an)
easy in your tongue. They may haply take a warning.

59. So you wait. They are also waiting.

45 Kneeling

Al-Jāthiyah: Makki

In the name of Allah, most benevolent, ever-merciful.

H̄Ā MĪM.

2. The revelation of this Book is from God,
the mighty and all-wise.

3. Indeed there are signs for believers
in the heavens and the earth.

4. In creating you and spreading all the moving things (on earth)
are signs for people firm of faith,

5. As there are signs in the alternation of night and day,
and in rain that God sends
with which He revives the earth once dead,
as there are in the changing of the winds,
for people who can understand.

6. These are revelations of God
which we recite to you correctly:
In what other lore but God and His manifestations
would they then believe?

7. Alas the woe for every dissembling sinner

8. Who hears the revelations of God
being recited to him, yet persists in denying with arrogance
as though he had never heard them!
So warn him of a painful punishment.

9. When he comes to know something of Our messages
he makes fun of them:
For them is shameful punishment.

10. There is Hell before them; and whatever they have earned
will not avail them in the least,
nor those whom they take as friends
apart from God. There is great chastisement for them.

11. This is guidance. Those who deny
the revelations of their Lord
will suffer a dreadful doom.

It is God who subjugated the ocean for you

so that ships may ply through it
by His command, and you may seek His bounty,
and may haply be grateful.
13. He subjugated for you whatsoever is
in the heavens and the earth, each and every thing.
Verily there are signs in this for those who reflect.
14. Tell the believers to forgive those
who do not fear the visitations of God,
so that He may requite the people for their deeds.
15. He who does good does so for himself;
and he who does evil suffers the consequence thereof.
You have then to go back to your Lord.
16. We gave the children of Israel
the Book, and the judgemnt and the prophethood,
provided them with good things,
favoured them over other people,
17. And gave them a clear exposition of Our laws.
And they did not differ until after knowledge came to them,
through mutual jealousies.
Verily your Lord will judge between them on the Day of
        Judgement
in what they differed about.
18. We have put you on the right way
in the matter (of divine law).
So follow it, and do not follow
the wishes of those who are ignorant.
19. They will not avail you in the least against God.
Surely the wicked are each other's friends,
but God befriends those who fear and follow the right path.
20. These are precepts of wisdom for men,
and guidance and grace for people who believe with certainty.
21. Do those who seek evil think
that We shall make them equal
in life and death to those
who believe and do good?
How bad is the judgement that they make!

God has created the heavens and the earth
with reason, so that He may reward
each soul in accordance with what it has done;
and no wrong will be done to them.
23. Just think: Who apart from God can show the way to him
who deifies his ego into his god,
whom God allows to go astray knowingly,
and seals his ears and heart, and covers over
his eyes with a veil?

Al-Jathiya   428

Why then do you not contemplate?

24. Yet they say: "There is nothing but the life of this world.
We die and we live, and only time annihilates us."
Yet they have no knowledge of this:
They only speculate.

25. When Our clear revelations are recited to them,
their only argument is to say:
"Bring our ancestors back, if what you say is true."

26. Say: "God, who gives you life and makes you die,
will (raise the dead) then gather you (and your ancestors)
together on the Day of Resurrection of which there is no
doubt."
And yet most men do not understand.

God's is the kingdom of the heavens and the earth.
The day the Hour is proclaimed
the liars will be losers.

28. You will see each community kneeling down;
and each community will be summoned
to its ledger (of good and evil deeds).
You will receive upon that day
your recompense for what you had done.

29. This, Our record, will speak about you truthfully.
We had every thing you did recorded in it.

30. So, those who believed and did good things
will be admitted to His favour by their Lord.
This will be a clear triumph.

31. As for the infidels, (it will be said).
"Were not My messages read out to you?
But you behaved with self-conceit, and became
a sinful people.

32. Whenever it was said: 'God's promise is certainly true,
and there is no doubt about the Hour,' you replied:
'We know not what the Hour is.
We have only a vague idea, but are not certain.' "

33. The evil of what they had done
will become clear to them,
and they will be seized by what they had scorned.

34. "We shall ignore you today," they will be told,
"as you had forgotten the meeting of this Day.
Your dwelling-place is Hell, and there is none to save you:

35. This because you laughed at God's revelations
and were taken in by the life of the world."
So they will neither be taken out of it,
nor will be asked to seek God's favour
on that day.

Al-Jathiyah

429

الجاثية ٤٥ الميه يرى ٢٥

فَلِلَّهِ الْحَمْدُ رَبِّ السَّمَوَاتِ وَرَبِّ الْأَرْضِ رَبِّ
الْعَالَمِينَ ۝
وَلَهُ الْكِبْرِيَاءُ فِي السَّمَوَاتِ وَالْأَرْضِ وَهُوَ
الْعَزِيزُ الْحَكِيمُ ۝

36. All praise be to God,
Lord of the heavens, Lord of the earth,
Lord of all the worlds.
37. His is the supremacy in the heavens and the earth;
and He is the all-mighty and all-wise.

46 Al-Ahqāf

Al-Ahqāf: Makki

In the name of Allah, most benevolent, ever-merciful.

HĀ MĪM.

2. The revelation of this Book is from God,
the mighty and all-wise.
3. We have not created the heavens and the earth
and all that lies between them
but with a purpose for an appointed time.
Yet the unbelievers turn away
from the warning.
4. Say: "Have you thought of those you invoke apart from God?
Show me what they have created of the earth,
or, do they have a share in the heavens?
Bring me an earlier Book than this,
or inherited knowledge, if you are truthful."
5. Who is more astray than he
who calls on those, apart from God,
who cannot answer their prayers
till the Day of Resurrection,
and are even unaware of being called.
6. When all men are gathered together (on that Day)
they will become their enemies
and deny their worship.
7. When Our clear revelations are read out to them,
the infidels say of the truth,
when it has come to them: "This is pure magic."
8. Do they say: "He has fabricated it?"
Tell them: "If I have fabricated it,
you have no power to save me from God.
He knows what you are busy with concerning this.
He is sufficient as witness between you and me;
yet He is forgiving, ever-merciful."
9. Say: "I am not a new Messenger to come,
nor do I know what is to be done to me or you.
I only follow what is revealed to me.
My duty is only to warn you clearly."

10. Tell them: "Think (of the consequence) if this is from God and you deny it
when a witness from the people of Israel
had testified to the like of it and come to believe,
while you spurn it?"
Assuredly God does not guide a wicked people.

Those who deny say of those who believe:
"Had there been any good in it
they would not have preceded us in coming to it."
Since they have not taken guidance from it,
they will say: "This is the same old lie."
12. There was the Book of Moses before this,
a guide and a mercy; and here is this Book
confirming it in lucid language,
warning those who are wicked,
and giving happy tidings to the righteous.
13. Surely for those who say, "God is our Lord,"
and then remain firm, there is no fear or regret.
14. They are men of Paradise
where they will abide for ever
as a recompense for what they had done.
15. We have enjoined on man to be good to his parents:
His mother carries him in her womb with hardship,
and gives birth to him in pain.
Thirty months is the period of her carrying and weaning him.
When he attains to manhood and the age of forty,
he says: "O Lord, guide me
to thank You for the favours You have bestowed on me
and my parents, and to do things good as may please You,
and give me a righteous offspring.
I turn to You in penitence and submit."
16. They are those from whom We accept
the very best of what they have done,
and overlook their faults.
They will be among the inmates of Paradise:
A true promise they have been made.
17. But he who says to his parents: "Shame on you:
You intimidate me
that I will be resurrected
when many generations will have passed before me?"
And (the parents) would implore God's help: "Woe to you.
You better believe. The promise of God is certainly true."
Yet he answers: "These are only fables of long ago."
18. They are those on whom the sentence of God would
     be justified

as on communities of jinns and men before them.
They will surely perish.
19. Each will have a position in accordance with his deeds;
and no wrong will be done to them.
20. The day the unbelievers are brought to the Fire,
(it will be said): "You wasted all your good deeds
in the life of the world, and enjoyed them to the full.
You will now be requited with a shameful punishment,
for you behaved with arrogance for no reason on the earth,
and acted wickedly."

Remember (Hud) the brother of 'Ad.
When he warned his people in Ahqaf —
though many a warner had come and gone before and after
    him:
"Do not worship any one but God,
for I fear the punishment of an awful day for you,"
22. They said: "Have you come
to turn us away from our gods?
Then bring upon us what you predict for us,
if you are a man of truth."
23. He said: "Only God has the knowledge.
I only convey to you what I have been sent with.
But I see you are a foolish people."
24. So when they saw it as a cloud
advancing towards their valleys, they said:
"This is just a passing cloud that will bring us rain."
"No. It is what you were trying to hasten:
The wind which carries the grievous punishment!
25. It will destroy every thing at the bidding of its Lord."
So in the morning there was nothing
but their empty dwellings to be seen.
That is how We requite the sinners.
26. We had strengthened them as We have not strengthened
    you,
had given them ears and eyes and hearts;
but nothing stood them in good stead,
neither their ears nor eyes nor hearts,
for they rejected the signs of God,
and were seized by what they had mocked.

We have destroyed habitations all around you,
having explained Our signs in different ways to them
that they may turn back.
28. Why then did the gods they had taken apart from God
as propitiators, not come to their aid?

In fact they strayed away from them.
It was all a lie what they had contrived!
29. And (remember), when We turned a company of jinns
towards you to listen to the Qur'an,
they arrived when it was being recited,
and they said: "Keep silent."
When it was over they came back to their people, warning
    them:
30. "O our people:" they said: "we have listened to a Book
which has come down after Moses,
confirming what was (sent down) before it,
showing the way to the truth and a path that is straight.
31. O our people, hearken to the summoner of God,
and believe in him, so that He may forgive you your sins
and save you from a painful doom.
32. He who does not listen to the summoner of God
cannot weaken (the power of) God on earth,
nor will he have protectors other than Him.
They are clearly in the wrong."
33. Do they not realise that God
who created the heavens and the earth,
and did not tire creating them,
is able to bring the dead to life?
And why not? He has the power over every thing.
34. The day the unbelievers will be stood
before the Fire, (they will be asked:)
"Is this not the reality?"
They will answer: "In truth, by our Lord!"
It will be said: "Then taste the torment
of what you had denied."
35. So bear with patience, as the apostles who were constant,
    bore;
and do not be hasty (in demanding punishment) for them.
On the day they see what they had been foretold,
(they will realise) that they did not stay in the world
but only an hour of the day.
This is the message to be conveyed:
Shall any perish but the ungodly?

47 Muhammad

Muhammad: Madani

In the name of Allah, most benevolent, ever-merciful.

Tʜᴏsᴇ ᴡʜᴏ ᴅɪsʙᴇʟɪᴇᴠᴇ
and obstruct (others) from the way of God
will have wasted their deeds.
2. But those who believe and do the right,
and believe what has been revealed to Muhammad,
which is the truth from their Lord,
will have their faults condoned by Him
and their state improved.
3. That is because those who refuse to believe
only follow what is false; but those who believe
follow the truth from their Lord.
That is how God gives men precepts of wisdom.
4. So, when you clash with the unbelievers,
smite their necks until you overpower them,
then hold them in bondage.
Then either free them graciously
or after taking a ransom,
until war shall have come to end.
If God had pleased
He could have punished them (Himself),
but He wills to test some of you through some others.
He will not allow the deeds
of those who are killed in the cause of God
to go waste.
5. He will show them the way,
and better their state,
6. And will admit them into gardens
with which he has acquainted them.
7. O you who believe, if you help (in the cause of) God
He will surely come to your aid,
and firmly plant your feet.
8. As for the unbelievers, they will suffer misfortunes,
and their deeds will be rendered ineffective.
9. That is so as they were averse

Muhammad

to what has been revealed by God,
and their actions will be nullified.
10. Have they not journeyed in the land
and seen the fate of those before them?
Destroyed they were utterly by God;
and a similar (fate) awaits the unbelievers.
11. This is so for God is the friend of those who believe
while the unbelievers have no friend.

Verily God will admit those who believe and do the right
into gardens with streams of water running by.
But the unbelievers revel and carouse
and subsist like beasts, and Hell will be their residence.
13. How many were the habitations,
mightier than your city which has turned you out,
which We destroyed;
and they did not have a helper.
14. Can one who stands on a clear proof from his Lord,
be like one enamoured of his evil deeds
and follows his inane desires?
15. The semblance of Paradise promised the pious and devout
(is that of a garden) with streams of water that will not go
         rank,
and rivers of milk whose taste will not undergo a change,
and rivers of wine delectable to drinkers,
and streams of purified honey,
and fruits of every kind in them, and forgiveness of their Lord.
Are these like those who will live for ever in the Fire
and be given boiling water to drink
which will cut their intestines to shreds?
16. There are some who listen to you; but as soon as they go
from you they say to those who were given knowledge:
"What is this he is saying now?"
They are those whose hearts
have been sealed by God, and they follow their own lusts.
17. But those who are rightly guided will be given
greater guidance by Him, and they will have their intrinsic
         piety.
18. Do they wait for any thing but the Hour (of change),
that it may come upon them suddenly?
Its signs have already appeared.
How then will they be warned when it has come upon them?
19. Know then, therefore, there is no god but He,
and ask forgiveness for your sins
and those of believing men and women.
God knows your wanderings

Muhammad

436

and your destination.

Those who believe say: "How is it no Surah was revealed?"
But when a categorical Surah is revealed
that mentions war, you should see those
who are sceptical
staring at you like a man in the swoon of death.
Alas the woe for them!
21. Obedience and modest speech (would have been more
becoming).
And when the matter has been determined
it is best for them to be true to God.
22. Is it possible that if placed in authority
you will create disorder in the land
and sever your bonds of relationship?
23. They are those who were condemned by God,
whose ears were blocked by Him and their eyes blinded.
24. Do they not ponder
on what the Qur'an says?
Or have their hearts been sealed with locks?
25. Those who turn their backs
after the way of guidance has been opened to them,
have been surely tempted by Satan
and beguiled by illusory hopes.
26. This was so because they said to those
who disdain what God has revealed:
"We shall obey you in some things."
But God knows their secret intentions well.
27. How will it be when the angels draw out their souls
striking their faces and their backs?
28. Because they followed what displeases God,
and they were averse to pleasing Him.
So We nullified their deeds.

Do they whose minds are filled with doubt, think
that God will not expose their malice?
30. Had We pleased We could have shown them to you
that you could know them by their marks,
and recognise them from the way
they twist their words.
Yet God knows all your deeds.
31. We shall try you in order to know
who are the fighters among you,
and who are men of fortitude,
and verify your histories.
32. Surely those who do not believe, and obstruct others

Muhammad

from the path of God, and oppose the Prophet
after the way of guidance has been opened to them,
will not hurt God in the least,
and He will nullify all that they have done.
33. O you who believe, obey God and the Prophet,
and do not waste your deeds.
34. Those who do not believe and obstruct others
from the way of God, and die disbelieving,
will not be pardoned by God.
35. So do not become weak-kneed and sue for peace,
for you will have the upper hand
as God is with you and will not overlook your deeds.
36. Verily the life of this world
is no more than a sport and frivolity.
If you believe and fear God,
He will give you your reward,
and will not ask for your possessions.
37. If He asks for all you possess and insist upon it,
you will become niggardly,
and it will bring out your malevolence.
38. Beware! You are called to spend in the way of God,
yet some among you close their fists.
But he who is niggardly is so for his own self:
God is above need, and it is you who are needy.
If you turn away then God
will bring other people in your place
who, moreover, will not be like you.

48 Victory

Al-Fath: Madani

سُوْرَةُ الْفَتْحِ مَدَنِيَّةٌ

اٰیَاتُهَا ۲۹ رُكُوْعُهَا

In the name of Allah, most-benevolent, ever-merciful.

بِسْمِ اللّٰهِ الرَّحْمٰنِ الرَّحِيْمِ ۞

WE HAVE GIVEN you a splendent victory

2. That God may save you from earlier and subsequent blames,
and complete His favours on you,
and guide you on the straight path,

3. And help you with surpassing help.

4. It is He who sent down the sense of security
into the hearts of believers
so that their faith may increase with belief, —
God's are the armies of the heavens and the earth;
and God is all-knowing and all-wise; —

5. And that He may admit men and women who believe
into gardens with rivers running by,
to live for ever there,
and absolve their evil, —
This, in the sight of God, will be the great fulfilment —

6. And that He may punish men and women (who are)
        hypocrites,
and idolaters and idolatresses who entertain
evil notions of God: It is against them
that the wheel of misfortune will turn,
and God will be wroth with them, and condemn them.
For them He has prepared Hell,
an evil destination!

7. For God's are the armies of the heavens and the earth;
and God is all-knowing and all-wise.

8. We have sent you as witness (of the truth)
and harbinger of good news and a warner,

9. So that (men) may believe in God and His Apostle,
and honour Him and revere Him,
and sing His praises morning and evening.

10. Those who swear allegiance to you
indeed swear allegiance to God;
and God's protection is over them.
Then whosoever breaks the promise

إِنَّا فَتَحْنَا لَكَ فَتْحًا مُّبِيْنًا ۞

لِيَغْفِرَ لَكَ اللّٰهُ مَا تَقَدَّمَ مِنْ ذَنْبِكَ وَمَا
تَأَخَّرَ وَيُتِمَّ نِعْمَتَهُ عَلَيْكَ وَيَهْدِيَكَ صِرَاطًا
مُّسْتَقِيْمًا ۞

وَّيَنْصُرَكَ اللّٰهُ نَصْرًا عَزِيْزًا ۞

هُوَ الَّذِيْ أَنْزَلَ السَّكِيْنَةَ فِيْ قُلُوْبِ الْمُؤْمِنِيْنَ
لِيَزْدَادُوْا إِيْمَانًا مَّعَ إِيْمَانِهِمْ وَلِلّٰهِ جُنُوْدُ السَّمٰوٰتِ
وَالْأَرْضِ وَكَانَ اللّٰهُ عَلِيْمًا حَكِيْمًا ۞

لِيُدْخِلَ الْمُؤْمِنِيْنَ وَالْمُؤْمِنٰتِ جَنّٰتٍ تَجْرِيْ
مِنْ تَحْتِهَا الْأَنْهٰرُ خٰلِدِيْنَ فِيْهَا وَيُكَفِّرَ
عَنْهُمْ سَيِّاٰتِهِمْ وَكَانَ ذٰلِكَ عِنْدَ اللّٰهِ فَوْزًا
عَظِيْمًا ۞

وَّيُعَذِّبَ الْمُنٰفِقِيْنَ وَالْمُنٰفِقٰتِ وَالْمُشْرِكِيْنَ
وَالْمُشْرِكٰتِ الظَّانِّيْنَ بِاللّٰهِ ظَنَّ السَّوْءِ عَلَيْهِمْ
دَائِرَةُ السَّوْءِ وَغَضِبَ اللّٰهُ عَلَيْهِمْ وَلَعَنَهُمْ وَ
أَعَدَّ لَهُمْ جَهَنَّمَ وَسَاءَتْ مَصِيْرًا ۞

وَلِلّٰهِ جُنُوْدُ السَّمٰوٰتِ وَالْأَرْضِ وَكَانَ اللّٰهُ
عَزِيْزًا حَكِيْمًا ۞

إِنَّا أَرْسَلْنٰكَ شَاهِدًا وَّمُبَشِّرًا وَّنَذِيْرًا ۞

لِّتُؤْمِنُوْا بِاللّٰهِ وَرَسُوْلِهِ وَتُعَزِّرُوْهُ وَتُوَقِّرُوْهُ وَ
تُسَبِّحُوْهُ بُكْرَةً وَّأَصِيْلًا ۞

إِنَّ الَّذِيْنَ يُبَايِعُوْنَكَ إِنَّمَا يُبَايِعُوْنَ اللّٰهَ
يَدُ اللّٰهِ فَوْقَ أَيْدِيْهِمْ فَمَنْ نَّكَثَ

breaks it to his own loss;
but whosoever fulfills the promise made to God
will receive a great reward from Him.

The Arabs of the desert who had stayed behind
will now say to you: "We were occupied
with our flocks and herds and families,
so ask forgiveness for us."
They say with their tongues what is not in their hearts.
Tell them: "Who can prevail with God for you
if He wish you harm or benefit?
Surely God is well aware of what you do.
12. In fact you imagined that the Prophet and the faithful
would never come back home;
and this seemed pleasing to your hearts,
and you entertained evil thoughts.
You are a people lost.
13. He who does not believe in God and His Apostle (should
     know)
We have prepared for unbelievers a blazing fire."
14. To God belongs the kingdom of the heavens and the
     earth;
He may forgive whosoever He please,
and afflict whosoever He will.
Yet God is forgiving and kind.
15. Those who had stayed behind will say:
"When you depart for taking the spoils,
allow us to follow you."
They wish to change the word of God.
Tell them: "You will not follow us.
That is what God has already said before."
They will say: "You are envious of our gain."
The fact is they understand but little.
16. Say to the desert Arabs who had stayed behind:
"You will be called against a formidable people.
You will fight them till they surrender.
If you obey, then He will give you a good reward;
but if you turn back, as you had done before,
He will punish you with a grievous affliction."
17. It is not binding on the blind,
the lame or the sick (to follow this command);
but those who obey God and His Apostle
will be admitted by God to gardens with running streams;
but those who turn back will suffer a painful doom.

God was pleased with the believers

when they swore allegiance to you under the tree,
for He knew well what was in their hearts,
and sent down tranquility on them,
and rewarded them with an expeditious victory
19. And the many spoils that they were to take.
God is all-mighty and all-wise.
20. God had promised you many spoils that you would
    capture;
so He gave this soon enough to you,
and stayed the hands of men from you
that it may serve as a sign for believers,
and guide you on the straight path;
21. And other (benefits) which you have not yet obtained,
are within the compass of God,
for God has power over every thing.
22. Had the unbelievers fought you
they would have turned their backs
and not found a protector or helper.
23. This is the law of God, effective as before:
You will not find any change in the law of God.
24. It was He who restrained their hands from you
in the heart of Makkah, and your hands from them,
after He had given you victory over them,
as God sees all that you do.
25. It were those who disbelieved who hindered you
from (going to) the Holy Mosque, preventing your offerings
from arriving at the place of sacrifice.
Had it not been for (the presence of) believers, men and
    women,
(among the unbelievers) of whom you were unaware,
and whom you might have trampled and thus incurred guilt
unknowingly on account of them,
(the matter would have been settled).
(But this was not done) so that God
may admit into His favour whom He willed.
If these (believers) had been separated from them,
He would have inflicted a grievous punishment on the
    unbelievers.
26. When the unbelievers fostered a sense of honour in their
    hearts,
a sense of pagan honour, God sent down
a sense of tranquility on His Apostle and the believers,
and obliged them to an act of self-restraint,
for they were deserving and worthy of it.
God is cognisant of every thing.

God has truly made the vision of His Apostle come true:
You will surely enter the Holy Mosque in security
if God please, without any fear,
having shaved your heads and cut your hair.
He knew what you did not know,
and has vouchsafed you, apart from this, a victory near at
hand.
28. It is He who has sent His Apostle
with the guidance and the true faith,
so that He may exalt it over every other creed.
God is sufficient as a witness.
29. Muhammad is the Prophet of God;
and those who are with him are severe with infidels
but compassionate among themselves.
You may see them kneeling and bowing in reverence,
seeking His favour and acceptance.
Their mark is on their foreheads
from the effect of prostrations.
Their likeness in the Torah,
and their likeness in the Gospel, is like a seed
that sends out a stalk, then makes it firm,
and it becomes strong and rises straight
upon its stem, gladdening the cultivator's heart,
in order to fill the unbelievers with dismay.
God has promised those who believe and do the right
forgiveness and a great reward.

49 Apartments

Al-Hujurāt: Madani

In the name of Allah, most benevolent, ever-merciful.

O YOU WHO believe,
do not forestall the judgements of God and His Apostle,
and have fear of God.
Verily God hears all and knows every thing.
2. O you who believe, do not raise your voices
above the voice of the Prophet,
and do not speak loudly to him
as you do with one another
lest your deeds are nullified unconsciously.
3. They who speak in a low voice in the presence of God's
        Apostle,
have had their hearts tried by God for reverence.
There is forgiveness for them and a great reward.
4. Many of those who call you from outside the apartments
are not considerate.
5. If they had waited for you to come out
it would have been better for them.
But God is forgiving and kind.
6. O you who believe, if a dissolute person brings some news,
verify it first lest you attack a people ignorantly
and later regret what you had done.
7. Know that the Apostle of God is among you:
If he agreed with you in most matters
you would surely come to grief.
But God has made faith more desirable to you,
and attractive to your hearts,
and rendered disbelief and sin and disobedience repugnant.
They are those who are well directed
8. By God's benevolence and His grace.
God is all-knowing and all-wise.
9. If two groups of believers come to fight one another,
promote peace between them.
Then if one of them turns aggressive against the other,
fight against the aggressive party

till it returns to God's authority.
If it does so, make peace among them equitably
and be impartial.
Verily God loves those who are just.
10. The faithful are surely brothers;
so restore friendship among your brothers,
and fear God that you may be favoured.

O you who believe, men should not laugh at other men,
for it may be they are better than them;
and women should not laugh at other women,
for they may perhaps be better than them.
Do not slander one another,
nor give one another nick-names.
After believing, it is bad to give (another) a bad name.
Those who do not repent behave wickedly.
12. O you who believe, avoid most suspicions:
Some suspicions are indeed sins.
So do not pry into others' secrets and do not backbite.
Would any of you like to eat a dead brother's flesh?
You would surely be revolted by it.
Then fear God. He is certainly forgiving and kind.
13. O men, We created you from a male and female,
and formed you into nations and tribes
that you may recognise each other.
He who has more integrity
has indeed greater honour with God.
Surely God is all-knowing and well-informed.
14. The Arabs of the desert say: "We believe."
Tell them: "You do not believe.
Better say: 'We submit'; for belief
has not yet penetrated your hearts."
If you begin to obey God and His Apostle,
He will not withhold the least (of the recompense) of your
        labour.
Verily God is forgiving and kind."
15. They alone are believers who come to believe
in God and His Apostle, then never doubt again,
and struggle wealth and soul in the way of God.
They are the truthful and sincere.
16. Say: "Are you trying to convince God of your faithfulness?
But God knows all there is in the heavens and the earth,
for God has knowledge of every thing."
17. They impress upon you that they have submitted.
Tell them: "Do not favour me with your submission.
In fact God has favoured you by showing you the way to

belief,
if you are men of truth."

18. Verily God knows the unknown of the heavens and the earth;
and God perceives all you do.

اِسْلَامَكُمْ بَلِ اللّٰهُ يَمُنُّ عَلَيْكُمْ اَنْ هَدٰىكُمْ
لِلْاِيْمَانِ اِنْ كُنْتُمْ صٰدِقِيْنَ ۝
اِنَّ اللّٰهَ يَعْلَمُ غَيْبَ السَّمٰوٰتِ وَالْاَرْضِ ۚ وَاللّٰهُ
بَصِيْرٌۢ بِمَا تَعْمَلُوْنَ ۝

50 Qāf

Qāf: Makki

In the name of Allah, most benevolent, ever-merciful.

Q̄ĀF. I CALL to witness the glorious Qur'an.
2. They are rather surprised that a warner
from among themselves has come to them.
So the unbelievers say: "This is astonishing:
3. When we are dead and turned to dust,
this returning (to life) is most far-fetched."
4. We know what the earth consumes of them,
for We have the Book that preserves every thing.
5. But no! They called the truth a lie when it came to them;
so they are in a confused state.
6. Have they not looked at the sky above them,
how We have fashioned and adorned it,
and it has no flaw?
7. We stretched the earth and placed upon it
firm stabilisers and We made
every kind of splendid thing to grow upon it
8. As instruction and reminder to every penitent creature.
9. And We send down water as a blessing from the sky,
and grow gardens with it and the grain for harvest,
10. And tall date-palms with their spathes pile on pile
11. As a provision for men, and enlivened
a region that was dead.
Even thus will be the life after death.
12. The people of Noah, Ar-Rass and Thamud
denied before you,
13. As did the people of 'Ad and Pharaoh and the brethren of
Lot,
14. And the dwellers of the Wood and people of Tubba'.
Each of them denied the apostles.
So My threat became a reality.
15. Were We exhausted by the act of the first creation?
And yet they are confused about a new creation.

We created man and surely know

what misdoubts arise in their hearts;
for We are closer to him than his jugular vein.

17. When the two (angels) who keep the account,
one sitting on the right, one on the left, take it down,

18. There is not a word he utters but an observer
is ready (to make note of it).

19. The palsy of death will surely come.
This is what you wished to avert.

20. And the trumpet blast will sound:
It would be the Day of Doom.

21. Each soul will come with a driver and a witness.

22. (And the driver will say:) "You were oblivious of this,
so we have removed the veil,
and how keen is your sight today!"

23. His companion will say: "Here is (the record)
I have ready with me."

24. "Cast each stubborn unbeliever into Hell," (they will
be told),

25. "Every obstructor of good, transgressor, and the sceptic,

26. Who had set up another god with God.
Cast him into severe torment."

27. His companion will say: "O Lord,
I did not lead him to wickedness,
but he was himself far astray."

28. "Do not argue in My presence. I had announced
the promise of doom in advance.

29. There is no changing of My word,
nor am I unjust to My creatures."

We shall ask Hell that day: "Are you full?"
It will answer: "Are there still more?"

31. And Paradise will be brought near, not far from those
who took heed for themselves and feared God.

32. "This is what you had been promised," (will be said)
to every penitent who remembered (his duty),

33. Who feared Ar-Rahman in secret,
and came with a penitent heart:

34. "Enter it in peace. This is the day of life abiding."

35. Theirs will be whatsoever they wish:
And with Us there is more.

36. How many generations have We destroyed before them
who were mightier in power than they.
Then they searched throughout the land
to see if there was a way of escape.

37. Surely there is a reminder in this
for whosoever has a heart (to feel), or takes heed.

38. We created the heavens and the earth
and all that lies between them, in six spans,
and no weariness came upon Us.
39. So you bear with patience what they say,
and sing the praises of your Lord
before the rising of the sun and its setting,
40. And glorify Him for some portion of the night,
and additional adorations.
41. Take heed that the day
the crier calls from a place close (to every one),
42. The day they actually hear the blast,
will be the Day of rising of the dead.
43. We are the one who give life and death,
and to Us will be the destination.
44. The day the earth will split asunder
they will come out hurriedly.
This gathering together is easy for Us.
45. We are cognisant of what they say;
but it is not for you to compel them.
So keep on reminding through the Qur'an
whoever fears My warning.

51 The Dispersing

Adh-Dhāriyāt: Makki

سورة الذٰریٰت مکیة (٥١)

ایاتها ٦٠ رکوعها

In the name of Allah, most benevolent, ever-merciful.

بِسْمِ اللهِ الرَّحْمٰنِ الرَّحِیْمِ ٥

I CALL TO witness those who scatter (dust) by dispersing,

وَالذّٰرِیٰتِ ذَرْوًا ٥ فَالْحٰمِلٰتِ وِقْرًا ٥

2. And those who bear the load (of rain),
3. And those who move (on the water) gently,

فَالْجٰرِیٰتِ یُسْرًا ٥ فَالْمُقَسِّمٰتِ اَمْرًا ٥

4. And those who distribute (it) by command,
5. Verily the promise made to you is true:

اِنَّمَا تُوْعَدُوْنَ لَصَادِقٌ ٥

6. The Judgement will indeed take place.

وَاِنَّ الدِّیْنَ لَوَاقِعٌ ٥

7. The heavens webbed-with-tracks is witness

وَالسَّمَآءِ ذَاتِ الْحُبُكِ ٥

8. You are surely caught in contradictions,

اِنَّكُمْ لَفِیْ قَوْلٍ مُّخْتَلِفٍ ٥

9. From which only he turns who is turned away.

یُّؤْفَكُ عَنْهُ مَنْ اُفِكَ ٥ قُتِلَ الْخَرّٰصُوْنَ ٥

10. Perish will those who just guess and speculate,
11. Who are lost in deception.

الَّذِیْنَ هُمْ فِیْ غَمْرَةٍ سَاهُوْنَ ٥

12. They ask: "When is the Day of Judgement?" —

یَسْئَلُوْنَ اَیَّانَ یَوْمُ الدِّیْنِ ٥

13. The day they will be burnt in the Fire,

یَوْمَ هُمْ عَلَی النَّارِ یُفْتَنُوْنَ ٥

14. (And told:) "Taste your punishment.
This is what you were trying to hasten."

ذُوْقُوْا فِتْنَتَكُمْ هٰذَا الَّذِیْ كُنْتُمْ بِهٖ تَسْتَعْجِلُوْنَ ٥

15. Surely those who fear God and follow the straight path
will be amidst gardens and fresh springs of water,

اِنَّ الْمُتَّقِیْنَ فِیْ جَنّٰتٍ وَّعُیُوْنٍ ٥

16. Receiving what is given them by their Lord.
They were surely the virtuous before this.

اٰخِذِیْنَ مَا اٰتٰهُمْ رَبُّهُمْ اِنَّهُمْ كَانُوْا قَبْلَ ذٰلِكَ مُحْسِنِیْنَ ٥

17. They slept little in the night,

كَانُوْا قَلِیْلًا مِّنَ الَّیْلِ مَا یَهْجَعُوْنَ ٥

18. And every morning asked forgiveness,

وَبِالْاَسْحَارِ هُمْ یَسْتَغْفِرُوْنَ ٥

19. In whose wealth the suppliant and the deprived had a share.

وَفِیْ اَمْوَالِهِمْ حَقٌّ لِّلسَّآئِلِ وَالْمَحْرُوْمِ ٥

20. There are signs in the earth
for those who are firm in their faith,

وَفِی الْاَرْضِ اٰیٰتٌ لِّلْمُوْقِنِیْنَ ٥

21. And within yourselves. Can you not perceive?

وَفِیْ اَنْفُسِكُمْ اَفَلَا تُبْصِرُوْنَ ٥

22. There is in the heavens your sustenance,
and whatever has been promised you.

وَفِی السَّمَآءِ رِزْقُكُمْ وَمَا تُوْعَدُوْنَ ٥

23. By the Lord of the heavens and the earth,
this is certainly true even as you speak.

فَوَرَبِّ السَّمَآءِ وَالْاَرْضِ اِنَّهٗ لَحَقٌّ مِّثْلَ مَا اَنَّكُمْ تَنْطِقُوْنَ ٥

Has the story of Abraham's honoured guests come to
you?

هَلْ اَتٰىكَ حَدِیْثُ ضَیْفِ اِبْرٰهِیْمَ الْمُكْرَمِیْنَ ٥

25. When they came to him, they said: "Peace."
He answered: "Peace."

اِذْ دَخَلُوْا عَلَیْهِ فَقَالُوْا سَلٰمًا قَالَ سَلٰمٌ قَوْمٌ

قال فاخطبكم ٢٧ الذٰريٰت۱۱٥

They were a people he did not recognise.

26. So he hurried to the house and brought a fatted calf,

27. And placing it before them said: "Won't you eat?"

28. He felt afraid of them; but they said:
"Have no fear," and gave him the good news of a wise son.

29. His wife came out lamentng, striking her forehead,
and said: "I, an old and barren woman?"

30. They said: "Thus said your Lord.
He is indeed all-wise and all-knowing."

31. He said: "What is then your business, O messengers?"

32. They said: "We have been sent to a wicked people

33. So as to let loose clods of clay on them

34. Marked by your Lord for those who waste their substance."

35. So We evacuated everyone who was a believer there,

36. But did not find more than a single family of believers.

37. We left a sign in this for those
who fear the grievous punishment,

38. As (there was) in Moses when We sent him to the Pharaoh
with clear authority.

39. But he turned to his counsellors, and said:
"He is a magician or lunatic."

40. So We seized him and his armies,
and threw them into the sea, for he was worthy of blame.

41. In 'Ad (also is a sign), when We sent
a blasting wind against them,

42. Which turned every thing it touched to ashes.

43. And in Thamud, when We said to them:
"Enjoy yourselves for a while;"

44. But they disobeyed the command of their Lord;
so they were destroyed by a thunderbolt,
and they could only gape,

45. And neither stand up nor defend themselves.

46. (So had We destroyed) the people of Noah before them:
They were surely a sinful people.

We built the heavens by Our authority;
and We are the Lord of power and expanse.

48. We spread the earth a carpet;
what comfort We provide!

49. And We created pairs of every thing
that you may contemplate.

50. So turn to God. I give you a clear warning from Him.

51. Do not set up another god with God.
I give you a clear warning from Him.

52. Even thus no apostle came to those before them
but they said: "He is a sorcerer or a mad man."

قال فما خطبكم ٢٧   الذٰريٰت ٥١

53. Is this the legacy they have passed down from one to the
   other?
In fact, they are a rebellious people.
54. Turn away from them. You will not be blamed.
55. But go on reminding them, as reminding
benefits the believers.
56. I have not created the jinns and men but to worship Me.
57. I want no sustenance from them
nor do I want them to feed Me.
58. God is certainly the great provider,
Lord of strength and power.
59. Those who do wrong will indeed
come to the same end as their fellows (of old).
So let them not ask Me to hasten (the punishment).
60. Alas the woe for those who refuse to believe
in the Day which has been promised them.

أَتَوَاصَوْا بِهٖ بَلْ هُمْ قَوْمٌ طَاغُوْنَ ۞

فَتَوَلَّ عَنْهُمْ فَمَا أَنْتَ بِمَلُوْمٍ ۞

وَذَكِّرْ فَاِنَّ الذِّكْرٰى تَنْفَعُ الْمُؤْمِنِيْنَ ۞

وَمَا خَلَقْتُ الْجِنَّ وَالْاِنْسَ اِلَّا لِيَعْبُدُوْنِ ۞

مَا أُرِيْدُ مِنْهُمْ مِّنْ رِّزْقٍ وَّمَا أُرِيْدُ اَنْ

يُّطْعِمُوْنِ ۞

اِنَّ اللّٰهَ هُوَ الرَّزَّاقُ ذُو الْقُوَّةِ الْمَتِيْنُ ۞

فَاِنَّ لِلَّذِيْنَ ظَلَمُوْا ذَنُوْبًا مِّثْلَ ذَنُوْبِ اَصْحَابِهِمْ

فَلَا يَسْتَعْجِلُوْنِ ۞

فَوَيْلٌ لِّلَّذِيْنَ كَفَرُوْا مِنْ يَّوْمِهِمُ الَّذِيْ

يُوْعَدُوْنَ ۞

52 The Mount

At-Tūr: Makki

In the name of Allah, most benevolent, ever-merciful.

I CALL TO witness the Mount Sinai,

2. And the Scripture inscribed

3. On a parchment scroll unrolled,

4. The house ever-peopled,

5. The roof raised high,

6. And the swollen sea,

7. The punishment of your Lord is certain to come.

8. There is none who could avert it.

9. The day the sky will tremble,

10. The mountains move and fly away,

11. Will be the day of woe for those

12. Who, ignoring the Reality, engage in pleasantries.

13. The day they are dragged and pushed into Hell,

14. (And told:) "This is the fire which you denied.

15. Is it magic, or you cannot see?

16. Roast in it. Bear it with patience or impatience,
it will be the same for you.
You will be requited for what you had done."

17. Those who fear God and follow the straight path
will surely be in gardens and in bliss,

18. Rejoicing at what their Lord has given them;
and their Lord will preserve them from the torment of Hell.

19. "Eat and drink with relish," (they will be told),
(as recompense) for what you had done."

20. They would recline on couches set in rows,
paired with fair companions (clean of thought and) bright of
eye.

21. And those who believed, and whose progeny
also followed them in their faith,
will be united with their offspring.
We will not deprive them of their labour in the least.
Every man is bound to what he does.

22. We shall give them fruits and meats,
and what they desire.

23. They will exchange cups of wine
free of (incitement to) pleasantry or sin.
24. And young attendants like pearls within their shells,
will go round.
25. They will ask each other questions,
26. Saying: "We were also once
full of fear at home.
27. But God has been gracious to us,
and has saved us from the torment of scorching wind.
28. We used to pray to Him erstwhile;
He is the just and merciful.

Remind them, therefore, that by the grace of your Lord
you are neither a soothsayer nor possessed.
30. Do they say: "He is a poet for whom we expect
an adverse turn of fortune?"
31. Tell them: "Keep on expecting, I am expecting with you."
32. Does their reasoning prompt them to this,
or they are a people rebellious?
33. Or do they say: "He has fabricated it?"
In fact, they will never believe.
34. So let them bring a discourse like it, if they are truthful.
35. Or were they created of themselves?
Or are they the creators?
36. Or have they created the heavens and the earth?
In fact they are certain of nothing.
37. Do they possess the treasures of your Lord?
Or are they the treasurers?
38. Or do they have a ladder (climbing which)
they can hear (the secrets of heaven)?
Let one who has heard then bring a clear proof.
39. Has (God) daughters and they sons?
40. Or do you demand any wages from them
so that they are burdened with expense?
41. Or do they have knowledge of the Unknown which they
     write down?
42. Or do they want to stage a deception? —
Then only those who do not believe
will be the ones who will be tricked.
43. Or do they have a god apart from God?
He is too exalted for what they associate with Him!
44. If they should see a segment falling from the sky,
they would say: "It is only a massive cloud."
45. So, leave them until they face their day (of doom)
when they will be stunned.
46. Their deception will not avail them in the least on that day,

At-Tur

nor will they be helped.

47. Surely there are other torments besides this for those who are wicked, though most of them do not know.

48. Await the judgement of your Lord,
for you are always before Our eyes,
and glorify your Lord with praises when you rise,

49. And glorify Him in the night
and when the stars begin to wane.

 يُنْصَرُونَ ۞

وَإِنَّ لِلَّذِينَ ظَلَمُوا عَذَابًا دُونَ ذٰلِكَ وَلٰكِنَّ
أَكْثَرَهُمْ لَا يَعْلَمُونَ ۞

وَاصْبِرْ لِحُكْمِ رَبِّكَ فَإِنَّكَ بِأَعْيُنِنَا وَسَبِّحْ
بِحَمْدِ رَبِّكَ حِينَ تَقُومُ ۞

وَمِنَ الَّيْلِ فَسَبِّحْهُ وَإِدْبَارَ النُّجُومِ ۞

53　The Star

An-Najm: Makki

In the name of Allah, most benevolent, ever-merciful.

I CALL TO witness the star of the pleiades when it has dipped
2. That your companion is not confused,
nor has he gone astray,
3. Neither does he speak of his own will.
4. This is only revelation communicated,
5. Bestowed on him by the Supreme Intellect,*
6. Lord of power and wisdom.
So he acquired poise and balance,
7. And reached the highest pinnacle.
8. Then he drew near and drew closer
9. Until a space of two bow (arcs)**
or even less remained,
10. When He revealed to His votary what He revealed.
11. His heart did not falsify what he perceived.
12. Will you dispute with him what he saw?
13. He saw Him indeed another time
14. By the Lote-tree beyond which none can pass,***
15. Close to which is the Garden of Tranquility,
16. When the Lote-tree was covered over
with what it was covered over;
17. Neither did sight falter nor exceed the bounds.
18. Indeed he saw some of the greatest signs of His Lord.
19. Have you considered Lat and 'Uzza,
20. And Manat, the other third (of the pagan deities)?****
21. Are there sons for you, and daughters for Him?
22. This is certainly an unjust apportioning.
23. These are only names which you and your fathers
have invented. No authority was sent down by God for them.
They only follow conjecture and wish-fulfilment, even though
guidance had come to them already from their Lord.
24. Can ever man get what he desires?
25. To God belong the End and the Beginning.

---

*to*** see notes 1,2 & 3 respectively on p. 457. **** Called by them 'daughters of God.'

Many as the angels be in heaven
their intercession will not avail in the least
without God's permission for whomsoever He please and
    approve.
27. Those who do not believe in the Hereafter
give the angels names of females.
28. Yet they have no knowledge of this,
and follow nothing but conjecture,
but conjecture cannot replace the truth.
29. So you turn away from him who turns away
from Our rememberance
and wants nothing but the life of this world:
30. This is the farthest limit of their knowledge.
Surely your Lord alone knows best
who has strayed away from the path
and who has come to guidance.
31. To God belongs whatever is in the heavens and the earth,
that He may requite those who do evil,
in accordance with their deeds,
and those who do good with good.
32. As for those who avoid the greater sins and shameful acts,
except minor trespasses,
your Lord's forgiveness surely has great amplitude.
He is fully knowledgeable of you
as He produced you from the earth,
and since you were a foetus in your mother's womb.
So do not assert your goodness;
he is better who takes heed and preserves himself.

Have you seen him who turns his back,
34. Who gives but little, and is niggardly?
35. Has he knowledge of the Unknown
that he perceives everything?
36. Has he not heard what is contained
in the Book of Moses,
37. And of Abraham who fulfilled his trust? —
38. That no one who carries a burden bears another's load;
39. That a man receives but only that
for which he strives;
40. That his endeavours will be judged,
41. And only then
will he receive his recompense in full;
42. And that to your Lord is your returning;
43. That it is He who makes you happy and morose,
44. And He who ordains death and life;
45. That He created pairs, male and female,

46. From a drop of semen when emitted;
47. That the second creation is incumbent on Him;
48. That it is He
who makes you rich and contented;
49. That He is the Lord of Sirius;
50. That it was He who destroyed
the 'Ad of old,
51. And Thamud, and did not leave them,
52. Like the people of Noah before them,
who were surely oppressors and rebellious;
53. And He overthrew the Cities of the Plain,
54. So that they were covered over
by what they were covered over.
55. How many favours of your Lord
will you then deny?
56. He who warns you is one of the warners of old.
57. What is to come is imminent.
58. There is no one to unveil it
apart from God.
59. Are you astonished at this news,
60. And keep laughing and do not weep,
61. Indulging in pleasantries?
62. Bow instead in adoration before God
and worship Him.

---

1. Note on vv. 1-5. These verses deal with the highest of all mystical experiences which only the most spiritually exalted could have and emphasise the spiritual elevation of the Holy Prophet. "This" in v. 4 refers to the Qur'an which, Surah 55, vv. 1-4, affirms, was taught by no one but God, the Supreme Intellect.

2. Note on v. 9. To understand the meaning of *qaba qausain*, we have to bear in mind the custom of pagan Arabs who, when making a pact, joined two bows, and stretching them together, shot one arrow to show that they were one in their resolution, and united in carrying out all decisions. The prophets and God are similarly united in carrying out the divine resolve. . . . If taken literally, two bows would mean the arcs of the two enlarged to form one wider arc. The relative positions of the Prophet and 'what he saw' (the object) would, thus, be on either side of the sphere so that the Prophet could behold what he saw only in refraction. And who could behold the Supreme Reality directly? The example of Moses is there, 7:143.

3. Note on v. 14. *Sidrat al-muntaha*, the Lote-tree beyond which none could pass, marks the limit of man's reach, the sphere of Relativity, beyond which lies the realm of the Absolute.

54 The Moon

Al-Qamar: Makki

بِسْمِ اللهِ الرَّحْمٰنِ الرَّحِيْمِ ۟

In the name of Allah, most benevolent, ever-merciful.

THE HOUR HAS come and split is the moon.*
2. But if they see a sign they turn away,
and say: "This is the same old lie continuing,"
3. And deny, and follow their own vain desires;
but every matter is determined at its time.
4. Messages deterring them from evil had come to them,
5. Containing consummate wisdom;
yet warnings were of no avail.
6. So turn away from them.
When on the Day the crier calls to the painful business,
7. They will come out of the graves with downcast eyes
like an expanding swarm of locusts.
8. They will hasten forward to the caller, gazes fixed.
And the unbelievers will say: "This is the day of untold woe."
9. The people of Noah had denied before them,
and had called Our votary a liar, and said:
"He is possessed," and repulsed him.
10. So he prayed to his Lord: "I am helpless, deliver me."
11. And We opened up the flood gates of the sky
with water pouring down in torrents,
12. And We opened up the springs of the earth;
and the waters met for a decreed end.
13. But We bore him on a (vessel made) of planks and oakum,
14. Which sailed right under Our eyes:
A recompense for him who had been denied.
15. And We left it as a sign. Is there any one who will be warned?
16. How was then My punishment and My commination!
17. Easy have We made the Qur'an to understand:
So is there any one who will be warned?
18. The 'Ad had also disavowed.
How was then My punishment and My commination!
19. We let loose against them a violent roaring wind

----

* See note at the end of the Surah.

on a day of ill omen, continuous,
20. Which snatched away men as though
they were palm trees pulled out by the roots.
21. How was then My punishment and My commination!
22. Easy have We made the Qur'an to understand:
So is there any one who will pay heed?

The Thamud rejected the warnings,
24. And said: "Should we follow only one man among us?
In that case we shall be in error and insane.
25. Was he the one of all of us to have been given the
exposition?
He is surely an impudent liar."
26. "Tomorrow they will know who is the impudent liar!
27. We shall send the she-camel to try them.
So watch them, and be constant.
28. Tell them that the water is to be apportioned
between them (and her); and every turn of drinking
will be fixed (for each)."
29. But they called their commander,
who seized and hamstrung her.
30. How was then My punishment of which they had been
warned?
31. We sent a single blast against them,
and they were reduced to husks of a decayed fence.
32. Easy have We made the Qur'an to understand:
So is there any one who will be warned?
33. The people of Lot rejected the warnings.
34. We sent a stone-hurtling storm against them,
except the family of Lot whom We saved
in the early hours of the morning
35. As a favour from Us.
That is how We reward the grateful.
36. He had warned them of Our might,
but they passed over the warnings.
37. They lusted after his guests,
so We put out their eyes (and said):
"Taste My punishment and My commination."
38. And early in the morning
the decreed punishment came upon them.
39. So now taste My punishment and My commination!
40. Easy have We made the Qur'an to understand:
So is there any one who will be warned?

The warnings came to the people of Pharaoh.
42. They rejected each one of Our signs.

So We seized them with the grip of one
mighty and powerful.
43. Are the unbelievers among you any better than they?
Or is there immunity for you in the Scriptures?
44. Or do they say: "We are a well-accoutred army?"
45. The army will be routed and put to flight.
46. Surely the Hour will be the moment of their promise,
and that moment will be calamitous and distressing.
47. Surely the sinners are misguided and insane.
48. On that Day they will be dragged into the fire
faces foremost, (and told:) "Taste the feel of Hell."
49. We have indeed created all things by measure;
50. And Our command is but one (word)
swift as the winking of an eye.
51. We have destroyed the likes of you in the past:
So is there any one who will be warned?
52. All things they do are (recorded) in the books;
53. All things small or great have been written down.
54. Surely those who fear God and follow the straight path
will be amidst gardens and light,
55. At the still centre
in the proximity of the King all-powerful.

---

* Note on v. 1. *Shaqqa* includes 'opposition' in its basic meanings, which is also implied by 'split' in English. The moon was the emblem of the Quraish. Raghib, however, says in his *Mufridat* that the flag of the Arabs consisted of the moon, even as the sun was the emblem of neighbouring Iran. The Quraish being the dominant tribe of Arabia, it was their emblem that represented the Arabs as a whole. After the advent of Islam there was a split among the Quraish, some accepting Islam, others remaining pagan and opposed to it. *Shaqq al-qamar,* therefore, stands, in the metaphor of the Qur'an, for this split in the ranks of the Quraish. Otherwise, the meaning of Surah 105, The Quraish, would not be brought out effectively, exhorting the Quraish to become united in the worship of one God. For use of *shaqqa* in the sense of opposition see 4:35; 4:115; 38:2; 59:4. After the victory of Makkah the 'split' was healed.

55 Ar-Rahmān

Ar-Rahmān: Madani

In the name of Allah, most benevolent, ever-mericful.

AR-RAHMĀN
2. Bestowed the Qur'an,
3. Created man,
4. And taught him to express clearly.
5. The sun and moon revolve to a computation;
6. And the grasses and the trees
bow (to Him) in adoration.
7. He raised the sky and set the Balance
8. So that none may err against the scales,
9. And observe correct measure, weigh with justice,
and not cheat the balance.
10. He positioned the earth for all the creatures:
11. There are fruits of all kinds on it,
and date-palms with their clusters sheathed,
12. Grain with husk, and fragrant grasses.
13. How many favours of your Lord
will then both of you deny?
14. He created man
of fermented clay dried tinkling hard
like earthen ware,
15. And created jinns from the white-hot flame of fire.
16. How many favours of your Lord
will you then deny?
17. Lord of the two Easts, Lord of the two Wests.
18. How many favours of your Lord
will then both of you deny?
19. He has set two seas in motion
that flow side by side together,
20. With an interstice between them
which they cannot cross. —
21. How many favours of your Lord
will then both of you deny? —
22. Out of them come pearls and coral.
23. How many favours of your Lord

will you then deny?
24. His are the high-sailed vessels
in deep ocean like the mountains.
25. How many favours of your Lord
will then both of you deny?

All that is on the earth is passing,
27. But abiding is the glory of your Lord,
full of majesty and beneficence.
28. How many favours of your Lord
will you then deny?
29. All those there are in the heavens and the earth
turn to Him with solicitation,
intent on His purpose all the time.
30. How many favours of your Lord
will you then deny?
31. We shall soon be free to turn to you,
O weary caravans,
32. How many favours of your Lord
will you then deny?
33. O society of jinns and men,
cross the bounds of the heavens and the earth
if you have the ability,
then pass beyond them;
but you cannot
unless you acquire the law.
34. How many favours of your Lord
will you then deny?
35. Let loose at you
will be smokeless flames of fire
so that you will not be able
to defend yourselves.
36. How many favours of your Lord
will then both of you deny?
37. When the sky will split asunder,
and turn rosy
like the dregs of annointing oil,
38. Which of the favours of your Lord
will you then deny?
39. Neither man nor jinn will be questioned
on that day about his sin.
40. How many favours of your Lord
will you then deny?
41. The sinners will be recognised
by their marks, and seized
by the forelock and their feet.

Ar-Rahman

42. Which of the favours of your Lord
will you then deny?
43. This is Hell
the sinners called a lie.
44. They will go round and around
between it and boiling water.
45. Which of the favours of your Lord
will you then deny?

But for him who lived in awe
of the sublimity of his Lord,
there will be two gardens —
47. How many favours of your Lord
will then both of you deny?
48. Full of overhanging branches —
49. Which of the favours of your Lord
will you then deny? —
50. With two springs of water flowing
through them both. —
51. Which of the favours of your Lord
will then both of you deny?
52. In both of them there will be
every kind of fruits in pairs. —
53. Which of the favours of your Lord
will then both of you deny? —
54. Reclining there on carpets lined with brocade,
fruits of the garden hanging low
within reach.
55. How many favours of your Lord
will then both of you deny?
56. In them maidens with averted glances,
undeflowered
by man or by jinn before them, —
57. Which of the favours of your Lord
will then both of you deny? —
58. As though rubies and pearls.
59. Which of the favours of your Lord
will then both of you deny?
60. Should the reward of goodness be
aught else but goodness? —
61. How many favours of your Lord
will then both of you deny? —
62. And besides these two other gardens —
63. Which of the favours of your Lord
will then both of you deny? —
64. Of darkest verdant green —

65. How many favours of your Lord
will then both of you deny? —
66. With two fountains gushing constantly, —
67. How many favours of your Lord
will then both of you deny? —
68. With fruits in them,
and dates and pomegranates. —
69. How many favours of your Lord
will then both of you deny? —
70. In them good and comely maidens —
71. How many favours of your Lord
will you then deny? —
72. Houris cloistered in pavilions —
73. How many favours of your Lord
will you then deny? —
74. Undeflowered
by man or by jinn before them, —
75. How many favours of your Lord
will then both of you deny? —
76. Reclining on green cushions
and rich carpets excellent.
77. How many favours of your Lord
will you then deny?
78. Blessed be the name of your Lord,
full of majesty
and beneficience.

56 The Inevitable

Al-Wāqi'ah: Makki

In the name of Allah, most benevolent, ever-merciful.

WHEN WHAT IS to happen comes to pass —
2. Which is bound to happen undoubtedly —
3. Degrading (some) and exalting (others);
4. When the earth is shaken up convulsively,
5. The mountains bruised and crushed,
6. Turned to dust, floating in the air,
7. You will become three categories:
8. Those of the right hand —
how (happy) will be those of the right hand!
9. Then those of the left hand —
how (unhappy) will be those of the left hand!
10. Then the foremost, how pre-excellent,
11. Who will be honoured
12. In gardens of tranquility;
13. A number of the earlier peoples,
14. And a few of later ages,
15. On couches wrought of gold,
16. Reclining face to face.
17. Youths of never-ending bloom
will pass round to them
18. Cups and decanters,
beakers full of sparkling wine,
19. Unheady, uninebriating;
20. And such fruits as they fancy,
21. Bird meats that they relish,
22. And companions
with big beautiful eyes
23. Like pearls within their shells,
24. As recompense
for all they had done.
25. They will hear no nonsense there or talk of sin,
26. Other than "Peace, peace" the salutation.
27. As for those of the right hand —
how (happy) those of the right hand —

28. They will be in (the shade)
of thornless lote
29. And acacia
covered with heaps of bloom,
30. Lengthened shadows,
31. Gushing water,
32. And fruits numberless,
33. Unending, unforbidden,
34. And maidens incomparable.*
35. We have formed them
in a distinctive fashion,
36. And made them virginal,
37. Loving companions matched in age,
38. For those of the right hand.

A crowd of earlier generations
40. And a crowd of the later.
41. But those of the left hand —
how (unhappy) those of the left hand —
42. Will be in the scorching wind
and boiling water,
43. Under the shadow of thick black smoke
44. Neither cool nor agreeable.
45. They were endowed with good things
46. But persisted in that greater sin,
47. And said: "What! When we are dead
and turned to dust and bones,
shall we then be raised again?
48. And so will our fathers?"
49. Say: "Indeed, the earlier and the later generations
50. Will be gathered together
on a certain day which is predetermined.
51. Then you, the erring and the deniers,
52. Will eat of the tree of Zaqqum,
53. Fill your bellies with it,
54. And drink over it scalding water,
55. Lapping it up like female camels
raging of thrist with disease."
56. Such will be their welcome
on the Day of Judgement.
57. It is He who created you, then why
do you not affirm the truth?
58. Just consider (the semen) that you emit,
59. Do you create it, or We are its creator?

_____

* See note on page 468.

60. We have incorporated death in your constitution,
and We shall not be hindered
61. From replacing you with others
or raising you
in a way you do not know.
62. You have known the first creation,
then why do you not reflect?
63. Just ponder over what you sow:
64. Do you give it its increase,
or are We the giver?
65. We could turn it, if We pleased,
into straw;
then you would rue the day,
66. (And say:) "We have fallen into debt;
67. Indeed, we have been deprived
of the fruits of our labour."
68. Consider the water that you drink.
69. Do you send it down from the clouds,
or We send it down?
70. We could make it brackish, if We pleased;
so why do you not acknowledge thanks?
71. Consider the fire that you strike
(and get by friction).
72. Have you raised its tree,
or We have raised it?
73. We have made it as a reminder and convenience
for the needy.
74. So glorify your Lord, the most supreme

So I call the placement of the stars to witness —
76. And this surely is great evidence
if you can understand —
77. That this is indeed the glorious Qur'an
78. (Inscribed) in the well-kept Book.
79. Only they can reach it who are clean (of mind).
80. It has been revealed
by the Lord of all the worlds.
81. Then why do you dissimulate this Revelation?
82. You live by calling it a lie.
83. Then how is it that when
the (dying) breath is withdrawn into the throat (and rattles),
84. And you wait for the moment (of death),
85. We are closer to him than you,
even though you cannot see?
86. Then why, if you are not
indebted (to Us for life),

87. Can you not bring him back?
(Answer) if you are truthful.
88. Then, if he is one of the honoured,
89. There will be peace and plenty,
and gardens of tranquility for him.
90. If he is of those of the right hand,
91. There will be the salutation
by those of the right hand: "Peace on you."
92. But if he is of the deniers
and the errants,
93. The welcome will be boiling water
94. And the roasting in Hell.
95. This is indeed the ultimate truth.
96. Then praise your Lord, the most supreme.

---

* Note on v. 34. *Furush,* Plural *farash,* in this verse has been generally translated as 'beds' or 'couches,' and *Marfu'ah* as 'raised high.' In fact, *furush* means maidens of Paradise according to *Taj al-'urus.* Raghib says that *farash* metaphorically means consort or companion, and wife and husband are called each other's *farash. Marfu'ah* means far above or higher than earthly maidens in beauty and elegance: *Taj.* Otherwise the meaning of vv. 35, 36 and 37 that follow would be lost and become incongruous.

Al-Waqi'ah   468

57 Iron

Al-Hadīd: Madani

In the name of Allah, most benevolent, ever-merciful.

WHATSOEVER IS IN the heavens and the earth
sings the praises of God.
He is all-mighty and all-wise.
2. His is the kingdom of the heavens and the earth,
He is the giver of life and death,
and He has power over every thing.
3. He is the first and He the last,
the transcendent and the immanent;
and He has knowledge of every thing.
4. It is He who created the heavens and the earth
in six stages, then assumed the throne.
He knows whatsoever enters the earth,
and whatsoever comes out of it,
and what comes down from the sky
and what goes up to it;
and He is with you wheresoever you may be,
and He perceives whatsoever you do.
5. His is the kingdom of the heavens and the earth,
and all things will go back to Him.
6. He turns night into day,
and turns day into night;
and He knows whatsoever is in your hearts.
7. Believe in God and His Apostle,
and spend of what He has given you as His trustee.
And those of you who believe and spend in charity
will have a great reward.
8. What has come upon you that you believe not in God,
though the Prophet is calling you to believe in your Lord?
And He has already taken your pledge, if you are believers.
9. It is He who sends down
splendent revelations to His votary
that he may take you out of darkness into light;
for surely God is gracious and kind to you.
10. What has come upon you that you do not spend

بِسْمِ اللهِ الرَّحْمٰنِ الرَّحِيْمِ ۞
سَبَّحَ لِلّٰهِ مَا فِى السَّمٰوٰتِ وَالْأَرْضِ وَهُوَ
الْعَزِيْزُ الْحَكِيْمُ ۞ لَهُ مُلْكُ السَّمٰوٰتِ
وَالْأَرْضِ يُحْيٖ وَيُمِيْتُ وَهُوَ عَلٰى كُلِّ شَىْءٍ
قَدِيْرٌ ۞ هُوَ الْأَوَّلُ وَالْأٰخِرُ وَالظَّاهِرُ
وَالْبَاطِنُ وَهُوَ بِكُلِّ شَىْءٍ عَلِيْمٌ ۞
هُوَ الَّذِىْ خَلَقَ السَّمٰوٰتِ وَالْأَرْضَ فِىْ سِتَّةِ
أَيَّامٍ ثُمَّ اسْتَوٰى عَلَى الْعَرْشِ يَعْلَمُ مَا يَلِجُ
فِى الْأَرْضِ وَمَا يَخْرُجُ مِنْهَا وَمَا يَنْزِلُ مِنَ
السَّمَاءِ وَمَا يَعْرُجُ فِيْهَا وَهُوَ مَعَكُمْ
أَيْنَ مَا كُنْتُمْ وَاللهُ بِمَا تَعْمَلُوْنَ
بَصِيْرٌ ۞
لَهُ مُلْكُ السَّمٰوٰتِ وَالْأَرْضِ وَإِلَى اللهِ تُرْجَعُ
الْأُمُوْرُ ۞
يُوْلِجُ الَّيْلَ فِى النَّهَارِ وَيُوْلِجُ النَّهَارَ فِى الَّيْلِ
وَهُوَ عَلِيْمٌ بِذَاتِ الصُّدُوْرِ ۞
اٰمِنُوْا بِاللهِ وَرَسُوْلِهٖ وَأَنْفِقُوْا مِمَّا جَعَلَكُمْ
مُسْتَخْلَفِيْنَ فِيْهِ فَالَّذِيْنَ اٰمَنُوْا مِنْكُمْ وَأَنْفَقُوْا
لَهُمْ أَجْرٌ كَبِيْرٌ ۞
وَمَا لَكُمْ لَا تُؤْمِنُوْنَ بِاللهِ وَالرَّسُوْلُ يَدْعُوْكُمْ
لِتُؤْمِنُوْا بِرَبِّكُمْ وَقَدْ أَخَذَ مِيْثَاقَكُمْ إِنْ كُنْتُمْ
مُؤْمِنِيْنَ ۞
هُوَ الَّذِىْ يُنَزِّلُ عَلٰى عَبْدِهٖ اٰيٰتٍ بَيِّنٰتٍ لِّيُخْرِجَكُمْ
مِّنَ الظُّلُمٰتِ إِلَى النُّوْرِ وَإِنَّ اللهَ بِكُمْ لَرَءُوْفٌ
رَّحِيْمٌ ۞
وَمَا لَكُمْ أَلَّا تُنْفِقُوْا فِىْ سَبِيْلِ اللهِ وَلِلّٰهِ مِيْرَاثُ

in the way of God, when the heritage
of the heavens and the earth belongs to God?
Those of you who spent before the victory and fought,
are not equal (to those who did not).
They are higher in position than those
who spent after (the victory) and fought.
To each one God has made the promise of excellence,
for God is aware of all you do.

Who will give a goodly loan to God
which He will double for him, and be
for him a splendid reward?

12. The day you see the believers, men and women,
with their light advancing ahead and to the right of them,
(they will be told:) "There is good news for you this day,
of gardens with rivers flowing by
where you will live for ever."
This will be the great attainment.

13. The day the hypocrites, men and women, will say
to the believers: "Wait for us that we may borrow
a little light from your light,"
they will be told: "Go back, and look for your light."
A wall shall be raised between them in which
there will be a door.
Within it will be benevolence and retribution without.

14. They will call to them: "Were we not with you?"
They will answer: "Certainly;
but then you let yourselves be tempted,
and waited in expectation but were suspicious
and were deceived by vain desires,
till the decree of God came to pass,
and the deceiver duped you in respect of God.

15. So no ransom will be accepted of you on this day,
or of those who refused to believe.
Hell will be your refuge and the only friend —
and how evil a destination!"

16. Has the moment not yet come when the hearts
of believers should be moved by the thought
of God and the truth that has been sent down,
so that they should not be like those
who received the Book before them but whose hearts
were hardened after a lapse of time,
and many of them turned disobedient?

17. Know that God enlivens the earth even after it has died.
We have explained to you clearly Our signs
that you may understand.

18. Surely the men and women who spend in charity
and give a goodly loan to God,
will have it doubled for them
and will receive a generous reward.
19. Those who believe in God and His apostles
are true of word and deed;
and by their Lord are considered
testifiers of the truth.
They have their guerdon and their light.
As for those who do not believe and reject
Our revelations, are the people of Hell.

Know that the life of this world
is only a frolic and mummery, an ornamentation,
boasting and bragging among yourselves,
and lust for multiplying wealth and children.
It is like rain so pleasing
to the cultivator for his vegetation
which sprouts and swells, and then begins to wither,
and you see it turn to yellow
and reduced to chaff.
There is severe punishment in the Hereafter,
but also forgiveness from God, and acceptance.
As for the life of this world,
it is no more than merchandise of vanity.
21. Hasten for the forgiveness of your Lord and Paradise
whose expanse is as wide
as that of the heavens and the earth,
which has been prepared for those who believe
in God and His apostles.
This is the bounty of God which He bestows
on whosoever He please;
and the bounty of God is infinite.
22. There is no calamity that befalls the earth or your own selves
but in accordance with the law (of causation)
before We make it evident.
This is indeed how the law of God works inevitably.
23. Lest you grieve for what you missed,
or rejoice at what you received.
God does not love the egoist and the braggart,
24. Who hold back what they possess
and enjoin stinginess on others.
Whoever turns away (from God, should remember)
that God is self-sufficient, worthy of praise.
25. We have surely sent apostles with clear signs,
and sent with them the Book and the Balance,

فال فما خطبكم ٢٧   الحديد ٥٧

so that men may stand by justice;
and We sent down iron which causes much distress
but also has advantages for men,
so that God may know
who helps Him and His apostles in secret.
Verily God is all-powerful and all-mighty.

We sent Noah and Abraham,
and gave prophethood to their progeny and the Book,
and some of them are well-directed,
but many of them are disobedient.
27. Then in their train We sent Our apostles,
and succeeding them Jesus, son of Mary,
and gave him the Gospel, and put into the hearts
of his followers compassion and kindness.
But they created monasticism
which had not been prescribed for them by Us
except for seeking the pleasure of God;
yet they did not observe it
as it should have been rightly observed.
So We gave those among them who were believers
their reward; but most of them are disobedient.
28. O you who believe, have fear of displeasing God,
and believe in His Prophet.
He will give you twice as much of His bounty
and place a light for you to walk in,
and forgive you, for God is forgiving and kind;
29. So that the people of the Book may know
that they have not the least power over the bounty of God,
and that the bounty is wholly in the hands of God
to give whosoever He please,
for God is the master of infinite bounty.

الْكِتَٰبَ وَالْمِيزَانَ لِيَقُومَ النَّاسُ بِالْقِسْطِ
وَأَنزَلْنَا الْحَدِيدَ فِيهِ بَأْسٌ شَدِيدٌ
وَمَنَٰفِعُ لِلنَّاسِ وَلِيَعْلَمَ اللَّهُ مَن
يَنصُرُهُ وَرُسُلَهُ بِالْغَيْبِ إِنَّ اللَّهَ قَوِيٌّ
عَزِيزٌ ۝
وَلَقَدْ أَرْسَلْنَا نُوحًا وَإِبْرَٰهِيمَ وَجَعَلْنَا فِي
ذُرِّيَّتِهِمَا النُّبُوَّةَ وَالْكِتَٰبَ فَمِنْهُم مُّهْتَدٍ
وَكَثِيرٌ مِّنْهُمْ فَٰسِقُونَ ۝
ثُمَّ قَفَّيْنَا عَلَىٰ ءَاثَٰرِهِم بِرُسُلِنَا وَقَفَّيْنَا بِعِيسَى
ابْنِ مَرْيَمَ وَءَاتَيْنَٰهُ الْإِنجِيلَ ۖ وَجَعَلْنَا فِي
قُلُوبِ الَّذِينَ اتَّبَعُوهُ رَأْفَةً وَرَحْمَةً وَرَهْبَانِيَّةً
ابْتَدَعُوهَا مَا كَتَبْنَٰهَا عَلَيْهِمْ إِلَّا ابْتِغَآءَ
رِضْوَٰنِ اللَّهِ فَمَا رَعَوْهَا حَقَّ رِعَايَتِهَا فَـَٔاتَيْنَا
الَّذِينَ ءَامَنُوا مِنْهُمْ أَجْرَهُمْ وَكَثِيرٌ مِّنْهُمْ
فَٰسِقُونَ ۝
يَٰٓأَيُّهَا الَّذِينَ ءَامَنُوا اتَّقُوا اللَّهَ وَءَامِنُوا بِرَسُولِهِ
يُؤْتِكُمْ كِفْلَيْنِ مِن رَّحْمَتِهِ وَيَجْعَل لَّكُمْ
نُورًا تَمْشُونَ بِهِ وَيَغْفِرْ لَكُمْ وَاللَّهُ غَفُورٌ
رَّحِيمٌ ۝
لِّئَلَّا يَعْلَمَ أَهْلُ الْكِتَٰبِ أَلَّا يَقْدِرُونَ عَلَىٰ
شَيْءٍ مِّن فَضْلِ اللَّهِ وَأَنَّ الْفَضْلَ بِيَدِ
اللَّهِ يُؤْتِيهِ مَن يَشَآءُ وَاللَّهُ ذُو الْفَضْلِ
الْعَظِيمِ ۝

58 The Disputant

Al-Mujādalah: Madani

In the name of Allah, most benevolent, ever-merciful.

بسم الله الرحمن الرحيم ۞

GOD CERTAINLY HEARD what the woman
who argued with you about her husband, said,
and complained to God;
and God heard your interrogation.
Verily God hears all, and sees every thing.

2. Those of you who divorce your wives by calling them
        'mothers,'
cannot (make them) their mothers.
Their mothers are only those who gave birth to them.
They surely utter what is unseemly and a lie.
But God is forbearing and forgiving.

3. Those who call their wives their mothers
then revoke what they had said,
should free a slave before having physical contact (with them).
This is to warn you,
as God is aware of what you do.

4. If one does not have the means (of doing so)
then he should fast for two months continuously
before he has physical contact;
but any one who is unable to do so,
should feed sixty needy persons.
This (is enjoined) so that you
may be faithful to God and His Apostle.
These are the limits set by God.
As for the unbelievers, there is painful punishment for them.

5. Those who oppose God will be disgraced,
as those before them were.
We have sent down very clear signs.
For unbelievers there is a shameful punishment.

6. On the day when God will raise them up together,
He will tell them what they did.
God takes account of it although they forget,
for all things are evident to God.

Have you not considered that God knows
whatever is in the heavens and the earth?
No three persons confer secretly
but He is the fourth among them,
and no five but He is the sixth;
and neither fewer nor more
but He is with them wheresoever they be.
And on the Day of Judgement He will announce
their deeds to them.
Verily God has knowledge of every thing.

8. Have you not considered those
who were forbidden to conspire,
but reverted after a time to what was forbidden them,
and conspired evil, rebellion and disobedience to the Prophet?
Yet when they come to you they greet you with a greeting
even God does not greet you with; and say to themselves,
"Why doesn't God punish us for what we say?"
Hell is sufficient for them, in which they will be burnt:
And what an evil consequence!

9. O you who believe, when you converse privately,
do not talk of iniquity, rebellion, and disobedience to the
        Prophet,
but talk of goodness and piety,
and fear God before whom you will be gathered.

10. Surely scheming is the work of Satan
that he may cause the faithful grief;
but he cannot harm them unless God dispense.
So in God should the believers place their trust.

11. O you who believe, when you are told
to make room in the assemblies, then make room;
God will give you more room to spread.
When you are told to rise, then rise;
God will raise those of you who believe,
and those who have knowledge, in position.
God is aware of what you do.

12. O you who believe, if you confer
with the Prophet in private,
give alms in the name of God before you go to confer.
This is better for you and becoming.
If you do not have the means,
then surely God is forgiving and kind.

13. Are you afraid of giving alms before confering?
Then, if you cannot do this, and God forgives you,
be constant in your devotional obligations
and pay the due share of your wealth for the welfare of others,
and obey God and His Prophet.

God is aware of all you do.

Have you not seen those who have taken
a people who have roused the wrath of God, as friends?
They are neither of you nor of them,
and swear to a lie, and knowingly.
15. God has reserved a severe punishment for them.
Evil indeed are the things they do!
16. They have made their oaths a shield,
and obstruct people from the way of God.
There is shameful punishment for them.
17. Neither their wealth nor children
will avail them against God.
They are the people of Hell,
and there will abide for ever.
18. On the day that God will raise them together,
they will swear before Him as they swear before you,
and imagine they are on the right path.
Is it not they who are liars?
19. Satan has got the better of them.
and made them forget to remember God.
Indeed they belong to Satan's faction.
Will not Satan's faction perish?
20. Surely those who oppose God and His Prophet
will be among the vilest.
21. God has decreed: "I will prevail, I and My apostles."
Verily God is powerful and all-mighty.
22. You will not find those who believe
in God and the Day of Resurrection, loving those
who oppose God and His Prophet, even though they be
their fathers, sons, or brothers or their kin.
God has inscribed on their hearts belief,
and has succoured them with His own grace,
and will admit them to gardens with rivers flowing by,
where they will abide for ever,
God accepting them, and they
happy in the pleasure of God.
They are verily the army of God.
Will not the army of God be victorious?

59 Confrontation

Al-Hashr: Madani

In the name of Allah, most benevolent, ever-merciful.

WHATEVER IS IN the heavens and the earth
sings the praises of God.
He is all-mighty and all-wise.
2. It is He who drove those among the people of the Book
who refused to believe, from their homes
for the first confrontation.
You did not think that they would go away,
and they imagined that their forts would protect them against
   God.
But God came upon them from where they did not suspect,
and filled their hearts with terror,
so that they destroyed their homes with their own hands
(or were destroyed) by the hands of believers.
So take heed, O men of sight!
3. Had God not decreed the expulsion for them
He would have punished them in this world,
and in the next the punishment of Hell would have been theirs.
4. For they had opposed God and His Apostle;
and whosoever opposes God, then God is severe in retribution.
5. The palm trees that you cut down or left standing intact
was by God's dispensation,
so that He might disgrace the transgressors.
6. You did not charge with horse or camel
for whatever (spoils) God gave His Apostle from them.
In any case, God gives authority to His Apostle
over whomsoever He please.
God has power over every thing.
7. Whatever booty God gives to His Apostle
from the people of the cities, is for God and His Apostle,
the near relations, the orphans, the needy and wayfarers,
so that it does not concentrate
in the hands of those who are rich among you.
Accept what the Apostle gives you,
and refrain from what he forbids,

and take heed for yourself and fear God.
Surely God is severe of retribution.
8. The spoils are also for the poor emigrants
who were deprived of their homes and possessions
and are seeking the bounty and protection of God,
and are helping God and His Apostle.
They are the ones who are true of word and deed.
9. Those who came to the city and to faith before them,
love those who take refuge with them,
and do not feel for themselves any need for what is given them,
and give them preference over themselves
even if they are indigent.
Whoever preserves himself from his own greed
will be prosperous.
10. (And the spoils are for) those
who came after them, who say: "O Lord,
forgive us and our brothers who came to faith before us,
and do not put a grudge in our hearts against those who believe.
O Lord, You are compassionate and kind."

Have you never considered the hypocrites?
They say to their brethren among the people of the Book
who do not believe:
"If you are driven out we shall go with you,
and will not listen to any one in what concerns you;
and if there is war against you, we shall aid you."
But God is witness they are liars.
12. If they are driven out, they will not go with them;
and if they are attacked, they will not aid them.
And even if they aided them, they will turn their backs,
then they will not be helped.
13. Surely they have greater fear of you in their hearts
than of God, because they do not understand.
14. They will not fight you in a body
except in fortified cities, or from behind the walls.
Their enmity among themselves is great.
You think they are united, but divided are their hearts.
That is because these people are devoid of sense,
15. Like those who had tasted
the gravity of their actions a little before them.
There is a grievous punishment for them.
16. (They are) like Satan who says to man: "Do not believe;"
and when he becomes a disbeliever, he says:
"I have nothing to do with you.
I fear God, the Lord of all the worlds."
17. Both of them will end up in Hell,

Al-Hashr

where they will abide for ever.
This is the punishment for the wicked.

فَ ذٰلِكَ جَزٰٓؤُا الظّٰلِمِيْنَ ۞

O you who believe, be fearful of God.
Let each soul consider
what it has sent (of good deeds) in advance for the morrow,
and fear God.
Surely God is aware of what you do.

يٰٓاَيُّهَا الَّذِيْنَ اٰمَنُوا اتَّقُوا اللّٰهَ وَلْتَنْظُرْ نَفْسٌ مَّا قَدَّمَتْ لِغَدٍ وَّاتَّقُوا اللّٰهَ اِنَّ اللّٰهَ خَبِيْرٌ بِمَا تَعْمَلُوْنَ ۞

19. And be not like those who have forgotten God,
so that God has made them forget themselves.
Such are the reprobates.

وَلَا تَكُوْنُوْا كَالَّذِيْنَ نَسُوا اللّٰهَ فَاَنْسٰىهُمْ اَنْفُسَهُمْ اُولٰٓئِكَ هُمُ الْفٰسِقُوْنَ ۞

20. Alike are not the inmates of Hell
and the residents of Paradise.
The men of Paradise will be felicitous.

لَا يَسْتَوِيْ اَصْحٰبُ النَّارِ وَاَصْحٰبُ الْجَنَّةِ اَصْحٰبُ الْجَنَّةِ هُمُ الْفَآئِزُوْنَ ۞

21. If We had sent down this Qur'an to a mountain
you would have seen it turn desolate
and split into two for fear of God.
We offer these examples to men
that they may think and reflect.

لَوْ اَنْزَلْنَا هٰذَا الْقُرْاٰنَ عَلٰى جَبَلٍ لَّرَاَيْتَهٗ خَاشِعًا مُّتَصَدِّعًا مِّنْ خَشْيَةِ اللّٰهِ وَتِلْكَ الْاَمْثَالُ نَضْرِبُهَا لِلنَّاسِ لَعَلَّهُمْ يَتَفَكَّرُوْنَ ۞

22. He is God; there is no god but He,
the knower of the unknown and the known.
He is the benevolent, ever-merciful.

هُوَ اللّٰهُ الَّذِيْ لَا اِلٰهَ اِلَّا هُوَ عٰلِمُ الْغَيْبِ وَالشَّهَادَةِ هُوَ الرَّحْمٰنُ الرَّحِيْمُ ۞

23. He is God; there is no god but He,
the King, the Holy, the Preserver,
Protector, Guardian, the Strong, the Powerful, Omnipotent.
Far too exalted is God
for what they associate with Him.

هُوَ اللّٰهُ الَّذِيْ لَا اِلٰهَ اِلَّا هُوَ اَلْمَلِكُ الْقُدُّوْسُ السَّلٰمُ الْمُؤْمِنُ الْمُهَيْمِنُ الْعَزِيْزُ الْجَبَّارُ الْمُتَكَبِّرُ سُبْحٰنَ اللّٰهِ عَمَّا يُشْرِكُوْنَ ۞

24. He is God, the Creator, the Maker, the Fashioner.
His are all the names beautiful.
Whatever is in the heavens and the earth
sings His praises.
He is all-mighty and all-wise.

هُوَ اللّٰهُ الْخَالِقُ الْبَارِئُ الْمُصَوِّرُ لَهُ الْاَسْمَآءُ الْحُسْنٰى يُسَبِّحُ لَهٗ مَا فِى السَّمٰوٰتِ وَالْاَرْضِ فَ وَهُوَ الْعَزِيْزُ الْحَكِيْمُ ۞

60 The Woman Tried

Al-Mumtahanah: Madani

In the name of Allah, most benevolent, ever-merciful.

O YOU WHO BELIEVE, do not take My enemies
and your enemies as friends.
You show kindness to them, but they reject
the true way that has come to you.
They expelled the Prophet and you, for you believe
in God your Lord.
If you have come out to struggle in My cause
having sought My acceptance,
(do not be) friendly with them in secret.
I know what you hide and what you disclose.
Whoever of you does this will have gone astray
from the right path.
2. If they gain ascendancy over you,
they will become your enemies,
and employ their hands and tongues with evil designs,
and wish that you also became disbelievers.
3. Neither your blood relations nor your children
will be of any avail to you on the Day of Resurrection.
He will judge between you,
for God sees what you do.
4. You have an excellent model in Abraham
and those who were with him,
when he said to his people: "We are through with you,
and those you worship other than God.
We reject you. Enmity and hate
have come between you and us for ever,
unless you believe in God the One," —
except for what he said to his father:
"I shall ask forgiveness for you,
but I have no power to prevail with God for you."
"O Lord, we place our trust in You, and turn to You in
        penitence,
and to You is our returning.
5. O Lord, make us not an example of punishment

for infidels, and forgive us, O Lord.
You are all-mighty and all-wise."
6. Those of you who have hope in God and the Last Day
have certainly a good example in them.
But whosoever turns away,
then surely God is above concern, worthy of praise.

It may be that God will create love
between you and your enemies. God is all-powerful,
and God is forgiving, ever-merciful.
8. God does not forbid you from being kind and acting justly
towards those who did not fight over faith with you,
nor expelled you from your homes.
God indeed loves those who are just.
9. He only forbids you from making friends
with those who fought over faith with you and banished you
from your homes, and aided in your exile.
Whoever makes friends with them is a transgressor.
10. O believers, when believing women come over to you
as refugees, then examine them.
God alone is cognisant of their faith.
If you find that they are believers,
do not send them back to unbelievers.
They are not lawful for them,
nor are infidels lawful for believing women.
Give the unbelievers what they have spent on them.
There is no sin if you marry them provided
you give their dowers to them.
Do not retain your (marriage) ties with unbelieving women.
Ask for the return of what you have spent (on them);
and the unbelievers should ask
for the return of what they have spent.
This is the judgement of God.
He judges between you.
God is all-knowing and all-wise.
11. If any of your women go away to the unbelievers,
and you succeed in your turn (and have a chance of getting
    spoils),
then give to those whose wives have so gone away
as much as they had spent on them;
but take heed and fear God in whom you believe.
12. O Prophet, when believing women come to you and swear
    on oath
that they will not associate anything with God,
nor steal, nor fornicate, nor kill their children,
nor accuse others for what they have fabricated themselves,

Al-Mumtahanah

nor disobey you in any rightful thing,
then you should accept their allegiance,
and ask forgiveness of God for them.
Certainly God is forgiving and kind.
13. O you who believe, do not make friends with those
who have suffered the anger of God
by having become despondent
of the life to come like those unbelievers
who are despondent of those who are in the graves.

61 Formations

As-Saff: Madani

سورة الصف مدنية (٦١)

اياتها ... ركوعها

In the name of Allah, most benevolent, ever-merciful.

بِسْمِ اللهِ الرَّحْمٰنِ الرَّحِيمِ ۝

ALL THAT IS in the heavens and the earth
sings the praises of God.
He is all-mighty and all-wise.
2. O you who believe, why do you profess what you do not
practise?
3. Saying what you do not practice is odious to God.
4. Surely God loves those who fight in His cause
in full formations as though they were a compact wall.
5. When Moses said to his people: "O my people,
why do you afflict me
though you know that I have been sent to you by God?"
But when they turned aside
God made their hearts turn farther away;
for God does not show the transgressors the way.
6. And when Jesus, son of Mary, said:
"O children of Israel, I am sent to you by God
to confirm the Torah (sent) before me,
and to give you good tidings of an apostle
who will come after me, whose name is Ahmad (the praised
one)."
Yet when he has come to them with clear proofs,
they say: "This is only magic."
7. Who is more unjust than he
who invents a lie against God when he is called to submit?
God does not show the evil-doers the way.
8. They want to extinguish the light of God
by uttering blasphemies.*
But God wills to perfect His light,
however the unbelievers may dislike it.
9. It is He who sent His Apostle with the guidance
and the true way
to raise it above all faiths,
however the idolaters may dislike it.

سَبَّحَ لِلّٰهِ مَا فِى السَّمٰوٰتِ وَمَا فِى الْاَرْضِ وَهُوَ الْعَزِيزُ الْحَكِيمُ ۝
يٰٓاَيُّهَا الَّذِينَ اٰمَنُوا لِمَ تَقُولُونَ مَا لَا تَفْعَلُونَ ۝
كَبُرَ مَقْتًا عِنْدَ اللهِ اَنْ تَقُولُوا مَا لَا تَفْعَلُونَ ۝
اِنَّ اللهَ يُحِبُّ الَّذِينَ يُقَاتِلُونَ فِى سَبِيلِهِ صَفًّا كَاَنَّهُمْ بُنْيَانٌ مَرْصُوصٌ ۝
وَاِذْ قَالَ مُوسٰى لِقَوْمِهِ يٰقَوْمِ لِمَ تُؤْذُونَنِى وَقَدْ تَعْلَمُونَ اَنِّى رَسُولُ اللهِ اِلَيْكُمْ فَلَمَّا زَاغُوٓا اَزَاغَ اللهُ قُلُوبَهُمْ وَاللهُ لَا يَهْدِى الْقَوْمَ الْفٰسِقِينَ ۝
وَاِذْ قَالَ عِيسَى ابْنُ مَرْيَمَ يٰبَنِىٓ اِسْرَآئِيلَ اِنِّى رَسُولُ اللهِ اِلَيْكُمْ مُصَدِّقًا لِّمَا بَيْنَ يَدَىَّ مِنَ التَّوْرٰىةِ وَمُبَشِّرًا بِرَسُولٍ يَّاْتِى مِنْ بَعْدِى اسْمُهُ اَحْمَدُ فَلَمَّا جَآءَهُمْ بِالْبَيِّنٰتِ قَالُوا هٰذَا سِحْرٌ مُّبِينٌ ۝
وَمَنْ اَظْلَمُ مِمَّنِ افْتَرٰى عَلَى اللهِ الْكَذِبَ وَهُوَ يُدْعٰٓى اِلَى الْاِسْلَامِ وَاللهُ لَا يَهْدِى الْقَوْمَ الظّٰلِمِينَ ۝
يُرِيدُونَ لِيُطْفِئُوا نُورَ اللهِ بِاَفْوَاهِهِمْ وَاللهُ مُتِمُّ نُورِهِ وَلَوْ كَرِهَ الْكٰفِرُونَ ۝
هُوَ الَّذِىٓ اَرْسَلَ رَسُولَهُ بِالْهُدٰى وَدِينِ الْحَقِّ لِيُظْهِرَهُ عَلَى الدِّينِ كُلِّهِ وَلَوْ كَرِهَ الْمُشْرِكُونَ ۝

O you who believe, may I offer you a bargain
which will save you from a painful punishment?
11. Come to believe in God and His Apostle,
and struggle in the cause of God, wealth and soul.
This will be good for you, if you can understand.
12. He will forgive you your sins and admit you
to gardens with rivers flowing by,
and excellent mansions in the garden of Eden.
This will be a great fulfilment.
13. And (He will give you) what is dearest to you —
help from God and early victory.
So give good tidings to those who believe.
14. O you who believe, be helpers of God,
as Jesus, son of Mary, had said to the disciples:
"Who will help me in the way of God?"
and they had answered: "We are the helpers of God."
Then a section among the children of Israel believed,
but a section among them did not.
So We helped those who believed
against their enemies,
and they prevailed over them.

يَـٰٓأَيُّهَا ٱلَّذِينَ ءَامَنُوا هَلْ أَدُلُّكُمْ عَلَىٰ تِجَـٰرَةٍ تُنجِيكُم
مِّنْ عَذَابٍ أَلِيمٍ ۝
تُؤْمِنُونَ بِٱللَّهِ وَرَسُولِهِۦ وَتُجَـٰهِدُونَ فِى سَبِيلِ
ٱللَّهِ بِأَمْوَٰلِكُمْ وَأَنفُسِكُمْ ذَٰلِكُمْ خَيْرٌ لَّكُمْ إِن كُنتُمْ
تَعْلَمُونَ ۝
يَغْفِرْ لَكُمْ ذُنُوبَكُمْ وَيُدْخِلْكُمْ جَنَّـٰتٍ تَجْرِى مِن
تَحْتِهَا ٱلْأَنْهَـٰرُ وَمَسَـٰكِنَ طَيِّبَةً فِى جَنَّـٰتِ عَدْنٍ
ذَٰلِكَ ٱلْفَوْزُ ٱلْعَظِيمُ ۝
وَأُخْرَىٰ تُحِبُّونَهَا نَصْرٌ مِّنَ ٱللَّهِ وَفَتْحٌ قَرِيبٌ
وَبَشِّرِ ٱلْمُؤْمِنِينَ ۝
يَـٰٓأَيُّهَا ٱلَّذِينَ ءَامَنُوا كُونُوٓا أَنصَارَ ٱللَّهِ كَمَا قَالَ
عِيسَى ٱبْنُ مَرْيَمَ لِلْحَوَارِيِّينَ مَنْ أَنصَارِىٓ إِلَى
ٱللَّهِ قَالَ ٱلْحَوَارِيُّونَ نَحْنُ أَنصَارُ ٱللَّهِ فَـَٔامَنَت
طَّآئِفَةٌ مِّنۢ بَنِىٓ إِسْرَٰٓءِيلَ وَكَفَرَت طَّآئِفَةٌ
فَأَيَّدْنَا ٱلَّذِينَ ءَامَنُوا عَلَىٰ عَدُوِّهِمْ فَأَصْبَحُوا
ظَـٰهِرِينَ ۝

----

* Note on v. 8. Literally, by blowing with their mouths.

62 The Congregation

Al-Jumu'ah: Madani

In the name of Allah, most benevolent, ever-merciful.

ALL THAT IS in the heavens and the earth
sings the praises of God
the King, the Holy, Omnipotent, the Wise.
2. It is He who raised among the gentiles
an apostle from amongst them,
who recites His revelations to them,
reforms them and teaches them the Scripture and the Law,
for before him they were clearly in error.
3. And for others among them who have not joined them yet.
He is all-mighty and all-wise.
4. This is the bounty of God, He gives whosoever He please.
God is master of great bounty.
5. The likeness of those who were charged
with (the law of) the Torah which they did not observe,
is that of a donkey who carries a load of books
(oblivious of what they contain).
How wretched the semblance of the people
who deny the words of God!
God does not show an unjust people the way.
6. Say: "O you Jews, if you claim
that you are the favourites of God apart from all men,
then wish for death, if you speak the truth.
7. But they will never wish for death
because of what they had done in the past,
and God knows the sinners well.
8. Tell them: "Death from which you run,
will surely come to you.
You will then be sent back to Him
who knows the unknown and the known,
who will tell you what you used to do.

O you who believe, when the call to prayer is made
on the day of congregation, hasten to remember God,
putting aside your business.

Al-Jumu'ah

484

This is better for you if you can understand.

10. And when the service of prayer is over
spread out in the land, and look for the bounty of God,
and remember God a great deal
that you may prosper.

11. Yet when they see some buying and selling, or some sport,
they go for it, leaving you standing.
Tell them: "What is with God is better
than your sport and commerce.
And God is the best of providers."

خَيْرٌ لَّكُمْ اِنْ كُنْتُمْ تَعْلَمُوْنَ ۞

فَاِذَا قُضِيَتِ الصَّلٰوةُ فَانْتَشِرُوْا فِى الْاَرْضِ
وَابْتَغُوْا مِنْ فَضْلِ اللّٰهِ وَاذْكُرُوا اللّٰهَ كَثِيْرًا
لَّعَلَّكُمْ تُفْلِحُوْنَ ○

وَاِذَا رَاَوْا تِجَارَةً اَوْ لَهْوَا ۨ انْفَضُّوْۤا اِلَيْهَا وَ
تَرَكُوْكَ قَآئِمًا ۭ قُلْ مَا عِنْدَ اللّٰهِ خَيْرٌ مِّنَ
اللَّهْوِ وَمِنَ التِّجَارَةِ ۭ وَاللّٰهُ خَيْرُ الرّٰزِقِيْنَ ۞

63 The Hypocrites

Al-Munāfiqūn: Madani

بِسْمِ اللهِ الرَّحْمٰنِ الرَّحِيْمِ

In the name of Allah, most benevolent, ever-merciful.

WHEN THE HYPOCRITES come to you,
they say: "We affirm that you are the Apostle of God."
God indeed knows you are His Apostle.
God bears witness that the hypocrites are indeed liars.
2. They have made their oaths a shield
in order to obstruct others from the way of God.
It is certainly evil what they do.
3. That is because they came to believe, and then renounced
(their faith).
So their hearts were sealed;
and now they do not understand.
4. Pleasing seem their persons when you look at them;
and when they talk, you listen to their speech.
Yet they are like the wooden panelling of a wall.
They imagine every rebuke to be directed against them.
They are the enemies, beware of them.
May God damn them, how pervert are they!
5. When you tell them: "Come, let the Apostle of God
ask forgiveness for you," they turn their heads,
and you see them turning away with arrogance.
6. Whether you ask forgiveness for them or do not ask,
it is all the same; God will not forgive them.
Surely God does not show a disobedient people the way.
7. They are the ones who say: "Do not spend
on those who are with the Apostle of God
till they break away (from him)."
To God belong the treasures of the heavens and the earth;
but the hypocrites do not understand.
8. They say: "If we now go back to Madina,
the stronger will turn the weaker out."
But power belongs to God, His Apostle and the faithful,
though the hypocrites do not know.

O you who believe, let not your wealth and children

make you negligent of the remembrance of God.
Those who do so will be losers.
10. Spend of what We have given you
before death comes to one of you, when he will say:
"O Lord, why did you not defer my term for a while
that I could give alms and be among the doers of good?"
11. But God does not grant a soul respite
once its term has come to end.
And God is aware of what you do.

فَأُولَٰئِكَ هُمُ الْخَاسِرُونَ ۝
وَأَنفِقُوا مِن مَّا رَزَقْنَاكُم مِّن قَبْلِ أَن يَأْتِيَ
أَحَدَكُمُ الْمَوْتُ فَيَقُولَ رَبِّ لَوْلَا أَخَّرْتَنِي
إِلَىٰ أَجَلٍ قَرِيبٍ فَأَصَّدَّقَ وَأَكُن مِّنَ
الصَّالِحِينَ ۝
وَلَن يُؤَخِّرَ اللَّهُ نَفْسًا إِذَا جَاءَ أَجَلُهَا ۚ وَاللَّهُ
خَبِيرٌ بِمَا تَعْمَلُونَ ۝

64 Exposition

At-Taghābun: Madani

In the name of Allah, most benevolent, ever-merciful.

ALL THAT THERE is in the heavens and the earth
sings the praises of God.
His the sovereignty and His is the praise,
and He has power over every thing.
2. It is He who created you,
though one of you is an infidel
and one of you a believer;
yet God perceives what you do.
3. He created the heavens and the earth with deliberation,
and gave you form, and shaped you well;
and to Him is your returning.
4. He knows what is in the heavens and the earth,
and knows what you hide and what you disclose;
God knows what is in the hearts.
5. Has not the account of those who disbelieved before come
to you,
who tasted the torment of their action,
and for whom is grievous punishment?
6. This was so because their apostles came to them with clear
proofs,
but they said: "What! Can a mortal show us the way?"
And they denied and turned away;
but God was unconcerned.
God is all-sufficient, worthy of praise.
7. The unbelievers claim that they will not be raised again.
Tell them: "Why not? By my Lord,
you will certainly be raised again, and then informed
of what you had done.
That is how the law of God works inevitably."
8. So believe in God, His Apostle and the Light
We have sent down.
God is well aware of what you do.
9. The day He will gather you together on the Day of
Gathering,

At-Taghābun

will be the day of Judgement.
He who believed and did the right,
will have his evil deeds expunged by God and admitted
to gardens with rivers flowing by,
and abide there perpetually.
This will be the great achievement of success.
10. Those who did not believe and denied Our revelations
will be inmates of Hell, where they will abide for ever,
and how evil a journey's end!

No calamity befalls
unless God dispenses.
He guides the heart
of whosoever believes in God;
and God has knowledge of every thing.
12. Obey God and obey His Apostle.
If you turn away,
the duty of the Apostle is to convey the message clearly.
13. God: There is no god but He;
and in God should believers place their trust.
14. O believers, some of your spouses and children
are your enemies, so beware of them!
Yet if you forbear, overlook, and forgive,
God is indeed forgiving and kind.
15. Your wealth and children are surely meant as trial for you:
But with God is the great reward.
16. So fear God as much as you can,
and listen and obey, and spend in charity
for your own good.
He who is saved from his own avarice
will be successful.
17. If you lend a goodly loan to God,
He will double it for you, and forgive you.
God knows the worth of good deeds and is clement,
18. The knower of the unknown and the known,
all-mighty and all-wise.

65 Divorce

At-Talāq: **Madani**

In the name of Allah, most benevolent, ever-merciful.

بِسْمِ اللهِ الرَّحْمٰنِ الرَّحِيمِ۞

O PROPHET WHEN you divorce women,
divorce them at their appointed period,
and calculate that period,
and fear God, your Lord.
Do not expel them from their houses,
nor should they go away themselves,
unless they are openly guilty of adultery.
These are the limits set by God.
Any one who exceeds the limits set by God
sins against his own self.
You never know that God may perchance lead
to a new situation after this.
2. When they have reached their appointed time,
then either keep them lawfully or let them go honourably;
but have two witnesses from among you,
and give truthful evidence for (being acceptable to) God.
This is to warn him who believes in God and the Last Day.
God will furnish a way out for him who fears Him,
3. And provide for him from where he does not reckon.
God is sufficient for him who places his trust in Him.
Certainly God fulfills His purpose.
God has indeed fixed a measure of every thing.
4. As for your women who have lost hope of
      menstruation,
and in case you have a doubt,
the prescribed period (of waiting) for them is three months,
as also for those who have not menstruated yet.
As for those who are pregnant,
their prescribed period is until the delivery of the child.
God will make things easy for him who is mindful of God.
5. This is the commandment of God that is sent down to you.
God will forgive the ills of those who fear Him,
and increase their reward.
6. House the (divorced) women where you live,

يَا أَيُّهَا النَّبِيُّ إِذَا طَلَّقْتُمُ النِّسَآءَ فَطَلِّقُوهُنَّ لِعِدَّتِهِنَّ
وَأَحْصُوا الْعِدَّةَ وَاتَّقُوا اللهَ رَبَّكُمْ لَا تُخْرِجُوهُنَّ
مِنْ بُيُوتِهِنَّ وَلَا يَخْرُجْنَ إِلَّا أَنْ يَأْتِينَ بِفَاحِشَةٍ
مُبَيِّنَةٍ وَتِلْكَ حُدُودُ اللهِ وَمَنْ يَتَعَدَّ حُدُودَ
اللهِ فَقَدْ ظَلَمَ نَفْسَهُ لَا تَدْرِي لَعَلَّ اللهَ
يُحْدِثُ بَعْدَ ذٰلِكَ أَمْرًا۞

فَإِذَا بَلَغْنَ أَجَلَهُنَّ فَأَمْسِكُوهُنَّ بِمَعْرُوفٍ أَوْ
فَارِقُوهُنَّ بِمَعْرُوفٍ وَأَشْهِدُوا ذَوَيْ عَدْلٍ مِنْكُمْ
وَأَقِيمُوا الشَّهَادَةَ لِلّٰهِ ذٰلِكُمْ يُوعَظُ بِهِ مَنْ كَانَ يُؤْمِنُ
بِاللهِ وَالْيَوْمِ الْآخِرِ وَمَنْ يَتَّقِ اللهَ يَجْعَلْ لَهُ مَخْرَجًا۞

وَيَرْزُقْهُ مِنْ حَيْثُ لَا يَحْتَسِبُ وَمَنْ يَتَوَكَّلْ عَلَى
اللهِ فَهُوَ حَسْبُهُ إِنَّ اللهَ بَالِغُ أَمْرِهِ قَدْ جَعَلَ
اللهُ لِكُلِّ شَيْءٍ قَدْرًا۞

وَاللَّائِي يَئِسْنَ مِنَ الْمَحِيضِ مِنْ نِسَآئِكُمْ إِنِ ارْتَبْتُمْ
فَعِدَّتُهُنَّ ثَلَاثَةُ أَشْهُرٍ وَاللَّائِي لَمْ يَحِضْنَ وَأُولَاتُ
الْأَحْمَالِ أَجَلُهُنَّ أَنْ يَضَعْنَ حَمْلَهُنَّ وَمَنْ يَتَّقِ
اللهَ يَجْعَلْ لَهُ مِنْ أَمْرِهِ يُسْرًا۞

ذٰلِكَ أَمْرُ اللهِ أَنْزَلَهُ إِلَيْكُمْ وَمَنْ يَتَّقِ اللهَ يُكَفِّرْ
عَنْهُ سَيِّئَاتِهِ وَيُعْظِمْ لَهُ أَجْرًا۞

أَسْكِنُوهُنَّ مِنْ حَيْثُ سَكَنْتُمْ مِنْ وُجْدِكُمْ وَلَا

according to your means;
but do not harass them
so as to reduce them to straitened circumstances.
If they are pregnant, then spend on them
until they give birth to the child.
And if they suckle the child for you,
then make the due payment to them,
and consult each other appropriately.
But if you find this difficult,
let some other woman suckle (the child) for her.

7. Let the man of means spend according to his means,
and he whose means are limited,
should spend of what God has given him.
God does not burden a soul beyond what He has given him.
God will bring ease after hardship.

How many habitations rebelled against their Lord's
        command
and His apostles;
but We took them to severe task,
and punished them with the harshest punishment.
9. So they tasted the pain of their actions;
and the consequence of their deeds was ruin.
10. God has prepared for them severe punishment.
So, you men of wisdom, and those who believe,
take heed for yourselves and fear God.
God has indeed sent down a Reminder for you,
11. An Apostle who recites before you
the explicating revelations of God
that He may bring those who believe and do the right
out of darkness into light.
Whosoever believes in God and does the right,
He will admit into gardens with rivers flowing by,
where they will abide for ever.
How excellent a provision has God made for him!
12. It is God who created several skies,
and as many earths.
The commandment is sent down among them
so that you may know
that God has power over every thing,
and every thing is held within the knowledge of God.

66 Prohibition

At-Tahrīm: Madani

سُوْرَةُ التَّحْرِيْمِ مَدَنِيَّةٌ ٦٦

اياتها ٢٨ ركوعها

In the name of Allah, most benevolent, ever-merciful.

بِسْمِ اللهِ الرَّحْمٰنِ الرَّحِيْمِ ۞

O PROPHET, WHY should you forbid (yourself)
what God has made lawful for you,
in order to please your wives?
Yet God is forgiving and kind.
2. Surely God has sanctioned the dissolution of your vows.
God is your Lord:
He is all-knowing, and all-wise.
3. When the Prophet told one of his wives
something in confidence and she disclosed it,
God revealed this to him. So he made
some of it known to her, and held back some.
When, however, he informed her about it, she asked:
"Who told you this?"
He said: "I was told this by the All-knowing, All-informed."
4. If both of you two (women) turn to God in penitence
(it would be better). Your hearts have been impaired;
and if you assist one another against him,
then surely his helper is God,
and Gabriel and the righteous believers,
and, besides them, the angels are his helpers.
5. In case he divorces you,
his Lord will give him better wives in return,
who will be modest, true believers,
obedient to God, repentant, observant of prayer and fasting,
both widows and virgins.
6. O you who believe, save yourselves and your families
from the Fire whose fuel is men and rocks,
over which are appointed angels stern and severe as wardens
who never disobey what God commands them,
and do what they are commanded;
7. (And say:) "O you who do not believe,
make no excuses today.
You will be requited only for what you had done."

O you who believe, turn to God truly in repentance.
Perhaps your Lord may forgive your ills
and admit you to gardens with rivers flowing by
on the day when God
will not humiliate the Prophet
and those who believe with him.
Their light will move in front of them and to their right,
and they will say: "O Lord, perfect our light and forgive us.
You have power over every thing."
9. O Prophet, fight the unbelievers and the hypocrites,
and be severe with them.
Their abode is Hell, an evil destination!
10. God advances the example of Noah's wife and the wife of
        Lot
for those who do not believe.
They were married to Our two pious devotees,
but they were unfaithful to them, and even (the apostles)
could not avail them in the least against God;
and it was said to them:
"Enter Hell with those (who are condemned) to enter it."
11. And God presents the example of Pharaoh's wife
for those who believe, when she said:
"O Lord, build me a house in Paradise,
and save me from Pharaoh and his deeds,
and save me from a wicked people;"
12. And of Mary, daughter of 'Imran,
who guarded her chastity,
so that We breathed into her a new life from Us,
and she believed the words of her Lord and His Books,
and was among the obedient.

67 The Kingdom

Al-Mulk: Makki

In the name of Allah, most benevolent, ever-merciful.

BLESSED BE HE who holds the (reins of) Kingship
        in His hand,
who has power over every thing,
2. Who created death and life in order to try you
to see who of you are best of deed.
He is all-mighty and forgiving,
3. Who created the seven skies one above the other.
Do you see any disproportion
in the creations of Ar-Rahman?
Turn your eyes again.
Do you see any fissures?
4. Turn your eyes again and again.
Your gaze turns back dazed and tired.
5. We have adorned the lowest sky with lamps,
and made them missiles against the devils,
for whom We have prepared a torment of most intense fire.
6. For those who believe not in their Lord
there is the punishment of Hell;
and what a wretched destination!
7. When they are cast into it, they will hear
it roar and raging
8. As though it would burst with fury.
Every time a crowd is thrown into it,
its wardens will ask:
"Did no warner come to you?"
9. And they will answer: "Surely; a warner came to us,
but we denied him, and said:
'God did not send down any thing;
you are greatly deluded, in fact.' "
10. They will say: "If we had listened and been wise,
we would not have been among the inmates of Hell."
11. So will they confess their guilt.
Deprived (of all joys) will be the inmates of Hell.
12. For those who fear their Lord in secret

is forgiveness and a great reward.

13. Whether you say a thing secretly or openly,
He knows the innermost secrets of your hearts.

14. Can He who has created not know (His creation)?
He is all-penetrating, all-aware.

It is He who made the earth subservient to you
that you may travel all around it,
and eat of things He has provided;
and to Him will be your resurrection.

16. Are you so unafraid that He who is in Heaven
will not open up the earth to swallow you,
when it will begin to tremble?

17. Or have you become so unafraid
that He who is in Heaven will not send
a violent wind to shower stones at you?
Then you will know the import of My commination!

18. Those before them had also denied.
And how was My punishment then!

19. Do they not see the birds above them
flying wings spread out or folded?
Nothing holds them aloft but God.
All things are within His purview.

20. What other army do you have to help you
apart from Ar-Rahman?
The unbelievers are surely lost in delusion.

21. Who is there to give you food
in case He withholds His bounty?
Yet they persist in rebellion and aversion.

22. Will he find the way who grovels flat on his face,
or he who walks straight on the right path?

23. Say: "It is He who raised you
and gave you ears and eyes and hearts.
How little are the thanks you offer!"

24. Say: "It is He who dispersed you all over the earth,
and to Him you will be gathered."

25. But they say: "When will this promise come to pass,
if what you say is true?"

26. Say: "God alone has knowledge.
My duty is only to warn you clearly."

27. When they realise it has come upon them,
distraught will be the faces of unbelievers.
They will be told: "This is what you asked for."

28. Say: "Just think: If God destroys me and those with me,
or is benevolent to us,
who will then protect the unbelievers

from a painful doom?"

29. Say: "He is the benevolent;
in Him do we believe,
and in Him do we place our trust.
You will now realise who is in manifest error."

30. Say: "Just think: If your water were to dry up in the
   morning
who will bring you water
from a fresh, flowing stream?"

اَلِيْمٍ ۞
قُلْ هُوَ الرَّحْمٰنُ اٰمَنَّا بِهٖ وَعَلَيْهِ تَوَكَّلْنَا ۚ
فَسَتَعْلَمُوْنَ مَنْ هُوَ فِيْ ضَلٰلٍ مُّبِيْنٍ ۞

قُلْ اَرَءَيْتُمْ اِنْ اَصْبَحَ مَآؤُكُمْ غَوْرًا فَمَنْ
يَّأْتِيْكُمْ بِمَآءٍ مَّعِيْنٍ ۞

68 The Pen

Al-Qalam: Makki

In the name of Allah, most benevolent, ever-merciful.

بِسْمِ اللهِ الرَّحْمٰنِ الرَّحِیْمِ ۞

NŪN. I CALL to witness the pen
and what they inscribe,

نٓ وَالْقَلَمِ وَمَا یَسْطُرُوْنَ ۞

2. You are not demented by the grace of your Lord.

مَا أَنْتَ بِنِعْمَةِ رَبِّكَ بِمَجْنُوْنٍ ۞

3. There is surely reward unending for you,

وَإِنَّ لَكَ لَأَجْرًا غَیْرَ مَمْنُوْنٍ ۞

4. For you are verily born of sublime nature.

وَإِنَّكَ لَعَلٰى خُلُقٍ عَظِیْمٍ ۞

5. So you will see, and they will realise,

فَسَتُبْصِرُ وَیُبْصِرُوْنَ ۞

6. Who is distracted.

بِأَیِّیكُمُ الْمَفْتُوْنُ ۞

7. Verily your Lord knows those
who have gone astray from His path,
and He knows those who are guided on the way.

إِنَّ رَبَّكَ هُوَ أَعْلَمُ بِمَنْ ضَلَّ عَنْ سَبِیْلِهِ وَ
هُوَ أَعْلَمُ بِالْمُهْتَدِیْنَ ۞

8. So do not comply with those who deny:

فَلَا تُطِعِ الْمُكَذِّبِیْنَ ۞

9. They only want that you should relent,
so that they may come to terms.

وَدُّوْا لَوْ تُدْهِنُ فَیُدْهِنُوْنَ ۞

10. Do not heed a contemptible swearer,

وَلَا تُطِعْ كُلَّ حَلَّافٍ مَهِیْنٍ ۞

11. Or backbiter, calumniator, slanderer,

هَمَّازٍ مَشَّاءٍ بِنَمِیْمٍ ۞

12. Who hinders men from (doing) good,
the transgressor, the iniquitous,

مَنَّاعٍ لِلْخَیْرِ مُعْتَدٍ أَثِیْمٍ ۞

13. Crude, and above all, mean and infamous,

عُتُلٍّ بَعْدَ ذٰلِكَ زَنِیْمٍ ۞

14. Simply because he possesses wealth and children.

أَنْ كَانَ ذَا مَالٍ وَبَنِیْنَ ۞

15. When you recite Our revelations to him,
he says: "These are fables of long ago."

إِذَا تُتْلٰى عَلَیْهِ اٰیَاتُنَا قَالَ أَسَاطِیْرُ الْأَوَّلِیْنَ ۞

16. We shall brand him on the muzzle.

سَنَسِمُهُ عَلَى الْخُرْطُوْمِ ۞

17. We have tried you as We tried
the owners of the garden
when they vowed to gather the fruits in the morning

إِنَّا بَلَوْنَاهُمْ كَمَا بَلَوْنَا أَصْحَابَ الْجَنَّةِ إِذْ أَقْسَمُوْا
لَیَصْرِمُنَّهَا مُصْبِحِیْنَ ۞

18. But did not add: "If God may please."

وَلَا یَسْتَثْنُوْنَ ۞

19. Then a calamity from your Lord
fell upon it,
but they remained fast asleep.

فَطَافَ عَلَیْهَا طَائِفٌ مِنْ رَبِّكَ وَهُمْ نَائِمُوْنَ ۞

20. So by the morning it seemed as though picked clean.

فَأَصْبَحَتْ كَالصَّرِیْمِ ۞

21. At daybreak they called to each other:

فَتَنَادَوْا مُصْبِحِیْنَ ۞

22. "If you want to gather the fruits,
let us go early to the plantation."

أَنِ اغْدُوْا عَلٰى حَرْثِكُمْ إِنْ كُنْتُمْ صَارِمِیْنَ ۞

23. So they departed, talking in low voices:

فَانْطَلَقُوْا وَهُمْ یَتَخَافَتُوْنَ ۞

24. "Let no needy person come to you within it today."
25. They left early in the morning
bent on this purpose.
26. When they saw (and did not recognise it) they said:
"Surely we have lost the way.
27. No. In fact we have been deprived of it."
28. One who was temperate among them, said:
"Did I not say: 'Why don't you priase God?' "
29. "Glory to our Lord," they said;
"we were really in the wrong."
30. Then they started blaming one another,
31. Saying: "Alas the woe, we were iniquitous.
32. Maybe our Lord will give us better than this.
We turn to our Lord in supplication."
33. Such is Our chastisement;
and the punishment of the Hereafter will be greater,
if only they knew!

For those who fear God
there are pleasure gardens with their Lord.
35. Should We treat those who submit and obey
in the same way as those who are culpable?
36. What has come upon you that you judge in such a wise?
37. Or have you a Book in which you read
38. That you can surely have whatever you choose?
39. Or have you taken a binding promise from Us
which would hold till the Day of Judgement,
that you will get whatever you demand?
40. Ask them: "Which of you is able to vouch for this?"
41. Or have they any partners?
Let them bring their partners then,
if what they say is true.
42. On the day the great calamity befalls,
and they are called to bow in homage,
they will not be able to do so.
43. Lowered will be their eyes,
disgrace overwhelming them.
They had indeed been called to bow in homage
when they were free of blame.
44. So leave those who deny this Discourse to Me.
We shall lead them step by step to (ruin)
in a way they will not know.
45. Yet I will give them respite:
Surely My plan is compact.
46. Do you ask for any compensation from them
that they are burdened with want?

47. Or do they have knowledge of the unknown
which they copy down?
48. So wait with patience for the judgement of your Lord,
and do not be like (Jonah) of the fish
who called (to his Lord) when he was choked with anger.
49. Had it not been for a favour from his Lord
he would have been cast
blame-worthy on a barren plain.
50. Then his Lord chose him and placed him among the
upright.
51. But the unbelievers would like
to stare you out of balance when they hear the warning,
and say: "Surely he is possessed;"
52. Whilst it is no more than reminder
for the people of the world.

69 The Concrete Reality

Al-Ḥāqqah: Makki

تبارك الذى ۲۹؏

(۶۹) سُوْرَةُ الْحَآقَّةِ مَكِّيَّةٌ

اٰيَاتُهَا ٥۲ رُكوُعُهَا

In the name of Allah, most-benevolent, ever-merciful.

بِسْمِ اللهِ الرَّحْمٰنِ الرَّحِيْمِ ۵

THE CONCRETE REALITY.

2. What is the concrete reality?

3. What do you comprehend by the concrete reality?

4. The Thamud and 'Ad denied the consequential calamity.

5. So destroyed were the Thamud
by a storm of thunder and lightning;

6. And the 'Ad were destroyed
by the furious cold blast of roaring wind

7. Which He sent to assail them
for seven nights and eight days running.
You should have seen the people prostrate
like the decayed trunks of date-palm trees.

8. Do you see any trace of them?

9. Then came the Pharaoh, and those before him
whose habitations were overthrown
while they were committing crimes.

10. When they disobeyed the apostle of their Lord
He seized them with an overwhelming punishment.

11. When the water rose in flood,
We bore you in the ark,

12. In order to make it a warning for you,
and that the ear retentive may preserve it.

13. When the single blast is sounded on the trumpet,

14. And the earth and mountains heaved and crushed
to powder with one levelling blow,

15. On that Day will come
what is to come.

16. The sky will cleave asunder on that day
and fall to pieces.

17. On its fringes will be angels, eight of them,
bearing their Lord's throne aloft.

18. You will then be set before Him,
and not one of you will remain unexposed.

19. He who is given his ledger in his right hand,

اَلْحَآقَّةُ ۵

مَا الْحَآقَّةُ ۵

وَمَآ اَدْرٰىكَ مَا الْحَآقَّةُ ۵

كَذَّبَتْ ثَمُوْدُ وَعَادٌ بِالْقَارِعَةِ ۵

فَاَمَّا ثَمُوْدُ فَاُهْلِكُوْا بِالطَّاغِيَةِ ۵

وَاَمَّا عَادٌ فَاُهْلِكُوْا بِرِيْحٍ صَرْصَرٍ عَاتِيَةٍ ۵

سَخَّرَهَا عَلَيْهِمْ سَبْعَ لَيَالٍ وَّثَمٰنِيَةَ اَيَّامٍ حُسُوْمًا فَتَرَى الْقَوْمَ فِيْهَا صَرْعٰى كَاَنَّهُمْ اَعْجَازُ نَخْلٍ خَاوِيَةٍ ۵

فَهَلْ تَرٰى لَهُمْ مِّنْ بَاقِيَةٍ ۵

وَجَآءَ فِرْعَوْنُ وَمَنْ قَبْلَهُ وَالْمُؤْتَفِكٰتُ بِالْخَاطِئَةِ ۵

فَعَصَوْا رَسُوْلَ رَبِّهِمْ فَاَخَذَهُمْ اَخْذَةً رَّابِيَةً ۵

اِنَّا لَمَّا طَغَا الْمَآءُ حَمَلْنٰكُمْ فِى الْجَارِيَةِ ۵

لِنَجْعَلَهَا لَكُمْ تَذْكِرَةً وَّتَعِيَهَآ اُذُنٌ وَّاعِيَةٌ ۵

فَاِذَا نُفِخَ فِى الصُّوْرِ نَفْخَةٌ وَّاحِدَةٌ ۵

وَّحُمِلَتِ الْاَرْضُ وَالْجِبَالُ فَدُكَّتَا دَكَّةً وَّاحِدَةً ۵

فَيَوْمَئِذٍ وَّقَعَتِ الْوَاقِعَةُ ۵

وَانْشَقَّتِ السَّمَآءُ فَهِىَ يَوْمَئِذٍ وَّاهِيَةٌ ۵

وَّالْمَلَكُ عَلٰى اَرْجَآئِهَا وَيَحْمِلُ عَرْشَ رَبِّكَ فَوْقَهُمْ يَوْمَئِذٍ ثَمٰنِيَةٌ ۵

يَوْمَئِذٍ تُعْرَضُوْنَ لَا تَخْفٰى مِنْكُمْ خَافِيَةٌ ۵

فَاَمَّا مَنْ اُوْتِيَ كِتٰبَهُ بِيَمِيْنِهِ فَيَقُوْلُ هَآؤُمُ اقْرَءُوْا كِتٰبِيَهْ ۵

will say: "Here, read my ledger.

20. I was certain I'll be given my account."

21. So he shall have an agreeable life

22. In high empyrean

23. With fruits hanging low within reach,

24. (And told:) "Eat and drink to your fill
as reward for (good) deeds you had done
in days of yore."

25. But whosoever gets his ledger in his left hand,
will say: "Would that I were never given my ledger,

26. And not known my account!

27. I wish death had put an end to me.

28. Of no use was even my wealth.

29. Vanished has my power from me."

30. "Seize him and manacle him,

31. Then cast him to be burnt in Hell;

32. And string him to a chain seventy cubits long.

33. He did not believe in God the supreme,

34. Nor urged others to feed the poor.

35. That is why he has no friend today,

36. Nor food other than suppuration

37. Which none but the hellish eat."

So, I call to witness what you see

39. And what you do not see,

40. That this is indeed the word of the noble Messenger,

41. And not the word of a poet.
How little is it that you believe!

42. Nor is it the word of a soothsayer.
Little is it that you reflect!

43. It has been sent down by the Lord of all the worlds.

44. Had he attributed falsely any words to Us,

45. We would have seized him by his right hand,

46. Then cut off his aorta,

47. And not one of you would have been able to stop (Us).

48. It is really a reminder for those who fear God
and follow the straight path.

49. We certainly know
that some among you do deny it.

50. It is surely the nemesis of unbelievers.

51. And He, He is indeed the ultimate Reality.

52. So glorify your Lord, the most supreme.

70 The Steps

Al-Ma'ārij: Makki

In the name of Allah, most-benevolent, ever-merciful.

بِسْمِ اللهِ الرَّحْمٰنِ الرَّحِيْمِ ۞

AN INQUIRER ASKED for the affliction that is to come
2. Upon the infidels — which none would be able to repel —
3. From God, the Lord of the steps (of progression),*
4. To whom the angels and the soul
take a day to ascend, whose length
is fifty thousand years.
5. So persevere with becoming patience.
6. They surely take it to be far away,
7. But We see it very near.
8. The day the sky becomes like molten brass,
9. The mountains like the tufts of (carded) wool,
10. And no friend inquires after friend
11. Though within sight of one another.
The sinner would like to ransom himself
from the torment of that Day
by offering his sons,
12. His wife and his brother,
13. And his family who had stood by him,
14. And all those who are on the earth,
to save himself.
15. But never. It is pure white flame
16. That would skin the scalp.
17. It will summon whoever turns his back and flees,
18. Who amasses and then hoards.
19. Surely man is greedy by nature.
20. If evil befalls him he is perturbed;
21. If good comes to him he holds back his hand,
22. Except those who closely follow (the Book of God),
23. Who persevere in devotion,
24. In whose wealth a due share is included
25. For the needy and those dispossessed,
26. And those who believe in the Day of Judgement,
27. And those who fear the punishment of their Lord, —
28. Surely no one can be secure from the punishment of his

سَأَلَ سَائِلٌ بِعَذَابٍ وَّاقِعٍ ۞
لِّلْكٰفِرِيْنَ لَيْسَ لَهٗ دَافِعٌ ۞
مِّنَ اللهِ ذِي الْمَعَارِجِ ۞
تَعْرُجُ الْمَلٰئِكَةُ وَالرُّوْحُ اِلَيْهِ فِيْ يَوْمٍ كَانَ
مِقْدَارُهٗ خَمْسِيْنَ اَلْفَ سَنَةٍ ۞
فَاصْبِرْ صَبْرًا جَمِيْلًا ۞
اِنَّهُمْ يَرَوْنَهٗ بَعِيْدًا ۞ وَّنَرٰهُ قَرِيْبًا ۞
يَوْمَ تَكُوْنُ السَّمَآءُ كَالْمُهْلِ ۞
وَتَكُوْنُ الْجِبَالُ كَالْعِهْنِ ۞
وَلَا يَسْئَلُ حَمِيْمٌ حَمِيْمًا ۞
يُبَصَّرُوْنَهُمْ يَوَدُّ الْمُجْرِمُ لَوْ يَفْتَدِيْ مِنْ عَذَابِ
يَوْمِئِذٍ بِبَنِيْهِ ۞ وَصَاحِبَتِهٖ وَاَخِيْهِ ۞
وَفَصِيْلَتِهِ الَّتِيْ تُؤْوِيْهِ ۞
وَمَنْ فِي الْاَرْضِ جَمِيْعًا ثُمَّ يُنْجِيْهِ ۞
كَلَّا ۭ اِنَّهَا لَظٰى ۞ نَزَّاعَةً لِّلشَّوٰى ۞
تَدْعُوْا مَنْ اَدْبَرَ وَتَوَلّٰى ۞ وَجَمَعَ فَاَوْعٰى ۞
اِنَّ الْاِنْسَانَ خُلِقَ هَلُوْعًا ۞
اِذَا مَسَّهُ الشَّرُّ جَزُوْعًا ۞
وَّاِذَا مَسَّهُ الْخَيْرُ مَنُوْعًا ۞ اِلَّا الْمُصَلِّيْنَ ۞
الَّذِيْنَ هُمْ عَلٰى صَلَاتِهِمْ دَائِمُوْنَ ۞
وَالَّذِيْنَ فِيْ اَمْوَالِهِمْ حَقٌّ مَّعْلُوْمٌ ۞
لِّلسَّائِلِ وَالْمَحْرُوْمِ ۞
وَالَّذِيْنَ يُصَدِّقُوْنَ بِيَوْمِ الدِّيْنِ ۞
وَالَّذِيْنَ هُمْ مِّنْ عَذَابِ رَبِّهِمْ مُّشْفِقُوْنَ ۞
اِنَّ عَذَابَ رَبِّهِمْ غَيْرُ مَأْمُوْنٍ ۞

Lord, —

29. And those who guard their sex
except from their wives and women slaves of old

30. Are free of blame,

31. But those who seek more than this
will be transgressors;

32. And those who fulfil their trusts and covenants,

33. Who uphold their testimonies,

34. And those who are mindful
of their moral obligations.

35. They will live in gardens with honour.

What is the matter with unbelievers that they stare at
you
with fixed gazes and hasten towards you

37. In crowds, right and left?

38. Does every one of them wish
to enter the garden of tranquility?

39. Never so. We have created them
from what they know.

40. So I swear by the Lord of the Easts and the Wests
that We are certainly able

41. To bring better people than they in their place;
and they will not be able to thwart Us.

42. So leave them to their vain disputes and amusement
till they meet their day (of reckoning) promised them,

43. The day when they will come out of their graves
in all haste as though rushing to their altars,

44. Eyes lowered, shame attending.
That is the day they have been promised!

---

* Note on v. 3. *al-ma'arij*. Though literally 'Lord of steps;' metonymically it means the Lord of progression, one who raises things from a starting point to their perfection. See 32:5 where it has been used in its verbal form *ya'ruj* to signify this evolution, thus affirming the dynamic principle of the human psyche — progression and ascension, which, spiritually, would imply nearness, or drawing close, to the Supreme Being.

71 Noah

Nūh: Makki

سورة نوح ٢٩

In the name of Allah, most-benevolent, ever-merciful.

WE SENT NOAH to his people to warn them
before the painful punishment came upon them.
2. He said: "O my people, I warn you clearly
3. That you should worship God and fear Him,
and follow me
4. That He may forgive some of your sins
and prolong your term till an appointed time.
Surely when God's appointed time is come
it will not be put off, if only you knew!
5. He said: "O Lord, I called my people night and day,
6. But the more I called they only ran the farther away.
7. And every time I called them
that You may forgive them,
they thrust their fingers into their ears,
and covered themselves with their garments,
and became wayward, and behaved with downright insolence.
8. Then I called them loudly and more openly,
9. And declared to them in public and in private,
10. And I told them: 'Ask your Lord to forgive you.
He is verily forgiving.
11. He will send you abundant rain from the sky,
12. And will give you increase of wealth and sons,
and give you gardens and springs of water.
13. What has come upon you
that you do not fear the majesty of God,
14. Knowing that He has created you by various stages?
15. Do you not see how God has fashioned
seven skies one above the other,
16. And has placed the moon therein, an illumination,
and has placed the sun, a lighted lamp?
17. God produced you from the earth like a vegetable growth; *
18. He will then return you back to it,
and bring you out again.
19. God has made the earth for you a spreading,

20. So that you may walk upon its spacious paths.'

But they did not listen to me," Noah said,
"and followed him whose wealth and children
only added to his ruin.
22. And they contrived a plot of great magnitude,
23. And said: 'Do not abandon your gods,
and do not abandon Wadda or Suwa',
or Yaghuth, Ya'uq or Nasr.'
24. And they misled many.
So do not give the evil-doers increase but in error."
25. They were drowned because of their habitual sinfulness,
and sent to Hell, and did not find any helper other than God.
26. Noah said: "O Lord, do not leave
a single habitation of unbelievers on the earth.
27. If you leave them, they will lead Your creatures astray,
and beget but iniquitous and ungrateful offspring.
28. O Lord, forgive me, my parents, and any one
who enters my house as a believer,
and all believing men and women,
and do not give the evil-doers increase save in ruin."

لِّتَسْلُكُوا مِنْهَا سُبُلًا فِجَاجًا ۝
قَالَ نُوحٌ رَّبِّ إِنَّهُمْ عَصَوْنِي وَاتَّبَعُوا مَن لَّمْ
يَزِدْهُ مَالُهُ وَوَلَدُهُ إِلَّا خَسَارًا ۝
وَمَكَرُوا مَكْرًا كُبَّارًا ۝
وَقَالُوا لَا تَذَرُنَّ ءَالِهَتَكُمْ وَلَا تَذَرُنَّ وَدًّا وَلَا
سُوَاعًا وَلَا يَغُوثَ وَيَعُوقَ وَنَسْرًا ۝
وَقَدْ أَضَلُّوا كَثِيرًا وَلَا تَزِدِ الظَّالِمِينَ إِلَّا ضَلَالًا ۝
مِّمَّا خَطِيئَاتِهِمْ أُغْرِقُوا فَأُدْخِلُوا نَارًا فَلَمْ يَجِدُوا
لَهُم مِّن دُونِ اللَّهِ أَنصَارًا ۝
وَقَالَ نُوحٌ رَّبِّ لَا تَذَرْ عَلَى الْأَرْضِ مِنَ الْكَافِرِينَ
دَيَّارًا ۝
إِنَّكَ إِن تَذَرْهُمْ يُضِلُّوا عِبَادَكَ وَلَا يَلِدُوا
إِلَّا فَاجِرًا كَفَّارًا ۝
رَّبِّ اغْفِرْ لِي وَلِوَالِدَيَّ وَلِمَن دَخَلَ بَيْتِيَ
مُؤْمِنًا وَلِلْمُؤْمِنِينَ وَالْمُؤْمِنَاتِ وَلَا تَزِدِ
الظَّالِمِينَ إِلَّا تَبَارًا ۝

---

* Note on v. 17. Read with verses 30:54, 4:1, 6:2, 7:26, 3:59, 22:5 etc., this would confirm matter to be the basic element in man's make-up. He is, however, distinguished from the rest of creation by having something supernal in his being. Having fashioned his body from fermented clay (15:28) God breathed into him of His spirit (15:29), thus giving him the participating energy with nature. Yet the metaphorical use of words as 'clay' with its suggestion of matter, and 'spirit' with that of breath, expresses an inner and deeper transcendental reality, as words are used for thoughts, thought implying a higher order above transcending all limitations. The conceptual phrases, thus, acquire primary authority, the elemental process of physical formation and reproductive processes of conception and growth being common to all animals, as germination is to vegetables, man alone possessing the discriminating quality of the divine spirit. The primary concept that is thus established through the metonymy of words is the omnipotence of God.

72 The Jinns

Al-Jinn: Makki

In the name of Allah, most benevolent, ever-merciful.

SAY: "I HAVE been informed that
a number of jinns had listened,
then said: 'We have heard the wondrous Qur'an,
2. Which guides to the right path;
and we have come to believe in it,
and will not associate any one with our Lord.
3. Exalted is the glory of our Lord;
He has neither wife nor son.
4. Certainly the foolish among us say preposterous things of
        God.
5. We had in fact thought that men and jinns
would never speak a lie about God,
6. But some men used to seek refuge with some jinns,
and this increased their waywardness;
7. So they began to think, even as you do,
that God would not resurrect any one.
8. We sought to pry into the secrets of the heavens,
but found it full of fierce guards
and shooting flames.
9. We sat in observatories to listen;
but any one who listened found
a shooting star in wait for him.
10. We do not know if this means ill
for the dwellers of the earth,
or their Lord wishes guidance for them.
11. For some of us are upright
and some otherwise:
Surely we follow different ways.
12. We realised that we could not weaken the power of God
        on earth,
nor outpace Him by running away.
13. So when we heard the guidance we believed in it;
and he who believes in his Lord
will neither fear loss nor force.

Al-Jinn

506

14. Some of us have come to submission,
and some of us are iniquitous.' "
Those who have submitted
have taken the right course;
15. But those who are iniquitous
will be fuel for Hell.
16. (Say): "If they keep to the right path
We shall give them water in abundance to drink
17. In order to try them through it.
But whoever turns away from the remembrance of his Lord,
will be given increasing torment by Him."
18. All places of worship are for God;
so do not invoke any one with God.
19. When the devotee of God stood up
to invoke Him (the jinns) crowded upon him (to listen).

Say: "I call on my Lord alone
and I do not associate any one with Him."
21. Say: "Neither is your loss within my power
nor bringing you to guidance."
22. Say: "No one can save me from God,
nor can I find a place of refuge apart from Him,
23. Unless I convey from God and deliver His message."
For those who disobey God and His Apostle
is the fire of Hell, where they will abide for ever;
24. Until they see what they are promised,
when they will understand
who is weaker in aid and poorer in numbers.
25. Say: "I do not know if what is promised you is near,
or if my Lord prolongs its term.
26. He is the knower of the Unknown,
and He does not divulge His secret to any one
27. Other than an apostle He has chosen,
when He makes a sentinel walk in front of him
and a sentinel behind,
28. So that He may know if they have delivered
their Lord's messages.
He comprehends all that has been given them,
and keeps count of every thing.

73 The Enwrapped

Al-Muzzammil: Makki

In the name of Allah, most benevolent, ever-merciful.

O YOU ENWRAPPED in the cloak (of prophethood),

2. Keep watch all the night except some,

3. A half of it or a little less

4. Or a little more, and recite the Qur'an
slowly and distinctly.

5. We shall soon entrust to you a message
heavy (with solemnity).

6. Surely in the watches of the night
the soul is most receptive
and words more telling.

7. Indeed during the day
you have a long schedule of occupations.

8. But recite the name of your Lord
withdrawing yourself from everything,
devoting yourself exclusively to Him.

9. He is the Lord of the East and the West.
There is no god but He.
So take Him alone as your protector.

10. Bear with patience what they say,
and gracefully come away from them.

11. Leave those to Me who deny, —
the lovers of ease and comfort; —
and bear with them for a while.

12. Verily We shall have fetters with Us,
and a roaring furnace,

13. And food that will stick in the throat,
and painful torment

14. On the day the earth and mountains will rock violently,
and the mountains turn to a heap of poured-out sand.

15. We have sent an Apostle to you
as a witness against you, as We had sent
an apostle to the Pharaoh.

16. But the Pharaoh disobeyed the apostle;
so We seized him with a grievous punishment.

17. How then, if you disbelieve,
will you preserve yourselves on the day
which will even turn the children hoary?
18. The heavens itself will be rent asunder (on that day).
His promise is bound to be fulfilled.
19. Verily this is a reminder.
So let him who desires take the way to his Lord.

Your Lord surely knows that you are occupied
with your devotions for nearly two-thirds of the night,
or half the night, or one-third of it,
as do many others with you.
Yet God prescribes the measure of night and day.
He knows you cannot calculate it,
and so turns to you in benevolence.
So recite as much of the Qur'an as you can easily.
He knows some among you will be sick,
and some will be travelling over the earth
in search of the bounty of God,
and some fighting in the way of God.
So read as much from it as you can easily,
and be firm in devotion, pay the zakat,
and lend a goodly loan to God.
And what you send for yourself of the good,
you will find it with God better and greater in reward.
So ask for God's forgiveness.
Indeed God is forgiving and kind.

74 The Enfolded

Al-Muddaththir: Makki

In the name of Allah, most benevolent, ever-merciful.

O YOU, ENFOLDED in your mantle (of reform),

2. Arise and warn,

3. Glorify your Lord,

4. Purify your inner self,

5. And banish all trepidation.

6. Do not bestow favours
in expectation of return,

7. And persevere
in the way of your Lord.

8. For when the trumpet blows

9. It will be a day of distress,

10. Dolorous for the unbelievers.

11. Leave him to Me whom I
created alone,

12. And gave him abundant wealth

13. And sons always present by his side,

14. And made things easy for them.

15. Yet he wants
that I should give him more.

16. Never.
He is refractory of Our signs.

17. I shall inflict on him hardship,

18. For he had thought and calculated.

19. May he be accursed,
how he planned!

20. May he then be accursed,
how he plotted!

21. Then he looked around,

22. And frowned and puckered his brow,

23. Then turned his back
and waxed proud,

24. And said: "This is nothing
but the magic of old,

25. Nothing more than the speech of a man!"

Al-Muddaththir

26. I will cast him into the fire of Hell.
27. What do you think Hell-fire is?
28. It leaves nothing, nor does it spare;
29. It glows and burns the skin.
30. Over it are nineteen (guards).
31. We have not appointed any one but angels
as keepers of Hell, and their number that We have fixed
is to make it a means of contention for disbelievers,
so that those who were given the Book may be certain,
and the faith of the believers may have greater increase,
and the people of the Book and believers may not be deceived,
and the sceptics and infidels may say:
"What does God mean by this parable?"
That is how God leads whosoever He will astray, and
guides whosoever He will.
None knows the armies of your Lord save Himself.
This is no more than reminder for mankind.

I say the truth, and call the moon to witness,
33. And the night when on the wane,
34. The morning when it is unveiled,
35. That (Hell) is surely one of the greater (signs),
36. A warning for people —
37. Whoever of you desires to progress or lag behind.
38. Every soul is pledged to what it does,
39. Except those of the right hand
40. Sitting in the gardens, asking
41. Of evil doers:
42. "What was it that brought you to Hell?"
43. They will answer: "We did not fulfil
our devotional obligations,
44. And did not feed the needy,
45. And plunged into useless things with those who were
obstinate,
46. And rejected the Day of Judgement as a lie
47. Until the certainty (of death) had come upon us."
48. So, the intercession of intercessors will not avail them.
49. Why then do they turn away from the admonition
50. As though they were frightened asses
51. Fleeing from a lion?
52. In fact every one of them wants
to be given open books (like the prophets).
53. By no means. In fact they do not fear the Hereafter.
54. Never so, as this is a reminder.
55. Let him then who heeds remember it.
56. But they will not remember except as God wills:
He is worthy to be feared, and He is worthy of forgiving

75 The Resurrection

Al-Qiyāmah: Makki

تبرك الذى ٢٩

(٧٥) سورة القيمة مكية

اياتها ٤٠ ركوعها ٢

In the name of Allah, most-benevolent, ever-merciful.

I CALL TO WITNESS the Day of Resurrection,
2. And I call the reprehensive soul to witness:
3. Does man think
We shall not put his bones together?
4. Surely We are able to re-form even his finger-tips.
5. Yet man is sceptical
of what is right before him.
6. He asks: "When will the Day of Resurrection be?"
7. Yet when the eyes are dazzled,
8. The moon eclipsed,
9. And the sun and moon are conjoined,
10. That day man will say:
"Where can I find escape?"
11. Never so, for there will be no escape.
12. With your Lord alone
will be the retreat on that day.
13. Then man will be told
what he had sent ahead (of good)
and what he had left behind.
14. In fact man is a witness against himself,
15. Whatever the excuses he may offer.
16. Do not forestall (the revelation
before its completion) by acting in haste.
17. Surely its collection and recitation
are Our responsibility.
18. So, as We recite it, follow its reading.
19. The exposition of its meaning surely rests on Us.
20. But no. You love this transient life,
21. And neglect the Hereafter.
22. How many faces will be refulgent on that Day,
23. Waiting for their Lord.
24. And how many faces on that Day will be woe-begone
25. Fearing that a great disaster
is going to befall them.

لَآ اُقْسِمُ بِيَوْمِ الْقِيٰمَةِ ۙ

وَلَآ اُقْسِمُ بِالنَّفْسِ اللَّوَّامَةِ ؕ

اَيَحْسَبُ الْاِنْسَانُ اَلَّنْ نَّجْمَعَ عِظَامَهٗ ؕ

بَلٰى قٰدِرِيْنَ عَلٰٓى اَنْ نُّسَوِّيَ بَنَانَهٗ

بَلْ يُرِيْدُ الْاِنْسَانُ لِيَفْجُرَ اَمَامَهٗ ۚ

يَسْئَلُ اَيَّانَ يَوْمُ الْقِيٰمَةِ ؕ

فَاِذَا بَرِقَ الْبَصَرُ ۙ

وَخَسَفَ الْقَمَرُ ۙ

وَجُمِعَ الشَّمْسُ وَالْقَمَرُ ۙ

يَقُوْلُ الْاِنْسَانُ يَوْمَئِذٍ اَيْنَ الْمَفَرُّ ۚ

كَلَّا لَا وَزَرَ ؕ

اِلٰى رَبِّكَ يَوْمَئِذِ ِالْمُسْتَقَرُّ ؕ

يُنَبَّؤُا الْاِنْسَانُ يَوْمَئِذٍ بِمَا قَدَّمَ وَاَخَّرَ ؕ

بَلِ الْاِنْسَانُ عَلٰى نَفْسِهٖ بَصِيْرَةٌ ۙ

وَّلَوْ اَلْقٰى مَعَاذِيْرَهٗ ؕ

لَا تُحَرِّكْ بِهٖ لِسَانَكَ لِتَعْجَلَ بِهٖ ؕ

اِنَّ عَلَيْنَا جَمْعَهٗ وَقُرْاٰنَهٗ ۚ

فَاِذَا قَرَاْنٰهُ فَاتَّبِعْ قُرْاٰنَهٗ ۚ

ثُمَّ اِنَّ عَلَيْنَا بَيَانَهٗ ؕ

كَلَّا بَلْ تُحِبُّوْنَ الْعَاجِلَةَ ۙ

وَتَذَرُوْنَ الْاٰخِرَةَ ؕ

وُجُوْهٌ يَّوْمَئِذٍ نَّاضِرَةٌ ۙ

اِلٰى رَبِّهَا نَاظِرَةٌ ۚ

وَوُجُوْهٌ يَّوْمَئِذٍ بَاسِرَةٌ ۙ

تَظُنُّ اَنْ يُّفْعَلَ بِهَا فَاقِرَةٌ ؕ

Al-Qiyāmah 512

26. Never so, for when
life withdraws into the clavicula,

كَلَّا إِذَا بَلَغَتِ التَّرَاقِىَ ۞

27. And it is asked:

وَقِيلَ مَنْ رَاقٍ ۞

"Is there any reciter of charms and amulets?"

وَظَنَّ أَنَّهُ الْفِرَاقُ ۞

28. He will then realise it is the parting,

وَالْتَفَّتِ السَّاقُ بِالسَّاقِ ۞

29. And anguish will be heaped upon anguish:

إِلَىٰ رَبِّكَ يَوْمَئِذٍ الْمَسَاقُ ۞

30. To your Lord then will be the driving.

فَلَا صَدَّقَ وَلَا صَلَّىٰ ۞

For he neither believed nor prayed,

وَلَٰكِن كَذَّبَ وَتَوَلَّىٰ ۞

32. But only disavowed and turned away;

ثُمَّ ذَهَبَ إِلَىٰ أَهْلِهِ يَتَمَطَّىٰ ۞

33. Then he strutted back to his people.

أَوْلَىٰ لَكَ فَأَوْلَىٰ ۞

34. Alas the woe for you, alas!

ثُمَّ أَوْلَىٰ لَكَ فَأَوْلَىٰ ۞

35. Alas, the woe for you!

36. Does man think that he will be left
alone to himself, free?

أَيَحْسَبُ الْإِنسَانُ أَن يُتْرَكَ سُدًى ۞

37. Was he not an emitted drop of semen,

أَلَمْ يَكُ نُطْفَةً مِّن مَّنِىٍّ يُمْنَىٰ ۞

38. Then formed into an embryo?
Then He fashioned, shaped
and proportioned

ثُمَّ كَانَ عَلَقَةً فَخَلَقَ فَسَوَّىٰ ۞

39. And assigned it sexes, male and female.*

فَجَعَلَ مِنْهُ الزَّوْجَيْنِ الذَّكَرَ وَالْأُنثَىٰ ۞

40. Cannot such as He
bring the dead to life?

أَلَيْسَ ذَٰلِكَ بِقَادِرٍ عَلَىٰ أَن يُحْيِىَ الْمَوْتَىٰ ۞

---

* That is, after the formation of the foetus, when the sex can be determined.

76 Time

Ad-Dahr: Madani

(٧٦) سورة الدهر مكيّة

اياتها ٣١ ركوعها ٢

In the name of Allah, most benevolent, ever-merciful.

بِسْمِ اللهِ الرَّحْمٰنِ الرَّحِيْمِ ۟

WAS THERE NOT a time in the life of man
when he was not even a mentionable thing?
2. Verily We created man from a sperm yoked (to the ovum)*
to bring out his real substance,
then gave him hearing and sight.
3. We surely showed him the way
that he may either be grateful or deny.
4. We have prepared for unbelievers
chains and collars and a blazing fire.
5. Surely the devotees will drink cups
flavoured with palm blossoms
6. From a spring of which
the votaries of God will drink
and make it flow in abundance.
7. Those who fulfil their vows and fear
the Day whose evil shall be diffused far and wide,
8. And feed the needy for the love of Him,
and the orphans and the captives,
9. (Saying): "We feed you for the sake of God,
desiring neither recompense nor thanks.
10. We fear the dismal day calamitous from our Lord."
11. So God will protect them from the evil of that day,
and grant them happiness and joy,
12. And reward them for their perseverence
Paradise and silken robes,
13. Where they will recline
on couches feeling neither heat of the sun
nor intense cold.
14. The shadows will bend over them,
and low will hang the clusters of grapes.
15. Passed round will be silver flagons
and goblets made of glass,
16. And crystal clear bottles of silver,
of which they will determine the measure themselves.

17. There will they drink a cup flavoured with ginger
18. From a spring by the name of Ever-flowing–Salsabil.
19. And boys of everlasting youth will go about
attending them.
Looking at them you would think
that they were pearls dispersed.
20. When you look around, you will see
delights and great dominion.
21. On their bodies will be garments
of the finest green silk and brocade,
and they will be adorned with bracelets of silver;
and their Lord will give them a purest draught to drink.
22. "This in truth is your recompense,
and acceptance of your endeavours."

We have revealed the Qur'an to you gradually;
24. So wait for your Lord's command, and do not follow
any sinner or disbeliever among them.
25. Meditate upon the name of your Lord
morning and evening;
26. And bow in homage part of the night,
and glorify Him far into the night.
27. Surely men love what hastes away
and forget the grievous day (ahead).
28. We created them and fixed their bones and joints;
and We could replace them when We like
with others like them.
29. This surely is a reminder;
Therefore whosoever desires
may take the way to his Lord.
30. But you will not desire except as God wills.
Verily He is all-knowing and all-wise.
31. He admits whosoever He will
to His benevolence.
But for the evil-doers
He has prepared a painful punishment.

---

* Note on v. 2. The first step in human reproduction is the forming of the zygot by the yoking of the sperm to the ovum, the union of two gametes. The next step is the formation of the embryo. In the Arabic text *amshaj* (root MSHJ) means mixed, joined or yoked. See 22:5 and 25:53-54, and notes on pp. 96 and 311 to get the full picture. This has generally been translated as 'mingled fluids.'

77 The Emissaries

Al-Mursalāt: Makki

In the name of Allah, most benevolent, ever-merciful.

بسم الله الرحمن الرحيم ۝

I CALL TO WITNESS those who are sent
consecutively,

والمرسلات عرفا ۝

2. And those that strike
violently,

فالعاصفات عصفا ۝

3. And those that revive
by quickening,

والناشرات نشرا ۝

4. And those that distinguish
distinctly,

فالفارقات فرقا ۝

5. And those that bring down the Reminder

فالملقيات ذكرا ۝

6. To end all argument
or to warn.

عذرا او نذرا ۝

7. What is promised will surely come to pass.

انما توعدون لواقع ۝

8. When the stars are obliterated,

فاذا النجوم طمست ۝

9. The heavens split asunder,

واذا السماء فرجت ۝

10. The mountains reduced to dust
and blown away,

واذا الجبال نسفت ۝

11. And when the time comes for raising
the little girls (buried alive)* —

واذا الرسل اقتت ۝

12. For what day is that time fixed?

لاى يوم اجلت ۝

13. The Day of Judgement.

ليوم الفصل ۝

14. How will you comprehend
what the Day of Judgement is?

وما ادراك ما يوم الفصل ۝

15. Alas the woe that day for those who deny!

ويل يومئذ للمكذبين ۝

16. Have We not destroyed
the earlier generations?

الم نهلك الاولين ۝

17. So shall We make the later ones
to follow them.

ثم نتبعهم الاخرين ۝

18. That is what We shall do to those
who are guilty of crime.

كذلك نفعل بالمجرمين ۝

19. Alas the woe that day for those who deny!

ويل يومئذ للمكذبين ۝

20. Did We not create you from contemptible water?

الم نخلقكم من ماء مهين ۝

21. Then We lodged you in a secure place (the womb)

فجعلناه فى قرار مكين ۝

22. For a certain appointed time,

الى قدر معلوم ۝

23. Then We facilitated (your birth).

فقدرنا فنعم القادرون ۝

Al-Mursalāt

How well do We calculate!
24. Alas the woe that day for those who deny!
25. Have We not made the earth
a repository
26. For the living and the dead,
27. And placed in it lofty and broad stablisers,
and gave you sweet water to drink?
28. Alas the woe that day for those who deny!
29. "Go to what you used to deny;
30. Go to the shadow with three ramifications, **
31. Neither shady nor protecting
against the blazing Fire.
32. It will throw out sparks
as logs of wood
33. So like golden camels."
34. Alas the woe that day for those who deny!
35. They will not be able to speak that day,
36. Nor given leave to make excuses.
37. Alas the woe that day for those who deny!
38. That will be the Day of Reckoning.
Gathered will be (you) and the earlier (generations).
39. So if you have any plot to devise against Me,
then devise it.
40. Alas the woe that day for those who deny!

Those who take heed for themselves and fear God,
will be amidst shade and springs of water,
42. And such fruits as they desire.
43. "Eat and drink with relish as reward
for what you had done."
44. That is how We reward the good.
45. Alas the woe that day for those who deny!
46. Eat and enjoy for a while:
You are certainly sinners.
47. Alas the woe that day for those who deny!
48. When it is said to them: "Bow in homage,"
they do not bow.
49. Alas the woe that day for those who deny!
50. In what other lore after this
will they then believe?

---

* Note on v. 11. *Rusul* here is not the plural of *rasul*, but is a singular feminine noun, and means the
little girl who does not yet cover her head. See *Taj al 'urus* which says that *jariyatun rusul* means this
little girl. See also 81:8-9 where the questioning of such innocent girls is mentioned. Here its time is
determined.
** The white cloud gathering through which the fire will strike, from three sides – above, below and
sides. Or, shadow of the grave – life, death and resurrection – the three shadows.

78 The Announcement

An-Nabā': Makki

بِسۡمِ اللهِ الرَّحۡمٰنِ الرَّحِيۡمِ

In the name of Allah, most benevolent, ever-merciful.

O**F WHAT ARE** they asking one another?

2. (Is it) of the great announcement

3. About which they have been differing?

4. Indeed they will come to know soon;

5. They will indeed come to know soon.

6. Did We not make the earth a spreading,

7. The mountains tent-pins?

8. We created you in pairs,

9. And made sleep for you to rest,

10. The night
a covering,

11. And the day
for seeking livelihood.

12. We raised over you
several secure (skies),

13. And placed a lamp therein
brightly burning.

14. And We sent down rain from water-laden clouds
pouring in torrents

15. That We may produce from it grain and vegetation,

16. And orchards full of trees and interlacing boughs.

17. Surely a time is fixed for the Day of Judgement.

18. The day the trumpet blast is sounded
you will come in hordes;

19. The heavens will be opened wide and turn
into so many doors,

20. The mountains put in motion
turning into a mirage.

21. Certainly Hell lies in wait,

22. The rebels' abode,

23. Where they will remain for aeons,

24. Finding neither sleep
nor any thing to drink

25. Except boiling water and benumbing cold:

26. A fitting reward.
27. They were those
who did not expect a reckoning,
28. And rejected
Our signs as lies.
29. We have kept account of every thing in a book.
30. So taste (the fruit of what you sowed),
for We shall add nothing but torment.

As for those who preserve themselves from evil
and follow the straight path,
there is attainment for them:
32. Orchards and vineyards,
33. And graceful maidens of the same age,
34. And flasks full and flowing.
35. They will hear no blasphemies there or disavowals:
36. A recompense from your Lord, a sufficient gift,
37. The Lord of the heavens and the earth,
and all that lies between them,
most benevolent, to whom none may dare address a word.
38. The day the Spirit* takes its stand,
with the angels ranged in rows.
None will speak except who is permitted
by Ar-Rahman and says what is right.
39. That day is certain. So whosoever likes
may prepare a way to his Lord.
40. We have indeed warned you of a calamity near at hand, —
a day when man will see
what he had sent (of his deeds) ahead,
and the unbeliever will say:
"Woe alas. Ah would that I were dust!"

---

* See 89:22 for the meaning of Spirit here.

79 Those Who Pull and Withdraw

(٧٩) سُوْرَةُ النَّزِعٰتِ مَكِيَّةٌ

An-Nāzi'āt: Makki

اٰیَاتُهَا ٤٦ وُرُوْعُهَا

In the name of Allah, most benevolent, ever-merciful.

بِسْمِ اللهِ الرَّحْمٰنِ الرَّحِيْمِ ۝

I CALL TO WITNESS those who dive
and drag,

وَالنّٰزِعٰتِ غَرْقًا ۝

2. And those who undo the bonds gently,

وَالنّٰشِطٰتِ نَشْطًا ۝

3. And those who glide swimmingly,

وَالسّٰبِحٰتِ سَبْحًا ۝

4. Then outpace the others swiftly

فَالسّٰبِقٰتِ سَبْقًا ۝

5. And direct affairs by command,

فَالْمُدَبِّرٰتِ اَمْرًا ۝

6. The day the convulsive (first blast)
shatters convulsively

يَوْمَ تَرْجُفُ الرَّاجِفَةُ ۝

7. Followed by the second blast,

تَتْبَعُهَا الرَّادِفَةُ ۝

8. Hearts will pound loudly on that day,

قُلُوْبٌ يَوْمَئِذٍ وَّاجِفَةٌ ۝

9. Eyes be lowered in submission.

اَبْصَارُهَا خَاشِعَةٌ ۝

10. They say: "Shall we go back
to our original state

يَقُوْلُوْنَ ءَاِنَّا لَمَرْدُوْدُوْنَ فِى الْحَافِرَةِ ۝

11. After having turned to carious bones?"

ءَاِذَا كُنَّا عِظَامًا نَّخِرَةً ۝

12. They say: "Then this returning
will be a dead loss."

قَالُوْا تِلْكَ اِذًا كَرَّةٌ خَاسِرَةٌ ۝

13. It will only be a single blast,

فَاِنَّمَا هِىَ زَجْرَةٌ وَّاحِدَةٌ ۝

14. And they will wake up suddenly.

فَاِذَا هُمْ بِالسَّاهِرَةِ ۝

15. Has the story of Moses come to you

هَلْ اَتٰىكَ حَدِيْثُ مُوْسٰى ۝

16. When his Lord called to him in Tuwa's holy vale?

اِذْ نَادٰىهُ رَبُّهُ بِالْوَادِ الْمُقَدَّسِ طُوًى ۝

17. "Go to the Pharaoh who
has become refractory,

اِذْهَبْ اِلٰى فِرْعَوْنَ اِنَّهُ طَغٰى ۝

18. And say: 'Would you like to grow (in virtue)?

فَقُلْ هَلْ لَّكَ اِلٰى اَنْ تَزَكّٰى ۝

19. Then I will guide you to your Lord
that you may come to fear Him.' "

وَاَهْدِيَكَ اِلٰى رَبِّكَ فَتَخْشٰى ۝

20. So he showed him the greater sign;

فَاَرٰىهُ الْاٰيَةَ الْكُبْرٰى ۝

21. But (the Pharaoh) disavowed
and disobeyed

فَكَذَّبَ وَعَصٰى ۝

22. Then he turned away, deliberating,

ثُمَّ اَدْبَرَ يَسْعٰى ۝

23. And assembled (his council)
and proclaimed,

فَحَشَرَ فَنَادٰى ۝

24. Saying: "I am alone your lord,
the highest of them all."

فَقَالَ اَنَا رَبُّكُمُ الْاَعْلٰى ۝

25. So God seized him for the punishment

فَاَخَذَهُ اللهُ نَكَالَ الْاٰخِرَةِ وَالْاُوْلٰى ۝

of the Hereafter and this world.
26. Truly there is a lesson in this
for those who fear (the consequences).

Are you more difficult to create or the heavens?
He built it,
28. Raised it high, proportioned it,
29. Gave darkness to its night,
and brightness to its day;
30. And afterwards spread out the earth.
31. He brought out its water
and its pastures from it,
32. And stabilized the mountains
33. As convenience for you and your cattle.
34. When the great calamity comes,
35. The day when man remembers
all that he had done,
36. And Hell made visible
to him who can see,
37. Then he who had been rebellious
38. And who preferred the life of the world,
39. Will surely have
Hell for his abode.
40. But he who feared standing
before his Lord,
and restrained his self from vain desires,
41. Will surely have Paradise for abode.
42. They ask you. "When will the Hour be?
When is its time fixed?"
43. What do you have to do
with explaining it?
44. The extent of its knowledge goes to your Lord.
45. Your duty is only to warn him who fears it.
46. The day they see it, it will seem
they had stayed in the world
but only an evening
or its turning into dawn.

80 He Made a Wry Face

'Abasa: Makki

(۸۰) سورة عبس مكية

اياتها ۳۶ ركوعها

In the name of Allah, most benevolent, ever-merciful.

بِسْمِ اللهِ الرَّحْمَنِ الرَّحِيمِ

HE FROWNED AND turned away,

عَبَسَ وَتَوَلّٰى ۞

2. Because a blind man came to him.

اَن جَآءَهُ الْاَعْمٰى ۞

3. What made you think that he will not grow in virtue,

وَمَا يُدْرِيكَ لَعَلَّهُ يَزَّكّٰى ۞

4. Or be admonished, and the admonition profit him?

اَوْ يَذَّكَّرُ فَتَنْفَعَهُ الذِّكْرٰى ۞

5. As for him who is not in want of any thing,

اَمَّا مَنِ اسْتَغْنٰى ۞

6. You pay full attention,

فَاَنْتَ لَهُ تَصَدّٰى ۞

7. Though it is not your concern if he should not grow (in fulness).

وَمَا عَلَيْكَ اَلَّا يَزَّكّٰى ۞

8. As for him who comes to you striving (after goodness),

وَاَمَّا مَنْ جَآءَكَ يَسْعٰى ۞

9. And is also fearful (of God),

وَهُوَ يَخْشٰى ۞

10. You neglect.

فَاَنْتَ عَنْهُ تَلَهّٰى ۞

11. Assuredly this is a reminder

كَلَّا اِنَّهَا تَذْكِرَةٌ ۞

12. For any one who desires to bear it in mind,

فَمَنْ شَآءَ ذَكَرَهُ ۞

13. (Contained) in honoured pages,

فِيْ صُحُفٍ مُّكَرَّمَةٍ ۞

14. Exalted and holy,

مَّرْفُوْعَةٍ مُّطَهَّرَةٍ ۞

15. In the hands of scribes

بِاَيْدِيْ سَفَرَةٍ ۞

16. Noble and pious.

كِرَامٍ بَرَرَةٍ ۞

17. Accursed is man. How ungrateful is he!

قُتِلَ الْاِنْسَانُ مَا اَكْفَرَهُ ۞

18. Of what substance God created him?

مِنْ اَيِّ شَيْءٍ خَلَقَهُ ۞

19. From a single sperm He created, then proportioned him,

مِنْ نُطْفَةٍ خَلَقَهُ فَقَدَّرَهُ ۞

20. Then made his passage easy (at birth);

ثُمَّ السَّبِيْلَ يَسَّرَهُ ۞

21. He will then send him to death and have him laid in the grave.

ثُمَّ اَمَاتَهُ فَاَقْبَرَهُ ۞

22. Then He will raise him up again when He please.

ثُمَّ اِذَا شَآءَ اَنْشَرَهُ ۞

23. But no. He has not fulfilled what was enjoined on him.

كَلَّا لَمَّا يَقْضِ مَا اَمَرَهُ ۞

24. Let man therefore consider
(the sources of) his food.
25. We poured down rain abundantly,
26. Then We cracked the earth open
under pressure (of germination)
27. And We made corn grow,
28. And grapes and herbage,
29. Olives and dates,
30. Orchards thick with trees,
31. And fruits and fodder:
32. A provision for you
and your cattle.
33. But when the great calamity comes
34. Man will fly
from his brother,
35. Mother and father,
36. As well as his wife and children.
37. Each man will have enough cares that day.
38. Many faces will that day
be bright,
39. Laughing and full of joy,
40. And many will be dust-begrimed,
41. Covered with the blackness (of shame):
42. They will be the unbelievers,
transgressors.

فَلْيَنْظُرِ الْإِنْسَانُ إِلَى طَعَامِهِ ۞
أَنَّا صَبَبْنَا الْمَاءَ صَبًّا ۞
ثُمَّ شَقَقْنَا الْأَرْضَ شَقًّا ۞
فَأَنْبَتْنَا فِيهَا حَبًّا ۞ وَعِنَبًا وَقَضْبًا ۞
وَزَيْتُونًا وَنَخْلًا ۞
وَحَدَائِقَ غُلْبًا ۞
وَفَاكِهَةً وَأَبًّا ۞
مَتَاعًا لَكُمْ وَلِأَنْعَامِكُمْ ۞
فَإِذَا جَاءَتِ الصَّاخَّةُ ۞
يَوْمَ يَفِرُّ الْمَرْءُ مِنْ أَخِيهِ ۞
وَأُمِّهِ وَأَبِيهِ ۞
وَصَاحِبَتِهِ وَبَنِيهِ ۞
لِكُلِّ امْرِئٍ مِنْهُمْ يَوْمَئِذٍ شَأْنٌ يُغْنِيهِ ۞
وُجُوهٌ يَوْمَئِذٍ مُسْفِرَةٌ ۞
ضَاحِكَةٌ مُسْتَبْشِرَةٌ ۞
وَوُجُوهٌ يَوْمَئِذٍ عَلَيْهَا غَبَرَةٌ ۞
تَرْهَقُهَا قَتَرَةٌ ۞
أُولَٰئِكَ هُمُ الْكَفَرَةُ الْفَجَرَةُ ۞

81 The Folding Up

At-Takvir: Makki

In the name of Allah, most benevolent, ever-merciful.

بِسْمِ اللهِ الرَّحْمٰنِ الرَّحِيْمِ

WHEN THE SUN is folded up,

اِذَا الشَّمْسُ كُوِّرَتْ ۝

2. The stars turn dim and scatter,

وَاِذَا النُّجُوْمُ انْكَدَرَتْ ۝

3. The mountains made to move,

وَاِذَا الْجِبَالُ سُيِّرَتْ ۝

4. The ten-month pregnant female camels
are abandoned,

وَاِذَا الْعِشَارُ عُطِّلَتْ ۝

5. The wild beasts stampede
on the run,

وَاِذَا الْوُحُوْشُ حُشِرَتْ ۝

6. When the oceans surge and swell,

وَاِذَا الْبِحَارُ سُجِّرَتْ ۝

7. When souls are reunited
(with the bodies)

وَاِذَا النُّفُوْسُ زُوِّجَتْ ۝

8. And the little girl buried alive
is asked

وَاِذَا الْمَوْءُدَةُ سُئِلَتْ ۝

9. For what crime she was put to death;

بِاَيِّ ذَنْبٍ قُتِلَتْ ۝

10. When the ledgers are laid open,

وَاِذَا الصُّحُفُ نُشِرَتْ ۝

11. The curtain drawn back from the skies,

وَاِذَا السَّمَاءُ كُشِطَتْ ۝

12. When Hell is set ablaze,

وَاِذَا الْجَحِيْمُ سُعِّرَتْ ۝

13. And Paradise brought near,

وَاِذَا الْجَنَّةُ اُزْلِفَتْ ۝

14. (Then) every soul will know
what it had prepared (for itself).

عَلِمَتْ نَفْسٌ مَّا اَحْضَرَتْ ۝

15. So, I call the receding stars to witness,

فَلَا اُقْسِمُ بِالْخُنَّسِ ۝

16. The planets withdrawing
into themselves,

الْجَوَارِ الْكُنَّسِ ۝

17. The closing night,

وَالَّيْلِ اِذَا عَسْعَسَ ۝

18. The rising dawn,

وَالصُّبْحِ اِذَا تَنَفَّسَ ۝

19. That this is indeed the word
of an honoured Messenger,

اِنَّهُ لَقَوْلُ رَسُوْلٍ كَرِيْمٍ ۝

20. Full of power, well-established (in position)
with the Lord and Master of the Throne,

ذِيْ قُوَّةٍ عِنْدَ ذِي الْعَرْشِ مَكِيْنٍ ۝

21. Obeyed and worthy there of trust.

مُطَاعٍ ثَمَّ اَمِيْنٍ ۝

22. Your companion is not mad.

وَمَا صَاحِبُكُمْ بِمَجْنُوْنٍ ۝

23. He had surely seen Him
on the clear horizon.

وَلَقَدْ رَاٰهُ بِالْاُفُقِ الْمُبِيْنِ ۝

24. He is not chary of making public
what is unknown.

وَمَا هُوَ عَلَى الْغَيْبِ بِضَنِيْنٍ ۝

25. This is not the utterance of an accursed devil.
26. So whither do you stray?
27. This is a reminder for all the peoples of the world,
28. For those of you who desire
to walk the path that is straight,
29. Though you cannot desire
except as God will,
the Lord of all the worlds.

وَمَا هُوَ بِقَوْلِ شَيْطٰنٍ رَّجِيمٍ ۝

فَأَيْنَ تَذْهَبُونَ ۝

إِنْ هُوَ إِلَّا ذِكْرٌ لِّلْعٰلَمِينَ ۝

لِمَنْ شَاءَ مِنكُمْ أَن يَسْتَقِيمَ ۝

وَمَا تَشَاءُونَ إِلَّا أَن يَشَاءَ اللهُ رَبُّ الْعٰلَمِينَ ۝

82 The Splitting

Al-Infitār: Makki

In the name of Allah, most benevolent, ever-merciful.

بِسْمِ اللهِ الرَّحْمٰنِ الرَّحِيْمِ ۞

WHEN THE SKY is split asunder,

2. And the stars dispersed,

3. When the oceans begin to flow,

4. When the graves are overturned,

5. Each soul will know
what it had sent ahead
and what it had left behind.

6. O man, what seduced you
from your munificent Lord

7. Who created you
then formed your symmetry,
then gave you right proportion,

8. Shaping you into any form He pleased?

9. Even then you deny the Judgement.

10. Surely there are guardians over you,

11. Illustrious scribes

12. Who know what you do.

13. The pious will surely be in heaven,

14. The wicked certainly in Hell:

15. They will burn in it on the Day of Judgement,

16. And will not be removed from it.

17. How can you comprehend
what the Day of Judgement is?

18. How then can you comprehend
what the Day of Judgement is?

19. It is the day when no soul
will have power to do the least for a soul,
and God's alone will be done.

83 The Defrauders

Al-Mutaffifin: Makki

بِسۡمِ اللهِ الرَّحۡمٰنِ الرَّحِیۡمِ

In the name of Allah, most benevolent, ever-merciful.

WOE TO THOSE who give short measure,

2. Who insist on being given full
when they take from others,

3. Whilst when they measure or weigh for them, give less.

4. Do they not think they will be raised
(to life) again

5. On a grievous day,

6. The day all mankind will stand
before the Lord of all the worlds?

7. Indeed the ledger of the wicked
will be in (the lowest depths) Sijjin.

8. How will you comprehend
what Sijjin is?

9. It is a (repository of) distinctly written record.

10. Ah the woe that day for those who deny,

11. Who call the Day of Judgement a lie!

12. None denies it but the sinful
transgressors.

13. When Our revelations are recited before him,
he says: "These are fables of long ago."

14. No. In fact what they have been doing
has rusted their hearts.

15. Therefore they will be screened off
from their Lord that day,

16. Then they will indeed burn in Hell.

17. They will then be told:
"This is what you had denied."

18. Surely the ledger of the pious
will be in 'Illiyun
(heights above the heights).

19. But how will you comprehend
what 'Illiyun is?

20. It is a (repository of) distinctly written record

21. Witnessed by those who are honoured.

Al-Mutaffifin 527

22. Verily the pious will be in heaven,

23. On couches face to face.

24. On their faces you will see
the glow of beatitude.

25. They will be served the choicest wine, sealed

26. With a sealing of musk,
which those who aspire for the best
should desire, —

27. Blended with the water of Tasnim, (heights ultimate
      of evolution),*

28. A fountain from which only they
who are honoured drink.

29. The sinners indeed laughed at believers

30. And winked at one another as they passed by them;

31. And when they went back to their people
turned to make fun of them;

32. And when they saw them, they said:
"They have indeed gone astray."

33. But they were not sent
to be guardians over them!

34. So, the believers will laugh at the infidels
on that day,

35. Regarding them from their cushioned seats.

36. Will not the infidels pay for what they had done?

---

* Root SNM, *Sanam*, which has a sense of exaltation and explained by the next verse 28. See also verse
19 of Surah, 84, opposite page.

84 The Cleaving

Al-Inshiqāq: Makki

عـــر ٣٠

(٨٤) سُوْرَةُ الْاِنْشِقَاقِ مَكِّيَّةٌ

اٰيَاتُهَا ٢٥ رُكُوْعُهَا

In the name of Allah, most benevolent, ever-merciful.

بِسْمِ اللهِ الرَّحْمٰنِ الرَّحِيْمِ ۞

WHEN THE SKY is cleft asunder,

2. And hearkens to its Lord and is dutiful,

3. When the earth is stretched out taut

4. And throws out whatever it contains
and is empty,

5. And hearkens to its Lord and is dutiful,

6. O man, you have to strive and go on striving
towards your Lord,
then will you meet Him.

7. And he who is given his ledger
in his right hand

8. Will have an easy reckoning,

9. And will return to his people full of joy.

10. But he who is given his ledger
from behind his back

11. Will pray for death,

12. But will be roasted in the fire.

13. He lived rejoicing among his people,

14. Never thinking he will return.

15. Why not? His Lord was always watching him.

16. So indeed I call to witness
the evening twilight,

17. And the night and all it gathers,

18. And the moon when at the full,

19. That you will climb from stage to stage.

20. So, wherefore do they not believe?

21. And when the Qur'an is recited to them
do not bow in adoration?

22. In fact the unbelievers disavow.

23. But God knows what they harbour
in their breasts.

24. So give them news of painful punishment,

25. Except those who believe and do the right:
For them there is reward unending.

اِذَا السَّمَآءُ انْشَقَّتْ ۞

وَاَذِنَتْ لِرَبِّهَا وَحُقَّتْ ۞

وَاِذَا الْاَرْضُ مُدَّتْ ۞

وَاَلْقَتْ مَا فِيْهَا وَتَخَلَّتْ ۞

وَاَذِنَتْ لِرَبِّهَا وَحُقَّتْ ۞

يٰۤاَيُّهَا الْاِنْسَانُ اِنَّكَ كَادِحٌ اِلٰى رَبِّكَ كَدْحًا

فَمُلٰقِيْهِ ۞ فَاَمَّا مَنْ اُوْتِيَ كِتٰبَهٗ بِيَمِيْنِهٖ ۞

فَسَوْفَ يُحَاسَبُ حِسَابًا يَّسِيْرًا ۞

وَّيَنْقَلِبُ اِلٰۤى اَهْلِهٖ مَسْرُوْرًا ۞

وَاَمَّا مَنْ اُوْتِيَ كِتٰبَهٗ وَرَآءَ ظَهْرِهٖ ۞

فَسَوْفَ يَدْعُوْا ثُبُوْرًا ۞

وَّيَصْلٰى سَعِيْرًا ۞

اِنَّهٗ كَانَ فِيْۤ اَهْلِهٖ مَسْرُوْرًا ۞

اِنَّهٗ ظَنَّ اَنْ لَّنْ يَّحُوْرَ ۞

بَلٰۤى اِنَّ رَبَّهٗ كَانَ بِهٖ بَصِيْرًا ۞

فَلَاۤ اُقْسِمُ بِالشَّفَقِ ۞ وَالَّيْلِ وَمَا وَسَقَ ۞

وَالْقَمَرِ اِذَا اتَّسَقَ ۞

لَتَرْكَبُنَّ طَبَقًا عَنْ طَبَقٍ ۞

فَمَا لَهُمْ لَا يُؤْمِنُوْنَ ۞

وَاِذَا قُرِئَ عَلَيْهِمُ الْقُرْاٰنُ لَا يَسْجُدُوْنَ ۞

بَلِ الَّذِيْنَ كَفَرُوْا يُكَذِّبُوْنَ ۞

وَاللهُ اَعْلَمُ بِمَا يُوْعُوْنَ ۞

فَبَشِّرْهُمْ بِعَذَابٍ اَلِيْمٍ ۞

اِلَّا الَّذِيْنَ اٰمَنُوْا وَعَمِلُوا الصّٰلِحٰتِ لَهُمْ

اَجْرٌ غَيْرُ مَمْنُوْنٍ ۞

85 Signs of the Zodiac

Al-Burūj: Makki

In the name of Allah, most benevolent, ever-merciful.

بِسْمِ اللهِ الرَّحْمٰنِ الرَّحِيْمِ ۞

I CALL TO witness the sky
(bespangled) with the signs
of the Zodiac,
2. And the promised day,
3. And the witness and the witnessed,
4. That accursed are the men of the trench
5. Full of fire fed by faggots,
6. As they sat around it
7. Witnessing what they had done
to the believers!
8. They had no other reason for hating them
except that they believed in God
the mighty, worthy of praise,
9. Whose kingdom spreads over the heavens and the earth.
God is witness over every thing.
10. Surely for those who persecute believers, men and women,
and do not repent afterwards,
is the punishment of Hell,
and the punishment of burning.
11. Surely for those who believe and do the right
are gardens with rivers running by.
That is the greatest success.
12. The grip of your Lord is severe indeed!
13. It is verily He who initiates
and repeats.
14. He is the forgiving and the loving,
15. The Lord of the glorious Throne,
16. Who does as He pleases.
17. Has the story of the hordes
18. Of Pharaoh and Thamud come to you?
19. Yet the infidels persist in denial.
20. But God surrounds them from all sides.
21. This is indeed the glorious Qur'an
22. (Preserved) on the guarded tablet.

وَالسَّمَآءِ ذَاتِ الْبُرُوجِ ۞
وَالْيَوْمِ الْمَوْعُوْدِ ۞ وَشَاهِدٍ وَمَشْهُوْدٍ ۞
قُتِلَ اَصْحٰبُ الْاُخْدُوْدِ ۞
النَّارِ ذَاتِ الْوَقُوْدِ ۞ اِذْ هُمْ عَلَيْهَا قُعُوْدٌ ۞
وَّهُمْ عَلٰى مَا يَفْعَلُوْنَ بِالْمُؤْمِنِيْنَ شُهُوْدٌ ۞
وَمَا نَقَمُوْا مِنْهُمْ اِلَّا اَنْ يُّؤْمِنُوْا بِاللهِ الْعَزِيْزِ
الْحَمِيْدِ ۞
الَّذِيْ لَهٗ مُلْكُ السَّمٰوٰتِ وَالْاَرْضِ ۗ وَاللهُ عَلٰى
كُلِّ شَيْءٍ شَهِيْدٌ ۞
اِنَّ الَّذِيْنَ فَتَنُوا الْمُؤْمِنِيْنَ وَالْمُؤْمِنٰتِ ثُمَّ
لَمْ يَتُوْبُوْا فَلَهُمْ عَذَابُ جَهَنَّمَ وَلَهُمْ عَذَابُ
الْحَرِيْقِ ۞
اِنَّ الَّذِيْنَ اٰمَنُوْا وَعَمِلُوا الصّٰلِحٰتِ لَهُمْ جَنّٰتٌ
تَجْرِيْ مِنْ تَحْتِهَا الْاَنْهٰرُ ۗ ذٰلِكَ الْفَوْزُ
الْكَبِيْرُ ۞ اِنَّ بَطْشَ رَبِّكَ لَشَدِيْدٌ ۞
اِنَّهٗ هُوَ يُبْدِئُ وَيُعِيْدُ ۞
وَهُوَ الْغَفُوْرُ الْوَدُوْدُ ۞
ذُو الْعَرْشِ الْمَجِيْدُ ۞
فَعَّالٌ لِّمَا يُرِيْدُ ۞
هَلْ اَتٰىكَ حَدِيْثُ الْجُنُوْدِ ۞
فِرْعَوْنَ وَثَمُوْدَ ۞
بَلِ الَّذِيْنَ كَفَرُوْا فِيْ تَكْذِيْبٍ ۞
وَّاللهُ مِنْ وَّرَآئِهِمْ مُّحِيْطٌ ۞
بَلْ هُوَ قُرْاٰنٌ مَّجِيْدٌ ۞
فِيْ لَوْحٍ مَّحْفُوْظٍ ۞

Al-Burūj

86 The Night Star

At-Ṭāriq: Makki

In the name of Allah, most benevolent, ever-merciful.

I CALL TO witness the heavens and the night star —
2. How will you comprehend
what the night star is?
3. It is the star that shines
with a piercing brightness —
4. That over each soul there is a guardian.
5. Let man consider what he was made of:
6. He was created of spurting water
7. Issuing from (the pelvis)
between the backbone and the ribs.
8. God has certainly power to bring him back
(from the dead).
9. The day all secrets are examined
10. He will have no strength or helper.
11. So I call to witness
the rain-producing sky,
12. And the earth which opens up
(with verdure),
13. That this (Qur'an) is a decisive word
14. And no trifle.
15. They are hatching up a plot,
16. But I too am devising a plan.
17. So bear with unbelievers with patience,
and give them respite for a while.

87   The Most High

Al-A'lā: Makki

In the name of Allah, most benevolent, ever-merciful.

بِسْمِ اللهِ الرَّحْمٰنِ الرَّحِيْمِ

GLORIFY THE NAME of your Lord, most high,

سَبِّحِ اسْمَ رَبِّكَ الْاَعْلَى ۝

2. Who creates and proportions,

الَّذِیْ خَلَقَ فَسَوّٰی ۝

3. Who determines and directs,

وَالَّذِیْ قَدَّرَ فَهَدٰی ۝

4. Who brings out the pastures

وَالَّذِیْۤ اَخْرَجَ الْمَرْعٰی ۝

5. Then reduces them
to rusty rubbish.

فَجَعَلَهُ غُثَآءً اَحْوٰی ۝

6. We shall make you recite (the Qur'an)
so that you will not forget it,

سَنُقْرِئُكَ فَلَا تَنْسٰۤی ۝

7. Unless God may please.
He knows the visible
and knows what is hidden.

اِلَّا مَا شَآءَ اللهُ ۙ اِنَّهٗ یَعْلَمُ الْجَهْرَ وَمَا یَخْفٰی ۝

8. We shall take you slowly towards ease.

وَنُیَسِّرُكَ لِلْیُسْرٰی ۝

9. So remind them
if reminder is profitable:

فَذَكِّرْ اِنْ نَّفَعَتِ الذِّكْرٰی ۝

10. Those who fear will understand.

سَیَذَّكَّرُ مَنْ یَّخْشٰی ۝

11. Only the wretch will turn aside,

وَیَتَجَنَّبُهَا الْاَشْقَی ۝

12. Who will burn
in the terrible Fire,

الَّذِیْ یَصْلَی النَّارَ الْكُبْرٰی ۝

13. In which he will neither die nor live.

ثُمَّ لَا یَمُوْتُ فِیْهَا وَلَا یَحْیٰی ۝

14. Surely he will succeed
who grows in goodness,

قَدْ اَفْلَحَ مَنْ تَزَكّٰی ۝

15. And recites the name of his Lord
and serves with devotion.

وَذَكَرَ اسْمَ رَبِّهٖ فَصَلّٰی ۝

16. But no, you prefer the life of the world,

بَلْ تُؤْثِرُوْنَ الْحَیٰوةَ الدُّنْیَا ۝

17. Though the life to come
is better and abiding.

وَالْاٰخِرَةُ خَیْرٌ وَّاَبْقٰی ۝

18. This is surely in the earlier Books,

اِنَّ هٰذَا لَفِی الصُّحُفِ الْاُوْلٰی ۝

19. The Books of Abraham and Moses.

صُحُفِ اِبْرٰهِیْمَ وَمُوْسٰی ۝

88 The Overpowering

Al-Ghāshiyah: Makki

In the name of Allah, most benevolent, ever-merciful.

HAS NEWS OF the Overpowering
Event reached you?
2. Many faces will be contrite on that day,
3. Labouring, wearied out,
4. Burning in the scorching fire,
5. Given water from the boiling
spring to drink.
6. They will have no food
except bitter thorn,
7. Neither nourishing nor
banishing hunger.
8. Many faces will be joyous on that day,
9. Well-pleased with their endeavour,
10. In the high empyrean,
11. Never hearing idle talk.
12. There is a stream of running water in it;
13. And within it are couches
placed on high,
14. Goblets set,
15. Cushions arranged,
16. And rich carpets spread.
17. Do they not then ponder
how the clouds were formed;
18. And the heavens,
how it was raised high;
19. And the mountains,
how they were fixed;
20. And the earth,
how it was spread out?
21. Remind them;
you are surely a reminder.
22. You are not a warden over them,
23. Other than him
who turns his back and denies,

24. In which case
he will be punished by God
with the severest punishment.

فَيُعَذِّبُهُ اللهُ الْعَذَابَ الْأَكْبَرَ ۝

25. To Us is surely their returning;

إِنَّ إِلَيْنَا إِيَابَهُمْ ۝

26. Ours is surely then
to reckon with them.

ثُمَّ إِنَّ عَلَيْنَا حِسَابَهُمْ ۝

89 The Dawn

Al-Fajr: Makki

بِسْمِ اللهِ الرَّحْمٰنِ الرَّحِيْمِ

سُوْرَةُ الْفَجْرِ مَكِّيَّةٌ (٨٩)

In the name of Allah, most benevolent, ever-merciful.

I CALL TO witness the dawn
2. And the Ten Nights,*
3. The multiple and the one,
4. The night as it advances,
5. Is there not an evidence in this
for those who have sense?
6. Have you not seen what your Lord
did to the 'Ad
7. Of Eram ** with lofty pillars
(erected as signposts in the desert),
8. The like of whom
were never created in the realm;
9. And with Thamud
who carved rocks in the valley;
10. And the mighty Pharaoh
11. Who terrorised the region,
12. And multiplied corruption.
13. So your Lord poured a scourge
of punishment over them.
14. Your Lord is certainly in wait.
15. As for man,
whenever his Lord tries him
and then is gracious
and provides good things for him,
he says: "My Lord has been gracious to me."
16. But when He tries him by restraining his means,
he says: "My Lord despises me."
17. No. In fact you are not
generous to the orphans,
18. Nor do you urge one another to feed the poor,
19. And you devour (others') inheritance greedily,
20. And love wealth with all your heart.

---

* See note on p.536. ** Fabulous gardens said to have been built by Shaddad bin 'Ad.

21. Surely when We pound the earth to powder
grounded, pounded to dust,
22. And comes your Lord, and angels row on row,
23. And Hell is brought near,
that day will man remember,
but of what avail
will then remembering be?
24. He will say: "Alas the woe!
Would that I had sent ahead
something in my life."
25. None can punish as He will punish
on that day,
26. And none can bind as He will bind.
27. O you tranquil soul,
28. Return to your Lord, well-pleased
and well-pleasing Him.
29. "Enter then among My votaries,
30. Enter then My garden."

كَلَّا إِذَا دُكَّتِ الْأَرْضُ دَكًّا دَكًّا ۞
وَجَاءَ رَبُّكَ وَالْمَلَكُ صَفًّا صَفًّا ۞
وَجِيءَ يَوْمَئِذٍ بِجَهَنَّمَ ۚ يَوْمَئِذٍ يَتَذَكَّرُ
الْإِنْسَانُ وَأَنَّى لَهُ الذِّكْرَى ۞

يَقُولُ يَالَيْتَنِي قَدَّمْتُ لِحَيَاتِي ۞

فَيَوْمَئِذٍ لَا يُعَذِّبُ عَذَابَهُ أَحَدٌ ۞
وَلَا يُوثِقُ وَثَاقَهُ أَحَدٌ ۞
يَا أَيَّتُهَا النَّفْسُ الْمُطْمَئِنَّةُ ۞
ارْجِعِي إِلَى رَبِّكِ رَاضِيَةً مَرْضِيَّةً ۞
فَادْخُلِي فِي عِبَادِي ۞
وَادْخُلِي جَنَّتِي ۞

---

* The first ten nights of the lunar month when the moon is on the rise, and the last ten nights when
she is on the wane. The Surah deals with the law of opposites, light and darkness, rise and fall, as in
Nature so in the lives of men and nations.

90 The Earth

Al-Balad: Makki

(٩٠)سُوْرَةُ الْبَلَدِ مَكِّيَّةٌ

اٰیَاتُهَا رُكُوْعُهَا

In the name of Allah, most benevolent, ever-merciful.

بِسْمِ اللهِ الرَّحْمٰنِ الرَّحِيْمِ ۞

I CALL THIS earth to witness —

2. And you are free to live upon it, —

3. And the parent and the offspring,

4. That We created man
in toil and trouble.

5. Does he think that no one
has power over him?

6. He says: "I have wasted
a great deal of wealth."

7. Does he think that no one sees him?

8. Did We not give him two eyes,

9. One tongue, and two lips,

10. And showed him two highways
(of good and evil)?

11. But he could not scale the steep ascent.

12. How will you comprehend
what the steep ascent is? —

13. To free a neck
(from the burden of debt or slavery),

14. Or to feed in times of famine

15. The orphan near in relationship,

16. Or the poor in distress;

17. And to be of those who believe,
and urge upon one another to persevere,
and urge upon each other to be kind.

18. They are the people of the right hand
(and will succeed).

19. But those who deny Our revelations
are the people of the left hand:

20. The Fire will vault them over.

لَاۤ اُقْسِمُ بِهٰذَا الْبَلَدِ ۞

وَاَنْتَ حِلٌّ بِهٰذَا الْبَلَدِ ۞

وَوَالِدٍ وَّمَا وَلَدَ ۞

لَقَدْ خَلَقْنَا الْاِنْسَانَ فِیْ كَبَدٍ ۞

اَیَحْسَبُ اَنْ لَّنْ یَّقْدِرَ عَلَیْهِ اَحَدٌ ۞

یَقُوْلُ اَهْلَكْتُ مَالًا لُّبَدًا ۞

اَیَحْسَبُ اَنْ لَّمْ یَرَهٗۤ اَحَدٌ ۞

اَلَمْ نَجْعَلْ لَّهٗ عَیْنَیْنِ ۞

وَلِسَانًا وَّشَفَتَیْنِ ۞

وَهَدَیْنٰهُ النَّجْدَیْنِ ۞

فَلَا اقْتَحَمَ الْعَقَبَةَ ۞

وَمَاۤ اَدْرٰىكَ مَا الْعَقَبَةُ ۞

فَكُّ رَقَبَةٍ ۞

اَوْ اِطْعٰمٌ فِیْ یَوْمٍ ذِیْ مَسْغَبَةٍ ۞

یَّتِیْمًا ذَا مَقْرَبَةٍ ۞

اَوْ مِسْكِیْنًا ذَا مَتْرَبَةٍ ۞

ثُمَّ كَانَ مِنَ الَّذِیْنَ اٰمَنُوْا وَتَوَاصَوْا بِالصَّبْرِ وَتَوَاصَوْا بِالْمَرْحَمَةِ ۞

اُولٰٓئِكَ اَصْحٰبُ الْمَیْمَنَةِ ۞

وَالَّذِیْنَ كَفَرُوْا بِاٰیٰتِنَا هُمْ اَصْحٰبُ الْمَشْئَمَةِ ۞

عَلَیْهِمْ نَارٌ مُّؤْصَدَةٌ ۞

91 The Sun

Ash-Shams: Makki

In the name of Allah, most benevolent, ever-merciful.

I CALL TO witness the sun
and his early morning splendour,
2. And the moon as she follows in his wake,
3. The day when it reveals his radiance,
4. The night when it covers him over,
5. The heavens and its architecture,
6. The earth and its spreading out,
7. The soul
and how it was integrated
8. And given the faculty
of knowing what is disruptive
and what is intrinsic to it.
9. He who nourishes it
will surely be successful,
10. And he who confines it
will surely come to grief.
11. The Thamud denied (the truth) in their perverseness
12. When among them the great wretch arose,
13. And the apostle of God had to tell them:
"This is God's she-camel, let her drink."
14. But they called him a liar and hamstrung her.
So God obliterated them for their crime,
and (destroyed) all of them alike.
15. He does not fear the consequence.

92 The Night

Al-Lail: Makki

In the name of Allah, most benevolent, ever-merciful.

I CALL THE night to witness
when it covers over,
2. And the day
when it shines in all its glory,
3. And Him who created
the male and female,
4. That your endeavour is for different ends.
5. Yet he who gives to others
and has fear,
6. And affirms goodness,
7. We shall ease
the way of fortune for him.
8. But he who does not give
and is unconcerned,
9. And rejects goodness,
10. For him We shall ease
the way of adversity,
11. And his riches will not avail him
when he falls headlong (into the Abyss).
12. It is indeed for Us to show the way,
13. And to Us belong
the End and the Beginning.
14. So, I warn you of the blazing Fire.
15. No one will burn in it
but the most wretched,
16. Who denied (the truth) and turned away.
17. But save him who fears
18. And gives of his wealth
that he may grow in virtue,
19. And is under no one's obligation
to return his favour,
20. Other than
seeking the glory of his Lord, most high,
21. Will surely be gratified.

Al-Lail

93 Early Hours of Morning

سُورَةُ الضُّحٰی مَكِّیَّة (۹۳)

عـم ۳۰

آیاتُها ۱۱ رُکوعُها ۱

Ad-Duhā: Makki

In the name of Allah, most benevolent, ever-merciful.

بِسْمِ اللهِ الرَّحْمٰنِ الرَّحِیْمِ ۰

I CALL TO witness
the early hours of morning,

وَالضُّحٰی ۰

2. And the night when dark and still,

وَالَّیْلِ اِذَا سَجٰی ۰

3. Your Lord has neither left you,
nor despises you.

مَا وَدَّعَكَ رَبُّكَ وَمَا قَلٰی ۰

4. What is to come is better for you
than what has gone before;

وَلَلْاٰخِرَةُ خَیْرٌ لَّكَ مِنَ الْاُوْلٰی ۰

5. For your Lord will certainly give you,
and you will be content.

وَلَسَوْفَ یُعْطِیْكَ رَبُّكَ فَتَرْضٰی ۰

6. Did He not find you an orphan
and take care of you?

اَلَمْ یَجِدْكَ یَتِیْمًا فَاٰوٰی ۰

7. Did He not find you perplexed,
and show you the way?

وَوَجَدَكَ ضَآلًّا فَهَدٰی ۰

8. Did He not find you poor
and enrich you?

وَوَجَدَكَ عَآئِلًا فَاَغْنٰی ۰

9. So do not oppress the orphan,

فَاَمَّا الْیَتِیْمَ فَلَا تَقْهَرْ ۰

10. And do not drive
the beggar away,

وَاَمَّا السَّآئِلَ فَلَا تَنْهَرْ ۰

11. And keep recounting the favours of your Lord.

وَاَمَّا بِنِعْمَةِ رَبِّكَ فَحَدِّثْ ۰

Ad-Duhā

540

94 The Opening Up

Al-Inshirah : Makki

In the name of Allah, most benevolent, ever-merciful.

HAVE WE NOT opened up
your breast
2. And removed your burden*
3. Which had left you
devoid of hope,
4. And exalted your fame?
5. Surely with hardship there is ease.
6. With hardship indeed there is ease.
7. So when you are free
work diligently,
8. And turn to your Lord
with all your love.**

---

* This refers to the opposition faced by the Prophet, as well as to verses 6, 7 and 8 of the previous Surah, *Ad-Duha*, which, in itself, prophesies the opening up of the bounties of the Lord on the Prophet.

** Al-Hallaj explains it thus: "Allah enunciated my knowledge with me from my heart. He drew me near to Him after I had been far from Him. He made me His intimate and chose me." 'The Ta-Sin of Purity.'

95 The Fig

سورة التين مكية (٩٥)

At-Tīn: Makki

اياتها ٨ ركوعها

In the name of Allah, most benevolent, ever-merciful.

بِسْمِ اللهِ الرَّحْمٰنِ الرَّحِيْمِ ۝

I CALL TO witness the Fig and the Olive,

وَالتِّيْنِ وَالزَّيْتُوْنِ ۙ۝

2. The Mount Sinai,

وَطُوْرِ سِيْنِيْنَ ۙ۝

3. And this Soil Secure,*

وَهٰذَا الْبَلَدِ الْاَمِيْنِ ۙ۝

4. That We created man
of finest possibilities,

لَقَدْ خَلَقْنَا الْاِنْسَانَ فِيْ اَحْسَنِ تَقْوِيْمٍ ۫۝

5. Then brought him down
to the lowest of the low,

ثُمَّ رَدَدْنٰهُ اَسْفَلَ سَافِلِيْنَ ۙ۝

6. Except those who believe
and do the right,
for whom there is reward undiminished.

اِلَّا الَّذِيْنَ اٰمَنُوْا وَعَمِلُوا الصّٰلِحٰتِ فَلَهُمْ
اَجْرٌ غَيْرُ مَمْنُوْنٍ ۝

7. Who should then make you deny
the Judgement after this?

فَمَا يُكَذِّبُكَ بَعْدُ بِالدِّيْنِ ۝

8. Is not God the most equitable of all judges?

اَلَيْسَ اللهُ بِاَحْكَمِ الْحٰكِمِيْنَ ۞

----

* The Olive, Mount and Soil Secure are identifiable with the Mount of Olive, Mount Sinai and the Valley of Makkah, that is, Jesus, Moses and Muhammad. From the context of the struggle between good and evil which is perpetual, the Fig stands for the mount of Fig (see Raghib and *Taj al-'Arus*) where Noah, the earliest of the prophets, first preached his gospel. Historically the order should have been the Fig, Mount Sinai, Olive and then Soil Secure. Geographically, however, and viewing from North to South, the names would occur as in the Surah. Rhythmically too the order marks a perfect example of the parallelism of words and thought underlining the perfect statement of the unity of outward form and inner meaning that parallelism represents.

96 The Embryo

Al-'Alaq: Makki

سورة العلق مكية

آياتها ١٩ ركوعها ١

In the name of Allah, most benevolent, ever-merciful.

READ IN THE name of your Lord
who created,
2. Created man from an embryo;
3. Read,
for your Lord is most beneficent,
4. Who taught by the pen,
5. Taught man what he did not know.
6. And yet,
but yet man is rebellious,
7. For he thinks he is sufficient in himself.
8. Surely your returning is to your Lord.
9. Have you seen him who restrains
10. A votary when he turns to his devotions?
11. Have you thought,
if he had been on guidance
12. Or had enjoined piety,
(it would have been better)?
13. Have you thought that if he denies
and turns away,
14. Does he not know that God sees?
15. And yet indeed if he does not desist
We shall drag him by the forelock,
16. By the lying, the sinful forelock.
17. So let him call his associates,
18. We shall call the guards of Hell.
19. Beware! Do not obey him,
but bow in adoration
and draw near (to your Lord).

Al-'Alaq

543

97 Determination

Al-Qadr: Makki

(٩٧)سُوْرَةُ الْقَدْرِمَكِّيَّةٌ

اٰيَاتُهَا رُكُوْعُهَا

In the name of Allah, most benevolent, ever-merciful.

بِسْمِ اللهِ الرَّحْمٰنِ الرَّحِيْمِ ۞

TRULY WE REVEALED it *
on the Night of Determination.
2. How will you know what the Night
of Determination is?
3. Better is the Night of Determination
than a thousand months.
4. On (this night) the angels and grace descend
by the dispensation of their Lord,
for settling all affairs.
5. It is peace
till the dawning of the day.

اِنَّآ اَنْزَلْنٰهُ فِيْ لَيْلَةِ الْقَدْرِ ۞

وَمَآ اَدْرٰىكَ مَا لَيْلَةُ الْقَدْرِ ۞

لَيْلَةُ الْقَدْرِ خَيْرٌ مِّنْ اَلْفِ شَهْرٍ ۞

تَنَزَّلُ الْمَلٰٓئِكَةُ وَالرُّوْحُ فِيْهَا بِاِذْنِ رَبِّهِمْ مِّنْ كُلِّ اَمْرٍ ۞

سَلٰمٌ هِيَ حَتّٰى مَطْلَعِ الْفَجْرِ ۞

---

* It clearly refers to the Qur'an, confirmed by 44:3-4. This night falls during the month of Ramadan,
vide 2:185. It is the Qur'an, called 'the custodian of all laws' elsewhere, by which all affairs are settled.

98 The Clear Proof

Al-Bayyinah: Madani

In the name of Allah, most benevolent, ever-merciful.

THOSE AMONG THE people of the Book
who disbelieve, and the idolaters,
would not have been freed (from false beliefs)
until the clear proof came to them —
2. An Apostle from God, reading out hallowed pages
3. Containing firm decrees.
4. The people of the Book were not divided among themselves
till after the clear proof had come to them.
5. They were commanded only to serve God
with all-exclusive faith in Him,
to be upright, and to fulfil their devotional obligations,
and to give zakat; for this is the even way.
6. Surely the unbelievers among the people of the Book
and the idolaters, will abide in the fire of Hell.
They are the worst of creatures.
7. But those who believe and do the right
are surely the best of created beings,
8. Whose reward is with their Lord —
gardens of Eden with rivers flowing by,
where they will abide for ever,
God pleased with their service, they with obedience to Him.
This (awaits) him who stands in awe of his Lord.

99 The Earthquake

Al-Zilzāl: Madani

In the name of Allah, most benevolent, ever merciful.

WHEN THE WORLD is shaken up
by its cataclysm,
2. And the earth throws out its burdens,
3. And man enquires:
"What has come over it?"
4. That day it will narrate its annals,
5. For your Lord will have commanded it.
6. That day people will proceed separately
to be shown their deeds.
7. Whosoever has done
even an atom's weight of good
will behold it;
8. And whosoever has done
even an atom's weight of evil
will behold that.

100   The Chargers

Al-'Ādiyāt: Makki

In the name of Allah, most benevolent, ever-merciful.

I CALL TO witness the chargers,
snorting, rushing to battle before the others,
2. Then those striking sparks of fire,
3. Then those charging in the morning
4. Raising clouds of dust,
5. Penetrating deep into the armies,
6. That man is ungrateful to his Lord
7. And is himself witness to it,
8. And is intractable in his love of worldly goods.
9. Does he not know when the contents
of the graves are laid bare
10. And the secrets of the hearts exposed,
11. Surely their Lord will be aware
of their (deeds).

101   The Calamity

Al-Qāri'ah: Makki

In the name of Allah, most benevolent, ever-merciful.

بِسْمِ اللهِ الرَّحْمٰنِ الرَّحِيْمِo

THE STARTLING CALAMITY.

2. What is the startling calamity?

3. How will you comprehend
what the startling calamity is? —

4. A Day on which human beings
would be like so many scattered moths,

5. The mountains like the tufts of carded wool.

6. Then he whose deeds shall weigh
heavier in the scale

7. Will have a tranquil life;

8. But he whose deeds
are lighter in the balance

9. Will have the Abyss for abode.

10. How will you comprehend
what that is?

11. It is the scorching fire.

102 Plenitude

At-Takāthur: Makki

عۣ۳۰

(۱۰۲)سورة التكاثر مكية

ایاتها ۸ رکوعها ۱

In the name of Allah, most benevolent, ever-merciful.

بسم الله الرحمن الرحيم ۞

THE AVARICE OF plenitude
keeps you occupied

اَلْهٰىكُمُ التَّكَاثُرُ ۞

2. Till you reach the grave.

حَتّٰى زُرْتُمُ الْمَقَابِرَ ۞

3. But you will come to know soon;

كَلَّا سَوْفَ تَعْلَمُوْنَ ۞

4. Indeed you will come to know soon.

ثُمَّ كَلَّا سَوْفَ تَعْلَمُوْنَ ۞

5. And yet if you knew
with positive knowledge

كَلَّا لَوْ تَعْلَمُوْنَ عِلْمَ الْيَقِيْنِ ۞

6. You have indeed to behold Hell;

لَتَرَوُنَّ الْجَحِيْمَ ۞

7. Then you will see it
with the eye of certainty.

ثُمَّ لَتَرَوُنَّهَا عَيْنَ الْيَقِيْنِ ۞

8. Then on that day
you will surely be asked
about the verity of pleasures.

ثُمَّ لَتُسْئَلُنَّ يَوْمَئِذٍ عَنِ النَّعِيْمِ ۞

549

103   Time and Age

Al-'Asr: Makki

In the name of Allah, most benevolent, ever-merciful.

TIME AND AGE are witness
2. Man is certainly in loss,
3. Except those who believe,
and do good and enjoin
truth on one another,
and enjoin one another
to bear with fortitude
(the trials that befall).

بِسْمِ اللهِ الرَّحْمٰنِ الرَّحِيْمِ ۟

وَالْعَصْرِ ۟

اِنَّ الْاِنْسَانَ لَفِىْ خُسْرٍ ۟

اِلَّا الَّذِيْنَ اٰمَنُوْا وَعَمِلُوا الصّٰلِحٰتِ وَتَوَاصَوْا
بِالْحَقِّ ەۙ وَتَوَاصَوْا بِالصَّبْرِ ۟

104   The Slanderer

Al-Humazah: Makki

عمر ٣٠

(١٠٤) سورة الهمزة مكية

اياتها ٩ ركوعها ١

In the name of Allah, most benevolent, ever-merciful.

بِسْمِ اللهِ الرَّحْمٰنِ الرَّحِيمِ ۞

WOE TO EVERY slanderer, back-biter,

وَيْلٌ لِّكُلِّ هُمَزَةٍ لُّمَزَةٍ ۞

2. Who amasses wealth
and hordes it.

الَّذِى جَمَعَ مَالًا وَّعَدَّدَهُ ۞

3. Does he think his wealth
will abide for ever with him?

يَحْسَبُ أَنَّ مَالَهُ أَخْلَدَهُ ۞

4. By no means.
He will be thrown into Hutama.

كَلَّا لَيُنْبَذَنَّ فِى الْحُطَمَةِ ۞

5. How will you comprehend
what Hutama is?

وَمَا أَدْرَاكَ مَا الْحُطَمَةُ ۞

6. It is the fire kindled by God

نَارُ اللهِ الْمُوقَدَةُ ۞

7. Which penetrates the hearts

الَّتِى تَطَّلِعُ عَلَى الْأَفْئِدَةِ ۞

8. (And) vaults them over

إِنَّهَا عَلَيْهِمْ مُّؤْصَدَةٌ ۞

9. In extending columns.

فِى عَمَدٍ مُّمَدَّدَةٍ ۞

105 The Elephants

Al-Fīl: Makki

سُوْرَةُ الْفِيْلِ مَكِّيَّةٌ (١٠٥)

اٰيَاتُهَا رُكُوْعُهَا

In the name of Allah, most benevolent, ever-merciful.

بِسْمِ اللهِ الرَّحْمٰنِ الرَّحِيْمِ ۞

Hᴀᴠᴇ ʏᴏᴜ ɴᴏᴛ seen how your Lord
dealt with the people of the elephants*?
2. Did He not make their plan go wrong,
3. And sent hordes of chargers flying against them,
4. (While) you were pelting them with stones
of porphyritic lava,
5. And turned them into pastured fields of corn?

أَلَمْ تَرَ كَيْفَ فَعَلَ رَبُّكَ بِأَصْحٰبِ الْفِيْلِ ۞
أَلَمْ يَجْعَلْ كَيْدَهُمْ فِيْ تَضْلِيْلٍ ۞
وَّأَرْسَلَ عَلَيْهِمْ طَيْرًا أَبَابِيْلَ ۞
تَرْمِيْهِمْ بِحِجَارَةٍ مِّنْ سِجِّيْلٍ ۞
فَجَعَلَهُمْ كَعَصْفٍ مَّأْكُوْلٍ ۞

---

* In 571 A.D. Abraha, the Christian viceroy of Sana' marched against Makkah with elephants and a large army with the intention of destroying the Ka'bah, but was routed in the battle that took place at dawn. This Surah contains a parabolic account of that battle, and uses another example from history as a lesson for mankind. Tradition has standardised the meaning of *tairan* (root TAR) used in v. 3 with *ababil* which means hordes, troops, swarms, as 'bird' in this surah, though it has many other forms, e.g., *ta-ir* pl. *at-tair, atarah, tayyarah, tayyar, mutar*, etc., and many meanings including bird. It is used in the Qur'an for omen or augury in 7:131, 36:18, for ledger of deeds in 17:13. It also means destiny or fortune, and swift-footed horse or charger, *tayyar*. See also note on pp. 322-23 and 386-87. Pertinent also is Surah 100 which describes the quality of these chargers. Contemporary evidence shows that cavalry was used in the battle which took place in the year of the Prophet's birth. Dhu'l-Rammah the famous Arab poet of the first century Hijarah, writes in an ode on the battle:

Wabrahma istadat sudur-e-mahana	Our lances hunted Abraha down
jahara wa'thnun al-'ijatah akdar	(While) the atmosphere was murky with gritty dust.
tanha lahu 'Umru fashakka dulu'aha	Charging with his lance 'Umru then smashed
binabidhtin bikhala' wa-l-khail-i tasbar	His ribs; and the chargers stood their ground.

In the murky atmosphere of the blowing dust storm the birds, whether large or small, would either fly high above it or take shelter on the ground. Since the people of Makkah had taken cover in the valleys and hills on the advice of 'Abd-al-Muttalib, the Prophet's grandfather who was the leader of Quraish, from there they could catapult stones, then a weapon of war, the horses charging from the valleys. The elephants would go amuck in such an attack, as those of Porus and Ibrahim Lodi had done under the charge of the cavalries of Alexander and Babur. If *tair* were to mean birds, the "winged ones" symbolised "the lords of the mighty ones". "Wings" in Babylonian legends symbolised kings, as bulls with extended wings from Nineveh or Persepolis did the Assyrian King. And the stretching forth of the Assyrian monarch's WINGS meant the overspreading of land by the "mighty ones," or hosts of armed men (*tairan ababeel*) the king of Babylon employed for his overflowing invasion. Besides, the language of verse 4 itself points to men throwing stones. The *t* of *tarmihim* refers to "you" — you were striking them with stones; and the verses 3 and 4 are separated by an *aya*, sign of both a punctuation and pause.

Al-Fīl

106 The Quraish

Al-Quraish: Makki

In the name of Allah, most benevolent, ever-merciful.

SINCE THE QURAISH have been united,*
2. United to fit out caravans
winter and summer,
3. Let them worship the Lord of this House,
4. Who provided them against destitution
and gave them security
against fear.

بِسْمِ اللهِ الرَّحْمٰنِ الرَّحِيْمِ ۝

لِاِيْلٰفِ قُرَيْشٍ ۙ۝

اٖلٰفِهِمْ رِحْلَةَ الشِّتَآءِ وَالصَّيْفِ ۚ۝

فَلْيَعْبُدُوْا رَبَّ هٰذَا الْبَيْتِ ۙ۝

الَّذِىْٓ اَطْعَمَهُمْ مِّنْ جُوْعٍ ۙ۬ وَّاٰمَنَهُمْ مِّنْ خَوْفٍ ۬۝

---

* See note at the end of Surah 54, p. 460 ante.

107　Things of Common Use

Al-Mā'ūn: Makki

In the name of Allah, most benevolent, ever-merciful.

بِسْمِ اللهِ الرَّحْمٰنِ الرَّحِيْمِ ۞

HAVE YOU SEEN him who denies
the Day of Judgement?

اَرَءَیْتَ الَّذِیْ یُکَذِّبُ بِالدِّیْنِ ۞

2. It is he who pushes the orphan away,

فَذٰلِكَ الَّذِیْ یَدُعُّ الْیَتِیْمَ ۞

3. And does not induce others
to feed the needy.

وَلَا یَحُضُّ عَلٰی طَعَامِ الْمِسْکِیْنِ ۞

4. Woe to those who pray

فَوَیْلٌ لِّلْمُصَلِّیْنَ ۞

5. But who are oblivious
of their moral duties,

الَّذِیْنَ هُمْ عَنْ صَلَاتِهِمْ سَاهُوْنَ ۞

6. Who dissimulate

الَّذِیْنَ هُمْ یُرَآءُوْنَ ۞

7. And withhold things
of common use (from others).

وَیَمْنَعُوْنَ الْمَاعُوْنَ ۞

108 Pre-eminence

Al-Kauthar: Makki

عـ ٣

(١٠٨) سُورَةُ الْكَوْثَرِ مَكِّيَّةٌ

اٰیَاتُهَا ٣ رُکُوعُهَا ١

In the name of Allah, most benevolent, ever-merciful.

بِسْمِ اللهِ الرَّحْمٰنِ الرَّحِیْمِ ۟

WE HAVE SURELY given you pre-eminence
(in numbers and following);

اِنَّاۤ اَعْطَیْنٰکَ الْکَوْثَرَ ۟

2. So serve your Lord
with full dedication and sacrifice.

فَصَلِّ لِرَبِّکَ وَانْحَرْ ۟

3. It is surely your opponents
whose line will come to end.

اِنَّ شَانِئَکَ هُوَ الْاَبْتَرُ ۟

109 The Unbelievers

Al-Kāfirūn: Makki

In the name of Allah, most benevolent, ever-merciful.

SAY: "O YOU unbelievers,
2. I do not worship
what you worship,
3. Nor do you worship
who I worship,
4. Nor will I worship
what you worship,
5. Nor will you worship
who I worship:
6. To you your way,
to me my way.

110 Help

An-Nasr: Madani

عـــو ٣.

(١١) سورة النصر مدنية

ايانها ركوعها

In the name of Allah, most benevolent, ever-merciful.

بِسْمِ اللهِ الرَّحْمٰنِ الرَّحِيُمِ ٥

WHEN THE HELP of God arrives
and victory,

إِذَا جَآءَ نَصْرُ اللهِ وَالْفَتْحُ ۞

2. And you see men enter God's discipline
horde on horde,

وَرَاَيْتَ النَّاسَ يَدْخُلُوْنَ فِيْ دِيْنِ اللهِ اَفْوَاجًا ۞

3. Then glorify your Lord and seek His forgiveness.
Verily He is relenting.

فَسَبِّحْ بِحَمْدِ رَبِّكَ وَاسْتَغْفِرْهُ ۗ اِنَّهٗ كَانَ
تَوَّابًا ۞

111   Abu Lahab

Al-Lahab: Makki

عۃ ٣٠

(١١١) سُوْرَةُ اللَّهَبِ مَكِّيَّۃٌ

اٰیَاتُهَا   رُکُوْعُهَا

In the name of Allah, most benevolent, ever-merciful.

بِسْمِ اللهِ الرَّحْمٰنِ الرَّحِيْمِ ۟

DESTROYED WILL BE
the hands of Abu Lahab,
and he himself will perish.

تَبَّتْ يَدَاۤ اَبِیْ لَهَبٍ وَّتَبَّ ۟

2. Of no avail shall be his wealth,
nor what he has acquired.

مَاۤ اَغْنٰی عَنْهُ مَالُهٗ وَمَا كَسَبَ ۟

3. He will be roasted in the fire,

سَيَصْلٰی نَارًا ذَاتَ لَهَبٍ ۟

4. And his wife,
the portress of fire wood,

وَّامْرَاَتُهٗ ۟ حَمَّالَةَ الْحَطَبِ ۟

5. Will have a strap of coir rope around her neck.

فِیْ جِيْدِهَا حَبْلٌ مِّنْ مَّسَدٍ ۟

112 Pure Faith

Al-Ikhlās: Makki

In the name of Allah, most benevolent, ever-merciful.

بِسْمِ اللهِ الرَّحْمٰنِ الرَّحِيْمِ ۞

SAY: "HE IS God
the one the most unique,

قُلْ هُوَ اللهُ اَحَدٌ ۞

2. God the immanently indispensable.

اللهُ الصَّمَدُ ۞

3. He has begotten no one,
and is begotten of none.

لَمْ يَلِدْ ۙ وَلَمْ يُوْلَدْ ۞

4. There is no one comparable to Him."

وَلَمْ يَكُنْ لَّهُ كُفُوًا اَحَدٌ ۞

113 The Rising Day

Al-Falaq: Makki

In the name of Allah, most benevolent, ever-merciful.

SAY: "I SEEK refuge with the Lord of rising day
2. From the evil of what He has created,
3. And the evil of evening darkness
when it overspreads,
4. From the evil of sorceresses
who blow incantations on knots,
5. From the evil of the envier
when he envies.

114 Men

An-Nās: **Makki**

عـ د ٣
(١١٤) سُورَةُ النَّاسِ مَكِّيَّة
اياتها ٦ رُكُوْعُهَا ١

In the name of Allah, most benevolent, ever-merciful.

بِسْمِ اللهِ الرَّحْمٰنِ الرَّحِيْمِ ۰

SAY: "I SEEK refuge with the Lord of men,

قُلْ اَعُوْذُ بِرَبِّ النَّاسِ ۙ

2. The King of men,

مَلِكِ النَّاسِ ۙ

3. The God of men,

اِلٰهِ النَّاسِ ۙ

4. From the evil of him
who breathes temptations
into the minds of men,

مِنْ شَرِّ الْوَسْوَاسِ الْخَنَّاسِ ۙ

5. Who suggests evil thoughts
to the hearts of men —

الَّذِيْ يُوَسْوِسُ فِيْ صُدُوْرِ النَّاسِ ۙ

6. From among the jinns and men.

مِنَ الْجِنَّةِ وَالنَّاسِ ۞

Index

Index of Names

INDEX OF NAMES

CERTIFICATE

This is to certify that I have read the Arabic
text of this copy of the Holy Qur'an word for
word, and have found no errors of any kind.

حافظ عبد الرؤف

Hafiz 'Abd-al-Rauf